PRIVATE LAW AND THE RULE OF LAW

Private Law and the Rule of Law

Edited by
LISA M AUSTIN
and
DENNIS KLIMCHUK

OXFORD
UNIVERSITY PRESS

OXFORD
UNIVERSITY PRESS

Great Clarendon Street, Oxford, OX2 6DP,
United Kingdom

Oxford University Press is a department of the University of Oxford.
It furthers the University's objective of excellence in research, scholarship,
and education by publishing worldwide. Oxford is a registered trade mark of
Oxford University Press in the UK and in certain other countries

First Edition published in 2014

Impression: 1

Published in the United States of America by Oxford University Press
198 Madison Avenue, New York, NY 10016, United States of America

British Library Cataloguing in Publication Data
Data available

Library of Congress Control Number: 2014945275

ISBN 978–0–19–872932–7

Printed and bound by
CPI Group (UK) Ltd, Croydon, CR0 4YY

Acknowledgements

We have incurred many debts in the course of working on this project. The first to David Dyzenhaus for suggesting that we organize a workshop around our shared interest in this book's theme. We'd also like to thank David, as well as Arthur Ripstein and Ernie Weinrib, for their encouragement and advice. In addition, we are indebted to the University of Toronto Faculty of Law for support provided for the workshop that we held to discuss early drafts of the contributors' papers. In producing this manuscript we were supported with first-rate research assistance by Sarah Bittman and Maeve Clougherty. And we would like especially to thank our contributors for their enthusiasm for the project and their excellent work.

Contents

List of Contributors

TRS Allan (Professor of Jurisprudence and Public Law, Cambridge University)

Lisa M Austin (Associate Professor of Law, University of Toronto)

Hanoch Dagan (Stewart and Judy Colton Professor of Legal Theory and Innovation, Tel-Aviv University)

David Dyzenhaus (Professor of Law and Philosophy, University of Toronto)

Evan Fox-Decent (Associate Professor of Law, McGill University)

John Gardner (Professor of Jurisprudence, University of Oxford)

Dennis Klimchuk (Associate Professor of Philosophy, The University of Western Ontario)

William Lucy (Professor, Durham Law School)

Gerald J Postema (Cary C Boshamer Professor of Philosophy and Professor of Law, University of North Carolina at Chapel Hill)

Margaret Jane Radin (Henry King Ransom Professor of Law, University of Michigan)

Arthur Ripstein (Professor of Law and Philosophy, University of Toronto)

Henry E Smith (Fessenden Professor of Law, Harvard University)

Stephen A Smith (James McGill Professor of Law, McGill University)

Benjamin C Zipursky (Professor of Law and James H Quinn '49 Chair in Legal Ethics, Fordham University School of Law)

Table of Cases

Introduction

Lisa M Austin and Dennis Klimchuk

1. Introduction

There is widespread agreement regarding the core elements of the rule of law. Most essential among these are the principles that a right to exercise power arbitrarily cannot be conferred or upheld by law, and that anything that claims the status of law must be able to guide action.[1] Different accounts of the rule of law connect these principles in different ways to a collection of institutional, formal, and procedural requirements—including, for example, that the powers of government be separated, that laws be public, stable and non-retroactive, and that courts be accessible and governed by principles of due process and natural justice—the list of which is itself an object of near consensus.

Beyond this, however, substantial disagreement begins, collecting around four main issues: How much more substantive is the ideal of the rule of law and what is its relation to other ideas and ideals such as freedom and equality? Does the rule of law express a kind of morality or justice of its own or is it of purely instrumental value? Are rule of law considerations categorical or is fidelity to the rule of law one value among many, such that different balances amongst these values may be struck in different circumstances? And, finally: Do the principles of the rule of law constitute conditions of legality or legal validity, or might a law or legal system violate these principles and yet still claim to be a law or a legal system?

Notwithstanding these points of disagreement—and cutting across the differences they represent—there is one further point of consensus, at times only implicit but no less widespread, namely that the rule of law is essentially a public law doctrine. We'll call this the *public law presumption*. This view is pervasive in contemporary work on the rule of law[2] and is expressed in the nineteenth- and twentieth-century accounts of the rule of law that set the context of that scholarship and of the articles in this volume.

[1] As we explain, it is a matter of debate whether this 'cannot' and this 'must' express conceptual claims about the conditions of legality, and so that a law that purports to confer a right to exercise power arbitrarily or that fails to guide action is therefore invalid or at least suspect in respect of its validity.

[2] See n 26.

Present-day discussion of the rule of law arguably gets its start with AV Dicey. On his view, the rule of law is particularly well exemplified by the English constitution owing to the fact that in England citizens' fundamental rights 'are with us the result of judicial decisions determining the rights of private persons in particular cases brought before the courts'.[3] The rule of law enjoys particular security in polities in which it has the status of a common law constitutional principle for two reasons. First, because in such a legal order the rights and principles the constitution protects (such as *nulla poena sine lege*) are secured by litigation, they are necessarily attached to remedies for their violation. Second, because the rights thereby protected by the constitution are not derived from a particular statute, they cannot be suspended without suspending the legal order itself.

Dicey draws the connection between the rule of law and public law on this view when he first introduces the section of his *Introduction to the Study of the Law of the Constitution* dedicated to the rule or, as he sometimes says, supremacy of law. Dicey glosses '[the] supremacy of law' that is characteristic of the English legal system as 'the security given under the English Constitution to the rights of individuals'.[4] The rights whose security Dicey implies is the upshot of the rule of law are those held by individuals against the government, such as freedom of discussion and freedom of assembly. And later as he unpacks the idea, Dicey contrasts the rule of law with 'every system of government based on the exercise of persons in authority of wide, arbitrary, or discretionary powers of constraint'.[5]

In contrast with Dicey, Friedrich Hayek argued that '[w]hether, as in some countries, the main applications of the Rule of Law are laid down in a bill of rights or in a constitutional code, or whether the principle is merely a firmly established tradition, matters little'.[6] What does matter, on Hayek's account, is that the government respect one's right to determine and, subject to consistency with the equality of others, pursue one's own ends. In governing other than by general rules fixed and announced beforehand, a government interferes with this form of individual liberty in two ways. First, it makes life unpredictable and, second, it arrogates to itself the right to determine which ends ought to be pursued by whom. In doing so a government violates what Hayek characterizes as the most important among the 'inalienable rights of the individual, inviolable rights of man'.[7] So a second point of disagreement between Hayek and Dicey concerns the foundation of the rule of law. While for Dicey it is a principle of the common law

[3] AV Dicey, *Introduction to the Study of the Law of the Constitution* (10th edn, Macmillan & Co 1959) 195.

[4] Dicey, *Introduction* (n 3) 184.

[5] Dicey, *Introduction* (n 3) 188.

[6] FA Hayek, *The Road to Serfdom* (University of Chicago Press 1944) 84. The disagreement between Dicey and Hayek on this point shouldn't be overstated. Dicey's claim was not that the link between right and remedy necessarily secured in a common law constitution was inconsistent with a written constitution or bill of rights. It is rather such documents could be and often were remedially hollow (the important exception being the American Bill of Rights). Dicey, *Introduction* (n 9) 200–1.

[7] Hayek, *Road* (n 6) 84.

constitution, for Hayek the rule of law is a moral constraint on the exercise of political authority.[8]

These are disagreements within the framework of the public law presumption. Echoing the contrast Dicey drew between government under the rule of law and arbitrary power, and drawing the connection to public law even more clearly, Hayek claims that:

> [n]othing distinguishes more clearly conditions in a free country from those in a country under arbitrary government than the observance in the former of all the great principles known as the Rule of Law. Stripped of all technicalities, this means the government in all its actions is bound by rules fixed and announced beforehand—rules which make it possible to foresee with fair certainty how the authority will use its coercive powers in given circumstances and to plan one's individual affairs on the basis of this knowledge.[9]

Linking it essentially to public law in another way, Hayek elsewhere tracks the history of the development of the rule of law by tracing the development of the principle of the separation of powers and the subjection of executive authority to law.[10]

A third influential account of the general nature and foundation of the rule of law is found in Lon Fuller's argument that the principles of legality often thought to form the core of the rule of law—generality, publicity, non-retroactivity, clarity, non-contradiction, possibility of compliance, stability, and congruence between official action and declared rule—constitute the 'inner morality' of the law.[11] For Fuller, Hayek's 'inalienable rights of the individual, inviolable rights of man', by contrast, form part of what he calls an external morality: a set of independent substantive moral principles to which a legal system may or may not in practice conform.

[8] This is not to suggest that for Dicey the principle of rule of law is just a matter of positive law, but rather that on his account it can be said to be a characteristic of a legal system just to the extent that it has a matter of common law established a set of individual rights and secured their protection and the remedies for their violation in a particular way.

[9] Hayek, *Road* (n 6) 72.

[10] See 'The Origins of the Rule of Law' in *The Constitution of Liberty* (Routledge & Kegan Paul 1960) ch 11.

[11] Fuller, *The Morality of Law* (rev edn, Yale University Press 1969) 33–94. We put the characterization of Fuller's account of the inner morality of law as an account of the rule of law slightly cautiously because in fact he does not explicitly say that the principles of legality collectively comprise the rule of law. Indeed, the phrase 'rule of law' does not come up during the discussion of the principles of legality. It does appear in the 'Reply to Critics' added to the Revised Edition, where Fuller identifies it principally with the last of the eight principles: 'Surely the very essence of the Rule of Law is that in acting upon the citizen (by putting him in jail, for example, or declaring invalid a deed under which he claims title to property) a government will faithfully apply rules previously declared as those to be followed by the citizen and as being determinative of his rights and duties. If the Rule of Law does not mean this, it means nothing' (Fuller, *Morality* 209–10). In an earlier paper, Fuller suggested that sense might be made of the variety of claims made on behalf of the rule of law if we emphasized in particular one aspect 'of the process by which a state of anarchy or despotism is converted into something we can call the "rule of law"', namely 'the process by which the party affected by a decision is granted a formally defined participation in that decision'. He gave two examples: establishing recognized voting procedures, and establishing a formal system of contracts. Lon Fuller, 'Adjudication and the Rule of Law' *Proceedings of the American Society of International Law* (1960) 1, 2.

This 'inner morality' of a legal system conditions the way in which a government should undertake what Fuller calls 'the enterprise of subjecting human conduct to the governance of rules'.[12] That he understands the form of this governance principally in public law terms is implicit in the very structure of the famous allegory with which Fuller introduces the principles of legality. Fuller asks us to imagine the inept rule of a king named Rex, who tries but fails to make law eight times, each failure being a failure to respect a different principle of legality. All are failures on the part of the King Rex to successfully legislate or administer the laws of his realm.[13]

Fuller's argument was partially responding to what he saw as the failure of legal positivism's ability to account for the nature of law. For Fuller, law can fail *as law* if the law fails to comply with the (for him moral) principles of legality even if it passes the positivist tests for legal validity. Owing to his claim that these principles are moral, Fuller classifies his view as falling in the natural law tradition, though in a qualified way.[14]

The now-classic positivist response to Fuller's rule-of-law argument is Joseph Raz's claim that the rule of law is like the sharp edge of a knife: an inherent virtue that makes the tool effective as a tool. The virtue of the rule of law 'is the virtue of efficiency; the virtue of the instrument as an instrument'.[15] Raz summarizes what he calls the literal sense of the rule of law as having two aspects: '(1) that people should be ruled by the law and obey it, and (2) that the law should be such that people will be able to be guided by it', glossing the second as holding that 'the law must be capable of being obeyed'.[16] An implicit connection to public law here is expressed by the centrality of the concept of obedience. This places criminal and hence public law at the paradigmatic centre of the rule of law. As Hart noted, we might say that the legal rules, for example, that define the ways in which contracts or wills are made may be, or may fail to be, 'complied' with. But compliance is not a kind of obedience.[17] The connection of this conception of the rule of law to public law is made explicit in the list of principles that Raz claims may be derived from it, all of which are directed toward legislation, the structure of government, and the administration of justice.[18]

Now, all of this is not to say that private law plays no role in the rule of law for Dicey, Hayek, Fuller, or Raz. On Dicey's account, one of the principal elements of the rule of law is the idea of legal equality, which requires that 'every man, whatever be his rank or condition, is subject to the ordinary law of the realm and amenable to

[12] Fuller, *Morality* (n 11) 106. [13] Fuller, *Morality* (n 11) 33–41.

[14] The qualification is that the principles of legality are not substantive principles of conduct. Fuller characterized them instead as procedural, though 'formal' might have been the better term for at least some. See Fuller, *Morality* (n 11) 96–106.

[15] Raz, 'The Rule of Law and its Virtue' in *The Authority of Law* (2nd edn, Oxford University Press 2009) 210, 226.

[16] Raz, 'Rule' (n 15) 213.

[17] HLA Hart, *The Concept of Law* (2nd edn, Clarendon Press 1994) 28.

[18] For example, 'All laws should be open, prospective and clear', 'The independence of the judiciary must be guaranteed', and 'The principles of natural justice must be observed', respectively. Raz, 'Rule' (n 15) 214, 216, 217.

the jurisdiction of the ordinary tribunals'.[19] Commitment in practice to legal equality understood this way is revealed in the principal institutional mechanism through which, on Dicey's telling, a government is held accountable to the ideal of the rule of law, namely by way of subjection to civil suit by those wronged by actions undertaken by officials 'in their official character but in excess of their lawful authority'.[20] For his part, Hayek argues that a polity that properly respects the rule of law is one that leaves matters of distribution to the private order.[21] It follows on his account that the rule of law is made possible through a system of private law structured by rules that are general and clear enough to allow persons to plan their activities and undertakings and to prevent their being used by officials to advance one particular set of interests or vision of the good over another.[22] As for Fuller, though he introduces the principles of legality by way of a story of a ruler's failed attempts to make law, in his discussion of those principles he draws on private law. For example, in his discussion of retroactivity, he argues that the same principle against retroactivity bears on private and on criminal law, but requires something different in each setting.[23] And, finally, in his discussion of the principle that law should be relatively stable, Raz says that

> though the rule of law concerns primarily private citizens as subject to duties and government agencies in the exercise of their powers . . . [i]t is also concerned with the exercise of private powers. Power conferring rules are designed to guide behaviour and should conform to the doctrine of the rule of law if they are capable of doing so effectively.[24]

Notwithstanding these important qualifications, however, a collective effect of these influential formulations of the rule of law, standing as they do in a long philosophical tradition that shares it,[25] is the implicit acceptance of the idea that at its heart the rule of law is an ideal concerning the manner in which a government exercises authority, and the institutional structures through which it may do so consistently with that ideal.[26]

[19] Dicey, *Introduction* (n 3) 193. [20] Dicey, *Introduction* (n 3) 193.

[21] Hayek, *Road* (n 6) 72–87. [22] On this idea see TRS Allan's contribution to this volume.

[23] Fuller, *Morality* (n 11) 51–62. Consider too the examples in the passages from 'Adjudication and the Rule of Law' discussed in n 11. For argument that for Fuller the rule of law was equally expressed in private and public law see TRS Allan's and David Dyzenhaus's contributions to this volume.

[24] Raz, 'Rule' (n 15) 215; see also Lisa M Austin's contribution to this volume, 'The Power of the Rule of Law'.

[25] Toward the end of his broad survey of treatments of the rule of law Brian Z Tamanaha says that '[t]he broadest understanding of the rule of law, a thread that has run for over 2000 years, often frayed thin, but never completely severed, is that the sovereign, and the state and its officials, are limited by the law.' Tamanaha, *On the Rule of Law* (Cambridge University Press 2004) 114.

[26] This acceptance is not without exception. For example Martin Krygier recently argued that '[w]hether or not the rule of law has claim in a society is a matter found in the extent and quality of its reach and effects there: in interactions between citizens and the state, of course, but of equal or more importance, between citizens themselves.' Martin Krygier,'Four Puzzles about the Rule of Law: Why, What, Where? and Who Cares?' in James E Fleming (ed), *Getting to the Rule of Law* (NYU Press 2011) 64, 89. But for the most part the public law presumption holds. For example, in an often-cited survey, Paul Craig sorts accounts of the rule of law according to whether they express formal or substantive conceptions of the ideal, but each on his reckoning holds that the rule of law is 'a central principle of constitutional governance'. Paul Craig, 'Formal and Substantive Conceptions of the Rule of Law: An Analytical Framework' (1997) *Public Law* 467, 487. More recently, Timothy Endicott argued that '[a]

The goal of this book is to explore the idea that the perception of the rule of law as an essentially public law doctrine is in fact a *mis*perception. We invited contributors to consider the idea that we should think of the rule of law as an important set of ideas about the nature of law generally and of the conditions under which any relationship—between citizens as well as between citizens and the state—becomes subject to law. This, we suggested, invites two complementary lines of enquiry.

First, one might ask whether our understanding of the rule of law is enriched by considering how and to what degree it is realized in private law. For example, if there is one idea or set of ideas common to its application in private and public law, then the classic formulations of the rule of law will turn out to be too narrow. What are the implications of the private law expression of the rule of law on our understanding of the more general principles of the rule of law? Second, one might ask whether our understanding of the private law is enriched by adding the principles of the rule of law to the traditional list of core private law concepts, such as ownership and promises. Are the principles of the rule of law expressed in the substantive and procedural doctrines of private law? Does the rule of law limit the sort of arrangements private law can uphold and constrain the ends to which its doctrines may be put?

While most contributors engaged both questions, we have sorted them according to which question they emphasized, as follows.

2. The Private Law Contribution to the Rule of Law

The rule of law, even in its canonical public law formulations, expresses an important set of ideas about the nature of law and legal order. By bringing an explicit focus on private law to rule-of-law debates, many of the chapters in this volume show that our understanding of legal order is at best incomplete and arguably also distorted if we only think about the rule of law in its public law guise.

One theme running through many chapters in this volume is the centrality of non-arbitrariness to our understanding of the rule of law and the ways in which private law relations can help enrich our understanding of this. In 'Fidelity in Law's Commonwealth', Gerald Postema argues that the rule of law 'promises protection and recourse against the arbitrary exercise of power through the distinctive offices

community attains the ideal of the rule of law when the life of the community is governed by law. So the rule of law can be opposed to anarchy, in which the life of the community is not governed. The rule of law can also be opposed to *arbitrary* government.' Timothy AO Endicott, 'The Impossibility of the Rule of Law' (1999) 19 *Oxford Journal of Legal Studies* 1, 2. Thus on Endicott's telling the rule of law is essentially connected to governance. So it is, as well, on Andrei Marmor's account, according to which 'the essence of the ideal of the rule of law is that people ought to be governed by law. This general ideal has at least two components. First, it requires that governments, namely, *de facto* political authorities, should rule, that is, guide their subjects' conduct, by law. Second, it requires that the law by which governments purport to rule should be such that it can actually guide human conduct.' Andrei Marmor, 'The Rule of Law and its Limits' (2004) 23 *Law and Philosophy* 1, 2. Examples could be easily multiplied.

and institutions of law'.[27] An exercise of power is arbitrary in the sense relevant to the rule of law when 'the agent answers only to his or her own *arbitrium*'.[28] This does not mean unreasoned or unpredictable, but unaccountable, 'exercised at the pleasure of its agent'.[29] This, Postema argues, is the core idea of the rule of law throughout history, and it also provides a coherent ideal that can unite the various elements traditionally associated with the rule of law.

Postema uses this understanding to argue for two important corrections to common treatments of the rule of law. First, he argues that in addition to observance of the principles of legality, the rule of law is only concretely realized within a polity where 'members of that polity embrace and practise a distinctive ethos'.[30] The core of his chapter is a defence of what he calls the 'fidelity thesis', which claims that the law rules in a polity only when its members embrace that ethos. Non-arbitrariness is linked, on Postema's account, to accountability and the fidelity thesis is, centrally, an account of mutual accountability whereby the responsibilities of accountability 'are owed *by all* who enjoy law's benefits *to all* who are subject to law's burdens'.[31] Second, Postema argues that the rule of law must attend to the social dimensions of power. This includes addressing power arbitrarily exercised by 'private' entities, understanding that the transactional lawyer may be more important than the courts for many, and that the legal norms that guide individuals must be understood in relation to their uptake by agents situated within a horizon of shared social understandings.

Whatever, on the best account, the rule of law *is*, William Lucy argues in 'The Rule of Law and Private Law', it is not arbitrary power. But what is meant by this is ambiguous. Lucy distinguishes among four different circumstances in which power can be said to be exercised arbitrarily. The first is when power is exercised 'without warrant and legitimacy'.[32] The second is when it is 'exercised without warrant by those who usually or sometimes have warrant to exercise power'.[33] The third is when power is exercised inconsistently. The fourth is when power is exercised unreasonably. Lucy argues that, while not all instances of arbitrariness involve the breach of rule-of-law principles and not all rule-of-law principles are directly connected to non-arbitrariness, adherence to the generally accepted rule-of-law principles, such as are articulated by Fuller, Hart, and Raz, protects members of a polity from subjection to arbitrary power in one or more of these senses.

Reflection on the senses of arbitrariness against which the rule of law protects us, Lucy argues, can help to decentre the primacy of the public law framing of the rule of law. His principal claim is that the doctrines that comprise the laws of property, tort, contract, and trusts promote just those values upheld by the rule of law but do so in the context of relations between individuals and not just in terms of relations

[27] Gerald J Postema, 'Fidelity in Law's Commonwealth' this volume ch 1, 17.
[28] Postema, 'Fidelity in Law's Commonwealth' (n 27) 18.
[29] Postema, 'Fidelity in Law's Commonwealth' (n 27) 18.
[30] Postema, 'Fidelity in Law's Commonwealth' (n 27) 20.
[31] Postema, 'Fidelity in Law's Commonwealth' (n 27) 21.
[32] William Lucy, 'The Rule of Law and Private Law' this volume ch 2, 46.
[33] Lucy, 'The Rule of Law and Private Law' (n 32) 46.

between individuals and the state. According to Hart, Raz, and Fuller, these rule-of-law values are freedom from interference, autonomy, and dignity. To these Lucy adds a fourth, freedom as non-domination. On Lucy's account, then, one way a polity manifests its commitment to the rule of law is by securing a regime of private law. An account of the rule of law cast exclusively in terms of constraints on government action is, to that extent, incomplete.

These are central claims in TRS Allan's contribution to this volume, as announced in its title, 'The Rule of Law as the Rule of Private Law', though for Allan the connection between the rule of law and private law is perhaps even deeper than it is for Lucy. '[P]rivate law', Allan argues, '*is* precisely the operation of the rule of law—the provision and enforcement of standards of legality in the context of civil society.'[34] And, again as for Lucy, for Allan it is the idea that the rule of law protects us from arbitrary exercises of power that provides the link to private law. Drawing on Hayek's account, Allan argues that the rule of law is not just about protection against the abuses of law, or the securing of predictability, but also involves securing a sphere of freedom as independence where individuals can pursue their own ends free from conscription into the public ends of the state or the ends of others. Allan goes even further, arguing that the demands of non-arbitrariness also imply a deep connection between the rule of law and both equality and justice. This places a robust sphere of private law at the heart of our understanding of the rule of law, and shows how the rule of law can limit the ends that the state can seek.

On Allan's account, then, there is a deep connection between the rule of law and the concept of law: it follows from the right understanding of what the rule of law requires, on his view, that the positivist separation of law and morality is cast into doubt. In 'Liberty and Legal Form', David Dyzenhaus draws the same link, borne as it is in Allan's view by reflection on the way the rule of law bears on private law. Dyzenhaus argues that the rule of law 'governs public and private law in the same way' and that 'its government ensures that the law has a moral quality to it, since law, in being (as it must) legal, constitutes a politically valuable condition of liberty—civil liberty'.[35] While Hayek's account of the rule of law serves as Allan's starting point, central to Dyzenhaus's argument is a defence of Fuller's understanding of the reciprocal and interactional dimensions of law as well as the republican understanding of liberty as non-domination, according to which law is both a necessary and sufficient condition of liberty. And, in contrast with Postema's account of both fidelity and the horizontal dimensions of the rule of law, for Dyzenhaus the role of the courts, and the institution of adjudication, is central.

Despite this connection between the rule of law and private law, Dyzenhaus denies that private law is *required* by the rule of law. In making this claim, Dyzenhaus also contests the view, held by Kantian corrective justice theorists, that the immanent morality of private law is fundamentally different from that of

[34] TRS Allan, 'The Rule of Law as the Rule of Private Law' this volume ch 3, 86 (emphasis added).
[35] David Dyzenhaus, 'Liberty and Legal Form' this volume ch 4, 92.

public law. Fuller's account of the immanent morality of law, Dyzenhaus argues, does not require us to make any such distinction and is in this sense superior to the Kantian position that distinguishes between private and public right.

In 'Unseating Unilateralism', Evan Fox-Decent argues that Hobbes offers us an account of legality that illuminates the shared fundamental organizing principles of private and public law. Unlike Dyzenhaus, who disputes the claim that private and public law exhibit different internal moralities, Fox-Decent claims that they may indeed express different forms of justice but they nonetheless 'co-habit the same overarching normative structure, with neither enjoying normative priority over the other'.[36] This normative structure is the prohibition on unilateralism, that is, the principle that 'no private party is ever entitled to dictate terms or enforce justice claims unilaterally against another'.[37]

The prohibition on unilateralism has two aspects for Hobbes, each of which has been taken up in subsequent rule-of-law literature. The first is its emphasis on the agency-enabling role that law and rule-of-law principles play in providing a public framework for interaction. As Fox-Decent points out, we can see this concern expressed in different ways in both Raz and Fuller. The second is the way in which rule-of-law principles (for Hobbes, 'equity') constrain the interpretation of statutes. According to Fox-Decent, Hobbes's views are echoed in Dicey's common law constitutionalism.

Zipursky takes a very different position regarding the relationship between the canonical expressions of the rule of law and the organizing principles underpinning private law in 'Torts and the Rule of Law'. He argues that tort law fails in relation to Fuller's principles of legality, such as generality, promulgation, non-retroactivity, and clarity, but that this is not a failure of tort law but should instead force us to revise our understanding of the rule of law.

According to Zipursky, Fuller's focus on legal systems and forms of governance threatens to overshadow other roles the law plays, to which the rule of law applies in distinctive ways. Tort law, the focus of his article, is not a form of governance but rather a system that empowers individuals to make enforceable demands of others as redress for wrongful injury. Looked at in this way, we can see that tort law's departures from Fuller's principles of legality are not necessarily departures from the rule of law.

Tort law constrains individual power in two principal ways. First, it protects plaintiffs from private power and domination in providing them a means of redress for wrongful injury. Second, it protects defendants through constraining the ways in which plaintiffs can use the power of the state in seeking redress, and it is here that we see tort instantiate rule-of-law principles that are distinct from though in ways analogous to the desiderata enumerated by Fuller. So, for example, the law of tort arguably fails the requirement of generality because (among other reasons)

[36] Evan Fox-Decent, 'Unseating Unilateralism' this volume ch 5, 117.

[37] Fox-Decent, 'Unseating Unilateralism' (n 36) 117. Note that Fox-Decent's account of unilateralism is broadly congruent with Postema's understanding of the kind of arbitrariness against which the rule of law is set.

'good fortune—the fact that misconduct that could easily cause injury happens not to do so—completely immunizes a tortious actor, so there is a gross disparity in the liability of those to behave identically'.[38] But once we recall that the point of tort 'is not to constrain conduct as such, but to protect against right-invasions'[39] we realize this shouldn't cause rule-of-law worries. Instead we can see that tort respects the rule of law by imposing the requirements that the plaintiff must have actually suffered some injury and that the defendant's conduct must have been wrongful in relation to her. These requirements collectively ensure that '[i]ndividuals who face the prospect of tort liability for their actions do not face [civil] actions for redress by everyone'[40] and thus serve to protect potential civil defendants in the way that traditional rule-of-law requirements protect potential criminal defendants.

In 'Private Law Pluralism and the Rule of Law', Hanoch Dagan addresses (among other things) the rule-of-law principle that the law must be able to guide conduct, and its relationship to determinacy in the law. As a contemporary defender of Legal Realism, Dagan's focus is on the indeterminacy debate that has animated the formalism v realism debate in its various iterations. For Dagan, it is not doctrinal landscape of black-letter law that renders law determinate but the 'broader social practice of law', including lawyers' understandings and the prevalent social understandings of the character of various private law institutions.[41] Unlike a number of the contributors to this volume who defend the main divisions of private law—property, tort, contract, and unjust enrichment—as involving core moral organizing principles, Dagan is a 'structural pluralist' who argues that each of these broad categories collects a heterogeneous group of relatively discrete smaller legal categories guided each by its own distinctive animating principle. Not only is this compatible with the rule of law, Dagan argues that it has a number of advantages over 'monist' conceptions of law because smaller discrete categories of the law that are more internally coherent than the broad categories to which they belong can be more determinate in practice. Moreover, having multiple private law institutions to choose amongst in ordering one's relationships can dilute concerns about the power of judges or legislatures, and thus structural pluralism can equally well account for the constraining function of the rule of law.

Unlike a number of other contributors to this volume, Dagan defends a perfectionist account of the law that, for him, is broadly Razian. The state has an obligation to promote human flourishing and 'to empower people to make choices among viable alternatives, and thus be the authors of their own lives'.[42] For him, such an account of autonomy is also better facilitated through multiple diverse private law institutions that express different values (or balances of values) among which individuals can freely navigate. This combination of perfectionism, pluralism, and realism, Dagan argues, operates in a manner that is not at odds with the

[38] Benjamin Zipursky, 'Torts and the Rule of Law' this volume ch 6, 144.
[39] Zipursky, 'Torts and the Rule of Law' (n 38) 150.
[40] Zipursky, 'Torts and the Rule of Law' (n 38) 151.
[41] Hanoch Dagan, 'Private Law Pluralism and the Rule of Law' this volume ch 7, 174.
[42] Dagan, 'Private Law Pluralism and the Rule of Law' (n 41) 159.

rule of law and might actually promote its values better than monist formalist accounts.

3. The Rule-of-Law Contribution to Private Law

Just as a focus on the private law can help us understand the nature of the rule of law, a focus on the rule of law can provide a source of insight and critique in relation to various aspects of the private law. Previous essays have already suggested, in a variety of ways, that since the rule of law applies to private law, it provides a set of norms against which to evaluate aspects of the private law. The following essays take up this theme. In doing so, they also provide general insights into the rule of law.

In 'Strict Duties and the Rule of Law', Stephen Smith argues that strict duties in private law run afoul of the rule of law. Smith focuses on strict legal *duties* rather than the more familiar category of strict liability since such liability is generally thought to follow upon the breach of a strict legal duty. For example, the duty not to trespass is a strict duty since even if I could not have reasonably known that I was trespassing, I breach the duty simply by entering another's land without her permission. He argues that such duties are incompatible with the rule of law because they provide individuals with too much guidance (rather than, as is the more common shortcoming, too little). They provide too much guidance because they instruct individuals to take more than reasonable care to avoid particular outcomes and the law cannot intend that individuals take 'unreasonable' care. This sends a mixed message, where the law cannot possibly mean what it appears to mean. And this is a problem for the rule of law.

Smith considers, and rejects, three possible responses: that strict duties support justified liabilities, that strict duties are not enforced, and that strict duties are substantively justified. Instead, Smith argues, the solution is to see these not as duties at all but as 'liabilities that arise without wrongdoing'.[43] We can therefore have strict legal liabilities, but not strict legal duties.

In 'Some Rule-of-Law Anxieties about Strict Liability in Private Law', John Gardner argues that some rule-of-law concerns might have more purchase in relation to criminal law than they do in relation to private law. In particular, Gardner argues against the claim that strict tort liability is objectionable on rule-of-law grounds, owing to the fact that one cannot follow a rule if one cannot find out if one is breaking it, or have a way of avoiding breaking it. Hart objected to strict criminal liability along these lines. Gardner argues that the objection does not apply to strict tort liability, and in making his case responds to Stephen Smith's arguments in his contribution to this volume.

Unlike criminal liability, with tort liability *both* the plaintiff and the defendant are affected by the legal rule: 'What the defendant gains from there being fault

[43] Stephen A Smith, 'Strict Duties and the Rule of Law' this volume ch 8, 189.

liability, the plaintiff loses; what the defendant loses from there being strict liability, the plaintiff gains.'[44] Plaintiffs and defendants share the same rule-of-law interest in having legal norms that conform to the principles of legality. Gardner argues that the plaintiff's complaint regarding strict liability is that the defendant's rule-of-law gain (from fault-based liability) is a loss to the plaintiff in some other way than a loss in rule-of-law values. It follows, then, that rule-of-law values can be more flexibly applied to the norms of private law. Gardner also adopts Fuller's understanding of strict liability as a kind of tax on some activities. So, for example, although liability associated with injuring people from blasting operations is strict, liability can be avoided by not engaging in the blasting business. This mitigates the rule-of-law concerns, at least in the context of what Gardner calls activity-specific strict liability. And it also shows, Gardner argues, that Smith is wrong to say that we can only understand strict liability as arising on the basis of a duty that cannot be understood to require what it seems to require of those subject to it.

In 'Property, Equity, and the Rule of Law', Henry Smith provides a rule-of-law defence of the role of equity in moderating the formality of private law. Smith argues that we should understand private law as a hybrid of formal law and equity, where equity offers a limited 'safety valve' that protects against the opportunistic exploitation of law's formality. In doing so, equity actually strengthens both the formal law and the rule of law.

According to Smith, with Legal Realism, equity 'slipped its bounds and became a preference for contextualized standards and discretion, in opposition to traditional formalism within private law and to the liberal notion of the rule of law'.[45] Traditional rule-of-law values, like generality, stability, and notice, are congruent with the features of private law that manage information costs. However, this formality can be exploited, both in relation to the private law and in relation to the rule of law more generally. In protecting against opportunistic evasion, Smith argues, equity has us look to the purpose of law outside the formal system, employing the language of morality and good faith, mediated through custom. This provides 'a reason to move one step toward thicker versions of the rule of law that incorporate morality and legitimacy'.[46]

In 'Equity and the Rule of Law', Dennis Klimchuk argues that at least those doctrines of the law of equity that can be understood to be equitable in Aristotle's sense uphold rather than undermine the rule of law. A doctrine is equitable in Aristotle's sense, according to Klimchuk, if it prevents someone from being, in Aristotle's words, a 'stickler in a bad way' by exploiting the generality of legal rules. (This is nearly the idea Smith describes in language of opportunism.) The law of equity responds to the stickler by imposing constraints on the exercise of her strict (historically common law) rights. Klimchuk considers four examples of equitable doctrines that, on his reconstruction, work this way: equitable estoppel, *laches*, the fiduciary obligations imposed on company directors, and trusts.

[44] John Gardner, 'Some Rule-of-Law Anxieties about Strict Liability in Private Law' this volume ch 9, 211.

[45] Henry E Smith, 'Property, Equity and the Rule of Law' this volume ch 10, 235.

[46] Smith, 'Property, Equity and the Rule of Law' (n 45) 226.

The doctrines through which these second-order constraints on the exercise of rights are imposed uphold the rule of law, Klimchuk argues, in a way analogous to the doctrines that serve to mark the point at which public office-holders abuse their powers. One who acts within but in abuse of her rights, in both contexts, acts arbitrarily in just the sense, on Klimchuk's account, against which the rule of law is set (a sense akin to but not quite identical with some of those identified by Postema and Lucy).

In 'The Power of the Rule of Law', Lisa Austin argues that the relationship between property and the rule of law is more complex than traditional accounts, such as Hayek's, suggest. According to Austin, private ownership does not protect a sphere of individual liberty from state interference so much as it provides individuals with legal powers to secure legal consequences not otherwise possible. Law must be able to guide, but not so that individuals can plan their activities in order to avoid legal sanctions; law guides so that individuals can follow the instructions necessary to exercise their property powers. These powers, and the guidance that make their exercise possible (and not merely effective), enlarge the scope of individual liberty through making future-oriented planning possible in a number of ways.

Although Austin argues that there is a constitutive relationship between property, when understood in terms of legal powers, and the rule of law, when understood in terms of its guidance function, there is another sense in which property and the rule of law are in potential tension. As many other contributors argue, a central meaning of the rule of law is that it constrains the arbitrary exercise of power. However, private ownership involves the conferral of private legal powers that look like they can be exercised arbitrarily. According to Austin, whether property powers express individual liberty or become the instruments of private domination depends on context; considerations of equality—both juridical equality and substantive equality—are central to any such contextual analysis.

In 'Boilerplate: A Threat to the Rule of Law?', Margaret Jane Radin suggests that the use of fine print (boilerplate) to delete basic background rights may undermine the rule of law when the deletions are used against wide swaths of the public, especially when they result in loss of the right of redress. She argues that the rule of law requires that some rights are 'permanently in the care of the polity' and non-waivable by individuals.[47] She focuses in particular on the waiver of remedies, arguing that '[t]hose in a position to deploy mass-market boilerplate deleting recipients' remedies against them are using and reinforcing their power over recipients by doing so.'[48] This is both arbitrary and contrary to the idea of equality before the law, and furthermore subversive of democratic rights, when and to the extent that rights erased by boilerplate have been secured through democratic processes.

Radin concludes, against both Legal Realist arguments that aim to collapse private law into public law and public choice theory arguments that aim to collapse

[47] Margaret Jane Radin, 'Boilerplate: A Threat to the Rule of Law?' this volume ch 13, 291.
[48] Radin, 'Boilerplate: A Threat to the Rule of Law?' (n 47) 297.

the public into the private, that 'some semblance of a public/private distinction' must be maintained, 'simply because some rules must remain in the care of the polity'.[49] According to Radin, the privatization of legal infrastructure 'becomes a scheme of arbitrary power'[50] and is not consistent with the ideals of the liberal state or the rule of law. Public law is necessary for a system of private ordering.

Like Radin, Arthur Ripstein, in 'The Rule of Law and Time's Arrow', argues that the rule of law demands a public legal system for there to be private rights. This is not just a claim about the need for effective enforcement, but is meant to be constitutive: a legal system makes rights determinate, not just secure. In order to have determinative rights, Ripstein argues, there must be a procedure for resolving disputes and the passage of time figures as an aspect of such procedure. In this way he argues both that limitation periods express an idea of the rule of law and that this account is superior to other familiar justifications, including accounts of rights 'fading', concerns about stale evidence, and claims about legal certainty.

Limitation periods, by providing closure to disputes, make rights determinate on a system-wide basis. In addition, according to Ripstein, this rationale connects with one of the basic organizing ideas of private law, which is the individual's 'right to his or her own good name'.[51] Individuals have the right to be free of accusations, which in turn requires a time limit for allegations of wrongdoing.

4. Conclusion

As the contributions to this volume show, the rule of law is not essentially a public law doctrine. A variety of themes emerge in these essays, all of them underscoring how reflection upon the rule of law can help us understand the relationship between public and private law in new ways. Many authors emphasize the role that private law plays in securing individuals from the arbitrary exercise of power, both from the state and from other individuals. This insight is sometimes marshalled to defend private law and sometimes marshalled to offer resources for critique. Other authors argue that understanding the ways in which the rule of law is expressed within private law requires a revision to some of the traditional ways of thinking about the rule of law, including our thinking about Fuller's principles of legality and formalist accounts of law. Still others argue that the rule of law can help us to understand what connects public law and private law as examples of law. And, finally, many offer examples of private law concerns that are usefully illuminated through rule-of-law themes, including strict liability, limitation periods, equity, and 'boilerplate'. It is our hope that these essays are just the beginning of a much larger enquiry into the relationship between private law and the rule of law.

[49] Radin, 'Boilerplate: A Threat to the Rule of Law?' (n 47) 301.
[50] Radin, 'Boilerplate: A Threat to the Rule of Law?'(n 47) 300.
[51] Arthur Ripstein, 'The Rule of Law and Time's Arrow' this volume ch 14, 316.

PART I

THE PRIVATE LAW CONTRIBUTION TO THE RULE OF LAW

1

Fidelity in Law's Commonwealth

Gerald J Postema

> [A] better kynde of Monorchie hathe byne by common Assent ordayned and establyshed, wherein the Prince (not by Lycentious will and Imoderate Assertions but by the Law, That is by the prudent Rules *and* Preceptes of Reason agreed vppon *and* made the Covenant of the Common Wealth) may Justly governe and commande, and the People in due obedience saeflie lyve and quyetly enioye their owne.[1]

Although it is widely contested, and sometimes thought to be indefinitely elastic, the rule of law, in its core notion, is a relatively straightforward ideal. Throughout its long history, the idea of the rule of law has been rooted in the twofold thought that (1) a polity is well ordered when its members are secured against the arbitrary exercise of power and that (2) law, because of its distinctive features, is especially if not uniquely capable of providing such security. That is, the rule of law promises protection and recourse against the arbitrary exercise of power through the distinctive offices and institutions of law.

Power, for purposes of this discussion, is a capacity to influence or control the practical decisions or actions of rational, self-directing agents. The control may involve more or less direct physical interference with an agent's actions (or capacity to act), or it may involve restructuring an agent's options. The control may be coercive, but it need not be, and it may be exercised through active interventions, but it might also do its work quietly in the background. As neo-republican political theorists remind us, one can be in the power, under the *dominion*, of another in a way that can decisively shape one's choices and actions, without the active intervention of the *dominus*.[2] Also, subjection to the power of another, again for purposes of this discussion, is not a 'natural' fact like being subject to the

[1] James Morice in lectures on the royal prerogative at the Middle Temple in 1579, BL Additional MS 36,081 fo 231, quoted by Christopher W Brooks in 'The Ancient Constitution in Sixteenth Century Legal Thought' in Ellis Sandoz (ed), *The Roots of Liberty: Magna Carta, Ancient Constitution, and the Anglo-American Tradition of the Rule of Law* (University of Missouri 1993) 71.

[2] See for example Philip Pettit, *A Theory of Freedom* (Polity Press 2001) 78, 137, Philip Pettit, *On the People's Terms* (Cambridge University Press 2012) 1–3, 7.

force of gravity or to threats from a menacing animal, that is, it is not a matter of the probability of the intervention or interference of some other force. Rather, it is an interpersonal, or second-personal, matter, a matter of decisions, choices, and actions of one responsible agent with respect to another, usually expecting or anticipating a response from that other agent. Exercising and responding to power are ways persons relate to each other; power relations are interpersonal, not merely objective, relations.

The rule of law sets its face against 'arbitrary' power and its exercise. But, as William Lucy observes,[3] there are many ways in which power or its exercise can be said to be 'arbitrary'. So, we must isolate the sense invoked by this understanding of the core aim of the rule of law. According to Raz, an exercise of power 'is arbitrary only if it was done either with indifference as to whether it will serve the purposes which alone can justify the use of that power or with the belief that it will not serve them'.[4] Sometimes we say an act is arbitrary if it is entirely without reason, or without sufficient reason, or under-determined by reason. However, the rule of law puts a relatively specific meaning of 'arbitrary' in view, which is only tangentially related to these. Closer to the rule of law's concern, an exercise of power may be said to be arbitrary if it is *ultra vires*, either in the sense of being entirely without warrant or being outside legitimately held warrant. But this does not quite capture the rule of law's concern either. Rather, an exercise of power is arbitrary in the rule-of-law relevant sense when it is the expression of the *libero arbitrium*, the free decision or choice, of its agent.[5] The act may be reasonable, reasoned, or otherwise justified, but it is still arbitrary if it is taken entirely at the will or pleasure of the agent. Actions of the *dominus* (master) or one who has *dominium* were in ancient times thought to be arbitrary in this sense. Although the actions might have been assessable in light of relevant norms or standards, the agent was not answerable for it. An arbitrary action, done at the pleasure of the agent, is a unilateral exercise of power: the agent answers only to his or her own *arbitrium*. The agent's judgment is the only relevant deliberative perspective. Leontes captured the idea: 'Our prerogative | Calls not your counsels . . . We need no more of your advice: the matter, | the loss, the gain, the ordering on't, is all | Properly ours.'[6] Arbitrary power is not necessarily unreasoned, or unpredictable, or even in a strict sense unruly; rather, it is unaccountable, exercised at the pleasure of its agent.

Pettit adds that an act of interference is arbitrary 'if it is chosen or rejected without reference to the interests, or opinions, of those affected. The choice is not forced to track what the interests of those others require according to their own judgements.'[7] And more recently he writes that interference is arbitrary if it is

[3] William Lucy, 'The Rule of Law and Private Law' in this volume ch 2, s 2.

[4] Joseph Raz, 'The Rule of Law and its Virtue' in *The Authority of Law* (2nd edn, Oxford University Press 2009) 219.

[5] 'An act is perpetrated on an arbitrary basis . . . if it is subject just to the *arbitrium*, the decision or judgment of the agent; the agent was in a position to choose it or not choose it, at their pleasure' (Philip Pettit, *Republicanism: A Theory of Freedom and Government* (Oxford University Press 1997) 55).

[6] William Shakespeare, *The Winter's Tale* (first published 1623; Oxford University Press 1914) II i 196–7, 201–3.

[7] Pettit, *Republicanism* (n 5) 55.

'uncontrolled by the person on the receiving end'.[8] These elaborations depart from the notion of arbitrariness lying at the heart of the rule of law's concern. First, the concern of the rule of law is not with the lack of controls in general, but lack of *answerability*. Second, the rule of law requires power to answer to norms of law to which the agent is otherwise bound, but not necessarily to the interests of those affected by the exercise of power. Third, the notion of answerability does not build reciprocity into it. I will argue below that law's rule requires mutual accountability—that is the core of the fidelity thesis—but this does not follow directly from the notion of arbitrariness. This mutuality thesis (I call it *Kant's Thesis* below) must be argued for, not built into the governing idea.

The rule of law, I maintain, promises protection and recourse against exercises of power that are arbitrary in this sense. This is its core, defining aim. Where law rules, power is systematically rendered non-arbitrary. The argument for this understanding of the orienting aim of the rule of law proceeds from two quarters. The first is historical: although other ideas sound as well, this is the dominant *motif* heard over the long history of thought and argument about the rule of law. The second is systematic: this core idea provides an illuminating and broadly attractive principle in terms of which the various, often contested, elements of the rule of law—its constituent standards, institutions, and conditions—can be selected and situated in a coherent and compelling conception of that political ideal. This principle makes clear the connection between an important political value and salient features of law in a way that disciplines and directs debate over constituent elements. However, I will not make this argument here. Neither will I enter the lists for the contests between relatively thin formal-procedural conceptions of the rule of law and the variety of more robust conceptions that build into the conception substantive equality, or civil, political, or welfare rights, or principles of democracy. Rather, taking the above core idea as a starting point, I will here address two issues that are rarely discussed by those who think seriously about the rule of law.

First, I wish to direct attention to the horizontal or societal dimension of law and its rule. The rule of law at its core promises protection and recourse against the arbitrary exercise of power, but such power can take many different forms: some are political, wielded by those who claim authority to govern or by those governed; some are societal, wielded by parties outside of government over others also outside of government. The rule-of-law ideal aspires to take all of forms of power exercised in a polity within its scope. It undertakes to 'bridle' the power of those who govern,[9] but it also promises to 'hedge' the exercise of societal power.[10] This

[8] Pettit, *On the People's Terms* (n 2) 58.

[9] 'The king must not be under man but under God and under the law, because law makes the king.... Let him, therefore, temper his power by law, which is the bridle of power, that he may live according to the laws' (Henry de Bracton, *On the Laws and Customs of England*, trans Samuel E Thorne (Belknap Press 1968) 33, 305).

[10] 'Laws are the people's Birth-right.... By this Hedge their All is secured against the Injuries of men' (Preamble, *Book of the General Lawes and Libertyes* (of Massachusetts) (1660), quoted in John Phillip Reid, *Rule of Law: The Jurisprudence of Liberty in the Seventeenth and Eighteenth Centuries* (Northern Illinois University Press 2004) 51).

essay will defend the centrality to the rule-of-law ideal of protecting individuals against power wielded by non-governmental individuals and entities.[11]

Second, I propose to explore the conditions of the realization of the rule-of-law ideal. For the rule of law to flourish in a polity, it is not enough that those in power rule *by* law—exercise their power for the most part through the instrumentality of the law—because the rule of law demands *reflexivity*: those who use law in their exercise of power must likewise be subject to it. The rule of law obtains in a community just when *law rules*. The thesis I shall defend, the 'fidelity thesis', maintains that law rules—that is, the rule of law is robust in a polity—only when members of that polity embrace and practise a distinctive ethos. Thus, I shall argue that, in addition to standards of *legality*—the formal, procedural, and institutional aspects of the ideal—the rule-of-law notion comprises a set of relationships and responsibilities rooted in core convictions and commitments, which are essential for the realization of this ideal. I associate this set of relationships, responsibilities, and commitments with the notion of *fidelity to law*. Fidelity involves a commitment of mutual accountability. The fidelity thesis is that a robust practice of holding each other accountable under the law is essential for the realization of law's rule. Taken together *legality* and *fidelity* constitute the ideal of the rule of law. That is to say, the rule-of-law ideal incorporates both standards of legality and standards of fidelity; and the rule of law is realized when laws and legal institutions by and large conform to the standards of legality and the convictions, commitments, and practices answering to the standards of fidelity are in place and healthy.

The two theses of this essay are complementary. Fidelity's commitments hold not just among the legal or ruling elite, or between citizens and officials of the state, but also among fellow members of the polity. Ultimately, fidelity is owed by individuals not *to law* or *to government*, but *to each other*, that is, to fellow members of law's commonwealth. Fidelity is the animating soul of law's commonwealth.

1. The Fidelity Thesis

Unlike legality, the focus of which is formal and institutional, the focus of fidelity is ethical. It is concerned with the ethos of a polity, the mutual understandings and associated practices of people in a community in which the rule of law is realized.

[11] A companion essay explores the political or vertical dimension of the rule of law. See Gerald J Postema, 'Law's Rule: Reflexivity, Mutual Accountability, and the Rule of Law' in Zhai Xiaobo and Michael Quinn (eds), *Bentham's Theory of Law and Public Opinion* (Cambridge University Press 2014) 7–39.

1.1 Fidelity as mutual accountability

Fuller's familiar argument for the moral character of his eight canons offers us orienting insight into the fidelity ethos.[12] The rule of law, he argued, presupposes and nurtures a partnership, a set of robust reciprocal commitments, between government officials and ordinary citizens. His eight canons, in his view, articulate this partnership: rulers pledge to rule with and to be ruled by law and ordinary citizens allow their conduct to be governed by those who so pledge. Reciprocal compliance with the law is at the core of Fuller's idea.

Adam Ferguson suggests a way to elaborate Fuller's notion. The law's capacity to rule (and hence protect liberty), he wrote, lies in 'the influence of men resolved to be free; of men, who, having adjusted in writing the terms on which they are to live with the state, and with their fellow-subjects, are determined, by their vigilance and spirit, to make these terms be observed.'[13] Fidelity, this suggests, is expressed not only in compliance with law and the standards of legality, but also in active taking of responsibility for the lawful condition. In particular, it involves taking responsibility for holding partners in the relationship to their respective duties. Fidelity involves mutual accountability as well as reciprocal compliance. Thus, we must think of the rule of law not (merely) as a set of standards for law-making and law-enforcing, but also as an ordering of relationships by mutual commitment to a shared and common law and reciprocal responsibilities with respect to it. Primary among these responsibilities is the mutual responsibility to hold each other accountable under this law. The fidelity thesis holds in part that the rule of law is robust in a polity just when its members, and not merely the legal or ruling elite, take responsibility for holding each other and especially law's officials to account under the law.

But the fidelity thesis pushes the Fuller–Ferguson notion further. It maintains that the relevant mutual commitments hold among members of the polity and not just between people and government officials; fidelity has an essential societal–horizontal as well as a political–vertical dimension. Moreover, the scope of fidelity's responsibilities is community wide, extending over the full reach of the law. Fidelity's responsibilities are owed *by all* who enjoy law's benefits *to all* who are subject to law's burdens.

1.2 Infidelity

Justice Khanna of the Supreme Court of India wrote, 'There can, indeed, be no greater indication of decay in the rule of law than a docile bar, a subservient judiciary and a society with a choked and coarsened conscience.'[14] The behaviour

[12] For a reconstruction of Fuller's argument, see Gerald J Postema, *A Treatise of Legal Philosophy and General Jurisprudence* xi: *Legal Philosophy in the Twentieth Century: The Common Law World* (Springer 2011) 153–8.

[13] Adam Ferguson, *An Essay on the History of Civil Society* (first published 1767), ed Fania Oz-Salzberger (Cambridge University Press 1995) 249.

[14] Quoted in Geoffrey de Q Walker, *The Rule of Law: Foundation of Constitutional Democracy* (University of Melbourne Press 1988) 18.

of officials and citizens during the era of Jim Crow racial segregation in the American South manifested this kind of decay.[15] It offers an appalling example of the failure of fidelity and its consequences.

The American South, from the late 1870s until the 1960s, saw a legally supported regime of racial segregation, called 'Jim Crow'. Although in some of its institutional manifestations Jim Crow racial segregation may have been at least colourably legal at the time, the blatant, intentional, and publicly humiliating inequality of access to public facilities of all sorts was not and the systematic violence that reinforced the practices of Jim Crow segregation was not just brutally unjust, it was morally and legally criminal. Violence in support of racial domination involving rape, kidnapping, terror, and murder was common, involving not isolated acts of rogue individuals, but widespread and systematic activities by private citizens that were officially tolerated, sanctioned, and abetted. No argument could be made that these violent actions were legally permitted, or that the legal protections provided to white citizens did not extend to their intended black victims. The violence targeted a specific social group with the undisguised aim of securing and maintaining their subordination to the community wielding arbitrary power. Moreover, the law was systematically ignored or publicly flouted by citizens and by officials up and down the governmental ranks. 'Jim Crow was a systematic, officially entrenched, public practice of illegality.'[16]

In the Jim Crow South law did not count.[17] There was a failure of congruence between the law professed and the practice of citizens and legal officials alike. However, this failure was not due to a lethal mix of public and secret laws or the uncertainty of wide official discretion, as is often the case. This incongruity was entirely public and there was little indeterminacy or uncertainty about the imposition of power. The informal rules of Jim Crow culture accorded arbitrary power to white individuals and officials in defiance of existing law. This was a failure of law: law failed to rule. It failed not through a defect of the legal norms or procedures, but through a failure of fidelity, dishonouring what James Morice called the covenant of law's commonwealth. It failed in both political and societal dimensions of the law's rule. The rule of law was truncated by state agents and private citizens alike and its promise was denied to fellow citizens to whom they owed duties of fidelity.

Jim Crow practices illustrate the thesis that law does its job of constraining abuse of power only when there is in place a culture or ethos of the rule of law. This ethos of fidelity involves not only a general willingness to submit to law's governance and

[15] The next few paragraphs draw heavily on Gerald J Postema, 'Law's Ethos: Reflections on a Public Practice of Illegality' (2010) 90 *Boston University Law Review* 1847. The description of Jim Crow practices offered here is indebted to David Lyons, 'The Legal Entrenchment of Illegality' in Matthew H Kramer et al (eds), *The Legacy of H.L.A. Hart* (Oxford University Press 2008). For a chilling detailed account of life under Jim Crow, see Isabel Wilkerson, *The Warmth of Other Suns* (Vintage Books 2010) 17–179.

[16] Postema, 'Law's Ethos' (n 15) 1850.

[17] Krygier and Mason argue that 'the rule of law requires that law *count,* which in turn requires that it be widely expected and assumed to count' (Martin Krygier and Whit Mason, 'Violence, Development and the Rule of Law' in George Mavrotas (ed), *Security and Development* (Edward Elgar 2011) 137–8).

to give deference to its limits and requirements,[18] but also an active engagement of citizens and officials of holding each other to their responsibilities under the law. The history of Jim Crow teaches further that law's rule fails when power is held to account only when it serves the interest of those doing the holding. Where Jim Crow was firmly in place, law did not count in and for relations between the whites and blacks in the community. No doubt officials and citizens in the white community needed to see their behaviour as justified in light of existing social standards, but the law was not among those standards. The white community's commitment to law failed precisely at the point where its protections extended to the people they sought to subjugate.

1.3 Alienation versus infidelity

Law's rule fails when law becomes irrelevant, when it or some significant portion of it does not count. Alienation, apathy, and resigned acceptance of corruption sap the rule of law of its vitality. But we must be careful here. The widespread sense of the irrelevance of law to daily life may manifest a massive failure of fidelity, but it might also manifest a different failure of law. In conditions of legal pluralism, it may manifest the failure of formal, government-imposed law to root itself in the community it purports to govern. In communities where this is true, it is possible that a robust fidelity is directed to some other common, public, albeit informal norms. Recall, fidelity is not a matter of mutual faithfulness to government or the state, or to government's law, but faithfulness of members of the community to each other with respect to some common governing norms. Thus, widespread alienation from government's law in a community may not signal *anomy* and failure of fidelity, but *polynomy* and commitment to norms other than government's law. In some cases, then, a more accurate characterization of the community would be that *law* rules, but it is a *different law* that rules.

However, we must not be too quick in such cases to accept that the rule of (informal) law is robust in the community. For it is possible that the core standards of the rule of law, and in particular its promised protection and recourse against the arbitrary exercise of power, may not be honoured by this alternative, informal law. Just as government's law may fail to meet formal or procedural rule-of-law standards, so too may informal, customary modes of law fall short. Fidelity is a necessary condition of the realization of the rule of law, but it is not sufficient.

What do these caveats imply for our analysis of the culture of the American South in the Jim Crow era? It is true that white citizens ignored or defiantly disobeyed the law that promised protection against violence to all citizens. They treated it as irrelevant to their behaviour and to their assessments of their neighbours' behaviour insofar as it applied to and protected black citizens. In some respects they followed an informal code that supported and encouraged racial oppression. Nevertheless, their behaviour manifested a massive failure of fidelity

[18] See also Jane Stromseth, David Wippman, and Rosa Brooks, *Can Might Make Rights? Building the Rule of Law After Military Interventions* (Cambridge University Press 2006) 75–8, 310–46.

and in consequence a failure of law to rule for two reasons. First, the informal racist code which may have guided the white community itself failed to meet the fundamental test of protecting all members of law's commonwealth against the arbitrary exercise of power. But, second and more importantly, it was a failure of fidelity because the white citizens were not alienated from the law in general; rather, they defiantly refused to acknowledge its application to fellow citizens they sought to oppress. Law failed to rule because when it was needed to make good on its promise to protect those governed by it, those bound to each other to vigilant efforts to sustain it failed to take their responsibilities seriously. The rule of law failed not because the government's law failed to take root in the community, but rather because members of the white community failed to take their responsibilities with respect to that law seriously, responsibilities owed to all members of their community.

2. The Horizontal Dimension of the Rule of Law

Power comes in many forms and is exercised in many different contexts. Theoretical discussions of the rule of law tend to concentrate on its public law dimensions and the exercise of political power—power exercised by those who govern over the governed and, perhaps, power of the governed over those who govern. But the rule of law is no less concerned with the arbitrary exercise of societal power. 'Whether or not the rule of law has claim in a society', Martin Krygier writes, 'is a matter found in the extent and quality of its reach and effects there: in interactions between citizens and the state, of course, but of equal or more importance, between citizens themselves.'[19] Of course, non-governmental power wielders include corporations and collectivities as well as individual citizens; indeed, their power is often far more potent, equalling or exceeding that of many governments.

2.1 Law as a mode of association

The rule of law is typically regarded as a *mode of governance*, a distinctive manner of exercising political power, but in the first instance it indicates a *mode of association*, a distinctive social formation, a way in which members of a polity regard, recognize, and relate to each other. This is the thought implicit in the claim that the rule of law obtains in a community in which all members are subject to a common set of laws[20] and hence are equal before the law (or perhaps we should say *equal in and through* the law). To say that members of the political community are equal before the law is to express an important fact about, and constraint upon, a government's treatment

[19] Martin Krygier, 'Four Puzzles about the Rule of Law: Why, What, Where? And Who Cares?' in James E Fleming (ed), *Getting to the Rule of Law* (New York University Press 2011) 89.

[20] Locke speaks of 'freedom of men under government' as the condition of having 'a standing Rule to live by, common to every one of that Society'. John Locke, *Two Treatises of Government*, ed Peter Laslett (Oxford University Press 1988) 284 (bk II ch 4 para 22).

of the governed, but it also captures a fact about, and commitment implicit in, relations among co-members of the polity.

Talk of law as a 'mode of association' brings to mind Michael Oakeshott's discussion of the rule of law.[21] Although I borrow Oakeshott's language, I want to distinguish my use of the term from his. Oakeshott understands the rule of law as a mode of moral, rather than enterprise, association. Enterprise associations, in his view, have specific goals or aims and the rules of association are oriented to achieving those aims, but members of moral associations are related 'transactionally';[22] they are related not via some common identity or purpose, but rather through their interactions in the course of pursuing individual aims or goals.[23] These interactions are structured by 'non-instrumental' mandatory rules, which impose only 'adverbial conditions' in the 'performance of self-chosen actions'.[24] Rather than prescribing specific ends to be achieved, they only impose conditions on the manner of pursing an agent's (law- and community-independent) ends. Moreover, these rules are understood to bind solely in virtue of mutual recognition by members of their authenticity.[25] Rules of law must meet two conditions: (1) they must be properly enacted and (2) they must qualify as *jus*.[26] The second condition is determined by 'an appropriately argumentative form of discourse in which to deliberate the matter'.[27]

Oakeshott's is a highly formal and very limited mode of association. Johannes Althusius, the sixteenth-century 'federalist' political theorist, offers a richer and more appealing conception. On this view, law's mode of association is that of defining a public constitution, a largely explicit social ordering, of rational self-directing *symbiotici* pledged to mutual communication of reciprocal rights, duties, and responsibilities.[28] Law enables members to come together, rather than merely keeping them apart, providing them with public means of mutual recognition and a medium for common and public deliberation. James Morice suggests this relationship can be modelled by the (biblical) idea of covenant. He refers to law as 'the Covenant of the common Wealth'.[29] Law's covenant is a covenant among people *with respect to* law—a network of mutual commitments to regard their polity as ordered by that law and to take responsibility for it. This covenant is at the heart of law, for, as I will argue later, law can rule in a commonwealth only if law's covenant has taken hold, only if it is rooted in a community of mutual faithfulness to differentiated and interconnected responsibilities of fidelity to law.

[21] As suggested by Lisa M Austin, 'Possession and the Distractions of Philosophy' in James Penner and Henry E Smith (eds), *The Philosophical Foundations of Property Law* (Oxford University Press 2013); Michael Oakeshott, 'The Rule of Law' in *On History and Other Essays* (Barnes & Noble Books 1983) 119–64.

[22] Oakeshott, 'Rule of Law' (n 21) 132.

[23] Michael Oakeshott, *On Human Conduct* (Clarendon Press 1975) 121–2.

[24] Oakeshott, 'Rule of Law' (n 21) 132–3, 136.

[25] Oakeshott, 'Rule of Law' (n 21) 137.

[26] Oakeshott, 'Rule of Law' (n 21) 136, 140–4.

[27] Oakeshott, 'Rule of Law' (n 21) 143.

[28] Johannes Althusius, *Politica*, ed FS Carney (Liberty Fund 1995) ch 1; *Symbiotici* ('symbiotes') are interdependent people sharing their public life together.

[29] Morice lectures at the Middle Temple (1579), quoted in Brooks, 'Ancient Constitution' (n 1).

2.2 Law's modus operandi

To appreciate the law's essential role in the ordering of horizontal relations, we must reflect on two relatively uncontroversial claims about law and its typical mode of functioning. First, we begin with the plausible claim that law—ie positive, civil, or 'human' law, as opposed to 'natural' or moral law—exists just insofar as it is the law of some community and is in place in that community. A community's law is not only law *for* that community, but the law *of* that community in virtue of being in force in that community. What is involved in law's being in force in a community? We would not judge a community to have a legal system in place just in virtue of the fact that some number of people got together and constructed a set of norms for their conduct and the conduct of all the other members of a community whose boundaries are also defined by the norms, especially if the rest of the community is ignorant of or generally ignores the norms. We would make the same judgment even if the behaviour of most of the members of the community on the whole is not inconsistent with those norms. In that case, we might say that their behaviour weakly complies with the norms, but the norms are still not in force in that community, because the compliance appears to be entirely coincidental.

What must be true of the community if law is in force in it is that its norms must be widely (but, of course, not universally) used by members of the community *in the right way*. What is it for law to be 'used in the right way'?[30] It is not easy to say, but we know it must make some difference to the way that members navigate the complex networks of social relations they face and that it must do so in ways that answer to the kind of thing it is, that is, in ways that answer to its characteristic mode of operating. Legal philosophers of different stripes for centuries have agreed that fundamental to law's typical mode of operating is that it offers normative guidance to rational agents capable of grasping its norms and applying them to their own concrete circumstances. If we accept this proposal, then we can say that law will be used in the right way when it plays a key or at least common and appropriate role in the deliberative–normative economy of a substantial number of those whom law purports to direct.

Further, we know that law does its characteristic work *in* public and *addressed to* a public. Thus, in order to guide the conduct of individuals, law must take into account the fact that these individuals find themselves in complex networks of social interaction that are shaped by their own understandings, and the understandings of others (and others' understandings of one's own understandings . . .) of the law that seeks to offer normative guidance. The success of the laws' guiding law-subjects depends on the uptake by those agents, and that uptake is determined by the public in which they act and the shared or overlapping understandings which shape their individual understandings of the horizons of their conduct.

[30] See Gerald J Postema, 'Conformity, Custom, and Congruence: Rethinking the Efficacy of Law' in Matthew Kramer (ed), *The Legacy of Hart* (Oxford University Press 2008) 45–65.

In view of these two very general features of law's modus operandi, the familiar top-down model of law can be seen to be a distortion of law's ordinary functioning. Law cannot be a game constructed and played only by a legal elite, if the rules of that game are meant to govern the conduct of parties outside the elite. Of course, it is possible for an elite to create such a game and play it with all seriousness, but what they create is not strictly speaking a *law* game. Likewise, it is a mistake to model law as 'a one-way projection of power', to use Fuller's apt phrase, not because a one-way projection of power is impossible, which it is not, nor because it is morally objectionable, although it is, but because it fails to acknowledge the conditions of its offering normative guidance to a public of rational agents. This is just to say that the societal dimension of law—the interactions and mutual understandings of law-subjects—is essential to law's ordinary functioning. The 'partnership' that Fuller envisioned at the foundations of law must have a robust horizontal dimension.

This horizontal dimension takes on richer texture if we look more closely at the typical manner in which law offers normative guidance. The model of commands that has proved irresistible for centuries does capture one mode of normative guidance—guidance by immediate directives—but there are other, equally important, modes of normative guidance utilized by law. At least since Hart's influential discussion of legal powers and power-conferring rules,[31] philosophers have recognized a form of indirect normative guidance. The law offers indirect guidance, it has been argued, by providing law-subjects facilities with which they can adjust their legal relations and thereby manage their social relations. This was an important addition to our understanding of the typical tools for normative guidance that are at the law's disposal; however, with a little thought we can identify other forms of indirect guidance that are characteristic of law's normal mode of operating. Two are worthy of mention here.[32]

First, in addition to directive guidance, law offers what we might call *constitutive* guidance. The law defines or constitutes positions, statuses, and roles, and associated procedures, bundled together in complex combinations of rights, duties, powers, liabilities, disabilities, and responsibilities. Perhaps the most familiar such constituted bundle is that which defines the duties, powers, and responsibilities of government enshrined in a state's constitution. But no less important are statuses and relationship networks that are the work of family law, employment law, and the like, on one level, and the work of business partnerships, trust arrangements, and the like, on another. Sometimes, these networks of norms—whether broad, general, and public, or more tailored and private—offer direct normative guidance. But often they operate at a different level, defining the horizons within which practical reasoning of law-subjects takes place rather than directives directly addressed to that

[31] Long before Hart, Roman law and canon law commentators recognized the 'nullifying power' of law (*vis irritantes*, or nullifying laws—*leges irritantes*) and its important role in guiding action. For a sophisticated discussion of the debate over the nature of law's nullifying power, see Francisco Suarez, *Tractatus de legibus ac Deo legislatore* (1612), Book 5, chapters 19–34 (Madrid: Consejo Superior de Investigaciones Científicas, Instituto Francisco de Vitoria, 1971), i. 374–541.

[32] See Postema, 'Conformity, Custom, and Congruence' (n 30) 55.

practical reasoning. Such networks provide the infrastructure within which meaningful social interaction takes place.

Second, the law often offers normative guidance by providing those who are subject to it resources for evaluating and vindicating in public terms their own conduct and the conduct of others in the political community and resources for holding others accountable for their conduct as measured in these public terms. In this way, members of the community direct their own decisions and actions and manage their relations with others, protecting, promoting, and repairing them. While it may be useful at some points for members to call on officials to assist and underwrite these activities, the law could not provide some of its most valuable normative guidance if that guidance depended entirely on ready access to officials, courts, and other formal legal institutions. While the law may be most visible in the conduct of police, the most frequent point of contact with the law for ordinary people may well be in the office of the transactional lawyer where vital social interactions often take place.

So, law in its ordinary mode of operating offers normative guidance in a number of ways. It is not impossible for a legal system to utilize only command-modelled directive guidance, but a system severely limited in this way would be as unlike our familiar system as a system in which coercion played no role or a system lacking all first-order power-conferring rules would be. But, then, we can conclude that also in these respects ordinary-functioning law characteristically has a fundamental horizontal dimension. Law orders the social relations among members of the community. It does so on the wholesale level by defining the parameters of family relations, employment, business partnerships, and the like; and it does so on the retail level when individuals construct their relationships in public, legal terms.

2.3 Property, power, and law's rule

Societal power exists outside of law, but also in and through it. And since the rule of law is concerned with all forms of power exercised in a polity that it can appropriately reach, it must address power exercised in the horizontal dimension. Indeed, Robin West maintains that the rule of law is 'quintessentially, the solution to the problem of private power'.[33] 'Law does a lot of things,' she observes, 'but one of its core functions is to protect individuals against what would otherwise be undeterred privations against them—not by overreaching state officials, but rather by undeterred private individuals, corporations, or entities.'[34] Power arbitrarily exercised is no less problematic from the point of view of the rule of law when it is exercised by non-governmental agents or entities than when exercised by officials or agencies. Unaccountable power is no less arbitrary for being 'private'. And if this is so, then law *rules* not only when government officials are bound by and held accountable to the law, but also when ordinary citizens structure their relations by

[33] Robin West, 'The Limits of Process' in James E Fleming (ed), *Getting to the Rule of Law: NOMOS L* (New York University Press 2011) 45.

[34] West, 'The Limits of Process' (n 33) 47.

law and hold each other accountable to the common, public terms that law provides.

The widespread use of mass-market boilerplate provisions in commercial transactions discussed by Margaret Radin in this volume[35] is a good example of the kind of exercise of power that contravenes the core concern of the rule of law and warrants careful scrutiny. Firms using such boilerplate provisions attempt unilaterally to opt out of the existing legal regime of rights, duties, and protections. They are enabled to exert such power by a combination of market conditions and law-created normative powers. Unchecked, the use of such devices is a genuine threat to the rule of law. Property regimes more generally, especially private property regimes, also warrant scrutiny and control for the same reason.

Private property is often defended as a bulwark against the intrusion of the arbitrary power of government. And actual ownership of property sufficient to sustain a decent life (not the mere capacity for such ownership) can provide a significant degree of protection, usually in combination with a number of other conditions and protections. But private ownership of resources and wealth also poses a potential threat of arbitrary power, created by law. This is serious if we wish to secure law's rule in the commonwealth. Private property can be a bulwark, but it must itself be bridled. If we are truly concerned about providing protection and recourse against the arbitrary exercise of power, then law must rule in the private as well as the public domain.

The problem for law's rule posed by private property regimes is not incidental to those regimes; it arises from their very nature. Property regimes allocate decision-making power over the use of resources in a polity. This law-created and law-allocated normative power underwrites and amplifies social power. As Lisa Austin argues in this volume,[36] the owner gets to decide how resources are used. This gives the owner power; and in social contexts of vastly unequal ownership this can be very great power. Such power is valuable to the owner, of course, and can be valuable to the society as a whole; but it can also be problematic. Not only is such power capable of abuse, but it is a potent source of domination of the kind that the rule of law is most concerned to protect against. It is not surprising, then, that Judge J Skelly Wright in *Robinson v Diamond Housing Corporation*[37] invoked the rule of law to justify preventing a landlord from unilaterally terminating a tenancy agreement in retaliation against the tenants' attempt to use the law to enforce their housing rights in court. The law provided recourse to tenants against landlords to force them to make improvements in their houses. Unilateral termination of the tenancy by the landlord was a clear exercise of arbitrary power in an attempt to deny the tenants enjoyment of their legal rights. Thus, the same principled concern that is often offered as a justification for private property regimes as protection against governmental domination calls for legal limits on

[35] Margaret Jane Radin, 'Boilerplate: A Threat to the Rule of Law?' in this volume.

[36] Lisa M Austin, 'The Power of the Rule of Law' in this volume.

[37] 463 F 2d 853 (DC Cir 1972) at 871; discussed in Margaret J Radin, 'Reconsidering the Rule of Law' (1989) 69 *Boston University Law Review* 781, 782, 817–19.

the exercise of the decisional power created and allocated by the law. These limits are not imposed from the outside, by values or principles in conflict with those that properly and persuasively underlie property, but rather they arise from the very principles on which it rests, internal to the normative structure of property itself.

3. Fidelity and Law's Rule

The fidelity thesis holds in part that law rules in a polity just when its members take responsibility for holding each other and especially law's officials to account under the law. One might defend this thesis on empirical grounds, but the argument I offer here is conceptual and normative in character.

3.1 Accountability

To begin, a word should be said about the notion of accountability in use here. Accountability is a *normatively structured interpersonal relationship*. A is accountable *to* B *for* some X—where A and B are individual or collective agents, B is usually a relatively determinate party and X is an act (activity, performance, or pursuit of a policy) broadly construed. This relationship is normatively structured in three respects: (1) A is normatively *liable* to be called to account by B and B not only can expect but has the normative *power* to call for or demand an accounting from A for X, and B has a *claim* to that accounting which A is *obligated* to provide; (2) this nexus of liability, power, claim, and obligation presupposes norms which authorize or provide warrant for B's claim and underwrite A's obligation; (3) A's act is norm governed in the sense that the accounting offered is expected to be articulated in terms of norms that warrant and justify it. A's accountability to B may and often does involve A's liability to and B's authorization to use formal sanctions, but this is not an essential element of accountability. Answerability to a charge or count (cause of action) is at the heart of the notion of accountability. B is authorized to demand both an *explanation* and a *reckoning*, that is, both a narrative and reasons or arguments connecting the act to relevant standards that could provide warrant and grounds for the act. B also has standing to assess them and issue a judgment of the action in light of the assessment of the explanation and reckoning offered.

The fidelity thesis connects law's rule with commonwealth-wide mutual accountability. The argument for this thesis begins with unpacking the notion of being subject to law.

3.2 Aquinas vs Hobbes

For law to rule in a community, it is not enough that its norms apply to those whom it rules, or even that their conduct conforms to them; in addition, those whom law rules must be, and take themselves to be, *subject* to the law. They must undertake a commitment; they must acknowledge their subjection. But this is not a matter of *self*-imposition. To be bound by self-imposed resolves or by self-directed commands is not to be bound *by law*. To be subject to law is to be subject to the judgment of another. He that 'setteth the laws above the sovereign', Hobbes wrote, 'setteth also a judge above him'.[38] The commitment involved in acknowledging that one is subject to the law accords to another the power to demand accountability. I will call this *Hobbes's Thesis*.

Hobbes's Thesis was not original with Hobbes. It had support amongst medieval commentators on Justinian's *Code*, but it was controversial, because it threatened the prince's claim to sovereign authority, expressed most starkly in the Roman Law doctrine, *princeps legibus solutus est*. Trying to thread his way between the latter doctrine and what was in effect Hobbes's Thesis, Aquinas (and many other medieval and early modern jurists) argued that the prince is subject to the directive force of the law, but not to its coercive force.[39] The prince is bound by the law and is subject to its directive force 'by his own will',[40] he argued, but 'no one can pass sentence of condemnation on him . . . there is no man who can judge the deeds of a king'.[41] *Aquinas's Thesis* holds that it is possible to be subject to the law but accountable to no one.[42]

The first step in defence of the fidelity thesis requires that we show why we must reject Aquinas's Thesis in favour of Hobbes's. We must reject it, not because self-limitations are impossible as a psychological matter (we sometimes succeed in holding ourselves to personal resolutions); not because (as Aquinas argued) no one can coerce himself[43] (Ulysses succeeded); not because (as Hobbes argued) no one is limited by restrictions one can freely lift[44] (because the problem arises even for agents who are not empowered to make laws). We must reject it because the notion of self-imposed, and so self-authorized, law entails a contradiction, namely, that one can have exclusive standing to judge whether one's actions fall under the norm.

The claim that one has exclusive standing to judge whether some action, A, falls under a norm N* can be analysed into two claims. (1) One *judges* P: A falls under N*. One judges of some subject matter, namely the action A and the norm N* that A falls under N*. In so judging one avows the correctness of P, in virtue of A, N*, and the relationship that obtains between them. Judging necessarily points away from the party making the judgment to the matter judged of. It is in that sense, self-transcending. So it is possible to distinguish between one's making the

[38] Thomas Hobbes, *Leviathan* (first published 1625), ed R Tuck (Cambridge University Press 1996) ch 29 para 9. From this premise, Hobbes concludes that the Sovereign, although he rules *with* and *through* the civil law and finds it prudent to follow it himself, *cannot be* subject to it.

[39] See Brian Tierney, '"The Prince is Not Bound by the Laws": Accursius and the Origins of the Modern State' (1963) 5 *Comparative Studies in Society and History* 391; *Digest* 1.3.31; Thomas Aquinas, *Summa Theologiae* IaII q 96, a5, ad 3.

[40] Aquinas suggests that he is morally required to do so, quoting for support the *Decretales* principle: 'whatever law a man makes for another, he should keep himself.'

[41] Aquinas, *Summa Theologiae* IaII q 96 a5, ad 3.

[42] Of course, the prince might be accountable to God, but only relative to divine or natural law and not relative to positive law.

[43] Aquinas, *Summa Theologiae* IaII q 96 a5, ad 3.

[44] Hobbes, *Leviathan* (n 38) ch 26 para 6.

judgment—*taking* something *to be so*—and its *being so.* (2) One asserts or claims *exclusive standing* to make this judgment of A relative to N* and thus that no one else is in a position to assess one's judgment. Note that since N* is a norm, it must exert some constraint on the assignment of an action as falling under it, at least in the sense that it must be possible for those seeking to apply it to go wrong, to make a mistake. It must not be the case that anything one lights upon as falling under N* *is so* just in virtue of the fact one *says so.* The application must be warranted by the norm, rather than being an assignment made, as it were, at one's pleasure. That is, if the assignment is not to be arbitrary (ie merely a matter of whim), it must be warranted by the norm and so must be self-transcending.

Clearly, claim (2), the claim to exclusive standing to judge whether A falls under N*, undermines (1). From the point of view of any other possible judge, it amounts to the claim that one's judgment is right solely because one has made it; the making or taking, rather than the content of the judgment, alone claims warrant. Thus, one who claims exclusive standing to judge whether an action falls under a norm embraces a contradiction. Insofar as it is a judgment, P is content-oriented and judger-self-transcending; but insofar as one claims exclusive standing to judge in this way one claims warrant solely on the basis of one's making the 'judgment'. This is a judger-self-oriented claim, a direct denial of judger-self-transcendence. To refuse to accord others standing to judge is to undercut one's own claim to *judge*, as opposed to merely uttering something at one's pleasure.

One can avoid the contradiction by abandoning the self-transcending claim to *judge* and embracing the self-oriented positing. In that way, *taking something to be so makes it so*—taking A to fall under N* makes it the case that A falls under N*. But the result is disastrous as an account of what it is to be subject to law, that is, to a legal norm. First, it follows that N* is no longer a norm, because it cannot constrain one's assessment. From one's own point of view, the only point of view allowed to be considered, there is no difference between taking something to be so and its being so; one cannot go wrong. But then one cannot be bound by N*. Submitting to N* while reserving the exclusive standing to judge applications of N* is not to authorize N* as a norm for oneself. It is to fail to authorize anything. Self-authorization is failed authorization.

Second, N* could not function as a norm for others; so it could not warrant one's holding another party accountable. For if one has sole standing to judge whether an action falls under N*, then there is no logical space between one's merely *taking* something to be the case, and its being so. So for others, N* must reduce to a very different proposition, a prediction of one's (arbitrary, capricious) assessments. The norm is reduced to a prediction. Thus, if one's judging is reduced to one's mere *taking* something to be the case, then it is not norm warranted. The action is arbitrary in the strict sense of being an action for which the agent is not answerable, but it achieves this by abandoning its claim to be law warranted. Thus, contrary to Aquinas's Thesis, it is not possible to be subject to law and yet have sole standing to judge whether one's actions accord with that law. Hobbes was right.

Moreover, now we can see that the notion of an unaccountable accountability-holder is a self-contradiction. To claim standing to hold another accountable is to claim that one's accountability-holding is warranted by a norm to which one is subject, but entails that someone else has standing to hold one accountable warranting norm; for one to claim standing as an accountability-holder is in effect to accord others standing to judge one's accountability-holding. There can be no such thing as an unaccountable accountability-holder.

3.3 Kant's Thesis

To Hobbes's Thesis, Kant added that the accountability relationship is necessarily reciprocal. 'No one can bind another to something', he wrote in 'Perpetual Peace', 'without also being subject to a law by which he in turn can be bound in the same way by the other.'[45] Elsewhere he wrote even more to the point: 'Whoever is *subject* to laws is a subject within a state and is thus subjected to coercive right equally with all other members of the commonwealth.'[46] The fidelity thesis embraces a modified version of Kant's claim. It claims that accountability must be *mutual* if not strictly *reciprocal.* Thus, Kant's Thesis revised is: One party, A, is in a position or has standing to bind another party, S, and to hold S accountable to this obligation, only if A is also subject to a network of accountability to others in which network S also participates. The second lemma needed for a full defence of the fidelity thesis is Kant's Thesis.

We can begin our argument for Kant's Thesis by recalling our reflections on the notion of accountability. Accountability, we noticed, involves a normatively structured interpersonal relationship. For a person or agency to hold another party accountable is a paradigm case of the exercise of normative authority, of 'binding another' in Kant's sense. For A to exercise the normative power characteristic of acting with (the law's) authority to hold another accountable involves more than manipulating S, causing S to behave in a certain way, even if doing so is (legally) justified. It involves A's addressing reasons of a particular kind to S. A also presupposes a certain *uptake* on the part of S: A assumes that S can grasp the reasons, that S is relatively free to act on those reasons, and that S acknowledges that acting on these reasons (conforming to the authority's directive) is *owed to* A. It is not enough that S behaves in a certain way *as a consequence* of what A does, but rather S's conduct must (that is, A expects it to) be *a response* to A's direction.

The exercise of accountability-holding authority involves action in the middle voice, as it were.[47] It is a kind of action in which the nominal subject or agent is also at the same time the passive object or recipient. To bathe is an action in middle

[45] Immanuel Kant, 'Perpetual Peace' in *Practical Philosophy*, ed and trans M Gregor (Cambridge University Press 1996) n 323† (emphasis deleted).

[46] Immanuel Kant, 'On the Common Saying: that may be correct in theory but it is of no use in practice' in *Practical Philosophy* 292.

[47] The middle voice, not found in English but common in other languages like ancient Greek, combines both active and passive, the subject is also the object, or where the subject is plural but not collective the parties are both agents and recipients of the action. I am grateful to Lauren Winner for alerting me to existence of this middle voice. See Lauren Winner, *Still: Notes on a Mid-Faith Crisis* (HarperCollins 2012) 154–7.

voice—the bather is also the party bathed. Similarly, to greet or embrace or cooperate or agree with another are interpersonal actions in middle voice; agents of these actions are also, reciprocally, patients. In standard instances, to greet is to *exchange greetings*, each greets and is greeted. To embrace is also to be embraced. To cooperate with is also to be cooperated with. (Of course, the cooperative action of one party may be very different from the co-relative cooperative action of the other. The respective roles may be different.) Likewise, to exercise normative authority is, in this sense, action in the middle voice. It involves reciprocal recognition, although, as with cooperation, the respective roles may be different or even asymmetrical. Nevertheless, like embracing and greeting, exercising authority is both active and passive; it involves reciprocal recognizing and being recognized. In the absence of reciprocity, it is a broken or defective exercise of authority, just as, in the absence of reciprocity, an embrace or a greeting is broken or defective.

We might wish to conclude that, in a sound exercise of accountability-holding, A claims warrant and judges A's exercise to be *intra vires* and expects, anticipates, and presupposes S's reciprocal recognition of these judgments. This puts A in a position to assess S's performance, but it likewise puts S in a position to assess A's performance. The relationship appears to be reciprocal. However, this conclusion seems to be the artefact of the example used. Where only two parties are in view, Hobbes's Thesis implies that accountability-holding must be reciprocal, but this gets Kant's Thesis on the cheap. Hobbes, Aquinas, and many others were keen to argue that accountability-holding authority is necessarily hierarchical.[48] Hobbes argued that subjection to law entails submission to others and, *thereby, subordination* to others, because submission is *necessarily hierarchical.*[49]

Where S is subject (and accountable) to A, A may likewise be accountable to a third party, C. A might then direct his claim of warrant for his exercise of authority to C and acknowledge C's standing to hold him accountable, while refusing to acknowledge any such standing for S. A slaveholder, for example, might go to court (recognize the court's authority over his claim) to uphold his *absolute* right over his slave. On the *Hierarchy Thesis*, accountability relations are transitive and anti-reflexive. Thus, to establish our modification of Kant's Thesis, we must show that this third-party hierarchical alternative is not an eligible option.

The Hierarchy Thesis is, from the point of view of the rule of law, fundamentally defective in two respects. First, the claim of authority envisioned in the above scenario is broken-backed. The claim of authority is made against or *with respect to* S, but it is *addressed to* the third party, C. If A merely claims support and

48 Arendt, for example, wrote: 'Since authority always demands obedience, it is commonly mistaken for some form of power or violence. Yet authority precludes the use of external means of coercion; where force is used, authority itself has failed. Authority, on the other hand, is incompatible with persuasion, which presupposes equality and works through a process of argumentation. Where arguments are used, authority is left in abeyance. Against the egalitarian order of persuasion stands the authoritarian order, which is always hierarchical' (Hannah Arendt, *Between Past and Future* (Penguin Books 1977) 92–3).

49 Hobbes, *Leviathan* (n 38) ch 29 para 9; see also Thomas Hobbes, *On the Citizen*, ed R Tuck and M Silverthorne (Cambridge University Press 1998) ch 6 para 18.

vindication of his conduct with respect to S, then the relationship between A and S is not yet a relationship of authority—any more than is A's relationship to his workhorse. On the other hand, if A claims the distinctive normative relationship of authority, then he claims that S owes obedience *to A*, but the only obligation that is in view is an obligation that S owes *to C*. A imposes his will on S, and may do so with C's blessing, but that is not to exercise authority over S. It is, rather (at best), the justified imposition of A's will on S. This maintains a deep asymmetry between A and S at the cost of evacuating the relationship of its distinctive normative content as a relationship of authority.

Yet the defect is even deeper. Hobbes, again, is our unwitting guide to the dialectic at this point.[50] For, if we accept the Hierarchy Thesis, and if holding accountable entails being liable to be held accountable, then accountability must form a unidirectional chain. If A's claim to authority over S and hence warrant to hold S accountable is tethered to C, then C's holding of A accountable rests on a warrant and judgment of action *intra vires* which subordinates C to another party, D. S's subordination to A presupposes A's subordination to C, but also C's to D, etc. Given the Hierarchy Thesis, the fate of such accountability chains lies in one of two directions: either the chain proceeds ad infinitum, or it must stop at some point. An infinite regress of accountability would appear to be a conceptual or at least practical absurdity.[51] So, the chain must stop somewhere, but it will have to stop with one who holds others accountable, but is not in turn accountable—an *unaccountable accountability-holder*. This, of course, was Hobbes's solution: The sovereign holds all subjects in the commonwealth accountable, but is not subject to the law—*princeps legibus solutus est.*

Surprisingly, Kant, who articulated most compellingly the mutuality component of the fidelity thesis—so much so that we called it 'Kant's Thesis'—nevertheless, exempted 'the head of state' from this subjection to accountability, on the ground that 'if he could also be coerced he would not be the head of state and the sequence of subordination would ascend to infinity'.[52] But that leaves 'the head of state'—what Hobbes called 'the sovereign'—as an unaccountable accountability-holder.

However, we have shown that an unaccountable accountability-holder is a conceptual absurdity. Either the unaccountable accountability-holder makes no claim to act with warrant, and thus is truly unaccountable, or it claims to act with warrant. But if it makes no claim to act with warrant, it does not hold accountable; it merely exercises coercive power. It is not an unaccountable *accountability-holder*, but only an unaccountable *wielder of power*. But if the 'ultimate' accountability-holder claims warrant, it claims to be subject to the norm that grounds that warrant. But then it (logically) cannot be unaccountable. Law's rule is possible only where accountability-holders are themselves accountable. Moreover rule *by*

[50] Hobbes, *Leviathan* (n 38) ch 29 para 9.

[51] Hobbes argued that an infinite accountability chain would lead to a practical absurdity, namely, 'confusion, and [ultimately the] Dissolution of the Commonwealth' (*Leviathan* (n 38) ch 29 para 9); see also *Leviathan* ch 20 para 18.

[52] Kant, 'On the Common Saying' (n 46) 292.

law, which borrows its vaunted and necessary legitimacy from its false similitude to the rule *of* law, is based on a fraud and a veiled incoherence.

Thus, if the Hierarchy Thesis is true, the rule of law, properly speaking, is *impossible*.[53] Put the other way around: the concept of law's rule requires that we abandon the Hierarchy Thesis. The ideal of the rule of law is fundamentally opposed to hierarchy. We can avoid incoherence by embracing the modified version of Kant's Thesis: If the rule of law is conceptually possible, accountability must be at least *mutual*. S's submission to A does not preclude A's submission—direct or perhaps indirect—to S. It may not be that A is *reciprocally* accountable *to S*, but A and S must be participants in what we might call an *accountability loop* or *accountability network* (and hence, *pace* Kant, would not 'ascend to infinity'). If law is to rule in a polity, accountability under the law must be in this way broadly mutual.[54] This is the core of the fidelity thesis.

3.4 Responsibility for the whole: the ethics of fidelity

The above argument is not meant to be a piece of a priori political sociology; it is meant rather to articulate the *ethics* of the rule of law. The reciprocity at the centre of the thesis is captured nicely by Rousseau when in his *Letters from the Mountain* he wrote: 'freedom consists less in acting at will than in not being subjugated to the will of another; it also consists in not subjugating the will of another to our own.'[55] Kant (like Locke) captured this thought with the concept of equality: equality of status in law's commonwealth. A core element of the rightful condition (*rechtlicher Zustand*), he argued, is 'the equality of human beings as subjects within a commonwealth'.[56] But, although these notions resonate with the idea of fidelity, they leave unexpressed the positive responsibility each member bears to hold co-members of law's commonwealth accountable under their common law. Fidelity makes a powerful claim about the obligations and responsibilities of and in a community that aspires to realize the rule of law. The claim is that in a community characterized by a robust rule of law, accountability is a communicated—distributed and shared—normative power. But with standing to hold accountable comes the responsibility to do so. The fidelity thesis holds that all members of the community *have a mutual responsibility* to exercise this power. Commitment to law, mutual submission to

[53] This may, of course, have been the conclusion Hobbes sought to establish. Rule *by* law was, in his view, prudent and politically necessary; *law's rule* was impossible and pursuit of it politically suicidal. The above argument demonstrates that Hobbes was right: sovereignty (insofar as it bottoms out in an unaccountable accountability-holder) is logically incompatible with the rule of law. (This is true wherever such sovereignty is located, including sovereignty located in 'the people'. See Postema, 'Law's Rule' (n 11).) Hobbes thought this was a decisive argument against the rule of law; partisans of the rule of law, and the kind of liberty that it secures (absence of subjection to arbitrary power), will conclude that sovereignty is the ultimate loser.

[54] For some examples of this accountability loop, both formal-institutional and informal-social, see Postema, 'Law's Rule' (n 11).

[55] Quoted in James Miller, *Rousseau: Dreamer of Democracy* (Yale University Press 1984), 250.

[56] Kant, 'On the Common Saying' (n 46) 292–3. I am grateful to Dennis Klimchuk for reminding me of Kant's view of equality as an element of the rightful condition.

law's rule, entails taking responsibility to engage in this distinctive rule-of-law practice. This is an obligation that *each member owes to each other member and to all*—it is *mutual* and *general*.

The argument for this remaining part of the fidelity thesis proceeds from two assumptions. The first is that the normative power and associated liability of accountability-holding is necessarily bundled together with a responsibility on the part of the power-holder to exercise this power (in appropriate ways, under appropriate circumstances, of course). The second is that the moral aim underlying and structuring fidelity—secure protection and recourse against the arbitrary exercise of power through the instrumentality of law—is directed to a public good that can be realized only through commonwealth-wide cooperative efforts.

That the power to hold accountable is necessarily bundled with a responsibility to exercise it follows from what it is to accord standing to hold accountable. According this standing is a bilateral, or multilateral, activity: successful according of standing entails acceptance by the agent to whom it is offered. Moreover, the point of according standing to hold one to account is met only if one can have some reasonable expectation that one will be held to account by the partner to whom standing is accorded. So, the bundle that is offered must include responsibility on the part of the other partner to exercise the power offered. This is underwritten by the fact that the point of any person's according such status to another is rooted in the point of mutual submission to law's rule, namely, realization of protection against the arbitrary exercise of power. To paraphrase Ferguson, it is only through the vigilance and spirit of citizens resolved to be free and to live together under common laws governing their common and public relations that they can hope that the terms of those laws will be observed. Fidelity to law is a matter of commitment to take responsibility for holding each other accountable under this common law.

Moreover, the fidelity-responsibility of each is owed *to each* as members of law's commonwealth. This is due to the fact that the good of a robust rule of law is an essentially *public* good; its benefits can only be achieved through cooperation. Upholding law's rule is a cooperative endeavour; one's own efforts may contribute to that endeavour but their success will depend on the ordered cooperative efforts of others as well. We can think in two ways about the implications of this public-good understanding of the rule of law for the direction and scope of fidelity-responsibilities. They are complementary rather than competing perspectives on the good of law's rule and the joint endeavour to realize it.

The *fair-play* perspective regards the vigilant efforts to hold those who exercise power, whether public or private, accountable under the law as a paradigmatic cooperative enterprise for mutual benefit. Seen in this way, the responsibilities of fidelity are responsibilities of doing one's part in a common, cooperative endeavour, responsibilities owed to each other as members similarly committed and bound. Sharing the burdens of law's governing involves doing one's part in the cooperative enterprise of accountability-holding. Each bears this obligation and it is owed in fairness *to each other*.

We can look at this endeavour from a different angle. The *solidarity* perspective is suggested by the sixteenth-century Huguenot writer of *Vindiciae Contra Tyrannos*.

In the writer's view, the covenant of mutual obligation and accountability between king and people was rooted in and shaped by a deeper covenant between God and the two parties. While the king was needed to hold the people to their duties of piety and righteousness, God recognized that to leave the king unaccountable was 'hazardous' and so God also empowered the people 'to stand as surety'.[57] Each pledged, to God and to each other, 'jointly, not separately' and 'on that account they [were] bound for the whole sum'. Just as 'creditors are accustomed to do with unreliable debtors, by making many liable for the same sum, so that two or more promissory parties are constituted for the same thing, from each one of whom the sum can be sought as if from the principal debtor'.[58] Drawing on Roman Law doctrine of joint liability for debt, the author argued that God gave each party standing (and incentive) to hold the other accountable to God's laws of piety and righteousness by requiring of each of them commitment for the whole. Each was 'bound one for another and each for the whole'.[59]

By analogy, we can argue that the public good of protection against the arbitrary exercise of power promised by law's rule calls for a multilateral joint commitment among members of law's commonwealth 'each for the whole'. The good sought is public and so it is a good for each in and through its being a good for all. The responsibility of each is first of all responsibility for the whole in that sense, but, because that whole can only be achieved through cooperative efforts of the members, each is, first, bound to *do one's part*, and second, bound also *for one another*—that is, bound to encourage and empower each other and, where necessary, hold each other accountable. Hence, from this solidarity perspective, each is bound *to* each other and *for* each other.

The solidarity perspective has one important implication. Because the responsibilities of fidelity are responsibilities to participate in a cooperative endeavour, they will be limited to an extent by the reliable participation of other parties. That is, the obligations are in an important respect conditional. *Fiat fidelis ruat caelum* is not a rational principle. To attempt to hold another accountable under the law in the face of massive infidelity may not be rational. However, from the solidarity perspective the participation of others in the cooperative endeavour is not merely an exogenously given fact. Rather, the fidelity-responsibility of each extends to efforts to empower and encourage others to participate, to take their corresponding responsibilities seriously.

Thus, fidelity obligations are not absolute. They are limited to an extent by the participation of others. They are also limited in two other respects. First, other duties of decency, justice, or respect for rights may override them in particular cases. Second, the exercise of fidelity-responsibility is constrained by considerations

[57] *Vindiciae Contra Tyrannos* (first published 1579), ed and trans George Garnett (Cambridge University Press 1994) 38. This work was first published in Basel (1579) in Latin and French under the pseudonym Stephanus Junius Brutus. A facsimile edition of an English translation of 1689 by William Walker is available on-line at <http://archive.org/details/vindiciaecontrat00lang> and in a print version published by EEBO Editions.

[58] Garnett, *Vindiciae Contra Tyrannos* (n 57) 38.

[59] Walker, *Vindiciae Contra Tyrannos* (n 57) 27.

of appropriateness of time, place, and manner, which are themselves rooted in the ultimate aim of protecting against the arbitrary exercise of power. Any proposed exercise of accountability-holding that is incompatible with that aim or that cannot be seen to contribute to its promotion, must be rejected.

From each of these perspectives it follows that the scope of concern of fidelity-responsibility is commonwealth wide. Because it is an obligation to do one's part in supporting, promoting, and protecting a public good, it is not limited to exercises of accountability for one's own benefit only. Similarly, responsibility for the whole entails responsibility to all those who have a right to participate in the benefit of the whole. On the understanding articulated here of the rule of law in law's commonwealth, subjection to law involves participation in a civic partnership, with mutual benefits and burdens. Subjection to its obligations and responsibilities implies the reciprocal benefit of its protection. On this view, there is no burden of compliance without benefit of law's protection. But, the argument we have pressed entails that protections promised must be secured by the network of accountability. So, any one person's or group's fidelity-responsibility is not limited to securing law's benefits for that person or group, but rather extends to all those who fall within the scope of law's demands and hence law's protection.

For this reason, the failure of white citizens in the Jim Crow South to hold its officials and fellow members of that community accountable to laws that purported to protect blacks and whites alike was a failure of fidelity. Obligations of fidelity of members of the white community did not stop at the borders of the white community. Subject to law's rule, we are, as Martin Luther King Jr put it, 'caught in an inescapable network of mutuality'.[60] In this further sense, we are bound for each other and for the whole.

4. Conclusion

Thus, the rule of law has an essential horizontal–social dimension as well as a vertical–political dimension. The responsibilities of fidelity concern not only, or even most fundamentally, relations between individual citizens and government officials (or the people and the government), but also concern mutual relations among members of law's commonwealth. The mutual responsibilities of accountability-holding among citizens and officials are not only echoed, but also grounded, in mutual responsibilities of members to each other and for the whole.

The rule of law promises protection and recourse against the arbitrary exercise of power. The guiding aim of the rule-of-law ideal is served when law's rule extends to all forms of power in the polity, social as well as political. The rule of law is not robust in a polity if the powers created, allocated, and protected by a regime of private law themselves define domains of arbitrary and unaccountable power, as we noted in Section 2.3. Moreover, conditions of polynomy aside, if a private law

[60] Martin Luther King Jr, 'Letter from the Birmingham Jail' in *Why We Can't Wait* (Beacon Press 2010) 85–6.

regime formally in place *does not count* in the polity—if interpersonal (and in that sense private) relations among its members are carried on irrespective of that formal regime and legal resources for recourse against violations of its norms cannot be utilized, or are treated with contempt—then, again, the rule of law has failed to take root.

The rule of law is realized when law is planted firmly in a commonwealth of mutual faithfulness to the differentiated and interconnected responsibilities of fidelity to law. Law rules not only when government officials are held accountable for the discharge of their duties under law, but also when ordinary citizens structure their relationships by law and hold each other accountable to the common, public terms that the law provides.

2

The Rule of Law and Private Law

*William Lucy**

1. Starting Points

Let's begin with our loosely contemporary, vaguely canonical, generally jurisprudential statements of the rule of law—by which I mean those offered by Lon L Fuller, HLA Hart, and Joseph Raz.[1] At first glance, this starting point generates a pretty unpromising answer to the question 'what is the relation between private law and the rule of law?' The answer is unpromising because the relation, viewed from the perspective of these accounts of the rule of law, *seems* negligible. One reason for this is that private law itself is more or less absent from these accounts. As a general matter, private law is no more obviously in play in Fuller's jurisprudential work than in either Raz's or Hart's sole-authored work,[2] although we know contract law occupied a sizeable part of Fuller's professional life.[3] Private law appears hardly at all in those areas of these scholars' work that is most concerned with the rule of law. Fuller, we all recall, is preoccupied with law-giving and law-creating in ch 2 of *The Morality of Law* and that, possibly because of the example of Rex, looks to contemporary eyes a lot like the work of the state in general and the legislature in

* Thanks to Dennis Klimchuk, Lisa Austin, Hannoch Dagan, Catherine Valcke, Ernest Weinrib, and other participants at the Toronto workshop for helpful thoughts and questions. Thom Brooks, Phil Handler, John Murphy, Robert Schütze, Adam Tucker, Alex Williams, and colleagues at Durham also made many improvements to the paper.

[1] Lon L Fuller, *The Morality of Law* (rev edn, Yale University Press 1969); HLA Hart, 'Problems of the Philosophy of Law' in *Essays in Jurisprudence and Philosophy* (Clarendon 1983); HLA Hart, *The Concept of Law* (rev edn, Clarendon 1994) 206–7; Joseph Raz, 'The Rule of Law and its Virtue' (1977) 93 *Law Quarterly Review* 195. A more expansive discussion would have to add a fine recent account of the rule of law (NE Simmonds, *Law as a Moral Idea* (Clarendon Press 2007)) to this quartet, as well as FA Hayek's earlier contributions: *The Constitution of Liberty* (Routledge 1960), part II, and *Law, Legislation and Liberty* (Routledge 1973), vol i.

[2] But see HLA Hart and T Honore, *Causation in the Law* (2nd edn, Clarendon 1985).

[3] L Fuller and WR Perdue, 'The Reliance Interest in Contract Damages: 1' (1936) 46 *Yale Law Journal* 52 and 'The Reliance Interest in Contract Damages: 2' (1937) 46 *Yale Law Journal* 373 and L Fuller and M Eisenberg, *Basic Contract Law* (8th edn, West: St Paul 2006; 1st edn 1947). See also S Gerber, 'Corbin and Fuller's Cases on Contracts (1942?): The Casebook that Never Was' (2003) 72 *Fordham Law Review* 595 + Appendix, for an account of a book stillborn.

particular.[4] If you are in the business of making law, then attend to Rex's failures and the eight desiderata—generality, promulgation, non-retroactivity, clarity, non-contradiction, possibility, constancy, and congruence—they contravene. Private law is ready-made law and Rex's mistakes seem of little instructional value unless our task is to create private law anew (along the lines, perhaps, of a *supra*-national code).[5]

The impression that the rule of law is pre-eminently the business of law-makers—a view henceforth dubbed 'the public law perspective'—is reinforced when we turn to the discussions of Hart and Raz. Hart's principles of legality are clearly all of a piece with Fuller's eight desiderata, in the sense that the perspective animating the discussion is that of law-maker, on the one hand, and addressee of the law, on the other. The main difference between Hart and Fuller, setting aside their rather unhelpful discussion of the moral status of the eight desiderata, is that Hart's account of the rule of law is more expansive than Fuller's. For, in addition to Fuller's eight desiderata, Hart includes principles of natural justice and impartiality within the rule of law (or principles of legality). He also has a principle of 'congruence between judicial decisions and the enacted law'[6] which is different from, because prima facie narrower than, Fuller's desideratum of 'congruence between official action and declared rule'.[7]

Raz's account of the rule of law is similar to Hart's in two obvious ways. First, the perspective that predominates in his discussion is essentially the same as that which animates Hart's: the public law perspective, that of law-maker and addressee of the law. Raz is not, however, completely blind to possible connections between the rule of law and private law: 'though the rule of law concerns primarily private citizens as subject to duties and governmental agencies in the exercise of their powers . . . it is also concerned with the exercise of private powers . . . [p]ower-conferring rules are designed to guide behaviour and should conform to the doctrine of the rule of law if they are to be capable of doing so effectively.'[8] But he does not subject this likely connection to scrutiny.

Second, Raz follows Hart in increasing the number of rule-of-law principles and carries out an expansionary manoeuvre of his own. That is, Raz, like Hart, incorporates principles of natural justice within the rule of law but goes beyond Hart by adding four supplementary requirements to what is now a list of ten or eleven desiderata or principles. They are: that 'the courts should be easily accessible',[9] that 'the independence of the judiciary must be guaranteed',[10] that the courts have review powers over other rule-of-law desiderata, and, finally, that '[t]he

[4] Note also this oft-quoted remark: 'the very essence of the Rule of Law is that in acting upon the citizen . . . government will faithfully apply rules previously declared as those to be followed by the citizen', in Fuller, *Morality* (n 1) 209–10.

[5] For a step in the recent EU codification project, see the Draft Common Frame of Reference at <http://ec.europa.eu/justice/contract/files/european-private-law_en.pdf>. Corroborating evidence that the perspective of law-maker and addressee of the law dominates Fuller's discussion in *Morality of Law* can be found in K Rundle, *Forms Liberate* (Hart Publishing 2012), ch 1.

[6] Hart, 'Problems of the Philosophy of Law' (n 1) 115.

[7] Fuller, *Morality* (n 1) 81.

[8] Raz, 'The Rule of Law' (n 1) 199.

[9] Raz, 'The Rule of Law' (n 1) 201.

[10] Raz, 'The Rule of Law' (n 1) 200.

discretion of ... crime preventing agencies should not be allowed to pervert the law'.[11]

While these accounts of the rule of law are interestingly expansive, being nowhere near as 'thin' or 'formal' as some discussions would lead us to think, they are also uninteresting from the perspective of private law. It might be right that the requirements that courts must have review powers, that judges and courts should be independent, that there be easy access to the justice system, and that there be no wide discretionary powers, are part of the best understanding of the rule of law. But these requirements, along with Hart's three additional principles, don't speak in any *unique* way to private law. The approximately fifteen desiderata of the rule of law with which we are now faced are assuredly of general importance in our thinking about law and legal-institutional design. Yet what, if anything, do they say that is of pre-eminent salience to private law? At face value, not much.

These three canonical discussions of the rule of law can, however, become more explicitly relevant to private law, and the public law perspective on the rule of law thereby decentred, by taking three steps. The first might seem quite unrelated to the other two; it consists of bringing our thoughts about the rule of law, on the one hand, and arbitrary power, on the other, into closer relation. I think there are good reasons for doing this regardless of any interest in the relationship between private law and the rule of law: they amount, in sum, to the claim that a clear view of the nature of arbitrariness, which shows it to be neither a uniquely public law nor even a uniquely legal notion, generates a better understanding of the rule of law. Arbitrariness can flourish in non-legal contexts just as much as in private law and public law contexts, but it is usually equally objectionable in all. And what is objectionable about it is, in part although perhaps not in whole, that it subverts or undermines many of the values and conditions the rule-of-law ideal is alleged to serve.

The second step elucidates these values, but with a twist. The latter is prompted by the insights of those philosophers who have relatively recently attempted to disinter a lost or certainly somewhat overlooked strand of political thought addressed, in the main, to the ills of arbitrariness and domination. That revival project is not a vital part of my argument here, since I am uncertain—for reasons articulated below—whether or not a dispute about how the values served by the rule of law should be characterized is worth resolving. My argument is, rather, a defence of two claims: (1) that private law protects against arbitrariness in much the same way as does the rule of law; and (2) that the values served by the rule of law are also to some extent served by private law.[12]

The third step which brings the rule of law and private law into closer alignment involves a slight, but for some unacceptable, expansion of our understanding of the rule of law.[13] This expansion illustrates another deep similarity—found in the

[11] Raz, 'The Rule of Law' (n 1) 201.

[12] I also believe—although I make no attempt to support it here—that these same values are served by and embodied in public law.

[13] Note Raz's caution that the rule of law 'is not to be confused with democracy, justice, *equality* (*before the law or otherwise*)' in Raz 'The Rule of Law' (n 1) 196 (emphasis mine).

notion of juridical equality—between private law and the rule of law. The first two steps are taken in the following sections of this essay and in the order just sketched; the third step is, however, a task for another occasion.[14] So as to avoid any confusion with other, more expansive conceptions of the rule of law, and also for ease of exposition, I amalgamate Fuller's, Hart's, and Raz's conceptions of the rule of law into one in what follows and label it 'RoL1'. Note also that the two steps taken here are certainly not the only way of exploring the relationship between the rule of law and private law. Another obvious path has been eschewed and it is worth noting why. We could describe this path as the 'rule-of-law audit strategy', whereby some or other segment of private law is judged against some conception of the rule of law, the outcome of the audit being positive, negative, or neutral. That path is not pursued here for a very simple and prosaic reason: it is fruitfully and illuminatingly travelled by a number of other essays in this volume.

2. Arbitrary Power and the Rule of Law

My claim here is that it aids our understanding of the nature of the rule of law to compare it with what it is not, namely, arbitrary power.[15] More specifically, the aid is at least twofold. First, contrasting the rule of law with *something like* its opposite serves to highlight some of the standards against which any acceptable account of the rule of law should be judged. Among those standards we should include, at the outset at least, fit with common intuitions as well as ordinary vocabulary and modes of thought and speech. And I suggest that one uniquely relevant hunch exists in ordinary thought and speech that deserves close attention: the idea that if there is some 'thing' that the rule of law is certainly not, then that is arbitrary power.

Second, contrasting the rule of law with arbitrariness reminds us of a somewhat neglected value—freedom as non-domination—that the rule of law embodies or serves. It is unlikely that Fuller, Hart, and Raz were blind to this specific value, but they did not articulate it in anything like the perspicuous vocabulary now available to us. While this vocabulary is ancient, it was rediscovered only relatively recently. The value it articulates thus received scant explicit attention from Fuller, Hart, and Raz and has been somewhat neglected by jurists ever since. The other values embodied in the rule of law, while only incrementally sketched by Fuller, are explicitly articulated by Hart and Raz, even though they are often said to underestimate their worth. It is, however, more accurate to say that Hart and Raz have frequently been interpreted *as if* they underestimate the worth of these values. It is thought necessary for them to downplay these values because a wholehearted

[14] I have taken some steps toward delineating the relevant conception of juridical equality in 'Equality Under and Before the Law' (2011) 61 *University of Toronto Law Journal* 411.

[15] There is plainly a circularity here, of the unavoidable hermeneutic kind, which reminds us that, in the social world, we need to know what we are looking for (or talking about) and thus what we are not looking for (or talking about) before we begin the search (or conversation). Which is to say neither that we need to know every detail of what we are looking for in advance, nor that our search will not refine and perhaps even change its ostensible object.

statement of their worth supposedly imperils other jurisprudential theses Hart and Raz defend.[16] The values served by or embodied in the rule of law form one bridge between it, on the one hand, and private law, on the other, for those values are also served by and embodied in private law.

Although it has been claimed that '"[a]rbitrary power" is a difficult notion',[17] this should neither inhibit our interest in the idea nor reduce its role in any discussion of the rule of law. If arbitrary power is close to being the opposite of the rule of law, then an account of the former should illuminate the latter. So, our question is, what is arbitrary power? As soon as we pose this question another immediately demands attention: how should we go about answering that question?

We have neither time nor need to explore the methodological precepts and injunctions of jurisprudence and legal philosophy. Within that realm, as within many other social sciences, we require what is sometimes called a 'pre-reflective'—but better named a 'pre-theoretical'—understanding of the idea, domain, conduct, institution, or practice that constitutes our area of interest. If one's topic is the gift-giving practices of the Azande, or contemporary common law understandings of the rule of law, an obvious starting point is the understandings members of those subject groups have of the practice or notion in question. Those understandings are first revealed to us in the language of those groups. What, then, does our own language reveal to us about the notion of arbitrariness and its cognate, arbitrary power? There are at least two not necessarily incompatible ways of answering this question. First, by a large-scale empirical study in which this question is posed of a sample group, their answers collated and valued. Second, by asking any single competent user of the language in question not just this question, but closely related questions designed to elucidate 'what we should say when . . . '.[18] Answers to these questions can also be found indirectly, in the wider culture of these language users, such as commentary upon and reaction to contemporary events and in standard sayings, adages, exemplary stories, and other sources.

As a user of our language, it seems to me that fellow citizens and lawyers may have at least four slightly different scenarios in mind when sincerely making a claim of arbitrariness. Attending to these scenarios ensures that arbitrariness is indeed a fairly expansive notion which may need to be cut down to size in some circumstances. However, it is surely preferable to err in this direction as opposed to stipulatively reducing the notion's range, since a more expansive approach can alert us to nuances and differences we would otherwise miss.[19]

[16] A fine corrective to the common view that Raz and Hart regard the rule of law as only instrumentally valuable is M Bennett, 'Hart and Raz on the Non-Instrumental Moral Value of the Rule of Law: A Reconsideration' (2011) 30 *Law and Philosophy* 603.

[17] Raz, 'The Rule of Law' (n 1) 203.

[18] This echoes the very brief remarks on a certain kind of philosophical method in JL Austin, *Philosophical Papers* (Clarendon 1961) 130.

[19] The *OED* contains four meanings, all of which overlap with those outlined below. In our English public law textbooks, neither 'arbitrariness' nor 'arbitrary' exercises of power receive much sustained attention (for an exception, see T Endicott, *Administrative Law* (Clarendon 2009) 4–9), it seemingly being taken for granted that lawyers will know arbitrariness when they see it. The notion also sometimes crops up in jurisprudential discussions of the rule of law, albeit almost always rather

One situation in which the rebuke of arbitrariness is appropriate is when power (or control or force)[20] is deployed without warrant and legitimacy. The mugger taking my wallet at knife-point or the complete stranger chastising a child each count as instances, albeit at different points on a spectrum. The mugger has no claim at all to my wallet and no warrant for the threat of force she deploys. The complete stranger is in a similar situation with regard to the child—what distinguishes him from relatives or carers or teachers is that these have some normative warrant for becoming interested in and thus interfering with the child's conduct. Our judgments here suggest that, while it is in some circumstances entirely appropriate for parents and others to chastise children, it is almost never appropriate for strangers to do so. Equally, our judgments suggest that the non-consensual taking of another's holdings is almost never appropriate. Part of the sense of 'impropriety' in these two sentences is, of course, given by 'illegitimate', where we mean not just that some deed or conduct is impermissible but also that it is wrong. We can call this type of arbitrariness 'S1' arbitrariness.

There is a second, related but narrower scenario in which judgments of arbitrariness are at home. This scenario includes all those situations in which power is exercised without warrant by those who usually or sometimes have warrant to exercise power. This scenario differs from the first because there is at some point here a legitimately conferred or assumed power, but the power that is actually exercised goes beyond that conferral or is unrelated to it. The conferral of power and the power itself can be either juridical or non-juridical: the power's source can be a body of law or a specific legal rule, on the one hand, or some non-legal rule or body of rules, on the other. With regard to legal powers, AV Dicey was keen to point out that Englishmen (and presumably women) were not subject to this kind of arbitrariness, unlike their French counterparts. Voltaire, Dicey noted, had good reason to know the difference between being ruled by law and being the victim of 'caprice'.[21] It was the latter that led to Voltaire being beaten and subsequently imprisoned by the Regent's lackeys in 1717. Some of those lackeys—the guards at the Bastille, for example—and the Regent himself (Philippe II d'Orléans) did indeed have legal powers to do certain things. But in this instance they had no legal power at all to beat and imprison Voltaire. They did so in part because they could do so without running the risk of the law being applied to them. They thus

fleetingly. Two examples are David Dyzenhaus, *The Constitution of Law* (Cambridge University Press 2006) 2, and TRS Allan, *Constitutional Justice* (Oxford University Press 2001) 2–3, 11–12, and 15.

[20] There are distinctions worth drawing between the members of this trio ('force' might, for instance, be the exercise of 'power' that is resisted, and 'power' might be displaced without 'control'). In what follows I ignore these and use 'power' as a generic term to cover all three instances. I do not, however, use it to encompass either the 'conduct of conduct' or its allegedly close relative, bio-power/bio-politics: see N Rose, *Powers of Freedom* (Cambridge University Press 1999) for a superb overview of these issues.

[21] *Introduction to the Study of the Law of the Constitution* (10th edn, Macmillan and Co 1959) 184. Voltaire was imprisoned in the Bastille twice: once for eleven months, from May 1717, which is presumably the instance Dicey has in mind, and again for two weeks in 1726, as a result of the machinations of the Chevalier de Rohan.

had lawful warrant for some areas of their activity and *de facto* impunity in relation to others.

The security and immigration service personnel complicit in the abduction and rendition of Maher Arar similarly had lawful warrant for some of their activities. Just about all such personnel are legally empowered to do a range of things which, without legal warrant, would be unlawful. They are not, however, lawfully empowered to abduct suspected terrorists, mislead their lawyers, and then remove them from one jurisdiction to another, so that they can be imprisoned and tortured. Not only did those personnel lack lawful authority to do that, their doing so was contrary to a number of legal obligations they were required to uphold in the discharge of their duties.[22] Regrettably, these personnel have now been indirectly granted immunity for their misdeeds by the US Supreme Court.[23]

The second scenario has another slightly different juristic version which lawyers might well call the '*vires* version'. In English public law, bodies that hold and exercise public powers can sometimes exceed the authority they have been granted, almost always by an empowering statute or statutory instrument. When they do so, they act *ultra vires*. The conduct of the public body that exceeds its powers is usually related to that in which the body has lawful authority to engage, but comes about either because of a misunderstanding of the range or nature of their authority, or because of irregularities in the process of exercising it, or because the body made a decision that no reasonable body could have made.[24] There is a similarity between this instance and the kind of exercise of power without warrant that was characteristic of the US security services' dealings with Maher Arar: both bodies, after all, had legal warrant to do some things. However, the key difference is that the *vires* scenario is usually one in which a power is mistakenly or unwittingly exceeded; in the Arar type of case, power seems to be exercised deliberately and regardless of any warrant.

A final point about what is henceforth called 'S2 arbitrariness': it can occur in non-legal realms as well in the legal realm, even in its 'vires' guise. More or less formal bodies of rules—the FIFA rules of the game for association football, for example—confer powers, duties, and entitlements upon players of the game and officials and it is perfectly possible for power-holders to exceed their powers. It would be rare but is nonetheless conceivable for a referee to mistake the range of her powers. She might, for example, think that her power to insist that players take the field in appropriate and safe attire not only allows her to exclude from the field players wearing jewellery but also those with ponytails. A decision to exclude players

[22] Commission of Inquiry into the Actions of Canadian Officials in Relation to Maher Arar, *Report of the Events Relating to Maher Arar: Analysis and Recommendations* (Ottawa: Public Works and Government Services Canada 2006), and see D Cole, 'Getting Away with Torture' *The New York Review of Books* (New York, 14 January 2010) 39.

[23] See D Cole, 'He was Tortured but he Can't Sue' (*New York Review Blog*, 15 June 2010).

[24] See HWR Wade and C Forsyth, *Administrative Law* (10th edn, Clarendon Press 2009) part IV. Note that the last ground for judicial review, particularly in its irrationality guise, is probably best viewed as a form of S4 arbitrariness.

with ponytails would currently be regarded as an obvious instance of the referee exceeding her powers.

A third scenario—'S3 arbitrariness'—in which arbitrariness is a rebuke is that in which a decision-maker exercises power inconsistently. All referees in association football have the power, in some circumstances, to award a penalty kick and all parents have the legal and moral power to discipline their children in certain circumstances. The referee who awards a penalty against team Y in circumstances X, but who does not award a penalty against their opponents, team Z, in circumstances X, will assuredly be subject to accusations of arbitrariness or inconsistency. So, too, will the parent who disciplines child 1 for deed A but not child 2 for the same deed in the same circumstances.

The inconsistent exercise of a legitimately held power often leads to two additional and closely connected worries. One is the prospect of a failure of impartiality, the other the chance of improper differential treatment. Real life instances of the referee and parent examples would quickly generate accusations of favouritism or partiality and such partiality is often—invariably?—a way of treating two similarly situated parties differently. This differential treatment need not have, but often has, objectionable grounds. In the referee example, her partiality could be the result of more or less reprehensible bias: she could simply be a fan of team Y, but she might also be a racist, favouring team Y because it has more players of the ethnicity she prefers. Either way, there is a serious breach of her duty to interpret and apply the rules of the game impartially. That breach grounds the claim that her decision-making is arbitrary. It seems it is just this type of lapse that Raz has in mind when he says that 'an act which is the exercise of power is arbitrary *only* if it was done either with indifference as to whether it will serve the purposes which alone can justify its use or with belief that it will not serve them'.[25] The referee's decision to favour team Y with the award of a penalty in circumstances X, and to deny team Z the award of a penalty in the same circumstances, cannot in any circumstances accord with the purposes of the penalty rule. However, if the previous and following analysis is correct, then Raz is mistaken in thinking that this is the *only* scenario in which the exercise of power can be appropriately described as arbitrary. It is one such scenario of three (the following scenario does not, in some instances, entail an exercise of power).

The fourth kind of scenario—'S4 arbitrariness'—in which arbitrariness is a salient issue is that in which a decision, deed, or course of conduct is marked by a defect of reason. I use that term to highlight only two distinct rational shortcomings, not all possible rational defects that any particular deed or course of conduct might display. The first shortcoming, which might not actually be appropriately regarded as such, arises when a deed or course of conduct is under-determined by reason. We could imagine, for example, asking someone who had picked a particular car to drive, 'why did you choose a pink car?' and receiving the reply, 'no reason'. This is unlikely to be a statement affirming that there was no reason at

[25] Raz, 'The Rule of Law' (n 1) 203.

all to pick a car but, rather, an affirmation that there was no specific reason to pick that particular car, given that a choice of car had to be made. While there was reason to pick a car, there was no salient or compelling reason to pick that car. The choice of the pink car was therefore under-determined by reason. That very under-determination by reason informs the charge of arbitrariness; it highlights the fact that there was no better reason to pick the pink car than any other car—any other colour of car was equally likely to be chosen. Such instances, which are ones in which the selector is indifferent between options and thus selects in the absence of either compelling or particularly salient reasons, have been dubbed instances of 'picking'. 'Choosing', by contrast, is said to refer to those instances when options are selected on the basis of compelling or salient reasons.[26] If 'arbitrariness' does indeed rightly characterize the under-determined nature of instances of picking, it is worth noting that this charge is not quite as damning here as it might be in scenarios one, two, and three. For, rather than disclose objectionable partiality or the illegitimate exercise of power, instances of picking might simply mark the limits of reason in some contexts. It is this consideration that suggests we are not really dealing with a rational shortcoming here but with a truth about reason itself.

The second shortcoming is in some instances a genuine shortcoming. The charge of arbitrariness is prima facie appropriate here because the situation is one in which there are no reasons at all for some deed or course of conduct, the deed or course of conduct not being a 'mere' reflex or the like. Individuals whose conduct is often or always reasonless are perhaps best characterized as wantons, lacking autonomy.[27] Those whose conduct is sometimes or occasionally reasonless might well be either experimenting with acting on whim (some think this makes them so much more 'interesting' than their peers), chance, or unthinkingly following in everyone else's tracks.[28] They might even have reasons for not coming up with reasons for their conduct. I shave in the way I do because that's the way I've always shaved and it seems an absurd waste of time to think about this, never mind to come up with reasons why it is a good way of shaving, how it compares with other ways etc, etc... When Dicey speaks of Voltaire being subject to the Regent's 'caprice', this surely being a near relative of 'whim', it seems unlikely that he has in mind an instance of reasonless conduct. Rather, the caprice here is the unwarranted or illegitimate exercise of sheer physical power over Voltaire, for which the Regent and his lackeys certainly had reasons.[29] By contrast, when Raz says that '[a] ruler can promote general rules based on whim... without offending against the rule of law'[30], reasonless conduct must be exactly what he has in mind. For, if he has the

[26] 'Choosing is choosing for a reason': E Ullman-Margalit and S Morgenbesser, 'Picking and Choosing' (1977) 44 *Social Research* 757, 758.

[27] H Frankfurt, 'Freedom of the Will and the Concept of a Person' in *The Importance of What We Care About* (Cambridge University Press 1988).

[28] On trusting to chance, a fiction classic is L Rheinhart, *The Dice Man* (W Morrow 1971).

[29] The Gods, too, might have their reasons, but being in their power is nevertheless objectionable, as Gloucester lamented after a particularly bad day: 'As flies to wanton boys are we to th' gods, they kill us for their sport', in *The Tragedy of King Lear* Act IV sc i l 36.

[30] Raz, 'The Rule of Law' (n 1) 202–3.

kind of caprice involved in Voltaire's treatment in view, then that obviously offends rule-of-law principles. It is also worth noting that recent developments in administrative law in England suggest that reasonless exercises of power by public bodies are indeed antithetical to the rule of law.[31]

It is useful to note how many and which of the four types of arbitrariness matches up with which components of our three sample conceptions of the rule of law. This enterprise serves to illuminate the degree to which the hunch affirmed at the beginning of this section—that arbitrariness and the rule of law can be meaningfully contrasted—is plausible. Of the fifteen principles of RoL1—generality (1), promulgation (2), non-retroactivity (3), clarity (4), non-contradiction (5), possibility (6), constancy (7), congruence (8), natural justice (9), impartiality (10), adjudicative congruence (11), accessibility (12), judicial independence (13), power of review (14), and limited discretion (15)—almost none directly engage with S1 arbitrariness. The exercise of power without warrant is not something that rule-of-law principles regulate. But, by existing clearly beyond the range of those principles, such exercises of power usually advertise their own egregious nature: commitment to the rule of law, after all, requires living under and through law. Ostensibly legally legitimate exercises of power are usually genuinely legitimate if and when carried out in accord with principles 1, 2, 4, 5, 6, 7, 8, 9, and 10. That is to say, they are warranted by a general and intelligible public rule of some kind, exercised consistently and in accord with that rule, while also complying with the rules of natural justice and the requirements of possibility, non-contradiction, and impartiality. By contrast, the prior two requirements of possibility and non-contradiction are internal to the very enterprise of subjecting human conduct to the governance of rules. But neither RoL1, nor any other conception of the rule of law for that matter, can ensure that power is always exercised legitimately (although they might generate the assumption that it should be).

Legal instances of S2 arbitrariness are usually also determined to be such by reference to many of the same principles of RoL1 just listed: 1, 2, 4, 6, 7, and 8. We can only know if and when an exercise of power is within its grant when we know and understand the rule that grants it and its conditions. That the power exercised must require conduct that is possible follows from the fact that recourse to a rule-granted and rule-bounded power is intelligible only as an effort to subject human conduct to the governance of rules. Inconsistency is the core of S3 arbitrariness and thus principles 4, 7, 8, 9, and 10 are the salient ones here, 1 and 2 being taken for granted in the identification of the power-conferring rule or rules under which power is exercised or a decision taken. That the power must be exercised impartially and in accord with natural justice serves as a limited bulwark against inappropriate and thus possibly inconsistent decision-making. Principles 8, 9, and 10 of RoL1 are

[31] I have in mind the trend towards a *general* duty to give reasons which, although not universally recognized by the English courts, is regarded by some judges as lurking on the horizon of judicial possibility. The obvious starting point is *R v Ministry of Defence, ex parte Murray* [1997] EWHC Admin 1136. A recent analysis of the duty is *R (on the application of KM) (by his mother and litigation friend JM) (FC) (Appellant) v Cambridgeshire County Council (Respondent)* [2012] UKSC 23.

evidently necessary for diagnosis of and protection against S4 arbitrariness in the legal context. Whether or not decision-makers have a duty to give reasons for their decisions and exercises of power, their decisions must almost always be ostensibly impartial and congruent with the grant under which the power is exercised. To determine the latter, we are thrown back upon principles 1, 2, and 4.

Is it possible to say, as a result of this brief analysis, that there is a *significant* connection between arbitrariness and RoL1? The connection affirmed in the hunch at the beginning of this section and bolstered in the previous few paragraphs is this: in the juridical context the link is that arbitrariness is often the antithesis of the rule of law, telling us what is wrong when many RoL1 principles are breached. The objection to arbitrariness in the legal domain is that each of its instances almost always either directly or indirectly contravenes rule-of-law principles—when the latter are breached, arbitrariness is afoot. Is this a significant link between these two notions? Moreover, is the link such as to give good reason for maintaining that *all* accounts of the rule of law, and not just RoL1, must be answerable to some or all instances of arbitrariness? If we can identify arbitrariness without recourse to the principles of either RoL1 or of any other conception of the rule of law, then there seems to be little reason why the latter must be constructed with the former in mind.

That we can indeed identify arbitrariness without recourse to rule-of-law principles seems plain: not all instances of arbitrariness are legal. Setting aside the possibility of non-legal analogues of RoL1 principles, this means that the category of 'arbitrariness' exceeds both that of 'the rule of law', on the one hand, and 'the legal', on the other. Principles of RoL1, or of any other conception of the rule of law for that matter, are thus not necessary conditions of all instances of arbitrariness, especially as at least two instances of the latter (S1 and S4 arbitrariness) can be defined without recourse to rule-of-law principles. Furthermore, some RoL1 principles clearly do not speak directly and explicitly to any of the four instances of arbitrariness. Access to justice (12) and the power of review over other desiderata (14) might both serve indirectly to impede some instances of arbitrariness, but it seems misleading to say that this is their only burden. And even if non-legal equivalents to principles 1–10 of RoL1 are in play in non-legal manifestations of S1–S4 arbitrariness, this does not establish anything like a direct entailment between these principles and arbitrariness. For what stands between arbitrariness and rule-of-law principles is, of course, the category 'law'; only instances of arbitrariness that fall within the latter domain trigger a rule of law 'alert', with recourse to and interrogation of desiderata 1–15 of RoL1.

That the juxtaposition of rule-of-law principles and types of arbitrariness illustrates one of the important values that the rule of law serves, and that arbitrariness subverts or denies, is not on its own completely satisfactory. For, if this is part of an argument to show that there is a *significant* connection between arbitrariness and the rule of law, we might be accused of smuggling in a particular account of the value of the rule of law in an improper way. The charge is that this value only becomes salient because of our invocation of the various types of arbitrariness and not as a result of our account of the rule of law. So is there something else that might be said in favour of linking RoL1 (or other accounts of the rule of law) with an account of arbitrariness?

One suggestion is that, while RoL1 principles are not necessary conditions of non-legal arbitrariness, those principles and arbitrariness are related within the juridical realm because they function together as contrastive concepts. This much is implicit in the claim that arbitrariness tells us what is wrong when many rule-of-law principles are breached. If arbitrariness and RoL1 are contrastive concepts, then each automatically throws light on the other in any attempt to articulate one.[32] We have many concepts that function in this way: the darkness of a dark suit is usually only meaningful by reference to various degrees of lightness and these, of course, are determined by context. A dark suit for a flamboyant popinjay will presumably be quite different from an undertaker's dark suit. The contrast here is therefore not one between simple opposites but, rather, between a range of possible gradations any two of which can be contrasted. While some contrastive concepts plainly look like simple opposites (black/white; wet/dry; drunk/sober), many legal contrastive concepts are not straightforwardly opposites. Consider, for instance, a determination of the unreasonableness of conduct in negligence law. This is only possible by reference to some understanding of its opposite, namely, reasonable conduct, but, as with the concepts 'light' and 'dark', there is an unavoidable degree of imprecision in the delineation of the contrasting poles. We can speak about something being more or less light just as properly as we can talk of conduct (and the standard of care it embodies) being more or less reasonable; we are thus able to draw the salient contrast with various degrees of strength or vividity. There is, furthermore, a large dollop of context-sensitivity in drawing the distinction between this particular pair of legal contrastive concepts. A reasonable standard of care in a highly stressful, emergency situation might well be unreasonable in a relaxed, non-emergency environment.[33] Nor is our understanding of what is reasonable and unreasonable (and similar contrastive concepts) so static that the dividing line between them cannot change. What was once regarded as reasonable in situation X can come to be regarded as unreasonable in that same situation.

Another consideration in favour of linking arbitrariness and the rule of law is that the link generates a general, plausible account of what is wrong with breach of rule-of-law principles. Breaches of principles 1–10 of RoL1 are almost always instances of S1–S4 arbitrariness and this might well capture our general sense of what is wrong when most rule-of-law principles are breached. When faced with instances of breach of different principles, my students (i) often think that what is wrong in these various instances is more or less the same; and (ii) they frequently characterize this wrong as arbitrariness or one or more of its cognates (the most commonly

[32] Saussure made a similar observation about words: 'In a given language, all the words which express neighbouring ideas help to define one another's meaning . . . No word has a value that can be identified independently of what else there is in its vicinity,' in F de Saussure, *Course in General Linguistics*, translated and annotated by R Harris (Duckworth 1983) 114.

[33] Two instances: *Watt v Hertfordshire CC* [1954] 1 WLR 835 (CA) and *Daborn v Bath Tramways* [1946] 2 All ER 333 (CA).

articulated expressions being variations on 'being subject to another's power/control/whim'). The discovery of a general wrong in many instances of breach of rule-of-law principles is helpful and important when compared to the alternative: an incremental list of apparently discrete wrongs. My view is certainly not that there is only one single wrong when rule-of-law principles are breached, but nor is it that there are fifteen separate and discrete wrongs. Rather, one wrong—arbitrariness—is common to numerous instances of breach.

The most sceptical response to the claim that there is a link between arbitrariness and the rule of law—the former often telling us what is wrong when the latter is transgressed—is straightforward denial. Such a denial is problematic principally because it requires that there can be breaches of many (rather than just one or two) rule-of-law principles that do not in any way implicate S1–S4 arbitrariness. That the breach of some specific rule-of-law principles need not entail any form of arbitrariness is unremarkable; we have already noted that this is the case with regard to two such principles. But it seems impossible to breach the majority of RoL1 principles without arbitrariness of one form or another. Also, as a general matter, it seems strange to hold that talk of arbitrariness is utterly out of place when faced with breach of many rule-of-law principles, yet that follows from the hard-headed sceptical view. A more moderate sceptical view, holding that there is indeed a link or overlap between arbitrariness and the rule of law but that it is not particularly significant, seems altogether more plausible.

Given the argument so far, it is tempting to regard RoL1 principles, breach of which often embodies arbitrariness, as central instances of the rule of law. We might, alternatively, claim that they provide an accepted argumentative plateau upon which all other conceptions of the rule of law arise. But the argument here gives no warrant for either of these claims. We have established only a connection between arbitrariness and some of the principles of RoL1, such that the former tells us what is wrong in many breaches of the latter: arbitrariness=not the rule of law. That connection cannot of itself support the claim that those principles are more significant or more central than others, nor can it show that those principles must be accommodated—as an argumentative plateau or in some other way—by all accounts of the rule of law. The most our argument has established is a prima facie presumption that accounts of the rule of law tell us what is wrong, in relatively general terms, with breaches of the rule of law. That presumption can surely be rebutted, but a plausible rebuttable must discredit the account of that general wrong just offered: it must reject the claim that breaches of the rule of law often entail arbitrariness of one form or another.

We need now articulate the value or values of RoL1 in such a way as to inform our understanding of the wrong of arbitrariness. For, while hard-headed sceptics might deny that there is any link at all between the rule of law and arbitrariness, more moderate sceptics could question exactly what is wrong with arbitrariness in the first place. The discussion in Section 3 answers that specific question in the course of providing a general account of the value—or values—of RoL1. But before we turn to that account, one final point must be noted. It is that our elucidation of the different families of arbitrariness does not depend, for its intelligibility, upon the existence of the state in anything like its modern understanding. The fact that we can conceptualize arbitrariness without reference to the state serves as a reminder that we might also be able to conceptualize many of the principles of RoL1 without reference to the state. And that, of course, dislodges the public law perspective: it stops us thinking about the rule of law exclusively in terms of state-centred law-making. Our thinking should therefore perhaps always be initially informed by what Raz calls the rule of law in its literal sense—when '[t]he rule of the law . . . means that people should obey the law and be ruled by it'—rather than the rule of law 'in a narrower sense, that the government shall be ruled by the law and subject to it'.[34]

3. The Value of the Rule of Law and a Bridge to Private Law

The 'value' of RoL1 is most likely the sum total of all the particular values it serves or embodies: it seems improbable that there is only one such value and this view is shared by proponents of RoL1. Nor is there significant disagreement among those proponents as to which values are served by or embodied in the rule of law. More awkward is the question of which formulation—'served by' or 'embodied in'—best characterizes the relationship: are all the pertinent values here immanent within the very idea of the rule of law or are they independent of that idea but advanced, served, and protected by it? Or is it the case that some of the pertinent values are immanent while others are not? In what follows, I speak most often of the values 'served by' RoL1 but this is merely a matter of linguistic convenience. I remain agnostic here as to which view of the relationship between RoL1 and its salient values is correct; no argument I offer turns on this issue.

The most obvious candidates for the status of values served by RoL1 are the values of dignity, autonomy, and liberty (understood as freedom from interference).[35] I treat these values together not just because they overlap to some degree, but also so as to avoid an unfruitful discussion of either the relative merits of each or of which one is truly, genuinely, and exclusively compatible with the rule of law, on the one hand, and private law, on the other. So: how might these values be understood? My answer has two initial parts. First, I chart the contours of these values by letting proponents of RoL1 speak for themselves and then, second, introduce another value that RoL1 seemingly serves. I then, in the third part, broaden the discussion by attempting to show that these values are also advanced by or inform private law and that private law itself serves as a bulwark against arbitrariness in much the same way as does the rule of law.

[34] Raz, 'The Rule of Law' (n 1) 196.

[35] I regard liberty and freedom as synonyms here, even though there seem to be reasons against this (H Pitkin, 'Are Freedom and Liberty Twins?' (1988) 16 *Political Theory* 523; see 542–4 in particular).

3.1 In their own words

The advantage of allowing Fuller, Hart, and Raz to speak for themselves with regard to the values served by RoL1 is that we avoid the huge amount of secondary comment on their work. In that comment these proponents' own words often slip from view. It is therefore worth reminding ourselves of some of what they say in a relatively direct and unmediated way. Furthermore, allowing these jurists to speak for themselves serves as a corrective to some common misrepresentations of their views.

I begin with the least laconic statement of the values served by RoL1. Of the principles that constitute his 'formal' conception of the rule of law, Raz says this: '[i]t should... be remembered that in the final analysis the doctrine rests on its basic idea that the law should be capable of providing effective guidance. The principles do not stand on their own. They must be constantly interpreted in light of the basic idea.'[36] He adds that:

> ... there are ... reasons for valuing the rule of law. We value the ability to choose styles and forms of life, to fix long term goals and effectively direct one's life toward them. One's ability to do so depends on the existence of stable, secure frameworks for one's life and actions. The law can help secure such fixed points of reference in two ways: (1) by stabilising social relationships which but for the law may disintegrate or develop in erratic or unpredictable ways; (2) by a policy of self-restraint designed to make the law itself a stable and safe basis for planning. This last aspect is the concern of the rule of law.[37]

Raz elaborates this concern thus:

> The second virtue of the rule of law is often... identified as the protection of individual freedom. This is right in the sense of freedom in which it is identified with an effective ability to choose between as many options as possible. Predictability in one's environment does increase one's power of action... The rule of law may be yet another way of protecting personal freedom. But it has no bearing on the existence of spheres of activity free from governmental interference and is compatible with gross violations of human rights.
>
> More important than both these considerations is the fact that observance of the rule of law is necessary if the law is to respect human dignity. Respecting human dignity entails treating humans as persons capable of planning and plotting their future. Thus, respecting people's dignity includes respecting their autonomy, their right to control their future.[38]

And, in expanding this notion of dignity, he says:

> it is clear that deliberate disregard for the rule of law violates human dignity. It is the business of law to guide human action by affecting people's options.... Deliberate violation of the rule of law affects... one's very ability to decide, act or form beliefs about the future. A legal system which does in general observe the rule of law treats people as persons at least in the sense that it attempts to guide their behaviour through affecting the circumstances of their action. It thus presupposes that they are rational autonomous creatures and attempts to affect their actions and habits by affecting their deliberations.... Violations of the rule of law

36 Raz, 'The Rule of Law' (n 1) 202.
37 Raz, 'The Rule of Law' (n 1) 203.
38 Raz, 'The Rule of Law' (n 1) 203–4.

affect one's fate by frustrating one's deliberations, by making it impossible for a person to plan his future to decide on his action on the basis of a rational assessment of their outcome. The rule of law provides the foundation for the legal respect for human dignity.[39]

There are, then, at least three closely related values served or protected by RoL1 on Raz's view: liberty, dignity, and autonomy. The former is understood as the ability to choose combined with some degree of freedom from interference in this sense: adherence to RoL1 serves notice on citizens as to when they will run up against the law and thus, in part at least, enables them to avoid its maw. Dignity is a matter of respect for individuals' ability to choose, deliberate, and plan and autonomy seems to be the culmination of both:[40] thus 'respecting human dignity entails treating humans as persons capable of planning and plotting their future... [which] includes respecting their autonomy, their right to control their future'. Of course, these values can only flourish in the conditions of relative predictability, stability, and certainty that Raz rightly thinks RoL1 can bring about or maintain, but it is important not to mistake these conditions for values. For predictability, stability, and certainty are not always valuable and important in and of themselves; indeed sometimes, in some contexts, they are regarded as vices. Who has not heard those on the brink of ending long-term relationships complain about the staid predictability of their lives? Variety and spontaneity, they maintain, are the spice of life, change and uncertainty life-affirming challenges. By contrast, and save for quite exceptional circumstances, liberty, autonomy, and dignity are almost always valuable in and of themselves.

Fuller's account of the values served by RoL1 is not radically dissimilar to either Hart's or Raz's. Yet Fuller is less reticent than Hart in articulating these values while, somewhat surprisingly, being more oblique than Raz. Fuller's general view of law obviously informs his discussion of RoL1, but this only becomes absolutely clear in retrospect. It is touched upon late in his discussion of the eight desiderata[41] and made explicit thereafter. It is the idea, obvious but surprisingly often in need of restatement, that 'law is the enterprise of subjecting human conduct to the governance of rules'.[42] That being so, legal rules must have certain properties, many of which are manifest in Fuller's eight desiderata. Fuller claims that subjecting human conduct to the governance of rules which comply with the eight desiderata creates 'a kind of reciprocity between government and the citizen with respect to the observance of rules.... Government says to the citizen in effect, "These are the rules we expect you to follow. If you follow them, you have our

[39] Raz, 'The Rule of Law' (n 1) 205.

[40] The view that dignity is a status-concept rather than a value-concept would suggest that it occupies a different, more encompassing role than the other values in this company. In what follows I assume it is a value-concept, 'merely' one value among others, and that its meaning is more or less exhausted by the statements of Raz and Fuller in the text. For more nuanced views of dignity, see J Waldron, *Dignity, Rank and Rights* (Oxford University Press 2012) and M Rosen, *Dignity: Its History and Meaning* (Harvard University Press 2012). On dignity as a status-concept, see Waldron, *Dignity, Rank and Rights*, lecture 1, lecture 2, sc 6, and his 'How Law Protects Dignity' (2012) 71 *Cambridge Law Journal* 200, 202.

[41] Fuller, *Morality* (n 1) 91.

[42] Fuller, *Morality* (n 1) 106.

assurance that they are the rules that will be applied to your conduct . . . ".'[43] In addition to creating this bond of reciprocity between governments and the governed, the eight desiderata also implicitly assume a

> view of man . . . [for] [t]o embark on the enterprise of subjecting human conduct to the governance of rules involves of necessity a commitment to the view that man is, or can become, a responsible agent, capable of understanding and following rules, and answerable for his defaults.
>
> Every departure from the principles of the law's inner morality is an affront to man's dignity as a responsible agent. To judge his action by unpublished or retrospective laws, or to order him to do an act that is impossible, is to convey to him your indifference to his powers of self-determination. Conversely, when the view is accepted that man is incapable of responsible action, legal morality loses its reason for being. To judge his actions by unpublished or retrospective laws is no longer an affront, for there is nothing left to affront—indeed, even the verb 'to judge' becomes itself incongruous in this context; we no longer judge a man, we act upon him.[44]

Both the conditions and values that Raz identifies are obviously in play here, albeit sometimes only fleetingly and in a different idiom. Law's properties, as identified in the eight desiderata, in conjunction with the reciprocity Fuller claims is the essence of the relationship between law-makers and their addressees, undoubtedly establish and maintain some degree of predictability, stability, and certainty in the social environment. And in that environment, 'man' can become or continue to be a responsible agent, not just answerable for his defaults but also presumably free to formulate and pursue plans and conceptions of the good. 'Dignity' and 'self-determination' are Fuller's terms for this. While his articulation of the former is not identical to Raz's, they seem to have a roughly similar idea in mind. 'Self-determination' is surely Fuller's analogue to Raz's account of autonomy and, although Fuller says relatively very little about this idea, the likeness is hard to miss.

Hart provides the most laconic statement of the conditions maintained and values served by RoL1. This is not the sum total of what he has to say about RoL1 (or the principles of legality, as he often refers to the rule of law), but it is a significant portion:[45]

> [t]hese requirements [of legality] and the specific value conformity with them imparts to laws may be viewed from two different points of view. On the one hand, they maximise the probability that the conduct required by the law will be forthcoming and, on the other hand, they provide individuals whose freedom is limited by the law with certain information and assurances which assist them in planning their lives within the coercive framework of the law.[46]

43 Fuller, *Morality* (n 1) 39–40; see also 91. 44 Fuller, *Morality* (n 1) 162–3.

45 See also Hart, *Concept* (n 1); Jeremy Waldron, 'Positivism and Legality: Hart's Equivocal Response to Fuller' (2008) 83 *New York University Law Review* 1135 provides a full round up of Hart's remarks on the principles of legality (1147–57), along with some interesting suggestions as to why Hart was so reticent when writing about them (1157–67). Waldron tackled similar themes in 'Hart and the Principles of Legality' in M Kramer et al (eds) *The Legacy of HLA Hart: Legal, Political and Moral Philosophy* (Clarendon Press 2008).

46 Hart, 'Problems of the Philosophy of Law' (n 1) 114–15.

He further elucidates these thoughts by pointing out that

> [g]eneral rules clearly framed and publicly promulgated are the most efficient form of social control. But from the point of view of the individual citizen, they are more than that: they are required if he is to have the advantage of knowing in advance the ways in which his liberty will be restricted in the various situations in which he may find himself, and he needs this knowledge if he is to plan his life.[47]

As to the significance of the principles of legality, Hart is unambiguous:

> For any rational man, laws conferring these protections and benefits must be valuable, and the price to be paid for them in terms of limitations imposed by the law upon his own freedom will usually be worth paying.[48]

Although brief, nothing in this account is incompatible with those of Raz and Fuller. The conditions and values Raz identified are present in Hart's picture of RoL1 just as they are in Fuller's. Thus adherence to the rule of law, according to Hart, protects the ability to plan one's life by furnishing some degree of certainty and stability. Compliance with RoL1 principles provides notice as to when one's freedom is likely to be curtailed. But why are stability, certainty, and notice important, if not as ways of upholding or protecting autonomy and liberty? The main problem with Hart's account is thus not one of incompatibility with the others but of brevity: he leaves so much unsaid that we cannot be absolutely certain he would accept those aspects of Raz's and Fuller's accounts—the emphasis on autonomy, for example, or the 'view of man' invoked—that go beyond his. Only by turning to Hart's non-rule-of-law writings do we discover his views on matters such as this.[49]

3.2 A forgotten value?

Each of these accounts holds that RoL1 can enhance the stability of the environment in which agents exist. RoL1 therefore allows agents to go about their everyday lives with some degree of certainty and facilitates their more long-term planning, in the sense of setting and pursuing life goals. For Raz, adherence to RoL1 increases predictability and thus can 'increase one's power of action', while Fuller characterizes this in terms of reciprocity ('these are the rules we expect you to follow, if you follow them they will be applied to your conduct'). Hart terms this the 'advantage of knowing in advance the ways in which . . . [one's] liberty will be restricted', which allows one to plan one's life. We should not exaggerate RoL1's role here, for it surely cannot bring about conditions of relative predictability, certainty, and stability on its own—much will depend upon other conditions obtaining in the society in question. Yet, in two societies roughly comparable in terms of the broader social conditions that bring about and sustain order, Hart, Fuller, and Raz would

[47] Hart, 'Problems of the Philosophy of Law' (n 1) 115.

[48] Hart, 'Problems of the Philosophy of Law' (n 1) 116.

[49] See HLA Hart, *Punishment and Responsibility* (2nd edn, Clarendon Press 2008), chs II and IV–VIII; and *Law, Liberty and Morality* (Clarendon Press 1963).

probably maintain that that in which the rule of law obtains has a greater degree of stability, certainty, and predictability and thus facilitates better the planning and pursuit of everyday lives and life-goals.

The predictability, stability, and certainty enhanced by RoL1 assuredly provide fertile ground for one value not yet mentioned: freedom as non-domination. Contemporary civic republicans hold that this conception of freedom is distinct from both positive and negative conceptions. It is, according to Philip Pettit,

> negative to the extent that it requires the absence of domination by others, not necessarily the presence of self-mastery, whatever that is thought to involve [and] . . . positive to the extent that . . . it needs something more than absence of interference; it requires security against interference, in particular against interference on an arbitrary basis.[50]

Domination looks like this: '[o]ne agent dominates another if and only if they have a certain power over that other, in particular a power of interference on an arbitrary basis.'[51]

That arbitrariness is the core of domination on this account of freedom might make it particularly enticing as a statement of the value served by RoL1. The temptation is one of intellectual tidiness and symmetry: an account of the rule of law that sees a connection between it and arbitrariness, such that the latter tells us what is wrong when many rule-of-law principles are breached, is a neat fit with an account which holds that non-domination (in the sense of freedom from arbitrary power) is the value protected by the rule of law.[52] I do not think it completely wrong to succumb to this temptation, but at least two caveats must be noted before falling headlong in love. The first caveat in this intellectual pre-nuptial agreement involves noting that the temptation undoubtedly has other grounds. One such ground is that the idea of non-domination is consistent with the substance of what Fuller, Hart, and Raz actually say about the importance of stability, predictability, and certainty for human beings living in groups. Yet there might be an urge to put the point in stronger terms: what other concern or value, if not *something very like* non-domination, can inform these remarks? The second caveat is no less obvious. It reminds us that to accept non-domination as a value served by RoL1 does not, at first glance at least, commit us to the view that it is the only value served by RoL1.

And there are, for Raz, Fuller, and Hart, clearly other values in play. The predictability, stability, and certainty that RoL1 maintains allows autonomy to take root, understood as the power to formulate and pursue a general life plan. Autonomy is an expansive value, since it embraces not just liberation from

[50] Philip Pettit, *Republicanism* (Clarendon Press 1997) 51. See also Q Skinner, *Liberty Before Liberalism* (Cambridge University Press 1998) ch 2. Arthur Ripstein reminds us that what Pettit terms 'security against interference' looks very similar to the right of independence at the core of Kant's legal and political philosophy in Arthur Ripstein, *Force and Freedom: Kant's Legal and Political Philosophy* (Harvard University Press 2009), at 15 and ch 2.

[51] Pettit, *Republicanism* (n 50) 52.

[52] Note that for Pettit (Pettit, *Republicanism* (n 50) 55) arbitrariness is a much narrower notion than for us.

and control over some of one's wants and desires, but also some realm of non-interference from others such that one is free to pursue some of one's (second-order) wants and desires. While only Raz explicitly speaks of autonomy as a value protected by RoL1, Hart and Fuller implicitly accept its connection with RoL1 insofar as both recognize that the rule of law respects an agent's ability 'to plan his life'[53] (or 'his powers of self-determination'[54]). Furthermore, this ability and these powers surely explain Raz's invocation of dignity—'respecting human dignity entails treating humans as persons capable of planning and plotting their future'—and animates Fuller's statement of the 'view of man' implicit in RoL1. That view is one of humans as responsible agents, capable of self-determination. Hence '[e]very departure from the principles of the law's inner morality is an affront to man's dignity as a responsible agent.'[55] The value of freedom from interference is also significant for Hart and Raz. While neither seems to regard law as compatible with freedom in this sense, both nevertheless maintain that legal systems which adhere to the principles of RoL1 are valuable because they provide their addressees with notice as to when the law's coercive force will be felt (assuming that the law is consistently and assiduously enforced). Knowing when one's liberty will be restricted in this way allows one, as Hart notes, to better plan one's life. This knowledge, for Raz, adds to the predictability of one's environment and makes one's ability to choose between options 'effective'. It is in this sense that the rule of law 'may be yet another way of protecting personal freedom'.[56]

At this point the effort to show that the value of non-domination informs RoL1 seems foolish. Since autonomy, dignity, and freedom (as non-interference[57]) are undoubtedly in play, why attempt to shoehorn freedom as non-domination into this picture and portray Raz, Hart, and Fuller as unwitting civic republicans? That freedom as non-domination does not feature explicitly in RoL1 is not a conclusive objection to this effort since, if the story contemporary civic republicans tell of the invention, loss, and rediscovery of this value is plausible, then we should not expect it to figure in work of this vintage. We should nevertheless (the story goes) expect freedom as non-domination to make sense of many of our contemporary political and juristic idioms, since the notion exerts significant gravitational pull even though we have been blinded to its presence. But is there anything more that can be said of the effort to show that non-domination informs RoL1, than that it is not incompatible with the values and conditions proponents of RoL1 themselves emphasize?

[53] Hart, 'Problems of the Philosophy of Law' (n 1) 115.
[54] Fuller, *Morality* (n 1) 162.
[55] Fuller, *Morality* (n 1) 162.
[56] Raz, 'The Rule of Law' (n 1) 204.
[57] Fuller is a bad fit in a list of jurists interested in and committed to a conception of freedom as absence of interference. He is in general very quiet on the link between RoL1 and freedom (however understood) in *The Morality of Law*: the book has no index entries for the terms 'liberty', 'freedom', or 'coercion'. Other work suggests that Fuller's conception of freedom extends beyond simple freedom from constraint: see, for example, his 'Freedom: A Suggested Analysis' (1955) 68 *Harvard Law Review* 1305. A helpful overview of Fuller's position on freedom is KI Winston, 'Legislators and Liberty' (1994) 13 *Law and Philosophy* 389. For some interesting thoughts on another of Fuller's freedom papers see Rundle, *Forms Liberate* (n 5) 108–12.

One possibility is this: the value of non-domination is worth inserting into the picture of the values served by RoL1 because it synthesizes into a harmonious whole the apparently discrete values and conditions upheld by RoL1. The initial plausibility of this claim derives from the fact that non-domination is compatible with the values Raz, Hart, and Fuller emphasize. Moreover, freedom from interference, autonomy, and dignity all surely inform or can be seen as aspects of freedom as non-domination. The latter could therefore stand as the master-value served by RoL1. Yet this is to move far too quickly, since the compatibility between freedom as non-domination and the other values, and the former's synthesizing role, demand closer scrutiny. If the alleged compatibility relation is bogus, then freedom as non-domination can have no synthesizing role.

The compatibility claim appears reasonably plausible with regard to some of these values. Pettit's claim, for example, that freedom as non-domination and autonomy are closely connected—'it is bound to be easier for people to achieve autonomy once they are assured of not being dominated by others'[58]—seems undeniable. But an obvious sticking point for the compatibility claim is freedom as non-interference. For, although contemporary civic republicans have recognized this value either as an independent concern of the neo-republican tradition standing equal alongside other values, or as a subsidiary value important because of its possible effect upon freedom as non-domination, this inclusionary spirit is not displayed by many proponents of freedom as non-interference.[59] Those proponents usually regard freedom as non-interference as incompatible with freedom as non-domination, the former being, on their view, simply conceptually and normatively better as an account of freedom than any of the alternatives.[60] It is therefore no surprise to find them arguing that freedom as non-domination occupies no distinct conceptual space, there being no significant difference between it and freedom from interference.[61]

That this dispute must be resolved before freedom as non-domination could play its synthesizing, unifying role with regard to the other values that RoL1 upholds is obvious. Equally plain is that neither time nor space allows an attempt at resolution here. Furthermore, even if such a resolution were forthcoming, something must be said in addition in favour of synthesis and unity in this context. Neatness is not in and of itself a self-evident intellectual virtue and we might, therefore, have to illustrate the practical or other advantages of this strategy. For these reasons, then, the Scots law verdict of 'not proven' seems the most appropriate judgment to make upon freedom as non-domination's synthesizing role. Henceforth I'll assume that RoL1 serves at least four distinct and thus to some extent independent values: dignity, autonomy, freedom from interference, and freedom as non-domination.

[58] Pettit, *Republicanism* (n 50) 82.
[59] The former is Skinner's view, see Skinner, *Liberty Before Liberalism* (n 50) 82–7, while the latter is Pettit's, see Pettit, *Republicanism* (n 50) 300–2.
[60] See the story as told in Pettit, *Republicanism* (n 50), 297–9.
[61] See M Kramer, *The Quality of Freedom* (Clarendon Press 2003) ch 2.

3.3 Private law, values, arbitrariness

There is little doubt that, among the values informing and served by private law, autonomy, dignity, non-domination, and freedom from interference loom large. A reminder is provided by Charles Fried's elegant and entirely orthodox view of some of the key components of private law and the way they hang together:

> [t]he law of property defines the boundaries of our rightful possessions, while the law of tort seeks to makes us whole against violations of those boundaries, as well as against violations of the natural boundaries of our physical person. Contract law ratifies and enforces our joint ventures beyond those boundaries. Thus the law of torts and the law of property recognise our rights as individuals in our persons, in our labour, and in some definite portion of the external world, while the law of contracts facilitates our disposing of these rights on terms which seem best to us. The regime of contract law, which respects the dispositions individuals make of their rights, carries to its natural conclusion the liberal premise that individuals have rights.[62]

The law of tort and property thus protect a sphere within which agents are free from interference. Both bodies of doctrine, alongside the injunctions of the criminal law, set parameters within which law's addressees are in principle free from the coercive intervention of other addressees. Furthermore, this sphere serves as protection against the arbitrary power of other ordinary citizens *as well as* against that of corporate and government bodies (assuming the latter to be subject to the ordinary—private and criminal—law of the land).

The kinds of arbitrary power against which citizens are protected, to some degree at least, by these areas of private law are primarily instances of S1 and S2 arbitrariness (with the exception, in the latter case, of 'vires' arbitrariness). By delineating and stabilizing not only agents' holdings and the ways in which they can be legitimately transferred, but also by protecting the boundaries of the physical person, private law forms an obvious bulwark against the exercise of power without warrant. The scheme of rights and entitlements embodied in private law constitutes a prima facie hurdle, which must be surmounted through legal means or brazenly discarded, to the exercise of such force. And even when that hurdle is overcome, the overcoming remains either regrettable (as when such rights and entitlements are legally overridden) or plain wrong (when there is no such legal licence). Tort and property law do not provide any specific protection against S3 arbitrariness, save that the inconsistent exercise of power might run up against the parameter set by these rights and entitlements. If, for example, I am a particularly capricious power-wielder, I can only advance my friends and disadvantage my enemies in ways consistent with their equal bundles of private law protections. My inconsistency is thus to some degree disciplined and constrained but not, of course, eliminated.

[62] Charles Fried, *Contract as Promise* (Harvard University Press 1981) 1–2. For what I take to be an interesting statement of the same point, but in quite different language, see S Shapiro, *Legality* (Harvard University Press 2011) 134.

That these areas of private law putatively protect all legal persons against the arbitrariness of all other legal persons will surprise only those gripped particularly tightly by the public law perspective. From this perspective, the only worrisome sources of potentially arbitrary power in the world are law-makers and their executive functionaries. One common accompanying claim holds that these sources of power are particularly troubling because of the scale of the power deployed; it is so all-embracing as to make the holders and their use of it especially worthy of concern. Yet another, equally common supplementary claim insists that the rule of law's importance is that it 'cabins, cribs, and confines' this perhaps unique power.[63] But we need not deny that law-makers and their executive functionaries are vexing sources of potential arbitrariness, nor must we question some of the assumptions here—is the scale of this power truly unique? How might we measure it? With what should we compare it?—for this point to stand: that the world contains *other* worrisome sources of potentially arbitrary power. One such source is surely one's fellow citizens, as well as other legal (non-governmental or non-executive) persons.

If the sphere of freedom from interference that tort and property law create is relatively stable, then they serve to notify agents when they are likely to run up against, and when they will be free from, juridical interferences from others. That function, of course, is one that RoL1 also performs: both private law and RoL1 give addressees the 'advantage of knowing in advance the ways in which . . . [their] liberty will be restricted'.[64] That knowledge facilitates the pursuit of life goals and choices of the kind which mark an autonomous life, its provision—via relatively stable and enforced legal rules—embodying respect for human dignity as conceived by Raz and Fuller. The possibility of those choices is further protected and extended by facilitative areas of private law such as contract law and trusts. These bodies of law do not hold spheres of freedom steady, as tort and property law do, but allow law's addressees to embed plans in the future and thus extend their freedom across time. They therefore facilitate autonomy and embed respect for human dignity in a somewhat different way from tort, criminal law, and land law.

The exact degree of certainty contract and trusts give to future plans depends not just upon the details and means of enforcing these areas of law, but also on the general conditions obtaining in the particular society in question. Yet even if addressees are dependent solely upon the law for stability, that still seems better than a solitary, nasty, brutish, and short state of nature. That legal systems, when compliant with RoL1 principles and containing certain substantive private and criminal law components, facilitate the pursuit of life plans by their addressees is plainly not an insight. But repeating the point reminds us why talk of autonomy, as well as of liberty, and of non-domination, is appropriate here. The ability to formulate and pursue life plans is a vital component of all plausible accounts of the nature of autonomy; that that ability requires some realm of freedom from interference for its realization is equally obvious. The certainty that contract, trusts, and other facilitative areas of private law can confer on future plans and transactions

[63] I am, of course, echoing Macbeth: Act III sc iv l 23 (*The Tragedy of Macbeth*).
[64] Hart, 'Problems of the Philosophy of Law' (n 1) 115.

also serves as insurance against domination for, insofar as no one other than the transacting parties has the power to end contracts, trust arrangements, and other dispositions of holdings, those contracts, arrangements, and dispositions are secure against interference. If any or all of the contracts and other arrangements one enters into can be ended at the whim of another not privy to those transactions, then those transactions and, in a sense, one's self are in the thrall of that other. That is domination, not freedom.[65] By protecting against this particular form of domination, these areas of private law also act as bulwarks against S1, S2, and S3 arbitrariness.

Detailed examination of particular private law doctrines—those dealing with vitiating factors in contract, for example, or the various conditions for agency in tort—would disclose how deeply the values of non-domination, freedom from interference, and autonomy are embedded in the law.[66] But there is another way, noted by Raz, in which private law can uphold or facilitate these values. His observation that RoL1 functions as a 'policy of self-restraint to make the law itself a stable and safe basis for planning'[67] is surely undeniable. Also undeniable, and of obvious relevance to private law as it has developed and been understood in the common law world, is the claim that law can 'stabilise social relationships . . . which may disintegrate or develop in erratic or unpredictable ways'.[68] It is not Whig-ish to think that those areas of private law most commonly claimed to have developed from, and been associated with, customary norms and standards of behaviour might have played exactly this role. If that was the case, and possibly still is the case, then private law again engenders precisely the same values as RoL1. The values served by some degree of stability, predictability, and certainty in our collective and individual lives are the core of both RoL1 and private law.

Finally, it is important to stress the exact nature of my argument against the public law perspective in this subsection. I have claimed only (i) that there is a source of potential arbitrariness in addition to those (law-makers and their executive functionaries) that are the focus of that perspective; and (ii) that there are plausible senses in which private law addresses that source of arbitrariness. Once this is accepted, it becomes tempting to regard private law and public law as quite different forms of constraint upon power and arbitrariness. Private law can be viewed as a constraint upon 'horizontal' arbitrariness, by which is meant that it impedes the power (*de jure* and *de facto*) deployed by all addressees of the law. While those addressees might differ in many ways—they may be either human or

65 'What constitutes domination is the fact that in some respect the power-bearer has the capacity to interfere arbitrarily, even if they are never going to do so': Pettit, *Republicanism* (n 50), 63. For further thoughts on the nature of interference, see P Pettit, 'Law and Liberty' ch 1 of S Besson and JL Marti (eds), *Legal Republicanism* (Clarendon Press 2009) at 42–9 and ch 1 of his *On the People's Terms* (Cambridge University Press 2012).

66 I have quite rightly been reminded that the misuse of process and misuse of public power torts ought not to be overlooked here: see J Murphy and C Witting, *Street on Torts* (13th edn, Clarendon Press 2012) ch 23.

67 Raz, 'The Rule of Law' (n 1) 203.

68 Raz, 'The Rule of Law' (n 1) 203.

corporate legal persons, public or private legal persons, state or non-state legal persons—they are also assumed, in most modern legal systems, to have the same legal standing. They supposedly have equal bundles of the same legal rights, duties, liabilities, and powers, private law in part distributing and stabilizing those bundles as well as constraining their exercise. In guaranteeing the same bundle of rights for all addressees of the law, and by holding all addressees of the law (in principle at least) to respect the bundle of rights of all other addressees, private law establishes a form of horizontal juridical equality: all have the same legal standing.

Where some legal persons or actors have different legal standing, having for example greater legal powers or immunities than others, then that asymmetry is often regarded as especially worthy of attention. Lawyers may well come to think that these especial powers and immunities require unique forms of legal regulation: the power here looks exceptional because it is deployed by legal persons who do not stand equal with all other legal persons. The arbitrary power that such exceptional legal actors may exercise therefore looks like vertical rather than horizontal power, a potential juridical sword of Damocles hanging over all other legal persons. Within the common law world, public law is usually seen as the means of disciplining the vertical power deployed by the state, the state being conceived as an exceptional source of power in either *de jure* (its exceptional powers, duties, liabilities, and immunities being enshrined in law) or *de facto* (the power it displaces is simply unique among all other sources of power) terms.

Thus stated, the temptation of the vertical/horizontal distinction is clear but so, too, are its hazards.[69] One such is that of slipping from this helpful distinction into another thoroughly misguided distinction, namely, one holding that public law and private law have entirely different target domains, the former being concerned solely with the realm of the state and the latter with the realm of the private (or non-state). There are few helpful senses in which the state, understood in anything like a plausible way, is absent from modern systems of private law: at the very least, the state upholds the court structure, funds the judiciary, and the mechanisms of enforcement that those systems rely upon for their efficacy. Furthermore, various aspects of the state, from central to local government bodies, and all their cognates, are players in the system of private law just like other legal persons—they enter contracts, commit torts, overpay, and fail to pay bills. Whether or not the power of the state is either *de facto* or *de jure* unique, the latter point reminds us that in common law jurisdictions, at least, the state is merely one among other players in the private law system. The various roles the state plays with regard to private law have little or no bearing upon the distinction between vertical and horizontal power-cum-arbitrariness.

[69] There is a rough analogy between this version of the distinction and the direct effect of some EU law provisions. See *Defrenne v SABENA* (Case 2/74) [1974] ECR 631 for background. Gerald J Postema's chapter in this volume 'Fidelity in Law's Commonwealth' provides an altogether more sophisticated statement and deployment of the distinction than that in this essay.

4. Conclusion

The rule of law and private law are not strangers. They protect against the same ill—arbitrariness—maintain the same conditions, and serve the same values. The task of highlighting this functional similarity is neither an insight nor an advance, but a series of reminders about what we lawyers have long known. In the course of issuing these reminders I have tried to do two other things: (i) to show that there is a helpful and important link between the rule of law and arbitrariness, such that the latter often tells us what is wrong with breaches of the former; and (ii) to loosen the grip the public law perspective has upon our thinking about the rule of law. These various tilts at multiple windmills might well be mistaken; if so, my hope is that they are interestingly and informatively mistaken.

3

The Rule of Law as the Rule of Private Law

*TRS Allan**

1.

The rule of law is a principle or doctrine usually associated mainly with public law: it is regarded, primarily, as a barrier to certain sorts of arbitrary governmental power, designed to control the manner in which public ends or interests are furthered or secured. Implicit in this perspective on the rule of law is a mainly instrumentalist conception of law: law is intrinsically a tool in governmental hands; and the rule of law acts as a constraint on the way in which that tool is wielded, shielding individuals from the worst excesses of authorized state coercion. An instrumentalist conception—readily compatible, at least, with the legal positivist denial of any necessary connection between law and morality—makes law the product of a constitutional regime founded on the empirical realities of state power. In a democracy, the power of the majority, or at least a special majority, ultimately determines the content of law; the balance of public power and private right or interest depends, in the last resort, on what the majority chooses to make it. Private law must be viewed, in that perspective, as subservient to general public ends: the identification of individual domains of freedom, as regards interaction between private citizens, is finally the product of state policy, dependent on a fluid and fluctuating political agenda.

There is, however, a radically different perspective on the rule of law that moves private law to centre-stage, denying its supposed subservience (in the last analysis) to public law and governmental policy. From this perspective, the rule of law is not a check on the exercise of state power through law; it is instead a moral ideal of *legality*, underlying and informing our grasp of the concept of law itself. A determination of the content of law, on this view, is the conclusion of an enquiry into what, in all the circumstances, the rule of law demands: legal rights and duties reflect not merely formal legal sources, expressing recognized political authority, but also a judgment of the requirements of legality, understood as a moral ideal. Insofar as private law embodies a just scheme of rights, powers, and duties to

* The comments on earlier drafts by participants at the Toronto workshop, my colleague Nigel Simmonds, and the editors of this volume are all very gratefully acknowledged.

regulate the private sphere—the interaction of individuals, regarded as equal and autonomous, entitled to respect for their separate aspirations and projects—it constitutes the major substance of the rule of law. The ordinary civil law and criminal law together define the protected domains of liberty within which individuals can pursue their own ends in cooperation with others, each enjoying the same freedom. While the specific content of civil and criminal law will vary from jurisdiction to jurisdiction, the maintenance of a system of regulation that serves an existing order of interaction is a basic requirement of the rule of law.

It is an important feature of our concept of law that it should provide moral justification for state coercion: force is legitimately applied only insofar as state officials (including judges) are authorized to act by existing law. It is not sufficient that coercion would be conducive to the public good, according to an official view of the public interest or general welfare. Force must be employed only within the limits of, and in accordance with the specific conditions of, grants of public authority previously made, so that the law acts as a barrier between evolving public policy and its implementation by interference in the affairs of individuals. The same applies to an award of compensation or damages against a private defendant in an action based on tort or contract: the administration of justice means justice according to law, previously enacted or established and applicable to all similar cases (according to public and defensible criteria of similarity). Law cannot, then, be whatever is imposed or announced by senior officials, even if such officials are elected by a majority of citizens. Legal rights and duties cannot be identified without reflection on the basic requirements of the principle of the rule of law: they derive from a general scheme of regulation whose consistent and impartial enforcement serves such fundamental values as liberty, equality, and human dignity.

In this essay, I shall elaborate these ideas by reflection on FA Hayek's robust repudiation of legal positivism, emphasizing his identification of law, properly so called, with the ordinary private law—the *nomos*, or rules of just conduct, by contrast with *thesis*, the regulations governing public administration. Hayek's understanding of the rule of law matched AV Dicey's famous conception, which gave pride of place to the 'ordinary law' as a bulwark of individual freedom. We shall see that Joseph Raz's critique of Hayek, rooted in a positivist and instrumentalist conception of law, proceeds from an unduly narrow and impoverished account of the rule of law. Hayek's work helps us to see the manner in which private law exhibits the nature and meaning of the rule of law. Consisting in the regular and reliable enforcement of rules that reflect and confirm an independent order of actions—independent of governmental ends or the assertion of political authority—private law reveals the fundamental point of the rule of law. By defining the boundaries of each person's freedom of choice and action, private law (along with the ordinary criminal law) secures an inviolable domain of liberty. A basic autonomy (in a sense to be elucidated) is preserved as a condition of the legitimacy of the state's coercive authority.

2.

The rule of law is often equated by legal theorists with the precepts of formal legality that Lon Fuller placed at the heart of his own engagement with legal positivism.[1] Seeking to expose an intrinsic connection between law and justice, Fuller attempted to show that compliance with certain canons of formal justice was a necessary condition of effective governance. There could not be law, in the sense of legislation, unless it met the requirements of the 'inner morality of law': it must consist of general rules which were published, prospective, intelligible, free from conflict and contradiction, possible to comply with, and not constantly being changed; and there must be congruence between the rules declared and official action. These desiderata are not merely minimal requirements for the existence of law, but also formal features of law that can be satisfied to varying degrees: they identify elements of an ideal of legality towards which law, in its very nature, aspires. If law is an intrinsically moral phenomenon, it is so in virtue of that moral aspiration: instances of law count as such by the extent of their approximation to what Nigel Simmonds has dubbed the archetype of law.[2]

Consisting of general rules, as opposed to ad hoc commands to particular persons, law contains within itself an ideal form: it aspires to a form of excellence comprising high standards of compliance with each of the canons of formal legality. Lon Fuller's famous allegory, in which Rex attempts but fails to make law for his subjects, illustrates eight different violations of the inner morality of law; but beyond the 'morality of duty' lies the 'morality of aspiration':

> Corresponding to these [modes of failure] are eight kinds of legal excellence toward which a system of rules may strive. What appear at the lowest level as indispensable conditions for the existence of law at all, become, as we ascend the scale of achievement, increasingly demanding challenges to human capacity.[3]

We are not to imagine a utopia of legality in which all the formal precepts of the rule of law are fully satisfied, but the ideal of legality latent within the practice of law suggests 'eight distinct standards by which excellence in legality may be tested'.

While Fuller failed clearly to articulate the basis of the moral ideal of the rule of law—the moral value served by conscientious conformity to the canons of formal legality—Simmonds makes good the deficiency. Even if an oppressive regime invokes the law to curtail its subjects' freedom, in the sense of their range of choices of action or lifestyle, its observance of the rule of law (in Fuller's sense) serves the value of freedom in the sense of independence. We can draw on republican political thought in explicating the intimate, conceptual connection between law and liberty. A citizen who enjoys the protection of the rule of law is granted immunity from arbitrary interference, whether by state officials or other citizens, who may

1 Lon L Fuller, *The Morality of Law* (rev edn, Yale University Press 1969).
2 Nigel Simmonds, *Law as a Moral Idea* (Oxford University Press 2007) 64–8.
3 Fuller, *Morality* (n 1) 41.

object to his manner of exercise of whatever freedom of action the rules bestow. No one can obstruct his actions, or silence his speech, unless the general law permits it: public and private power alike must bow to law, administered by independent courts, insulated (as far as possible) from political or economic or social pressure.

The moral value of the rule of law lies chiefly, then, in its capacity to safeguard liberty as independence. The free citizen may be contrasted with the slave along precisely these lines. It is conceivable that a free man might have fewer options available to him than a slave, if the slave has a benevolent master:

> The connection between slavery and a restricted set of options is therefore purely contingent, yet we do not think that slavery is only contingently connected with freedom: we think of slavery as the very embodiment of unfreedom. Even when the slave has an extensive range of options available to him, we think of him as unfree. This is presumably because of the conditions under which he enjoys that extensive range of options, for they are fully dependent upon the will of the master.[4]

The rule of law, understood as the precepts of formal legality, is intrinsically linked to liberty in the sense in which slavery is regarded as intrinsically violative of liberty:

> When a citizen lives under the rule of law, it is conceivable that the duties imposed upon him or her will be very extensive and onerous, and the interstices between these duties might leave very few options available. Yet, if the rule of law is a reality, the duties will have limits and the limits will not be dependent upon the will of any other person.[5]

Even a relatively austere and spartan account of the rule of law, then, illuminates the conceptual connection between law and liberty. We can understand the most basic sense in which law is the antithesis of arbitrary power: a regime of law constitutes a bulwark against unregulated interference with each person's liberty, whether by public officials or private citizens; all such interference must be consistent with previously published and readily ascertainable general rules. A grasp of the nature of law as a safeguard of freedom as independence also points to further features of the rule of law, beyond Fuller's somewhat modest account. In the sphere of public law, the rule of law encompasses every aspect of legal doctrine necessary to ensure that, where administrative discretion is conferred on public officials or agencies, such discretion is not abused. The principles of natural justice (or procedural fairness) aim, above all, to ensure that people are treated fairly in accordance with whatever criteria the pertinent rules or policies provide; and requirements of rationality or reasonableness impose companion constraints of consistency, requiring public authorities to show that coercive action is genuinely and closely related to acknowledged and legitimate public ends.

Insofar as state officials adhere to the formal precepts of the rule of law, extended to include the precepts of legality applicable to the exercise of administrative discretion, they acknowledge the claims of individual freedom and human dignity: liberty as independence is preserved, at least insofar as the grant and exercise of discretionary governmental powers reasonably permit. An exclusive focus on public

[4] Simmonds, *Moral Idea* (n 2) 101.
[5] Simmonds, *Moral Idea* (n 2) 101.

law, however, diverts our attention from a body of legal doctrine that arguably has the prior claim to recognition as an instantiation of the rule of law. The principal doctrines and requirements of private law operate to guarantee liberty as independence, as regards the interaction of private persons and organizations. The ordinary civil and criminal law together provide a framework within which the citizen is free to pursue his own chosen ends, subject to constraints that afford a similar freedom to others. If there is a moral obligation to obey the law, it arises because universal adherence to the civil and criminal law provides the only conditions under which liberty, in the sense of independence, can be assured.[6] This characterization of private law is, it appears, implicit within a general account of constitutional governance, subject to the rule of law:

> Law represents the only possible set of conditions within which one can live in community with others while enjoying some domain of entitlement that is secure from the power of others. When a government pursues its objectives through the rule of law, it governs consistently with those conditions. To show that a rule is law is to show that it forms part of a system of universality, necessity and independence: that is to say, a system of general rules and principles (universality) that are given peremptory force and are reliably enforced (necessity) . . . Such a system of reliably enforced rules represents the only conditions within which one can live in political community and nevertheless enjoy a degree of freedom (independence).[7]

Insofar as state officials are required to act in conformity to previously announced general rules, being unable to assert an unfettered will as regards the treatment of particular persons or the disposition of specific cases, their position mirrors that of the ordinary citizen, obliged to honour established legal constraints in his relations with other persons. There would, moreover, be little point to such official self-restraint if the citizen were not assured of similar protection against arbitrary private power. Our efforts to bring governmental action within the limits of the rule of law presuppose that the relations between private citizens (and private groups or organizations) are already effectively regulated by law. Respect for human dignity and autonomy demands the consistent and reliable enforcement of both public and private law.

3.

Contrasting accounts of the rule of law reflect and embody competing conceptions of law. When the rule of law is viewed as an ideal to which any actual system of law inherently aspires—a moral ideal that expresses the nature of law itself—law is conceived as a form of governance associated with ideals of liberty and justice. A certain relationship between ruler and ruled, respectful of human freedom and

[6] Compare Arthur Ripstein, *Force and Freedom: Kant's Legal and Political Philosophy* (Harvard University Press 2009) especially ch 2.

[7] Simmonds, *Moral Idea* (n 2) 143.

dignity, is treated as a value to which law is necessarily and internally related. The generality of law is understood to provide a bulwark against any arbitrary exercise of power—arbitrary in the sense of subjecting identifiable persons to the will of those who can wield substantial political or economic power. When the law consists of general rules and principles, capable of being enforced by impartial and independent courts, no one is at the mercy of another's hostility or whim: he enjoys the protection of the rule of law. Even when the rules impose onerous constraints on freedom, inimical to individual autonomy, liberty in the sense of independence—freedom from domination or the threat of interference—is preserved by faithful adherence, whether by officials or private citizens, to those rules. When, however, the rules embody a legitimate scheme of mutual cooperation, securing compatible domains of freedom, law is linked to justice: liberty as independence attains the full protection of the rule of law.

A competing vision of the rule of law denies the moral nature of law, viewing it as essentially a tool in the hands of government for the implementation of policy. An instrument that may be wielded by autocratic and authoritarian regimes as readily as liberal and democratic ones, the law transmits the rulers' will to ensure their subjects' obedience. Conformity to the rule of law, in the sense of formal and procedural legality, remains a valuable safeguard against arbitrariness; but the rule of law in this conception is mainly a defence against the abuse of law, rather than a moral ideal informing the nature of law itself. If, moreover, the rule of law is only one of a number of competing political values, it may be sacrificed, when necessary, for other pressing public ends. It may even be thought that the rule of law—adherence to settled procedural rules and the security that stems from regular enforcement of general rules—must surrender to democracy, where democracy is equated with the temporary will of a current majority (or its elected representatives).

When the rule of law is understood, instead, as an ideal internal to the very nature of law, its integrity is a condition of the legitimacy of state coercion. If there is an important connection between rule through law and respect for human dignity, our conception of legality must be appropriately complex and nuanced. We should challenge the notion that the rule of law can be traded off against countervailing benefits, as if a departure from legality can be assuaged by the desirability of the outcome—the ends justifying the means. Admittedly, rule must sometimes surrender to discretion, allowing state authorities to tailor their policies to a variety of circumstances that may be hard to predict in advance; the application of vague or open-ended standards to particular cases will leave people reliant, to some degree, on the good faith, competence, and fairness of public officials. Public law, however, must enforce appropriate safeguards against abuse of discretionary power: the rule of law generates requirements of procedural fairness and substantive rationality that narrowly confine the boundaries of discretion, making official coercion subject to demanding constraints of due process. The substantive equality attained by consistent application of general rules, excluding arbitrary discrimination between persons, is secured instead by requirements of *justification*, pertinent to particular instances and enforced by independent courts.[8]

The divergent views of FA Hayek and Joseph Raz about the nature of law and the ideal of the rule of law perfectly illustrate these contrasting philosophical outlooks. Hayek distinguishes between law properly so called—the law identified by the principle of the rule of law—and the authoritative instructions given to officials as regards performance of their public duties, which are not law in the primary sense of the term. *Nomos*, comprising the 'rules of just conduct' that emerge to regulate and sustain a spontaneous order of actions, is contrasted with *thesis*, associated with legislation concerned with the direction and regulation of government. Far from law being imposed by political authority, political society is, on this account, the result of individuals observing common rules: authority derives from law (rather than the converse) in the sense that 'authority commands obedience because (and so long as) it enforces a law presumed to exist independently of it and resting on a diffused opinion of what is right'.[9] Whereas an order giving instructions to officials may be 'executed', a rule of just conduct 'merely limits the range of permitted action and usually does not determine a particular action; and what it prescribes is never accomplished but remains a standing obligation on all'.[10]

Raz acknowledges no such distinction between *nomos* and *thesis*, asserting that for the lawyer, if not the layman, 'anything is the law if it meets the conditions of validity laid down in the system's rules of recognition or in other rules of the system'.[11] But recognizing that this is at odds with the ideal of the rule of law, in contradistinction to rule by men and women, Raz proposes a different distinction. The layman's view of law, which reflects the ideal of the rule of law, consists in a sub-class of such valid rules: 'To him the law is essentially a set of open, general, and relatively stable laws.'[12] This attitude is taken as the basis of a distinction between the law, on the one hand, and the rule of law, on the other. The law is not confined to such general and stable rules but includes particular legal orders, 'an essential tool in the hands of the executive and judiciary alike'. What the rule of law requires is merely that the making of particular orders should be 'guided by open, stable, clear, and general rules', which will 'impose limits on the unpredictability introduced by the particular orders' of government officials and agencies.[13] In this account, the law is plainly the product of official authority: it is imposed by social institutions rather than, in any fundamental sense, constituting the society in which those institutions function.

In associating the rule of law with the universal application of settled rules of just conduct, Hayek invokes the same conception of liberty that explains the moral

[8] See further TRS Allan, *The Sovereignty of Law: Freedom, Constitution, and Common Law* (Oxford University Press 2013) especially chs 3, 6.

[9] FA Hayek, *Law, Legislation and Liberty* i: *Rules and Order* (Routledge & Kegan Paul 1982) 95.

[10] Hayek, *Law, Legislation and Liberty* (n 9) i. 127.

[11] Joseph Raz, 'The Rule of Law and its Virtue' in *The Authority of Law: Essays on Law and Morality* (2nd edn, Oxford University Press 2009) 213.

[12] Raz, *Authority* (n 11) 213.

[13] Raz, *Authority* (n 11) 215–16.

value of adherence to Fuller's precepts of formal legality. Adherence to legality, in the sense of compliance with the rules that reflect and sustain an established order of actions, generates a certain quality of freedom. Our freedom as independence is secured by other people's inability to interfere with our plans and actions except insofar as existing rules allow: we are accorded a protected sphere of deliberation and action, free from the fear of unpredictable, hostile intervention by other persons, whether citizens or officials. Hayek invokes John Locke's contention that political freedom 'is to have a standing rule to live by', common to everyone: it is the 'liberty to follow my own will in all things, where that rule prescribes not; and not to be subject to the inconstant, uncertain, arbitrary will of another man'.[14] It is primarily liberty as independence, or freedom from domination, that Hayek is defending:

> The [pertinent] conception of freedom under the law . . . rests on the contention that when we obey laws, in the sense of general abstract rules laid down irrespective of their application to us, we are not subject to another man's will and are therefore free. It is because the lawgiver does not know the particular cases to which his rules will apply, and it is because the judge who applies them has no choice in drawing the conclusions that follow from the existing body of rules and the particular facts of the case, that it can be said that laws and not men rule.[15]

While acknowledging that the rule of law is an ideal that may be hard fully to realize in practice, Hayek would not countenance deliberate departures from it in the pursuit of incompatible governmental ends. For Raz, by contrast, the rule of law is a political value that can be traded off against other public gains. Hayek's objections to the exercise of coercive administrative discretion, allowing officials to curtail people's liberty in ways not previously specified by general rules, are quickly dismissed: Hayek is alleged to have exaggerated the importance of the rule of law. Severance of the concept of law from the rule of law enables Raz to reconcile our insistence on legality, in the minimal sense that the law should be enforced against all, with the contention that we should not make an idol of the rule of law. According to Raz, the rule of law has only prima facie force:

> It has always to be balanced against competing claims of other values . . . Conformity to the rule of law is a matter of degree, and though, other things being equal, the greater the conformity the better—other things are rarely equal. A lesser degree of conformity is often to be preferred precisely because it helps realization of other goals.[16]

In Raz's instrumentalist conception, the law serves whatever purposes its authors envisage, and conformity to the rule of law makes it a more efficient tool. When the law is contained in relatively stable, open, clear, and prospective rules, it is easier for people to obey its instructions: 'if the law is to be obeyed *it must be capable of guiding the behaviour of its subjects*.'[17] The rule of law is thus the special virtue of law in the way in which sharpness is the special virtue of knives: 'It is of the essence of law to guide behaviour through rules and courts in charge of their application.

[14] John Locke, *Two Treatises of Government*, ed Peter Laslett (Oxford University Press 1988) 283 (bk II ch 4 para 22).

[15] FA Hayek, *The Constitution of Liberty* (Routledge & Kegan Paul 1960) 153.

[16] Raz, *Authority* (n 11) 228.

[17] Raz, *Authority* (n 11) 214.

Therefore, the rule of law is the specific excellence of the law.'[18] Conformity to the rule of law is nonetheless a moral good: it protects human dignity by curtailing the evils of uncertainty and frustration of expectations that accompany breaches of the rule of law. But the principal virtue of law, when it conforms to the requirements of the rule of law, is efficiency—efficiency for whatever purposes it is intended to serve: 'Thus the rule of law is an inherent virtue of the law, but not a moral virtue as such.'[19]

Even if the rule of law is a valuable safeguard of human dignity, it is disparaged, nevertheless, as a merely 'negative value', protecting us from abuse of the power enjoyed by those in charge of the legislative machine: 'It is merely designed to minimize the harm to freedom and dignity which the law may cause in its pursuit of its goals however laudable these may be.'[20] The idea here is that the law may be an instrument of arbitrary power, and the constraints of the rule of law—the requirements of publicity, stability, and clarity—serve as a defence against such arbitrariness, albeit only a partial and prima facie defence. The rule of law is thus a negative value in two senses: 'conformity to it does not cause good except through avoiding evil and the evil which is avoided is evil which can only have been caused by the law itself.'[21]

An extension of the precepts of legality to include those principles of administrative law designed to forestall abuse of official discretion, however, shows that the rule of law is not truly a defence against, or qualification of, law itself: rather, it is a defence against the abuse of power. While the various requirements of rationality and fairness serve to ensure that administrative agencies adhere to the terms of their statutory mandates, serving the effective implementation of public policy, they constitute at the same time a barrier to arbitrary power, asserted in defiance or disregard of jurisdictional limits. Here the rule of law performs a function similar to the prevention of arbitrary private power—the abuse of superior economic or political power, wielded by non-governmental bodies. So far from being merely a protection against the abuse of law, the rule of law instead constitutes a shield against arbitrary power from wherever it appears: it is the idea that law, properly understood, is the antithesis of arbitrary power, requiring all coercive interference to be authorized by existing general rules.[22]

Raz overlooks the critical role of law as the means whereby the differing needs, interests, and aspirations of individuals can be brought into stable equilibrium, allowing each to pursue his own ends with as much freedom as an equivalent entitlement in others permits. He ignores the fundamental place of law as guardian of civil society, where the essential role of government is simply the reliable enforcement of accepted general rules applicable to interaction between private citizens. That, at least, is the ideal of law envisaged by Hayek's conception of *nomos*, reflecting the structure of autonomous or spontaneous order. The state's authority

18 Raz, *Authority* (n 11) 225.
19 Raz, *Authority* (n 11) 226.
20 Raz, *Authority* (n 11) 226.
21 Raz, *Authority* (n 11) 224.
22 Compare Jeremy Waldron, 'The Concept of Law and the Rule of Law' (2008) 43 *Georgia Law Review* 1, 11.

underpins an order of private law, which need not be the product of formally enacted rules but may be rooted in custom and common law. Insofar as the rule of law may be understood as the unswerving and impartial enforcement of such a body of private law, it has nothing to do with the manner of implementation of discrete governmental ends. And its preservation is a moral good: it secures a kind of freedom or autonomy—liberty as independence—that could not otherwise exist.

Raz supposes that Hayek is defending freedom in the sense of 'an effective ability to choose between as many options as possible'; predictability serves one's freedom of action in that sense.[23] Political freedom consists, by contrast, of '(1) the prohibition of certain forms of behaviour which interfere with personal freedom and (2) the limits imposed on the powers of public authorities in order to minimize interference with personal freedom'.[24] Whereas the criminal offences against the person illustrate the first kind of protection of freedom, the government's disability to restrict freedom of movement is an example of the second:

> The rule of law may be yet another mode of protecting personal freedom. But it has no bearing on the existence of spheres of activity free from governmental interference and is compatible with gross violations of human rights.[25]

Even if we have in mind only the implementation of government policy through law, however, we should quarrel with this assertion. Although the various precepts of formal legality may not guarantee respect for human rights, compliance with these requirements does secure a basic freedom as independence: there are legal boundaries to permissible interference, and hence at least limited scope for private initiative and action. And in the broader, more substantive conception of the rule of law, that freedom is greatly enhanced. Understood as the maintenance of established rules of private law, the rule of law is an essential buttress of personal freedom; and to the extent that government itself is subservient to the rule of law—state officials being subject to the ordinary law in the same manner as private citizens—the law provides significant protection for individual liberty and human dignity. Constitutional constraints on government or Parliament supplement the protection of liberty inherent in the requirement of compliance with existing rules. It is not merely that such compliance furthers predictability; people are accorded a sphere of independent action in which they may act as they please, regardless of the disapproval of their fellow citizens or of public officials. It is the reliable enforcement of settled rules, inhibiting other people's attempts at interference, together with the absence of any governmental discretion to employ coercion on an ad hoc or *ad hominem* basis, that secures that fundamental freedom.

4.

Hayek's *nomos*, or law of liberty, is quintessentially the ordinary common law, in which the judge seeks to maintain the integrity of an existing order of relations built

[23] Raz, *Authority* (n 11) 220. [24] Raz, *Authority* (n 11) 220.
[25] Raz, *Authority* (n 11) 220–1.

on custom and reciprocal expectations. The judge is the servant of a 'spontaneous order', constructed on the basis of reasonable expectations, dependent on evolving practice: he is not concerned with the commands of authority, or with governmental ends, but only with the implications of a system of interaction already in place and awaiting repair or refinement. Hayek distinguishes between the system of rules and the 'existing order of actions' they serve to maintain: if the rules of just conduct are well chosen, they facilitate the coordination of individual action, preventing unnecessary interferences and enabling cooperation for mutually beneficial ends. While the rules will initially be the product of spontaneous growth, their perfection depends on judicial efforts to clarify and supplement them when necessary. But the task is purely intellectual. The judge seeks to resolve a conflict generated by the deficiencies of an ongoing order of actions; he is not concerned with particular ends or 'the plight of one of the contestants'; and he does not exercise choice or will: 'in most instances it will be difficult enough to find even one solution which fits all the conditions it must satisfy.'[26]

Hayek follows Locke in pointing to property as the basis of the individual domains of freedom that spontaneous order secures. We distinguish between legitimate expectations, entitled to judicial protection, and other lesser interests or desires, by the construction of boundaries that mark out the 'life, liberty, and estates' of each individual:

> Law, liberty, and property are an inseparable trinity. There can be no law in the sense of universal rules of conduct which does not determine boundaries of the domains of freedom by laying down rules that enable each to ascertain where he is free to act.[27]

The demarcation of respective domains of freedom is, of course, a complex matter that depends on many factors. Technological advances will pose new problems for the definition and conditions of enjoyment of different sorts of property; old rules may require adaptation or reform. Hayek, however, stresses the way in which such developments occur in the context of an existing order: we build on an established system of rules, attempting to maintain and improve its ability to coordinate people's actions for the benefit of all.

The system of private law, as Hayek describes and explains it, illuminates many of the features of the rule of law, viewed as a political ideal related to individual freedom. Far from being a tool in the hands of government, law in the pertinent sense forms a bulwark against governmental power: the law is sovereign in the sense of constituting a framework of rules which is resistant to manipulation for specific political ends. The independence of private law from specific governmental purposes—beyond the purpose of maintaining a flourishing market order—confirms our conviction that the law (strictly so called) must be separate and detached from merely temporary or political or partisan plans and projects. It must be an objective order of rules and principles, serving a genuine common good that embraces all projects and purposes insofar as they can be made

[26] Hayek, *Law, Legislation and Liberty* (n 9) i. 100–1.
[27] Hayek, *Law, Legislation and Liberty* (n 9) i. 107.

compatible. Formal equality, secured by the consistent application of the rules to all who come within their scope, has a substantive dimension: being blind to personal circumstance or rank or status, the system of rules treats all alike according to its own internal logic. Insofar as the system generates and sustains reasonable expectations, allowing all to pursue their own purposes without unnecessary interference, it amounts to a scheme of justice that treats everyone equally.[28]

In the perspective of legal positivism, in which law is characteristically or primarily a product of the will of the legislator (or secondarily, that of the judge), there can be no necessary connection between law and justice. If, then, the rule of law is regarded as a constitutional safeguard, it must be a largely formal principle governing the manner in which the legislative will is imposed or implemented. It has no bearing on the content of the law, which is purely a reflection of parliamentary intention or governmental decision. Raz is memorably clear on the point. The rule of law is not to be conflated with other virtues a legal system might possess:

> It is not to be confused with democracy, justice, equality (before the law or otherwise), human rights of any kind or respect for persons or for the dignity of man. A non-democratic legal system, based on the denial of human rights, on extensive poverty, on racial segregation, sexual inequalities, and religious persecution may, in principle, conform to the requirements of the rule of law better than any of the legal systems of the more enlightened Western democracies.[29]

In his challenge to legal positivism, however, Hayek forges a necessary link between law and justice: adherence to the rule of law secures for everyone the benefits of a system of private law based on values of freedom and equality. Justice consists in adherence to a customary regime of law that owes its coherence chiefly to the efforts of impartial adjudicators to resolve disputes, where the only overarching aim or goal is the effective coordination of people's various private ends. Justice is not, on this account, a blueprint for an ideal society, adopted and pursued by public authorities, but instead a customary morality constantly finessed in response to technological change and competing expectations. Hayek emphasizes the negative character of the relevant conception of justice:

> The test which the rules of just conduct have passed in the process of their evolution to become general (and usually negative) is itself a negative test which makes necessary a gradual reformulation of these rules so as to eliminate all references to particular facts or effects which cannot be known to those who are to obey the rules. Only those rules can pass this test which are end-independent and refer only to facts which those who are to obey them can know or readily ascertain.[30]

[28] It is a scheme of justice that exhibits what Ronald Dworkin, in the broader context of both public and private law, calls *integrity*: all are treated alike in the sense that they are governed by the same general principles, imposing constraints of justification on differential treatment: see Dworkin, *Law's Empire* (Belknap Press 1986).

[29] Raz, *Authority* (n 11) 211.

[30] FA Hayek, *Law, Legislation and Liberty* ii: *The Mirage of Social Justice* (Routledge & Kegan Paul 1982) 39–40. Hayek observes that rules of just conduct will themselves usually be negative in

It is, then, a test of universalizability: justice consists in the universal application of the rules of conduct, modified and extended only so as to eliminate conflict arising between them. Even the legislator, if he wishes to enhance the effective operation of the system of private law, must obey its constraints: 'Operating upon and within such a system, and faced with the task of improving the function of an existing order of actions, he will generally have little choice which rule to lay down.'[31]

While it is now customary to ridicule the notion that judges merely apply existing law and do not make it, the idea that a common law judge *discovers* the law—even in complex and contentious cases—makes perfect sense within Hayek's account of the system of private law. A judge seeks to articulate the principles that underlie the system of rules, attempting to resolve conflicts arising from novel and unanticipated circumstances:

> While the judge's starting point will be the expectations based on already established rules, he will often have to decide which of conflicting expectations held in equally good faith and equally sanctioned by recognized rules is to be regarded as legitimate. Experience will often prove that in new situations rules which have come to be accepted lead to conflicting expectations. Yet although in such situations there will be no known rule to guide him, the judge will still not be free to decide in any manner he likes. If the decision cannot be logically deduced from recognized rules, it still must be consistent with the existing body of such rules in the sense that it serves the same order of actions as these rules.[32]

The idea of discovering the real law through interpretation may seem far-fetched if the judge must choose between competing interests or projects; if we suppose that any solution must advance some specific goal and retard another, we will think instead of the judge as interstitial legislator, supplementing existing law. But insofar as the judge administers an order of private law that does not discriminate, in principle, between competing private purposes, he is genuinely the mouthpiece of a law he articulates but does not (in the pertinent sense) lay down. He merely improves and clarifies an order of relations he finds, and he does so only insofar as resolution of the particular case requires. In their efforts to apply the principles distilled from the precedents, neither the judge nor the parties involved 'need to know anything about the nature of the resulting overall order, or about any "interest of society" which they serve, beyond the fact that the rules are meant to assist the individuals in successfully forming expectations in a wide range of circumstances'.[33]

Hayek and Raz share a disdain for expansive conceptions of the rule of law that amount to what Raz calls a 'complete social philosophy'. Raz objects to the proposal that the rule of law underpins human dignity in the sense of requiring not only the

character: they rarely impose positive duties unless such duties have been voluntarily incurred. Hayek adds a reference to Kant's theory of law, the categorical imperative providing a negative test of universalizability, enabling us progressively to eliminate what is unjust (Hayek, *Law, Legislation and Liberty* (n 30) ii. 43).

[31] Hayek, *Law, Legislation and Liberty* (n 30) ii. 40.
[32] Hayek, *Law, Legislation and Liberty* (n 9) i. 115–16.
[33] Hayek, *Law, Legislation and Liberty* (n 9) i. 119.

recognition of the individual's civil and political rights, but also 'the establishment of the social, economic, educational and cultural conditions which are essential to the full development of his personality'.[34] We may compare Hayek's evident contempt for certain articles of the Universal Declaration of Human Rights 1948, which invokes a conception of rights that treats society 'as a deliberately made organization by which everybody is employed'.[35] What, Hayek demands to know, 'can be the legal meaning of the statement that everyone is "entitled to the realization . . . of the economic, social, and cultural rights indispensable for his dignity and free development of his personality" (Art. 22)?' Against whom, he fairly enquires, is everyone to have a claim to 'just and favourable conditions of work' and to 'just and favourable employment' (Art. 23)?

As regards the traditional civil and political liberties, however, there is very little correspondence between the two theorists. As we have seen, formal equality in Hayek's hands generates an equality of substance: the benefits of participation in a flourishing market order are available, in principle, to all.[36] Moreover, pernicious discrimination against particular groups of the sort envisaged by Raz would be simply arbitrary, and hence impermissible, from the perspective of a system of universal rules of just conduct. They are arbitrary, and hence *unjust*, because they have no connection with any legitimate governmental purpose. Distinctions between different groups must be related, at least indirectly, to the requirements of an order of private law, which is intended to serve the varied interests of individuals—persons whose aims and ambitions will intersect with those of others according to mutual interest, fostered by freely chosen relationships. Curtailments of freedom must be justified by reference to the general good in the sense of the preservation of equal independence; from that perspective racial, sexual, or religious discrimination is simply a perversion of state power, analogous to the arbitrary whim of the official who abuses the power conferred by a general rule. Laws against libel (for example) may strike an imperfect balance between free speech and the protection of personal honour; but if they apply to everyone in the same way there is no injustice of the kind that undermines the rule of law. Some such balance between freedom and constraint, as regards speech or expression, is a necessary safeguard of independence: it is consistent, in principle, with respect for the basic equality and dignity of persons. The law must seek to *minimize* social conflict, not promote or entrench it for partisan political advantage.

By permitting coercive interference only in accordance with established rules of just conduct, the 'basic clause' of Hayek's model constitution would (he contends) 'achieve all and more than the traditional Bills of Rights were meant to secure'; any separate enumeration of specially protected fundamental rights would be

[34] Raz, *Authority* (n 11) 210–11 (quoting International Commission of Jurists, report of Committee 1 of the International Congress of Jurists at New Delhi, 1959).

[35] Hayek, *Law, Legislation and Liberty* (n 30) ii. 104.

[36] And these benefits may be supplemented by provision of state-funded education and the relief of poverty: 'There is no reason why in a free society government should not assure to all protection against severe deprivation in the form of an assured minimum income . . . ' (Hayek, *Law, Legislation and Liberty* (n 30) ii. 87).

unnecessary.[37] Hayek observes that such basic rights as freedom of speech, religion, assembly, and association cannot be absolute rights, incapable of limitation by general legal rules. It follows that such rights enjoy protection against the legislature only if they must be limited by 'law' in the sense of abstract end-independent rules, not merely by any manner of rule adopted by the representative assembly.

> What the fundamental rights are intended to protect is simply individual liberty in the sense of the absence of arbitrary coercion. This requires that coercion be used only to enforce the universal rules of just conduct protecting the individual domains and to raise means to support the services rendered by government; and since what is implied here is that the individual can be restrained only in such conduct as may encroach upon the protected domains of others, he would under such a provision be wholly unrestricted in all actions which affected only his personal domain or that of other consenting responsible persons, and thus be assured all the freedom that can be secured by political action.[38]

No doubt, in practice, there would be scope for argument about whether a proposed rule actually made the grade as a universal rule of just conduct, indifferent to the aims and interests of particular persons or groups; we could hardly expect unanimous agreement about the justification for the necessary distinctions and boundaries. So Hayek has not abolished representative government or rendered democratic deliberation otiose; he has only imposed high standards of rationality and justification on measures intended to remedy defects in the inherited legal regime of private law. Hayek does not naively suppose that the ideal of equality is a simple matter of logical inference, noting that abstract classification can be made in ways that limit the class in view to known persons or even a single individual. The distinctions drawn by rules 'will not be arbitrary, will not subject one group to the will of others, if they are equally recognized as justified by those inside and outside the group'.[39] There need not be unanimity as to the desirability of any pertinent distinction, but we can presume that it serves the general interest if a person's views do not reflect his position within or outside the group.

We reach similar conclusions about fundamental rights if we consider the scope for 'horizontal effect' of a Bill of Rights designed chiefly to curb state power. There is much discussion about how English common law should adapt, if at all, to reflect the requirements of the European Convention on Human Rights: the Human Rights Act 1998, while giving the Convention rights domestic legal force against public authorities, says nothing about private law. Insofar as rights against torture, murder, slavery, and arbitrary detention extend to the private sphere, they are already enshrined in the ordinary civil and criminal law. And rights to freedom of speech, association, privacy, and other so-called 'qualified' rights—rights expressly subject to provisos for the protection of specified public interests—depend on development of a more specific jurisprudence for their definition and

[37] FA Hayek, *Law, Legislation and Liberty* iii: *The Political Order of a Free People* (Routledge & Kegan Paul 1982) 109–10.

[38] Hayek, *Law, Legislation and Liberty* (n 37) iii. 111.

[39] Hayek, *The Constitution of Liberty* (n 15) 154.

enforcement.[40] The rather limited scope for giving horizontal effect to Convention rights, as a process distinct from ordinary development of the common law in tune with its underpinning values of freedom and dignity, underlines Hayek's principal message. Maintaining the rule of law as a foundation of individual freedom means, above all, limiting the scope for coercion in pursuit of specific, temporary governmental objectives.

We have now reached conclusions similar to the oft-derided views of AV Dicey, whose conception of the rule of law is usually dismissed as a quaint, outdated, and parochial contrivance of Victorian liberalism. Dicey's emphasis on equality before the law, however, coupled with his insistence on the fundamental role of private law, generates a view broadly matching Hayek's vision. The subjection of 'every man, whatever be his rank or condition' to the 'ordinary law of the realm', administered by the 'ordinary tribunals', is an important principle of the rule of law.[41] In the context of a 'judge-made constitution', in which individual rights are the product of litigation at private law, there is at least a presumption against official coercion of individuals in the exercise of special administrative powers. Dicey's rule of law is explicitly opposed to the 'exercise by persons in authority of wide, arbitrary, or discretionary powers of constraint'.[42] It entails the subjection of officials to the same rules of private and criminal law applicable to ordinary citizens: 'the principles of private law have with us been by the action of the courts and Parliament so extended as to determine the position of the Crown and of its servants; thus the constitution is the result of the ordinary law of the land.'[43]

If we see the point of the rule of law as a safeguard of liberty—liberty in the sense of independence—we should hesitate before rejecting Dicey's conception. It is not, as usually assumed, necessarily antithetical to the modern welfare-regulatory state. It simply insists that public authorities must obey the ordinary law, in the same manner as private citizens, unless special powers are specifically granted for limited public purposes. The burden is thrown on to public officials to justify coercive action by establishing the legal basis of their statutory powers: any doubt must be resolved against a power to violate the ordinary protections against trespass, assault, or false imprisonment. Every invasion of private property is a trespass, requiring justification according to 'some positive law', subject to judicial scrutiny and interpretation; and 'with respect to the argument of state necessity, or a distinction that has been aimed at between state offences and others, the common law does not understand that kind of reasoning, nor do our books take notice of any such distinctions'.[44] In enforcing the principles of private law against state bodies, moreover, the courts can insist that any pertinent delegated powers are exercised fairly and reasonably. The grant of special powers is no defence to an action in tort

[40] For a helpful discussion, see Gavin Phillipson and Alexander Williams, 'Horizontal Effect and the Constitutional Constraint' (2011) 74 *Modern Law Review* 878, especially 895–900. Compare *Osborn v The Parole Board* [2013] UKSC 61, paras 54–63 (Lord Reed).

[41] AV Dicey, *Introduction to the Study of the Law of the Constitution* (10th edn, Macmillan 1964) 193.

[42] Dicey, *Law of the Constitution* (n 41) 188.

[43] Dicey, *Law of the Constitution* (n 41) 203.

[44] *Entick v Carrington* (1765) 19 St Tr 1030, 1073 (Lord Camden CJ).

if they have been asserted in ways that flout general principles of rationality and due process—constraints of legality treated as implicit conditions of any administrative jurisdiction.[45]

It is the fundamental constitutional role of the ordinary private law that explains Dicey's disparagement of 'those declarations or definitions of rights so dear to foreign constitutionalists'.[46] His point was not simply that a comparison of English and French political history suggested the greater security of English liberties; the idea is that the predominance of private law fosters a free society.[47] The juridical equality implicit in private law jurisprudence underpins and supports a constitutional culture inimical to arbitrary discrimination and oppression. If, we may fairly suppose, an evolution of ordinary common law has recognized a reasonably robust freedom of speech—subject only to reciprocal safeguards against defamation and incitement to crime—it may be a better defence against official encroachments than a formal bill of rights, which might be suspended on alleged grounds of public interest. The liberty of the press was, in England, a 'mere application of the general principle, that no man is punishable except for a distinct breach of the law'.[48] When constitutional rights are considered part of the ordinary law—the product of judicial reasoning in private law—they enjoy a certain immunity from political interference: such rights can 'hardly be destroyed without a thorough revolution in the institutions and manners of the nation'.[49]

There is here an echo of Hayek's observation that the constitution, so far from being the foundation of the legal system, is only a provisional political arrangement superimposed on the ordinary private law: 'a constitution is essentially a superstructure erected over a pre-existing system of law to organize the enforcement of that law.'[50] When the whole structure of government is overturned by revolutionary upheaval, most of the civil and criminal law remains in force: 'This is so because only by satisfying general expectations can a new government obtain the allegiance of its subjects and thereby become "legitimate".'[51] Private law, then, has a certain priority over public law: its integrity secures the foundation of the rule of law. Administrative law, for Hayek, means 'the rules regulating the activities of the various governmental agencies'; it should not extend to 'administrative powers over persons and property' that aim at 'particular foreseeable results', involving by necessity discrimination and discretion.[52] It is in that sense, as Hayek points out, that Dicey denied the existence in Britain of administrative law.

[45] See eg *Cooper v Wandsworth Board of Works* (1863) 14 CBNS 180 (1863) 143 ER 414 (requirements of natural justice implied by extensive power of demolition of a house built without proper notice to the district board).

[46] Dicey, *Law of the Constitution* (n 41) 197.

[47] Dicey invokes the treatment of Voltaire as exemplifying the arbitrariness of French law in the early part of the eighteenth century.

[48] Dicey, *Law of the Constitution* (n 41) 247–8.

[49] Dicey, *Law of the Constitution* (n 41) 201.

[50] Hayek, *Law, Legislation and Liberty* (n 9) i. 134.

[51] Hayek, *Law, Legislation and Liberty* (n 9) i. 135.

[52] Hayek, *Law, Legislation and Liberty* (n 9) i. 138.

5.

In much the same way as Fuller presents the rule of law as an ideal that we should strive to approximate, but are condemned to fall short of, Hayek acknowledges that government and politics will struggle to satisfy the standards of legality. He observes that, in rendering educational, health, and other services and providing financial and other assistance to particular trades or professions, there is great scope for illegitimate discrimination:

> It is evident that in connection with such measures the distinction between providing facilities to be used by unknown persons for unknown purposes, and providing facilities in the expectation that they will help particular groups, becomes a matter of degree, with many intermediate positions between the two extreme types.[53]

So there is always a danger that government ceases to lubricate the operation of what Hayek calls the 'Great Society' and instead manipulates it for the benefit or to the disadvantage of particular persons or groups. Official discretion inevitably arises, moreover, not merely in the provision of services but, more broadly, in maintaining public order and enforcing the criminal law. Hayek concedes, for example, that the police must be allowed a 'power of specific direction' in certain instances. In practice, then, we are obliged to accept a degree of coercive official discretion, exercised within the boundaries of published general rules and overseen by independent courts or tribunals.

As we have seen, Raz explains that the rule of law requires that the making of particular legal orders—a necessary governmental tool—should be guided by open, stable, clear, and general rules; predictability is enhanced when 'particular laws of an ephemeral status are enacted only within a framework set by general laws which are more durable'.[54] Hayek and Dicey would surely agree; but beyond this narrow area of agreement lies a fundamental divergence. For Raz, the rule of law regulates the manner in which governmental ends are sought, whatever the nature of those ends. For Hayek the rule of law limits such ends, making government subservient to a republican ideal of freedom as independence. There are many ways of sustaining and improving an established regime of private law, which include arrangements to remedy the kinds of social disadvantage that operate in practice to undermine equal access to the market economy; politics must play an important role in the regulation of civil society, supplementing the operation of private law. But there is no scope, within the rule of law, for the suppression of artistic, literary, or political expression that government deplores, or the persecution of members of despised religious or ethnic groups, or the punishment of homosexuals.[55] While

[53] Hayek, *Law, Legislation and Liberty* (n 9) i. 140.

[54] Raz, *Authority* (n 11) 216.

[55] Nor should the state enforce discrimination against particular groups through private law: freedoms of association and contract must be qualified by protection against arbitrary discrimination, irrelevant in principle to general commercial or employment purposes. Legislation prohibiting discrimination on such grounds as age, disability, race, religion, sex, and sexual orientation serves to bring

such ends might serve the narrow interests of a government faction, perhaps keen to elicit popular support, they are inimical to freedom in the sense of independence—freedom from domination, threatening the suppression of ordinary rights and liberties. The curtailment of freedom lacks any plausible *justification* by reference to a common good, capable in principle of eliciting general support. Applying Hayek's test of arbitrariness, a person's view of such measures would plainly *not* be independent of his membership of the pertinent group; the very threat of such interference amounts to an abrogation of the rule of law.[56]

Raz concedes the value of the rule of law as a bulwark against arbitrary power, in the sense of power asserted for improper purposes, irrelevant to the reasons for the original grant:

> The arbitrary use of power for personal gain, out of vengeance or favouritism, is most commonly manifested in the making of particular legal orders. These possibilities are drastically restricted by close adherence to the rule of law.[57]

But Raz cannot concede that the rule of law is a barrier to similar forms of discrimination, imposed by officially sanctioned general legal rules: it would then have the connections with justice and equality that he denies. Yet this distinction threatens the plausibility of his thesis. We cannot identify illicit 'vengeance or favouritism' without some background assumption about legitimate state objectives; there is a certain artificiality in distinguishing between vengeance and favouritism, on the one hand, and racial segregation, sexual discrimination, and religious persecution, on the other. How should we classify action that favours party associates over government critics when it comes to the grant of licences or permits, perhaps for activities that confer a certain social prestige or influence? What about administrative action based on assumptions (shared by senior officials) about the inferior capacities of women, Jews, or homosexuals?[58] Divorcing the concept of law from the ideal of the rule of law has generated very doubtful conclusions.[59]

As Jeremy Waldron observes, we recognize as law not just any commands issued by the powerful, for their own reasons, but rather norms that address matters of concern to society at large:

a common law order of private law closer to the ideal of the rule of law. It may be considered a requirement of what Hayek calls the 'Great Society'.

56 Compare Hayek, *Law, Legislation and Liberty* (n 30) ii. 57: 'Law serves a social order, ie the relations between individuals, and actions which affect nobody but the individuals who perform them ought not to be subject to the control of law, however strongly they may be regulated by custom and morals.'

57 Raz, *Authority* (n 11) 219.

58 The ministerial policy of excluding homosexuals from the British armed forces, which in part pandered to perceived homophobic prejudice within the forces, was arguably a violation not only of rights of privacy or personhood but, precisely by reason of the lack of any tenable justification (consistent with equal citizenship), a violation of the rule of law. See *Smith and Grady v United Kingdom* (1999) 29 EHRR 493; see further Allan, *The Sovereignty of Law* (n 8) 247–9.

59 For a further critique of this dualism, see Simmonds, *Moral Idea* (n 2) 47–51.

We recognize institutions as part of a legal system when they orient themselves in their public presence to the good of the community—in other words, to issues of justice and the common good that transcend the self-interest of the powerful. It strains our ordinary concept of law to apply it to norms that address matters of personal or partial concern, or to institutions that make no pretence to operate in the name of the whole community, presenting themselves as oriented instead to the benefit of the individuals who control them.[60]

If nothing is law unless it at least purports to promote the public good, we must condemn as an infringement of the rule of law any measure that asserts or assumes a wholly untenable view of the public good—one that denies, for example, the equal citizenship of some despised minority group, denying them rights accorded to others.

In condemning discriminatory, or 'irrational', assertions of power by officials in particular cases, we generally account them a violation of a basic equality of citizenship. We suppose, in other words, that forms of discrimination must be justified by reference to public ends that all could, in principle, endorse—ends that do not imply anyone's inferior status, less deserving of respect for his rights or interests. As Raz acknowledges, since 'it is universally believed that it is wrong to use public powers for private ends any such use is in itself an instance of arbitrary use of power'.[61] But the distinction between public powers and private ends becomes blurred unless we suppose that not all state ends are compatible with the rule of law. A state that freely discriminates against certain groups, treating their interests as less important than those of others, is arguably more analogous to a private organization than a government (in the sense in which government is subject to the rule of law). Its very existence is, we are entitled to think, a continuing infringement of the rule of law.

Once we recognize the important conceptual link between the rule of law (or legality) and the idea of law as a form of governance related to a common good of the whole community—as opposed to law as an instrument of government for any purposes whatever—we can also see the central connection with private law. For private law is precisely the operation of the rule of law—the provision and enforcement of standards of legality—in the context of civil society. It exists to serve the people as independent persons with their own lives to lead and their own projects to pursue, in collaboration as far as possible with others having similar aims and interests. The role of the state is chiefly to maintain the fabric of civil society, enforcing the rules of private law in a manner that serves the varied and intersecting ambitions of individuals—improving, updating, and preserving the scheme of justice that fosters and protects reciprocal expectations. Insofar as there are disagreements about how to improve or extend the regime of private law, requiring resort to collective political action, there must be arrangements for deliberation and decision that are fair and open: democracy is a means of refining and sustaining the rule of law. Contrary, then, to Raz's denial, the rule of law is closely related to

[60] Waldron, 'The Concept of Law and the Rule of Law' (n 22) 31.
[61] Raz, *Authority* (n 11) 220.

democracy, each value reflecting a fundamental idea of equality, or equal citizenship, which is in turn closely tied to liberty in the sense of non-domination or independence.[62]

As I have argued elsewhere, there is an irresolvable tension in Raz's discussion of the rule of law.[63] On the one hand, the rule of law is merely a technique for enhancing the efficiency of law for whatever purposes it serves; on the other, the rule of law is a safeguard of human dignity, limiting the scope for ad hoc official coercion that, however beneficial in terms of the ends in view, disrupts or destroys the possibility of independent private choice and action. It is far from clear that these divergent perspectives, expressing rival instrumentalist and idealist approaches to the rule of law, can be plausibly combined. Raz's account effectively admits a moral dimension to a concept of law regarded as morally neutral, conceding the moral value of compliance with a form of ordering supposedly as good for wicked as for virtuous ends. In acknowledging the importance of 'stable, secure frameworks for one's life and actions', enabling us 'to choose styles and forms of life, to fix long-term goals and effectively direct one's life towards them', Raz defends a view of law associated with individual autonomy or independence.[64] Here the rule of law is an important safeguard of human dignity:

> A legal system which does in general observe the rule of law treats people as persons at least in the sense that it attempts to guide their behaviour through affecting the circumstances of their action. It thus presupposes that they are rational autonomous creatures and attempts to affect their actions and habits by affecting their deliberations.[65]

The autonomy and rationality presupposed by governance through law is a theme in the work of Lon Fuller, whose delineation of the various canons of formal legality—the 'inner morality of law'—accompanies an emphasis on a certain reciprocity between lawgiver and subject as an essential element of law.[66] Governance by rule entails an implicit undertaking to honour a bargain: if people attempt in good faith to obey the rules, as published or proclaimed in advance of their conduct, they will be fairly treated in accordance with those standards. While much of Fuller's discussion shares the ambiguity that marks Raz's account—an unresolved tension between efficient direction, on the one hand, and respect for individual autonomy, on the other—in his 'Reply to Critics' (in the second edition of *The Morality of Law*) Fuller draws an important distinction between law, characterized by adherence to the rule of law, and 'managerial direction', to which many of the canons of formal legality are simply irrelevant. Here the tension

[62] Elsewhere, Raz offers a more subtle account of the connection between democracy and the rule of law, contending that, in ensuring the coherence of the law, the rule of law enhances the effectiveness of democratic rule: Joseph Raz, *Ethics in the Public Domain: Essays in the Morality of Law and Politics* (Clarendon Press 1994) ch 16. The connections between freedom as independence and constitutional democracy are explored in Philip Pettit, *Republicanism: A Theory of Freedom and Government* (Clarendon Press 1997).

[63] Allan, *Constitutional Justice: A Liberal Theory of the Rule of Law* (Oxford University Press 2001) 54–9.

[64] Raz, *Authority* (n 11) 220. [65] Raz, *Authority* (n 11) 222.

[66] Fuller, *Morality* (n 1) especially 39–40, 61–2, 137–40.

between instrumentalist and idealist accounts is resolved; the rule of law is a demand of human dignity rather than a powerful tool in the hands of government:

[I]f the law is intended to permit a man to conduct his own affairs subject to an obligation to observe certain restraints imposed by superior authority, this implies that he will not be told at each turn what to do; law furnishes a baseline for self-directed action, not a detailed set of instructions for accomplishing specific objectives.[67]

There is, however, an important ambiguity here concerning the nature of the autonomy or agency that respect for the rule of law secures. It is only a very minimal sense of autonomy that is satisfied by the enforcement of published rules rather than specific commands. Treating people as capable of a rational response to rules, where disobedience may provoke harsh sanctions, is not to be confused with respect for autonomy in the (more significant) sense of making law a stable and secure framework for purposive action.[68]

The respect for persons that Fuller attributes to law, when correctly conceived according to the ideal of legality, depends on his (largely implicit) identification of law with private law. Whereas the directives 'issued in a managerial context are *applied* by the subordinate in order to serve a purpose set by his superior', the 'law-abiding citizen' does not '*apply* legal rules to serve specific ends set by the lawgiver, but rather *follows* them in the conduct of his own affairs . . . '.[69] In substance, Fuller here draws a distinction between public and private law. By contrast with a 'managerial system', which we might think analogous, at least, to the execution of government policy, the rules of a legal system 'normally serve the primary purpose of setting the citizen's relations with other citizens and only in a collateral manner his relations with the seat of authority from which the rules proceed'.[70] In the same manner as Hayek, then, Fuller identifies the operation and maintenance of the regime of private law as central to our understanding of the rule of law:

[L]aw is not, like management, a matter of directing other persons how to accomplish tasks set by a superior, but is basically a matter of providing the citizenry with a sound and stable framework for their interactions with one another, the role of government being that of standing as guardian of the integrity of this system.[71]

In pointing to the existence of general and public norms as central to our idea of a legal system, Waldron pursues a similar line of thought, making reference to Fuller's work. Such general public norms, which present themselves as settled features of the social landscape, 'operate by using, rather than suppressing and short-circuiting, the responsible agency of ordinary human individuals'.[72] It is not

[67] Fuller, *Morality* (n 1) 210.

[68] Compare Matthew H Kramer, *In Defence of Legal Positivism: Law without Trimmings* (Oxford University Press 1999) 58–62, distinguishing between agency or autonomy as moral ideal and agency or autonomy qua cognitive fact.

[69] Fuller, *Morality* (n 1) 207.

[70] Fuller, *Morality* (n 1) 208.

[71] Fuller, *Morality* (n 1) 210. Incongruously, Kramer attributes Fuller's connection between legality and dignity to a preoccupation with American *constitutional* law (embracing both formal and substantive requirements): Kramer, *In Defence of Legal Positivism* (n 68) 62.

[72] Waldron, 'The Concept of Law and the Rule of Law' (n 22) 26.

simply (as Hart observed) that there could not be sufficient numbers of officials to inform each member of society individually of every act he is required to do.[73] The dimensions of generality and publicity are conceptually part of our idea of law: 'this pervasive emphasis on self-application is definitive of law', which is therefore 'sharply distinct from a system of rule that works primarily by manipulating, terrorizing, or galvanizing behaviour'.[74] A system of law therefore operates in accordance with the demands of human dignity: 'law is inherently respectful of persons as agents; it respects the dignity of voluntary action and rational self-control.'[75] But a similar objection applies: the (minimal) dignity of voluntary action, in the sense of self-conscious compliance with applicable rules, is not equivalent to autonomy in the sense of freedom of action, insulated from the threat of arbitrary interference.

By further reference to what he calls the 'systematicity' of law, Waldron extends his point about agency or rationality so as to encompass the scope for *argument* about the law's requirements, developing the connection with dignity. A legal system is not merely a heap of unrelated commands (as in a 'crude' positivist conception) but rather an organized body of requirements susceptible, in principle, of rational understanding. It is organized according to general principles, which illuminate and integrate the various elements of legislation and case law: 'The principles of a legal system are not part of its enacted law or its formal holdings, but they represent the underlying *coherence* of its enacted law and formal holdings.'[76] In that way, the law presents itself to its subjects as a 'unified enterprise of governance that one can make sense of', understanding how 'the regulation of one set of activities relates rationally to the regulation of another'. That susceptibility to rational analysis is a public resource on which people can draw in their arguments over the law's interpretation: 'In this way, the law pays respect to those who live under it, conceiving them now as bearers of individual reason and intelligence.'[77]

Now the argument has subtly altered: what began as implicit acknowledgement of mere agency or rationality has been transformed into respect for the freedom that only governance by law can guarantee. Some of these general norms and principles will, of course, be key elements of public law: they will, in particular, identify constitutional rights that impose general constraints on the manner in which public agencies can enforce their demands against recalcitrant citizens. But such general rules will also encompass the central features of private law, providing a stable structure within which people can pursue their own endeavours in collaboration with others and, when necessary, in the teeth of the opposition or disapproval of others. Insofar, moreover, as public law rights have an absolute character—independent of public policy requirements as they apply in specific instances—they will share a content with private law rights: rights to life, liberty, and security of

[73] HLA Hart, *The Concept of Law* (2nd edn, Clarendon Press 1994) 21.

[74] Waldron, 'The Concept of Law and the Rule of Law' (n 22) 27.

[75] Waldron, 'The Concept of Law and the Rule of Law' (n 22) 28.

[76] Waldron, 'The Concept of Law and the Rule of Law' (n 22) 34, citing Ronald Dworkin, *Taking Rights Seriously* (Harvard University Press 1977) 22–41.

[77] Waldron, 'The Concept of Law and the Rule of Law' (n 22) 35–6.

person and property will have substantial overlap in both fields. And insofar as public law rights, such as rights to freedom of speech, association, and assembly, or rights to natural justice or due process, have a variable content—dependent on an appraisal of conflicting considerations in a specific context—their contribution to the *corpus iuris* will rely on the interpretative efforts of independent courts, resistant (to a degree) to governmental demands for adherence to official policies and programmes. In that sense, at least, they possess a subsidiary status in respect of the role of law as a safeguard of liberty as independence: they are rights only to judicial oversight of the fairness and reasonableness—in all the circumstances—of one's treatment by governmental agencies.

When rights in public law protect substantially the same interests as their private law counterparts, they are in essence the same rights. We expect state officials and agencies to obey the ordinary rules of private law in their dealings with the citizen, except insofar as they are clearly and necessarily authorized to depart from these rules; excesses or abuses of jurisdiction entail liability for breach of private law rights. Other constitutional rights acknowledge the importance of erecting a barrier to the abuse of political power: they are constraints on the exercise of discretion, whether by the legislature in making new law or by the executive in pursuance of its policies and programmes. Such rights are supplementary to ordinary rights in private law in much the same manner as Raz conceives of the rule of law—as a protection against the arbitrary use of law itself (or the powers conferred by law on officials). When we appreciate their supplementary status, however, we can also see more clearly the problems with Raz's thesis. The central core of rules that constitute the legal order of a free people—people whose dignity and autonomy are properly respected by their government—are the principles of private law, applied for the most part without regard for government policy or specific political objectives. That is the primary sense in which the rule of law serves the value of freedom as independence: it means, above all, the reliable and impartial enforcement of the ordinary private law.

A non-instrumentalist view of law, which places the ordinary private and criminal law centre-stage, therefore has important implications for our grasp of the idea of the rule of law. It undermines the assumption that law is primarily an instrument in governmental hands and challenges the related notion that the rule of law is merely a safeguard against the abuse of law. If the rule of law affords protection against oppression, it is because it embodies the idea of law as a framework of rules that secures, so far as possible, the equal enjoyment of liberty. The principal function of the state is to maintain an order of relations between independent citizens, who choose their own plans and projects, cooperating with each other in mutually beneficial ways. It is not the function of the state to impose or enforce particular ways of life or further the interests of certain groups at the expense of others. Public law should be supplementary to private law, regulating the exercise of public powers ancillary to the continued operation of established rules of just conduct. The rule of law is not merely a principle of formal legality, applicable to legislation; it is the set of conditions under which freedom as independence is best preserved. While those conditions include enforcement of general principles constraining the exercise of discretionary governmental power, they entail—first and foremost—adherence to the principles that underpin and organize the ordinary civil and criminal law. In preserving the integrity of private law, the rule of law is a both a basic guarantee of liberty and an expression of fundamental equality.[78]

[78] While there must be provision for compensation for injuries inflicted by civil wrongs, defined by law, I do not insist on the priority of private law in the extended sense that David Dyzenhaus (in his essay in this volume) describes: a statutory insurance scheme, independent of fault, could legitimately replace common law tort rules in some field. Hayek's challenge to positivism, like Fuller's, points to an internal morality of law which is dependent neither on the claim that a legal order must be democratic nor on the claim that it must incorporate a bill of rights. Law may simply embody a customary order of relations between independent persons, reflecting their own disparate purposes. Law is fundamentally non-instrumental: the question is precisely (as Dyzenhaus says) whether the law conscripts an individual in order to achieve some goal or whether (consistently with the ideal of the rule of law) it makes it possible for him to select his own goals.

4

Liberty and Legal Form

*David Dyzenhaus**

1. Introduction

The topic of the rule of law in private law presents at least four puzzles. First, the rule of law is usually discussed in the public law context, where the problem is taken to be whether its constraints on the exercise of public power, whatever they are, operate effectively there. Does that mean that rule of law operates so effectively and without problem in the private law context that we don't even notice its presence, so that an enquiry into the rule of law in private law will merely make its operation explicit? I suspect that those who take the distinction between private and public law to be fundamental, marking a difference in domains or kinds of law, will want to resist the thought that both domains of law are characterized by the same normative structure and its apparent corollary that public law differs from private law only in that it has trouble living up to that structure.

That distinction raises the second puzzle. If private law and public law have different normative structures, and if the constraints we associate with the rule of law are at home only in public law, should we conclude that private law is not governed by the rule of law?

Since that conclusion seems most odd, we get the third puzzle: On the assumption that the rule of law does operate in private law, must we be pluralists about the rule of law because its requirements differ radically from domain to domain?

Finally, if such pluralism is right, is it not also odd that what we usually take to be the requirements of the rule of law are requirements only for public law, and thus for the domain that has such trouble living up to them?

I will argue that the rule of law or legality governs public and private law in the same way. Moreover, its government ensures that the law has a moral quality to it, since law, in being (as it must) legal, constitutes a politically valuable condition of liberty—civil liberty. Put differently, it shows that the rule of law should not be understood primarily as a set of constraints on state action. Rather, it should be

* I thank the participants in the conference for their discussion of this paper and Jacob Weinrib for both raising some fundamental challenges and providing me with references to material that I should take into account. I regard my responses to his challenges as highly provisional.

understood as constitutive of liberty, since the rule of law sets out formal criteria of legality that give law a freedom-enabling character, in that law enables individuals to interact in ways that conduce to them achieving their own ends. Law is, then, a necessary condition of a particular kind of liberty, the kind of liberty one enjoys under an order of *public laws.* I mean by this term not 'public law'—the contrast to 'private law'—but rather *publica lex* or all promulgated law. I will also suggest that where law is present, so there will be liberty of this kind.

My position thus contests legal positivism's claim that there is no necessary connection between law and morality. It also makes the distinction between private law and public law into something that does not mark any fundamental difference in kinds of law. As I will try to show, the position illuminates the four puzzles raised by the topic of the rule of law in private law. But it does not do so by 'solving' them. Rather, it seeks to undermine the two assumptions that generate them: first, that however we understand the rule of law, the distinction between public and private law is fundamental; second, that the rule of law is best understood as a set of constraints on public power.

2. Three Conceptions of Law's Immanent Morality

Ever since the 1958 exchange between HLA Hart and Lon L Fuller in the *Harvard Law Review*,[1] the central question of philosophy of law has been whether there is a necessary connection between law and morality. Hart, following his immediate predecessors in the legal positivist tradition, argued both that any relationships between the law of a jurisdiction and morality are entirely contingent and that recognition of this fact is morally beneficial. Legal positivism makes it clear to the citizen that the existence of law is one thing, its merit or demerit another.

In his last major treatment of this issue, Ronald Dworkin says that it was a mistake, one to which he himself had been prone, to think of the issue as about whether two systems could be bridged, the legal system with its contingent, changing content and the moral system with its universal norms that 'have imperative force for everyone'.[2] He proposed in place of the two-systems picture a one-system picture: 'Legal rights are political rights, but a special branch because they are properly enforceable on demand through adjudicative and coercive institutions without need for further legislation or lawmaking activity.'[3] In other words, Dworkin proposed that there is a morality immanent in law.

This proposal is not, however, altogether novel. Fuller drew a self-consciously one-system picture when he responded to Hart that if rulers are to rule through law they will find that they are required to abide by principles of legality that amount to

[1] HLA Hart, 'Positivism and the Separation of Law and Morals' (1958) 71 *Harvard Law Review* 593; Lon L Fuller, 'Positivism and Fidelity to Law—a Reply to Professor Hart' (1958) 71 *Harvard Law Review* 630.

[2] Ronald Dworkin, *Justice for Hedgehogs* (Harvard University Press 2011) 400–1.

[3] Dworkin, *Justice for Hedgehogs* (n 2) 407.

an 'internal morality' of law.[4] Indeed, Hart had anticipated this kind of response in his 1958 essay, and in later work he and other legal positivists developed his argument there—that at most compliance with legality can make law more effective. Since highly effective law can satisfy such requirements and yet be 'hideously oppressive',[5] legal positivists concluded that even if Fuller succeeds in showing that law to be such has to be legal, he fails to show that compliance with legality makes law moral.

Dworkin shared this view of Fuller's position and proposed in its place an account of the immanent morality of law as the substantive set of principles of political morality that emerge when judges in interpreting the law ask the question, 'What set of principles shows the law of my jurisdiction in its best light?' Dworkin meant by 'best' 'morally best' and he seems ultimately committed to supposing that the principles will turn out to be liberal, since only liberal principles are capable of justifying the state's claim to exercise justified coercion.[6]

One way of depicting the contrast between Dworkin's and Fuller's positions, which follows Fuller's own terminology, is to say that Dworkin presents a substantive natural law position, whereas Fuller presents a procedural one. But, as I will suggest below, Fuller's principles of legality are best understood as formal rather than as procedural, where 'formal' indicates the features of legality that an order has to possess in order to qualify as legal. However, 'formal' is not meant as a contrast with 'procedural' since procedural principles can figure among these formal features. In addition, that the features are formal does not mean that they lack moral substance. On the contrary, as Fuller emphasized, legality has substantive implications that are clearly liberal in character. In particular he claimed that compliance with law's internal or (as he later termed it) 'inner' morality will affirm 'man's dignity as a responsible agent'.[7]

If Fuller is best understood as proposing a formal natural law position, he has something in common with one of the most significant advances in philosophy of law in the late twentieth century, the account of the normativity of private law developed by my colleague Ernest Weinrib, in which he argues that attention to the formal features of a private law regime will bring to light the moral structure intrinsic to it. More recently, this kind of account has been firmly nested by another of my colleagues, Arthur Ripstein, within an exposition of Kant's political and legal philosophy.[8]

Together, Weinrib and Ripstein present yet a third version of a one-system picture of the relationship between law and morality, in which the formal features of private law presuppose an immanent morality organized around the Kantian idea

[4] Fuller, 'Positivism and Fidelity to Law' (n 1) 645.

[5] Hart, 'Separation of Law and Morals' (n 1) 624.

[6] In response to the challenge posed to his position by 'wicked legal systems', Dworkin has expressed some ambivalence about whether the principles that figure among the 'grounds' of law also justify law's 'force'. See Ronald Dworkin, *Law's Empire* (Belknap Press 1986) 108–13.

[7] Lon L Fuller, *The Morality of Law* (rev edn, Yale University Press 1969) 162.

[8] Ernest J Weinrib, *The Idea of Private Law* (Harvard University Press 1995); Arthur Ripstein, *Force and Freedom: Kant's Legal and Political Philosophy* (Harvard University Press 2009).

of the purposive agent whose freedom to enact his own purposes has to be made consistent with the same freedom of all other agents. Only such consistency can achieve the ideal that each individual is to be his own master, not subject to the will of any other, and legal institutions have to be in place for the ideal to be realized. They also suppose that the same Kantian idea can underpin public law, but that the two domains of law have their own immanent moralities or normative structures, respectively, public right or distributive justice, and private right or corrective justice.

I will argue that an idea of liberty as independence is indeed the core idea of the immanent morality of law. But I will also argue that it does not entail, as Weinrib and Ripstein think, the distinction between private law and public law they take to be fundamental to political and legal philosophy. To suppose that the distinction is fundamental is, as legal positivists have argued against Dworkin, to rely too much on what legal positivists rightly suppose is a contingent incorporation of a substantive political morality into law. In the case of the Kantian position, such reliance undermines its formalism even in the private law part of law in which it is most at home. In this regard, Fuller's formal theory of legality seems more satisfactory, in that it articulates an account of the immanent morality of law that is not tied to the contingencies of historical incorporation.

More particularly, I will explore the idea in the evocative title of Kristen Rundle's recent book on Fuller, *Forms Liberate*.[9] As she explains, these words appear in Fuller's notes that were the basis for his Reply to Critics in the revised edition of *The Morality of Law*. Their appearance is rather dramatic. Fuller had blacked out the previous longer sentence, which one can just make out started with 'Legal morality'. He subsequently drew a ring around 'Forms liberate' and connected those typed words via an arrow to a handwritten note—'cf negative concept of freedom'.[10] But Fuller seemed to gesture at a rather different conception of liberty when in the same set of notes he contrasted a condition of liberty with the condition of being part of 'a subservient populace ready to do what they are told to do'. As Rundle says, the idea here is that to be a legal subject is 'to be a participant in a distinctly constituted social condition in which one is respected as an agent'.[11]

Put differently, when relationships between individuals or between individuals and state take a legal form, those individuals will find themselves in a condition of liberty. And the kind of liberty they will experience, the condition of not being subservient, seems closely akin to the kind elaborated most recently by Republican thinkers as liberty as independence or non-domination,[12] which is also akin to the

[9] Kristen Rundle, *Forms Liberate: Reclaiming the Jurisprudence of Lon L Fuller* (Hart Publishing 2012). For a full exploration of this idea in Fuller, see Nigel Simmonds, *Law as a Moral Idea* (Oxford University Press 2007) especially 141–3 and TRS Allan's chapter in this volume, 'The Rule of Law as the Rule of Private Law'.

[10] The page is reproduced as the frontispiece of Rundle, *Forms Liberate* (n 9) 1–2.

[11] Rundle, *Forms Liberate* (n 9) 2.

[12] See Philip Pettit, *On the People's Terms: A Republican Theory and Model of Democracy* (Cambridge University Press 2012).

sense of freedom defended by Weinrib and Ripstein in their elaboration of a Kantian legal theory.

My claim is not that Fuller, the Republicans, and the Kantians advance exactly the same conception of liberty. Nor do I claim that they offer a common justification for their conceptions. But they do share the idea that law should not be seen, as it often is by liberal thinkers in the negative liberty tradition, as a necessary constraint on negative liberty, but (as Republicans emphasize) as a necessary condition of liberty. What my chapter seeks to add is the insight that where law is present, so there will be liberty. In other words, I will suggest that legal form is not merely necessary for liberty of this kind but also sufficient.

My argument proceeds in three parts. In Section 3, I will explore the debate within legal philosophy in a way that addresses some of the main themes of a collection on the rule of law and private law by setting out the views of Fuller, Hart, and Hans Kelsen on legality and the public/private law distinction. As we will see, Hart's argument about the control of legality in public law proceeds from private law to public law, whereas Kelsen denies the salience of the private/public distinction for understanding legality. Fuller also does not make his account of legality depend on that distinction but nevertheless argues that an element of private law relations that Hart identified as bilateralism characterizes public law relationships as well.[13] In Section 4, I will sketch a Fullerian legal theory that links a formal account of legality with a conception of legal liberty, or liberty under an order of public laws, where (as I indicated above) 'public' means simply that the laws have been appropriately promulgated. Government in accordance with the rule of law produces law that has a particular form and that form makes possible liberty as non-domination. This connection is made concrete within the institutional framework of adjudication, at the moment when an impartial judge or other adjudicator 'converts', in Fuller's words, the legal issues into 'claims of right'.[14]

However, as I will show in Section 5, the idea of liberty and thus of the immanent morality of law is much thinner or less substantive than the Kantian one. Fuller was clear that the internal morality of law did not rule out substantive purposes that we might for good reason deem immoral, and he could be understood as relegating to 'external morality' questions such as polygamy, the progressive income tax, the 'subjugation of women',[15] or whether, to add an example, legality requires that there be a domain of private law. But I will suggest by way of a general conclusion that there is much to be said for this thinner version of legality.

[13] I will take terms such as 'bilateral', 'reciprocal', and 'correlative' to connote more or less the same thing—a two-way relationship of mutual accountability between the parties. This tactic may neglect certain nuances, but I take these not to affect my discussion here.

[14] Lon L Fuller, 'The Forms and Limits of Adjudication' in Kenneth I Winston (ed), *The Principles of Social Order: Selected Essays of Lon L. Fuller* (Hart Publishing 2001) 101, 111.

[15] Fuller, *Morality* (n 7) 96; see also 132–3, 153.

3. A Public or a Private Law Conception of the Rule of Law?

The Morality of Law is best known for Fuller's discussion of the eight 'desiderata' of legality that together make up the 'inner morality' of law. Fuller developed these in the course of an analysis of the all-powerful but hapless monarch Rex, whose bungled attempts to make law reveal that the activity of law-making is constrained by the need to attempt to live up to the desiderata: generality, promulgation or publicity, non-retroactivity, clarity, non-contradiction, possibility of compliance, constancy through time, and, the one Fuller took to be the most complex, congruence between official action and declared rule.[16]

Fuller said of the last principle that it was the 'most complex', both because congruence could be destroyed or impaired in various ways and because the 'procedural devices designed to maintain it take, of necessity, a variety of forms'.[17] In the United States of America, he noted, it was chiefly the judiciary that was entrusted with preventing discrepancy between rules and administrative action, though he also said that there would be 'serious disadvantages' in any system that looked solely to the courts 'as a bulwark against the lawless administration of the law'.[18]

Despite this qualification, Fuller was anxious in other work to emphasize the importance of impartial adjudicators in a rule of law order, in which the issues submitted to the adjudicators '[tend] to be *converted* into a claim of right or an accusation of guilt. This conversion is effected by the institutional framework within which both the litigant and the adjudicator function.'[19] The process of reasoned argument requires the person making the argument to present it as more than a 'naked demand'. It has to be presented as a 'claim of right', that is, as 'supported by a principle'. And that has the consequence that 'issues tried before an adjudicator tend to become claims of rights or accusations of fault'.[20] Thus Fuller regards courts and other adjudicative institutions as 'essential to the rule of law'. The 'object of the rule of law is to substitute for violence peaceful ways of settling disputes. Obviously peace cannot be assured simply by treaties, agreements, and legislative enactment. There must be some agency capable of determining the rights of the parties in concrete situations of controversy.'[21]

Fuller's desiderata are often taken to be an account of the rule of law or legality constraints that operate in a public law context, a view that aligns with the fact that the rule of law is generally taken to be a concern for public rather than private law because public law is about the limits on state action. Though many philosophers of law reject Fuller's claim that the desiderata make up any kind of morality, they have by and large accepted that the desiderata provide a more or less accurate, although perhaps partial, account of the rule of law.

[16] Fuller, *Morality* (n 7) 38–41.
[17] Fuller, *Morality* (n 7) 81.
[18] Fuller, *Morality* (n 7) 81.
[19] Fuller, 'Forms and Limits' (n 14) 111 (emphasis added).
[20] Fuller, 'Forms and Limits' (n 14) 111.
[21] Fuller, 'Forms and Limits' (n 14) 114.

I suspect that Fuller would reject this train of thought because he did not regard his conception of legality as one appropriate only for public law. While he developed his account of the inner morality of law in a discussion of legislation, the point of that way of proceeding was polemical. He wanted to show why even the legislature in a system of parliamentary supremacy is subject to the rule of law, a fact that he thought that Hart's legal positivism had to, but could not properly, confront.

In other words, the implicit structure of the problem as Fuller sets it up might seem to presuppose that the model of the rule of law that is taken for granted in the private law context applies also in the public law one. And that structure becomes wholly explicit in his 'Reply to Critics', especially at the many points where Fuller emphasizes the horizontal or interactional nature of the rule of law. For Fuller took legal positivism to be able to account for law only as a vertical phenomenon, as a 'managerial order' in which 'one-way' projections of authority are directed from top to bottom.[22] Law, he argued, 'is not, like management, a matter of directing other persons how to accomplish tasks set by a superior, but is basically a matter of providing the citizenry with a sound and stable framework for their interactions with one another, the role of government being that of standing as a guardian of the integrity of this system'.[23]

Fuller did not think, however, that this framework arose merely because the state is constrained in making law by the rule of law. Rather, he saw the law that provides the framework as itself arising out of an interactive process. Here he had in mind not only the way in which the institutions of private law make it possible for individuals to make law for themselves, but also that legislation, addressed as it is to responsible agents, is the product not of a 'one way projection of authority', but of 'an interplay of purposive orientations between the citizen and his government'.[24]

It is in this set of claims that the puzzles about the rule of law sketched above begin to emerge. Private law might well appear to be easily understood as both horizontal and reciprocal in nature, the latter because it consists of relationships of correlative, individual rights and duties. Fuller himself said that legal (and moral) duties become 'most acceptable' when created out of a 'voluntary agreement', in which the performance of the parties is 'equal in value', and 'reversible' so that I could owe you tomorrow the duty that you owe me today.[25] And he continued that his analysis suggested 'the somewhat startling conclusion that it is only under capitalism that the notion of moral and legal duty can reach its full development'.[26] However, the point of the Rex allegory is to show that law in general is reciprocal even when the political order is monarchical. Further, that legal duties are 'most acceptable' when in the private law form does not establish that they have to be in that form to be acceptable as legal duties.

The focus on the rule of law in the public law domain is not, in my view, for Fuller the result of the fact that the constraints of the rule of law are especially

[22] Fuller, *Morality* (n 7) 191–2.
[23] Fuller, *Morality* (n 7) 210.
[24] Fuller, *Morality* (n 7) 204.
[25] Fuller, *Morality* (n 7) 23.
[26] Fuller, *Morality* (n 7) 24.

appropriate in that context. Rather, it comes about because the apparently vertical, top-down relationships in that context make it hard to see how legality governs in a way that we take for granted in the private law context, so for granted that we often don't notice its operation there. His argument is that an aspect of legality that we take for granted in the private law context—reciprocity—must also be present in the public law context.

I will come back to the issues of the relationship between reciprocity, internal morality, and liberty below. For the present, I want to point out again that Fuller's main target in both the implicit and the explicit critiques of legal positivism was Hart, especially *The Concept of Law*. But that was because Hart was the most recent important figure in a tradition that Fuller claimed stretched from 'Hobbes through Austin to Kelsen' that sees 'the essence of law in a pyramidal structure of state power'.[27] Fuller's claim is at odds with Hart's understanding of his own contribution to philosophy of law, and in particular to the legal positivist tradition. For Hart had argued that the principal error of that tradition lay in its command model of law, a model which Hart attributed in 1958 to Bentham and Austin, though later he took, as Fuller did, Hobbes to be its founder. The model assumes that the sovereign, the ultimate legal authority, is legally unlimited and that the law consists of the commands of that sovereign to which a sanction attaches.

Moreover, Hart's argument on this score both in 'Positivism and the Separation of Law and Morals' and in *The Concept of Law*[28] proceeds from private to public law. The first step in Hart's argument serves to cast doubt on the tenet of his tradition that the form of all law is a command of a legally unlimited commander backed by threats. It does so by pointing out that there are 'other legal rules' that are 'presented to society in quite different ways and have quite different functions. They provide facilities more or less elaborate for individuals to create structures of rights and duties for the conduct of life within the coercive framework of the law.'[29]

The second step involves pointing out that such 'power-conferring'[30] rules are not confined to rules that confer power on private individuals, since they are to be found also in public law in the rules that confer power on public officials to legislate, adjudicate, and administer.[31] In the public law context, if officials are to legislate, adjudicate, and administer, they must abide by these rules, just as a private individual has to act in accordance with the law of contracts to succeed in contracting. It follows, so Hart argued, that even the highest legislative authority has to be understood as legally constituted.

[27] Fuller, *Morality* (n 7) 110, 191–2. In my view, Fuller not only misunderstood Hobbes, but Hobbes in many respects does a better job than Fuller of articulating the relationship between law and liberty. See David Dyzenhaus, 'Hobbes on the Authority of Law' in Dyzenhaus and Thomas Poole (eds), *Hobbes and the Law* (Cambridge University Press 2012) 186. Note that on the argument of that paper, Gerald Postema is wrong to suppose that Hobbes thought the sovereign is unaccountable to law. See Postema, 'Fidelity in Law's Commonwealth', this volume. But otherwise I am in general agreement with Postema.

[28] HLA Hart, *The Concept of Law* (2nd edn, Clarendon Press 1994).

[29] Hart, 'Positivism' (n 1) 60–1; Hart, *Concept* (n 28) 27–9.

[30] Hart, 'Positivism' (n 1) 33.

[31] Hart, 'Positivism' (n 1) 28–33, Hart, 'Positivism' (n 1) 58–9.

Hart thought that this kind of rule can explain not only the way that legislation is a rule-bound or legally regulated activity in the same way that promising is, but also how legislation can be self-binding in the same way as promising. He did note some differences. The rules governing legislation

are very much more complex and the bilateral character of a promise is not present. Moreover, there is no person in the special position of the promisee *to whom* the promise is made and who has a special, if not the only claim, to its performance. In these respects, certain other forms of self-imposition known to English law, such as that whereby a person declares himself trustee of property for other persons, offer a closer analogy to the self-binding aspect of legislation. Yet, in general, making of law by enactment is something we shall understand best by considering such private ways of creating particular legal obligations.[32]

Hart continued:

The legislator is not necessarily like the giver of orders to another: someone by definition outside the reach of what he does. Like the giver of a promise he exercises powers conferred by rules: very often he may, as the promisor *must*, fall within their ambit.[33]

Thus Hart wished to analogize public to private law, minus the element of reciprocity or bilateralism that one finds in private law, and that Fuller seems to claim pervades public as well as private law. And in both works, Hart is anxious to emphasize that the constraints of legality on public officials do not in themselves impose moral limits on what the officials may do, and hence do nothing to legitimize political power that operates in accordance with such constraints.

Fuller was aware of the nuances and complexities of Hart's theory. However, he still regarded Hart as wedded to the image of law as a one-way projection of authority, just one of a set of several positivistic assumptions that together ruled out seeing the 'lawgiver and the citizen in interaction with one another, and by virtue of that failure . . . that the creation of an effective interaction between them is an essential ingredient of law itself'.[34]

Curiously, Hart had much the same view of Kelsen. He argued that Kelsen remained in the grip of the command model of law, a 'vertical or "top-down" image of law-making' required to understand law if law has to be conceived of as orders backed by threats. Kelsen's conception of law thus remained trapped in the primitive, 'pre legal world' unable to account for the kind of rule whose 'introduction into society . . . is a step forward as important to society as the invention of the wheel'.[35]

Here Hart emphasized Kelsen's insistence that 'the content of the law' is not addressed primarily to 'ordinary citizens'. Rather, it is:

merely the antecedent of an if-clause in a rule which is directed not to them but to officials, and orders them to apply certain sanctions if certain conditions are satisfied. All genuine laws, on this view, are conditional orders to officials to apply sanctions. . . . By greater and

[32] Hart, *Concept* (n 28) 43–4.
[33] Hart, *Concept* (n 28) 44.
[34] Fuller, *Morality* (n 7) 193.
[35] Hart, *Concept* (n 28) 41–2.

greater elaboration of the antecedent or if-clauses, legal rules of every type, including the rules conferring and defining the manner of the exercise of private or public powers, can be restated in this conditional form.[36]

In my view, Hart's criticism of Kelsen might not do justice to Kelsen's position. For Kelsen is even more anxious than Hart to show that the state is legally constituted, especially in the first edition of *The Pure Theory of Law*.[37] There Kelsen argues against what he sees as the prevailing dualism associated with the distinction between public and private law. That distinction, he says, 'tends to take on the import of an opposition between law and power . . . the opposition, especially, between law and state'. 'Typical' of the 'autocratic' public law relation is a 'unilateral expression of will (a directive or a command)', hence one in which 'the party who is subject to obligation plays no role whatsoever in creating the norm that imposes obligations'.[38]

In contrast, 'typical' of the 'democratic' private law relation is a 'reciprocal transaction' in which 'the parties who are subject to obligation participate in creating the norm that imposes obligations'.[39] However, Kelsen denies the significance of the contrast for philosophy of law, since both the private law transaction and the authoritative directive are individualizations of a general norm—'of a provision of the civil code in one case, of an administrative regulation in the other'. Both are therefore 'acts of state . . . imputable to the unity of the legal system'.[40]

In bringing us this insight, the Pure Theory, Kelsen claims, undermines what he takes to be the 'ideology' associated with a strong distinction between public and private law, one which wishes to 'create the illusion' that in the field of public law, 'in particular in the politically significant fields of constitutional and administrative law', the *Rechts-Prinzip* or 'legality principle'[41] does not obtain 'in the same sense or with the same intensity as in the field of private law, regarded, so to speak, as the proper realm of law'. This ideology has it that, while in private law the 'application of statutes to particular cases' is constrained by the law, in public law, as long as the framework of the statute is observed, realization of the 'state purpose' is 'unhampered'.[42] Not only, says Kelsen, are both realms equally subject to the legality principle, it is also the case that the realm of private law is no less political than public law.

What we call private law . . . is simply . . . the form corresponding to the capitalist economic system of production and distribution; its function, then, is the eminently political function of exercising power. Another form of law would suit a socialist economic system, not the

[36] Hart, *Concept* (n 28) 36.

[37] Hans Kelsen, *Introduction to the Problems of Legal Theory*, trans Bonnie Litchewski Paulson and Stanley L Paulson (Clarendon Press 1992).

[38] Kelsen, *Problems* (n 37) 92–3.

[39] Kelsen, *Problems* (n 37) 92–3.

[40] Kelsen, *Problems* (n 37) 94.

[41] The translators have 'principle of law', but, in line with my argument about legality and the law, I prefer this translation.

[42] At most Kelsen is willing to concede that in the realm of public law, public officials have more discretion than do the courts in private law.

autonomous democratic form represented by present private law, but—presumably—a heteronomous, autocratic form closer to the form of our present administrative law.[43]

Note that Kelsen is not suggesting that administrative law has to have this autocratic form, only that, in his day, this is the form it has. The subjective, democratic rights associated with the capitalist form of private law might or might not be morally appropriate—a question on which the Pure Theory takes no stance. All that the Pure Theory does is point out that these rights are legal when and only when 'normatively' regulated by the 'objective law'.[44] A subjective right exists 'only in so far as the objective law is at the disposal of a concrete subject'.[45] Correspondingly, in a democratic political system the law gives subjective rights of participating in the creation of legislation to the citizenry.[46] It thus follows that administrative law could be made more participatory or democratic by legislating subjective rights for those affected by the decisions of the administrative state. But it also follows that every state is a rule of law state, a *Rechtsstaat*, given the Pure Theory's claim that the state is no more than the entity that exists when a legal system 'has achieved a certain degree of centralization'.[47] Hence, that a state is a *Rechtsstaat* does not in any way legitimize it.[48]

Kelsen, in my opinion, has a more sophisticated view than Hart's. Hart seems to argue that public law has to be understood by analogy to private law since his amendment to the command model of the positivist tradition depends on an argument from private law to public law. If one sees how contracting is a rule-bound activity, one can also see how legislating is rule bound. But Hart then adds that there is a big difference in that there is a bilateral relationship in contract that does not exist in public law, that is, the element of reciprocity that one can take more or less for granted in private law is missing in public law.

Kelsen, in contrast, need not deny that if legal relationships between individuals were to be structured as bilateral relationships, they would have to take a particular form, the one we associate with private law. But he argues that legal theory has no view about that being the best way to order things. That question can only be answered ideologically, that is, by political or moral philosophy. However, if it were decided to structure such individual-to-individual relationships along lines associated with public law, they would still be subject to legality, the *Rechts-Prinzip*. Similarly, one can make public law, including administrative law, more private law in nature, that is, more reciprocal or bilateral. It seems to follow for Kelsen that there is a principle of legality that underpins both public law and private law that is more basic than what we might otherwise suppose is the immanent morality of bilaterally organized private law or of unilaterally organized public law.

Moreover, there are two potential advantages to Kelsen's position over Hart's, at least from a perspective that regards it as normatively appropriate that all acts of state are legally authorized, so that a defect in authorization makes an official's act

[43] Kelsen, *Problems* (n 37) 96.
[44] Kelsen, *Problems* (n 37) 44.
[45] Kelsen, *Problems* (n 37) 44.
[46] Kelsen, *Problems* (n 37) 45–6.
[47] Kelsen, *Problems* (n 37) 99.
[48] Kelsen, *Problems* (n 37) 105.

ultra vires. First, on Kelsen's picture of law, law never runs out. While Kelsen thought that officials often had to exercise discretion when it came to interpreting and applying the law, and that in public law there was probably more discretion than in private law, for him any legal situation, even a situation of emergency, would be fully controlled by legality in a *Rechtsstaat*. In contrast, for Hart, that an official has to exercise discretion does mean that law has run out, and in extreme situations, all that he can offer is the slogan: 'All that succeeds is success.'[49]

One might think that Hart's view is more realistic, in that the more an official has discretion, the less legally constrained he is by the law, no matter what authority he has from the law to exercise his discretion as he sees fit. However, we should note that for Hart law runs out when the content of a particular law is indeterminate, whilst for Kelsen control by the determinate content of particular laws does not make up the full or even the most important part of control by law, because for him the *Rechtsstaat* is the rule of legality, not the rule of positive law. Indeed, a point I will come back to in a moment, one might suppose that Hart's equation of control by law with the determinate content of particular laws reveals his own inability to escape from the command model of law.

Second, and relatedly, I want to suggest that there is something to Kelsen's argument that, as Hart portrays it, the content of the law is merely the antecedent of an if-clause in a rule which is directed not to citizens but to officials, and that orders them to apply certain sanctions if certain conditions are satisfied. Indeed, in the passages in Kelsen's *General Theory of Law and the State* to which Hart refers in the longer Notes at the end of *The Concept of Law*, Kelsen introduces this conditional concept of law in the course of his criticism of Austin.[50] Kelsen's criticism is that Austin supposes that law is a matter of the determinate content of particular positive laws, in which one person tells another what to do. Indeed, despite his rejection of the command model, Hart seems to rely precisely on this model when he criticizes Kelsen for rejecting the view that 'the content of the law' is addressed primarily to 'ordinary citizens'.

Without going into the details of Kelsen's position, his central claim is that a complete picture of law cannot stop with a command of determinate content addressed by a legislative body to a subject; there is still the moment when a public official has to decide whether and how the law applies to that individual. Put differently, no act of legislation is complete for Kelsen before its moment of application to the legal subject by the official authorized to do so. Now, Kelsen conceives of that moment as the issuance of another command, one that will involve some degree of discretion. However, the point, as above, is that Kelsen, in contrast to Hart, wishes to understand the legal relationship in terms of legality rather than in terms of the communication of the predetermined content of particular laws.

[49] Hart, *Concept* (n 28) 153.

[50] Hart, *Concept* (n 28) 286, Hans Kelsen, *General Theory of Law and State*, trans Anders Wedberg (Harvard University Press 1945) 58–63.

Kelsen thus seems closer to Fuller than to Hart in these regards. For both Fuller and Kelsen there is more to legal government than the content of particular positive laws, since public officials have to take account of legality in order to determine what that content is. The difference between Fuller, on the one hand, and both Kelsen and Hart, on the other, is that Fuller argues that reciprocity between ruler and ruled and between individuals is immanent in legality, although it can take different forms. And we have seen that Hart, although he proceeds from private law to public law in order to explain why legal authority is always at least partially legally regulated, regards the public law relationship as not having the character of bilateralism or reciprocity that characterizes private law.

Kelsen differs from Hart, then, not only because he thinks that legality governs legal activity more comprehensively, but also because he thinks that any normative character we impute to private law in contrast to public law is politically contingent. In fact, Hart is not committed to denying this claim, since, like Kelsen, he must as a legal positivist suppose that the law can be given any content. It is not that the bilateral form of private law relationships has any normative priority in his explanation, simply that if we attend to the way that private law as it contingently happens to be constitutes private power, we can also understand how law constitutes public power. That tells us that all legal authority, whether bilateral or unilateral, is (at least partially) legally regulated.

I will now set out Fuller's position that whatever the contingent content of the law, and whether it seems more private or more public, law is reciprocal in nature. Since the claim that private law is reciprocal in nature is relatively uncontroversial, I will focus on the public law, legislative context, where reciprocity comes about in the following way: the requirement that law to be legal must comply with principles of legality has the result that law constitutes a condition of civil liberty.

4. Reciprocity and Liberty

Fuller's natural law position seems to me to pose a fundamental challenge to legal positivism since it sets out formal features of legality such that even when a tyrant decides to use the law as a mere instrument of policy, he will find that his use of law is conditioned by the internal morality of law, the immanent morality of legality. In other words, if Fuller's challenge works, it does so despite the fact that it relies neither on a claim that a legal order has to be democratic, nor on the claim that it must incorporate a bill of rights. The positivist response to Fuller has been, by and large, to concede that law has to be consistent to some degree with legality, but then to argue that such consistency only makes law into a better or more effective instrument of extra-legally determined value. In my view, Fuller's position, especially when it is understood as a formal rather than a procedural natural law position, resists this debunking response.

However, I wish to note first that I do not think the worth of this exercise is exhausted by the issue of whether or not it can respond to another position in legal theory. Rather, it seems to me that legal positivists, perhaps Kelsen more than (or at least more explicitly than) his anglophone counterparts, have undertaken to explain something about law that has to be explained in an era in which the primary modes of law are statutes that delegate authority to officials and the law that is made by such officials as they exercise their authority. In other words, legal positivism's great virtue has been that it has taken as its task the explanation of what is legal about the way in which enacted law regulates our lives, whether in question are statutes that regulate private relationships between individuals or statutes that regulate the public relationship between state and individuals.[51]

The problem is not, then, in positivism's insight that it is this kind of legality that has to be investigated but with the way positivism articulates that insight. With Kelsen, the problem manifests itself in the way in which legality gets reduced to compliance with criteria for valid enactment, with the consequent claim that the form of law can embrace any content. The anglophone legal positivists, notably Hart and Joseph Raz, have been compelled by Fuller's challenge to see that there is more to legality than such compliance, since legality also requires some consistency with Fuller's desiderata, understood as principles or criteria of legality. But, as I just suggested, they still wish to make the claim that the form of law can embrace any content.[52]

Recall that I said that Fuller's allegory of King Rex was designed to show why even the legislature in a system of parliamentary supremacy is subject to the rule of law, a fact that he thought that Hart's legal positivism had to, but could not properly, confront. Recall also Hart's remark that power-conferring rules can explain not only the way that legislation is a rule-bound or legally regulated activity in the same way that promising is, but also how legislation can be self-binding in the same way as promising. Hart did, as we saw, note some differences, mainly the missing element of the bilateral character of the promise, but said that in these respects, 'certain other forms of self-imposition known to English law, such as that whereby a person declares himself trustee of property for other persons, offer a closer analogy to the self-binding aspect of legislation'.[53]

It is worth noting in this respect that Fuller prefaced his chapter in which he introduced his principles of legality with the following quote from John Lilburne, the Leveller, and parliamentary rights activist, from his 1645 pamphlet *England's Birth-Right Justified*:

It is desired that our learned lawyers would answer these ensuing queries . . . whether ever the Commonwealth, when they chose the Parliament, gave them a lawless unlimited power, and

[51] My claim is not, however, that all particular legal positivists are aware of this. See further Michael Oakeshott's claim that his formal account of the rule of law, one 'superbly pioneered, in modern times, by Bodin and Hobbes', 'hovers over the reflections of many so-called "positivist" jurists'. Michael Oakeshott, 'The Rule of Law' in *On History and Other Essays* (Liberty Fund 1999) 129, 175.

[52] Joseph Raz, 'The Rule of Law and its Virtue' in *The Authority of Law: Essays on Law and Morality* (2nd edn, Oxford University Press 2009) 210; for an illuminating discussion of this issue see Jeremy Waldron, 'Positivism and Legality: Hart's Equivocal Response to Fuller' (2008) 83 *New York University Law Review* 1135.

[53] Hart, *Concept* (n 28) 43–4.

at their pleasure to walk contrary to their own laws and ordinances before they have repealed them?[54]

Fuller came back to this quote in his 'A Reply to Critics', at the point where he claimed that Hart had in *The Concept of Law* recognized that there had to be some voluntary cooperation on the part of citizens in creating the authority of law, but not 'a corresponding cooperative effort on the part of government', that is, that 'maintaining a legal system in existence depends upon the discharge of interlocking responsibilities—of government toward the citizen and of the citizen toward government'.[55] Fuller rejected the idea of a social contract for explaining the commitment by the lawgiver 'implicit in the concept of law', and suggested in its place the 'old fashioned legal term' 'intendment'—that is, that 'our institutions and our formalized interactions with one another are accompanied by certain interlocking expectations that may be called intendments'.[56] He took Lilburne to be suggesting 'that underlying the institution of parliamentary government there is an intendment—that is, a generally shared tacit expectation—that parliament will act towards the citizen in accordance with its own laws so long as those laws remain unrepealed'.[57]

By intendment, Fuller had in mind that the law has to be interpreted in light of these expectations, in particular the expectation that the law when so interpreted will manifest a relationship of reciprocity between ruler and ruled or individual and individual. Had Fuller noticed at this point Hart's remark about the trustee as the 'closer analogy to the self-binding aspect of legislation' he might have had to be less scathing in his criticism of Hart for failing to recognize that government has its responsibilities. But Fuller would probably have thought, and rightly so, that Hart failed utterly to follow through on the idea of the legislator as trustee, one which goes beyond Fuller's point of being bound to one's previous commitments. However, this kind of idea was precisely the one at which Lilburne's argument was aimed,[58] and one which Fuller clearly had in mind when he spoke of government as the 'guardian of the integrity' of a system in which law provides citizens 'with a sound and stable framework for their interactions with one another'.[59]

Moreover, Lilburne, like Fuller, thought that the judiciary and other adjudicative institutions had an essential role to play through interpretation of statutes in bringing the immanent morality of the legislative office—analogized to private law doctrines such as trusteeship or guardianship—to the surface.[60] In this regard, they both looked to Coke's invocation of the common law as a repository of principles for interpreting statutes in such a way as to ensure that this immanent

[54] Fuller, *Morality* (n 7) 33.

[55] Fuller, *Morality* (n 7) 216. Fuller is referring to the discussion in Hart, *Concept* (n 28) 201.

[56] Fuller, *Morality* (n 7) 217.

[57] Fuller, *Morality* (n 7) 218.

[58] See Diane Parkin-Speer, 'John Lilburne: A Revolutionary Interprets Statutes and Common Law Due Process' (1983) 1 *Law and History Review* 276.

[59] Fuller, *Morality* (n 7) 210.

[60] For a Fullerian account of public law along these lines, see Evan Fox-Decent, *Sovereignty's Promise: The State as Fiduciary* (Oxford University Press 2011) as well as his chapter in this volume.

morality was realized.[61] Finally, both thought that the civil condition which government under the rule of law brings about is one characterized by a particular kind of liberty, civil liberty or liberty under an order of *publica lex*. For Fuller, the principles of the internal morality of law amount to the *jus* of that *lex* that explains what makes a legal condition also a condition of liberty.

Fuller's position can be reconstructed as follows. The eight principles of the internal morality of law are, as Jeremy Waldron has argued, not well described as procedural. Rather, they are 'formal and structural in character: they emphasize the forms of governance and the formal qualities . . . that are supposed to characterize the norms on which state action is based'.[62] They apply, that is, to law-making and to the implementation of law, to the activity of the legislature and to the executive administration. But they are applied not by the legislature and the administration to themselves, but by the impartial official who is charged with converting the law into something that can be presented as a 'claim of right', as 'supported by a [legal] principle'.[63]

Of course, in order for the law to be so convertible, it has to have the appropriate form; and different legal orders provide an array of institutional mechanisms for dealing with the pathologies that are generated when an official cannot in good faith make the law so conform. Hence, the formal principles of legality include procedural principles that will govern both law-making and adjudication, the former so that it is clear when an artefact has a claim to be law, the latter so that it is possible for that artefact to be converted into a claim of right.

Notice that on this view it does not matter that, as Hart pointed out, when the legislature makes a law there is 'no person in the special position of the promisee *to whom* the promise is made and who has a special, if not the only claim, to its performance'.[64] For the commitment is to all those in the legal community, so that any one of them who has standing to challenge the application of a law is entitled to ask an impartial official to demonstrate to that individual, and thus to the legal community at large, that the content of that law—its intendment—lives up to the promise of law.

The content of the promise is that the law will present itself to the individual as a vehicle for his or her purposes, as facilitating rather than dictating civil interaction. Fuller said of law that conceived in this way it provides 'guideposts for human

[61] Fuller, *Morality* (n 7) 82–3, 99–102; Parkin-Speer, 'John Lilburne' (n 58) 282–6.

[62] Jeremy Waldron, 'The Concept and the Rule of Law' (2008) 43 *Georgia Law Review* 1, 7.

[63] In the kinds of cases where individuals get to the point of raising a claim of right before an impartial adjudicator, the process of conversion is not always or even often a matter of the adjudicator identifying a content to the law that could have guided the individual in advance of the decision. Statutory guidance can never be total, and is sometimes left deliberately vague in order to permit officials to develop and adapt the law to changing circumstances. Liberty is protected in such situations by ensuring that officials act in accordance with both a justifiable interpretation of the statute and the relevant principles of the rule of law. Thus while individuals in such situations cannot predict the exact content of the decision, they may expect that the content will bear a rational relationship to the purposes of the statute and that it will be consistent with the rule of law.

[64] Hart, *Concept* (n 28) 43.

interaction'.[65] But the most felicitous philosophical description of this conception of law is Michael Oakeshott's, when he said of the rule of law that 'taken precisely, [it] stands for a mode of moral association exclusively in terms of the recognition of the authority of known, non-instrumental rules (that is, laws) which impose obligations to subscribe to adverbial conditions in the performance of the self-chosen actions of all who fall within their jurisdiction'.[66] In other words, these are the conditions that attach to performing actions that the law makes possible, but which are ultimately up to the individual to choose.

That the law provides such guideposts could, of course, be said to be the purpose of which the law is the instrument. But the point of the claim about non-instrumentality is not that law has no general purpose, or that particular laws must be purposeless. It has to do with whether the law conscripts an individual in order to achieve some goal or whether it makes it possible for an individual to select his own goals. This idea of a non-instrumental law is, I think, an advance over the positivist distinction between power-conferring and duty-imposing rules. It tells us that an authentic law—one that has authority—is a law that through setting out conditions for purposive activity makes it possible for such activity to take place under conditions of security and stability. The move away from the command model of law does not require, as Hart thought, simply noticing that there are power-conferring rules as well as commands or duty-conferring rules and that the commander has to comply with rules in order to make rules.

It requires seeing, first, that the idea of law as the command to which a sanction attaches does not even describe the criminal law, since the criminal law consists of general laws that set out conditions for successful interaction, just as the law of contracts does. When the sovereign uses commands instead of such laws, that is, he exploits the legislative form to command that a punishment be visited on a particular individual, he runs the risk of finding that he has made not a law, but a bill of attainder. In such a case, the failure to make criminal law in general form, so that the subject can in advance know what the conditions are that attach to lawful interaction with his fellow subjects, has the result that the judge at the point of conversion is faced with a pathology so severe that even in a legal order where there is no entrenched bill of rights, he or she will have to contemplate refusing to recognize this validly produced artefact as a law. In other words, compliance with criteria of validity is in some cases insufficient for a law to have authority in any legal order, whatever institution of judicial review it has.

Second, it requires seeing that the commander is not legally regulated only in that he has to comply with power-conferring rules in order to make law. For law to have authority it must comply in addition with the principles of legality that ensure the non-instrumental nature of law. It is in this regard that Fuller's idea of conversion plays a role.

Legislation requires the reduction of a political programme to the explicit terms of a statute and thus converts policy into public standards, which produces a kind of

[65] Fuller, *Morality* (n 7) 222. [66] Oakeshott, 'Rule of Law' (n 51) 148.

legal surplus value. By this I mean that the legitimacy of official action in compliance with the statute is not simply that of compliance with a political policy that the demos has determined to be appropriate. It is also the case that this conversion process adds value because it brings into being a particular type of *public* standard, one that permits the operation of the principles identified by Fuller as the desiderata of the inner morality of law, and which enables claims of right based on legal principle to be adjudicated.

Legal form liberates, then, because of the form particular enacted laws have to take, though questions about whether they have that form will arise concretely only at the point of interpretation. At that point, the law has to be converted into a claim of right, which is to say that it must be shown to be answerable to the principles of the internal morality of law, which will in turn ensure the legal subject's 'dignity as a responsible agent'[67] is affirmed. 'Responsible' means here that the individual is enabled to take responsibility for setting his own goals. Hence, in conforming to the principles of legality, a sovereign ensures the possibility of a reciprocal relationship obtaining between state and subject or citizen and citizen.

Of course, for that to happen the enacted law must be convertible. But if it is not, it will appear to be legally flawed law, as it fails to comply with the formal attributes of law, and consequently the individuals to whom it applies will have difficulty understanding why that law has a justified claim on their obedience. Hence, even when the positive law of a legal order does not accord any participatory rights to the subject other than the right to ask a judge to give an authoritative interpretation of the law that applies to the subject, the bare commitment of rulers to govern by law establishes a liberty-constituting relationship of reciprocity between sovereign and subject.

Indeed, as Kelsen argued, the sovereign state is nothing more than the sum total of the legally authorized power of the officials who staff a legal order. Fuller's important addition to this argument is that legally authorized power is not simply power that can be shown to have a warrant in a validly enacted law, since it is also power whose exercise is conditioned by the formal principles of legality. While it is not, as I will now show, conditioned to the same degree as the Kantian position on the immanent morality of law seems to demand, I will conclude that its very sparseness redounds to its advantage, since the Kantian position accords a problematic place in its understanding of legality to the idea of corrective justice.

5. The Normative Priority of Private Right

I mean by the normative priority of private right, first, that the argument begins in private right, so that public right and hence an order of public laws or *publica lex* comes into being primarily in order to make it possible for individuals to interact rightfully; second, that any order of public laws must include the domain of private

[67] Fuller, *Morality* (n 7) 162.

law, that is, the domain where horizontal relationships between individuals are governed by corrective, not distributive justice. It is, as I will now argue, only the second aspect of the priority of private right that is problematic from the perspective of legality.[68]

If the only task for public right were to make it possible for private right to govern, it would be not only illegitimate but also illegal for institutions of public right—the state—to go beyond securing a public condition of private right.[69] There would be public laws, *publica lex*, but no, or at least no significant, public law. That version of the Kantian position would be highly controversial from the perspective of any political theory that sees distributive justice as a legitimate task for the liberal state, but it would be internally consistent.

However, while Weinrib and Ripstein both argue that public right, an order of public laws with an effective separation of powers between the legislative, judicial, and executive authorities, is an essential precondition of private right, they also argue that the Kantian idea can underpin public law, this time as the contrast with 'private law'. Both domains of law have to be part of *publica lex*, but they have their own immanent moralities or normative structures, respectively, public right or distributive justice, and private right or corrective justice. Distributive justice is required to ensure that individuals are not in a condition of dependence on the will of others. Thus, its juridical basis is in the same idea of the freedom of the purposive agent that animates corrective justice, but its legal form is different. In the case of corrective justice, the idea involves the wrongdoer correcting a wrong so as to restore the wronged party to the position he would have been in but for the wrong, whereas distributive justice requires a less determinate and more political judgment about how to allocate a pool of resources so as to reduce the dependence of the worse off in a society on the better off.

Of course, an argument is needed about why it is justified at all to establish and distribute that pool, since its existence requires taking assets from the better off. But both Weinrib and Ripstein suppose that the same Kantian idea of freedom that justifies the institution of private property can justify its taxation.[70] Since private right protects the property of those who have it from takings by the poor who need access to these resources to subsist, private right makes possible a relationship of dependence of the poor on the property owners, and so the same right of independence that argues for private right to be made effective by public right also requires that public right see to it that the state redistributes resources to the poor to

[68] Hence, I would dispute also the main argument in Allan, 'The Rule of Law as the Rule of Private Law' (n 9).

[69] As Kant himself seems to suggest at 6.306 of *The Doctrine of Right* when he says that '[The condition of public right] contains no further or other duties of men among themselves than can be conceived in the former state; the matter of private Right is the same in both. The laws of the condition of public Right, accordingly, have to do only with the rightful form of men's association (constitution), in view of which these laws must necessarily be conceived as public.' See Immanuel Kant, *Practical Philosophy* (Cambridge University Press 1996) 451.

[70] See Ernest J Weinrib, 'Poverty and Property in Kant's System of Rights' in *Corrective Justice* (Oxford University Press 2012) ch 8; Ripstein, 'Public Right III: Redistribution and Equality of Opportunity' in *Force and Freedom* (n 8) ch 9.

reduce their potential dependence. In Weinrib's elegant summary, 'one may say that the distributive justice of taxing to support the poor is the conceptual concomitant of establishing a legally effective system of corrective justice'.[71]

However, if, as Weinrib and Ripstein argue, the liberal state not only may but must engage in redistribution, the claim of the normative priority of private right, or so I will argue, becomes tenuous. Put differently, I want to address a dilemma that the Kantian position knows that it faces.[72] Either it stands its ground on the priority of private right and insists that its normative structure is the immanent morality of legality, which confines the role of the legislature to securing private right both by declaring its requirements and by providing resources without which private rights holders could not interact, for example, a system of roads that connect private properties as well as rules that coordinate traffic flow on the roads.[73] Alternatively, it recognizes the need for a legislature to make decisions that go beyond this restriction, for example, decisions to alleviate substantive inequalities, and that recognition gives up its grip on the priority of private right. As I will show, this dilemma manifests itself in the position's understanding of legality.

Let me start with the question why the Kantians suppose that the state requires legislative, judicial, and executive institutions when only the last two might be necessary to secure private right. We clearly need judges, since it is the case that the content of private right cannot be authoritatively determined in a state of nature, where each individual's interpretation has the same status as any other's, making the rights of each prey to the interpretations of others. Hence, private law has to be made part of *publica lex*. In addition, the executive is obviously necessary because judgments of private right require enforcement.

Thus far we have in place reasons to establish an executive to enforce private right and a court to provide authoritative determinations of what private right requires. But notice that we do not yet have reason to require a legislature, nor do we get one from Weinrib's main writing so far on the relationship between private law and public right. There the legislature gets mentioned. Judges, however, do almost all the work in explaining the relationship between private law and public right. The judiciary thus seems perfectly capable of settling problems about the indeterminacy of private rights in accordance with the requirement that their determinations be instances of a universal law, that is, omnilaterally authorized, even on occasion 'adopting a principle inconceivable in the state of nature'.[74]

In *Force and Freedom*, however, Ripstein suggests that one could not make do with an executive and a court because 'without a legislature omnilaterally authorizing the laws that they apply and enforce would simply be an exercise of unilateral choice by officials'.[75] Legislation, he explains following Kant, is the 'major premise' in a practical syllogism, with the minor premise being executive enforcement, 'the

[71] Weinrib, *Corrective Justice* (n 70) 296.

[72] See Ripstein, *Force and Freedom* (n 8) 270–1; Weinrib, *Corrective Justice* (n 70) 264–5.

[73] See Ripstein, 'Public Right II: Roads to Freedom' in *Force and Freedom* (n 8) ch 9.

[74] Ernest J Weinrib, 'Private Law and Public Right' (2011) 61 *University of Toronto Law Journal* 191, 198.

[75] Ripstein, *Force and Freedom* (n 8) 173–4.

means available for giving effect to the legislation', and the judicial verdict the conclusion, 'the making-determinate of the authorization to use force in a particular case'.[76]

But this claim seems to make the common law of torts, contract, and property, that is the very systems of private law that form the raw material of Weinrib's theory of corrective justice, the product of judicial arbitrariness. In addition, if the only cure for judicial arbitrariness is that the legislature render determinate the content of private law so that judges simply supply the conclusion of a practical syllogism, we would need an explanation of why the legislature is not playing the same role in this Kantian legal theory as it does in a version of legal positivism in which the legislature is considered to have a monopoly of the determination of what is morally right. It thus becomes unclear why Ripstein rejects the attribution of such a view to Kant.[77]

The problem here is not conceptual, as Weinrib and Ripstein find in Kant a conceptually sequenced argument that shows the logical progression from the establishment of private right in the state of nature to the public securing of private right in a civil condition to the public law redistribution of privately held resources. Rather, the problem arises in practice with what we can think of as public law intrusions into the realm of private law, understood as the realm of corrective justice, for example, when the legislature more or less does away with tort law in an area of private interaction by introducing a system of no-fault public insurance to compensate individuals for the harms they suffer, perhaps matched with a separate system that inflicts penalties on those that bring about certain classes of harms in a way calculated to deter similar behaviour.

The Kantian position is committed to preserving the distinction between private law/corrective justice and public law/distributive justice, and to asserting the primacy of the former over the latter. It must thus suppose (despite some hesitations of Kantian legal theorists in this regard) that such intrusions are moral mistakes. But it is unclear that it can suppose them to be legal mistakes, in the sense that it would be illegal to take this step—that this new regime is inherently incapable of being governed by legality or public right.[78] And if I am right about

[76] Ripstein, *Force and Freedom* (n 8) 174.

[77] Ripstein, *Force and Freedom* (n 8) n 34 at 69, referring to Jeremy Waldron's work on legislatures and also his 'Kant's Legal Positivism' (1996) 109 *Harvard Law Review* 1535.

[78] See Ernest J Weinrib, 'The Insurance Justification of Private Law' (1985) 14 *The Journal of Legal Studies* 681, 687:

> Now an assertion of the integrity of private law supplies no ground for preferring private to public law: both modes of ordering can have their own integrity.... Public law does not require the existence of private law as a positive reality of the legal system, but the intelligibility of public law requires at least the recognition that private law too must have the status of, in Kant's words, an idea of reason.... This is because public law, inasmuch as it is law, must no less than private law actualize freedom in man's external relationships, and the freedom that law actualizes—the recognition of a person's status as a self-determining entity—is the same for law in both its public and its private aspects. Orientation of the plaintiff's suit to an extrinsic purpose reflects badly on the commitment of legal institutions to the ideal of law they supposedly serve. Proponents of public law have no reason to rejoice in the warping of the realm of private right.

For further discussion along the same lines, see Weinrib, *Idea of Private Law* (n 8) 36–42.

that, then it seems to follow that Kelsen is correct to assert an idea of legality that is more fundamental than the immanent morality of corrective justice and that has a normative force for public officials and legal subjects that needs exploration.

Indeed, if the Kantian position wishes to stick to the claim that corrective justice is part of the immanent morality of law, so that the distinction between private law and public law is fundamental, it is hard to see why it does not fall within the camp of the 'traditional jurisprudence'[79] against which Kelsen argues—a substantive natural law position which establishes a universal class of *mala prohibita* and regards law as the instrument of that class.[80] As in his argument against Austin described above, Kelsen wishes to move philosophy of law away from the idea that law is merely the instrument of extra-legally determined moral content towards describing what is immanent in legality.

Notice in this regard that there is significant agreement between a substantive natural law position that says that law is the instrument of the one true morality, and a positivist position that says that law is the instrument of extra-legal value. The only difference between the two is that the substantive natural law position seems driven to the conclusion that law is not law when it implements immorality, and that conclusion seems so implausible that positivism has always seemed to have the better of this debate.

But positivism only has the better of this debate if law is conceived in this way,[81] and I believe, though I cannot provide the argument here, that any substantive natural law position will end up faced with this dilemma, because such a position is driven to taking an instrumental view of the relationship between law and morality. Indeed, this dilemma manifests itself most fundamentally in the architecture of the Kantian position in its distinction between a constitutive principle of authority, which accords *de jure* or legitimate authority to the law enacted by any established legal order, and a regulative principle of justice, which imposes a duty on the state to regulate the private realm in accordance with corrective justice and the public realm in accordance with distributive justice.[82] For that distinction creates an irresolvable tension.

The constitutive principle supposes that it is sufficient for law to have fully legitimate authority that it is valid or enacted in accordance with the *de facto*

[79] Hans Kelsen, *The Pure Theory of Law*, trans Max Knight (The Law Book Exchange 2009) 111–12.

[80] Weinrib is not, I think, correct to claim that the main dispute between him and Kelsen is over their view of remedies. See Weinrib, 'Remedies' in *Corrective Justice* (n 70) ch 3, 81–6. Kelsen's position is not inconsistent with the claim that legal orders that *contingently* have bilaterally structured systems of private law will contain the morality of private law that Weinrib describes in his work.

[81] Consider the problems Dworkin's theory of law encounters when legislators have used the law so overwhelmingly as an instrument of immorality that the moral mistakes embedded in the law seem to require that the set of principles that show the law of the jurisdiction in its 'best light' are the principles of an immoral ideology. In the face of this scenario, Dworkin has shown considerable ambivalence between the claim that there is no law because the purported law is so unjust or the positivistic response that the law is law but too unjust for the judge to apply it; Dworkin, *Justice for Hedgehogs*, 410–12.

[82] For detailed discussion and a defence of these two principles, see Jacob Weinrib, *Authority, Justice, and Public Law: A Unified Theory* (PhD thesis, Department of Philosophy, University of Toronto, 2013).

accepted procedures for making law. In other words, its account of law is positivistic with the significant qualification that validity suffices for legitimacy. This makes the Kantian position highly authoritarian, akin to the position often attributed to Hobbes's absolutist conception of political sovereignty.[83] That the position then argues that the regulative principle is one internal to law and which moderates the constitutive principle by imposing a duty on rulers to govern justly seems to display the tension, not to resolve it. As legal positivists would respond, it would be more candid to speak plainly and to say that a valid law might be too evil to be obeyed, in which case we should recognize its validity but deny that it has *de jure* authority.[84]

In contrast, the Fullerian position argues that there is only one principle—a constitutive principle of authority—but that it includes criteria of legality that law has to satisfy to be considered authoritative. In a slogan, law has to be legal. Moreover, in being legal law will constitute a condition of civil liberty for its subjects. The position is open to an argument that the optimal way to construct such a civil condition is by designing it on Kantian lines, thus preserving a distinct domain of private law governed by corrective justice. But it enters a sceptical note that such a design is plausible in an age of statutes and of the administrative state. This is not only because statutes and the administrative state are facts on the ground, as it were. It is also because the age of statutes and that state came about in large part as a response to the problem of personal dependence on the arbitrary will of others in a world of material inequality that was regulated mainly by private law.

As we have seen, the Kantian position recognizes that the injustice of such personal dependence is in some sense the result of the way in which a commitment to the normative priority of private right protects the beneficiaries of material inequality. I also pointed out that there are two aspects to such priority: first, that the argument for it begins in private right, so that public right and hence an order of public laws or *publica lex* comes into being primarily in order to make it possible for individuals to interact rightfully; second, that any order of public laws must include the domain of private law, that is, the domain where horizontal relationships between individuals are governed by corrective, not distributive justice. Finally, I suggested that it is the second aspect of the priority of private right that is problematic from the perspective of legality.

On the basis of my argument in this section, I want to make a further suggestion—that this second aspect is also problematic from the perspective of morality. Indeed, so much is recognized by the Kantian position insofar as it would find what we might think of a *Lochneresque* entrenchment of private right unjust, that is, a world in which the legal protection of private right immunized the beneficiaries of material inequality against legislative attempts to bring about a more just distribution of resources. I have not provided here anything like the full

[83] Though this is a mistaken view of Hobbes, in my view; see Dyzenhaus, 'Hobbes on the Authority of Law' (n 27).
[84] Hart, 'Separation of Law and Morals' (n 1) 620.

argument that would be required to show that compliance with Fullerian legality is sufficient to constitute the condition of legal or civil liberty that ensures individual independence.[85] But if natural law theory is to have a purchase in the age of statutes and of the administrative state, it will be because of the way in which an order of public laws makes it possible for individuals to interact rightfully, and not because of an implicit or quasi-implicit entrenchment of the immanent morality of corrective justice.

6. Conclusion

I started this chapter with four puzzles about the topic of the rule of law in private law. I have suggested that the puzzles are generated by two assumptions that drive each, first, that however we understand the rule of law, the distinction between public and private law is fundamental, second, that the rule of law is best understood as a set of constraints on power. I have taken from Kelsen the view that the distinction between private law and public law is not fundamental to an understanding of law or the rule of law and that the idea of legality is. I have also suggested that Fuller shared this view, though he differed from both Kelsen and the tradition of legal positivism in general in that he took legality to entail an immanent morality of reciprocity between ruler and ruled that is constitutive of a certain kind of liberty, civil liberty, or liberty under an order of public laws.

My argument here has been that any hard and fast distinction between public and private law and their corresponding immanent moralities is both legally implausible and recognized even by those who make it to be morally suspect. Yet, this argument does not require us to adopt legal positivism since the Fullerian view both does not depend on this distinction and indicates why we might suppose that law in being legal does display an immanent morality, since such law is constitutive of a politically valuable condition of liberty.

Hence, Fuller does not so much solve the puzzles as undermine their assumptions. He thus sets the task for legal theory of an elaboration not of discrete moralities that contingently underpin the distinct domains of private and public law, but of a more fundamental immanent morality of legality that underpins all law—*publica lex*.

[85] For a more elaborate argument, see Dyzenhaus, 'Hobbes on the Authority of Law' (n 27) and David Dyzenhaus, 'Freedom under an Order of Public Law: From Hobbes through Hayek to Republicanism' in Andras Sajo and Renata Uitz (eds), *The Tragedy of Liberty* (Eleven Publishing forthcoming).

5

Unseating Unilateralism

*Evan Fox-Decent**

1. Introduction

Two sets of literature dominate academic discussion of the rule of law. The first is the Fuller/Hart/Raz literature of legal philosophy that focuses on Fuller's internal morality of law and the framework it supplies for the exercise of agency. The second is the public law literature descended from AV Dicey that celebrates the rule of law as an equity-working bulwark against arbitrary executive power. According to Dicey, judges uphold the rule of law by interpreting statutes against the backdrop of common law rights and principles. Long before these literatures developed a life of their own, however, Thomas Hobbes articulated a conception of legal order that featured core elements of both. Hobbes's legal order is structured by an internal morality that foreshadows Fuller's, and is partially governed by an equity-laden theory of statutory interpretation that anticipates Dicey's. The combination of these elements is the public law dimension of Hobbes's theory.

Given this rich public law content, it is striking that Hobbes's account of authority in *Leviathan* begins with the fact situation that is characteristic of private law: a dispute between two private parties.[1] Hobbes claims that the equitable resolution of such disputes requires an impartial third party, such as an arbitrator or judge. Hobbes thereby sets out a private law model of adjudicative authority. This private law dimension of Hobbes's legal theory raises a question: what, if anything, is the relationship between private law and public law in Hobbes? For many legal scholars, the two domains are treated as separate spheres that respond to two categorically distinctive modes of justice: private law answers to corrective

* I thank for comments Evan Criddle, Andrew Gold, Steve Smith, Daniel Viehoff, the editors of this volume, the participants at the Private Law and the Rule of Law Workshop held at the University of Toronto's Faculty of Law, 19–20 September 2012, the participants of a Work-in-Progress workshop of the Research Group on Constitutional Studies, McGill University, held 24 January 2012, and the participants of the Private Law Theory Symposium held at Bar-Ilan's Faculty of Law, held 26–7 June 2013. I owe a similar debt to Ian Dahlman, Michaël Lessard, and Katie Saulnier for excellent research assistance and comments, and a further debt to the Social Science and Humanities Research Council for financial support.

[1] Thomas Hobbes, *Leviathan with Selected Variants from the Latin Edition of 1668* (first published 1651), ed Edwin Curely (Hackett Publishing 1994) 23 (ch v para 3).

justice, while public law answers to distributive justice.[2] While not disputing that corrective and distributive justice have different internal structures of justification, I argue that Hobbes offers a persuasive account of private law and public law in which both can be seen to share the same fundamental organizing principle. Hobbes thereby articulates a unified account of legality wherein the relationship between private law and public law is one of mutual presupposition and accommodation. In other words, private law and public law may express different modes or forms of justice, but they nonetheless manifest the same organizing principle, and so they co-habit the same overarching normative structure, with neither enjoying normative priority over the other.

For Hobbes, law is necessarily a public and institutional phenomenon. He begins with private law because it allows him to express most vividly the fundamental organizing principle he sees underlying the institutions of public as well as private law: the prohibition on unilateralism. This principle affirms that no private party is ever entitled to dictate terms or enforce justice claims unilaterally against another. It is reflected in Hobbes's private law model of adjudicative authority under which public authorities alone are entitled to resolve private disputes. But the prohibition on unilateralism is reflected as well in the public law dimension of Hobbes's legal theory. The principle is embodied in various laws of nature that inform both the structure and norms of legal institutions, including his aforementioned internal morality and equity-laden theory of statutory interpretation. The prohibition on unilateralism thereby explains both the public and private law dimensions of Hobbes's legal theory, revealing public law and private law as a unity.

2. Hobbes and the Rule of Law

Much contemporary legal philosophy on the rule of law begins with Lon Fuller's internal morality of law and his debate with HLA Hart and Joseph Raz.[3] Fuller's internal morality sets out formal desiderata that, Fuller thought, ordinarily guide

[2] See eg Ernest J Weinrib, 'Corrective Justice in a Nutshell' (2002) 52 *University of Toronto Law Journal* 349, 351 ('Corrective and distributive justice embody categorically different structures of justification').

[3] Lon L Fuller, *The Morality of Law* (rev edn, Yale University Press 1969); HLA Hart, 'Review the Morality of Law' (1965) 78 *Harvard Law Review* 1281; Joseph Raz, 'The Rule of Law and its Virtue', in *The Authority of Law: Essays on Law and Morality* (2nd edn, Oxford University Press 2009) 210. For the literature on this debate, see eg TRS Allan, *Constitutional Justice: A Liberal Theory of the Rule of Law* (Oxford University Press 2001); Daniel Brudney, 'Two Links of Law and Morality' (1993) 103 *Ethics* 280; Paul Craig, 'Formal and Substantive Conceptions of the Rule or Law' (1997) *Public Law* 467; David Dyzenhaus, 'Fuller's Novelty' in W Witteveen and W van der Burg (eds), *Rediscovering Fuller: Essays on Implicit Law and Institutional Design* (Amsterdam University Press 1999) 78; Kristen Rundle, *Forms Liberate: Reclaiming the Jurisprudence of Lon L Fuller* (Hart Publishing 2012); Andrei Marmor, 'The Rule of Law and its Limits' (2004) 24 *Law and Philosophy* 1; Colleen Murphy, 'Lon Fuller and the Moral Value of the Rule of Law' (2005) 24 *Law and Philosophy* 239; Jennifer Nadler, 'Hart, Fuller and the Connection between Law and Justice' (2007) 27 *Law and Philosophy* 1; Gerald J Postema, 'Implicit Law' in Witteveen and van der Burg (eds), *Rediscovering Fuller* (this note) 255; Margaret Jane Radin, 'Reconsidering the Rule of Law' (1989) 69 *Boston University Law Review* 781; Kristen Rundle, 'The Impossibility of an Exterminatory Legality: Law and the Holocaust' (2009) 59 *University of*

(and should guide) lawgivers as they make and apply law. The desiderata are principles of generality, publicity, non-retroactivity, clarity, consistency, stability, feasibility of performance, and congruence between law as written and law as implemented. At its strongest, Fuller's claim was that if a lawgiver failed entirely to abide by one or more of the principles of the internal morality, then she had not made bad law, but rather had failed to make law at all.[4] His basic idea was that a wholesale failure to live up to the demands of the internal morality would leave the individual without a stable framework of rules to guide her conduct. Since having such a framework for interaction is morally valuable, and general compliance with the internal morality is necessary for such a framework to exist, Fuller inferred that the internal morality disclosed a necessary connection between law and morality.

Hart and Raz accepted that any system of rules, to function as such, would have to have more or less the features of Fuller's internal morality. But they disputed Fuller's claim that those rule of law features revealed a necessary connection between law and morality, since substantively wicked rules could take the forms prescribed by the internal morality. Raz acknowledged that the basic point of the rule of law is to let the law guide people's conduct, and that as a general matter subscription to the rule of law is necessary to respect the subject's autonomy.[5] He argued, however, that slavery is consistent with the rule of law, and concluded that compliance with the rule of law is neither sufficient to respect autonomy nor evidence of a necessary connection between law and morality.

My purpose at this juncture is not to rehash Fuller's debate with his rivals, but to suggest that for both sides the virtue of the rule of law is connected to human agency. For Raz, the value of the connection is contingent on the merits of the law. The rule of law just avoids certain forms of abuse that would not be possible but for the existence of law itself. In other words, law's monopoly on the use of force makes abuse possible, so the fact that the rule of law may limit or mitigate abuses does not show that law or legal order has intrinsic moral worth.[6] If the law is a slave law that conforms to the internal morality, then it may be capable of guiding the conduct of those it oppresses, but Raz would say it deserves no moral credit for doing so. To draw on a well-known metaphor from Raz, we would not say that a four-inch knife is morally praiseworthy because it cannot be used to cut an innocent person six inches deep. We would simply say that the knife's instrumental value is limited in part by the knife's sharpness and size.[7] For Raz, *mutatis mutandis*, the same is true of law. Law's specific virtue, he claimed, is the morally neutral virtue of efficiency with respect to the good or bad purposes to which law may be put.

Fuller, on the other hand, relying on the internal morality alone, appears committed to another view of slave laws. Assume that the law under consideration

Toronto Law Journal 65; Nigel E Simmonds, *Law as a Moral Idea* (Oxford University Press 2007); Jeremy Waldron, 'Why Law—Efficacy, Freedom, or Fidelity?' (1994) 13 *Law and Philosophy* 259.

[4] Fuller, *Morality* (n 3) 33–8.

[5] Raz, 'Rule of Law and its Virtue' (n 3) 222.

[6] For trenchant critique of this view, see Marmor, 'Rule of Law and its Limits' (n 3) 40.

[7] Raz, 'Rule of Law and its Virtue' (n 3) 225–6.

merely indicates which classes of people are subject to slavery by whom, and that slaves are not persons but the property of their masters. Arguably for Fuller there would be an important sense in which this law is not really a law for the slave. The slave law does not guide the slave's conduct as a system of rules, but rather identifies a class of people who can own and use others as they wish, with or without standing rules. Laws of this sort give slaves a meta-level rule of recognition and implicit notice of the unrestrained abuse they may face if they disobey their masters. But such laws supply no object-level rules susceptible to the internal morality and capable of guiding the slave's conduct. The master's will alone guides the slave's conduct. And so the slave is not really subject to law, properly understood, since the slave is not subject to a system of rules conformable to the internal morality. Fuller never actually said as much explicitly, preferring instead to insist that in practice the rule of law would never function as more than a *modus vivendi* in a tyranny, since the rule of law serves the people and, by definition, tyrants serve themselves first and the people only to the extent it is convenient for them to do so.

The point to underline, however, is that for both Raz and Fuller the value of the rule of law is explained by the framework it establishes for the individual's independent exercise of her agency. Without such a framework in place, the rule of law is either stripped of its value (Raz) or simply does not apply (Fuller). Intriguingly, Hobbes's conception of legal order anticipates this agency-enabling feature of the rule of law, just as it anticipates the protection the rule of law affords against executive arbitrariness.

The last principle of Fuller's internal morality—congruence between the law as written and the law as implemented—speaks directly to the idea of protection against executive arbitrariness. Fuller relied on this principle heavily in his reply to Hart in the second edition of *The Morality of Law*. Generally, however, the literature that explores in greatest depth and doctrinal sophistication the rule of law's limits on executive power is the public law literature on administrative law rather than the Fuller-inspired scholarship of legal philosophy.[8]

The public law literature from the commonwealth draws on AV Dicey's foundational work on British constitutionalism. Dicey claimed that the unwritten British constitution rested on two principles: parliamentary sovereignty and the rule of law. By parliamentary sovereignty, Dicey meant that Parliament, and Parliament alone, was free to make and repeal any law whatsoever. Thus, no Parliament could have its law-making hands tied by a predecessor. To underscore

[8] Fuller, *Morality* (n 3) 187; See eg Christopher Forsyth (ed), *Judicial Review and the Constitution* (Hart Publishing 2000), Murray Hunt, *Using Human Rights Law in English Courts* (Hart Publishing 1997), David Mullan, *Administrative Law* (Irwin Law 2001), Michael Taggart (ed), *The Province of Administrative Law* (Hart Publishing 1997), William Wade and Christopher Forsyth, *Administrative Law* (10th edn, Oxford University Press 2009); There are some notable exceptions that combine legal philosophy with public law doctrinal analysis: see eg Allan, *Constitutional Justice* (n 3), Craig, 'Formal and Substantive Conceptions' (n 3), David Dyzenhaus, 'Schmitt v. Dicey: Are States of Emergency Inside or Outside the Legal Order?' (2009) 27 *Cardozo Law Review* 2005.

the scope of Parliament's authority, Dicey pointed to amnesty laws that made legal that which hitherto had been illegal.[9]

By the rule of law, Dicey meant that individuals could not be punished except for a breach of law determined by independent judges of courts of inherent jurisdiction, and that public officials as well as private citizens were subject to the 'ordinary' law of the land and the jurisdiction of independent courts. Moreover, he claimed that all statutory powers 'however extraordinary . . . are never really unlimited, for they are confined by the words of the Act itself, and, what is more, by the interpretation put upon the statute by the judges'. This interpretative exercise, Dicey thought, was to be guided by common law rights such as personal liberty and the right of assembly, with the effect that interpretations consistent with such rights were to be preferred: rights could be violated only if the statute expressly authorized their violation. Elsewhere, Dicey indicated that he thought Parliament would be hard pressed to draft statutory language sufficiently clear to violate fundamental rights, saying that 'the right of individual freedom is part of the constitution because it is inherent in the ordinary law of the land', and hence 'the right is one which can hardly be destroyed without a thorough revolution in the institutions and manners of the nation'. He traced these constitutional rights to judge-made private law, declaring that they are 'the result of judicial decisions determining the rights of private persons in particular cases brought before the courts'.[10] By tempering parliamentary sovereignty with this common law conception of the rule of law, Dicey articulated a version of what public lawyers now call common law constitutionalism.

In its modern form, common law constitutionalism affirms a principle of legality that borrows from Dicey's rule of law interpretative principle. The principle of legality (or clear statement principle) affirms that fundamental rights, including human rights and more traditional common law rights, are not to be infringed by executive action in the absence of clear and unequivocal statutory authorization.[11] Parliament is presumed to legislate cognizant of these rights and on behalf of their bearers, so judges will not ascribe to Parliament an intent to violate them unless Parliament makes that intention plain. Hobbes adopts a similar principle of legality.

[9] AV Dicey, *Introduction to the Study of the Law of the Constitution* (10th edn, Macmillan 1959) 47.

[10] Dicey, *Introduction* (n 9) 188, 193, 413, 201, 195; Dicey leaves no doubt that the principles of private law occupy the apex of constitutional authority: '[W]ith us the law of the constitution . . . [is] not the source but the consequence of the rights of individuals, as defined and enforced by the courts; that, in short, the principles of private law have with us been by the action of the courts and Parliament so extended as to determine the position of the Crown and of its servants' (Dicey, *Introduction* (n 9) 203).

[11] *R v Secretary for the Home Department, Ex parte Simms* [2000] 2 AC 115, 131 (Lord Hoffman): 'The principle of legality means that Parliament must squarely confront what it is doing and accept the political cost. Fundamental rights cannot be overridden by general or ambiguous words. This is because there is too great a risk that the full implications of their unqualified meaning may have passed unnoticed in the democratic process. In the absence of express language or necessary implication to the contrary, the courts therefore presume that even the most general words were intended to be subject to the basic rights of the individual.'

It is important to note as a preliminary matter, however, that laws for Hobbes are of two kinds: the laws of nature and civil laws. Although Hobbes at one point claims that these laws 'contain each other, and are of equal extent', they have distinctive properties.[12] One important difference is that the laws of nature alone are precepts of reason and thus are knowable in the state of nature. The civil law is the law in force in civil society, which includes both the laws of nature and the sovereign's positive law. Hobbes sets out some twenty laws of nature, several of which we canvass below. A number of these laws direct individuals to do what Hobbes thinks is best for their self-preservation, such as to seek peace when others are so willing, and to develop moral virtues conducive to peace, such as gratitude and modesty.[13] At another juncture Hobbes says that these laws are really just 'conclusions and theorems concerning what conduceth to the conservation and defence of themselves, whereas law, properly, is the word of him that by right hath command over others'.[14] Many of Hobbes's readers have concluded that the laws of nature are merely prudential maxims that express a hypothetical imperative of the structure: 'If you want peace (your best chance at self-preservation) and others are like-minded, then do x', where x is the substantive content of a law of nature.[15] Yet, Hobbes's laws of nature also include principles such as equity and equality aimed at the institutions of legal order. These principles are difficult to explain through private self-interest because their exclusive role is to demarcate a public space that the sovereign alone, in his public capacity, is charged with securing. With this much of the civil law/law of nature distinction in view, let us turn to Hobbes's legal theory and its remarkable anticipation of contemporary scholarship on the rule of law.

2.1 Hobbes's internal morality and agency

In his discussion in *Leviathan* of what makes a law a good law, Hobbes writes that the point of law 'is not to bind the people from all voluntary actions, but to direct and keep them in such a motion as not to hurt themselves by their own impetuous desires, rashness, or indiscretion, as hedges are set, not to stop travellers, but to keep them on their way'.[16] In the 1668 Latin version of *Leviathan* he clarifies that the point of law-as-hedges is 'to prevent [individuals] from wandering off, with injury

[12] Hobbes, *Leviathan* (n 1) 174 (ch xxvi para 8).

[13] Hobbes, *Leviathan* (n 1) 80 (ch xiv paras 4–5); 95–7 (ch xv paras 16–22).

[14] Hobbes, *Leviathan* (n 1) 100 (ch xv para 41).

[15] See eg Jean Hampton, *Hobbes and the Social Contract Tradition* (Cambridge University Press 1988), Norberto Bobbio, *Thomas Hobbes and the Natural Law Tradition*, trans Daniela Gobetti (University of Chicago Press 1993).

[16] Hobbes, *Leviathan* (n 1) 229 (ch xxx para 21); Locke would later use a similar hedge metaphor to explain how law does not constitute domination, with Philip Pettit applauding this characterization as evidence of how, for republicans, law is 'creative of freedom'. Philip Pettit, *Republicanism: A Theory of Freedom and Government* (Oxford University Press 1997) 40. The passage to which Pettit is referring is John Locke, *Two Treatises of Government*, ed Peter Laslett (Cambridge University Press 1988) 305 (bk II ch 6 para 57).

to their fellow citizens'.[17] As with hedges that mark off public spaces from private domains, law on Hobbes's reading is a public phenomenon designed to allow each of us to choose our own paths without trespassing against others or suffering their trespasses against us. Law, in other words, supplies a public framework for interaction that lends mutual security to the exercise of agency.

Through their concern for agency, the formal requirements of Hobbes's theory parallel Fuller's internal morality. Hobbes foreshadows Fuller's principle of generality—that lawgiving takes the form of rules and not ad hoc commands—when he claims that civil law consists in rules, and that the commonwealth 'prescribes and commandeth the observation of those rules we call law'. While Hobbes allows that some laws are addressed to only some classes of subjects, and even some 'to particular men', the civil law is nonetheless expected to take the form of general rules capable of guiding the conduct of its addressees.[18]

Hobbes also adopts a principle of publicity akin to Fuller's when he claims that civil law must be published by a known public authority to be obligatory. The laws of nature need not be published, since they are knowable through reason. Positive laws, however, must be published because 'the command of the commonwealth is law only to those that have means to take notice of it'. So the commonwealth's commands are not laws to 'natural fools, children or madmen', nor to anyone who has lost the ability to take notice of the law. But the notice requirement constrains the sovereign too, requiring him to provide the means necessary for people of ordinary cognitive ability to know his will. Hobbes's argument, then, is that individuals cannot be subject to conventional obligations they have no reasonable means of knowing; positive law imposes conventional obligations; therefore, if an individual has no reasonable means of knowing a particular law, then he cannot be subject to its obligations. And for Hobbes, to say that someone is not subject to a law's obligations is to say that this law 'is no law to him'.[19]

Hobbes likewise insists that a good law must be '*perspicuous*', or, in Fuller's terms, clear. Perspicuity is achieved by the legislator declaring the purpose for which the law is made, and drafting the law as concisely and unambiguously as possible, 'in as proper and significant terms, as may be'.[20] From this idea of perspicuity we can also infer Fuller's principle of internal consistency, since inconsistency is a form (perhaps the severest form) of ambiguity. A law whose ambiguity crystallized in two inconsistent meanings would frustrate the subject's ability to know her legal obligations and be guided by the law. The same can be said of laws that demanded the impossible or changed too frequently for subjects to keep themselves apprised of their content.

Finally, Hobbes takes on board Fuller's non-retroactivity in his discussion of crime, claiming that '[n]o law made after a fact done can make it a crime; because if

[17] Hobbes, *Leviathan* (n 1) 229 n 11 (ch xxx para 21) providing the Latin version of this passage in *Leviathan*.

[18] Hobbes, *Leviathan* (n 1) 173 (ch xxvi para 5); 173 (ch xxvi para 4).

[19] Hobbes, *Leviathan* (n 1) 177–80 (ch xxvi paras 12–19); 177 (ch xxvi para 12).

[20] Hobbes, *Leviathan* (n 1) 229 (ch xxx para 20); 230 (ch xxx para 22).

the fact be against the law of nature, the law was before the fact; and a positive law cannot be taken notice of before it be made, and therefore cannot be obligatory'. Similarly, when discussing punishment, Hobbes writes that 'harm inflicted for a fact done before there was a law that forbade it is not punishment, but an act of hostility'.[21] In other words, a sovereign who enforced retroactive punishment would act as an enemy toward her subjects by subjecting them to naked force rather than law.[22] In this conception of law, subjects are implicitly regarded as agents held liable solely for those wrongs for which they are responsible, where a necessary condition of responsibility is fair notice of the relevant rule. If such notice is lacking, Hobbes seems to agree with Fuller that a putative law, in the ordinary case, is not really a law.

Hobbes also shares Fuller's reason for thinking that lack of fair notice disqualifies a putative law from counting as such. It is not that a candidate law for which there is no fair notice fails to count as law merely because it expresses indifference to the agency of the subject and therefore is not morally binding. Substantively wicked laws would arguably satisfy this indifference-to-agency criterion, and for Fuller and Hobbes (other things being equal), wicked laws still count as laws. For example, consider a clearly drafted statute that barred a particular ethnic group from holding public office. The statute is patently offensive to the agency of members of the group; it arbitrarily limits the practical scope of their agency while communicating that they are not able or worthy to hold public office. There may be other grounds for disputing the legality of such legislation,[23] but unlike putative laws for which there is no fair notice, the wicked legislation under consideration can still guide the conduct of the group's members.

Putative laws for which there is no fair notice express indifference to the subject's agency in a special way; they deny that the subject's agency must be the ground of his liability for any breach of the rules the laws posit. Such a law 'is no law to him' because its lack of notice decouples the liability that agency ordinarily makes possible from the content of the posited rule, and it is the content of the posited rule under which liability is supposed to be determined. As a general matter, rules presuppose the agency of their intended subjects, but here the purposive exercise of agency is short-circuited by the rule's defective form. And so the rule, shorn of its presupposition of agency, 'is no law to him', and its enforcement, 'an act of hostility'.

[21] Hobbes, *Leviathan* (n 1) 192 (ch xxvii para 9); 205 (ch xxviii para 11).

[22] *Hostis* is the Latin root for enemy.

[23] For instance, if Raz is correct in claiming that legal systems necessarily claim legitimacy and must be capable of doing so, then arguably such a statute is suspect from a legal point of view vis-à-vis the targeted group, assuming the statute cannot be read to purport to claim legitimacy over the group (though Raz may not agree: 'Nazi rules may not be authoritatively binding, but they are the sort of thing that can be authoritatively binding, whereas statements about volcanoes cannot.' Joseph Raz, 'Authority, Law, and Morality' in J Raz (ed), *Ethics in the Public Domain* (Oxford University Press 1994), 210, 218). See Kristen Rundle, 'Form and Agency in Raz's Legal Positivism' (2013) 32 *Law and Philosophy* 767, 787 ('it is difficult to see how the precondition of the capacity for legitimate authority over a subject that Raz suggests is part of the nature of law... could be satisfied if the law designated that subject as a slave').

2.2 Hobbes's principle of legality

Hobbes's legal theory also anticipates common law constitutionalism's principle of legality, though Hobbes's view of the position of the judge differs from Dicey's. Whereas Dicey championed an independent judiciary, Hobbes defended a subordinate judiciary that serves at the sovereign's pleasure. In principle, Hobbes's sovereign could sit in final judgment of any case. Nonetheless, while Hobbes was suspicious of the common law as a possible rival of the sovereign's law-making power, he nonetheless envisioned equity playing a role in legal order akin to the role played by the common law within common law constitutionalism.[24] That is, equity in Hobbes operates as a substantive norm of statutory interpretation and adjudication so as to remedy iniquities that otherwise would be authorized by the law itself.

In setting out the 'things that make a good judge (or a good interpreter of the laws)', Hobbes first points to '*a right understanding* of that principal law of nature called *equity*'. In interpreting the law, a proper understanding of equity is important because 'the intention of the legislator is always supposed to be equity; for it were a great contumely for a judge to think otherwise of the sovereign'. Thus, 'if the word of the law do not fully authorize a reasonable sentence', the judge ought to 'supply it with the law of nature'. Hobbes gives the hypothetical case of a man who voluntarily leaves his house empty and upon returning is kept out by force. The written law says only that if someone is put out of his house by force he shall be restored by force. Hobbes claims that although 'there is no special law ordained' that expressly governs the dispute, its resolution nonetheless 'is contained in the same [written] law; for else there is no remedy for him at all, which is to be supposed against the intention of the legislator'.[25]

Hobbes offers the case to show how equity can 'supply' a 'reasonable sentence' when the written law alone cannot do so. The judge must rely on the idea that the 'intention of the legislator is always supposed to be equity', and this reliance on equity implies that the judge must adopt one of two approaches to cases such as this. The first is that equity on its own, as a norm of substantive justice, requires the 'reasonable sentence' in light of the lacuna in the written law. As Henry Smith might put it, equity intervenes to prevent the wrongdoer from opportunistically taking advantage of the law's failure to prescribe a remedy tailored to the specific facts of the case.[26] Or in Dennis Klimchuk's formulation, equity intervenes to prevent the trespasser from insisting on a strict application of the letter of the law so as to be 'a stickler for her rights in a bad way'.[27] The second approach Hobbes's judge could take is to invoke equity as a ground for moving beyond a literal interpretation of the statute so as to query its general purpose—in this case,

[24] Hobbes, *Leviathan* (n 1) 181–3 (ch xxvi paras 24–5).
[25] Hobbes, *Leviathan* (n 1) 84 (ch xxvi para 28); 183 (ch xxvi para 26).
[26] Henry E Smith, 'Property, Equity, and the Rule of Law' in this volume; 'An Economic Analysis of Law versus Equity' (unpublished manuscript).
[27] Dennis Klimchuk, 'Equity and the Rule of Law' in this volume.

provision of a remedy to wrongfully dispossessed homeowners—which in turn warrants reading a remedy into the law so as to hand down a 'reasonable sentence'.

Similarly, if a judge has no positive law from which to take guidance, equity will fill in the gaps, for in those circumstances the judge's sentence 'ought to be according to the reason of his sovereign (which being always understood to be equity, he is bound to it by the law of nature)'. Equity also plays this gap-filling role whenever the sovereign's administrative agents lack statutory instructions. Administrative officials as much as judges are 'obliged to take for instructions the dictates of reason... which [is] always understood to be equity'.[28]

In Hobbes as much as in common law constitutionalism, it is a vexed question whether the sovereign is legally entitled to pass laws which, if sufficiently clear and unambiguous, can ground a violation of equity (Hobbes) or fundamental rights (common law constitutionalism). I cannot resolve this question here. The orthodox reading of Hobbes is that the sovereign possesses absolute legislative power that entitles him to pass any legislation whatsoever, unfettered by equity or any other of Hobbes's laws of nature.[29] Yet time and again Hobbes insists that the sovereign cannot abrogate the laws of nature, while at the same time, as we have seen, claiming that legislation must be read so as to render it consistent with equity.[30] In *Behemoth*, Hobbes's history of the English Civil War, he gives a dramatic example of how equity can be deployed to nullify the effect of even clearly stated legislation.

During the tumultuous times of late 1640, under great pressure and (according to Hobbes) fearing for his life, Charles I signed a bill that purported to give Parliament authority to decide the timing of its dissolution, a power that hitherto resided with the King. Hobbes saw in this bill a dangerous transfer of sovereign power from the King to Parliament, and looked to equity to undo it:

> And I think that even by the law of equity, which is the unalterable law of nature, a man that has the sovereign power cannot, if he would, give away the right of anything which is necessary for him to retain for the good government of his subjects, unless he do it in express words, saying that he will have the sovereign power no longer. For giving away that, which by consequence only, draws the sovereignty along with it, is not (I think) a giving away of the sovereignty; but an error, such as works nothing but an invalidity in the grant itself. [31]

Hobbes uses equity here as an 'unalterable' criterion for assessing and denying the validity of an explicit grant of power that, presumably, could be entrenched in otherwise valid legislation. Equity, in other words, seems to limit what the

[28] Hobbes, *Leviathan* (n 1) 177–8 (ch xxvi para 14).

[29] See eg Bobbio, *Thomas Hobbes* (n 15), Quentin Skinner, 'Hobbes and the Purely Artificial Person of the State' in *Visions of Politics: Hobbes and Civil Science* (Cambridge University Press 2002 vol iii).

[30] Hobbes, *Leviathan* (n 1) 100 (ch xv para 38); 147 (ch xxii para 7); 188 (ch xxvi para 41); 213 (ch xxix para 9).

[31] Thomas Hobbes, *Behemoth or The Long Parliament* (first published 1682), ed Ferdinand Tönnies (University of Chicago Press 1990) 118, 74, where Hobbes laments that Parliament was able to obtain 'a continuance of their own sitting as long as they listed: which amounted to a total extinction of the King's right, in case that such a grant were valid; which I think it is not, unless the Sovereignty itself be in plain terms renounced, which it was not'.

sovereign can do through express legislation. Using unambiguous words, the sovereign cannot, 'if he would', transfer a power of sovereignty that 'by consequence only, draws sovereignty along with it'. If he really wishes to transfer his sovereignty he can do so, with an express grant in which his sovereignty-transferring purpose is made clear. But the King cannot validly grant away an element of sovereign power that is constitutive of it, unless he states categorically that his intent is to transfer the whole of sovereignty to another person or entity. Hobbes is plainly of the view that a judge tasked with interpreting legislation that purported to grant away a constitutive aspect of sovereign power would have to read down the legislation consistent with equity and declare the grant invalid.

Equity constrains the effect of the sovereign's legislative power in this instance in much the same way the principle of legality regulates parliamentary sovereignty in commonwealth jurisdictions. In both cases, if the law-maker wishes to compromise principle, then the relevant legislation must use terms that unambiguously express an intent to do so.[32] And in both Hobbes's legal order and commonwealth jurisdictions, where equity and other legal principles are called on to fills gaps in positive law and supply reasonable sentences, the subjection of legislation to principled interpretation gives subjects protection against arbitrary executive action.

Hobbes's understanding of law, then, appears to include core aspects of both Fuller's internal morality and common law constitutionalism. One set of ideas posits formal presuppositions necessary to establishing a system of rules as a legal system, while the other set concerns principles of statutory interpretation. On the surface these ideas may appear unconnected to one another. In Hobbes's legal theory, however, we shall see that they are both manifestations of the prohibition on unilateralism. This principle receives its most explicit articulation in Hobbes's discussion of the arbitrator or judge.

3. The Prohibition on Unilateralism Underlying Private Law

Hobbes introduces the prohibition on unilateralism as a precept of 'right reason'. In the event of a controversy over even simple facts or mathematics, Hobbes writes, it is always possible for one side or the other to be in error. Where the error is made in

[32] For clarity, I do not mean to imply that this particular case establishes that Hobbes's sovereign either can or cannot lawfully enact and interpret a law that manifestly violates equity. On the orthodox reading of Hobbes, the sovereign can do so *either* because the laws of nature place no constraints on him *or* because he has final interpretative authority, and in any event, on the orthodox reading, the sovereign has prerogative power that he is entitled to exercise extra-legally however he wishes. See eg Thomas Poole, 'Hobbes on Law and Prerogative' in D Dyzenhaus and T Poole (eds), *Hobbes and the Law* (Cambridge University Press 2012) 68. I suggest in Section 4 that a flagrant violation of equity would jeopardize the sovereign's claim to the subject's obedience by subverting the 'mutual relation between protection and obedience', a relation, in my view, that lies at the heart of Hobbes's account of authority (Hobbes, *Leviathan* (n 1) 497 (Review & Conclusion para 17)). For more extended discussion see Evan Fox-Decent, 'Hobbes's Relational Theory: Beneath Power and Consent' in D Dyzenhaus and T Poole (eds), *Hobbes and the Law* (Cambridge University Press 2012) 118.

good faith, the parties reach an impasse, since 'no one man's reason, nor the reason of any one number of men' can itself dispel the error with demonstrable certainty. And so 'the parties [to a controversy] must by their own accord set up for right reason the reason of some arbitrator or judge to whose sentence they will both stand, or their controversy must either come to blows or be undecided, for want of a right reason constituted by nature'. Put slightly differently, since nature is not constituted so as to yield dispute-resolution authority to those who 'think themselves wiser than all others', right reason is necessarily institutional in that it can flow only from an adjudicator who occupies a public (or public-like) position vis-à-vis the disputants.[33]

There is as yet, however, an important ambiguity in Hobbes's argument. Hobbes could be read as claiming merely that the parties need an arbitrator because their knowledge of the relevant facts is necessarily uncertain and prone to error, whereas the arbitrator is more likely to assess the relevant facts dispassionately and get them right. That is, in any given controversy there is some crucial fact of the matter out there (moral or non-moral, legal or non-legal), and the impartial arbitrator alone has privileged epistemic access to it. On this reading, the justification of the arbitrator's authority hinges on her disinterested expertise.[34]

Another interpretation of the passages above is that the arbitrator's authority rests on the distinctively public nature of her office. That Hobbes's conception of authority is a public rather than expertise conception is suggested by the contempt he expresses toward those who would insist that their reason could stand as right reason. This self-aggrandizing view, he writes, 'is as intolerable in the society of men as it is in play, after trump is turned, to use for trump on every occasion that suit whereof they have most in their hand'. Private parties who assert authority over others, Hobbes says, do no less than betray 'their want of right reason by the claim they lay to it'. One could read these passages as evincing a concern for the bias of parties who are judges of their own causes, but this is too narrow. As we shall see now, Hobbes means to claim that those who demand to be judges of their own causes engage in a form of conduct that is wrongful per se because it implicitly denies the equality of legal subjects.[35]

Hobbes insists that it is a law of nature '*that they that are at controversy, submit their right to the judgment of an arbitrator*', and that it is a further such law that '*no man is a fit arbitrator in his own cause*'.[36] While Hobbes elsewhere lampoons the teachings of the common law's great champion Sir Edward Coke, he nonetheless incorporates into the foundation of his legal theory the very common law principle enshrined in Sir Edward's most famous decision, *Dr Bonham's Case*; that is, the

[33] Hobbes, *Leviathan* (n 1) 23 (ch v para 3).

[34] Compare Joseph Raz, *The Morality of Freedom* (Oxford University Press 1986) 53 (setting out the 'normal justification thesis' according to which someone is an authority if and only if following her directives allows their addressee to comply better with reasons that apply to her than she would by following her own judgment directly).

[35] Raz, *Morality* (n 34) 53.

[36] Hobbes, *Leviathan* (n 1) 98 (ch xv para 30); 98 (ch xv para 31).

principle that no one is entitled to be judge and party of the same cause.[37] Hobbes's argument for this principle stems from perhaps the central sense of equity on which his legal theory relies: equality before the law.[38] Hobbes lays down as a law of nature that '*every man acknowledge other for his equal by nature*', and from this precept infers another: '*that at the entrance into conditions of peace, no man require to himself any right which he is not content should be reserved to every one of the rest.*' To entrench this idea of reciprocity and equality in civil society, Hobbes prescribes an institutional norm of equity that implicitly affirms the legal equality of law's subjects: '*if a man is trusted to judge between man and man*, it is a precept of the law of nature that *he deal equally between them.*'[39]

With these principles in view, we can now piece together Hobbes's argument for the claim that 'no man is fit arbitrator in his own cause'. Hobbes invites us to imagine the consequences that would follow if an individual *were* a fit arbitrator of his own cause. If this were so, Hobbes says, then because equity allows 'to each party equal benefit', it would follow that 'if one is admitted to be judge, the other is to be admitted also; and so the controversy, that is, the cause of war, remains, against the law of nature'.[40] But it is unclear what Hobbes means at this juncture when he says that equity gives 'each party equal benefit'. Equal benefit of what?

He cannot mean, at this stage of the argument, that equity gives each party the benefit of legal equality before existing legal institutions, since the point of explicating the laws of nature is to establish the structure of those institutions and the respective roles of their actors and the parties subject to them. He must mean, instead, that equity gives each party equal benefit of the normative presuppositions that are necessary to the constitution of legal institutions. Put another way, equity gives each party equal benefit of the idea of law, understood here as the idea that disputes are to be settled by impartial institutions guided by public reason. One of law's presuppositions cannot be that a private party is entitled to sit in judgment of its own disputes, since were this presupposition applied equally to the other side, then the parties would be in the same position from which they started, and so 'their controversy must either come to blows or be undecided'.

It is important to underscore, however, that the fundamental wrongfulness of unilateralism lies not in the possibility of unresolved disputes, nor even the prospect of disputes decided by the will of the stronger. While these concerns are serious, they are not fundamental; unresolved disputes and the will of the strong are mere symptoms. Tellingly, they miss why unilateralism is wrongful in the state of nature, particularly where an individual seeks to enforce her rights or inflict punishment that the state would enforce or inflict were she in civil society. These instances of

[37] See eg Thomas Hobbes, *A Dialogue Between a Philosopher and a Student of the Common Laws of England* (first published 1681; University of Chicago Press 1971); *Dr Bonham's Case* (1610) 8 Co Rep 107a, 118a, 77 ER 638 (CP).

[38] For argument that a concern for equality animates most of Hobbes's uses of equity, see Dennis Klimchuk, 'Hobbes on Equity' in David Dyzenhaus and Thomas Poole (eds), *Hobbes and the Law* (Cambridge University Press 2012).

[39] Hobbes, *Leviathan* (n 1) 97 (ch xv para 21); 97 (ch xv para 22); 97 (ch xv para 23).

[40] Hobbes, *Leviathan* (n 1) 98 (ch xv para 31).

unilateralism are wrongful because they implicitly deny the equality of the parties to a dispute by giving to one, but not the other, adjudicative and executive authority. This is the fundamental wrong of unilateralism.

3.1 Objection I: unilateralism is permissible if one but not both of the parties is an excellent judge

One might object that this argument errantly presupposes that the parties are necessarily symmetrically situated, where one party's claim to authority would always carry with it an entitlement of the other party to make the same claim. To sketch a response, let us suppose that feature F is necessary and sufficient for authoritative dispute resolution. Perhaps feature F is fair-mindedness combined with a robust understanding of the relevant norms. Party A possesses feature F but party B does not, and both A and B recognize this. Under these assumptions, it would not seem to follow that if A is entitled to be the arbitrator then so is B, since A but not B possesses feature F. There appears to be a relevant difference between A and B that undoes the presumption of symmetry.[41] If so, why can A not rightfully claim authority to settle the dispute?

Hobbes has two replies; one formal, the other substantive. The formal reply is that 'feature F' is necessarily relational, and that A and B do not stand in the appropriate relation to one another. The appropriate relationship between the decision-maker and the parties is one in which the decision-maker is under a juridical duty, inherited from the law of nature, to 'deal equally between them'. But if A is the decision-maker for A and B, A cannot be seized of this duty. The problem is that because the relevant duty is a legal duty, it presupposes the existence of separate legal persons (the right holder and the duty bearer). But A is one person, not two, and so A cannot owe the duty to herself. She might, as a matter of fact, be able to treat herself and B impartially, and if given the chance she may do so. But this is a contingent matter, whereas the duty to 'deal equally between them' is partially constitutive of the decision-maker's authority.[42] Unbeholden to this duty, A is not in the appropriate relationship of authority to A and B, and therefore she lacks authority to resolve their dispute.

We might imagine that A-the-decision-maker could act as an artificial person and arbitral representative vis-à-vis the private parties A and B. Splitting A into two distinct persons in this manner may appear to finesse the separate persons problem, but it would do so at the cost of admitting that A-the-private-party has no authority to settle her dispute with B. The underlying difficulty is that even though, by hypothesis, A is uniquely capable of rendering a just decision, it does not follow that B is under an obligation to treat the decision as binding, since there is no relationship of authority between them.

41 I am indebted to Daniel Viehoff for pointing out this worry.
42 I defend this interpretation of Hobbes's conception of authority in Fox-Decent, 'Hobbes's Relational Theory' (n 32).

The substantive reply to A's purported authority trades on the common law maxim that justice should not only be done, but should also be seen to be done.[43] The maxim reflects the idea that even if a conflicted arbitrator were to render judgment impartially, it is impossible to demonstrate her impartiality because the operation of her mind as she comes to judgment is opaque to others (and, possibly, to herself).[44] Because judgment is inscrutable, the law generally proscribes conflicted decision-making. Hobbes affirms this principle when he writes that 'no man in any cause ought to be received for arbitrator, to whom greater profit, or honour, or pleasure apparently ariseth out of the victory of one party, than the other; for he hath taken (though an unavoidable bribe, yet) a bribe; and no man can be obliged to trust him'.[45] Hobbes assumes that the arbitrator's conflict is innocent, yet insists that it amounts to a bribe which vitiates the arbitrator's authority. In short, the impartiality of a judgment must be publicly demonstrable if the decision is to bind the parties. Thus, although A may possess all the necessary attributes of a fine arbitrator, her conflict necessarily corrupts the judgment she is capable of giving. It follows that her claim to unilateral authority fails to regard the parties as equals by arrogating to A alone a purported authority that cannot be exercised with demonstrable impartiality.

3.2 Objection II: unilateralism is permissible if limited to rights' violations

A liberal-minded objector might contend that unilateralism does not deny the equality of the parties, since it gives *both* parties unilateral authority, but this authority may be exercised *only if* the party exercising it is the victim of a rights violation. Even under this assumption, however, many issues cloud the apparent justice of private redress. The right at issue may be somewhat indeterminate, such as the right to the quiet enjoyment of one's property. Who gets to delineate the scope of this right? There may be questions about whether the alleged rights-infringing conduct breached the relevant duty. Who decides, for instance, whether music played audibly but not loudly on a Saturday afternoon infringes the right to quiet enjoyment? The wrongdoer may have a series of defences at her disposal (lapse of time, waiver, frustration, and so on). Who decides their effect? In a tort case, who decides whether the victim can recover pure economic loss? Who decides the test for causation and how it applies to the facts? Assuming a breach of duty has occurred, causation is not in doubt, and there are no applicable defences, who decides the appropriate remedy? In a contract case, can the breachee elect for damages or specific performance at her discretion? Can the remedy include aggravated or punitive damages? The point is that even if there is no doubt that a victim has suffered a rights violation at the hands of a particular wrongdoer, a variety of contestable issues may need to be resolved, and in every case a suitable remedy

[43] *R v Sussex Justices, Ex parte McCarthy* [1924] 1 KB 256, [1923] All ER Rep 233.
[44] I thank Lionel Smith bringing this point to my attention in another context.
[45] Hobbes, *Leviathan* (n 1) 98 (ch xv para 32).

would have to be fashioned. To let the victim decide any of these matters unilaterally would fail to respect the equal standing of the parties.

But, the objector may continue, we can imagine cases in which the facts and norms are determinate, and the remedy selected is reasonable in light of the breach of duty. Suppose we are in the state of nature and I pay you a bushel of wheat to build a table. You build it, but then renege and refuse to deliver. A few days later I notice you have left the bushel of wheat in a common field. I take back the bushel, believing it is mine since you openly breached our agreement. Let us assume there are no reasonably contestable issues of fact or law, and the breach of contract can be remedied without coercion. This moderate unilateralist's position, then, is that if a private party is able to redress a wrong without resort to force, and there are no reasonably contestable issues of law or fact, she is entitled to redress the wrong privately. After all, why should an injustice be allowed to stand if it can be cured without coercion?

Now, I have tried to state the moderate unilateralist's view as persuasively as possible. But it is misleading to suggest that the remedy postulated is 'without coercion'. I am able to repossess the bushel without using force against you personally (assuming you were to resist) only because I take it from you surreptitiously. Furthermore, my ongoing right to the bushel, if my right is at all like a legal right, is one that I can presumably defend with force (eg if you come to take the bushel back). So maintenance of the remedy relies implicitly on the threat of force. This is significant, as I will argue that moderate unilateralism rests ultimately on a false equation between the presence of incontestable facts and legal norms, on the one hand, and the authority of a private party to enforce legal norms unilaterally, on the other.

An immediate difficulty with the position staked out by moderate unilateralism is that there may be a good faith disagreement over whether the facts of a given case disclose a contestable issue. To let the victim's will prevail with respect to this preliminary matter would again fail to respect the equal standing of the parties, since the wrongdoer can claim with equal justice that her will should carry the day. Moreover, if the wrongdoer is indeed entitled to raise a good faith objection as to whether there is a contestable issue, then the victim's purported right to exercise unilateral authority will depend on the wrongdoer's willingness to forgo her objection. And because good faith tracks sincerity of belief rather than an objective standard, any objection the wrongdoer claims to make in good faith is inscrutable. Consequently, under moderate unilateralism, every possible exercise of the victim's unilateral authority is subject to the good will of the wrongdoer. In the bushel-of-wheat case, this aspect of the parties' interaction is effaced because the victim's surreptitious repossession of the bushel denies the wrongdoer any opportunity to participate in the process leading to the remedy, contrary to the principle that the parties must be treated as equals throughout.

The moderate unilateralist might reply that only good faith objections based on reasonable grounds have any standing, and that in the class of cases under consideration, by hypothesis, there are no reasonably contestable issues in play. But this reply begs the question, since it implicitly presupposes that the victim is entitled to specify the relevant facts and legal norms, and is likewise entitled to apply them authoritatively and unilaterally to her case. The illicit move the moderate unilateralist makes is to suppose that the presence of incontestable facts and norms implies that the victim of a rights violation has unilateral authority to enforce the legal norms relevant to her case. The presence of an applicable norm, however, does not in itself imply that a given party has authority to enforce it. Suppose the norm 'children should eat their vegetables' is true. It does not follow that a stranger has authority to enforce this norm against an unfamiliar child sitting across from a plate of vegetables. Only the child's parents (or people occupying a suitably parental role, such as teachers) have this authority.

The deep structural problem with moderate unilateralism is that, in its attempt to use substantive requirements of justice to dictate the nature of authority relations, it commits a category error. As the children-should-eat-their-vegetables example suggests, there is no obvious conceptual connection between the substantive requirements of justice, which specify the content of justice claims and to whom they are directed, and the question of who has standing to enforce such claims.

Moreover, the problem of unilateralism remains even if the parties are amicable, highly ethical, and reach a negotiated settlement while maintaining a good faith disagreement on the merits of their dispute. To settle, one party, or possibly both, would have compromised their position, letting the will of the other party dictate (at least partially) the outcome of the dispute. In the actual world, such settlements are commonplace given the high cost and risk associated with litigation. But there is a qualitative difference between negotiation conducted against the background threat of impartial adjudication, and negotiation conducted on a desert island inhabited by just the parties to the dispute. In the former case, the subjection of the weaker party to the stronger is tempered by the possibility of the weaker seeking redress through the impartial third party. In the latter, the subjection of the weaker to the stronger is unalloyed, since the position of the weaker depends on the will of the stronger. The desert-island parties could, of course, agree to various impartial dispute-resolution mechanisms (taking turns making decisions that affect both, flipping a coin, setting up an auction, and so on). But the purported authority of any such mechanism will rely always on the individual willingness of the parties to accept that the mechanism is authoritative, a willingness that can at any time be suspended. So on the desert island, as in the state of nature, unilateralism is inevitable.

3.3 Objection III: unilateralism does not arise if there is no contest of wills

One might reply that unilateralism is inevitable only if one of the desert-island parties actually tries to enforce her rights or will against the other, and the other person resists.[46] Suppose instead that the second party always submits freely to the will of the dominant individual. Perhaps they are friends, the submissive party

[46] I thank Andrew Gold for raising this objection.

doesn't like conflict, and in any event the dominant party is the wiser of the two and she always takes account of the submissive party's interests. With an ongoing consensual relationship of this nature, it may appear that no unilateralism is present because there is no contest of wills. The lack of conflict, however, simply masks the unrelenting fact that the parties remain subject to each other's unilateral wills, a subjection that could turn to oppression at any time. Their *modus vivendi* is necessarily insecure given its dependence on their separate wills. It may well be that the two friends can cohabit the island indefinitely in a consensual but dominant/submissive relationship such that an actual dispute never arises. But without the security and equality of legal order, they are still subject to the vicissitudes of each other's private wills. Without law's reciprocal limits and impartial dispute resolution, they are subject to unilateralism.

The evil of unilateralism, then, operates on two planes. First, it encompasses situations where one party actually interferes with another, such as when a stronger person forcibly imposes her will on someone weaker. But second, unilateralism also refers to cases of domination; that is, cases where one party has the power to interfere arbitrarily with the choices or interests of another, but may or may not exercise this power. The slave–master relationship is the classic example of domination's unfreedom, since the slave remains unfree even if the master never actually interferes with any of the slave's choices or interests. The power of arbitrary interference is enough, and on my construal its possession counts as a case of unilateralism. On the desert island, as in the state of nature, the interactions of individuals are governed by their private wills alone. Whichever person happens to be ascendant at any given time stands in a position of domination over the other. She dominates the vulnerable party whether or not she is disposed to take advantage, since at any moment she could. When unilateralism is understood to include domination, we can readily see that unilateralism would be endemic as well as inevitable on the desert island, even if one party habitually submits to the other such that there is no actual conflict. Unilateralism would be endemic because in the ordinary course of events there will always be times during which one of the two parties is vulnerable to the other's unfettered discretion, whether the ascendant party chooses to exercise her discretion wrongfully or not.

We have seen that from the outset Hobbes takes unilateralism to be inimical to public reason, and so inimical to legal order. We have also seen that Hobbes's starting point in his argument against unilateralism is the basic fact situation addressed by private law; ie a dispute between two private parties. Finally, we have canvassed some of the laws of nature Hobbes enlists to explicate the constitution of the legal order supplied by private law, such as equality before the law and the prohibition on being judge and party to the same cause. We turn now to how the prohibition on unilateralism that informs the constitution of private law also underlies Hobbes's internal morality of law and equity as an interpretative principle of statutory interpretation.

4. The Prohibition on Unilateralism Underlying Public Law

The prohibition on unilateralism establishes a categorical distinction between public and private spheres of authority that the principles of Hobbes's internal morality institutionalize. In so doing, the prohibition on unilateralism, I argue, explains both the principles of Hobbes's internal morality and the reciprocal limits on private liberty within the commonwealth.

Consider first the public sphere and the proscription on retroactive punishment. This principle is justified on the grounds that punishment is exclusively an act of public authority, and that retroactive punishment is inconsistent with the nature of public authority. As noted above, by characterizing retroactive punishment as 'an act of hostility', Hobbes is signalling that it is the action of an enemy. In effect, retroactive punishment places the sovereign in the state of nature vis-à-vis the subject. He confronts the subject as a hostile private party rather than a public authority, contrary to both the prohibition on unilateralism and the constitutive requirements of his office (the laws of nature) that flow from the prohibition.

The same can bc said of the other formal requirements of Hobbes's internal morality. A secret law or a law that is hopelessly unclear or inconsistent gives the subject inadequate guidance regarding the content of his legal obligations, and so 'is no law to him'. For the sovereign to enforce such a law against the subject would be for him to treat her in the same way she would be treated through the enforcement of a retroactive sanction. In both cases, the subject has inadequate means to take notice of her legal obligations, and so in both cases the sovereign acts as an enemy toward her, as a hostile private party in the state of nature rather than as a public authority.

For Hobbes, the private sphere of authority is the space made available for self-directed action within the public framework structured by the internal morality. The liberty of the subject comprehends all actions not proscribed by law.[47] Hobbes thought that typically it would include 'the liberty to buy, and sell, and otherwise contract with one another; to choose their own abode, their own diet, their own trade of life, and institute their children as they themselves think fit; and the like'. Notably absent from Hobbes's catalogue of liberties is the freedom to enslave, inflict cruelty, dictate terms, or contract on behalf of another without prior authority. The absence of such freedoms is explained by the feature that thematically unites the liberties in Hobbes's catalogue: in principle they may all be held

[47] Hobbes also refers to a smaller class of actions as the 'true liberty of a subject', which is the liberty to act on the inalienable right of self-preservation, such as the liberty to refuse to kill oneself at the sovereign's command (Hobbes, *Leviathan* (n 1) 141 (ch xxi para 10)). This liberty is 'true' in the sense that it is not subject to the sovereign's authority. As such, the true liberty of the subject demarcates a conceptually ineliminable sphere of private authority vis-à-vis the sovereign whereas the private liberties permitted by law are subject to restriction. Nonetheless, it is through the exercise of these latter liberties that individuals interact with one another (true liberty applies to sovereign-subject interactions only), and so from the perspective of an enquiry into unilateralism it is important to determine, as the subsequent text attempts to do, whether the ordinary liberties of the subject either permit or foreclose unilateralism.

and exercised equally by everyone, and without their possession leading to the subjection of anyone to the will of another.[48] Hobbes prepares the way for liberties of this character with his second law of nature. When others are likewise disposed, Hobbes says, individuals should '*lay down their right to all things, and be contented with so much liberty against other men, as he would allow other men against himself*'. Strikingly, the liberty with which we must 'be contented' is the same civic freedom as we would allow to others. The implication is that the liberty the sovereign is authorized to procure through law is none other than equal liberty. And because we cannot claim for ourselves a greater liberty than we would allow for others, we cannot expect the law to confer on us a legal power or status that would entitle us to dictate terms unilaterally to others.[49]

The public/private distinction resulting from the prohibition on unilateralism also explains the role of equity as a principle of statutory interpretation. When Hobbes insists that judges charged with interpreting statutes must assume that the sovereign's intent is equity, he is making an expressly normative claim. The claim is that the sovereign is entitled to make law in exclusively his public capacity as representative of the commonwealth, and that this entitlement is constituted and limited in part by the laws of nature, most notably by the principle of legal equality. Put another way, because subscription to the laws of nature is constitutive of what it means to be a public law-making authority, the laws of nature enable the sovereign to act as a public representative rather than a private party when he makes law. This explains why Hobbes says that judges *must* presume that the sovereign's will is equity. For them to do otherwise would be for them to deny the public character of the sovereign's law-making power and treat his declared will as an expression of private interest rather than public law.

Now, Hobbes does at times suggest that the sovereign can, in his public capacity, breach the laws of nature, and that the subject cannot complain of injustice because she is deemed to have authorized all the laws he makes. But this in no way mitigates the duty of the judge, who is still to strive to read the sovereign's laws through the prism of equity. Moreover, Hobbes acknowledges that such laws would constitute iniquity. If in a limit case those laws stripped legal institutions of their public character such that they came to serve sectional interests, arguably the oppressed subjects' duty to obey would disintegrate, since the duty remains in place 'as long, and no longer, than the power lasteth by which [the sovereign] is able to protect them'. Hobbes concluded *Leviathan* saying that he wrote it 'without other design than to set before men's eyes the mutual relation between protection and

[48] The institution of property within a market economy may lead to the subjection of non-owners to the will of owners. Hobbes worried about individuals who 'by accident inevitable, become unable to maintain themselves by their labour', and advised that they 'ought not to be left to the charity of private persons', but must 'be provided for by the laws of the commonwealth'. Hobbes, *Leviathan* (n 1) 228 (ch xxx para 18). To force such persons to beg for their subsistence from others would be 'to expose them to the hazard' of 'uncertain charity'. Hobbes, *Leviathan* (n 1) 228. The better off would be able to dictate terms unilaterally to the disadvantaged. Hobbes arguably requires the commonwealth to provide for the disadvantaged in order to protect them from this form of unilateralism.

[49] Hobbes, *Leviathan* (n 1) 138 (ch xxi para 6); 80 (ch xiv para 5).

obedience'. And as with laws that infringe Hobbes's internal morality, laws that violate the laws of nature would risk placing the sovereign in the state of nature vis-à-vis the subject since, by hypothesis, they would pit the sovereign's private interest against the subject's, rekindling the problem of unilateralism.[50]

5. Mutual Presupposition and Accommodation

I have argued that in Hobbes's legal theory the prohibition on unilateralism is the fundamental organizing principle of both private and public law. I suggest now that this sharing of conceptual resources allows us to see how public law and private law stand in a relationship of mutual presupposition and accommodation to one another. They stand in this relationship notwithstanding that they operate in different spheres and with distinctive internal structures of justification. Whereas Hobbes's private law of contract is known through reason and can operate independently of statute in accordance with the bilateral norms of corrective justice, public law is established by legislation governed by Hobbes's internal morality and equity as a principle of statutory interpretation.[51]

A relationship of mutual presupposition obtains when two or more ideas, principles, concepts, doctrines, rules, institutions, etc rely on the same underlying organizing principle. Consider, for example, the rules governing offer and acceptance and the rules governing remedies in the common law of contract. The two sets of rules answer to an underlying theory of contract that affirms as its organizing principle—let us stipulate—that the common law empowers individuals to enter into enforceable agreements. Neither set of rules is reducible to the other, and both are explicable as constitutive aspects of an institution—contract—that takes its structure from its organizing principle. The rules on offer and acceptance control formation, while the rules on remedies establish the enforceable consequences in the event of breach. Both sets of rules presuppose our stipulated organizing principle (or one much like it) because both play a constitutive role in the institution of contract. In this sense, the two sets of rules stand in a relationship of mutual presupposition to one another; they mutually presuppose the organizing principle of contract. And because they play complementary constitutive roles in the same institution, their relationship is also one of mutual accommodation. Neither possesses normative priority over the other since both are independently

[50] Hobbes, *Leviathan* (n 1) 162 (ch xxiv para 7); 112–13 (ch xviii paras 6–7); 144 (ch xxi para 21); 497 (Review & Conclusion para 17).

[51] Hobbes had a somewhat idiosyncratic view of corrective and distributive justice. He understood corrective justice to bear on the primary rights and duties of private parties, whereas distributive justice he identified with equity and 'the justice of the arbitrator, that is to say, the act of defining what is just'. Hobbes, *Leviathan* (n 1) 94–5 (ch xv para 14). Whereas some modern commentators see private law as species of distributive justice, Hobbes saw distributive justice as the embodiment of private law's public dimension. See eg Anthony T Kronman, 'Contract Law and Distributive Justice' (1979–80) *Yale Law Journal* 472. But Hobbes plainly thought that contract could give rise to rights and duties without the prompt of statute because the obligation to perform one's contractual obligations is a law of nature and known though reason. Hobbes, *Leviathan* (n 1) 89 (ch xv para 1); 177 (ch xxvi para 13).

necessary to the common law of contract. Because the relations of mutual presupposition and accommodation described above flow from a single organizing principle, they allow us to see contract as a single, unified institution.

The same analysis applies to private law, public law, and the prohibition on unilateralism in Hobbes. But instead of the institution of contract, the larger conceptual framework in which private law and public law participate is legal order. For Hobbes, private law and public law both answer to a conception of legal order that affirms the prohibition on unilateralism as its underlying organizing principle. Neither private law nor public law is reducible to the other, and both are explicable as constitutive aspects of a conception of legal order that takes its overarching normative structure from the prohibition on unilateralism. Both necessarily presuppose this organizing principle because both are constitutive of legal order. Thus, they stand in a relationship of mutual presupposition to one another; they mutually presuppose the prohibition on unilateralism. And because they play complementary constitutive roles in legal order, they also stand in a relationship of mutual accommodation to one another. Neither enjoys normative priority over the other since both occupy space in legal order on the same normative basis. And because the relations of mutual presupposition and accommodation flow from a single organizing principle, they reveal that Hobbes articulates a unified theory of law and legal order.

This is not to say that public law in Hobbes cannot displace private law. Hobbes thought, for example, that the sovereign could limit the enforceability of contracts formed under duress, and he conceded no restriction on the sovereign's authority to tax for the good of the commonwealth.[52] In his contribution to this volume, David Dyzenhaus observes that Kantians are hard pressed to explain the legitimacy of public law programmes that oust tort law and corrective justice in favour of no-fault insurance schemes that reflect the norms of distributive justice.[53] Dyzenhaus's main argument attacks the Kantian justification offered for the legislature, a justification which asserts that the legislature is necessary because laws must enjoy an omnilateral authorization that only the legislature can provide. Dyzenhaus claims that this justification turns statute-independent private law into the product of judicial arbitrariness, since the judge who adjudicates matters not contemplated by statute is just imposing her will unilaterally. To resist this conclusion, the Kantians must commit to the normative primacy of private law, and then it is difficult for them to defend, as Ernest Weinrib tries to do,[54] an attitude of indifference to the choice between tort law and no-fault insurance.

[52] Hobbes, *Leviathan* (n 1) 86 (ch xiv para 27); 162 (ch xxiv para 8).

[53] David Dyzenhaus, 'Liberty and Legal Form' in this volume, citing *inter alia* Ernest J Weinrib, 'Poverty and Property in Kant's System of Rights' in *Corrective Justice* (Oxford University Press 2012) and Arthur Ripstein, 'Public Right III: Redistribution and Equality of Opportunity' in *Force and Freedom: Kant's Legal and Political Philosophy* (Harvard University Press 2009).

[54] See eg Weinrib, *The Idea of Private Law* (Harvard University Press 1995) 68–75 (describing corrective and distributive justice as comprehensive and fundamental as well as categorically distinctive forms of justice, with neither enjoying any sort of normative primacy over the other).

Hobbes faces no such challenge, since his conceptions of private law and public law are, from the outset, structured by the same organizing principle, ie the prohibition on unilateralism. While Hobbes's most explicit expression of this principle is in the context of a private dispute, even there the principle operates so as to vindicate the authority of a public (or public-like) adjudicator. Likewise, in the context of public law, the principle emerges to distinguish public acts of authority from private counterfeits. So long as public law incursions into private law respect the prohibition on unilateralism and its implications, there is, on Hobbes's account, no compromise of legal order's immanent morality. Yet it would be a mistake to conclude that Hobbes's legal theory gives normative primacy to public law, for while it may displace at least some private law given public law's institutional supremacy in legal order, it must do so consistent with the prohibition on unilateralism that underlies both it and private law.[55]

6. Conclusion

I have argued that Hobbes's conception of legal order anticipates core elements of the rule of law that orient, on the one hand, the Fuller/Hart/Raz literature, and on the other, commonwealth public law scholarship. Hobbes develops an internal morality of his own which, like Fuller's, is designed to secure a stable framework for the exercise of equal freedom. Hobbes also develops a principle of legality akin to the principle inherited from Dicey that animates common law constitutionalism. At the foundation of his legal theory, however, is the prohibition of unilateralism, which he articulates in the first instance as a principle of private law, but which also serves as an organizing principle of public law. It does so by explicating legal authority as a distinctively public phenomenon constituted in part by the laws of nature, in part by Hobbes's internal morality, and in part by Hobbes's principle of legality, all of which resist unilateralism on the part of the sovereign. The prohibition on unilateralism that runs throughout Hobbes's legal theory thus reveals a unified conception of private and public law: each branch of law stands in a relationship of mutual presupposition and accommodation to the other, and both answer ultimately to the same organizing principle.

[55] It is unclear, for example, that the sovereign could eliminate contract altogether, since contract is implicit in Hobbes third law of nature (see n 51).

6

Torts and the Rule of Law

Benjamin C Zipursky

1. Introduction

Those who ask whether 'the rule of law' obtains in a certain political community are often presupposing the proposition that there are abstract structural constraints on how legal systems operate such that, in at least one dimension of political morality, legal systems that satisfy such constraints are better than legal systems that do not.[1] Rule of law assessments, on such a view, pertain to attributes of a legal system or putative legal system. I suggest later in this chapter that this perspective taps into one aspect of the concept of the 'rule of law', but is in basic respects incomplete: the rule of law is an ideal that pertains not only to the constraint of government power, but also to the constraint of individual power. Even within this perspective, however, rule of law evaluations sometimes presuppose the stronger proposition that there are certain structural features of legal systems such that they are *required* for the political legitimacy and political morality of the putative legal system. Hayek's classic *Road to Serfdom* effectively treated generality, promulgation, prospectivity, and clarity as key constituents of the list.[2] Constitutions, including but not limited to the United States Constitution, often turn many such normative requirements into legal requirements.

Lon Fuller famously depicted several of these rule-of-law attributes as desiderata for a legal system, and in fact argued that a sufficiently great shortcoming in any of these attributes could disqualify a putative legal system from counting as such a system.[3] His first pass at the argument was intuitive and was rooted in the power of the parable of King Rex in *The Morality of Law*. That classic work used the intuition to develop an argument for an analytical claim about the nature of law: law is

[1] See Joseph Raz, 'The Rule of Law and its Virtue' in Joseph Raz, *The Authority of Law: Essays on Law and Morality* (2nd edn, Oxford University Press 2009) 210–32. Raz's important article stands for the position that the rule of law is one among several possible virtues of a legal system (and that its possession does not preclude injustice or other vices in the same legal system).

[2] FA Hayek, *The Road to Serfdom* (University of Chicago Press 1944).

[3] Lon L Fuller, *The Morality of Law* (rev edn, Yale University Press 1969).

governance of a political community by subjecting its members to enforceable rules of conduct.

The common law of torts constitutes a deep and powerful counterexample to Fuller's analytical claim about law. As I have argued elsewhere, tort law spectacularly fails to satisfy Fuller's desiderata—generality, promulgation, proactivity, and clarity, among others—but nevertheless is plainly a form of law.[4] Generality: Far from being general, tort law prides itself in its particularistic nature. Promulgation: The common law of torts that applies to a new case is not necessarily a law that has been promulgated already; courts try to derive conclusions from what they understood to be implicit in the common law, and part of its 'spirit'. Moreover, tort decisions do not necessarily apply already articulated rules of conduct. Judges pride themselves on bringing out what is latent in the law. Proactivity: There is no *ex post facto* clause for tort law; indeed, it is commonplace for a court to recognize liability based on duties that it itself had never articulated before. Tort law blatantly violates a principle of non-retroactivity. Clarity: Tort law is plainly not particularly transparent for subjects, and there remain many different disagreements amongst tort scholars about what the law actually says. To some extent it is true in every area of law, but in torts it is perhaps more dramatically clear than elsewhere. Notions like 'duty', 'ordinary care', 'proximate cause', and 'offensiveness' are palpably normative, and they leave a great deal of discretion to those who apply the law. Courts, in applying and articulating tort law, sometimes express frustration at the unclarity of the concepts in it, but virtually never entertain the possibility that tort law's unclarity undermines its status as law.

Tort law's failure is not surprising, I argue, for tort law is not—at least not in its most straightforward institutional embodiment—a system for governing by subjecting individuals to primary rules of conduct; it is institutionally entrenched as a system for empowering individuals to redress wrongs done to them.[5] That is another thing that law can be. Whether one wants to call law of this form a kind of 'governance' is a discretionary terminological choice; it is not governance in anything like the sense that the creation of criminal or regulatory schemes is. In any event, satisfaction of Fuller's desiderata is not a necessary condition for being law.

Even if one were to accept that I had refuted Fuller's claims about necessary conditions for law and about the concept of law, tort law's failure to satisfy Fuller's desiderata would not necessarily be something to accept uncritically. For these constraints are virtually coextensive with well-accepted *moral* conditions on coercive law. And so the question arises whether tort law should be viewed as *normatively* legitimate even if it is, conceptually, a form of law. Relatedly, should we say that a legal system that includes the common law of torts to that extent fails to live

[4] Benjamin C Zipursky, 'The Inner Morality of Private Law' (2013) 58 *American Journal of Jurisprudence* 27.

[5] Although tort law is most plainly institutionally realized as a set of rules empowering individuals to redress wrongs done to them, there is an important sense in which tort law also includes primary rules of conduct. See eg Benjamin C Zipursky, 'Rights, Wrongs, and Recourse in the Law of Torts' (1998) 51 *Vanderbilt Law Review* 1 and John CP Goldberg and Benjamin C Zipursky, 'Seeing Tort Law from the Internal Point of View: Holmes and Hart on Legal Duties' (2006) 75 *Fordham Law Review* 1563.

up to *the rule of law* because it is highly particularized, non-explicit, retroactive, and unclear?

The recognition that tort law is not a form of *governance* in the same sense as (for example) criminal law provides the first step in an answer to this. Fuller's conceptual argument about law borrowed, in the first instance, from the normative argument. The Fullerian vices do present legitimacy problems for a system of governance of the sort he had in mind. But, since tort law is not this type of system, it is not obvious why it should be required to have these features in order to be legitimate.

The argument cannot be so quickly dismissed, of course. Indeed, there is a sense in which the claim that tort law is not such a system of governance makes the legitimacy problems even worse. Consider the setback to liberty that comes from being held to certain rules and the setback to well-being that comes from being sanctioned for failure to comply with such rules: these setbacks tend to be deemed acceptable for contractarian and utilitarian reasons *combined* with a conception of freedom and choice that the Fullerian notion of governance respected. In other words, one can say from a contractarian and utilitarian perspective that there are reasons to have some system of enforceable rules of conduct with negative consequences for non-compliance attached, but then add that vulnerability to the rules and the sanctions must be domesticated by the requirement that the rules be put there in advance in a digestible, clear, and consistent form. Actors are then able to choose whether to comply or not. If tort liability (and the risk of tort liability) is said to be exempt from structural requirements like these because it is not even 'trying' to be the sort of system of rules that would need to meet these requirements (but it nevertheless produces setbacks to liberty and well-being), that would seem only to exacerbate the legitimacy problem rather than solving it.

This seemingly theoretical nest of normative complaints about tort law is not only academic. The tort reform movement that began in the 1980s has very much this flavour; President Ronald Reagan's Secretary of Health and Human Services said of medical malpractice law that 'it has become more a lottery than a rational system for compensating the injured'.[6] Punitive damages are said to be arbitrary, unpredictable—like a bolt of lightning.[7] Companies complained that there is no way to win in tort law; they are damned if they do and damned if they don't. The norm in tort law is a radically underspecified liability trigger, leaving legal actors in a guessing game. And the impact of all of this is to squash liberty, the arguments often conclude.

If tort law is not rendered illegitimate by these shortcomings in form, we need to know why. Why is tort law not rejected as an unpredictable and largely unwritten system for sanctioning those who act in ways that juries and judges decide to condemn? Is the truth that we are just winking at tort law's shortcomings, either because we are glad to have the extra revenue around for compensation of accident

[6] Otis R Bowen, Congressional Testimony on Senate Bill S 1804, 257 JAMA 816, 818 (1987).

[7] Ruth Marcus, 'Are Punitive Damage Awards Fair to Firms? Supreme Court Finally Agrees To Referee High-Stakes Dispute' *Washington Post* (Washington, 23 September 1990) H1.

victims without having to burden taxpayers, because it is a bit of backdoor distributive justice that carries an impressive historical pedigree, or because it offers some regulatory clout against big corporations that they are less able to finesse through lobbying and politics? *Aren't all of these really ways of circumventing the rule of law for what are thought by some to be worthwhile consequences?* If that is so, then either the rule of law is not the crowning set of values and constraints it is often said to be, or tort law (and indeed other branches of common law) must be condemned, as critics dating at least back to Hobbes have long maintained.

2. The Crime/Tort Distinction and the Realist Rejoinder

These challenges to tort law put great pressure on our earlier question: if tort law is not a form of governance in the sense that criminal and regulatory law are, what is it?

Tort law is part of private law; it is the part of private law that involves empowering individuals to make enforceable demands of others as redress for having been wrongfully injured. When a court issues a judgment against a defendant, the court is not punishing the defendant for having violated a legal prohibition; it is holding the defendant responsible for having wrongfully injured the plaintiff.

Both Legal Realists and small 'r' realists will bridle at this distinction. The normative Fullerian challenge to tort law might be put as follows: Why is there any less need for rule of law protections like non-retroactivity and the other Fullerian desiderata when the state enters a money judgment against a defendant in favour of a plaintiff for having committed a tort than there is when the state imposes a criminal fine against a defendant for having committed a crime? After all, it is not uncommonly the case that the same conduct can be both a crime (murder) and a tort (battery), and that criminal conduct can be sanctioned with an order directing the defendant to pay money (a fine) that at least resembles a judgment directing a tort defendant to pay compensation.

My first answer to the normative Fullerian challenge—and the focus of much of the remainder of this essay—is that tort law has an alternative set of rule of law protections, quite unlike the Fullerian desiderata, but equally capable of protecting individual liberty. The general point is that a relaxation of the Fullerian requirements is conditioned on the satisfaction of a parallel, and similarly protective set of alternative constraints.

A second answer is that, even if a monetary penalty is among possible criminal punishments, it is not necessarily the paradigm of such punishment: deprivation of liberty with substantial reputational opprobrium is the paradigm, and it is in fact more serious in several respects that being required to pay money. The fact that criminal punishments can be scaled down to something roughly equivalent to a tort liability payment does not mean they are typically the same. There may be (and, as we shall see, there indeed are) sets of protections that apply to *kinds* of liabilities and treatments by our legal system; the criminal package applies equally to the paradigmatic sanction and to something in fact less onerous in important ways. The prospect of liberty deprivations for crimes is one of the reasons that crimes require greater notice. The requirement being in place, it does not necessarily shift even if a lesser penalty is being applied.

The third answer to the normative Fullerian challenge to tort law is that the question falsely presupposes that vulnerability to remedial action through the courts is the sole basis for having rule of law constraints on criminal law. This point requires further elaboration.

In setting out criminal prohibitions, the state is not merely forewarning that it will engage in punishment for certain conduct or asserting that it takes the position that such punishment would be warranted. Rather it is enjoining people from behaving in certain ways; it is declaring primary rules of conduct. Moreover, the state's power to render certain ways of behaving *criminal* is quite broad, and includes domains of conduct that have often been viewed as entirely permissible, from a moral point of view: drinking alcohol, declining to send one's children to school, driving a motorized vehicle one has purchased (regardless of whether one has a licence), and so on. The police power is very broad indeed. If these ways of behaving are going to be removed from the set of liberties one enjoys, the sovereign must go through the process of specifying a rule announcing that these ways of behaving have become illegal. When the state converts something one has licence to do into something forbidden, for which the state may prosecute and punish and with respect to which one becomes a lawbreaker, it bears the onus of clearly identifying what conduct will now count as criminal and subject an actor to punishment.

A fourth response to the Fullerian challenge to tort law is that the state—qua prosecutor or regulatory enforcer—is and always has been a uniquely intimidating antagonist in litigation. Notwithstanding the formal and (typically) reasonably realized separation of powers, the state is the only plaintiff that is also the adjudicator and the law-maker. The state's resources know virtually no bounds. Its capacity to find facts, change law, and alter the system in which adjudication takes place is unmatched.

I hope that by recognizing several unusually daunting aspects of the structure of criminal law, I have at least temporarily neutralized the Realists' bridling at a distinction between punishment in criminal law and civil liability in tort. Nonetheless, this chapter does not mean to give tort law a pass. The thesis is *not* that rule of law concerns apply to criminal law but have no application to tort law. It is that they apply differently to tort law. Indeed, as mentioned above, a principal reason why generality, promulgation, prospectivity, and clarity do not apply to tort law is that there is an alternative set of constraints that do apply.

3. Generality, Promulgation, Non-Retroactivity, and Clarity

Let us examine more closely the apparently basic rule of law shortcomings of tort law: generality, promulgation, non-retroactivity, and clarity. We will take them in turn.

Generality: Dispelling the Superficial Concerns. It is of course misleading to say that tort law fails to be general. It fails on generality for reasons that have little to do with those attributes that superficially suggest a problematic particularity—the individualization of fact-finding and the absence of a general legislative command. Tort cases are decided one at a time, but so are criminal cases; individualized adjudication of facts applies to both as a value. Moreover, realistically, the world of settlement in tort and plea-bargaining in criminal law lead us to a broader, more wholesale view of the area. Most fundamentally, the absence of a legislative or regulatory command in lieu of judicial holdings is not necessarily an obstacle to generality, for high court holdings are intended to be general and their legal meaning *is* general. We shall return to this point below.

Generality: The Serious Shortfalls. Tort law is distinctively uneven and non-general in at least five different ways. First, good fortune—the fact that misconduct that could easily cause injury happens not to do so—completely immunizes a tortious actor, so there is a gross disparity in the liability of actors who behave identically (eg negligent driving that leads to no injury generates no liability, but identical negligent driving that injures someone generates liability). Second, it is left to putative tort victims to determine whether any case is brought at all. Third, the sanctions faced by a tortfeasor differ dramatically depending on the happenstance of how much harm there is. Fourth, affirmative defences are relevant to whether there is tort liability, and some affirmative defences (for example contributory negligence) are relevant in ways that have nothing to do with the justifiability of the conduct of the defendant. Finally, and in some ways most importantly, the standard of conduct that applies in many tort cases is deliberately left to the fact-finder. In negligence cases, for example, the jury is usually left to decide whether the defendant's conduct was careless. For all of these reasons, there is a dramatic hit-and-miss quality to liability imposition of tort law, one that virtually guarantees that at least several important versions of the desideratum of generality are not satisfied.

Promulgation: The promulgation problem is arguably the most blatant, the most severe, and the most antithetical to common sense. Take *Nickerson v Hodges*, in which the defendants played an elaborate practical joke on the plaintiff by burying a pot full of rocks where the plaintiff believed a treasure was buried, and then arranged for the plaintiff to be publicly humiliated when her belief in the existence of the 'treasure' was revealed to be delusional.[8] To be sure, the plaintiff was deeply upset by this practical joke. Moreover, it seems plausible to say that the defendants' penchant for humour passed beyond insensitivity into mean-spiritedness. Nonetheless, the defendants might have complained, with great plausibility, '*Where is it written* that one cannot play a practical joke on someone?' And the answer would have been it is written nowhere; it was never legislated or ruled upon in advance. Nonetheless, Nickerson recovered in this case, which came to be a prototype of the tort of intentional infliction of emotional distress.

Part of the promulgation concern may well be based on notice (which we will discuss below), but part of it goes beyond notice to something arguably more

[8] *Nickerson v Hodges*, 84 So 37 (La 1920).

fundamental: the absence of an explicit imperative. To see the difference, imagine that practical jokes like the one in *Nickerson* began occurring with some regularity and—before any lawsuits had been brought—the legislature enacted a law forbidding such practical jokes, imposing liability upon anyone who plays such a joke, and announcing that it is retroactive. In this scenario, a judgment entered on a pre-legislation act would still suffer from a retroactivity/notice problem, even if the promulgation problem would disappear. In the actual case, both problems existed: not only did *the alleged wrongful conduct* pre-date the articulation of the legal pronouncement according to which it is deemed wrongful, but *the plaintiff's allegation to the court that the defendant had violated a norm of right conduct* pre-dated the articulation of that norm of conduct. The concern is that the determination of whether there is liability is not made with reference to any rule of conduct that has been authoritatively announced. It is as if judges are simply using their opinions about whether the conduct in question 'crossed a line' or went 'too far'. This is a prototypical rule-of-law complaint, stating, essentially, 'It is not law, but judicial fancy, that determines whether or not the defendant will be forced to pay because of how he behaved'.

Non-retroactivity. The non-retroactivity component of rule-of-law norms is the one most plainly articulated by the US Constitution. Article 1, Section 9 and Article 1, Section 10 both contain laws prohibiting the enactment of *ex post facto* laws. Their point is that one cannot sanction someone for violating a rule of law that was not put in place as law until after the actor engaged in the conduct said to violate the rule. The reason is that the law breaking triggering the sanction is not the action itself; it is the fact that, in acting, the defendant violated an extant law. If the law according to which the conduct was wrongful had not yet been made law, then in acting the defendant could not have violated it. Our system surely relies upon moral reasons in enacting norms of conduct, but the crime is the breaking of the rule that has been put there.

A different way of thinking about non-retroactivity is that the defendant must have had an opportunity to obey the law if he or she is to be sanctioned for failing to obey it. If the law proscribing the conduct did not exist at the time the defendant engaged in that conduct, then there was no opportunity to obey it.

Our legal system not only tolerates the non-prospectivity of tort law, it takes pride in it. The evolution of the common law is built into what Judge Cardozo famously called 'the nature of the judicial process'. An appellate court determining whether a cause of action exists in a category of case must respect precedent and draw from it, but need not be limited by it. Indeed, a court that categorically stated that it *could not* expand the domain of causes of action because it lacked the institutional competency to do so would be making a mistake. So too would a court that recognized a new cause of action emerging from prior causes of action, but declined to enforce it in the case before it.[9]

[9] This is not to say that courts could not decline to expand causes of action or could not decline to enforce a newly articulated rule in the cases before them. The point is that they would be disingenuous

To a significant extent, lawyers and legal actors have generally taken these features of tort law in their stride. When a cutting-edge issue of tort law arises that threatens to expand the domain of actionable legal duties as it has been understood, the defendant (and often interested parties) fights against it, just as the plaintiff (and often interested parties) fights for it. Once a case is decided, industry participants, lawyers, and journalists typically cover the decision as they would cover a new piece of legislation—as informing the legal duties of which actors in the area will need to be aware. However, the decision only counts as truly resolving an issue if it is in fact ruled upon and one litigant wins or loses. Retroactivity of new duty recognition is in the sense virtually built into the structure of appellate adjudication.

Lastly, and perhaps most controversially, there is the desideratum of clarity. Tort law in many areas does not speak clearly; it sometimes speaks in vague terms, and it often utilizes moral and non-moral predicates whose content is highly contentious. None of this is controversial; what is controversial is the suggestion that any area of law—including criminal law—has managed to sidestep this criticism. If all of law is unclear, then either all of law has a serious legitimacy problem, or the selection of clarity as a desideratum was ill informed.

There are several reasons to be less reductive than this, and to suppose that tort law is unclear and vague to an extent considerably beyond criminal law. First, it bears mention that many of those scholars who have addressed the topic of open-ended legal concepts—including, but not limited to, both Hart and Fuller—typically select tort law as the emblem of 'standards' that have the attributes of unclarity and open-endedness.[10] Conversely, courts are often explicit in their requirement that criminal law not be vague, in a way that they are not with tort law. In the third place, it is by design that tort law gives juries the opportunity to make value judgments, and yet the very same idea is typically rejected in criminal law. Finally, we need not ignore the fact that a great deal of the reductive, realist, and instrumentalist jurisprudence in American legal thinking made its home in tort law; these movements were plainly motivated, in significant part, by a perception of a shortfall in clarity in the common law (including, prominently, the law of torts).

Even where there is no retroactivity problem, tort law's unclarity arguably creates a major rule of law difficulty. Consider, for example, a manufacturer trying to ascertain which risks of a drug require warning, and what kind of warning is appropriate. It is far from clear whether there is a standard catchphrase or slogan that captures what is required. Nor—so far as tort law goes—is there any official situated to clarify the standard prior to any action by the manufacturer. A rough estimate of what products liability law says is as follows: a failure to warn claim lies where the risk is one such that a failure to warn of it renders the product unreasonably unsafe. So indefinite is this standard that the United States Supreme Court was nearly persuaded to engage in a peremptory, across-the-board

(to the point of being untruthful) if they described themselves as lacking the proper legal power to expand causes of action or to apply a newly declared rule.

[10] HLA Hart, *The Concept of Law* (2nd edn, Clarendon Press 1994); Fuller, *Morality* (n 3).

immunization of drug companies that complied with all federal regulations. Part of the reason that it declined to do so was its (correct) perception that it is in the nature of the common law of torts within each of the states that it allocates to the jury the judgment call on the adequacy of the warning (and many similar questions).

4. Beyond the Constraint of Government Power

As indicated in the beginning of this chapter, there is something seriously incomplete about a conceptualization of rule of law qualities that pertains only to the attributes of legal systems or putative legal systems. There is a larger picture here that is suppressed by the Fullerian focus on legal systems. The concept of the rule of law is often utilized to evaluate *political communities*, not legal communities. Indeed, the question often is whether a given political community has the rule of law or enjoys rule-of-law attributes. Of course, one is often drawn in the next instant to evaluate whether what is patently a putative legal system enjoys various attributes, not only those indicated above but also, more generally, the attribute of efficacy. One wants to know whether the series of laws and structured legal institutions (such as courts) are sufficiently entrenched in the political community and respected by its members as to count as *their* legal system. Yet it would be a mistake to insist that the concept of the rule of law is really just about attributes of putative legal systems. It is, in very substantial part, about attributes of political communities.

When we look first at political communities to ask whether the rule of law applies, we tend to be asking a question that does not focus only upon *constraints on government power*; we are also looking at whether there are *constraints on individual behaviour*. Likewise, we are not only looking at *whether individuals are protected against the overreaching of governmental actors and institutions*, but also *whether individuals are protected against the violent, oppressive, or licentious behaviour of other private parties*. A political community that did not suffer from an *overreaching government* could still lack the rule of law if it were a Hobbesian chaos of each against the world, or a stable community of private domination by a mighty few. Rule of law values are of course partly about the discipline of government by legal and constitutional norms, but they are also about the discipline of individuals. In other words, there needs to be law that rules, even if the law itself needs to be constrained in various important ways. A state cannot necessarily ride to the top on rule of law values by shearing away its laws to leave a minimum of laws—only those that score high on generality, promulgation, and the other Fullerian desiderata. It needs to have thick enough, broad enough, and substantive enough laws so that individuals enjoy the kind of security and freedom that rule of law values hold up as ideals. In Dicey's classic exposition of the rule of law, he recognized that an important side of the rule-of-law ideal was a conception of individual rights, a conception according to which the individual's rights against the government was a critically important inclusion of the individual's rights against others more broadly.[11]

When the rule of law is understood more broadly in terms of the constraint of private power *and* the constraint of government power, the ideal of the rule of law as we know it from criminal law of course looks much more robust. The state, through criminal law, prohibits certain acts and punishes individuals for so acting. The state must do so in a general and consistent manner in order for the rule of law to be in place. The generality is of double value: it ensures that the individuals (qua potential victims of individual violence) are not underprotected by virtue of inconsistent or patchy articulation (or enforcement) of the law, and it ensures that individuals (qua potential victims of government power) are not randomly or unequally targeted for punishment. Clear, prospective, promulgated prohibitions also have a double aspect: the law can be more efficacious and therefore more protective of and beneficial to the average citizen if those expected to comply with the law are told in advance what the rules are: potential targets are better protected against government overreaching with these rule of law desiderata in place.

5. Two Aspects of Tort Law

The rule of law in tort law, as in criminal law, has two interlocking aspects. First, tort law protects individuals against the overreaching of other private parties by articulating norms of conduct and empowering individuals to redress wrongs done to them by other private parties. The accountability of private parties to other private parties through tort law is a fundamental constraint on the exercise of private power and domination. In this sense, potential tort victims are protected by tort law—both before the fact by the articulation of norms of conduct and the deterrent of liability, and after the fact by the reality of redress. Individuals are thereby protected against the insecurity of injury and attack by other private parties.[12]

Second, however, tort law is also designed to protect individuals (qua tort defendants) against the power and aggression of putative victims and against the power of the state acting on their behalf. For one thing, the very availability of a civil form of recourse through courts is a critically important protection of individuals against private non-civil aggression: people are less likely to engage in retaliatory violence if there is a mode of civil recourse available. For another, the structure of tort law ensures that the state's power, and the power the state affords to private individual litigants, is not used simply against the scapegoats of the day, or used in a manner that undercuts the capacity to plan or to live securely.

[11] AV Dicey, *Introduction to the Study of the Law of the Constitution* (9th edn, Macmillan and Co 1939).

[12] John CP Goldberg, 'The Constitutional Status of Tort Law: Due Process and the Right to a Law for the Redress of Wrongs' (2005) 115 *Yale Law Journal* 524.

Areas as diverse as nuisance law and medical malpractice illustrate both aspects of this point. One's right to the use and enjoyment of property is, among other things, a kind of security and liberty; the infringements of such a right are infringements of security and liberty. When one actually has a possessory interest in real property, one is entitled to use and enjoy it. An intrusion of a polluter or a farm or an airport may well be an unreasonable interference with that right. There is a sense in which living in a community with a rule of law means that one should not be subject to that kind of intrusion, dependent as it is on the typically unpredictable decisions of others. In this sense, the availability of a right of action, and the concomitant knowledge that it is real invasion, are in part rule of law protections. Similarly, medical malpractice liability is available when one has entrusted one's well-being to someone who holds himself out as a professional and one has been injured by a failure of that person to carry through on a competent performance of those professional duties—a performance one is entitled to expect. The physician can be held accountable for failure to deliver adequate performance and thereby injuring the plaintiff.

The rule of law in torts protects each against the private wrongs of others, but it also protects each against the overreaching of the state and of private parties with respect to the possible misuse or overuse of rights of redress. Just as the rule of law in criminal law means not only the criminalization of certain invasions of others' rights, but also the constraint of the government in carrying out punishment, so the rule of law in torts means not only the understanding that one has enforceable duties not to wrong others, but also that the state, in allowing redress to putative victims, will be subject to constraints in how it holds private individuals responsible and liable. Hence, in nuisance law, for example, an interference—even a significant interference with the use and enjoyment of property—is not sufficient for liability. It must be an unreasonable interference and it must be continuous. Money damages are also constrained, and although injunctions are available, they are subject to equitable restrictions. Various defences are available in a nuisance action, too. Similarly, a medical malpractice claim will not succeed simply because the jury believes the physician could or should have done better; there must be experts who attest to the physician's failure to live up the standard of care, and the jury must give credence to those experts even after they have listened to the experts for the other side.

A key distinction between tort law (on the one hand) and criminal and regulatory law (on the other) pertains to the ground of an individual's vulnerability to the power of the state to impose liability. Punishments and regulatory sanctions are what I have called 'non-compliance sanctions'. The state's authority to punish and sanction, in such cases, is derivative from its power to set out rules of conduct punishable by sanction for non-compliance.[13] Of course, there are a variety of kinds of limits on what rules can be issued and what sanctions can be imposed for

[13] The distinction set forth in the remainder of this paragraph was developed in Zipursky, 'Inner Morality' (n 4) 27, 36–40. Also see Benjamin C Zipursky, '*Palsgraf*, Punitive Damages, and Preemption' (2012) 125 *Harvard Law Review* 1757, 1777–84.

non-compliance with them. The larger point is that an individual's proper vulnerability to such sanction by the state is derivative of the state's correlative power to impose liability, which is in turn derivative of the state's power to make enforceable rules in this domain of conduct.

Tort liability works differently. The individual's vulnerability to tort liability turns on the individual's having wrongfully injured someone. It is because the defendant wrongfully injured someone that the victim has a claim on the state to permit redress from the harmed individual. Liability is not a sanction for what the state has announced to be prohibited conduct. Liability is rather the court's ratification of a plaintiff's assertion of a right to redress against someone who wronged her. It is the wrongful injuring of the plaintiff, not the violation of an announced rule, that generates liability in tort.

6. Alternative Structural Norms

The failure of tort law to live up to Fullerian desiderata now looks both less surprising and less concerning. Consider the critique offered above of tort law's failure to live up to a generality norm: liability turns on whether a wrongful act ripened into an actual injury; the amount of the liability turns on the happenstance of how great the injury was, not how risky or intentional the conduct was; the right to bring a case turns on the discretionary choices of private parties, not the deliberative choices of a central prosecutor. Affirmative defences apply and the jury gets to do fact-finding on whether the conduct fell below the standard of ordinary care.

None of these attributes of tort law should cause rule of law worries. Torts are not actionable without a realized wrong because the point of the law is not to constrain conduct as such, but to protect against rights invasions, and to empower individuals whose rights are invaded to redress the injury. That norm is perfectly general, once so understood.[14] Absent the requisite injury, the rights invasion has not occurred. Similarly, the protection offered to the individual includes the right to damages that will compensate him or her—the choice of liability level should not be understood as a deviation from generality in sanctioning, but rather as an intelligible feature of the kind of constraint on conduct and the kind of protection of right-holders tort law provides.

There is a sense in which this response may seem quite non-responsive. The fact that there are rights-protecting reasons to structure tort law in this manner may remove the concern that such structural features are arbitrary, but it does not (one might argue) remove the worry that a certain kind of protection for defendants is absent from tort law. Insofar as at least part of the conception of the rule of law does relate to the constraints to which the government must be subjected before

[14] John CP Goldberg and Benjamin C Zipursky, 'Tort Law and Moral Luck' (2007) 92 *Cornell Law Review* 1123.

individuals are sanctioned, one may still wonder why the absence of such constraints in tort law would not and does not constitute a massive rule of law problem.

An answer suggested much earlier is that, in imposing tort liability, the state is not sanctioning the defendant but rather enabling a victim of a wrongful injuring to hold the defendant responsible for having wrongfully injured him or her. I admitted above that this distinction might sound contrived in a post-legal-realist world. But now we can see that the distinction is an important one, and not just because it relieves the state of satisfying certain structural burdens. It also *adds* certain structural burdens. Tort law is structured so that only certain persons—victims—are actually entitled to seek the imposition of tort liability. Indeed, the point is stronger than it appears. Tort law does not so much involve the state imposing liability, as it does the state empowering private parties to obtain redress. Not any private party is so entitled, however. Rather, tort law insists that only persons who are able to establish that they themselves were wrongfully injured are allowed to bring a tort claim.

Tort law actually contains two conceptually distinct 'standing-like' requirements, which are easy to confuse. One is a requirement that the plaintiff *have actually* suffered some injury and is not simply bringing her claim to impose liability for acting in a manner that *might have* hurt the plaintiff; this is an injury requirement.[15] The second—which I have elsewhere referred to as a 'substantive standing' requirement[16]—is a requirement that the defendant's conduct have been wrongful in relation to the plaintiff.

Although plainly quite different from a generality requirement, the injury and substantive standing requirements are in a sense abstract desiderata that our tort law satisfies, which in some sense constitute a rule of law virtue or at least an alternative to the generality norms that tort law does not meet. Individuals who face the prospect of tort liability for their actions do not face such actions for redress by everyone. The state cannot permit a defendant to be vulnerable to such claims unless the claimant is herself or himself proved to be a victim of this conduct. One is vulnerable only to those one has wronged and only to those who were actually injured.

Turn now to the Fullerian requirement that the rule itself have been promulgated or made explicit in a rule. The point of this principle is that what triggers vulnerability to sanction is the breaking of a certain kind of legal rule. The state qua prosecutor goes to see who broke one of the rules that the state said was not to be broken. It is the non-compliance with an actual imperative that kicks the prosecutor in gear, and so there should not be any liability to sanction if no written rule was broken. That is, of course, simply the reverse of the point that if there is a prosecution, there had better be a promulgated rule that was broken.

15 John CP Goldberg and Benjamin C Zipursky, 'Unrealized Torts' (2002) 88 *Virginia Law Review* 1625; Arthur Ripstein and Benjamin C Zipursky, 'Corrective Justice in an Age of Mass Torts' in Gerald J Postema (ed), *Philosophy and the Law of Torts* (Cambridge University Press 2001).

16 Benjamin C Zipursky, 'Rights, Wrongs, and Recourse in the Law of Torts' (1998) 51 *Vanderbilt Law Review* 1.

Tort law lacks this protection, but it has a different protection which criminal law lacks. The state has no entitlement to allow redress unless the defendant actually injured the plaintiff. If the individual opens himself up to criminal liability by breaking an express rule, the individual opens himself up to tort liability by actually injuring the plaintiff. The rule of law value constrains government action in both cases, making liberty from courts imposing liability the baseline in each. Part of having such a baseline be meaningful is that there is a kind of thing one must have done to become vulnerable to such attacks by others through the court. In criminal law (and, indeed, in public regulatory law), one must have broken an actual written and promulgated rule.[17] In tort law, one must actually have injured the person. The distinction of course matches the distinction between being sanctioned and being held responsible to a tort victim. One is sanctioned for having broken a legal rule and one is held responsible for having wrongfully injured someone. The rule of law partly involves protecting individuals against the state's overreaching in terms of its system of imposing liability, be it criminal, regulatory, or tort. But it partly involves having those norms and institutions that allow individuals to be secure against the rights invasions of others.

The criticism tort law has received for the insufficient promulgation of its norms of conduct is perhaps exceeded by the criticisms voiced about the insufficient boundedness of the extent of liability; this criticism has been particularly marked with regard to punitive damages. Here, too, a careful examination reveals that tort law does not lack structural protections, but simply has different ones. As I have argued elsewhere in detail, the common law of torts contains a requirement that the magnitude of liability must be anchored in the magnitude of the injury inflicted upon the plaintiff.[18]

Tort law quite dramatically lacks a prospectivity requirement, but, as with the discussion of other desiderata, one can locate quite different structural requirements that tort law possesses but criminal law lacks. Superficially, at least, criminal law's prospectivity requirement is aimed at rendering it fair to sanction someone for breaking a rule. The rule must be one which the putative wrongdoer was given notice of in advance. One cannot expect someone to live up to a rule without having given them a chance to know what the rule is.

As many scholars have pointed out, the argument is not as strong as it appears. That is because our legal system is fully aware that prospective announcement does not generally mean—and does not generally secure—knowledge of the law. Our law does not require that the defendant actually have known, but that the system have published the rule in advance of the conduct that is putatively unlawful. While it is true that we hold citizens responsible to know the law, that is in part a question-begging way of saying that what we care about with notice is not actual knowledge

[17] The prior sentence of course understates the preconditions of criminal liability, as conventionally conceived; *mens rea* is also a precondition for criminal liability. The intention is to contrast tort law not simply with a criminal law, but also with regulation; regulatory liability carries no *mens rea* requirement.

[18] Zipursky, '*Palsgraf*' (n 13) 1757; Benjamin C Zipursky, 'A Theory of Punitive Damages' (2005) 84 *Texas Law Review* 105.

but the in-principle obtainability of it. The position seems more palatable if one focuses on the normative aspect of the concept of an 'expectation'. It is, one might argue, unfair to 'expect' someone to live up to a rule one has not even announced in advance, but it is not unfair to expect someone to live up to a rule one has announced in advance, so long as the rules are in some systematic way publicly available.

In tort law, courts are willing to hold defendants responsible for having wrongfully injured others through failure to live up to tort duties one owes them, *even if those tort duties were not announced in advance.* However, tort law is rooted in both precedent (in connection with *stare decisis*) and custom (in connection with the content of tort concepts). Legislators in announcing the criminal law are not bound by precedent or custom. Precedent and custom do not ensure that legal actors know in advance what their duties are, but neither does prospective announcement; it allows (we shall assume) that one *could* know. But why is that relevant? I have suggested above that it is unfair to expect someone to comply with duties of which they were not told in advance, and of which they could not have become aware; and it is arguably fair if it was announced in advance and they could have become aware, to expect them to act in accordance with such duties. In tort law, the duties one has to others, the breach of which generates responsibility, need not be duties expressly announced in advance. On the other hand, the courts articulating such duties must do so in the context of mining our customary understanding of what we owe to one another, as fleshed out through precedent.[19] The intellectual exercise of ascertaining whether some way of curtailing one's conduct so as not to interfere with others is *customary*, or is implicit in a customary norm of conduct, is, in substance, connected to the exercise of ascertaining what kind of forbearance from interfering with others can be *expected* of each of us. There is thus a sense in which *linkage to custom* substitutes for *prospective announcement* as a value.[20] Of course, it is probably somewhat anachronistic to put matters this way, given that the common law pre-dates extensive non-common law criminal legislation, at least in the English legal system from which ours derived; the need for prospective announcement arguably arose when linkage-to-custom was abandoned.

The tradeoff of prospective announcement for custom-linkage and precedent-rootedness needs greater examination, as does the tradeoff of generality for standing and the tradeoff of promulgation for injury-causation. One further desideratum should be discussed before we evaluate the full picture. Fuller insisted that the law be tolerably clear. The idea is really that the law be rule-like, with sharp edges, so

[19] This argument is put forward in greater detail in Benjamin C Zipursky, '*Snyder v. Phelps*, Outrageousness and the Open Texture of Tort Law' (2011) 60 *DePaul Law Review* 473.

[20] Fuller makes what appears to be a similar point at a number of junctures (see eg Fuller, *Morality* (n 3) 51–62), where he notes that anti-retroactivity concerns in common law are, in part, satisfied by a background of shared norms. As indicated, I do not accept that the most basic principle is one of anti-retroactivity and that the common law of torts fumbles into nearly satisfying it because it is custom based. It is just as likely that the need for prospective announcement arises most urgently when the break from custom is the sharpest; the priority of the criminal/legislative model should not be assumed.

that it can be understood. Norms of conduct that depend too heavily upon standards and principles, rather than categories, are a threat to liberty. If there is really no clear idea that has a clear articulation, then one cannot be expected to grasp the permissible boundaries of conduct *ex ante*.

Tort law lacks this desideratum just as it lacks the others mentioned above. On the other hand, the law is unclear for at least two interrelated reasons, which are themselves related to the rule of law. The first is that a defendant is not liable unless the plaintiff's right was invaded; *liability therefore tracks plaintiff's rights, as conventionally understood.* As suggested above, however, the concept of a right in the common law is conceptually linked to what we may fairly expect of one another. It falls to courts to articulate the extent of the rights and the extent of what we may fairly expect of one another. In this context, what makes the tort system unclear is in part its willingness to protect those who are the object of legal claims quite robustly against demands for compensation of injury. As Calabresi emphasized in a quite different theoretical context, strict liability cuts down on the costs associated with ascertainment of fault-based liability. It does so, however, by removing an important level of protection against the assertion of claims by others through the state's judicial apparatus. Defendants are only subject to such claims when they have invaded a plaintiff's rights, and rights are understood in a way that tracks embedded moral concepts.[21] The rights-tracking feature of tort law that reduces its clarity offers individuals, in return, freedom from responsibility or accountability where they have not violated anyone's rights as conventionally understood, even if their conduct has caused injury.

One could arguably blunt the aforementioned problem by using a bright line rule to protect defendants where there is unclarity in rights definitions. This is in fact what the United States Supreme Court has done for constitutional tort claims against government actors: qualified immunity shields defendants from liability unless the right alleged violated was 'clearly established'. These protections obviously come at a cost to other interests. Quite obviously, in the constitutional tort case, it is a sacrifice in our protection against wrongful government action, and our capacity to hold the government accountable when it so invades individuals' rights. More generally, the contraction of tort liability is concomitantly a contraction of the rights of individuals to hold others accountable for violating their rights. It is thus far from obvious that rule of law values demand that the state adopt such liability-shielding rules, even if they increase clarity and predictability. The aspiration to be rights-tracking is thus a feature of tort law that in some ways counterbalances its failure to offer greater clarity, but does so without eviscerating the power to hold others responsible for wronging us.

Finally, some of tort law's unclarity in practice pertains to the adjudicative role given to fact-finders—in America, juries. Courts ask juries to opine on a variety of questions that are central to the substance of the cause of action. The reasonably-

[21] See Dennis Klimchuk, 'Equity and the Rule of Law' in this volume (arguing that Equity's rejection of overbroad, 'stickler'-like interpretations of legal rights in favour of interpretations that more accurately capture moral rights is in fact a rule of law respecting virtue).

prudent-person standard of negligence law is the most oft-cited example of this; but almost every tort has its own version, which is central to the very definition of the wrong. Of course, many elements of offences and defences in the criminal law also require what might be called normative fact-finding, but the weighty role of such concepts in torts dwarfs that in criminal law. We shall call this institutional feature of tort law its 'normative particularism'.

Like its rights-tracking feature, tort law's normative particularism is part of why tort law is unclear and arguably less predictable than other areas. Yet its normative particularism is also protective in several respects. It is far from clear that defendants in negligence cases lose more often than they win because a fact-finder is invited to engage in a relatively fine-grained analysis of the reasonableness of the care used (or, in other torts, on parallel issues). More importantly, perhaps, tort law allows for a relatively ample set of reasons to be provided in defence against liability. What the defendant understands, pre-legally, to be normatively relevant is more likely to find a place in the fact-finders' deliberations about whether the defendant wrongfully injured the plaintiff. It bears mention that civil law's placement of the burden of proof on the plaintiff carries over to mixed questions of law and fact, so while it is true that plaintiffs are allowed to include more factors in their arguments *for* the unreasonableness of the defendant's conduct (in a negligence case), it would be a mistake to suppose that the addition of normative particularism is a wash.

It should not be surprising that tort law's rights-tracking feature and its normative particularism work hand in glove, both excluding cases where there really was no rights invasion notwithstanding first appearances and including cases where there was. The resulting unclarity means that legal actors do not always have a good way to ascertain whether a certain course of conduct will lead to legal liability, which is at least a prima facie shortcoming regarding the rule of law. However, what goes along with the synergy of rights-tracking and normative particularism is a remarkable kind of commitment of the legal system to protecting the rights of individuals against the invasions of others, and allowing redress for the invasions of those rights.[22] The commitment is remarkable because it is not limited by extant express definitions of the wrongs and rights. If there is an added vulnerability to individuals qua defendants, there is an added protection to individuals qua rights holders.

7. Conclusion

Generality, promulgation, non-retroactivity, and clarity constitute a cluster of rule of law virtues that come together in an ideal of law as a clear, crisp, rule-like imperative that is published and widely available prior to a defendant's decision to act. The prior section has enumerated a series of alternative virtues: standing, actual injury, anchoring, custom-rootedness and precedent-rootedness, rights trackingness, and normative particularism. These alternative virtues, moreover, are related

[22] See Margaret Jane Radin, 'Boilerplate: A Threat to the Rule of Law?' in this volume (identifying as part of the rule of law a commitment to allow individuals to redress grievances).

to one another—they form an integrated scheme. The ideal they embody is of a defendant free from liability unless a plaintiff proves to a fact-finder examining all of the circumstances that she was wronged by the defendant, that the wrong caused her injury, and that the wrong was a rights violation. The extent of liability, moreover, is anchored in the plaintiff's injury. This ideal has a second aspect: it is also an ideal of an individual whose rights against others' wrongs are protected by law, who is empowered to redress the invasions of such rights through the courts, and whose right of redress is connected in certain ways with her underlying primary rights.

The identification of these qualities in tort law—standing, injury, anchoring, custom, precedent, rights-trackingness, and particularism—raises a series of broader questions: whether it is the *private law* nature of torts that demands these requirements, whether it is tort's *common law* nature, or whether these features are actually unique to tort law itself.

These questions would take us beyond the scope of this chapter, but I have begun answering them elsewhere: the short answer is that the standing, rights-trackingness, and anchoring are critical to all of the private law of obligations, that custom and precedent are critical to all of the common law, and that a certain conception of injury is critical to the law of torts in particular.[23]

It remains to ask why one should call the aforementioned features of tort law 'rule of law' qualities, even if one recognizes (or concedes for the purposes of argument) that there is much to be said for them from a normative point of view. I shall conclude by offering several reasons for doing so.

First, and most broadly, the principal point of limiting structural features of the law is that once the machinery for the imposition of sanction or liability is in place, there is a huge risk that the state will abuse that machinery. The concept of the rule of law contemplates that there are proper and improper uses of such state power and that, while law and legal institutions are certainly important for human flourishing, it is critical that there be structural criteria to help sort the proper from the improper use of state power. Indeed, part of how we distinguish law from brute political force is whether the power is systematically used in accordance with these criteria. The alternative criteria set out with respect to tort law do just this; they are structural criteria that allow us to distinguish authentic and systematic legal uses of the government power to impose liability-to-a-private-party on someone from arbitrary or oppressive uses of this power. Overwhelmingly, the question is whether the state is simply using its power to redistribute wealth or to favour some over others, or whether it is actually implementing a system of legal rights and duties.

Second, as Dicey remarked and as I have discussed throughout this chapter, a critical component of the rule of law is respect for individual rights. The Fullerian desiderata of promulgation and clarity are compelling only against a roughly liberal backdrop according to which the default is freedom to act and freedom from

[23] Zipursky, 'Inner Morality' (n 4) 27; Benjamin C Zipursky, 'Civil Recourse and the Plurality of Wrongs' (2014) *New Zealand Law Review* 145 (forthcoming).

sanction. Hayekians are wholly unwilling to suppose that because the government is the government, it has a broader latitude of intrusion than others would. Indeed, the conception of the rule of law found from Dicey to Hayek and Fuller—and indeed found in the American and English constitutional traditions—is one according to which the government is not above the law, ie it must refrain from infringing on individuals' rights, too. Implicit in this ideal is a conception of individual rights against intrusions by others. The rights are not a product of legislative authority, but prior to it. In this way, the rule of law ideal presupposes a common law conception of rights against intrusion by others, and presupposes that this conception must be made real.

Finally, and relatedly, from John Marshall to Albert Dicey to Hayek and Fuller and, today, Waldron,[24] rule of law ideals put courts in a central place. The rule of law becomes real only when courts are willing to be there to shear away the state assertion of its power, if it is an abuse of power. In this sense, the rule of law is a concept that courts use to police the workings of legal institutions so as to monitor overstepping and abuse, and so as to counterbalance the exercise of power by political actors. In the context, the role of courts in empowering private parties to seek remedies for abuses and wrongs they have suffered is core to our rule-of-law notions.

It is tempting to say that tort law and criminal law are fundamentally aimed at the same goal—to protect individual rights against intrusion—and that rule-of-law norms in both domains are fundamentally about ensuring that, in enforcing such rights-protective norms, the state does not itself infringe individual rights. These observations are indeed among the themes of this chapter, but it is critical to see that they depict only part of the landscape of law and the rule of law. Focusing on what is distinctive about the rule of law in torts allows us to see much more.

As HLA Hart famously explained, legal rules can be power-conferring, not simply duty-imposing. The standard conception of the rule of law—the one most conspicuously evident in criminal law but also evident in state regulation—is essentially about making sure that our legal and political system adequately constrains the power of the government to enforce its duty-imposing rules; inadequate constraint of government power can itself be rights-invasive, and can undermine the integrity of the whole legal and political system. We have seen above that the constraint of power in tort law works in different ways. Let us not lose sight of a larger point, however: attending to rule of law concerns in torts does not merely require the *adequate constraint* of power, it also requires the *adequate conferral* of power. The accountability of wrongdoers to those whom they have injured—the principle that where there is a right there is a remedy—is a critical component of our legal system's self-conception as a rule of law. In tort law—and more generally in private law—the rule of law secures the possibility of accountability and rejects the prospect of private powerlessness.

[24] Jeremy Waldron, 'The Concept and the Rule of Law' (2008) 43 *Georgia Law Review* 1.

7

Private Law Pluralism and the Rule of Law

*Hanoch Dagan**

1. Introduction

My previous work characterizes private law as structurally pluralist and moderately perfectionist. Its pluralism implies that property, contracts, torts, and unjust enrichment are merely broad umbrellas for narrower private law institutions sharing some thin common denominators. Property law, for example—my central example in this chapter—is composed of a set of diverse doctrines that cannot be reasonably described as being governed by one coherent regulative principle, at least if that principle is to be robust enough to play a meaningful role in the development of this heterogeneous body of law. Thus the search for property's core is futile. But a careful study of various property institutions (such as fee simple absolute, co-ownership, common-interest communities, marital property, copyrights, patents, and the like) is valuable because the regulative principles of *these* institutions express our society's ideals for core categories of interpersonal relationships regarding various resources and consolidate people's expectations in their regards.

I hold that this structural pluralist account fits private law better than its monist counterparts and is also normatively superior to these alternative understandings, such as the exclusion conception of property. By facilitating a diverse set of interpersonal relationships, a pluralist conception of private law participates in

* Thanks to Einat Albin, Katya Assaf, Lisa Austin, Shyam Balganesh, Jane Baron, Ilan Benshalom, Eyal Benvenisti, Richard Briffault, Mauro Bussani, David Carlson, Margit Cohn, Guy Davidov, Nestor Davidson, Avihay Dorfman, Shai Dotan, Chris Essert, Stanley Fish, Charles Fried, David Gliksberg, Andrew Gold, Guy Goldstein, Michael Graetz, Philip Hamburger, Assaf Hamdani, Alon Harel, Michael Heller, Adam Hofri-Winogradov, Larissa Katz, Dennis Klimchuk, Roy Kreitner, Sudhir Krishnaswamy, David Lametti, Amnon Lehavi, Daphna Lewinsohn-Zamir, Mark Lotman, Tom Merrill, Trevor Morrison, James Penner, Eduardo Peñalver, Ariel Porat, Dan Priel, Amit Pundik, Andrzej Rapaczynski, Alex Reinert, Fred Schauer, Elizabeth Scott, Tony Sebok, Yuval Shany, Henry Smith, Stewart Sterk, Martin Stone, Ernest Weinrib, Leif Wenar, Elkow Yankah, and participants at the Harvard Law School Conference on Progressive Property, the University of Toronto Workshop on Private Law and the Rule of Law, the NYU Property Theory Workshop, and faculty workshops at Cardozo Law School, Columbia Law School, and the Hebrew University Faculty of Law for their helpful comments. This chapter recapitulates and builds upon chapter 9 of Hanoch Dagan, *Reconstructing American Legal Realism & Rethinking Private Law Theory* (Oxford University Press 2013).

the state's obligation to empower people to make choices among viable alternatives, and thus be the authors of their own lives. One implication of the perfectionist nature of private law is that its institutions are subject to ongoing normative re-evaluation and possible, even if properly cautious, reconfiguration. They are thereby forced to live up to their promise as valuable options of human flourishing, thus making a significant contribution to worthwhile life plans.

I assume in this chapter that this understanding of private law, which is summarized in Section 2, fits our legal practice and is normatively appealing. My current mission is to examine whether this understanding, despite its multiplicity, dynamism, and disavowal of neutrality, complies with the rule of law. There are, or at least so I argue, two key aspects to the rule of law—the requirement that the law be capable of guiding its subjects' behaviour and the prescription that law may not confer on officials the right to exercise unconstrained power[1]—and they are both connected to people's autonomy. On its face, my account of private law is vulnerable on both fronts. If this first impression is correct, defending this conception of private law would require a choice between downplaying the significance of the rule of law for private law, and showing that the rule-of-law deficit generated by a pluralist and perfectionist private law is dwarfed by its normative virtues.

Fortunately, as I hope to show, there is no real friction between private law pluralism and the guidance and constraint strands of the rule of law. Private law pluralism neither requires nor should it imply adopting the dubious nominalistic approach of case-by-case adjudication, which indeed undermines guidance. Rather, because private law institutions are supposed to consolidate expectations and express ideals of interpersonal relationships, private law pluralism supports, even requires, relatively stable and internally coherent—albeit properly narrow—doctrinal categories. Each such private law institution is governed by fairly precise rules alongside informative standards founded on the regulative principles of these institutions, enabling people to predict the consequences of future contingencies and to plan their lives accordingly. These private law institutions are shaped and developed through both legislation and adjudication. Courts are appropriately involved in many of these processes because (at least insofar as private law is concerned) they typically enjoy no less legitimacy, from either a participation or accountability perspective, than legislatures. Likewise, while the plurality of values involved in the moulding of our private law institutions' regulative principles makes this a challenging endeavour, we have no grounds for assuming that the requirement of normative contextual enquiry typifying common law adjudication does not reliably constrain this judicial power.

Consequently, no comparison is now required between the virtues of the rule of law and those of my account of private law. To be sure, it is not my claim that no private law system would have scored better than private law pluralism in terms of

[1] In this respect I join Martin Krygier's meta-claim whereby, in order to understand the rule of law, we must begin with its telos. See Martin Krygier, 'Four Puzzles about the Rule of Law: Why, What, Where? and Who Cares?' in James E Fleming (ed), *Getting to the Rule of Law* (NYU Press 2011) 64, 67–73.

guidance or constraint. But if the claims just mentioned (which are elaborated in Sections 3 and 4) are correct, private law pluralism seems to score quite high on both fronts. Thus, if one supports a threshold conception of the rule of law, private law pluralism would probably pass it. Even barring such a threshold—meaning a situation wherein the rule of law and substantive virtues must always be balanced—my conclusions imply (assuming that private law pluralism is indeed worth endorsing substantively) that adding the concerns of the rule of law to the picture is unlikely to lead to its abandonment, at least when compared with alternative (that is: monist) approaches to private law.[2]

Reconciling private law pluralism and the rule of law does not vindicate the conventional perception that the rule of law is only marginally interesting to private lawyers, quite the contrary. Much of the resistance of private law theorists to embracing pluralism and perfectionism, despite their saliency in the practice of our private law, rests implicitly on rule-of-law concerns. Explicitly articulating these worries in the language of the rule of law and demonstrating why a pluralist and perfectionist private law neither fails to guide people's behaviour properly nor sanctions unconstrained judicial power may thus allow private law theorists to celebrate these core features of private law instead of marginalizing or suppressing them. Moreover, this exercise is also useful to our understanding of the rule of law. Tracing how a pluralist and perfectionist private law complies with the rule of law may enrich our perspective on both the guidance and the constraint aspects of the rule of law.

2. Structural Pluralism in Private Law

Private law is canonically divided into property, contracts, torts, and unjust enrichment, and nothing in what follows will necessarily challenge this division. Yet, legal actors—judges, practising lawyers, academics, lobbyists, and the like—sometimes assume that this division carries some important justificatory burden. To take one example, consider the analysis that many lawyers apply to the question of whether copyright is property. Notwithstanding the vigorous debate between advocates of the information industry and champions of the public domain, many players on both sides seem to assume that classifying copyright as a species of property is bound to bolster the claims of the former at the expense of the latter. The (usually implicit) presupposition of both sides to this debate is that property is a more or less monist concept that, at its core, is the owner's right to exclude. Thus

2 While conformity with the rule of law is an inherent value of law, my understanding of the rule of law implies that Joseph Raz is correct when insisting that (1) it is a matter of degree and (2) it may conflict with other values, so that less conformity may at times be preferable because it helps to realize these values. See Joseph Raz, 'The Rule of Law and its Virtues' in *The Authority of Law: Essays on Law and Morality* (2nd edn, Oxford University Press 2009) 210, 222, 225, 228–9. See also eg John Gardner, *Law as a Leap of Faith: Essays on Law in General* (Oxford University Press 2012) 33, 192, 195–6. But see Ernest J Weinrib, 'The Intelligibility of the Rule of Law' in Allan Hutchinson and Patrick Monahan (eds), *The Rule of Law: Ideal or Ideology* (Carswell 1987) 59.

they imply that this exclusion principle is significant to the point of affecting real life consequences concerning the scope of authors' rights. Rather than the innocuous cohabitation of various property doctrines under the broad category of property, it is these presuppositions that are the target of my critique because I consider them both wrong and misleading.[3] Just like its sister categories of contracts, torts, and unjust enrichment, property is far too heterogeneous a field to be guided by one regulative principle (such as exclusion), at least when defined as one that generates significant doctrinal prescriptions. Therefore, classifying copyright as property does not necessarily imply an expansion of the scope of authors' rights.[4]

The starting point of structural pluralism in private law, which is part of the legacy of American legal realism, is that broad legal categories like property, contracts, torts, or unjust enrichment are merely convenient 'umbrellas' for a more diversified landscape.[5] Along these lines, Herman Oliphant celebrated the traditional common law strategy of employing narrow legal categories, which 'divided and minutely subdivided the transactions of life for legal treatment', with the desirable result of a significant 'particularity and minuteness in the [legal] classification of human transactions'. Such narrow categories help to produce 'the discrimination necessary for intimacy of treatment', thus encouraging lawyers to shape law 'close and contemporary' to the human problems they deal with. The traditional common law strategy thereby facilitates one comparative advantage of lawyers (notably judges) in producing legal norms: their daily access to actual human situations and problems in contemporary life.[6] Similar convictions led Karl Llewellyn to insist that wholesale legal categories, such as property, contracts, or torts, are 'too big to handle' because they encompass too 'many heterogeneous items' and, accordingly, to recommend '[t]he making of smaller categories', which allow lawyers to develop the law while 'testing it against life-wisdom'. To pre-empt certain responses, let me clarify that the claim (at least Llewellyn's claim—and mine) is *not* that 'the equities or sense of the particular case or the particular parties' should be determinative. Rather, it is that decision-making should benefit from 'the sense and reason of some significantly seen *type* of life-situation'.[7]

[3] For similar expressions of these presuppositions in the context of the so-called new property and in regard to body parts, which are thus subject to the very same line of criticism, see, respectively, JW Harris, *Property & Justice* (Oxford University Press 1996) 151, 304, Alan Hyde, *Bodies of Law* (Princeton University Press 1997) 73.

[4] See Hanoch Dagan, *Property: Values and Institutions* (Oxford University Press 2011) ch 4.

[5] See generally Hanoch Dagan, *Reconstructing American Legal Realism & Rethinking Private Law Theory* (Oxford University Press 2013) chs 6, 8.

[6] Herman Oliphant, 'A Return to Stare Decisis' (1928) 14 *American Bar Association Journal* 71, 73–4, 159.

[7] Karl N Llewellyn, 'A Realistic Jurisprudence: The Next Step' in *Jurisprudence: Realism in Theory and in Practice* (University of Chicago Press 1962) 3, 27–8, 32; Llewellyn, 'Some Realism about Realism' in *Jurisprudence* 42, 59–60; Llewellyn, 'The Current Recapture of the Grand Tradition' in *Jurisprudence*, 215, 217, 219–20. Frederick Schauer has argued that the concrete examples faced by judges distort their judgment rather than illuminate it because they systematically trigger certain cognitive biases. See Frederick Schauer, 'Do Cases Make Bad Law?' (2006) 73 *University of Chicago Law Review* 883. But as Jeff Rachlinski shows, alongside the cognitive weaknesses of adjudication, courts also have several cognitive advantages over legislatures, which might facilitate superior

Property law follows the prescriptions of structural pluralism by setting up a number of distinct property institutions. Each governs a specific social context or a given resource and is typified by a particular configuration of property owners' entitlement corresponding to a particular property value or balance of such values serving as its regulative principle. Thus, some property institutions, such as the fee simple absolute, are structured along the lines of the Blackstonian view of property as sole and despotic dominion. These institutions are atomistic, competitive, and vindicate people's negative liberty. Liberal societies justifiably facilitate such property institutions, which serve both as a source of personal well-being and as a domain of individual freedom and independence. In other property institutions, such as marital property, a more communitarian view of property may dominate, with property as a locus of sharing. There are many others along the strangers–spouses spectrum, thus shades and hues of these property institutions will be found. In these various categories of cooperative property institutions, both liberty and community are of the essence, and the applicable property configuration includes rights as well as responsibilities. This variety is rich both between and within contexts: it provides more than one option for people who want, for example, to become homeowners, engage in business, or enter into intimate relationships.[8]

Thus, alongside more atomistic property institutions, property law supports a wide range of institutions that facilitate the economic and social gains made possible by cooperation. Some of these institutions, such as a close corporation, are mostly about economic gains, including securing efficiencies of economies of scale and risk-spreading, with social benefits merely a (sometimes pleasant) side-effect. Other institutions, such as marriage, are more about the intrinsic good of being part of a plural subject, where the *raison d'être* of the property institution refers more to identity and interpersonal relationships, while the attendant economic benefits are perceived as helpful by-products rather than the primary good of cooperation. The underlying character of the divergent relationships proves to be the key to explaining the particular property configuration that serves as the default for the property institution at hand.[9]

Property institutions vary not only according to the social context but also according to the nature of the resource at stake. The resource is significant because its physical characteristics crucially affect its productive use. Thus, for example, the fact that information consumption is generally non-rivalrous implies that, when the resource at hand is information, use may not always necessitate exclusion.[10] The nature of the resource is also significant in that society approaches different

law-making. See Jeffrey J Rachlinski, 'Bottom-Up Versus Top-Down Lawmaking' (2006) 73 *University of Chicago Law Review* 933, 950–61.

[8] See generally Dagan, *Property* (n 4) chs 1, 3–4, 8, 10. For a structural pluralist account of contract law, see Hanoch Dagan, 'Autonomy, Pluralism, and Contract Law Theory' (2013) 76 *Law & Contemporary Problems* 19.

[9] See Dagan, *Property* (n 4) ch 10.

[10] See Mark A Lemley, 'Ex Ante versus Ex Post Justifications for Intellectual Property' (2004) 71 *University of Chicago Law Review* 129, 143.

resources as variously constitutive of their possessors' identity.[11] Accordingly, resources are subject to different property configurations: whereas the law vigorously vindicates people's control of their constitutive resources, the more fungible an interest, the less emphasis property law will need to place on its owner's control.[12]

To be sure, the similarities among the various property institutions (or the various types of torts, contracts, or unjust enrichments) justify studying them together and treating them as the subject matter of unified scholarly analysis. Often, however, these similarities merely mean that studying the various institutions of property law requires us to ask similar questions, such as: What is the appropriate scope of an owner's exclusion? Or what is the optimal governance regime for this property institution? At times, these similarities imply some overlap in the pertinent values that affect the regulative principles of these diverse institutions. For example, personhood concerns inform a certain subset of property institutions, while utility is significant in another subset. These similarities ensure that reflecting on the variety of property institutions (or the diverse families of contracts, torts, or unjust enrichments) is likely to yield some useful cross-fertilization. They do not imply, however, the type of normative coherence needed to justify making membership in one of these wide areas of law a reason for any concrete prescriptive consequence.[13]

Accordingly, the pluralist conception of property as institutions takes the heterogeneity of our existing property doctrines seriously. It understands property as an umbrella for a limited and standardized set of property institutions, which serve as important default frameworks of interpersonal interaction. All these institutions mediate the relationship between owners and non-owners regarding a resource, and in all property institutions owners have some rights to exclude others. This common denominator derives from the role of property in vindicating people's independence. Alongside this important property value, however, other values also play crucial roles in shaping property institutions. As briefly indicated above, property can and does serve our commitments to personhood, desert, aggregate welfare, social responsibility, and distributive justice.[14] Different property institutions offer differing configurations of the entitlements constituting the contents of an owner's rights vis-à-vis others, or a certain type of others, with respect to a given resource. At least at its best, this plurality allows property law to vindicate differing balances among these property values according to their characteristic settings, namely, the type of social relationship in which they are situated and the nature of the resource at stake. While the cohabitation of different property values and divergent property institutions within property is contentious, property law—again, at its best—offers principled ways of accommodating this happy plurality.

[11] See Margaret J Radin, 'Property and Personhood' (1982) 34 *Stanford Law Review* 957, 992, 1013.

[12] See Hanoch Dagan, *Unjust Enrichment: A Study of Private Law and Public Values* (Cambridge University Press 1997) 40–9, 63–108.

[13] See n 4 and accompanying text.

[14] See Gregory S Alexander and Hanoch Dagan, *Properties of Property* (Aspen Publishers 2012) pt I.

Although from a monist viewpoint the heterogeneous landscape of property law looks like a random mess, it turns out to be a rich mosaic once a perspective of structural pluralism is applied. This mosaic is valuable, indeed indispensable, for people's autonomy.[15] The fee simple absolute, the property institution that is at the core for exclusion theorists, facilitates people's independence and is indeed crucial for liberal societies. But law's support for other property institutions is just as crucial for autonomy, which is precisely why the conception of property as institutions resists the way exclusion theory privileges this one property institution—the fee simple absolute—and suppresses the others as variations on a common theme, or marginalizes them as peripheral exceptions to a robust core. As Joseph Raz explains, autonomy understood as the ideal that people should, to some degree, be the authors of their own lives, requires not only appropriate mental capabilities and independence but also 'an adequate range of options'. For autonomy to be meaningful, there must be (other things being equal) 'more valuable options than can be chosen, and they must be significantly different', so that choices involve 'tradeoffs, which require relinquishing one good for the sake of another'. Thus, autonomy admits and indeed emphasizes 'the value of a large number of greatly differing pursuits among which individuals are free to choose'.[16]

Given the diversity of acceptable human goods from which autonomous people should be able to choose as well as their distinct constitutive values, the state must recognize a sufficiently diverse set of robust frameworks for people to organize their life. And because many of these plural values cannot be realistically actualized without the active support of viable legal institutions,[17] law should actively facilitate them. Hence, although the global coherence in monistic conceptions of broad private law fields such as property is appealing, law should adopt more than one set of coherent doctrines.[18] Accordingly, a structurally pluralist property law includes diverse types of institutions, each incorporating a different value or different balance of values. Boundaries between these institutions are open, enabling people to freely choose their goals, principles, forms of life, and associations by navigating their way among them. Only in this way can law recognize and promote the individuality-enhancing role of multiplicity.[19]

Implicit in this account is the twofold role of property institutions (and of the institutions of the other branches of their private law). These institutions consolidate people's expectations when, for example, entering a joint tenancy or a common-interest community, or, for that matter, using another person's copyrighted work. They may also perform an expressive and cultural function, affecting

[15] See Dagan, *Reconstructing American Legal Realism* (n 5) ch 8.

[16] See Joseph Raz, *The Morality of Freedom* (Oxford University Press 1986) 372, 381, 395, 398–9; cf Robert Nozick, *Anarchy, State, and Utopia* (Basic Books 1974) 309–12. The ideal of personal autonomy should be strictly distinguished from Kant's conception of personal independence. See Arthur Ripstein, *Force and Freedom: Kant's Legal and Political Philosophy* (Harvard University Press 2009) 14, 34, 45.

[17] See Hanoch Dagan, 'Inside Property' (2013) 63 *University of Toronto Law Journal* 1, 8–10.

[18] See Joseph Raz, 'The Relevance of Coherence' in *Ethics in the Public Domain: Essays in the Morality of Law and Politics* (Oxford University Press 1994) 261, 281–2, 291–304.

[19] See Raz, *Morality* (n 16) 417–18, 425.

people's ideals and consequently their preferences regarding these categories of relationships. Both roles require some measure of stability. To form effective frameworks of social interaction and cooperation, property law can recognize a necessarily limited number of categories of relationships and resources. This prescription of standardization, enshrined in property law as the *numerus clausus* principle, is particularly acute with regard to the expressive role. This role mandates limiting the number of property institutions because law can effectively express only so many ideal categories of interpersonal relationships.[20]

Moreover, our private law institutions do not supply merely an assortment of disconnected choices. Rather, they offer a repertoire that responds to various forms of valuable human interaction. Admittedly, regarding many private law institutions, law often falls short of the human ideals they represent. But these gaps only mean that, rather than searching for unifying normative accounts of property, contracts, torts, or unjust enrichment in their entirety, the main task of private law theory is twofold: first, to distil the distinct human ideals of the various private law institutions in order to elucidate the ways each of them contributes to human flourishing. And second, to offer reform, if needed, that would force these private law institutions to live up to their own implicit promises; and if these promises themselves turn out to be disappointing or, worse, unjust, or if the repertoire of private law institutions is not sufficiently diverse, to call, respectively, for amending these promises or adding institutions that can enrich its inventory.

The pluralist understanding of private law is thus inherently dynamic. While existing private law institutions are and should be the starting point of any analysis of private law questions, they are never frozen. Rather, as institutions structuring people's relationships, they are subject to ongoing—albeit properly cautious—re-evaluation and possible reconfiguration. The conservative baseline of this approach derives not only from the pragmatic reality that existing rules cannot be abandoned completely, but also from the recognition that existing law represents a cumulative judicial and legislative experience that deserves respect. In turn, the forward-looking perspective of this endeavour is premised on an understanding of law as a dynamic enterprise. Its content unfolds through challenges to the desirability of normative underpinnings in private law institutions; their responsiveness to their social context; their effectiveness in promoting their contextually examined, normative goals; and the sufficiency of the repertoire private law offers for any given type of activity. In this way, this understanding of private law follows the common law method described by Llewellyn as 'a functioning harmonization of vision with tradition, of continuity with growth, of machinery with purpose, of measure with need', mediating between 'the seeming commands of the authorities and the felt demands of justice'.[21]

At times, this process helps to fill gaps in the law by prescribing new rules that further bolster and vindicate these goals. At other times, it points out 'blemishes' in the existing doctrine, rules that undermine the most illuminating and defensible

[20] See Dagan, *Property* (n 4) 31–5.
[21] Karl N Llewellyn, *The Common Law Tradition* (Little Brown 1960) 37–8.

account of such a private law institution, which should be reformed so that an institution lives up to its own ideals.[22] This reformist potential has actually yielded different types of legal reforms throughout the history of property. In some cases, the reform is relatively radical—the abolition of a property form (as was the case with the fee tail form)[23] or an overall reconstruction of its content (as with leaseholds).[24] Sometimes more moderate options are in order, such as restating the doctrine pertaining to a property form in a way that brings its rules closer to its underlying commitments and, in the process, removing indefensible rules. The best recent example for such moderate reform is probably the transformation of the property form of servitudes, discussed in some detail below.

3. The Rule of Law as Guidance

Henry Smith has recently argued that this pluralist conception of property can hardly be distinguished from the bundle understanding of property. Accordingly, he has claimed, this conception irreparably undermines stability. Referring to my book *Property: Values and Institutions*, where I developed this conception of property, Smith argues that stability is not 'yet another detachable feature or lever to be dialled up or down' or 'a factor to be balanced whenever we are deciding on the supposedly separable sticks in the bundle', but is rather 'a feature that can only be evaluated as an aspect of the system'. And while it may be important for the system to serve 'values like community, autonomy, efficiency, personhood, labor, and distributive justice', we must reject '[t]he idea that doctrines are part of an issue-by-issue balancing of [these values]'. Smith's claims rely on the view that the only alternative to the exclusion school of property is 'to invoke a plethora of general principles to be balanced as specific situations present themselves'. And given that 'ad hocery itself is not a feature that can easily be dialed down', Smith concludes that nothing separates my account of property from the understanding of property as 'an ad hoc, unstructured bundle'.[25]

To understand Smith's critique of ad hocery, consider his defence of concepts in property. Concepts 'pick out categories' and thus serve as 'mental shortcuts', which are essential given 'people's cognitive limitations' 'for prediction, communication, and abstract thought'. Conceptualism, which he claims is rightly associated with formalism, is thus helpful precisely because of its 'relative indifference to context': 'To be useful, the concept has to pick out enough facts to serve the purpose in question but not so many that it entails too much complexity.' Smith argues that the objection of legal realists (like me) to defining exclusion 'as any baseline or starting point', which is reminiscent (in his view) of the realists' 'nominalistic

[22] See Ronald Dworkin, *Taking Rights Seriously* (Harvard University Press 1977) 118–23.

[23] See Dukeminier et al, *Property* (7th edn, Aspen Publishers 2010) 200–1.

[24] See generally Edward H Rabin, 'The Revolution in Residential Landlord–Tenant Law: Causes and Consequences' (1984) 69 *Cornell Law Review* 517.

[25] Henry E Smith, 'Property Is Not Just a Bundle of Rights' (2011) 8 *Econ Journal Watch* 279, 287; Henry E Smith, 'Property as the Law of Things' (2012) 125 *Harvard Law Review* 1691, 1705–6.

impulse', is misguided because it downplays and may undermine the important function of concepts 'in reducing information costs and building the overall architecture of property'. Thus, rejecting the exclusionary conception of property might replace rigidity with 'near-chaos'. Exclusion is 'the baseline for delineation purposes', not because it is 'the moral "core" of property' but rather because 'it is the general case, and governance is special'. Only the presumption of exclusion, Smith insists, can assure that we keep the bundles 'lumpy' and 'opaque', allow property to function as 'something more that high transaction costs prevent us from fully achieving by contract', and avoid 'hard-to-predict ripple effects through the entire system'.[26]

This critique of property pluralism, and hence of private law pluralism more generally, must be taken seriously. The conception of property as a formless bundle of sticks open to ad hoc judicial adjustments bears no resemblance to the law of property as lawyers know it or as citizens experience it. More generally, and more significantly for my purposes, if—as Smith contends—property (or private law) pluralism necessarily collapses into such unstable nominalism it necessarily undermines the rule of law.

Indeed, Smith's critique can be recast in terms of one of the most prominent understandings of the rule of law. In this view, associated mostly with Raz, the rule of law is organized around the idea that 'the law should be such that people will be able to be guided by it'; that law should 'provide effective guidance'.[27] While seemingly thin, the guidance conception of the rule of law, which is often broken up into lists of formal requirements,[28] is intimately connected with people's autonomy understood as self-authorship. By requiring that 'government in all its actions [be] bound by rules fixed and announced beforehand', the rule of law enables people 'to foresee with fair certainty how the authority will use its coercive power in given circumstances, and to plan [their] affairs on the basis of this knowledge'.[29] Only a relatively stable and predictable law can serve as a 'safe basis for individual planning', which is a prerequisite to people's ability to 'form definite expectations' and plan for the future. Law's participation in securing stable 'frameworks for one's life and action' increases '[p]redictability in one's environment', and therefore 'one's power of action', thus facilitating people's 'ability to

[26] Henry E Smith, 'On the Economy of Concepts in Property' (2012) 160 *University of Pennsylvania Law Review* 2097, 2100–2, 2105–6, 2113, 2116–17, 2123, 2128.

[27] Raz, 'Rule of Law and its Virtues' (n 2) 213, 218. Whereas the requirement of law's guidance is important because of law's coercive power, the emphasis here is not on limiting this power and thus its potential abuse, but rather on circumscribing its detrimental effects on people's self-authorship. This is also why the desirability of predictability to autonomy may be disputed in more benevolent authority settings, such as parenthood.

[28] See eg Lon L Fuller, *The Morality of Law* (rev edn, Yale University Press 1969) 39.

[29] FA Hayek, *The Road to Serfdom* (University of Chicago Press 1944) 54. To be sure, in general, Hayek's account of the rule of law is more amenable to the constraint conception. See TRS Allan, 'The Rule of Law as the Rule of Private Law' in this volume. Furthermore, relying on Hayek for the conception that founds the rule of law on our commitment to self-authorship is somewhat ironic. Hayek gives no significance to non-government factors, which can deprive people of control over their life in ways as debilitating as those implemented by governments; his views are also alien to the Razian notion that government is responsible for actively ensuring a range of choices.

choose styles and forms of life, to fix long-term goals and effectively direct one's life towards them'.[30]

The guidance conception of the rule of law is often associated with the idea that the rule of law is the law of rules.[31] According to this view, in order to 'provide maximally effective guides to behavior', the preferred form of the law must be that of 'a "rule," conceived as a clear prescription that exists prior to its application and that determines appropriate conduct or legal outcomes'.[32] Open-ended standards that allow judges to consult law's underlying commitments in each case jeopardize, so the argument goes, this virtue of 'the rule of rules': rules 'are designed to translate the implications of normative values into concrete prescriptions' and must therefore be 'sufficiently determinate' so as to be followed by their appliers 'without first resolving the very normative questions [they] are designed to settle' or 'considering whether the local outcome of the rule conforms to the values [they are] supposed to advance'.[33]

On its face, the 'normative dynamism' of the pluralist conception of private law threatens the rule of law as guidance. In line with the common law tradition, private law pluralism conceptualizes adjudication as 'a process that allows judges to remake the existing doctrinal propositions in the process of applying them'. But if rules 'are defeasible when direct application of their background rationales would generate a different result' then 'the constraint of the rule *qua* rule seems to disappear'. If normative commitments can always upset existing doctrinal propositions and require that they be discarded or modified, then these propositions seem to be no more than rules of thumb. As Frederick Schauer argues in criticizing the common law tradition, '[r]ules of this sort, capable of modification at the time of application and thus incapable of constraining that application, differ so much from our ordinary conception of rules as guides and constraints that it hardly pays to speak of them as rules at all.'[34]

I claim that, properly interpreted, private law pluralism conforms to the prescriptions of the guidance conception of the rule of law and also fits this conception's emphasis on rule-based decision-making insofar as this emphasis is indeed justified (which, as will be shown, it not always is). An example demonstrating many of the characteristics I find in private law pluralism will be helpful.

[30] Raz, *Authority* (n 2) 220, 222; see David Dyzenhaus, 'Liberty and Legal Form' in this volume.

[31] See Antonin Scalia, 'The Rule of Law as a Law of Rules' (1989) 56 *University of Chicago Law Review* 1175.

[32] Richard H Fallon Jr, '"The Rule of Law" as a Concept in Constitutional Discourse' (1997) 97 *Columbia Law Review* 1, 14–15.

[33] Emily Sherwin, 'Rule-Oriented Realism' (2005) 103 *Michigan Law Review* 1578, 1589, 1590, 1591. See generally Larry Alexander and Emily Sherwin, *The Rule of Rules* (Duke University Press 2001).

[34] Frederick Schauer, 'Is the Common Law Law?' (1989) 77 *California Law Review* 455, 455–6, 464, 467. To be sure, Schauer admits that 'rules of thumb are useful guides for prediction and useful to consult when time is short', but he insists that because rules of thumb can only indicate 'the result likely to be reached by the rationales or justifications lying behind the rule . . . they are intrinsically unweighty' (467).

Neponsit Property Owners' Ass'n v Emigrant Industrial Savings Bank[35] is the first major decision on the enforceability of the assessment covenant, whose validity at that time (1938) was in doubt.[36] This makes *Neponsit* a significant milestone in one of the most important developments of American land law in the last century: the emergence of common-interest communities, a property institution that by now is a major form of land ownership. My choice of this property institution and of this particular case are not fortuitous: no one can hope to provide a reasonable account of common-interest communities without considering governance, which is obscured in the exclusionary conception of property with its excessive focus on property's foreign affairs.[37] *Neponsit* is the landmark decision that enlisted servitudes law into facilitating the governance of this property institution.[38]

As Justice Lehman noted when delivering the decision of the New York Court of Appeals, Neponsit had unquestionably intended that the covenant should run with the land. The difficulties posed by this case were elsewhere, in the 'age-old essentials of a real covenant' set by 'ancient rules and precedents', according to which 'a covenant will run with the land and will be enforceable against a subsequent purchaser' only if it 'is one "touching" or "concerning" the land with which it runs', and if 'there is "privity of estate" between the promisee or party claiming the benefit of the covenant and the right to enforce it, and the promisor or party who rests under the burden of the covenant'.[39]

Does 'an affirmative covenant to pay money for use in connection with, but not upon, the land which it is said is subject to the burden of the covenant' indeed touch or concern the land? The 'touch and concern' test developed by old English cases is, says the court, 'too vague to be of much assistance' and, as such, leaves the enforceability question 'for the court to determine in the exercise of its best judgment upon the facts of each case'. The court mentioned that some prior cases may imply that only negative covenants 'which compel the covenanter to submit to some *restriction on the use* of his property, touch or concern the land' and, therefore, affirmative covenants do not run with the land. It also noted, however, the cases that, notwithstanding this seemingly bright line distinction, enforce 'promises to pay money... as covenants running with the land, against subsequent holders of the land who took with notice of the covenant'. Acknowledging the difficulty of classifying these exceptions or formulating 'a rigid test or definition which will be entirely satisfactory or which can be applied mechanically in all cases', the court moves on to state 'a reasonable method of approach' to such cases, namely: 'that a covenant which runs with the land must affect the legal relations—the advantages and the burdens—of the parties to the covenant as owners of particular parcels of land.' While the results of this test may still be 'a matter of degree', it is—the court insists—superior to the negative/affirmative

[35] 15 NE 2d 793 (NY 1938).

[36] See Dukeminier et al, *Property* (n 23) 872.

[37] To be sure, *Neponsit* (n 35) relied on the prior relaxation of the requirements for the enforcement of covenants in equity in cases such as *Tulk v Moxhay* (1848) 41 ER 1143.

[38] See generally Dagan, 'Inside Property' (n 17) 6–7.

[39] *Neponsit* (n 35) 795.

distinction because it does not 'exalt technical form over substance', and because it also accounts well for quite a few prior cases.[40]

Applying this test to the question at hand allows the court to conclude with a rather bright line rule regarding the specific issue of assessment covenants. While the payments at hand serve 'public purposes' upon land other than the land conveyed to a grantee's predecessors in title, through that conveyance grantees obtain 'not only title to particular lots, but an easement or right of common enjoyment with other property owners in roads, beaches, public parks or spaces and improvements in the same tract'. In order for the 'property owners of these easements or rights' to fully enjoy them in common, these public improvements 'must be maintained'. This happy outcome can be achieved only if the burden of paying this cost is 'inseparably attached to the land which enjoys the benefit'.[41]

The court had to pass yet another hurdle. Although '[v]arious definitions have been formulated of "privity of estate" in connection with covenants that run with the land... none of such definitions seems to cover the relationship' between a property owners' association, which 'has been organized to receive the sums payable by the property owners and to expend them for the benefit of such owners', and a subsequent purchaser. The *Neponsit* court alluded to the rather tortuous privity doctrine, but refused to have its analysis obscured by its technical details:

> Only blind adherence to an ancient formula devised to meet entirely different conditions could constrain the court to hold that a corporation formed as a medium for the enjoyment of common rights of property owners owns no property which would benefit by enforcement of common rights and has no cause of action in equity to enforce the covenant upon which such common rights depend.

Thus, the court held that a corporate plaintiff like Neponsit, which 'has been formed as a convenient instrument by which the property owners may advance their common interests', should be able to enforce the covenants at hand.[42]

Neponsit set bright line rules on the standing of property owners' associations and the validity of the assessment covenant. It also prescribed the standard articulating the regulative principle underlying the property form of covenants, thereby serving as the springboard for the development of common-interest communities, which are the fastest growing property institution in America. On both fronts, *Neponsit* demonstrates the happy cohabitation of private law pluralism and the guidance conception of the rule of law.

Consider first *Neponsit*'s bright line rules establishing the validity of assessment covenants and the standing of homeowners' associations,[43] which were (almost literally) necessary preconditions for the subsequent flowering of common-interest communities. This simple observation attests that, notwithstanding Smith's assertion to the contrary, a pluralist conception of property or of private law can, and

[40] *Neponsit* (n 35) 795–7. [41] *Neponsit* (n 35) 797. [42] *Neponsit* (n 35) 797–8.

[43] Later cases indeed show that *Neponsit* is standing for such rules. See eg *Riverton Cmty Ass'n v Myers*, 142 AD 2d 984, 985 (NY App Div 1992); *Lincolnshire Civic Ass'n v Beach*, 64 NYS 2d 248 (NY App Div 1975).

indeed should, distance itself from the dubious nominalist approach of case-by-case adjudication. Private law pluralism neither requires nor should it imply focusing on the equities of the particular case or the particular parties. By the same token, private law pluralism should not imply rule-sensitive particularism allowing judges to depart from rules whenever the outcome of a particular case so requires, while taking into account both substantive values and the value of preserving the rule's integrity.[44] Private law pluralism does not suggest replacing clear rules with open-ended discretionary decision-making. Instead, it stands for the proposition that reasoning about property rules should involve reasoning about the normatively appropriate character of the property institution at hand—given the social context of the relevant property institution and the nature of the resource at hand—and not about property (or contracts, torts, or unjust enrichment) writ large. Given that the number of property institutions is limited and the role of the property values in their regard is confined to a few deliberative moments, we need not assume that private law pluralism cannot, to a significant extent, be rule based.[45] More importantly, given the significance of stability and predictability in the institutions of private law to function in consolidating expectations and expressing ideals of interpersonal relationships,[46] private law pluralism is not only capable of setting bright line rules, but is in fact, if properly executed, inclined to do so.

Indeed, the identification of legal realism with nominalism, although prevalent,[47] is mistaken. While a small minority among realists does endorse the dubious ad hoc approach of case-by-case adjudication,[48] most realists take a very different position.[49] They realize that law's use of categories, concepts, and rules is unavoidable, even desirable,[50] and that many legal reasoners should in most cases simply follow rules, which is why realists indeed take pains to improve legal rules.[51] Thus, for example, the property values of autonomy, personhood, utility, labour, community, and distributive justice neither are nor should be invoked as reasons for particular outcomes of specific property cases, but rather as reasons for property rules or standards. Recognizing these values as the normative infrastructure of property law should advise *some* legal actors—notably, judges of

[44] See Sherwin, 'Rule-Oriented Realism' (n 33) 1591–4. Interestingly, Smith's conception of equity, discussed in his contribution to this volume, seems to follow this strategy which, as the text implies, tends to undermine the stability and predictability of any system of rules.

[45] Cf Michael Lobban, 'Legal Theory and Judge Made Law in England, 1850–1920' (2011) 40 *Quaderni Fiorentini* 553, 580; Jeremy Waldron, 'Stare Decisis and the Rule of Law: A Layered Approach' (2012) 111 *Michigan Law Review* 1. See also Larry Alexander and Emily Sherwin, 'Judges as Rule Makers' in Douglas E Edlin (ed), *Common Law Theory* (Cambridge University Press 2007) 27.

[46] See text accompanying n 20.

[47] See eg Dworkin, *Taking Rights Seriously* (n 22) 15–16; Morton Horwitz, *The Transformation of American Law, 1870–1960* (Harvard University Press 1992) 202.

[48] See eg Fred Rodell, *Woe Unto You, Lawyers!* (Reynal and Hitchcock 1939) 169–74, 201–2.

[49] See eg Andrew Altman, 'The Legacy of Legal Realism' (1986) 10 *Legal Studies Forum* 167, 171–2.

[50] See eg Llewellyn, 'A Realistic Jurisprudence' (n 7) 27, Walter Wheeler Cook, 'Scientific Method and the Law' in William W Fisher III et al (eds), *American Legal Realism* (Oxford University Press 1995) 242, 246.

[51] Karl Llewellyn, the most important legal realist, was of course the principal draftsman of article 2 of the Uniform Commercial Code.

appellate courts—to *occasionally* use new cases as triggers for an ongoing refinement of the doctrine and as opportunities for both revisiting the normative viability of existing rules qua rules and re-examining the adequacy of the legal categorization that organizes these rules. In fact, much of *Property: Values and Institutions* is similarly devoted to the identification of property rules that best promote the property values underlying the property institutions to which they belong.

Besides prescribing rules regarding the validity of assessment covenants and the standing of homeowners' associations, *Neponsit* significantly transformed the doctrinal analysis of covenants more generally. Although not formally overruling the complex requirements of touch and concern and of privity, *Neponsit* criticized the technical niceties of these doctrines. It pointed out that, even where they took the form of a rule (as in the affirmative/negative covenants distinction) courts have tended to use such a rule merely as a rule of thumb, arguably because of its undue detachment from any reasonable understanding of the regulative principle that should guide this area of the law. Thereby, *Neponsit* paved the way for the substitution of the old (vague) tests of touch and concern and of privity with more substantive elements focusing on the role of covenants in the landowners' endeavour to pre-regulate their relationships qua landowners—or, more precisely, in their capacity[52] as participants in the property institution of common-interest communities—so as to facilitate their common enjoyment of certain public improvements and advance their common interests. Both the critical and the reconstructive sides of this part of *Neponsit* are relevant for my purposes.

In criticizing the pre-existing doctrinal rules, the court reminds us that, at times, a complex set of rules may fail to adequately serve as a guide for action. Regulating a wide range of conduct is complex, and technical non-intuitive complexity may undermine the guidance value of rules.[53] In such circumstances (and *Neponsit*'s reconstructive side comes into play here), vague standards may be needed, such as *Neponsit*'s focus on the role of covenants in facilitating landowners' ability to enjoy the potential benefits of common-interest communities. Even though such standards do not provide bright line instructions, they may still guide people's actions. As Jeremy Waldron claims, although complying with such a vague standard 'may be more onerous than' complying with a bright line rule, a standard can still be action-guiding, channelling and directing people's behaviour. People aware of this kind of standard (or their lawyers who are actually the active players at the relevant moments of common-interest community formation) can '[t]ake it on board', make for themselves 'the evaluative judgment that the norm requires', and thus monitor and modify their behaviour accordingly.[54]

[52] See Christopher Essert, 'The Office of Ownership' (2013) 63 *University of Toronto Law Journal* 1.

[53] See Richard A Posner, *The Problems of Jurisprudence* (Harvard University Press 1990) 48; Timothy Endicott, 'The Value of Vagueness' in Andrei Marmor and Scott Soames (eds), *Philosophical Foundations of Language in the Law* (Oxford University Press 2011) 14, 23, 28, 30.

[54] See Jeremy Waldron, 'Vagueness and the Guidance of Action' in *Language in the Law* (n 53) 58, 65–6, 69.

This conceptualization of standards as appeals to people's practical reasoning also sheds light on the types of issues wherein standards can be particularly guidance-friendly, as well as on the kind of legal reasoning that can accentuate the guidance potential of standards. It explains the truism that, given normative consensus on the pertinent issue, one may expect broad agreement regarding the application of a standard, and thus expect it to be particularly helpful as a guide.[55] Furthermore, in cases lacking such social agreement, the guidance capacity of standards as appeals to people's practical reasoning can rely on the significance of judicial reasoning in the common law tradition. Because 'the justification of a common law rule is as important as the norm itself',[56] refining the justification of a norm (or, for my purposes, explaining the role of a regulative principle in promoting the social ideal underlying its private law institution) helps its addressees figure out its intended content and realm of application. Finally, in addition to the benefits these vague standards can provide 'as is', they can, and usually do, create over time more bright line rules to implement their prescriptions.[57]

Both of these aspects are at work regarding property institutions generally and the *Neponsit* doctrine more particularly. To see why, recall that by structuring property as a limited number of identifiable and standardized forms and dividing the other fields of private law along similar lines,[58] private law facilitates stable categories of human interaction.[59] Unlike the broad and heterogeneous private law fields to which they belong, each of these private law institutions is internally coherent, meaning it is more or less guided by one regulative principle, one value or balance of values. Thus, given social consensus as to this regulative principle, or even without it but with the law clarifying (in constitutive cases such as *Neponsit*) what this regulative principle is and making it sufficiently stable (meaning it is not revisited so frequently as to make law incapable of guiding behaviour), legal subjects or their lawyers are likely to be aware of the 'character' of an institution and form their expectations accordingly.[60] (Recall that 'the rule of law does not require that law's guidance never change. It requires that the prospect of change should not make it impossible to use the existing law as a guide.'[61])

Therefore, insofar as private law cannot use only bright line rules but must also rely on vague standards, using the various private law institutions as its building blocks seems optimal from a guidance perspective. This comforting conclusion is

[55] See Fuller, *Morality* (n 28) at 50, 92; Fallon, '"The Rule of Law" as a Concept' (n 32) 49–50; John Gardner, 'Rationality and the Rule of Law in Offences against the Person' (1994) 53 *Cambridge Law Journal* 502, 513, 515–17.

[56] Douglas E Edlin, 'Introduction' in Douglas E Edlin (ed), *Common Law Theory* (Cambridge University Press 2007) 1, 3.

[57] See Carol M Rose, 'Crystals and Mud in Property Law' (1988) 40 *Stanford Law Review* 577.

[58] See eg Roy Kreitner, 'Multiplicity in Contract Remedies' in Nili Cohen and Ewan McKendrick (eds), *Comparative Remedies For Breach of Contracts* (Hart Publishing 2005) 19, 19–20, 38.

[59] See text accompanying n 20.

[60] This does not mean, of course, that such guidance is always effective. Thus, even the New York Court of Appeals failed at times to rely on and properly apply *Neponsit*'s reformulation of the regulative principle of covenant law. See eg *Eagle Enters v Gross*, 349 NE 2d 816 (NY 1976).

[61] Timothy AO Endicott, 'The Impossibility of the Rule of Law' in *Vagueness in Law* (Oxford University Press 2000) 185, 193; see also eg Gardner, *Law as a Leap of Faith* (n 2) 41.

particularly valid by comparison to the alternative that private law monism presents of resorting to the principles underlying property, contracts, torts, or unjust enrichment, which—given the heterogeneity of these fields[62]—are inevitably thin, and thus hardly informative.[63]

My claims regarding the guidance potential of private law pluralism that, as I mentioned in Section 1, are inspired by legal realism, are ostensibly threatened by the legal realist critique of doctrinal determinacy.[64] Legal realists argued that the irreducible choice among the many potentially applicable doctrinal sources competing to control any given case, all of which can be expanded, contracted, or variously interpreted or elaborated, means that legal doctrine is always open to multiple readings.[65] Unlike their image in some caricatures of legal realism, however, most realists did not challenge the predictability of legal doctrine. While insisting that legal doctrine qua doctrine cannot constrain decision-makers, they recognized that the convergence of lawyers' background understandings at a given time and place generates a significant measure of stability.[66] Thus, rather than threatening the compatibility of private law pluralism with the guidance conception of the rule of law, legal realism merely insists that such guidance does not inhere in the doctrine as such and rests instead on the broader social practice of law.[67] In the present case, guidance rests on the prevalent understanding of the private law institution's character, which reflects the regulative principle governing its constitutive rules.

Llewellyn thus argued that, although adjudication is necessarily creative, it is invariably constrained by legal tradition. Cases are decided with 'a desire to move in accordance with the material as well as within it . . . to reveal the latent rather than to impose new form, much less to obtrude an outside will'. The case law *system* imposes 'a demand for moderate consistency, for reasonable regularity, for on-going conscientious effort at integration'. The instant outcome and rule must 'fit the flavor of the whole'; it must, as we have seen in *Neponsit*, 'think with the feel of the body of our law' and 'go with the grain rather than across or against it'. Legal realists

62 Smith acknowledges that '[o]ptimal concepts [. . .] have a medium level of generality' (Smith, 'Concepts in Property' (n 26) 2105), but nothing in his critique supports the assertion that the correct level of abstraction in private law is that of such broad and heterogeneous legal fields.

63 Thus, as Felix Cohen argued, whereas every property right involves *some* power to exclude others from doing something, this is a rather modest truism, which hardly yields any practical implications. Private property is also always subject to limitations and obligations, and 'the real problems we have to deal with are problems of degree, problems too infinitely intricate for simple panacea solutions.' Felix S Cohen, 'Dialogue on Private Property' (1954) 9 *Rutgers Law Review* 357, 362, 370–4, 379.

64 See Lisa M Austin, 'Pluralism, Context and the Internal Life of Property: A Response to Hanoch Dagan' (2013) 63 *University of Toronto Law Journal* 22.

65 See Dagan, *Reconstructing American Legal Realism* (n 5) 18–22.

66 Dagan, *Reconstructing American Legal Realism* (n 5) 26; see also eg Alexander and Sherwin, *The Rule of Rules* (n 33) 32–4.

67 See Frederick Schauer, 'Editor's Introduction' in Karl N Llewellyn, *The Theory of Rules*, ed Frederick Schauer (University of Chicago Press 2011) 1, 5, 7–8, 18, 20–4, Fallon, '"The Rule of Law" as a Concept' (n 32) 16–17; Margaret Jane Radin, 'Reconsidering the Rule of Law' (1989) 69 *Boston University Law Review* 781, 803.

begin with the existing doctrinal landscape because it may and often does incorporate valuable normative choices, even if implicit and sometimes imperfectly executed. They nonetheless recognize that the existing legal environment always leaves interpretive leeway. Furthermore, they believe that law's potential dynamism, as long as properly cautious and not too frequent, is laudable because it represents our perennial quest 'for better and best law' and, therefore, our judges' 'duty to justice and adjustment', thus implying an 'on-going production and improvement of rules'.[68]

4. The Rule of Law as Constraint

However fortunate this conclusion may appear to be in terms of guidance, it seems to be alarming in terms of another understanding of the rule of law. The conception of the rule of law discussed so far has focused on the subjects of law and their guidance, whereas henceforth it will focus on the government.[69]

Consider the notion that the rule of law is the flip side of the rule of man. While its literal interpretation, as Albert Ven Dicey put it, is 'absurd' because '[p]olitical institutions . . . are made what they are by human voluntary agency', a more substantive understanding of this contrast implies that the rule of law stands for 'the absence of arbitrary power on part of the government'.[70] This characterization explains EP Thompson's spirited claim that the rule of law is 'an unqualified human good' since it represents 'the imposing of effective inhibitions upon power and the defense of the citizen from power's all-intrusive claims'.[71] Unrestrained power is frightening because of its potential devastating impositions; even more fundamentally, unrestrained power renders us mere objects, dominated by the power-wielder.[72] The conception of the rule of law as constraint seeks to address these grave concerns.

As Waldron explains, the rule of law in this conception stands for an 'aspirational idea', wherein law must purport to be guided by 'justice and the common good that transcend the self-interest of the powerful'. Its main mission, therefore, is 'to correct abuses of power',[73] and to 'take the edge off human political power, making it less objectionable, less dangerous, more benign and more respectful'.[74] Accordingly,

[68] Llewellyn, *The Common Law Tradition* (n 21) 36, 38, 190–1, 217, 222–3; Karl N Llewellyn, 'The Normative, the Legal, and the Law-Jobs: The Problem of Juristic Method' (1940) 49 *Yale Law Journal* 1355, 1385.

[69] This focus on the government, to be sure, is important because it affects people.

[70] V Dicey, *Introduction to the Study of the Law of the Constitution* (10th edn, Macmillan and Company 1959) 188, 196.

[71] EP Thompson, *Whigs and Hunters: The Origin of the Black Act* (Pantheon Books 1975) 266; Gardner, *Law as a Leap of Faith* (n 2) 213. But cf Raz, 'The Rule of Law and its Virtues' (n 2) 219 ('Many forms of arbitrary power are compatible with the rule of law.').

[72] See Krygier, 'Four Puzzles' (n 1) 79–80. Parenthetically, note that the conception of the rule of law as constraint is thicker than that of the rule of law as guidance, but serves a thinner understanding of individual autonomy.

[73] RR 1, 11, 32.

[74] Jeremy Waldron, 'Is the Rule of Law an Essentially Contested Concept (in Florida)?' (2002) 21 *Law and Philosophy* 137, 159.

the rule of law as constraint requires 'a particular mode of the exercise of political power: governance through law'. It thus maintains that 'people in positions of authority should exercise their power within a constraining framework of public norms, rather than on the basis of their own preferences, their own ideology, or their own individual sense of right and wrong'.[75]

In a sense, insofar as private law pluralism follows the guidance conception of the rule of law it also addresses the concerns of unconstrained judicial power, because the requirement to identify and articulate a general norm imparts *some* element of impersonality.[76] But is this an adequate answer to the challenge at hand? Consider the possibility of allowing property doctrines to rest on the pertinent property values (liberty, personhood, labour, well-being, community, and distributive justice) without a predetermined formula for measuring and balancing these values.[77] Would not such an option entail unbridled judicial discretion, inviting these unaccountable officials to apply their subjective (or self-serving) normative preferences?[78]

To appreciate this challenge, consider Duncan Kennedy's account of 'the experience of legal reasoning as an activity pursued in a medium that is at once plastic and resistant'. Somewhat along the lines of my claim regarding the conventional rather than doctrinal underpinnings of the guidance function of private law pluralism,[79] Kennedy argues that an interpreter of legal materials 'works to create or to undo determinacy, rather than simply registering or experiencing it as a given'. Rather than being '"qualities" or "attributes" inherent in the norm', this argument continues, determinacy or indeterminacy are effects 'produced contingently by the interaction of the interpreter's time, energy, and skill with an... "essential" nature of the rule [at hand]'. And therefore, Kennedy concludes, 'we predict a result *because we anticipate that no work will be done to destabilize the initial apprehension*'.[80]

Some may find this account an affront to the rule of law, posing 'the specter of the usurpation of power by an unaccountable elite', misrepresenting political decisions 'as if they were matters of law', and thus making 'the rule of law ideal... a fraud'.[81] Kennedy's response to this worry is that 'juristic work intended to inflect

[75] Waldron, 'Is the Rule of Law an Essentially Contested Concept' (n 74) 6, 31; see also eg Krygier, 'Four Puzzles' (n 1) 75–6, 78, 82, 88.

[76] See Waldron, 'Stare Decisis' (n 45) section 3; cf William Lucy, 'Abstraction and the Rule of Law' (2009) 29 *Oxford Journal of Legal Studies* 481.

[77] Notice that in these (not too many) deliberative moments in which judges rethink the regulative principles of a private law institution, they do not (and should not) solely rely on conventional morality, and thus cannot (solely) rely on prevalent social conventions.

[78] See Austin, 'Pluralism, Context and the Internal Life' (n 64).

[79] See text accompanying nn 65–7.

[80] Duncan Kennedy, *Legal Reasoning: Collected Essays* (The Davies Group Publishers 2007) 3, 159–61, 167.

[81] Brian Z Tamahana, *On the Rule of Law: History, Politics, Theory* (Cambridge University Press 2004) 125; Brian Z Tamahana, 'How an Instrumental View of Law Corrodes the Rule of Law' (2006) 56 *DePaul Law Review* 469, 493; see also eg Robert H Bork, *The Tempting of America* (Free Press 1990) 4–5; Martti Konskenniemi, 'Constitutionalism as Mindset: Reflections on Kantian Themes About International Law and Globalization' (2007) 8 *Theoretical Inquiries in Law* 9, 25.

the law in the judge's (or jurist's) preferred ideological direction' is legitimate.[82] But this defence seems far from comforting. We need not object to such 'judicial activism', Kennedy argues, because we should not expect that the notion of obedience or fidelity to law might help jurists to decide whether to employ 'ideologically oriented work strategies' to transform, or at least destabilize, 'initial apprehensions of what the materials require'. To think otherwise is to adhere to a 'fetishized or reified belief in the rule of law', rather than to maturely realize that the jurist's 'role constraint is no more than "do your best under all the circumstances to do something politically good"'.[83]

The anxieties that friends of the rule of law as constraint experience in light of statements that collapse law into politics inform many critiques of judge-made law and thus of the common law tradition.[84] These concerns cannot be easily dismissed even by those (like myself) who agree with Kennedy that law, like politics, cannot avoid addressing normative commitments and furthermore do not deny that politics, like law, must rely on the aspiration to constrain decision-makers' power. The reason for this is that the appropriate modes of constraining power in these two realms are different: 'participatory politics is . . . situated between the realm of the market (that focuses on preferences) and that of the law (that must always strive for public-regarding justification)', so that in politics—even in its ideal form—'neither convictions nor preferences should be excluded'.[85]

Taking the critical legal studies' critique of the rule of law seriously,[86] Ernest Weinrib, who is a friend of common law, proposes a radical but seemingly attractive understanding of private law purporting to be an adequate response to the challenge of preserving the distinction between law and politics.[87] Weinrib's account builds on a particularly demanding reading of the rule of law as constraint: Aristotle's claim that the rule of law is 'differentiated from the rule of men' by being 'the embodiment of intelligence without appetite'. In order to 'sustain the possibility' of this injunction, Weinrib argues, law must not be 'subservient to external ideals'; it must be 'conceptually sealed off from the interplay of extrinsic purposes'. Rather than promoting purposes such as the plural values that inform private law pluralism, the rule of law rests on the view that law 'constitutes, as it were, its own ideal, intelligible from within and capable of serving as [a] constraint upon the radical idealisms which postulate its depreciation'.

Private law, Weinrib claims, especially in the common law tradition, 'makes a show of [such] a self-contained rationality'. This is the case because the 'adjudicator

[82] Kennedy, *Legal Reasoning* (n 80) 163.

[83] Kennedy, *Legal Reasoning* (n 80) 6–8, 165, 168.

[84] See respectively Waldron, 'Rule of Law as Essentially Contested Concept' (n 74) 142–3, Frederick Schauer, 'The Failure of the Common Law' (2004) 36 *Arizona State Law Journal* 765, 781–2.

[85] Hanoch Dagan, 'Political Money' (2009) 8 *Election Law Journal* 349, 356.

[86] Ernest J Weinrib, 'Legal Formalism: On the Immanent Rationality of Law' (1988) 97 *Yale Law Journal* 949, 1015–16.

[87] Weinrib, 'Intelligibility of the Rule of Law' (n 2) 60, 63, 70–1, 78, 80–1, 83.

in a private law dispute [must] follow through and give specificity to the order implicit in the nature of the transactions, and his reasons for judgment are the public announcement of the intimations of this order in the context of a particular occurrence'. This is the case because, by being 'presented with two parties only, a plaintiff and a defendant', the court is 'structurally cut off from consideration of overall welfare' and is strictly confined to 'the litigants' assertions of right[s] arising out of particular courses of dealings'. In this way, '[t]he structural features of the form of corrective justice place it conceptually beyond the reach of political determination', thereby rendering 'law intelligible as its own end', and justifying 'the common law's self-understanding of the adjudicative process which regards the judge's decision not as the exercise of political choice but as an act of cognition'.

Weinrib's claim that the rule of law requires private law to adhere to corrective justice and exclude any collective or public values from our understanding of property (or of its sister private law doctrines) is, if successful, devastating to private law pluralism.[88] Fortunately, it is not. The main reason for its lack of success,[89] which I have discussed at some length elsewhere[90] and can only address briefly here, is anticipated by Weinrib himself when he notes that the integrity of this position 'depends upon whether [corrective justice is indeed] immune to the projection on to [it] of extrinsic purposes'.[91]

Weinrib illuminates the unique justificatory burden generated by the bipolar structure of private law litigation: private law is structured as a drama between plaintiff and defendant and must therefore require correlativity between the defendant's liability and the plaintiff's entitlement. But Weinrib's more ambitious claim (and the one that is relevant here) concerning private law's airtight insulation from collective values does not stand. Although private law is not just one of many strategies of regulation, it neither is nor can be dissociated from our social values. Quite the contrary, in order for the correlativity enquiry to even begin, and indeed be intelligible, we need to determine the content of the parties' rights, a determination that necessarily invokes our public values.[92] To be sure, not every value can

[88] Weinrib's thesis threatens, of course, not only private law pluralism, but also most (if not all) of the competing monistic conceptions of private law.

[89] Another significant shortfall of Weinrib's conception of the rule of law is that it does not properly address the significance of the prospective effects of every significant legal pronouncement, which must imply that judges should be able to justify their decisions to those who will be subject to them even if they are not participating in the judicial drama at hand. See Hanoch Dagan, 'Law as an Academic Discipline' in Shauna Van Praagh and Helge Dedek (eds), *Stateless Law* (Ashgate Publishing 2014).

[90] Hanoch Dagan, 'The Distributive Foundation of Corrective Justice' (1999) 98 *Michigan Law Review* 138; See Dagan, *Reconstructing American Legal Realism* (n 5) ch 5; Dagan, *Property* (n 4) 58–60, 63–6. The next two paragraphs draw on these sources.

[91] Weinrib, 'Intelligibility of the Rule of Law' (n 2) 75.

[92] Weinrib denies, of course, any reliance on such public values and derives his thesis of private law autonomy from the correlativity requirement by relying on the idea of property. Property, in his view, serves as a benchmark requiring no reference to collective values: while voluntary changes in the distribution of property cannot generate any legitimate grievance, involuntary changes both justify owners' complaints and specify the appropriate remedial response. See eg Ernest J Weinrib, 'Restitutionary Damages as Corrective Justice' (1999) 1 *Theoretical Inquiries in Law* 1, 6–7, 12, 24. But for property to serve as such a safe haven for private law autonomy, Weinrib must defend a conception of property that is securely detached from social values. Weinrib faces this challenge by advancing a regime in which the state functions both as a guarantor of people's robust property rights against one

qualify for the task. By and large, only values that participate in the regulative principle that underlies the private law institution at issue, meaning only values that inform our ideal vision of the interpersonal relationship at hand, can legitimately be taken into account. The implication is that the values underlying private law are not identical to those guiding public law, that not only one set of values underlies private law (or any one of its broad fields) in its entirety, and that in most cases these values are not to be directly engaged by judges deciding specific cases. At the same time, the implication is also that private law is deeply affected by our public values, so that corrective justice cannot render private law intelligible from within, sealed off from our social ideals.

Indeed, the pivotal role of private law in defining our mutual legitimate claims and expectations in our daily interactions undermines the legitimacy of a private law regime that ignores these values. The parties' *ex ante* entitlements, from which correlativity must be measured, are best analysed by reference to our social values. Rather than being divorced or abstracted from our social values, private law both reflects these values and at times even participates in their formation.

The fact that Weinrib's strategy is not a panacea able to set aside the concerns of the rule of law as constraint is insufficient to redeem private law pluralism, as it merely reinstates the challenge of constraint. There seem to be two aspects to this challenge: one from legitimacy and the other from determinacy.[93]

The sheer fact that judges, unlike legislators, are often unelected ostensibly suffices to condemn their significant impact on private law as illegitimate application of power. But the question of legitimacy should be examined in more nuanced and comparative terms.[94] To determine the proper domain of judicial creation and

another, and as the authority responsible for levying taxes in order to fulfil a public duty to support the poor so as to secure everyone's independence. Strong property rights and a viable welfare state, so the argument goes, cluster as a matter of conceptual necessity. See Ernest J Weinrib, 'Poverty and Property in Kant's System of Rights' in *Corrective Justice* (Oxford University Press 2012) 263. But such a strict division of labour between a libertarian private law and a robust welfare state wherein the threat of dependence is universally alleviated is quite implausible. As I show elsewhere (Dagan, *Property* (n 4) 63–6), the public law of tax and redistribution is unlikely to supplement private law with rules adequately remedying the injustices of a libertarian private law, if not in terms of distribution at least in terms of interpersonal dependence. The reason for this is threefold. *First*, the realities of interest group politics in the promulgation of tax legislation render egalitarian tax regimes, such as one based on Rawls's difference principle, a matter of political theory rather than of empirical reality. This difficulty is intrinsic to the concept of democracy, which respects people's preferences and not only their principles. *Furthermore*, because our understandings of the responsibilities of owners and the limits of what we perceive to be their legitimate interests are influenced by our legal conception of ownership, an extreme libertarian private law regime might undermine social solidarity and dilute people's responsiveness to claims from distributive justice. *Finally*, treating the propertyless as passive recipients of welfare and mere beneficiaries of the public duty to support the poor entrenches their dependent, subservient status rather than their dignity and independence. Shifting dependence from the context of private law to that of the individual's relationship with the state via the welfare bureaucracy does not solve the problem and, indeed, might actually exacerbate it.

93 Both aspects are raised by Austin, 'Pluralism, Context and the Internal Life' (n 64).

94 My discussion of legitimacy draws on Hanoch Dagan, 'Judges and Property' in Shyamkrishna Balganesh (ed), *Intellectual Property and the Common Law* (Cambridge University Press 2013) 17; see Gardner, *Law as a Leap of Faith* (n 2) 200–1; Scott J Shapiro, *Legality* (Belknap Press of Harvard University Press 2011) 331, 358.

modification of private law institutions, if any, we need to examine potential bases for the legitimacy of judicial rulemaking in private law matters. Though I could not possibly hope to provide an adequate account of legitimacy in a liberal democracy here, the following remarks should suffice to support the claim that the legitimate scope of judicial rulemaking in private law is in fact rather broad.[95]

Consider first the notion that state power can be legitimate only if it is a product of its citizens' co-authorship. To be meaningful, the ideal of co-authoring the normative commitments that serve as the foundation of our private law entitlements must not be axiomatically attached solely to the legislative process.[96] Rather, a commitment to co-authorship requires a comparative account of real participation and deliberation in legislation and in adjudication. This account can look at the participation of the citizens (directly or via elected representatives) or focus on the participation of the subset of citizens who are likely to be affected by the private law development at hand.

In general, participation and deliberation will more likely be found in legislation than in adjudication because law-making is legislation's only task, whereas in adjudication it emerges as part of the resolution of discrete disputes.[97] But the broad or representative participation that might significantly foster collective co-authorship does not seem typical of legislation on many private law matters. Take (again) property: some property doctrines, such as the law of common-interest communities, may seem too mundane as a subject for robust public deliberation.[98] By contrast, when the creation or modification of property institutions provides significant opportunities for rent seeking, as in the repeated extensions of the term and scope of copyright, the legislative process tends to be dominated by interest groups promoting narrow distributive goals,[99] and thus cannot meaningfully count as collective co-authorship.

The ideal of participation by parties affected by the proposed development of private law is a more realistic expectation. But insofar as this participatory ideal is concerned, adjudication fares quite well and, in some contexts, probably better than legislation. The adjudicatory adversarial process fares well because it invites disagreements on questions of facts, opinion, and law. It thereby creates a forum where the judges' normative and empirical horizons are constantly challenged by the conflicting perspectives of the participating parties, which present a microcosm

[95] Note that I do not make a claim for judicial supremacy, as in judicial review. My sole focus is on the legitimacy of judicial rulemaking where legislatures are silent.

[96] Even if one insists that such an axiom is justified in the discussion of democracy-based legitimacy, it is out of place in the discussion of legitimacy in a democracy. The latter, broader type of legitimacy that concerns me here accommodates differing types of citizens' participation and of decision-makers' accountability.

[97] Another reason relates to comparative costs: voters 'often face a far less expensive road [than litigants] to registering their needs . . . in the political process' (Neil K Komesar, *Imperfect Alternatives: Choosing Institutions in Law, Economics, and Public Policy* (University of Chicago Press 1991) 127).

[98] To pre-empt a possible objection, I may add that the notion that judicial passivity can upset the marginality of these topics within our public discourse does not seem particularly plausible.

[99] See generally Jessica Litman, *Digital Copyright* (Prometheus Books 2001).

of the social dilemma at hand.[100] Moreover, as Neil Komesar shows regarding tort law, adjudication sometimes provides a qualitatively better forum for the participation of affected parties. One instance is cases showing sharp 'distinction between *ex ante* and *ex post* stakes', so that the low *ex ante* probability of harm may obscure an important perspective rendered vivid in the *ex post* litigation triggered by the unfortunate realization of such harm.[101] Certain developments of property institutions, such as marital property, cohabitation, and leaseholds, by the judiciary may also fit well into this category.

But legitimacy should perhaps require only decision-makers' accountability rather than citizens' participation. Accountability is a more modest standard: it does not require active participation or deliberation but merely insists that decision-makers be responsive to citizens' values and preferences. As with participation, the accountability requirement may in the abstract appear as a trump in favour of elected legislators vis-à-vis unelected judges, given that re-election is a rather potent guarantee of responsiveness. But my previous observations regarding skewed participation in private law matters detrimentally affect legislators' responsiveness as well. If many private law matters are either politically marginal or dominated by interest groups, the legislators' expected responsiveness is likely to be rather limited. Likewise, an outright dismissal of judges' responsiveness seems exaggerated. As Llewellyn insisted, in their opinions judges need to 'account to the public, to the general law-consumer' on a regular basis and in detail. They must persuade not only their brethren but also the legal community 'that outcome, underpinning, and workmanship are worthy' and that their judgment was formed 'in terms of the Whole, *seen whole*'.[102] While real life adjudication falls short of these ideals, having these standards in place is nonetheless significant because it affects judges' utility function and thus informs judicial behaviour, as even the tough-minded portrayals of judges as maximizers of their utility function admit.[103]

Even if judges can legitimately affect our private law, is granting judges the power to apply a rather diverse set of collective values not tantamount to inviting them to apply subjective and thus illegitimate unbounded discretion? I do not think so. Different types of human interactions and, consequently, different categories of private law doctrines, call for different balances of the (indeed limited number of) values relevant to any given private law institution. Here, as elsewhere, the requirement to explicitly apply judgment, which needs to be normatively and contextually justified, is a real constraint.[104] In some categories of cases, this enquiry might

[100] See Dagan, *Reconstructing American Legal Realism* (n 5) 51–3; Matthew Steilen, 'The Democratic Common Law' (2011) *The Journal Jurisprudence* 437.

[101] See Komesar, *Imperfect Alternatives* (n 97) 135–6.

[102] Llewellyn, 'The Common Law Tradition' (n 21) 48, 132; Llewellyn, 'American Common Law Tradition and American Democracy' in *Jurisprudence* (n 7) 282, 309–10.

[103] See Richard A Posner, *How Judges Think* (Harvard University Press 2008) 11–12, 60–1, 371; Lawrence Baum, *Judges and their Audiences: A Perspective on Judicial Behavior* (Princeton University Press 2006) 16–21, 90, 106; Frederick Schauer, 'Incentives, Reputation, and the Inglorious Determinants of Judicial Behavior' (2000) 68 *University of Cincinnati Law Review* 615, 615–17, 619–21.

[104] See eg Michael Martin, *Legal Realism: American and Scandinavian* (P Lang 1997) 39–40, 76; Joseph William Singer, 'Normative Methods for Lawyers' (2009) 56 *UCLA Law Review* 899.

indeed lead to a standoff. The relevant question, however, is not whether such cases are possible. The sheer existence of hard cases scarcely undermines the determinacy or the integrity of our private law, especially given that purely doctrinal reasoning, the main alternative to openly normative legal reasoning, is hopelessly malleable and thus indeterminate.[105] Rather, the question is whether cases of contextual-normative deadlock are prevalent enough so that they threaten a conception of private law premised on these guidelines, that is, whether we are indeed unable to use reason as the arbiter for identifying the most normatively desirable regulative principle of the private law institution at hand. As I attempted to demonstrate in my books on property and on restitution,[106] a sufficiently robust contextual normative account can often have quite sharp doctrinal teeth. Although some of my analyses may be controversial, they can hardly be challenged by the sheer difficulty of measuring or balancing the private law values I employ or by the possibility that there are other pertinent values. To challenge my approach, a detailed demonstration of the superiority of a competing account is needed.[107] Furthermore, recall that private law pluralism is committed to provide a rich variety of institutions both between and within social contexts, so that people who want, for example, to become homeowners, engage in business, or enter into intimate relationships have more than one option. Thus, private law pluralism 'allows individuals to navigate their course so that they bypass certain legal prescriptions',[108] which means that judicial errors are less worrisome than they are in a monist private law regime.

Let me again take an example, then, from the law of common-interest communities. My example this time deals with another constitutive characteristic of this property institution, which is improperly marginalized in the exclusionary conception of property: inclusion. Since the landmark case of *Shelley v Kraemer* held that judicial enforcement of racially restrictive covenants is an exercise of state action that violates the Fourteenth Amendment,[109] some rights to entry in defiance of the property owners' will have become inherent in a significant segment of housing law in America. With the enactment of the Fair Housing Act,[110] discrimination in the sale or rental of residential dwellings on the basis of race, colour, religion, sex, familial status, national origin, or handicap is indeed currently prohibited.

Given its constitutional origin, the right to fair housing is usually analysed as an external qualification of the owner's exclusionary prerogative,[111] rather than as an internal entailment of the meaning of the right to property in common-interest

[105] See text accompanying n 65.

[106] See Dagan, *Property* (n 4), Hanoch Dagan, *The Law and Ethics of Restitution* (Cambridge University Press 2004).

[107] Cf Ronald Dworkin, *Law's Empire* (Belknap Press 1986) 76–86.

[108] See Dagan, *Reconstructing American Legal Realism* (n 5) 176.

[109] *Shelley v Kraemer*, 344 US 1 (1948).

[110] Fair Housing Act, 42 USC § 3601; see also Civil Rights Act of 1866, 42 USC §1982 and *Jones v Alfred Mayer Co*, 392 US 409 (1968).

[111] See Richard A Epstein, 'Covenants and Constitutions' (1988) 73 *Cornell Law Review* 906, 918–19; Stewart E Sterk, 'Minority Protection in Residential Private Governments' (1997) 77 *Boston University Law Review* 273, 281.

communities (or of landlords' property rights). But this seems to be wrong or at least incomplete because, as Carol Rose insisted, *Shelley* poses 'a state action enigma': both prior and later decisions show that the bare potential for judicial enforcement of private arrangements does not transform them into state action. While Rose's specific solution to this puzzle seems to me unsatisfactory,[112] her more general claim that *Shelley* presents 'some of the best instincts of property law' is precise.[113] The non-owners' right of entry to common-interest communities is indeed intrinsic to this property institution and should not be perceived as an external limitation or imposition.[114]

To see why, and to appreciate the constraining power of contextual normative reasoning regarding private law institutions, consider the way the right to entry to common-interest communities is grounded in the very reasons—the very same property values—that justify the support of our legal system for this property institution.[115] Consider, in other words, why *Shelley* is correct notwithstanding the state action enigma, and why the basic entry rule set by the Fair Housing Act should likewise be treated as a statutory specification of the regulative principle of common-interest communities (refined in *Neponsit*) rather than as a public law intervention.

Consider first the justification common to all property institutions as means for securing people's ability to be the authors of their lives. Limiting the opportunities of certain people to buy or lease houses or apartments in a certain geographical area undermines this role of property in facilitating people's self-determination. For this reason, exclusionary practices that unreasonably limit the mobility of the excluded persons (a mobility crucial to them in forming, revising, and pursuing their own ends) must be invalidated. In some settings, the concern for the autonomy of entrants is defeated by the autonomy and personhood concerns of property owners: the Fair Housing Act vigorously protects the right to exclude in intimate settings, where the personhood value of the owner (potential landlord) trumps any possible interest of potential tenants.[116] The Act, however, reverses this rule and recognizes a rather capacious right to entry where the lessor is a commercial entity. Because

[112] Rose suggested that this puzzle can be solved by reference to the welfarist commitment of property law to minimize negative externalities on third parties who may not share the preferences of the existing transactors. But, as Rose herself admits, making the protection of third parties from the idiosyncratic preferences of current transactors the core of property raises difficult questions for cases such as *Shelley*, where third parties are likely to share these current preferences. Carol Rose, 'Shelley v. Kraemer' in Gerald Korngold and Andrew P Morriss (eds), *Property Stories* (Foundation Press 2004) 169.

[113] Rose, 'Shelley v. Kraemer' (n 112) 169.

[114] See *Noble v Alley* [1951] SCR 64 (SCC), invalidating racially based restrictive covenants because they referred to the identity of users/owners rather than to any actual use of the pertinent land. Not only is this reasoning from within property, but it also (implicitly) relies on the *raison d'être* of the property institution of covenants as a means to facilitate landowners' ability to commonly enjoy the benefits of private land use controls along the lines discussed earlier (text accompanying nn 53–4). Understanding covenants in these terms does, on its face, make references to the identity of users and owners suspicious.

[115] The following paragraphs draw on Dagan, *Property* (n 4) ch 2; see also Sophia Moreau, 'What is Discrimination' (2010) 38 *Philosophy & Public Affairs* 143.

[116] See the Act's exceptions for intimate associations: single families (§3603(b)(1)) and small owner-occupied multiple unit dwellings (§3603(b)(2)).

negative liberty is not an ultimate value but rather a means for self-determination, a claim by one who wishes to establish her life in a certain locus must override that of someone who perceives that property as a fungible asset.

Thinking about common-interest communities as a property institution aimed at fostering the community value of property, thus conceptualizing covenants along the lines of the regulative principle identified in *Neponsit*, leads to similar conclusions. This perspective sanctions exclusionary practices of residential communities only in limited circumstances. In particular, it implies that law should not authorize such practices insofar as they are used against, rather than by, cultural minority groups.[117] It also requires that the law should make sure that the limits on entry applied by 'thin' common-interest communities are indeed necessary in order to ensure that 'bad co-operators' likely to jeopardize the success of the commons property are excluded. This means that courts need to supervise both the admissions criteria of such communities and the way they are practised on the ground. One implication of this prescription is that rejections of applicants for admissions must be reasoned, and that the reasons must be sufficiently detailed so that both their evaluative and factual components can be properly scrutinized.[118]

5. Conclusion

The most charitable explanation of private law theorists' resistance to embrace the structural pluralism typical of private law focuses on the worry that, by endorsing this feature, they could end up exacerbating private law's deficiencies concerning both the conception of the rule of law as guidance and its understanding as constraint. As I tried to show in the preceding pages, however, these concerns are exaggerated if not simply wrong.

Properly interpreted, private law pluralism does not endorse ad hoc decision-making, which is indeed detrimental to guidance, and is often supportive of rule-based decision-making. As any (sensible) understanding of the rule of law as guidance acknowledges, however, private law pluralism does need to resort to standards in certain cases. Rather than undermining guidance, however, its standards are frequently conducive to guidance because they build on the character of the private law institution at hand, which is typically the basis of most people's expectations.

[117] Or, for that matter, by other types of groups, such as where a common-interest community is organized around a commitment to, say, vegetarianism. But see Austin, 'Pluralism, Context and the Internal Life' (n 64) 27–9.

[118] And there is no way to avoid the hard questions of distinguishing appropriate goals of common-interest communities from illegitimate ones. But see Austin, 'Pluralism, Context and the Internal Life' (n 64) 27–9, who implies that common-interest communities can never relate to the identity of their members. Identifying the specific content of the minimal core to which private law pluralism must adhere is a significant task that cannot be undertaken here. For our purposes, it is enough to indicate that this core must be located around the maxim of treating every person as a human being whose dignity—or normative agency—fundamentally matters. See Dagan, *Reconstructing American Legal Realism* (n 5) 180.

Private law pluralism need not raise serious concerns of unconstrained judicial power either. To be sure, legislatures in a democracy can legitimately play a role in the development of private law, which shapes and reshapes our social order, adjusting it to new circumstances, challenges, and opportunities. In some contexts, judges should possibly refrain from taking part in this drama,[119] but in many others, courts enjoy no less legitimacy—from a participation or accountability perspective—in the shaping of our private law institutions.[120] Likewise, while the plurality of values involved in the moulding of these institutions' regulative principles makes the enterprise challenging, we have no grounds for assuming that a normative contextual enquiry cannot lead to just and principled results.

The compatibility of private law pluralism with the rule of law is not coincidental; rather, it is ingrained in its foundational features: its commitment to stability and predictability given its dual mission of stabilizing expectations and expressing ideals; and its even more fundamental commitment to employ multiple and relatively small categories, which are sufficiently distinct from one another and internally coherent, so as to facilitate autonomy as self-authorship. The former feature is crucial from a rule-of-law perspective because it requires private law to employ bright line rules whenever possible, and to otherwise resort to informative standards. The latter feature is even more critical both because only small categories can plausibly rely on regulatory principles that are sufficiently determinate so as to function as informative standards, and because the multiplicity of private law categories dilutes the power yielded by the carriers of private law, be they judges or legislatures. Indeed, the contrast to the large heterogeneous categories advocated by private law monists invites the question of whether monism, rather than pluralism, can plausibly comply with either the guidance or the constraint injunctions of the rule of law.

[119] Typical types of cases calling for significant deference are those of newly enacted private law legislation, as well as of private law innovations that require a regulatory structure, depend on specialized knowledge available elsewhere, or involve excessive widespread redistribution. See Dagan 'Judges and Property' (n 94) 36–7.

[120] There may also be cases in between these categories in which judges may legitimately begin a process of law reform, which would benefit from a further legislative intervention which can solidify that reform in a comprehensive scheme of rules. This may well be the full story of common-interest communities.

PART II

THE RULE-OF-LAW CONTRIBUTION TO PRIVATE LAW

8

Strict Duties and the Rule of Law

Stephen A Smith

1. Introduction

According to a common understanding, the rule of law requires that 'the law be capable of guiding the behaviour of its subjects'.[1] In this view, the rule of law demands that laws be clear, stable, prospective, and applied by impartial courts because laws which lack these qualities cannot be followed, or can be followed only imperfectly. The primary value of the rule of law, thus understood, is that it 'minimize[s] the harm to freedom and dignity which the law may cause in its pursuit of its goals'.[2]

In this chapter, I argue that a so-called strict legal duty—such as a duty 'not to trespass', a duty 'not to commit a battery', or a duty 'not to allow water to escape from one's property'—is inconsistent with the above conception of the rule of law. The inconsistency arises not because strict duties are incapable of guiding behaviour, but, to the contrary, because they provide too much guidance. In a legal system that not only recognizes but also accords a central role to duties to take reasonable care, the natural interpretation of strict duties is that the law wants citizens to take *more* than reasonable care to avoid the outcomes they contemplate. Yet the law cannot seriously intend that citizens take such care: that is to say, the law cannot intend that citizens take 'unreasonable' care. From a rule-of-law perspective, therefore, the objection to strict duties (or at least to their existence in a system that also recognizes duties to take reasonable care) is that they render the law unclear. Insofar as the law articulates strict duties, it appears to recommend actions that it does not want to recommend, thus sending mixed messages. Strict duties only become intelligible if one supposes that 'duty' means something different when prefaced by the word 'strict' from what it means in other legal contexts. The lesson to draw from these observations, I further argue, is that so-called strict duties should be reinterpreted as 'free-standing' strict liabilities: that is, as liabilities that arise without wrongdoing.

[1] Joseph Raz, 'The Rule of Law and its Virtue' in *The Authority of Law* (2nd edn, Oxford University Press 2009) 210, 214.
[2] Raz, *Authority*, 228.

This chapter is divided into four sections. Section 2 explains in more detail the concept of strict duties. Section 3 describes the 'rule-of-law objection' to such duties. Section 4 then examines—and rejects—three possible responses to the rule-of-law objection. Finally, Section 5 defends the view that apparent examples of strict duties should be interpreted as free-standing strict liabilities. It concludes by briefly discussing the nature of such a liability: that is, whether it should properly be understood as a liability to fall under a duty to pay compensation, or merely a liability to be ordered by a court to pay compensation.

2. The Concept of a Strict Duty

A strict duty is a duty to bring about a particular outcome.[3] To adopt John Gardner's helpful terminology, strict duties are 'duties to succeed'[4] because they can be breached even though one made reasonable efforts, or even extraordinary efforts, to try to achieve the stipulated outcome: all that matters in determining whether a strict duty is fulfilled is whether the outcome is achieved. Strict duties not to trespass, not to commit batteries, and not to allow water to escape from one's property are thus all examples of such duties. If I drive onto another's land without permission, I will have breached a duty not to trespass, regardless of whether I knew or could reasonably have known that I was trespassing, since trespass is defined as entering another's land without permission.[5]

Most lawyers appear to assume that the common law recognizes strict duties, and most would include within this category duties not to trespass, not to commit batteries, and not to allow water to escape from one's property.[6] Admittedly,

[3] The stipulated outcome is usually a negative state of affairs, such as that which exists when you have not committed a trespass.

[4] John Gardner, 'The Purity and Priority of Private Law' (1996) 46 *University of Toronto Law Journal* 459, 486. As Gardner notes, so-called 'fault-based' duties ('duties to try' in his terminology) are also, in part, duties to succeed because they are not just duties to take care, but also duties to take care not to bring about a stipulated result. To commit the tort of negligent misrepresentation, I must not only act carelessly, but the result of that carelessness must be a misrepresentation on which another person has detrimentally relied.

[5] WVH Rogers, *Winfield & Jolowicz on Tort* (16th edn, Sweet & Maxwell 2002) 487–8. For an entry to qualify as a trespass, it must be voluntary. I do not commit a trespass if I am forced onto your land against my will.

[6] These examples are all taken from tort law. The duty to perform a contract is the most important example of a non-tort private law duty that is generally assumed to be a strict duty. Some lawyers would also include within this category duties to pay damages and duties to reverse unjust enrichments. This chapter focuses on so-called 'strict' tort law duties. Contractual duties raise special issues (because contractual promises are arguably a kind of guarantee: see Stephen A Smith, *Contract Theory* (Oxford University Press 2004) 384–6). As for duties to pay damages or to reverse unjust enrichments, it is far from clear that the law recognizes such duties (as opposed to recognizing mere liabilities to being ordered to pay damages or reverse an unjust enrichment: see Stephen A Smith, 'Duties, Liabilities, and Damages' (2012) 125 *Harvard Law Review* 1727, 1741–9; and Stephen A Smith, 'A Duty to Make Restitution?' (2013) 26 *Canadian Journal of Law and Jurisprudence* 157, 169–70). Furthermore, even if it is assumed that the law recognizes strict duties to pay damages and to reverse unjust enrichments, such duties raise different issues from those stemming from strict tort duties because, *inter alia*, their breach does not give rise to a liability to pay damages nor to any other kind of liability.

lawyers often refer to the rules governing trespasses, batteries, escaping water, and so on as creating strict 'liabilities' rather than strict 'duties'. Liabilities are different from duties.[7] To say that you have a legal duty to do X means that, from the law's perspective, you must do X. In contrast, to say that you have incurred a legal liability to Y means that you may have Y done to you or imposed upon you if another person (or institution) exercises a legal power.[8] We thus say that citizens have duties not to steal, but we do not say that they have duties to punish themselves: rather, we say that criminals are liable to be punished. It seems clear, however, that the liabilities lawyers contemplate when they talk about strict liabilities—or at least when they talk about strict liabilities arising from events like trespasses, batteries, and escaping water[9]—are liabilities that arise because a legal wrong, or tort, has been committed.[10] The rules governing such liabilities are found in books on torts, the liabilities themselves are described as liabilities to pay damages for a tort, and the defendants, who have to pay strict liability damages, are described as wrongdoers. The conventional presentation appears to assume, therefore, that a strict liability to pay damages arises on proof of a trespass because there is a strict legal duty not to trespass.[11]

As I mentioned earlier, this assumption is questioned in Section 5, where I will also suggest that it is not coincidental that lawyers are more comfortable with the language of strict liabilities than that of strict duties. For the moment, however, I will assume that strict duties exist, and I will use as examples duties not to trespass, not to commit batteries, and not to allow water to escape from one's property. The question this chapter addresses is not whether judges or lawyers believe in strict duties, but whether such a belief is reasonable.

[7] The correlative of a duty is a right (as in your right that I not steal your property), while the correlative of a liability is a power (as in the law's power to punish me if I infringe your property rights): Wesley Hohfeld, 'Some Fundamental Legal Conceptions as Applied in Judicial Reasoning' (1913) 23 *Yale Law Journal* 16, 44–54.

[8] A liability may take the form of a liability to fall under a duty (for example, contractual offerors are liable to fall under contractual duties if their offers are accepted), but in such cases the liability remains distinct from the duty (thus if a contractual offer is not accepted, no duty arises).

[9] The qualification is important because some examples of strict liabilities (in the technical, though not everyday, sense of the term) are clearly not assumed to arise from a wrong. The obvious example is the liability incurred by the recipient of an unjust enrichment to reverse the enrichment. Though not discussed in this chapter, the strict liability that is conventionally assumed to stem from a breach of contract is also conventionally assumed to arise from a wrong (but see Smith, 'A Duty to Make Restitution' (n 6)).

[10] For present purposes, it does not matter whether the strict liability to pay damages is a liability to fall under a duty to pay damages or merely a liability to be ordered by a court to pay damages; it only matters that the liability is assumed to arise upon the breach of a legal duty. I briefly discuss the broader relevance of this distinction in Section 5.

[11] This assumption is often made explicit. For example, John Gardner writes that 'the law *asserts* the existence of unperformed obligations to succeed whenever it imposes strict liability': John Gardner, 'Obligations and Outcomes in the Law of Torts' in P Cane and J Gardner (eds), *Relating to Responsibility: Essays for Tony Honoré* (Hart Publishing 2001) 120.

3. The Rule-of-Law Objection to Strict Duties

The suggestion that strict duties are problematic is not new. The most common objection to strict duties, however, focuses not on the duties themselves but on the strict liabilities to pay damages that are assumed to arise upon their breach.[12] In broad terms, the objection is that strict liabilities are unfair because they penalize citizens for behaviour that is morally unimpeachable.[13] According to this perspective, it is unfair to hold citizens liable to pay damages unless they engaged in blameworthy behaviour: that is to say, unless they failed to take reasonable care to avoid the relevant injury (and where one way of failing to take reasonable care is to intentionally cause the relevant injury).[14]

The fairness objection is important, but as just mentioned it is an objection to strict liabilities rather than to strict duties. This objection is concerned with the unfairness that arises not from the law telling citizens 'do not trespass', but rather from the law telling citizens 'if you trespass, you will be liable to pay a sum of money'. Further, the substance of the objection is distinct from the rule-of-law concerns that are this chapter's focus: its validity turns on the merits of holding individuals responsible for the consequences of their blameless behaviour.

Admittedly, one could try to frame this objection in rule-of-law terms. In particular, it might be argued that strict liabilities make it difficult for citizens to plan their lives: if the law recognizes strict liabilities, then citizens who have done everything they can reasonably be expected to do to avoid incurring liabilities to pay damages may nonetheless incur such liabilities. This difficulty is easily exaggerated: as any traveller knows, there are many ways to mitigate the consequences of unexpected costs, such as obtaining insurance—or simply by not engaging in the relevant activity (eg by not travelling). But even accepting that the potential subjects of strict liabilities may find it difficult to plan their lives, this difficulty is not an objection to strict liabilities themselves but rather to the vagaries of life. It is not the law that causes the uncertainties that this objection targets. Rules that impose strict liabilities are (or at least can be) perfectly clear, stable, prospective,

[12] If it is assumed that strict liabilities to pay damages arise if, and only if, a strict duty has been breached, then an objection to strict liabilities is also an objection to strict duties. As I explain in Section 4.1, this assumption should not be made.

[13] A version of this critique is advanced by Ernest J Weinrib when he states that strict liabilities are inconsistent with the idea of human agency because they 'hold the agent liable merely for being active': Ernest J Weinrib, *The Idea of Private Law* (Harvard University Press 1995) 181; see also Alan Brudner, *The Unity of the Common Law: Studies in Hegelian Jurisprudence* (University of California Press 1995) 190. The unfairness critique is often joined to a critique of the broadly consequentialist justifications (eg 'loss-spreading', 'enterprise liability', 'deterrence') that defenders of strict liabilities typically invoke. It should not be assumed, however, that strict liabilities can only be justified on consequentialist grounds. The strict liabilities associated with intentional torts like trespass and battery are commonly defended on non-consequentialist grounds: see eg Robert Stevens, *Torts and Rights* (Oxford University Press 2007) 92–102.

[14] Unless otherwise indicated, all references in this chapter to 'reasonable care' (or to 'proper care', 'appropriate care', or just to 'taking care') assume that intentionally causing X can be equated with failing to take reasonable care to avoid causing X.

etc.[15] More to the point, the losses caused by blameless behaviour must (like all losses) be borne by someone. If careful trespassers are not liable for the injuries they cause, then landowners will bear the costs of those injuries. Eliminating a strict liability to pay for injuries caused by blameless trespassers might help potential trespassers plan their lives, but it would equally impinge on the ability of landowners to plan theirs.

Strict duties give rise to different concerns. From a rule-of-law perspective, strict duties are problematic because they provide misleading guidance. More concretely, the objection is that strict duties give citizens legal reasons to do things that the law clearly does not want them to do. Specifically, strict duties provide reasons for citizens to take extreme care—even to the point (as far as this is possible) of not acting at all.[16] Consider a strict duty not to trespass. It is true, as John Gardner notes, that this duty is not literally a duty to take extreme care.[17] Indeed, the duty says nothing about the level of care that citizens should take. It is irrelevant, when determining if a duty not to trespass has been breached, whether the defendant took extreme care, reasonable care, or no care at all: all that matters is whether or not a trespass has occurred. Further, it is not necessary, as a matter of empirical fact, to take extreme care in order to avoid trespassing. If I am lucky enough to reside on an extremely large property, I might live my entire life without committing a trespass, regardless of how little care I take to avoid trespassing.

From a rule-of-law perspective, however, the central question is what guidance strict duties provide to citizens. The answer to this question is that strict duties guide citizens to take extreme care to achieve the outcomes they stipulate. The existence of a strict duty not to trespass does not merely give me reasons not to trespass: it gives me reasons to do whatever will make it less likely that I will trespass.[18] This proposition does not deny that it is possible to fulfil a duty not to trespass without taking extreme care, or indeed any care at all; the point is simply that the best way to avoid trespassing is to take extreme care not to trespass.[19]

[15] If it is assumed that strict liabilities take the form of liabilities to fall under duties to pay damages (as opposed to liabilities merely to be ordered by a court to pay damages), then they raise a rule-of-law issue because, as I have explained elsewhere, citizens cannot reasonably be expected to know the content or, in some cases, even the existence of such duties prior to a judicial determination: see Smith, 'Duties, Liabilities, and Damages' (n 6) 1743–4. This objection, however, works against any duty to pay damages, not merely duties that arise upon the breach of a strict duty.

[16] Though not framed in terms of rule-of-law concerns, a similar objection to strict duties has been made by others: Brudner, *The Unity of the Common Law* (n 13) 190; Weinrib, *The Idea of Private Law* (n 13) 181–3.

[17] Gardner, 'Obligations and Outcomes' (n 11) 134.

[18] John Gardner agrees that, while a strict duty need not entail a reason to try to succeed let alone a reason to do one's utmost to succeed (as for example where success is impossible), a strict duty creates a derivative reason to do whatever will make it more likely that one succeeds: 'A reason to do something is not a reason to try to do it. One's reason to do something yields a derivative reason to try to do it only if, by trying to do it, one will help oneself to do it'; John Gardner, 'Reasons and Abilities: Some Preliminaries' (2013) 58 *American Journal of Jurisprudence* 63, 73.

[19] As part of his defence of strict duties, John Gardner argues that some goals are best achieved by taking less than extreme care or even by taking no care at all. As an example of the former Gardner mentions accident-free driving, suggesting that 'over-cautious' drivers may cause more accidents. As an example of the latter, he mentions the goal of walking over hot coals without burning one's feet ('If one

Indeed, taking this argument to its logical conclusion, the very best way for me to avoid trespassing is to move my body as little as possible. And if I have a duty to achieve a particular outcome—which is exactly what a strict duty entails—then it follows that I ought to do my best to achieve that outcome.[20]

As I explain in a moment, it is highly unlikely that the law actually wants citizens to take more than reasonable care to achieve the outcomes that strict duties mandate. Still, strict duties require citizens to achieve the specified outcome, without any qualification. Further—and this point is critical—it is not clear what other guidance a strict duty could provide. As we will see, strict liabilities might be defended on the ground that citizens should be responsible, at least in certain cases, for the consequences of their actions regardless of whether those actions are blameworthy. The question now under consideration, however, is what guidance strict duties provide. More precisely, the question is what guidance they provide in a legal system that also contains duties to take reasonable care. Nothing prevents the law from expressing the duty to avoid trespassing as a duty to take reasonable care not to trespass. The law contains many duties that are expressed as duties to take reasonable care. The natural conclusion to draw from the coexistence of strict duties with duties to take care is that strict duties ask citizens to take a different level of care than that required by duties to take reasonable care. More specifically, the natural conclusion is that strict duties guide citizens to take more than reasonable care (keeping in mind, again, that intentionally doing X is also an instance of failing to take reasonable care not to do X).

The rule-of-law objection to strict duties is therefore not that, taken literally, they provide no guidance: strict duties guide citizens to take extreme care. The objection is that this guidance is only apparent because the law cannot possibly want citizens to take extreme (that is, 'unreasonable') care. It hardly seems necessary to prove the latter proposition since, as far as I am aware, no one has ever argued to the contrary.[21] It is however worth noting that a duty to take extreme care is

must walk across a bed of hot coals it is probably best, as a rule, to be entirely careless where one places one's feet' (Gardner, 'Obligations and Outcomes' (n 11) 116)). It may be queried whether driving too cautiously is an example of taking extreme care (it seems rather to be an example of a misguided attempt to take extreme care), or that successful coal-walkers take no care (taking care when walking on coals would seem to be taking care not to place one's feet slowly or precisely); but even if we accept Gardner's point, it is undeniable that many goals are best pursued by taking extreme care and, further, that the goals contemplated by most strict duties fall into this category. For example, the best way to make sure that one does not trespass is to avoid moving one's body at all.

[20] It might be thought that this objection applies to all legal duties, including duties to take reasonable care. For example, it might be argued that the best way to make sure that I never infringe a duty to take reasonable care not to harm others would be to never interact with others. If I avoid all contact, I avoid the chance of inadvertently failing to take reasonable care not to injure another person. However, this objection does not apply because a duty to take reasonable care specifies exactly the behaviour that the law desires—namely, to take reasonable care. In the case of strict duties, which specify only a result and not a particular kind of behaviour, citizens must determine what behaviour will best bring about the results the law requires. As I have suggested, the only behaviour consistent with a strict duty is to do everything possible to achieve the stipulated result.

[21] It is not part of John Gardner's defence of strict duties that it is desirable for citizens to take extreme care in any case where taking such care would make compliance with strict duties more likely. To the contrary, Gardner's repeated insistence that strict duties can be fulfilled without extreme care

arguably inconsistent with the very concept of a legal duty. Legal duties are meant to reflect moral duties.[22] This does not mean that legal duties actually reflect such duties, but it does mean that, when we try to explain legal duties, our explanation should show how they could plausibly be presented as reflecting moral duties. A duty that gives citizens reasons to take extreme care, extending to the point of providing reasons not to act at all, is not conceivable as a moral duty. Of course, the law might reasonably want citizens to avoid certain kinds of activities altogether: for example, the law might think that some activities, while not harmful in themselves, are too risky even if the requisite care and precautions are taken. But the usual and appropriate way for the law to prevent an activity from occurring is to make it illegal, rather than articulating a duty to take extreme care when engaging in that activity.

To be clear, the objection to strict duties now under consideration is not that they actually lead citizens to undertake excessive precautionary measures. It is unlikely that even the most law-abiding citizens, on being told by their lawyers that there is a strict legal duty not to trespass, would conclude that they ought to take extreme care not to trespass. These citizens would suppose that their lawyers were using the term 'duty' in a specialized sense. This supposition, however, highlights the rule-of-law objection to strict duties. From the law's perspective, legal duties are moral duties: the term 'duty' is not meant to have a specialized legal meaning.[23] Generally speaking, the term 'duty' means in law what it appears to mean. Citizens who are told by their lawyers that they have a duty to take reasonable care not to injure others would straightforwardly, and correctly, understand that the law expects them to take reasonable care to avoid injuring others. But when the law says there is a strict duty not to trespass, it cannot mean what it appears to mean. And whenever the law does not mean what it appears to mean, the rule of law is threatened.

4. Three Possible Responses to the Rule-of-Law Objection

The strictness of strict duties is evident. It might be asked, then, why most judges and lawyers appear to accept strict duties largely without comment. The answer, I suggest, lies in various misunderstandings about the nature of legal duties and, in particular, about their relationship to legal liabilities. These misunderstandings are conveniently explored by considering three possible responses that defenders of strict duties might make to the rule-of-law objection: (1) strict duties are required to

appears to be premised on the assumption that one could validly object to such duties if they could only be satisfied by taking extreme care.

[22] See Raz, *Authority* (n 1) 3–232; Joseph Raz, *Ethics in the Public Domain* (Oxford University Press 1994) 210–37.

[23] Raz, *Authority* (n 1) 3–232; Raz, *Ethics* (n 22) 210–37. It does not follow that legal duties are in fact moral duties: the point is merely that the law regards legal duties as moral duties.

support strict liabilities; (2) strict duties are not enforced; and (3) strict duties are substantively justified.

4.1 Strict duties support justified liabilities

One possible response to the rule-of-law objection to strict duties is to defend the strict liabilities that arise from their breach. I mentioned earlier that while strict liabilities are often criticized, they are also defended by many writers.[24] To the extent that such defences are valid, it might be thought that they count equally as defences of strict duties, on the basis that strict liabilities cannot exist without strict duties.[25] Admittedly, this suggestion is not a direct response to the rule-of-law objection. But if accepted, it identifies a justificatory reason that might outweigh that objection.

I will say something later about the substantive merits of strict liability. For the moment, it is sufficient to note that, whatever those merits might be, the premise of the above suggestion—that strict liabilities cannot exist without strict duties—is unfounded. To be sure, if it is assumed that the strict liabilities in question are strict liabilities to pay damages and, further, that damages are only available if a duty has been breached, then the premise is true by definition. But this assumption need not be made—or at least it need not be made when critically analysing the law. This chapter seeks to understand the substance, not the technical label, of what courts are doing when they require defendants to pay sums of money to plaintiffs whom they have blamelessly injured. Viewed from this perspective, there is no reason to assume that a strict liability to pay a sum of money can arise only upon the breach of a strict duty. The law recognizes many 'free-standing' strict liabilities. For instance, the strict liability incurred by the recipient of a mistaken transfer to return the transferred property or its value does not arise from the breach of a prior duty—it arises automatically upon the transfer. Nor is the Criminal Injuries Compensation Board's liability to pay compensation to victims of crime dependent on the Board's wrongdoing—rather, the liability arises from the injury.[26] There is no reason that a liability to pay compensation for an injury or loss caused by a faultless trespass or battery could not be understood in a similar way. Of course, free-standing liabilities must be justified. But there is no reason to assume that such justifications are unavailable. Indeed, justifying free-standing strict liabilities is in principle easier than justifying strict duties, as evinced by the justifications for strict liabilities (and not strict duties) found in the tort literature.

[24] See eg Tony Honoré, 'Responsibility and Luck: The Moral Basis of Strict Liability' (1988) 104 *Law Quarterly Review* 530; Richard Epstein, 'A Theory of Strict Liability' (1973) 2 *Journal of Legal Studies* 151, 165.

[25] See eg Gardner, 'Obligations and Outcomes' (n 11) 120.

[26] Sections 4–9, The Criminal Injuries Compensation Scheme 2012 (UK).

4.2 Strict duties are not enforced

A second possible response to the rule-of-law objection is that its target is illusory because strict duties are not legally enforced. Courts never order defendants to take extreme care. Of course, courts are perfectly willing to, for example, order trespassers to cease trespassing. Furthermore, they are willing to sanction defendants who fail to comply with such orders by imprisoning or fining them. However, such orders are only made against defendants who are already trespassing or, exceptionally, who have shown a clear intention to trespass in the immediate future. Furthermore, and crucially, failing to comply with an order not to trespass is only sanctioned if it is blameworthy. A failure to comply that is merely 'casual or accidental or unintentional' is not a contempt of court, and so will not lead to a sanction.[27] Nor do courts sanction defendants for failing to take extreme care. Of course, citizens who breach strict duties will incur liabilities to pay damages that are enforced in the usual way: that is, by seizing and selling their assets if they fail to pay after being ordered to do so. But it is the failure to comply with an order to pay damages—not the failure to comply with a strict duty—that is sanctioned by execution against the defendant's assets. Stated more simply, notwithstanding the law's apparent recognition of strict duties, the law never forces citizens to take extreme care. In terms of enforcement, the existence of a strict duty merely means that the law will enforce the liability to pay damages that arises when this duty is breached. Whether or not citizens employ extreme care is thus entirely up to them.

The fact that strict duties are not directly enforced helps to explain why writers who are critical of such duties focus their attention on strict liabilities rather than on the strict duties that (it is assumed) ground these liabilities. Nonetheless, the non-enforcement of strict duties does not justify their existence. If strict duties are genuine duties, they should be complied with—and if the best way of complying with them is to take extreme care, then citizens should take extreme care. Duties to take reasonable care are also rarely, if ever, directly enforced.[28] Yet it has never been suggested that such duties are not meant to be followed.

Strict liability defenders might attempt to buttress the no-enforcement response by arguing that not only are strict duties not enforced, they are not even intended to provide guidance. It might be argued, in other words, that the law recognizes strict duties merely to provide a formal legal ground or legal explanation for strict liabilities, and that it is only the rules setting up the latter that are substantively important. As will later become clear, I think this explanation is broadly correct. The best explanation as to why (some) judges and lawyers say that the law recognizes strict duties is that they assume that the law cannot impose the strict liabilities it wants to unless a strict duty has been breached. However, this revised response admits rather than rebuts the rule-of-law objection that strict duties are not what they appear to be: that is to say, they are not actually duties. Both in law

[27] Adrian Zuckerman, *Zuckerman on Civil Procedure* (2nd edn, Sweet & Maxwell 2006) 819.

[28] See Nicholas McBride, 'Duties to Take Care—Do They Really Exist?' (2004) 24 *Oxford Journal of Legal Studies* 417.

and morality, to say that you have a duty to do X means that you ought to plan your actions so that you do X. The Holmesian 'bad man' may care only about the possible sanctions imposed by the law, but the law itself supposes that citizens should accept legal duties as duties: that is, as guides for behaviour in and of themselves. Thus, to admit that strict duties are not intended to guide behaviour (or at least to admit that they are not intended to guide behaviour in a different way from duties to take care) is to suppose, consistent with the rule-of-law objection, that the concept of a duty means something different when prefaced by the word 'strict' from what it means in other legal contexts.

4.3 Strict duties are substantively justified

The final and most important response to the rule-of-law objection to strict duties supposes that strict duties—and not just strict liabilities—are themselves substantively justified. As we will see, this response is, again, not strictly a response to the rule-of-law objection. But insofar as strict duties are substantively justified, one might think that the rule-of-law objection must be flawed. How can it be contrary to the rule of law to require citizens to perform duties that they have good reasons to fulfil?

John Gardner provides the most sophisticated attempt to justify strict duties in this way.[29] Reduced to its essentials, Gardner's argument is that strict duties are justified because the outcomes contemplated by such duties are desirable. Consider a strict duty not to trespass. It goes without saying that, from the law's perspective, the outcome contemplated by such a duty—not trespassing—is desirable. Of course, the law might reasonably suppose that certain kinds of trespasses are acceptable (such as those undertaken to avert a serious injury);[30] but in the normal case, the law clearly prefers that trespasses not occur. More specifically, and exceptional cases aside, trespasses are presumed to be undesirable regardless of the reasons for which they occur. From the law's perspective, all trespasses—innocent, careless, or intentional—are bad: that is why they are called trespasses. Indeed, even if the existing strict duty to avoid trespassing were reduced to a duty to take reasonable care to avoid trespassing, the same conclusion would follow. As Gardner observes, there is no reason to dissuade careless trespasses unless trespassing itself—regardless of how it is caused—is undesirable.[31] If this conclusion is accepted, it follows naturally, Gardner suggests, that a strict duty not to trespass is in principle entirely appropriate. Such a duty simply makes explicit the law's view that it would be better if no trespasses occurred, period.

[29] See Gardner, 'Obligations and Outcomes' (n 11); John Gardner, 'The Mark of Responsibility' (2003) 23 *Oxford Journal of Legal Studies* 157; Gardner, 'Reasons and Abilities' (n 18). Gardner's argument builds on Honoré's (see Honoré, 'Responsibility and Luck' (n 24)).

[30] Whether the perpetrator of a justified trespass should pay damages is a different question. The rules governing the defence of necessity demonstrate that the law generally holds even justified trespassers liable to pay damages.

[31] John Gardner says, rightly, that 'the *intelligibility* of reasons to try depends on the *independent intelligibility* of reasons to succeed' (Gardner, 'Obligations and Outcomes' (n 11) 138).

Does it follow from this argument that all legal duties should be framed as strict duties? It does, though Gardner suggests otherwise.[32] Gardner rightly notes that the question of what duties the law should impose is different from the question of what consequences should flow from failing to comply with a duty. For example, when the law contemplates whether breaching a duty should support a liability to pay damages, new issues arise for consideration. Thus, Gardner argues that it may be unfair to impose a liability for breaching a strict duty in situations where citizens might not expect the liability, or where there is no reasonable way for them to avoid incurring the liability. For this author, such 'external' considerations explain why many legal duties are framed as duties to make reasonable efforts to achieve a desired outcome ('duties to take care') rather than strict duties to achieve a desired outcome. In Gardner's account, then, all duties are prima facie strict duties, although some of them are then reduced to duties to take care for external reasons.

It seems clear, however, that rather than supporting duties to take care (in some circumstances), Gardner's arguments merely support liabilities that are conditional on failing to take care ('fault-based' liabilities). The external considerations that Gardner invokes are considerations that pertain to the appropriateness of attaching consequences—liabilities—to blameless behaviour. These considerations have nothing to do with the reasons for imposing a duty. Gardner's argument supposes that a strict duty is justified by the desirability of the outcome specified by the duty. Yet the desirability of the outcome is unaffected by whether it is fair to hold a defendant liable for failing to achieve it. Gardner's external reasons are thus not reasons to reduce a strict duty, but instead to reduce the liability attached to such a duty. Gardner says as much himself: 'Once we have established that an action is obligatory, it remains to be discussed whether the obligation should be enforced, or more generally whether people should have to bear any adverse normative consequences of its nonperformance.'[33] In short, the conclusions to be drawn from Gardner's argument are that (1) all duties should be strict duties and (2) the liability imposed for breaching a duty should be conditional, in some cases, on fault or other factors.

I will consider the implications of these conclusions in a moment. First, however, I wish to consider the implications of Gardner's argument for the central question addressed in this chapter: what kind of guidance do strict duties provide? As Gardner makes clear, the legal recognition of a strict duty tells citizens that the law regards the outcome prescribed by the duty as desirable. Thus, the existence of a strict duty not to trespass tells citizens that the world would be a better place if trespasses did not occur. Further, because the duty is strict—it does not say, for example, that only trespasses that cause harm should be avoided—its existence tells citizens that it would be better if trespasses did not occur, regardless of all other factors. The question, however, is how citizens should use this information in planning their actions. What guidance does a strict duty not to trespass provide with respect to day-to-day decisions such as how to travel to work, where to have a

[32] Gardner, 'Obligations and Outcomes' (n 11) 125–6.
[33] Gardner, 'Obligations and Outcomes' (n 11) 140.

picnic, which kind of car to buy, what sorts of maps to purchase for a hiking trip, and so on?

One possible answer is that strict duties provide no guidance at all. All that strict duties do, it might be thought, is announce—and merely announce—that citizens have rights to have certain things happen (or not happen), and that when those things do not happen (or do happen), a legal wrong has been committed. This answer avoids the rule-of-law objection to strict duties but fails to explain why strict duties exist at all. It is true that the conventional explanation for why citizens who commit innocent trespasses incur liabilities to pay damages is that they have committed a legal wrong. It is also true that the explanation for why an innocent trespass is wrong is that the duty to avoid trespasses is strict. In the conventional view, then, strict duties are assumed to be a conceptual prerequisite for strict liabilities. As we saw earlier, however, this assumption is mistaken. There is nothing preventing the law from recognizing a strict liability to pay a sum of money that is not conditional on the payor committing a wrong. If the law wants citizens who blamelessly trespass to be liable to pay compensation for any injuries that arise from their trespasses, it can simply enact a rule to this effect. Such a rule would be similar in form to the common law rule that holds citizens who mistakenly receive money liable to return it. It is true that, under such an arrangement, payments made to compensate for innocent trespasses would not be regarded as redress for wrongs committed, nor would victims of innocent trespasses be able to assert that their rights were infringed. But it is not clear why these features of the current law are important. If the law's aim is simply to ensure that victims of innocent trespasses obtain compensation, then it seems more appropriate to describe victims' rights as rights to compensation for harms caused by innocent trespasses.

A second possible answer is that strict duties tell citizens that, where they have a choice, they should always choose to bring about the outcome required by the duty. In the case of a strict duty not to trespass, this interpretation supposes that such a duty informs citizens that—and only that—they should never choose to trespass. In this view, a strict duty not to trespass says nothing about how much care citizens should take to avoid accidental trespasses; it merely tells citizens never to choose to trespass. Duties of this kind are prima facie possible in Gardner's model. If a particular outcome is undesirable only when it is intended, then it is logical to have a duty that informs citizens not to intentionally bring about this outcome. If it is thought that, say, defamation is only undesirable when the defamer intends to defame, a duty directing citizens never to intentionally defame others is perfectly intelligible. Further, if this interpretation is adopted, then it is comprehensible for strict duties and duties to take care to coexist in one system. Duties to take care, in this understanding, focus on a different and larger class of actions, namely those that are undesirable even when performed accidentally.

It is interesting to consider whether there are actions that are undesirable only when they are motivated by a particular intention (and, if there are, whether such actions should ever be of concern to the law).[34] But even accepting that such

[34] It is clear in law that certain torts, such as the tort of inducing a breach of contract, require an intention to bring about a particular outcome (for example, a breach of contract). However, it is less

actions exist, they are different from the kinds of actions that Gardner or anyone else has in mind when they are talking about strict duties. Actions like trespassing, committing batteries, and letting water escape from one's property are undesirable even when done accidentally. More broadly, Gardner's defence of strict duties assumes that the outcomes they address are undesirable regardless of how they are brought about; indeed, it is their general undesirability that, in his view, explains why strict duties can be breached regardless of the care taken by the defendant.

This observation leads to the third possible answer, which is that strict duties direct citizens not just to avoid intentionally bringing about the specified outcome, but also to take reasonable care to avoid bringing about these outcomes. This interpretation is presumably how Gardner understands the guidance that strict duties provide, as he never suggests that the law might want citizens to take more than reasonable care. Given that Gardner defends strict duties and believes that they provide guidance (by providing reasons for action), it is hard to imagine how else he could interpret them. To take 'reasonable' care just means to take the appropriate amount of care in the circumstances (keeping in mind that what is reasonable is different when transporting dynamite from when transporting vegetables[35]). For the same reason, it seems natural to suppose that the law expects citizens to interpret strict duties as giving them reasons to take reasonable care. What other intention could the law sensibly have? When I tell my son 'don't hit your sister', I don't expect him to take extreme precautions to avoid ever hitting his sister (for example, by avoiding all contact with his sister); what I expect is that he will avoid intentionally hitting his sister and that he will take reasonable care to avoid accidentally hitting her. As noted earlier, to the extent that citizens believe the law contains strict duties, they appear to interpret such duties in the same manner.

The suggestion that a strict duty not to trespass should be understood as guiding citizens to take reasonable care not to trespass is therefore prima facie plausible. Specifically, it is prima facie plausible when strict duties are considered (as they have just been) in isolation. However, strict duties do not exist in isolation: rather, they are part of a legal system that recognizes duties that explicitly direct citizens to take reasonable care to bring about specified outcomes. The duty that forms the core of the law of negligence is a duty to take reasonable care not to interfere with the persons, property, or liberty of others. As we have seen, such a duty makes clear (as do strict duties) that the actions it directs citizens to avoid are undesirable. Further, the duty that is at the core of negligence law explicitly directs citizens to take the level of care that the above interpretation supposes is entailed by strict duties. The natural inference to be drawn from the law's recognition of duties to take care, therefore, is that strict duties are meant to provide additional or different

clear whether the requirement of intentionality shows that the law regards the same outcome, when brought about unintentionally, as a neutral event. Instead, the law might simply believe that defendants should not be held responsible for the specified outcome unless they intended to bring it about.

[35] I also leave aside the question of whether individuals with special abilities might be required to take more care than the 'average' person. The preceding argument for a 'reasonable care' standard applies regardless of whether reasonableness is interpreted objectively or subjectively.

guidance from that provided by duties to take care. What kind of guidance could this be? The only possible answer is that strict duties are meant to guide citizens to take *more* than reasonable care: that is, to take extreme care.

As previously mentioned, no one, including Gardner, supposes that the law actually wants citizens to take more than reasonable care. Our exploration of Gardner's argument thus leads us back to where we started, namely that the law cannot mean what it appears to mean. The natural implication to be drawn from the different ways in which strict duties and duties to take care are formulated is that these duties are meant to provide different kinds of guidance. Yet as we have seen, on any reasonable interpretation of the law's intentions in this regard, the guidance intended by the law is the same in each case, namely that citizens should take reasonable care to try to achieve the desired outcome.

In principle, this resulting ambiguity could be remedied in two ways. The first option, which Gardner's argument implicitly recognizes, is to reframe all duties as strict duties and, at the same time, to specify that the liability to pay damages for breaching a duty is conditional, in certain cases, on proof that the breach was intentional, or that the defendant acted carelessly. Such proof would be required in the sub-set of cases where the duty in question is currently specified as a duty to take care. This first option, by eliminating duties to take care, removes the main impediment to interpreting the guidance provided by strict duties in the way Gardner's argument suggests, namely as a guidance to take reasonable care. At the same time, it allows the liability to be contingent, in some cases, on proof of fault. This option thus ensures that the rules governing the consequences attached to breaching a duty consider, among other external factors, issues of fairness, in line with Gardner's position.

The second option is the mirror image of the first. It reframes all duties as duties to take care but then specifies that, in addition to the liabilities to pay damages that arise from breaching a duty, citizens may also be liable, in certain circumstances, to pay sums of money even if they have not breached a duty. The circumstances in which these 'free-standing' liabilities arise would be those currently described as the innocent or blameless breach of a strict duty. Consistent with the first suggestion, this solution removes any ambiguity surrounding the guidance provided by the law: if all duties are explicitly duties to take reasonable care, then it is obvious that citizens should take reasonable care. Simultaneously, by introducing new free-standing liabilities, the law would clarify that, in certain circumstances, citizens will be held responsible (that is to say, liable) for the consequences arising from their blameless actions.

In principle, either of these solutions could remedy the ambiguity found in the current law, and each could therefore address the rule-of-law concerns that motivated this chapter. However, in practice, the second solution is preferable for three reasons. First, conventional usage favours it. As mentioned earlier, while lawyers sometimes refer to the rules governing trespasses, batteries, escaping water, and so on as creating 'strict duties', it is more common for lawyers to say—and only say—

that these rules give rise to 'strict liabilities'. In contrast, while lawyers are admittedly perfectly happy to talk about the law of, say, negligence creating a 'fault-based liability', they are also perfectly happy to describe this law as creating a duty to take care. Indeed, identifying the circumstances in which 'duties of care' arise is one of the central concerns of negligence law.

The second solution is also preferable because duties to take care, when compared to strict duties, occupy a more central role in the way lawyers think about the private law. Two hundred years ago these roles were reversed. Yet today it is generally assumed that the dominant example of a private law duty is a duty to take care. Tort law courses are devoted primarily to the law of negligence,[36] and strict duties are typically presented as exceptions to the general rule. Some authors regret this movement (usually for reasons unrelated to this chapter's concerns),[37] but there are no signs that it will change direction.

The final and most important argument for reframing strict duties as duties to take care is that the latter explicitly direct citizens to take the care that the law wants them to take. We have seen that it is possible to interpret strict duties as implicitly guiding citizens to take reasonable care to achieve the outcomes they specify. However, we have also seen that other interpretations, both more and less strict, are possible. By contrast, it is impossible to interpret a duty to take reasonable care as guiding citizens to do anything other than to take reasonable care, since the desired level of care is made explicit. The unsatisfactory state of the present law derives precisely from its ambiguity. Thus, a solution that states clearly the behaviour the law desires is preferable to one that only implies that such behaviour is desired.

Does it matter that, under the solution proposed above, the circumstances that give rise to strict liabilities will cease to be described as 'wrongs'? It might be thought that the current terminology has the advantage of making clear that trespasses, batteries, escaping water, and other such outcomes are undesirable, regardless of how they are caused. If blameless trespasses and batteries merely give rise to liabilities, will they not come to be regarded as morally neutral events akin to, say, income-generating behaviour (which attracts a free-standing liability in the form of a liability to pay tax, but is otherwise considered neutral, if not positively beneficial, behaviour)? This consequence seems unlikely. To be sure, if the law eliminated not just strict duties to avoid trespasses but, in addition, all duties to avoid trespasses, then it would indeed send the message that trespassing is a neutral event. But the suggestion now under consideration is merely to reframe strict duties to avoid trespasses, and other similar outcomes, as duties to take care to avoid these outcomes. As we have seen, it is implicit in the meaning of a duty to take care that the outcome that one is meant to try to avoid is undesirable.

[36] Contract law is different, though even here the language of 'strict duties' is largely absent; rather, what is normally said—and it is normally only said when discussing the consequences of a breach—is that liability in contract law is strict.

[37] See, for example, Stevens, *Torts and Rights* (n 13) 2.

5. Conclusion

Two conclusions may be drawn from the foregoing discussion. First, the arguments that seem to support strict duties turn out in every case to be arguments for strict liabilities. The second conclusion follows from the first: it is unnecessary and misleading for the law to recognize strict duties. It is unnecessary because all the work that strict duties might be thought to do, both in law and theory, can be done by strict liabilities. Admittedly, if we jettison the concept of a strict duty, we must come up with a different name for the kind of liability contemplated by a strict liability. The conventional description of this liability as a liability to pay damages implies that the liability arises upon the breach of a legal duty. Current terminology aside, however, there is no reason that a legal rule requiring citizens to pay a sum of money in the event that they injure another or damage another's property (regardless of fault) cannot stand alone. Structurally, such a rule is similar to the rule that holds citizens who have received property by mistake liable to pay the transferor a sum of money. The only alternative solution would be to continue asserting the existence of strict duties, but then to explain that, unlike duties to take care, they are not meant to guide behaviour, or at least that they are not meant to provide guidance that is any different from the guidance provided by duties to take care. It is here that the charge that strict duties are misleading comes to the fore. Specifically, it is misleading to use a basic legal term like 'duty' in two radically different senses. And given that duties to take care state more clearly the kind of guidance the law actually wants to give, it seems clear that the strict duty sense is the one that should be dropped.

I end with three observations. First, nothing I have said shows that strict liabilities are themselves justified. My own view is that certain strict liabilities are justified, but it would take a chapter in another book to defend this proposition. Here, I have merely claimed that the arguments that might be used to justify strict duties are better interpreted as justifications for free-standing strict liabilities.

The second observation is that it may well be, as others have argued, that many apparent examples of strict duties are neither strict duties nor free-standing strict liabilities. For example, the best explanation of so-called vicarious liability may be that the acts of employees are properly attributed to their employers, so that an employer's liability is, in reality, an ordinary fault-based liability.[38] This, and other similar attempts to explain away particular examples of strict duties, is perfectly compatible with this chapter's argument. The concept of free-standing liabilities is only needed to explain examples of apparent strict duties that cannot be interpreted as ordinary duties to take care.

Thirdly and finally, it should be noted that I have said nothing about the legal form of strict liabilities. Specifically, I have not discussed whether a strict liability should be understood as a liability to fall under a substantive duty to pay a sum of

[38] As defended by Stevens, *Torts and Rights* (n 13) 259–67.

money, a liability to be ordered by a court to pay money, or a liability to something else. This question also merits another chapter. Briefly, however, it might be thought that if there are good reasons to require citizens who have, for instance, blamelessly damaged another's property to pay compensation, then there are good reasons to enact a legal duty to make such payments. An immediate difficulty with this suggestion is that alleged injurers cannot reasonably be expected to know how much to pay or even whether they should pay at all. As I have explained elsewhere,[39] the facts needed to determine the content and even the existence of a duty to compensate are in the hands of the injured party. It is thus not reasonable to assume or expect that the injurer will obtain these facts. Even if the injured party provides this information to the injurer, how is the injurer to know whether the injured party has told the truth? Only courts can accomplish the task of ascertaining the existence and content of a duty to pay compensation.

If the 'uncertainty' objection just described were the only objection to strict liability duties to compensate, then one would expect that, in the first instance anyway, courts would give effect to such duties by issuing declarations stating their existence and content in particular cases. The obvious and appropriate way for courts to fix a previously uncertain duty is by issuing a declaration.[40] Duty-declaring declarations are the individualized counterparts of duty-declaring rules. Only if the injurer fails to comply with the now-specified duty would it be appropriate for a court to order or force compliance with the duty.

There is, however, another potential objection to imposing strict liability-based duties to pay compensation: it may be that such payments are not even in principle an appropriate subject matter for a legal duty. As I mentioned earlier, legal duties are meant to express moral duties. Of course, many legal duties do not, in fact, express moral duties, since the law is often mistaken. Nonetheless, it is part of the very meaning of a legal duty that it is intended to reflect reasons—moral reasons—that apply to the subject. This feature of legal duties places limits on the kinds of actions that may appropriately be the object of substantive legal duties, since not all the things that legal officials want citizens to do are things that such officials think citizens have moral duties to do.[41] One clear example is where a judge wants a defendant to perform an action by way of punishment, such as paying a fine. When judges issue fines, they do not suppose that they are telling defendants to do something that they have a moral duty to do. This helps to explain why the law does not enact substantive duties to pay fines at all: such duties would be unintelligible. The law merely authorizes judges to *order* defendants to pay fines. Orders, not rules, are used in the case of fines because orders do not carry the same moral message as rules. An order is essentially a command, and although orders may be based on moral reasons that apply to the subject (as is the case where an order confirms an existing legal duty), it is not part of the meaning of orders that they carry this message.

[39] Smith, 'Duties, Liabilities, and Damages' (n 6).
[40] Smith, 'Duties, Liabilities, and Damages' (n 6) 1746–9.
[41] See Smith, 'A Duty to Make Restitution?' (n 6) 60–5.

Whether liabilities to pay compensation should be given legal effect initially by declarations or, instead, merely by court orders, therefore depends on whether such liabilities are meant to express moral duties. This second question cannot be answered without determining the substantive justification—if any—for strict liabilities. I will not attempt that task here, but instead limit myself to noting that many of the best-known justifications for certain kinds of strict liabilities (such as liability for the escape of water from one's property or liability for harm arising from dangerous activities) do not appear to be based on moral reasons that apply to the subject. The most common justifications given for such liabilities—such as deterrence, loss-spreading, or enterprise liability—are, broadly speaking, social welfare justifications. To the extent that strict liabilities are justified in this way, they are appropriately given effect by court orders.

9

Some Rule-of-Law Anxieties about Strict Liability in Private Law

*John Gardner**

1. Strict Liability: Why Worry?

In legal parlance, strict liability is liability regardless of fault. 'Fault' here has a technical lawyers' meaning. Unpacking that meaning: strict liability is liability that attaches to someone (call her D) for something she did (call it φing), irrespective of any steps that she took in order not to φ and irrespective of whether she knew or had reason to know that she was φing.[1] Never mind that D did all that it was reasonable for her to do to avoid φing, all that she was personally capable of doing, even all that it was humanly possible to do. Never mind that she could not reasonably, possibly, imaginably have known that she was φing. She is still stuck with her strict liability for having φed. 'Liability' here, in turn, bears its lawyers' meaning. To say that D is liable is to say that another has a normative power to burden her, eg by imposing extra duties on her or taking away some of her rights. She is liable *for* φing if her having φed grounds her liability, that is, if her having φed is (a) a complete (but not necessarily conclusive) reason[2] for her to be liable, and (b) a necessary condition of her being liable. And, to repeat, her liability for φing is *strict* if and only if her having φed grounds the liability irrespective of what she could have known or done about her φing and thereby incurring the liability.

Strict liability plays a significant role in many legal systems, in both criminal law and private law. Its occasional use attracts a weary toleration from legal thinkers, but few stand up for it with enthusiasm, and few argue for its extension. Common anxieties about strict liability fall under two main headings. Some writers worry most about the suboptimal incentives or spurs to action that, in their view, a strict liability rule creates for those who might, or think they might, fall foul of it in the

* Earlier versions of this chapter were presented at the University of Toronto, King's College London, and the University of Oxford. I am grateful to the many who commented at each meeting, and especially to Andy Burrows, Dennis Klimchuk, Joseph Raz, Prince Saprai, Irit Samet, Stephen Smith, and Robert Stevens.

[1] Including any steps she took to find out whether she was about to φ.

[2] On complete reasons, see Joseph Raz, *Practical Reason and Norms* (Hutchinson 1975) 22–5. On conclusive reasons, see the same book at 25–8.

future. Others worry more about how the rule treats the particular person who has already fallen foul of it, the D who has φed. To express the difference in a familiar, if not entirely happy, terminology: some people fret mainly about the supposed *inefficiency* of strict liability, while others fret mainly about the supposed *injustice*. One reason why the terminology is not entirely happy is that it is possible for a rule to be inefficient *at* doing justice.[3] Another reason is that we might object to the way the rule treats D not because it is unjust but because it is (say) cruel or petty. Still, the terminology is revealing enough that we can live with it for now. We will return to inefficiency below. But let's start with injustice.

Injustice challenges to strict liability take more than one form. Here I will focus on those that portray the injustice of strict liability as bound up with a failure, on the law's part, to conform to the ideal of the rule of law. These challenges can be contrasted with others that point to the supposed injustice of attaching liability to morally blameless actions. Although strict liability is no-fault liability in a special lawyers' sense of 'fault', it also extends in the process to many who are not at fault in the ordinary moral sense of 'fault', ie many whose actions are morally blameless. Some people think that, whatever consequences the law may attach to them, one's morally blameless actions cannot change one's moral situation for the worse; unwelcome moral consequences cannot descend upon one in the absence of moral culpability. Thus, writes Nagel, 'strict liability may have its legal uses but seems irrational as a moral position'.[4] This view gives rise, in turn, to a simple moral critique of the legal uses of strict liability. Such uses are unjust, some say, because they do not treat us as moral agents. Treating someone as a moral agent means holding him liable for what he does only if he is morally culpable in doing it.

In my view, this line of thought harbours an accumulation of errors. Most importantly, the view of moral agency that Nagel tempts us to endorse (in the end he does not endorse it himself[5]) is wrong. Morally blameless actions often do change their agent's moral situation for the worse. Often their agent is morally bound to repair, to mitigate, to apologize, or to explain.[6] Ironically, we think otherwise only if we are in the thrall of what HLA Hart calls 'a legalistic conception of morality'.[7] We project back onto morality our moral expectations of the law. And one moral expectation we have of the law is that it will live up to the ideal of the rule of law. It was Kant, first and foremost, who lured us into thinking that morality itself ('the moral law') somehow lives up to this ideal. Not so. We need law, and law that lives up to the ideal of the rule of law, partly in order to help us

[3] For further explanation see John Gardner, 'What is Tort Law For? Part 1. The Place of Corrective Justice' (2011) 30 *Law and Philosophy* 1, 21–2.

[4] Thomas Nagel, 'Moral Luck' in his *Mortal Questions* (Cambridge University Press 1979) 24, 31.

[5] Nagel, 'Moral Luck' (n 4) 38.

[6] Explaining includes offering a justification or excuse. Once we recognize being morally bound to offer a justification or excuse as a possible moral consequence of acting, it becomes hard to deny that morally blameless actions are capable of having unwelcome moral consequences for their agents. This is one theme of my essay 'The Mark of Responsibility', the authoritative version of which appears in John Gardner, *Offences and Defences* (Oxford University Press 2007).

[7] 'Intention and Punishment' in HLA Hart, *Punishment and Responsibility: Essays in the Philosophy of Law* (Oxford University Press 1968) 113, 125.

deal with the fact that morality often does not.[8] Here begins a quite separate kind of 'injustice' objection to strict liability, one that is specific to strict liability's 'legal uses'. It sees the injustice of strict liability as bound up with a failure on the law's part to conform to the ideal of the rule of law. This is the kind of complaint about strict liability on which—to repeat—I will focus here.

2. Guiding and Goading

The ideal of the rule of law is the ideal according to which the law should be capable of guiding those who are subject to it. People should not be ambushed by the law; it should be possible for them reliably to anticipate the legal consequences of their actions and reliably to obtain or to avoid those consequences by following the law. So understood, the ideal sets a wide range of disparate standards for all legal systems to live up to. The ones that mainly concern us here are standards for legal *norms* to live up to. Legal norms should not, according to the ideal of the rule of law, be secret, retroactive, unclear, impossible to conform to, or forever in a state of flux; and particular legal norms (rulings) should be applications of general legal norms (rules). Legal norms that do not live up to these standards, as Lon Fuller famously explained, are not truly capable of being *followed*.[9] That does not stop them from being legal norms (Fuller sometimes got this point wrong[10]), but it does make them deficient qua legal norms. One may try to follow them but, however hard one tries, one cannot be sure of avoiding their violation, and thereby avoiding the unwelcome legal consequences. If one conforms to them by trying to do so, then that is at least partly a stroke of luck.

Fuller himself argued that strict liability in the law is objectionable on rule-of-law grounds because it demands the impossible.[11] That was a slip on his part. Only very rarely is it impossible for people to do what it takes to avoid strict liability. If only D had bought less dynamite, which she had the option to do, there would have been no fatal blast; if only D had parked on a different street, which she could easily have done, nobody would have put up a 'no parking' sign in her absence; if only D had emptied the swimming pool for winter a week earlier, as she had seriously considered doing, there would have been no flood; if only D had let her home to a different tenant, and she had plenty of candidates to choose from, it would never have become a crack-den; if only D had sold her customers a different holiday, as she was poised to do, they would not have ended up in that flea-pit. In every case, a happy ending to D's misadventure was perfectly possible when she went into it. Her problem, from the point of view of the rule of law, was not one of impossibility but only of lack of assurance. It was always entirely possible that she

[8] For a detailed and memorable discussion, see Tony Honoré, 'The Dependence of Morality on Law' (1993) 13 *Oxford Journal of Legal Studies* 1, 1–17.

[9] Lon L Fuller, *The Morality of Law* (rev edn, Yale University Press 1969) 33–8.

[10] eg Fuller, *Morality* (n 9) 41.

[11] Fuller, *Morality* (n 9) 75–7.

would not φ but it was nevertheless, at the crucial time, impossible for her to *make sure* that she would not φ.

Where the law imposes strict liability on D for φing (for blowing people up, for parking in a 'no parking' zone, for flooding a neighbour's land, for permitting property to be used for drug dealing, for providing a holiday different from the one contracted for) there is no step D could have taken, at the moment when she φed, to make sure that she wouldn't incur the liability, or even to be sure whether she would incur it. Recall that when the law imposes strict liability on D for φing, it doesn't care which steps D took to avoid φing or even whether there was any way for her to know that φing was what she was doing. And that, it may be thought, puts strict liability radically at odds with the ideal of the rule of law. One cannot follow a rule, in the relevant sense, if the rule provides one with no mechanism by which one can reliably avoid breaking it, or even find out if one is breaking it, when the time to conform to it arrives.

This is essentially HLA Hart's argument against the legal imposition of strict liability. He writes:

> Consider the law not as a system of stimuli but as what might be termed a choosing system, in which individuals can find out, in general terms at least, the costs they have to pay if they act in certain ways. This done, let us ask what value this system would have in social life and why we should regret its absence. I do not of course mean that it is a matter of indifference whether we obey the law or break it and pay the penalty. Punishment is different from a mere 'tax on a course of conduct'. What I do mean is that the conception of the law simply as goading individuals into desired courses of behaviour is inadequate and misleading; what a legal system that makes liability generally [non-strict, fault-based] does is to guide individuals' choices as to behaviour by presenting them with reasons for exercising choice in the direction of obedience, but leaving them to choose.[12]

Hart goes on to divide into three the advantages of eschewing strict liability in favour of some kind of fault-based liability:

> First, we maximize the individual's power at any time to predict the likelihood that the sanctions of the criminal law will be applied to him. Secondly, we introduce the individual's choice as one of the operative factors determining whether or not these sanctions shall be applied to him. Thirdly, . . . we provide that, if the sanctions of the criminal law are applied, the pains of punishment will for each individual represent the price of some satisfaction obtained from breach of law.[13]

I have argued at length elsewhere that these passages should be read as (successfully) harnessing Hart's objection to strict liability to a wider defence of the ideal of the rule of law.[14] As well as militating against strict liability, the considerations Hart adduces also militate, in broadly Fullerian spirit, against a resort to retroactivity, obscurity, secrecy, impossibility, inconstancy, and so on. We could say that Hart

[12] 'Legal Responsibility and Excuses' in Hart, *Punishment and Responsibility* (n 7) 44.

[13] 'Legal Responsibility and Excuses' in Hart, *Punishment and Responsibility* (n 7) 47.

[14] See John Gardner, 'Introduction' in HLA Hart, *Punishment and Responsibility*, ed John Gardner (2nd edn, Oxford University Press 2008) xxxiv–xliv.

adds 'strict liability' to Fuller's list, as a distinct affront or challenge to the rule of law. Strict liability laws, like secret or retrospective ones, do not guide us towards conformity; they cannot really be *followed.*

3. From Criminal Law to Private Law

Hart focuses his attention on strict criminal liability, or at any rate on strict liability to be punished. Can his argument equally be extended to private law, for example to the law of torts or breach of contract, where the normal mode of liability is not punitive ('pay[ing] the penalty') but rather reparative or restitutionary?

Clearly the argument applies in both contexts. But the change of context equally clearly makes a difference to how much weight we should attach to the argument in evaluating the relevant legal norms. Litigation in private law, unlike criminal prosecution, is zero-sum. In the criminal court there may of course be a victim of the crime and he may feel aggrieved if he does not 'get justice'. But contrary to the impression given by such familiar complaints, the main task of the criminal court is not corrective. It is not to give to the victim of wrongdoing something that it extracts from the wrongdoer. Burdens imposed on the wrongdoer (years spent in prison, fines levied, etc) are not burdens that the victim would otherwise bear. Conversely, burdens *not* imposed on the wrongdoer (years not spent in prison, fines not levied, etc) are not thereby borne by her victim instead. In the civil courts, when dealing with the aftermath of torts and breaches of contract, things are very different. The main task of the court is corrective. It is to give to the wronged plaintiff something that it extracts from the wronging defendant, reversing so far as possible the wrongful transaction that took place between them. There is normally a burdensome consequence of the wrong to be borne by either the plaintiff or the defendant and the court has to determine, *inter alia*, which of them is to bear how much of it. What is not allocated to the defendant (by an award of damages) is left with the plaintiff (who must absorb the costs of the wrong that the award of damages would otherwise have covered). This means that not only the defendant but also the plaintiff can be unjustly treated, and moreover in a similar way, by the legal rule under which the defendant's liability is determined.[15] In particular, the more extra protections against liability that we give to the defendant in the name of upholding the rule of law in her case, the more the plaintiff loses the protection that a less defendant-protective regime would allow her. What the defendant gains from there being fault liability, the plaintiff loses; what the defendant loses from there being strict liability, the plaintiff gains.[16]

[15] I have argued elsewhere that this zero-sum feature inevitably brings distributive-justice questions to bear on the doing of corrective justice: 'What is Tort Law For? Part 2: The Place of Distributive Justice' in John Oberdiek (ed), *Philosophical Foundations of the Law of Torts* (Oxford University Press 2014).

[16] It may be thought that this fact already militates in favour of fault-based liability (using the negligence standard) because such liability somehow puts the parties on an equal footing in their zero-sum conflict in a way that strict liability would not. See Ernest J Weinrib, *The Idea of Private Law*

Some writers think that this difference between criminal law and private law may be less substantial than it seems. Contrary to first impressions, they say, the criminal trial is indeed zero-sum. True, burdens not imposed on the wrongdoer (years not spent in prison, fines not levied, etc) are not borne by his victim instead. They are, however, borne by various (usually indefinite) other people who will some day be the victims of crimes. By burdening today's wrongdoer less we are not doing our bit to prevent or deter these future crimes and so are burdening future victims more. Some say, indeed, that a necessary condition of just sentencing (although, most agree, not a sufficient one) is that no extra burdens should be imposed by the court on wrongdoers beyond those that future victims of crime can thereby be spared.[17] If that proposal is sound, should we not conclude that rule-of-law protections accorded to criminal defendants, like those accorded to private law defendants, necessarily come at the cost of protections that are thereby denied to others?

Maybe. But be that as it may, the criminal trial remains importantly different from its private-law counterpart. The burdens created by (as it were) criminal under-sentencing are generally diffuse. For the most part, they are spread thinly across a wider population of victims of later crimes, usually in unassignable proportions. True, loss-spreading among potential plaintiffs is also possible in private law, thanks to the availability and widespread use of insurance. But in private law, defendant-side burdens can also be spread thinly, and often are spread thinly, through liability insurance. Not so in criminal law. In criminal law, making the defendant personally bear the burdens of liability is an aim of the exercise, and liability insurance (or any contract of indemnification) is void.[18] The distinctive technique by which criminal law deters and prevents (and of course often punishes too) is that of the non-spreadable, and more generally non-transferable, burden. So the way in which criminal trials are zero-sum, if indeed they are, still leaves the criminal defendant uniquely exposed and in need of enhanced protection against the possibility of being ambushed by the law.[19] The civil trial remains, in the relevant respect, a more symmetrical one than its criminal counterpart, and hence

(Harvard University Press 1995) 177–83, and Alan Brudner, *The Unity of the Common Law: Studies in Hegelian Jurisprudence* (University of California Press 1995) 190. I do not agree, and this is not what I am arguing here. My argument here does not enable one to draw any positive conclusions about which standards for liability should be used where in the law. I am exclusively attending to the question of how the zero-sum feature of private law affects the relative importance of the ideal of the rule of law in evaluating private law standards of liability, whatever they may be.

[17] The latest and probably most philosophically ambitious defence of this view is in Victor Tadros, *The Ends of Harm: The Moral Foundations of Criminal Law* (Oxford University Press 2011). However a similar view was defended less ambitiously by Hart in 'Prolegomenon to the Principles of Punishment', chapter 1 in his *Punishment and Responsibility* (n 7). Hart was in turn moderating the positions of Bentham and Beccaria, who came close to embracing 'no extra burdens' as a sufficient condition of just sentencing (although they might both have favoured a word other than 'just').

[18] *Askey v Golden Wine Company Limited* [1948] 2 All ER 35, 38; for nuanced discussion of the limits of this common law doctrine, see *Gray v Thames Trains* [2009] UKHL 33, especially in the speech of Lord Hoffman.

[19] A possible *quid pro quo* is that if the law does not provide the relevant protection against ambush, then a contract of insurance covering criminal penalties should exceptionally be enforceable: *R v Northumbrian Water ex parte Newcastle and North Tyneside Health Authority* [1998] All ER (D) 733.

one in which the defendant-protective standards of the rule of law may well call for more compromise in the name of plaintiff protection.

I am not suggesting an exact symmetry here. Some talk as if, in a tort or breach of contract case, there is either defendant liability or plaintiff liability, so that the question is: liability for whom?[20] But there is no such thing as 'plaintiff liability'.[21] At the end of the trial there is either defendant liability or no liability. This makes a significant difference in many ways. In particular, the standards of the rule of law that we are focusing on here are standards for legal norms to live up to, including legal norms that impose liabilities. If there is no norm imposing liability, it cannot either meet or fail to meet the relevant rule-of-law standards. In respect of norms imposing liability, the plaintiff's rule-of-law interests are usually aligned with those of the defendant: both want legal norms that are open, clear, prospective and otherwise tolerably free from the potential to ambush the unwitting. That is a public good from which both sides stand to benefit. So the complaint from aggrieved plaintiffs that we are imagining, when we think about the civil trial, is not strictly speaking that the defendant's rule-of-law gain is their *rule-of-law* loss.[22] Rather it is that the defendant's rule-of-law gain is their loss *in other ways*; most obviously, it deprives them of a remedy for wrongdoing that the law would otherwise grant. And that consideration does militate in favour of less stringent adherence to rule-of-law standards in respect of private law norms than would be acceptable in respect of criminal law norms. Rigid adherence to the Hartian stance on strict liability (as to the related Fullerian stance on unclarity, inconstancy, retrospectivity, secrecy, etc) can make an otherwise symmetrical private law dispute unjustly asymmetrical. The standards that the ideal of the rule of law sets for legal norms to live up to therefore need to be less stringently or more flexibly applied to the norms of private law, or at any rate to those that make up the law relating to the treatment in court of torts and of breaches of contract.

This is not startling news. In the common law world we tolerate a radically indeterminate body of law governing the tort of negligence—a body of law that, were it transplanted into the criminal law, would constitute a grave departure from the most elementary requirements of the rule of law. One reason to have any law, as I mentioned in Section 1, is to help us cope with the various ways in which morality can trip us up. Law cannot do this where its purported norm only says: morality applies here; just do the right thing. That is not the rule of law. That is not even a

[20] Jules Coleman, 'The Morality of Strict Tort Liability' in his *Markets, Morals, and the Law* (Cambridge University Press 1988) 166, 175.

[21] I am disregarding the possibility of a counterclaim in which the plaintiff is cast as defendant. I am also ignoring any possible liability to pay legal costs.

[22] My view on this point would be different if I thought, with Robin West, that the imperative of protecting plaintiffs and plaintiff-classes by law against abuses of power must be an aspect of the rule of law: West, 'The Limits of Process' in James Fleming (ed), *Getting to the Rule of Law: Nomos Volume 50* (New York University Press 2011) 32 at 45. But I do not think that. Not all the things that law should do, not even all the things that law should do qua law, are aspects of the rule of law. The rule of law is one particular way of protecting people from abuses of power, namely by making the law such that people can use it for guidance and can have reliable recourse to it. I have defended this view in various places including in my book *Law as a Leap of Faith* (Oxford University Press 2012) ch 8.

legal norm. That is a legal vacuum.[23] Many propositions of the law governing the tort of negligence come surprisingly close to such legal vacuity. They pass the buck back, in large measure, to ordinary moral reasoning in its rawest form. They invite us to think and act reasonably, meaning just as we should quite apart from the law.[24]

In view of the relatively rudimentary level of attention to Fullerian rule-of-law standards in this ever more dominant part of the law of torts, it is perhaps slightly comic to be fretting, on Hartian rule-of-law grounds, about some relatively contained pockets of strict liability in the residue. Motes and beams come to mind. That is not, of course, a reason to think that strict liability in the law of torts, or anywhere else in private law, is nothing to worry about, or nothing to worry about so far as the rule of law is concerned. My point is only that, for reasons I have sketched out, we should and do expect less stringent compliance with the relevant rule-of-law standards for legal norms in private law than in criminal law. A Hartian rule-of-law critique of strict liability in private law should make much the same allowances that a Fullerian rule-of-law critique of the law of negligence, on the ground of its indeterminacy, would have to make for the more symmetrical setting of the private law trial.

4. Commanding and Commending

Stephen Smith offers a reoriented 'rule-of-law' objection to strict liability, one that is perhaps designed to have more force in private law settings than the Hartian objection.[25] He presents it as an objection under the 'clarity' heading, and to that extent remains faithful to the Fullerian account of the rule of law. The main thing that makes Smith's objection different from Hart's is that it is not (in the terms I introduced cautiously in Section 1) an injustice objection. It is an inefficiency objection. It focuses on the suboptimal spurs to action that, in Smith's view, a strict liability rule creates for those who might, or think they might, fall foul of it, rather than on how the rule treats those who have already fallen foul of it. In one way this focus is not surprising. The ideal of the rule of law is primarily an ideal for legal efficiency, demanding of the law that it be good at guiding action.[26] The injustices that can come of failure to conform to the rule of law, such as those on which Hart is dwelling, are in a way derivative. They are consequential unjust impositions *ex post* upon people to whom the law did not (as it were) efficiently address itself

[23] For what seems to me to be the decisive argument, see Joseph Raz, 'Incorporation by Law' in his *Between Authority and Interpretation: On The Theory of Law and Practical Reason* (Oxford University Press 2009).

[24] For a detailed explanation and defence of this 'exclusive legal positivist' view see my paper 'The Many Faces of the Reasonable Person', forthcoming.

[25] Stephen A Smith, 'Strict Duties and the Rule of Law' this volume.

[26] Joseph Raz, 'The Rule of Law and its Virtue' in his *The Authority of Law* (2nd edn, Oxford University Press 2009) 210, 226. This sounds odd to a contemporary theorist of private law only because we have unwisely allowed economists to monopolize the language of efficiency. Conformity to the rule of law does not of course make the law economically efficient. It only makes it legally efficient.

ex ante. Possibly Smith thinks that some such unjust impositions flow from the inefficiencies with which he is primarily concerned; but his emphasis throughout is on the inefficiencies themselves, not on the injustices.

In keeping with this shift in emphasis from the *ex post* to the *ex ante*, Smith tells us that he is not objecting to strict liability as such. He is objecting to strict liability only when it is strict liability for the supposed breach of a 'strict duty'.[27] That is his name for a supposed duty not to φ that D may supposedly breach irrespective of any steps that she took in order not to φ and irrespective of whether she knew or had reason to know that she was φing. This change of focus from the liability to the duty makes less difference than some may think. Strict liability is normally contrasted with fault-based liability, and fault-based liability, by its nature, can only be liability for one's own actions and omissions (including, of course, one's actions and omissions of contributing to the actions and omissions of another). To make the contrast with fault-based liability a contrast of like with like, strict liability too must be thought of as a species of liability for one's own actions and omissions. I defined it accordingly at the start of this essay: 'strict liability is [a type of] liability that attaches to someone (call her D) for something she did (call it φing)'. This means that an employer's vicarious liability for the tort of an employee, understood as arising irrespective of the employer's own contributions to the tort, does not qualify as strict.[28] Likewise an insurer's contractual liability to indemnify the torts of the insured, or of a third party, does not qualify as strict, for it does not depend on the insurer's having played a part in the commission of the tort. On the other hand, an insurer's legal liability for *breach* of the same insurance contract by *non-payment* of a sum validly claimed could be a strict liability. For now there is an action or omission by the insurer—not paying out on a valid claim—which serves as the ground of the liability.

Must D's φing always be a breach of duty if D is to be strictly liable, in law, on the ground of it? Clearly not. The plainest counterexample is the one that Hart foregrounds when he speaks of a 'tax on a course of conduct',[29] and that Fuller describes, in similar vein, as 'a kind of surcharge on the act'.[30] An import tax is levied on actions of importing and a sales tax on actions of selling. In each case the action is the ground of the liability to pay tax, and that liability is typically strict. Reasonable ignorance or reasonable effort may be defences to a further liability (eg a liability to pay administrative penalties for non-reporting of a taxable import or sale), but the liability to pay the tax itself is typically unaffected by such considerations. As Fuller explains, it is possible to think of some strict liabilities in private law on this model. Strict tort liability for an ultra-hazardous activity such as blasting, for example, can be understood as 'impos[ing] on [the] blasting operations

[27] Smith, 'Strict Duties and the Rule of Law' (n 25) 189.

[28] Compare Lord Nicholls in *Majrowski v Guy's Hospital* [2006] UKHL 34 [7]: 'Vicarious liability is a common law principle of strict, no-fault liability.' This strikes me as a category mistake. If it were fault liability it could not possibly be vicarious. Therefore it makes no sense to classify it as 'no-fault' either.

[29] 'Legal Responsibility and Excuses' in Hart, *Punishment and Responsibility* (n 7) 44.

[30] Fuller, *Morality* (n 9) 75.

a kind of tax in the form of a rule that [the operator] must respond for any damage that results from these operations, whether or not they can be attributed to any negligence on his part'.[31] And when the strict liability is so understood, Fuller goes on to say, then what is required of the law under the rule of law 'is not that it cease commanding [actions that one cannot be sure of avoiding], but that it define as clearly as possible the kind of activity that carries a special surcharge of legal responsibility'.[32]

These remarks help us to see what Smith means when he claims not to be objecting to strict liability as such. He is leaving open the possibility that what we think of as strict tort liability might turn out to meet the requirements of the rule of law when understood on Fuller's tax model. His thesis is only that it does not meet the requirements of the rule of law when understood on the *tort* model, ie as liability for a wrong, a breach of duty.

Smith's objection to the existence of such a duty, however, is not Fuller's. It is not that a strict liability rule (understood on the tort model) commands something that it should not command, but that it *commends* something that it should not *commend*. Or rather, in Smith's turn of phrase, that the law, so understood, 'appears to recommend actions that it does not want to recommend'.[33] Smith has something like the following in mind: When the law of trespass is held to impose a strict duty not to enter another's land without permission, those who fear falling foul of the law may go to ridiculous lengths not to trespass, for example by never going anywhere, or by neglecting other duties in order to avoid a trespass even when the other duties are much more important. The law clearly does not seek this kind of overkill by its users, which is on any view totally unreasonable; yet the law does give people a reason to engage in it. A duty not to enter another's land without permission gives one a reason to destroy all one's opportunities to enter another's land without permission, in the same way that a duty to destroy a wasp's nest in the attic gives one a reason to blow up the whole house. The law is not being sufficiently clear in this case, thinks Smith, because it is 'sending mixed messages'.[34] It is giving people a reason to go to lengths to which, as the law well knows, it would be unreasonable for them to go. If the law only wanted them to go to reasonable lengths not to enter another's land without permission, that is what it would tell them to do. It would tell them to take reasonable steps not to φ, and then the duty, by definition, would no longer be a strict one.

This argument itself contains an element of overkill. All laws give one reasons to do things that it would be unreasonable for one to do. Many cowardly people hide behind the law to do totally unreasonable things. They evasively cite 'legal reasons'. They make it sound as if they have a legal duty not to allow nut-eating at school, ice-skating in the park, or advice-giving on the phone. In fact they have no such

[31] Fuller, *Morality* (n 9) 75.

[32] Fuller, *Morality* (n 9) 75. I have substituted the square-bracketed words here for Fuller's words 'the impossible' to reflect the point, in Section 2, that Fuller confuses the impossibility of making sure that one will φ with the impossibility of φing.

[33] Smith, 'Strict Duties and the Rule of Law' (n 25) 189.

[34] Smith, 'Strict Duties and the Rule of Law' (n 25) 189.

duty. They only have a duty to take reasonable steps to avoid injuries or losses of one kind or another, under the law of tortious negligence. The problem is that this also gives them a reason to take unreasonable steps, since one way to avoid failing to take reasonable steps is to take every imaginable step, including daft ones like banning everyone from the school or the park or the phone. This shows that the problem of 'mixed messages' to which Smith is addressing himself is not specific to strict legal duties. It applies to all legal duties.

So Smith still needs to show some way in which strict duties are especially or distinctively prone to induce overkill. The way he tries to show this is by showing that what appear to be strict duties to φ in the law are in fact duties to go to every possible length not to φ. They do not only give one a reason to engage in crazy overkill but positively *require* it of one. If there is a duty, then 'go to all lengths not to φ' is the content of the duty.

I have argued elsewhere that the law is not telling anyone to 'go to all lengths not to φ' when it gives them a strict duty not to φ.[35] Far from telling them to go to all lengths not to φ, it is telling them that in the law's eyes it does not matter what lengths they go to. They can go to no lengths at all if they like, so long as they do not φ. And that is because, as I explained above, strict liability is liability that attaches to D for φing, irrespective of any steps that she takes not to φ. Smith resists this line of thought. He has some minor skirmishes with my previous writings along the way. He rejects my view, for example, that going to great lengths to do something is not always, or even reliably, the best way to do it. But his main resistance has deeper roots. For when Smith is faced with my affirmative view that the only thing a strict duty not to φ tells D to do is *not to* φ—ie that the law means exactly what it says—he does not regard that as even a candidate interpretation. He says that the law here 'cannot mean what it appears to mean'.[36] It can only mean that D has a duty to take *some set of steps towards* not φing. And if that is all it can mean, then in the name of the rule of law ('clarity') that is what it should say. It should not say to D: do not φ. It should say: take steps not to φ. Then we can openly discuss whether it should be saying 'all possible steps', or only 'all reasonable steps', or perhaps 'all the steps that D thinks reasonable', or whatever.

This explains why, when I first told you what a 'strict duty' is according to Smith, I told you that it is a *supposed* duty not to φ that D may *supposedly* breach irrespective of any steps that she took in order not to φ and irrespective of whether she knew or had reason to know that she was φing. All of this is only 'supposed' because, according to Smith, the duty cannot really be like this. Its content must be different from what we suppose.

Smith's refusal to even entertain my simple 'do not φ' interpretation of the duty seems to come most immediately of his unargued assumption that the meaning of a proposition of law can only be its meaning '[f]rom a rule of law perspective'.[37]

[35] John Gardner, 'Obligations and Outcomes in the Law of Torts' in Peter Cane and John Gardner (eds), *Relating to Responsibility* (Oxford University Press 2001) 111, 111–16.
[36] Smith, 'Strict Duties and the Rule of Law' (n 25) 195.
[37] Smith, 'Strict Duties and the Rule of Law' (n 25) 193.

In other words the content of the so-called 'strict duty' must be read in such a way as to satisfy Fuller's demand for followability, and hence cannot be read as a strict 'do not φ' duty. The law must be interpreted as guidance, and 'strict duties guide citizens to take more than reasonable care'.[38] For reasons that I gave in Section 3, this manoeuvre jumps the gun. In private law there are plaintiff-side considerations that compete systematically (albeit not simply) with Fullerian rule-of-law standards for legal norms, and this fact should lead us to contemplate interpretations of some private law norms which leave them scoring pretty badly on the Fullerian scale.

Can we *only* interpret the law that governs the tort of negligence, for example, in such a way that it is as determinate as it would need to be to satisfy the tough standards that Fuller sets, the ones that we rightly insist upon in the criminal law? To do that we would need to dismiss almost every modern case on the tort of negligence, at least since *Donoghue v Stevenson*. It cannot be that in order to judge whether and to what extent a body of legal norms meets the relevant standards of the rule of law we can only ever begin by interpreting the body of norms so that it already meets them. That would mean that there is no law that fails to meet the standards of the rule of law. And this view, with which Fuller flirted and to which Dworkin later became wedded,[39] has long been exposed as incoherent. There cannot be standards for somebody or something to meet such that, by its nature, that same somebody or something always meets them. That is at odds with the very idea of a standard for somebody or something to meet.[40]

Smith's resistance to the simple 'do not φ' interpretation of strict duties, then, rests partly on a Dworkinian mistake, the mistake of thinking that nothing in the law can be rule-of-law deficient. Yet there seems to lurk in Smith's paper a second, deeper, cause of resistance to the simple 'do not φ' interpretation. Smith shares my view that legal duties must be morally intelligible, meaning presentable and imaginable as moral duties. '[W]hen we try to explain legal duties,' he writes, 'our explanation should show how they could plausibly be presented as reflecting moral duties.'[41] Apparently, however, Smith does not think that moral duties can be strict duties of the 'do not φ' kind. At any rate, that seems to be the implication of the following passage:

> [T]he rule of law objection [to strict duties is] that strict duties are not what they appear to be: that is to say, they are not actually duties. Both in law and morality to say that you have a duty to do X means that you ought to plan your actions so that you do X.[42]

I think that this is false of both legal and moral duties. Smith explains why he thinks it is true of legal duties: for him they must, as we saw, be interpreted as already rule-of-law compliant. But he says nothing to explain why he thinks it is true of moral

[38] Smith, 'Strict Duties and the Rule of Law' (n 25) 194.

[39] For a notable statement, see Ronald Dworkin, 'Hart's Postscript and the Character of Political Philosophy' (2004) 24 *Oxford Journal of Legal Studies* 1, 25.

[40] See further Timothy Macklem and John Gardner, 'Provocation and Pluralism' in Gardner, *Offences and Defences* (n 6).

[41] Smith, 'Strict Duties and the Rule of Law' (n 25) 195.

[42] Smith, 'Strict Duties and the Rule of Law' (n 25) 197–8.

duties. The only hint he gives is in the very words just quoted. He says that his 'rule of law objection' is an objection to taking literally a supposed moral injunction ('strictly') not to do X. This suggests to me that Smith thinks that morality conforms to the requirements of the rule of law. I have already explained why I think this assumption is mistaken. The fact that moral norms are often inadequate as guides—that morality constantly ambushes us and sabotages even our well-laid plans—is one reason why we need to have law, and to live under the rule of law. Morality is rife with luck. In particular it includes many strict duties: duties not to φ, where φing is something that one cannot be sure not to do or even to know one is doing. When we φ, even totally innocently, we often owe apologies, accounts, and repairs.

The puzzle is why the same should not be true in the law. Hart gives an answer. He draws attention to one tension between strict liability and the requirements of the rule of law. Does Smith's argument draw attention to another tension between strict liability and the requirements of the rule of law? Inasmuch as Smith's answer depends on an insistence that strict duties cannot possibly be what they seem, the answer is clearly no. One cannot show a rule-of-law problem with strict duties, or with the strict liabilities that are grounded in their breach, by denying that such duties are conceptually possible. If they are conceptually impossible, the question of their desirability does not arise.

5. Prophylaxis and Pricing

None of this goes to show that strict liability in private law is unobjectionable from the point of view of the rule of law. Smith's argument fails. But Hart's argument succeeds. It reveals genuine rule-of-law problems with strict liability, which I called assurance problems. All I added to Hart's argument was a caveat to the effect that, in the private law context, we may sometimes have to swallow our rule-of-law scruples and tolerate some assurance problems that we would not tolerate in criminal law, because in private law we have to think of extra assurance for the defendant in a zero-sum way, as extra hazard for the plaintiff.

This way of presenting what is at stake assumes that we are already at the stage where a zero-sum conflict exists, where plaintiff and defendant are locked together in the grim embrace of pending or imminent litigation. A merit of Smith's argument is that it draws our attention back to the earlier *ex ante* point at which there is still, for the potential defendant, a question of whether to risk becoming part of such a grim embrace.

Those writing about strict liability sometimes write as if the only relevant question of what to do facing the potential defendant *ex ante* is the question of whether to φ, where φing is the breach of duty that grounds the strict liability. But for the most part strict liability for φing exists, in the private law of all legal systems known to me, only where the φing takes place in the course of some specified activity or relationship—call it ψing. And in general, in such legal systems, ψing is an activity or relationship that one cannot but know one is engaged in, and moreover that one could (with enough effort) avoid getting into. So for the most part the law does provide an assurance of no liability to potential defendants at an earlier time, via a prophylactic measure, if they are willing to take the trouble to use it. Want to avoid strict liability for injuring people with your blasting operations? Fine: just don't go into the blasting business. Want to avoid strict liability for flooding your neighbour's land? Fine: just don't transport water onto your land. Want to avoid strict liability for breaches of contract? Fine: just don't enter into contracts that impose strict duties on you; undertake contractual duties only when they are of a 'best endeavours' variety. More generally, want to avoid strict liability for φing in the course of your ψing? Fine: just don't start ψing.

The law in these cases makes the strict liability a predictable cost, we might want to say, of doing certain avoidable kinds of business, or in Fullerian terms 'a kind of tax in the form of a rule that [the ψer] must respond for any damage that results from [φing in the course of ψing]'.[43] Don't want to bear the cost of φing? Fine: just stay out of the ψing business. This kind of prophylactic assurance device, in my view as in Fuller's, is capable of going a long way to meeting the assurance requirements of the rule of law, and in the process tends to mitigate, although maybe not eliminate, the Fuller–Hart rule-of-law anxieties we might otherwise experience about the use of strict liability in private law contexts. Moreover, the device does so without significantly shifting the risks of the regulated activities in question onto potential plaintiffs. By hypothesis, those who help themselves to the relevant prophylactic assurance devices do not embark on the regulated activities in question, and so do not impose the risks of those activities on any potential plaintiff. They might still be sued, of course—anyone at all can be sued for anything at all—and dispute might still arise in such a suit over whether their activity was, in spite of appearances, the regulated one. So the prophylactic assurance device does still create an obstacle for future plaintiffs. Nothing can save us altogether from the zero-sum quality of litigation in private law. But the addition of a prophylactic assurance device generally gives rise to less complex and speculative probative challenges than arise from the addition of a requirement to prove fault. And it also does more to guide plaintiffs into choosing different (more suitable) defendants to sue. So as a measure to bring greater rule-of-law conformity into private law without hobbling plaintiffs, the use of prophylactic assurance devices has some advantages over the use of fault standards. If fault liability in private law is nevertheless (at least sometimes) morally preferable to activity-specific strict liability, that can only be on other grounds. It is not because of the assurance demands of the rule of law.

Or at least not directly. Maybe indirectly, in the following way. Where ψing is a very specialized activity, giving rise to a small pocket of strict liability in a sea of potential liabilities that are otherwise fault based, it is relatively easy to steer clear of strict liability for ψing. There are plenty of other ways left to make a living, get around, engage in social activities, etc. As ψing gets less specific and the associated

[43] Fuller, *Morality* (n 9) 75.

pockets of strict liability grow, the force of the argument that one could have ruled them out at an earlier stage by simply not ψing diminishes. It is one thing to say: If you want to steer clear of strict liability, don't go into the blasting business. It is quite another to say: If you want to steer clear of strict liability, don't go into business at all. It is one thing to say: If you want to steer clear of strict liability, don't say anything about other people in the newspapers. It is quite another to say: If you want to steer clear of strict liability, don't say anything about other people. Activity-specific strict liability helps to satisfy the rule-of-law demand for assurance because and to the extent that it is genuinely specific. A regime of otherwise fault-based liabilities in private law is presupposed.

Since activity-specific strict liability, when it satisfies these conditions, makes certain liabilities in private law a predictable cost of doing certain kinds of business, it is tempting to read it as not regulating the action of φing at all (the killing by blasting, the flooding by importing water onto your land, the failure to deliver on the contractually specified date, etc). It is tempting to read it as only regulating, on the one hand, the wider activity of ψing (blasting, importing water onto your land, contracting) and, on the other hand, the legal liabilities that ensue when someone suffers harm or loss by one's ψing. On this view, when one is strictly liable in law, it is not really for one's wrongdoing. There is not really a tort or a breach of contract; those are just the lawyer's perhaps outmoded or fantastical *façons de parler*. There is no prior duty, breach of which grounds the liability. Nobody is suggesting, obviously, that one has a duty not to ψ, a duty that one breached by ψing. Rather, there is a free-standing liability that belongs to all ψers when certain harms or losses materialize from their ψing. In some ways, then, theirs is akin to the indemnity liability of an insurer, or the vicarious liability of an employer. It is a liability attached to their activities (employing, insuring) rather than their actions. In particular, there is no suggestion that they, as employers or insurers, have themselves done anything wrong. On this view the law attaches, as Fuller puts it, 'a special [kind of] liability to *entry* upon a certain *line* of conduct'.[44]

I do not doubt—in fact I have conceded already[45]—that it is possible to interpret some tort liabilities in this way, even though in doing so one awkwardly puts paid to the idea that tort liability is liability for torts, that is, for actions that the law holds to be wrongful. The question before us, however, is not whether the interpretation is (awkwardly) possible but whether one is forced to it as soon as one thinks of strict tort liability as a cost of doing certain types of business. It seems to me that one is not.

It is often suggested that one must choose between the following two ways of looking at any given tort liability. Either one thinks of it as a liability for a wrongful action of φing (the 'old' moralistic way of thinking about tort law) or one thinks of it as a mechanism for attaching a cost to the activity of ψing (the 'new' regulatory way of thinking about tort law). But these are not rival ways of thinking about the liability. They are fully compatible. Only an economist or accountant, or someone

[44] Fuller, *Morality* (n 9) 75.

[45] Text at n 31.

who should be an economist or accountant, would take it for granted that the cost of doing business we are talking about, when we describe strict liability as a cost of doing business, is the economic cost, meaning the price in pounds or dollars that the strictly liable ψer ends up paying. The cost that I had in mind, by contrast, was the fact of the strict tort liability itself, ie the fact that φing (whatever one did to avoid it and whether one knew of it or not) will now be a wrong, and a wrong recognized by law and actionable in law, because it will have been done in the course of ψing. The cost of doing business that we should be thinking of first, when we think about tort liability in the 'new' way as a mechanism for attaching costs to ψing, is the very fact of being subject to extra tort liability in the 'old' way, ie being at risk of committing wrongs of φing that would not qualify as wrongs were one not engaged in ψing. Any economic costs are mere consequences of that. They come and go according to the skill of one's lawyers, the scope of one's insurance policies, and the resources and resilience of those who launch proceedings against one. The tort liability, however, remains, and the non-awkward way to interpret it is as a liability for a tort of φing-while-ψing, and to think of potential liability for committing that tort as one of the costs of ψing. This is what Fuller gestures towards when he speaks of a 'special surcharge *of legal responsibility*'[46]—pointing not to the tax on ψing alone, but also to the distinctively tort-law ground for its falling due, namely that D tortiously φed in the course of ψing.

Different elements of this tort of φing-while-ψing come into the foreground depending on one's investigative preoccupations. If one is interested in how people might plan for their future liabilities, then one naturally focuses on the ψing element. If one is interested in the ground of the liability in tort, however, one naturally focuses on the φing element—the action, not the activity. The activity, ψing, is a necessary condition of liability but not, in itself, a ground of it (because not, in itself, a complete reason for it). It is perfectly understandable that many lawyers, immersed from the first day of their professional education in the ideology of the rule of law, are tempted to shift the focus of their analysis from the *ex hypothesi* unassurable φing element (killing, flooding, failure to deliver on the specified date, etc) to the *ex hypothesi* assurable ψing element (blasting, importing water onto land, contracting). It is also understandable that, in forging such a ψing-focused analysis, lawyers often find common cause with, or take comfort in the work of, micro-economists, who are immersed from the first day of *their* professional education in the stunted psychology of the self-interested 'rational' chooser who is out to maximize economic returns for himself. The economistic ideology agrees with the legalistic ideology in focusing attention on the ψing element as opposed to the φing element. In emphasizing the importance of the φing element, the action by D that grounds the liability, I am not suggesting that we can dispense with these specialized professional ideologies. The bewildering conditions of modern life unfortunately demand ever-greater bureaucratization, an ever-more pervasive parcelling up of rational labour into distinct professions, offices, and

[46] Fuller, *Morality* (n 9) 75.

disciplines. The occupants of such distinct professions, offices, and disciplines cannot but interpret the world so that it can be marshalled and rationalized according to the defining ideology of their role. Sometimes they are led to think and talk as if the ideals built into that ideology are the most important ideals for humanity, or society, or civilization. Sometimes they are led to think and talk, wishfully, as if the world of their work, or the world as a whole, already conforms to the ideals that they, as professionals, set for it. Most often they are led to focus professional attention on the data that do conform to those ideals, and to hold them up as some kind of vindication for their professional worldview.

This is well-known syndrome among lawyers, who naturally enough long to convince themselves and others of the nobility of what is often a murky and desolate professional life, raking and ploughing an endless 'field of pain and death'.[47] In this exercise of esteem-building, not only is the moral ideal of the rule of law casually endowed with too much importance as compared with the rest of morality; not only is the law often paraded too uncritically as already conforming to the ideal; but also the organizing categories of the law, and the relationships among them, are distorted by the urge to foreground those that conform to the ideal, and to background those that do not.[48] In the literature of the law of torts, especially but not only among those writers who self-identify as belonging to the new world of tort law as 'regulation', this syndrome is greatly in evidence in the premature rejection, marginalization, or reconstruction of strict liability, and in particular in the refusal to acknowledge (or even entertain) the existence of the strict duties, duties not to φ, the breach of which constitutes the tort.

[47] The famous phrase is Robert Cover's, from his 'Violence and the Word' (1986) 95 *Yale Law Journal* 1601, 1601.

[48] To see all three esteem-building engines whirring simultaneously without interruption, see Ronald Dworkin, *Law's Empire* (Belknap Press 1986).

10

Property, Equity, and the Rule of Law

*Henry E Smith**

1. Introduction

Property and the rule of law are often thought to be almost two sides of the same coin. The protection of property rights shields individuals from arbitrary state action, thereby giving substance to the rule of law. For those of a more procedural or formalist bent, the features of generality and stability often emphasized in property law are precisely at the core of the rule of law. Furthermore, property is in many ways more general and formal than other areas of private law, which again dovetails with the familiar rule-of-law criteria. Nevertheless, upon closer inspection, property law itself employs a variety of equitable standards, which give courts discretion and thus appear to raise concerns that property law might be undermining the rule of law. Is property the poster child for the rule of law or a Trojan horse of arbitrariness? Which is it?

Surprisingly, both, and in a surprising way. This chapter will argue that private law, and property in particular, exemplifies the rule of law on two scales, partly for reasons of information cost. On a micro level, property itself implements the rule of law, which reduces the information costs of coordinating the actions of large and indefinite sets of persons with respect to things. Property is at its core in rem. Especially where it sets up in rem rights and duties, it needs to be general, stable, and give proper notice on the widest possible basis—the familiar formal rule-of-law criteria.[1] Property law must satisfy these criteria because it must manage information: facilitating coordination on this scale requires simplicity and a degree of formalism precisely because the audience is in rem. Furthermore, in order to

* I would like to thank Lisa Austin, Lee Fennell,Andrew Gold, David Harper, Dennis Klimchuk, and participants at the Rule of Law and Private Law Workshop at the University of Toronto Faculty of Law, the Geneva–Harvard–Renmin–Sydney Conference on Property, the Workshop on Property Law and Theory at the New York University School of Law, and the New York University Colloquium on Market Institutions and Economic Processes for their helpful comments and discussions. All errors are mine.

[1] For a familiar list, see Lon L Fuller, *The Morality of Law* (rev edn, Yale University Press 1969) 38–91.

serve this coordinating function property must draw on a simple type of everyday morality against stealing and other forms of gross violation.

But property cannot stop there. Property governs both the relations of people in general and in a variety of more personal interactions. Some of these interactions can be formulated somewhat generally, as in the law of nuisance or in zoning. But at the most particularist end of the spectrum of property doctrines are those dealing with individual behaviour and whether it was done in good faith or with notice. Many of these doctrines trace back to the jurisdiction of the equity courts.

Equity protects the formal part of property that is congenial to rule-of-law proponents, or so I argue. The simple structures of the law are open to exploitation by opportunists. Formal law provides information about where the line exactly is, and evaders can use this information to take unforeseen advantage of the gap between the law's purpose and its literal terms. In order to prevent this opportunism, the law must employ a different set of moral standards that sound in anti-deception and anti-evasion. In previous work, I have argued that the equitable decision-making mode can serve this function of protecting the law against opportunistic evasion.[2] Interestingly, next to the tradition of legal rules and their formality and certainty there has always coexisted the notion of equity, which itself can be explained as largely directed at the problem of opportunism. Actual historical equity has been subjected to a number of different interpretations. It is commonly thought that the purpose of equity is to soften or modify the law when it fails owing to its generality. Here particularism and discretion hold sway because of the inherent difficulty of answering a host of questions before events as they occur. I will show that a constrained version of equity that focuses on opportunism does not undermine, but rather strengthens the formal law—and the rule of law that it implements. Situations of fraud, accident, and mistake—the traditional domain of equity—give rise to the problem of near fraud and exploitation of uncertainty, which call for the limited intervention of equity.

Equity helps maintain the structures within property called for by the rule of law, but something similar holds true of the legal system as a whole. The overall architecture of formal structures and equitable safety valves is replicated on a more macro level, in part for similar reasons of information cost. The rule-of-law criteria themselves are formal and can be evaded opportunistically. Evasion of the rule-of-law criteria is the most straightforward and thoroughgoing way in which a formal version of the rule of law is consistent with 'bad law'. Prevention of substantive evasion of the rule of law requires (limited) reference to norms outside the formal law, in a macro version of equity. Just as moral and information cost theories tend to converge at the level of legal doctrine, so too formal law and what used to be known as 'natural justice' or 'natural equity' can be seen to point in similar directions at the level of the law as a whole.

[2] For an extended argument that equity can be partly explained and justified in terms of anti-opportunism, see Henry E Smith, 'An Economic Analysis of Law versus Equity' (unpublished manuscript).

Information cost considerations shape the law of property consistently with the rule of law because both property and the rule of law itself respond to information cost constraints. In the following, I will start with the thinner and more formal notions of the rule of law and show how they must at least be supplemented by notions of equity in order to prevent evasion.[3] For this reason alone we have a reason to move one step toward thicker versions of the rule of law that incorporate morality and legitimacy. Anti-evasion requires the amount of intervention couched in moral terms that equity supplies.

Section 1 will show how information cost considerations lead private law, and property in particular, to exhibit the familiar features of the rule of law. It will also argue that a less formal safety valve, roughly identified with historical traditions of equity, is needed in order to protect formal law against evasion by opportunists. Section 2 will demonstrate that this micro equity and its functions scale up to the system of law itself: the rule of law is vulnerable to opportunistic evasion without some ability to invoke larger moral considerations in at least a limited way. This can be termed 'macro equity'. Section 3 draws out some implications of the convergence between the information cost theory and 'natural equity'.

2. Property and the Rule of Law

Property exemplifies the virtues and the perils of the rule of law. As I will show, considerations of information cost call for a high degree of formalism in property law, compared to contract. The in rem aspect of property in particular has to be communicated to a large and indefinite audience. However, a subset of that audience will probably find loopholes within bright line rules. Such opportunism calls for limited intervention traditionally associated with courts of equity and embodied in equitable maxims, defences, and remedial doctrines, all of which serve to bolster formal law in the face of misuse by opportunists.

2.1 Information cost and the rule of law

There is a reason why property exemplifies so well the rule of law, both in its regularity and in its limited need for open-endedness. Property governs both the relations of people in general and in a variety of more personal interactions. Especially where it sets up in rem rights and duties, property needs to be general, stable, and give proper notice on the widest possible basis. Achieving generality, stability, and notice requires managing information: facilitating coordination on

[3] For a taxonomy of notions of rule of law divided into formal and substantive and along a spectrum from thinner to thicker, see Brian Z Tamanaha, *On the Rule of Law: History, Politics, Theory* (Cambridge University Press 2004) 91; *see also* David Dyzenhaus, 'Form and Substance in the Rule of Law: A Democratic Justification of Judicial Review' in Christopher Forsyth (ed), *Judicial Review and the Constitution* (Hart 2000) 141.

this scale requires simplicity and a degree of formalism precisely because the audience is in rem.[4]

A good place to start in discussing the formalism of property law is the *numerus clausus* principle. Thomas Merrill and I have argued that the *numerus clausus* can be explained as implementing a rough version of optimal standardization.[5] Property comes in a standard set of forms, and courts will interpret people's attempts to create forms as falling in the pigeonholes the law provides. Thus, a lease 'for the duration of the war' will be taken to be a tenancy at will, and so on.[6] The catalogue of estates (fee simple absolute, defeasible fees, life estate, various future interests) is but the most obvious aspect of this standardization. By contrast, the law of contracts is hardly standardized at all. Other than high-level housekeeping, like providing for what counts as offer and acceptance, the law of contracts allows parties to customize their relations. Parties can, with sufficient clarity, even create their own vocabulary—something that is somewhere between difficult and impossible in property.

The greater degree of standardization in property can be traced back to a fundamental difference between property and contract: property at its core sets up in rem rights and corresponding duties, whereas contract is in personam. The duty bearers in property are numerous and indefinite and much less likely to be able to process idiosyncrasy at reasonable cost. In property, the in rem nature of duties has a substantive impact on widespread and non-consenting parties and gives rise to an informational externality: parties to a property transaction who wish for their own reasons to create idiosyncratic property rights with third party effects—these are sometimes called 'fancies'—will not take into account the costs these fancies pose for third parties. Those who encounter the property rights outside a contracting context, such as potential violators, will have burdens of processing information, which the transactors (unless altruistic) will not take into account. Furthermore, people transacting in similar property in general will have more types of information to be on the lookout for. There is no direct connection between these other market transactors and the creators of fancies. Thus, if A and B want to create a timeshare in watches, people transacting over other watches will have to make sure they are getting all the days they think they are getting, but will also have to be on the lookout for features of property rights that no one has even dreamed up yet—unless this open-endedness is cut off by the *numerus clausus*.

4 Henry E Smith, 'The Language of Property: Form, Context, and Audience' (2003) 55 *Stanford Law Review* 1105, 1148–57.

5 Thomas W Merrill and Henry E Smith, 'Optimal Standardization in the Law of Property: The Numerus Clausus Principle' (2000) 110 *Yale Law Journal* 1; see also Henry E Smith, 'Standardization in Property Law' in Kenneth Avotte and Henry E Smith (eds), *Research Handbook on the Economics of Property Law* (Edward Elgar 2011) 148.

6 See eg *National Bellas Hess, Inc v Kalis* 191 F2d 739 (8th Cir 1951), *Stanmeyer v Davis* 53 NE 2d 22 (Ill App 1944). *Lace v Chantler* 2 All ER 369 (KB 1944); Richard R Powell, *Powell on Real Property*, ed Michael Allan Wolf (Matthew Bender 2013) s 16.03[4][b] at 16-68–16-69; Merrill and Smith, 'Optimal Standardization' (n 5) 11–12; cf *Smith's Transfer & Storage Co v Hawkins* 50 A2d 267, 268 (DC 1946) (redefining definiteness requirement of the term of years).

The *numerus clausus* is also a rule of thumb about institutional choice. It directs courts to avoid innovating in the basic menu of property forms and to let legislatures take the lead instead. Without claiming that legislation is necessarily superior to judge-made law, Merrill and I did suggest that legislatures have certain advantages when it comes to innovations in the menu of property forms.[7] And in the history of property law, even in common law countries, legislatures have indeed been the main source of innovation in the menu of property forms, despite the common law nature of property law in the Anglo-American legal world. Thus, changes to the types of marital property stem from the Married Women's Property Acts, not from judicial modification of marital property.[8] Courts do innovate within the set of forms of property, but leave major changes in the menu like replacing dower and courtesy to legislation. The advantages of legislatures over courts as the source of innovation in property law stem in turn from the in rem nature of property rights. As Merrill and I noted, new property forms issuing from the legislature have a built-in advantage in terms of clarity, universality, comprehensiveness, stability, and prospectivity.[9] (They also can more easily be bundled with implicit compensation: the Married Women's Property Acts abolished dower and courtesy but also replaced them with the spousal elective forced share.) When the legislature announces a change, it is by its nature salient and locatable in one place, and thereby gains in clarity. Legislation applies across a jurisdiction, whereas courts' judgments apply to parties. And, depending on the court, judicial opinions may hold sway in only part of a jurisdiction. Legislatures, as is well known, can study a problem and take into account all sorts of factors and values bearing on a proposed change, in a way that courts cannot. Legislative change is difficult, and statutes might be expected to have more stability than court opinions. Finally, legislation tends not to be retroactive, whereas common law rule changes are often treated as having been the law all along.

Interestingly, these features of legislation in the property area are strikingly similar to the features on the typical list of criteria for the rule of law in its thinner versions. This is not to say that common law reasoning does not exemplify the rule of law.[10] But it does suggest that the rule of law gets an extra boost when the *numerus clausus* principle directs major changes to the menu of property forms to legislatures. Legislative innovation in basic property forms is more likely to possess Fuller's criteria of generality, clarity, non-contradiction, constancy, and non-retroactivity than is innovation in the menu by judges.[11] His generality and our universality are similar: legislation that is meant to be universal will tend to be couched in general terms. Indeed, universality is tightly connected to the reasons that generality is prized in the rule of law. And clarity, stability, and prospectivity are identical criteria. Indeed, the main apparent difference between Fuller's list and

[7] Merrill and Smith, 'Optimal Standardization' (n 5) 58–60.

[8] Merrill and Smith, 'Optimal Standardization' (n 5) 15, 65.

[9] Merrill and Smith, 'Optimal Standardization' (n 5) 60–8.

[10] Lisa Austin argues that common law reasoning can be explained in terms of the rule of law. Lisa M Austin, 'Property and the Rule of Law' *Legal Theory*, forthcoming.

[11] See Fuller, *Morality* (n 1) 38–91.

ours is that we emphasize comprehensiveness and he speaks of non-contradiction (and not requiring the impossible). Even these remaining criteria are not unrelated. Taking a comprehensive approach to a problem requiring innovation in property forms is likely to avoid contradiction and the requiring of the impossible.

Why does the rationale of the *numerus clausus* as a principle of institutional choice converge with the rule of law on the same set of criteria? Both the *numerus clausus* and the rule of law are shaped by considerations of information cost. If property rights were not in rem, they would not burden third parties informationally and substantively, and there would be less reason to worry about how efficiently and fairly the law has this impact.

One can generalize this point about the *numerus clausus* to property law in general and the rest of private law. Private law sets up a general platform for individuals in their interactions with each other. Property does this through an initial definition of things, which depersonalizes certain interpersonal relations.[12] The person walking through the parking lot need not know anything about the owners of the cars—whether the owner is morally worthy, has lent the car to his sister-in-law, has given a security interest to a bank, etc—in order for the actor to know that he has a duty not to steal or damage the car.[13] Even the law of torts, which does not have a *numerus clausus* in the way property does, employs modularity to reduce the costs of managing complex interactions between private actors.[14] Again, the tools employed by private law exhibit clarity, generality, and stability, in a fashion congruent with the rule of law. The rule of law as it plays out in private law helps contain information costs.

This aspect of private law—that it governs actors' relations in general—is sometimes referred to as the 'omnilaterality' of private law. Omnilaterality is at the heart of Kant's theory of public right that underpins private law, and it is important to Kant's understanding of the structure of property.[15] For Kant, the content of people's rights stems from the 'universal principle of right', under which people have rights that maximize their freedom consistent with a like freedom in others.[16] This approach builds in a form of the rule of law. It rightly points to the

[12] Henry E Smith, 'Property as the Law of Things' (2012) 125 *Harvard Law Review* 1691.

[13] JE Penner, *The Idea of Property in Law* (Oxford University Press 1997) 75–6. The civilian tradition divides private law into the law of persons, the law of things, and the law of obligations. What counts as a legal person and the consequences of this help manage interactions.

[14] Henry E Smith, 'Modularity and Morality in the Law of Torts' (2011) 4 *Journal of Tort Law* 1.

[15] Lisa M Austin, 'Possession and the Distractions of Philosophy' in James Penner and Henry E Smith (eds), *The Philosophical Foundations of Property Law* (Oxford University Press 2013): Austin argues that omnilaterality of legal relations is at the core of the law dealing with issues of possession. See also Alan Brudner, 'Private Law and Kantian Right' (2011) 61 *University of Toronto Law Journal* 279 (arguing that need for omnilaterality swallows up private nature of private law for Kant), Jeremy Waldron, 'Kant's Legal Positivism' (1996) 109 *Harvard Law Review* 1535, 1556–62 (arguing that plurality of moral views undermines role of omnilaterality for Kant).

[16] Immanuel Kant, *Doctrine of Right in The Metaphysics of Morals in Practical Philosophy*, trans Mary Gregor (Cambridge University Press 1996) 230, 237; see also Arthur Ripstein, *Force and Freedom: Kant's Legal and Political Philosophy* (Harvard University Press 2009) 57–106 (explicating Kant's philosophy of acquired rights and property in particular); Ernest J Weinrib, 'Poverty and Property in Kant's System of Rights' in *Corrective Justice* (Oxford University Press 2012) 263–96; NW Sage, 'Original Acquisition and Unilateralism: Kant, Hegel, and Corrective Justice' (2012) 25 *Canadian*

public aspects of private law. But in pointing to public right, sometimes the further implication is drawn that private law is simply a branch of public law.[17] This is an overstatement: even though the law (whether one wants to call it public or private) is an essential underpinning for the successful interaction of private actors, omnilaterality does *not* require specification of each potential connection between each actor in every respect. On the contrary, the modular architecture of private law, and of property law in particular, allows many of these interactions to be under- or unspecified. For private law to underpin the omnilateral interactions of actors, it has to be couched in fairly general terms and not in terms specific to particular parties. Again, doing the opposite would be intractable from an information cost point of view.

Interestingly, information costs form a link between two concepts for which Fuller is most known: the rule of law and polycentricity. The latter refers to tasks that involve a dense network of interactions. In such tasks the number of potential interactions increases much more than linearly, as is well known in complexity theory, the study of problems in terms of the minimum running time for programmes to solve them. Fuller gives the example of a will that leaves paintings to two museums but does not specify which paintings are to go to which museum.[18] The problem is that to the museums each painting's value depends on which other paintings that museum gets. This is reminiscent of the Knapsack Problem of complexity theory. In the Knapsack Problem, out of a given set of n items, with given weights and values, one must choose the combination that has the maximum value but a weight under a given limit. This problem requires exponential time and is probably intractable, requiring approximate methods.[19]

Property and private law in general are in part a solution to a similar potentially intractable problem, and the type of solution required is congruent with the rule of law. Private law deals with the interaction of persons (as opposed to the relation of the individual to the state). This is a classic polycentric problem. It is also potentially intractable. We could in theory specify every relation between every person and every other person with respect to every aspect of every resource. A 'complete' property system would be one in which each such relation is specified.[20] For a set C of all the possible claimants in the world, a set D of all the possible duty bearers, and a set A of all the possible actions with respect to a set R of all the possible resource attributes, a complete property system would take as its

Journal of Law and Jurisprudence 119, 120–4 (arguing that omnilaterality is not needed to solve the 'problem' of original acquisition).

[17] For discussion, see Brudner, *Kantian Right* (n 15) and Ernest J Weinrib, 'Private Law and Public Right' (2011) 61 *University of Toronto Law Journal* 191 (arguing that for Kant omnilaterality is an aspect of public right that transforms private law into a community of rights).

[18] Lon L Fuller, 'The Forms and Limits of Adjudication' in Kenneth I Winston (ed), *The Principles of Social Order: Selected Essays of Lon L. Fuller* (Hart Publishing 2001) 101, 126–36 (introducing the concept of polycentric tasks); see also Michael Polanyi, *The Logic of Liberty; Reflections and Rejoinders* (University of Chicago Press 1965) 171.

[19] That is, the Knapsack Problem is NP-complete.

[20] Brian Angelo Lee and Henry E Smith, 'The Nature of Coasean Property' (2012) 59 *International Review of Economics* 145.

domain the set P of all the quadruples: $P = C \times D \times A \times R$. Then the complete system would be a function from this domain to the set {0, 1}. And the function to be useful would take into account the relation of many of the pairs with respect to each other: C_1 controlling R_1 with respect to D_1 over action A_1 will naturally go along with C_1 controlling R_2 (and $R_3, \ldots$) with respect to D_2 (and $D_3, \ldots$) with respect to A_1 (and $A_2, \ldots$). And some pairs will conflict, etc. Instead of proceeding in this fully articulated fashion, property employs a massive short cut over this complete system by defining lumpy things (clusters of *R*s) and providing for in rem rights (making a right in C_i correspond in the first instance to duties in all the *D*s other than D_i). With such an exclusion strategy in place, it is possible to focus in through governance strategies on particularly important modifications, by making exceptions for certain *A*s to C_1's rights (or the rights of all *C*s), through nuisance, zoning, covenants, and so on.[21]

Notice, though, that we are on the road to the rule of law. The shortening of the complete system through bunching provides for generality. The modularity it allows permits stability: we need not worry about run-away and hard-to-foresee ripple effects when the system consists of lumpy components that interact in simpler ways. Finally, we can even begin to think about giving people notice of the short-cut system, whereas the list-style system of property and private law is a non-starter. Not coincidentally, our morality consists of broad-brush imperatives against stealing and injuring in impersonal contexts along with more articulated exceptions and affirmative obligations in more personal contexts. Morality itself is fully congruent with what a concern for information costs dictates. I do not argue that we can ground morality in information cost or vice versa, but they do reinforce each other. It is hard to see how human beings would adopt a morality that is too informationally demanding, and the fact that a system has been internalized and institutionalized as a moral system makes it easier to implement in terms of generality, stability, and notice. In 'in rem' contexts, satisfying the informational tradeoff involves piggybacking on a common denominator of morality. Thus, in the parking lot, 'thou shalt not steal' is a good guide. Correspondingly, in more personal contexts, the law can either draw on more localized customs or take a page from the dealings of the parties themselves. It can require more in the way of affirmative duties instead of depending primarily on negative duties of abstention—as property law does in the in rem context. Thus, neighbouring landowners can be subjected to duties of lateral support and the relatively complex governance regime of nuisance law, whereas trespasses, which can be committed potentially by anyone, are keyed to the *ad coelum* rule (that a landowner owns 'to the heavens above and the depths below') in an exclusionary strategy. Information cost, morality, and the rule of law work hand in glove.

Thus, the nature of the coordination provided by property law raises an informational problem that can be solved with the rule of law and its familiar formal features. The kind of morality needed likewise requires simplicity and publicity.

21 Henry E Smith, 'Exclusion Versus Governance: Two Strategies for Delineating Property Rights' (2002) 31 *Journal of Legal Studies* S453.

Information costs provide a reason why the rule of law has at least some relation to morality.

It is often pointed out that the rule of law does not ensure the morality of the law. I return to this question later, but consider for a moment how the formality of property relates to its morality. As with the rule of law generally, we cannot say that property, merely by virtue of its being formal, is thereby ensured to be good property law. As with the rule of law in general, the generality, stability, and non-retroactivity that serve the purpose of property can even be said to have a moral aspect. But this does not ensure that *any* formal property law would be desirable in terms of efficiency and autonomy, fairness, and distributional justice. The formality of property does make some demand on the type of morality which it can implement. In order to broadcast messages to duty holders who are far-flung, the law has to employ a basic everyday morality that is easy to communicate precisely because it is basic and everyday.[22]

2.2 Protecting the law through micro equity

One limit to formalism is its vulnerability to evasion by opportunists. This is one reason to allow for equitable intervention.

The simple structures of the law are open to exploitation by opportunists. What is opportunism? Some notion of deception is somehow involved. Nobel laureate Oliver Williamson defines opportunism as 'self-interest seeking with guile',[23] but this includes all sorts of outright lying and cheating. Others define opportunism to be behaviour that is not technically illegal but contravenes the spirit of an agreement or a law.[24] This definition is narrow in the sense of requiring technical legality, but the notion of the spirit of an agreement is left fairly open. At what level of generality is an agreement's or a law's spirit supposed to be invoked? Traditionally, equity concerned itself with 'near fraud', which is behaviour that is close to the line of fraud or may well be fraud but cannot be proved as such.[25] Picking up on this notion, I have defined opportunism as such:

[22] Thomas W Merrill and Henry E Smith, 'The Morality of Property' (2007) 48 *William & Mary Law Review* 1849.

[23] Oliver E Williamson, *The Economic Institutions of Capitalism* (Collier Macmillan 1985) 47.

[24] See eg George M Cohen, 'The Negligence-Opportunism Tradeoff in Contract Law' (1992) 20 *Hofstra Law Review* 941, 957 (defining opportunism as 'any contractual conduct by one party contrary to the other party's reasonable expectations based on the parties' agreement, contractual norms, or conventional morality') (footnote omitted), Timothy Muris, 'Opportunistic Behavior and the Law of Contracts' (1981) 65 *Minnesota Law Review* 521 (opportunism is conduct that is 'contrary to the other party's understanding of the contract, but not necessarily contrary to the agreement's terms'), and Samuel W Buell, 'Good Faith and Law Evasion' (2011) 58 *UCLA Law Review* 611, 623 ('In common parlance, the evasive actor is one whose project is to get around the law. She seeks to avoid sanction while engaging, in substance, in the very sort of behavior that the law means to price or punish.'). For a wider definition, see eg Richard A Posner, *Economic Analysis of Law* (5th edn, Aspen Law & Business 1998) s 4.1 103 (defining 'opportunism' in the contracting context as 'trying to take advantage of the vulnerabilities created by the sequential character of the contract').

[25] In the nineteenth-century view, 'unconscionability' referred to fraud that could not readily be proved; see eg *Seymour v Delancey* 3 Cow 445, 532, 15 AmDec 270 (NY Sup 1824) ('Inadequacy of price, unless it amount to conclusive evidence of fraud, is not itself a sufficient ground for refusing a

> [B]ehavior that is undesirable but that cannot be cost-effectively captured—defined, detected, and deterred—by explicit ex ante rulemaking.... It often consists of behavior that is technically legal but is done with a view to securing unintended benefits from the system, and these benefits are usually smaller than the costs they impose on others.[26]

Elsewhere I argue that a major theme of traditional equity was to counteract opportunism. To do so equity needs to go beyond *ex ante* bright line rules, because it is difficult to anticipate all the avenues of evasion. Plugging nine out of ten loopholes is useless if all the evaders can rush through the tenth. Equity employs *ex post* standards, emphasizes good faith and notice, couches its reasoning in terms of morals, and is sometimes vague rather than bright line. To cabin such a powerful tool, equity courts were only supposed to act in personam and not in rem, and the substantive doctrines of equity counselled caution in undermining the law. Equity was not designed to root out every last bit of opportunism and courts recognized that equitable doctrines and remedies, not least injunctions, themselves could be exploited by opportunistic litigants unless courts were on their guard and were willing to stay the hand of equity.

Equity often consists of structured rules of thumb and shifting presumptions rather than broad-brush rules that would override the law. For example, contrary to the Supreme Court's recent strange four-factor 'test' for injunctions starting with its opinion in *eBay Inc v MercExchange, LLC*,[27] the traditional approach was to consider whether inadequacy of the legal remedy, in terms of well-known categories—like difficulty of valuation and repeated violation—gave rise to a presumptive right to an injunction.[28] Then considerations like balance of the hardships, meaning not equipoise but gross imbalance, could overcome the presumption.[29] That is, if the injunction would be far more damaging to the defendant than it would benefit the plaintiff, the court could exercise its discretion and not enter an injunction. (For one thing, in such situations the movant might well be acting opportunistically.) However, if the defendant had violated the right in bad faith, then the injunction would be near-automatic after all. This approach to injunctions was highly structured and designed to counteract opportunism while dampening the uncertainty costs of the discretion. The '*eBay* test', by contrast, is highly uncertain and on its face does not even take bad faith into account.[30]

specific performance of an agreement'); James Gordley, 'Equality in Exchange' (1981) 69 *California Law Review* 1587, 1639. See also Richard A Epstein, 'Unconscionability: A Critical Reappraisal' (1975) 18 *Journal of Law & Economics* 293, 293–301.

[26] Smith, 'Law versus Equity' (n 2) 9–10. For an argument that equity's role as a court of conscience originally meant that the judge knew and could draw on facts not in evidence, see Mike Macnair, 'Equity and Conscience' (2007) 27 *Oxford Journal of Legal Studies* 659 (2007).

[27] 47 US 388, 390–1 (2006); see also *Monsanto Co v Geertson Seed Farms* 130 S Ct 2743, 2756–7 (2010) (applying the four-factor test from *eBay* for injunctions in a NEPA case).

[28] Mark R Gergen, John M Golden, and Henry E Smith, 'The Supreme Court's Accidental Revolution? The Test for Permanent Injunctions' (2012) 112 *Columbia Law Review* 203, 212–26.

[29] Gergen et al, 'Accidental Revolution?' (n 28) 226–30; Douglas Laycock, 'The Neglected Defense of Undue Hardship (and the Doctrinal Train Wreck in *Boomer v Atlantic Cement*)' (2012) 4 *Journal of Tort Law* 1, 4–5; Smith, 'Law versus Equity' (n 2).

[30] Gergen et al, 'Accidental Revolution?' (n 28) 240–1.

Practically speaking, what is important is to find proxies for unforeseeable exploitation of rules. Situations of fraud, accident, and mistake give rise to the problem of near fraud and exploitation of uncertainty. More particularly, proxies relating to bad faith and disproportionate hardship can be used to invalidate actions or to throw the burden of justification on a party who wishes to take advantage of them.[31] I have argued that historically equity courts and their special doctrines were loosely associated with anti-opportunism, such that it makes sense to identify countering opportunism as a function of the equitable decision-making mode (which is imperfectly correlated with equity jurisdiction of old).[32] What has been termed the 'Grand Style' and freewheeling natural law jurisprudence can be seen as serving this more modest safety-valve function.[33] The limited open-textured quality of the law (through equity or otherwise) is required by the ability of some actors to consciously exploit the rules the law lays down, or as Justice Story put it, '[f]raud is infinite' given the 'fertility of man's invention'.[34] Story was tapping into a long tradition of equity tracing back to Aristotle,[35] and this tradition does implicitly (and sometimes explicitly) sound in anti-opportunism. In the words of one court quoted by Story:

Now equity is no part of the law, but a moral virtue, which qualifies, moderates, and reforms the rigour, hardness, and edge of the law, and is an universal truth; it does also assist the law where it is defective and weak in the constitution (which is the life of the law) and defends the law from crafty evasions, delusions, and new subtilties, invented and contrived to evade and delude the common law, whereby such as have undoubted right are made remediless; and this is the office of equity, to support and protect the common law from shifts and crafty

[31] Smith, 'Law versus Equity' (n 2).

[32] Smith, 'Law versus Equity' (n 2); see also Henry E Smith, 'Rose's Human Nature of Property' (2011) 19 *William & Mary Bill of Rights Journal* 1047.

[33] See Robert Lowry Clinton, 'Classical Legal Naturalism and the Politics of John Marshall's Constitutional Jurisprudence' (2000) 33 *John Marshall Law Review* 935, 948 (discussing Carl Dibble's identification of a 'moderate Enlightenment' tradition of legal interpretation associated with Grotius, Blackstone, and Marshall, that emphasized the role of equity and located the need for interpreting laws not in the ambiguity of language but in the possibility 'that corrupt, duplicitous persons will "treat the law in a sophisticated manner" in order to advance their own individual interests'), quoting Carl M Dibble, *The Lost Tradition of Modern Legal Interpretation* (1994) 5 (unpublished essay prepared for delivery at the 1994 Annual Meeting of the American Political Science Association).

[34] Joseph Story, *Commentaries on Equity Jurisprudence: As Administered in England and America* (Hillard, Gray & Co 1836) § 186, at 196 (quoting a Letter from Lord Hardwicke to Lord Kames (30 June 1759)). Or, as Chancellor Ellesmere put the point: 'The Cause why there is a Chancery is, for that Mens Actions are so divers and infinite, That it is impossible to make any general Law which may aptly meet with every particular Act, and not fail in some Circumstances.' *The Earl of Oxford's Case* 21 Eng Rep 485, 486 (Ch 1615).

[35] Aristotle, *The Nicomachean Ethics*, ed David Ross, JL Ackrill, and JO Urmson (rev edn, Oxford University Press 1980) 132–4; Thomas Aquinas, *Summa Theologica* (American edn; Benziger Bros 1947–8) I–II q 96 art 6; TFT Plucknett and JL Barton (eds), *St. German's Doctor and student* (Seldon Society 1974) 94–107; see also eg *Riggs v Palmer* 22 NE 188, 189 (NY 1889) (quoting Aristotle on equity); Eric G Zahnd, 'The Application of Universal Laws to Particular Cases: A Defense of Equity in Aristotelianism and Anglo-American Law' (1996) 59 *Law & Contemporary Problems* 263, 270–5 (documenting influence of Aristotelian equity on Anglo-American law); but cf Darien Shanske, 'Four Theses: Preliminary to an Appeal to Equity' (2005) 57 *Stanford Law Review* 2053 (arguing that Aristotle's equity was not primarily legal).

contrivances against the justice of the law. Equity therefore does not destroy the law, nor create it, but assist it.[36]

The law needs a safety valve to deal with opportunists. The correlation between the equitable decision-making mode and historical equity jurisdiction is not perfect. Sometimes the old common law side employed moral standards (eg quasi-contract), and sometimes the equity side was more rule-like (eg tracing rules for constructive trusts). Still, the Aristotelian notion of equity as carried forward by equity courts did focus on countering opportunism.

An equitable safety valve does not require separate courts or even a separate jurisdiction, but the fusion of law and equity that reached its culmination in the Legal Realist era did lead to the polarized versions of both property and the rule of law we see today. On the one hand, equity in Legal Realism slipped its bounds and became a preference for contextualized standards and discretion, in opposition to traditional formalism within private law and to the liberal notion of the rule of law.[37] On the other hand, the backlash against this freewheeling approach seeks to reinvigorate formalism to the exclusion of even the traditional role for equity.[38]

Thus, different versions of equity have always been a foil of proponents of the rule of law. The common law lawyers accused the equity courts of exercising an intolerable level of arbitrary discretion, often associated with the notion that equity varied with the 'Chancellor's Foot'.[39] (Also, the need for consistency may have led to the understaffing that in turn caused the equity courts to become a Kafka-esque nightmare in nineteenth-century England.[40]) Equity courts were regarded with suspicion in America, partly for rule-of-law reasons: equity courts were associated with arbitrary royal prerogative.[41]

With the rise of Realism, one version of the context-sensitivity espoused by the Realists involved removing the jurisdictional and other restraints on equity.

36 *Dudley v Dudley* (1705) 24 Eng Rep 118, 119 (Ch) (UK), quoted in Story, 'Commentaries on Equity Jurisprudence' (n 34) § 17, at 18–19. Story endorses this account of equity's function, despite some reservations about the broad identification of equity with virtue.

37 See eg Robert G Bone, 'Mapping the Boundaries of the Dispute: Conceptions of Ideal Lawsuit Structure from the Field Code to the Federal Rules' (1989) 89 *Columbia Law Review* 1, 78–114.

38 For a good example of this polarization, see *Grupo Mexicano de Desarrollo, SA v Alliance Bond Fund, Inc* 527 US 308 (1999); Smith, 'Law versus Equity' (n 2) 52–3.

39 The most famous critique is Selden's humorous one: 'Equity is a Roguish thing: for law we have a measure, know what to trust to; Equity is according to the Conscience of him that is Chancellor, and as that is larger or narrower, so is Equity. 'Tis all one as if they should make the Standard for the measure we call a Foot, a Chancellor's Foot; what an uncertain Measure would be this. One Chancellor has a long Foot, another a short Foot, a Third an indifferent Foot: 'Tis the same thing in the Chancellor's Conscience' (John Selden, 'Equity' in *Table-Talk: being the discourses of John Selden, Esq.* (2nd edn, JM Dent & Co 1689) 43, 43–50). See generally JH Baker, *An Introduction to English Legal History* (3rd edn, Butterworths 1990) 112–33.

40 And a Dickensian one: Charles Dickens, *Bleak House* (first published 1853; Oxford University Press 1978).

41 Puritans had been on the common law and parliamentary side of the battles of the sixteenth century, and, according to Pound, 'always been a consistent and thorough-going opponent of equity'. Roscoe Pound, 'Puritanism and the Common Law' (1911) 45 *American Law Review* 811, 825, but cf Zechariah Chafee Jr, *The Suffolk County Court and its Jurisdiction, Introduction to 29 Publications of the Colonial Society of Massachusetts, Records of the Suffolk County Court 1671–1680* (1933) pt I l–lii.

A proto-Realist like Pound was quite explicit in noting that modern twentieth-century strains in jurisprudence were in some sense expanding equity.[42] The fusion of law and equity itself was adopted as a Realist project culminating in the federal rules of civil procedure in 1937. And the turn toward public law and court intervention with structural remedies was cast as a vindication or sympathetic expansion of traditional equity. The structural injunction was justified as part of a court's roving commission to do good.[43] And administrative law, which sceptics of the welfare state saw as undermining the rule of law, was sometimes thought of as 'the new equity'.[44]

The Realists were suspicious of the rule of law, and in turn classical liberals and conservatives accused Legal Realism (and the administrative welfare state) of undermining the rule of law. On their view, policy-oriented judging, and by the same token government by administration, necessarily involved too much discretion to be consistent with the rule of law.[45] But to the unsympathetic ear, appeals to natural law or natural rights do not sound very determinate and consistent with the rule of law either. In the twentieth century, proponents of the rule of law tended to take an increasingly narrow proceduralist approach to the rule of law. And, to the extent that these proponents of the rule of law also opposed positivism and Realism, they would invoke a thin, or in Fuller's terms 'internal', morality of the law, in a kind of procedural natural law.

The approach to micro (and macro) equity offered in this chapter allows one a way out of these classic dilemmas of hyper-formalism and hyper-realism. The question then becomes which hybrid of law and equity—of formalism and safety valve—is best, keeping in mind that all form or all contextualism is not possible. I will argue that a limited equity based on equitable rules of thumb has great advantages but only so long as it can draw on a common morality that cannot be fully captured within the law itself. It is no accident that traditional equity was identified with natural law or natural justice. It is an open question how much

[42] Roscoe Pound, 'The End of Law as Developed in Legal Rules and Doctrines' (1913) 27 *Harvard Law Review* 195, 226 ('Equity sought to prevent the unconscientious exercise of rights; today we seek to prevent the anti-social exercise of rights'); Pound, 'The End of Law as Developed in Legal Rules and Doctrines' 227 ('Equity imposed moral limitations. The law today is beginning to impose social limitations').

[43] See Owen M Fiss, 'The Supreme Court, 1978 Term—Foreword: The Forms of Justice' (1979) 93 *Harvard Law Review* 1, 2 ('The structural suit is one in which a judge, confronting a state bureaucracy over values of constitutional dimension, undertakes to restructure the organization to eliminate a threat to those values posed by the present institutional arrangements. The injunction is the means by which these reconstructive directives are transmitted'), but see *Bisciglia v Kenosha Unif Sch Dist No 1* 45 F3d 223, 228 (7th Cir 1995) (denying temporary injunction in suit over employment termination and stating: '[T]his court does not possess a roving commission to do good. It must make a decision based upon the record and the law'); Douglas Laycock, 'The Triumph of Equity' (1993) 56 *Law & Contemporary Problems* 53 (denying 'that a court of equity has a roving commission to do good once it identifies a threshold violation of law that justifies its intervention').

[44] See eg Leonard J Emmerglick, 'A Century of the New Equity' (1945) 23 *Texas Law Review* 244, 255 ('The administrative court, found in both the federal and state legal systems, is a corresponding effort to meet the need for specialized judicial administration of equity'); Michael J Hays, 'Where Equity Meets Expertise: Re-Thinking Appellate Review in Complex Litigation' (2008) 41 *University of Michigan Journal of Law Reform* 421, 434–5 (noting the parallels between administration and equity in terms of both benefits and perils).

[45] See Tamanaha, *On the Rule of Law* (n 3) 60–72.

consensus there is about the common morality required for an equity to support the rule of law. I return to the relation of equity and natural law later.

3. The Rule of Law and the Need for Macro Equity

The literature on the rule of law shows, one level up, the same dilemmas as we face in property and private law. Formalistic versions of the rule of law offer a set of criteria, often requiring law itself to be formalistic, in order to satisfy the rule of law. Fuller's ways for the law to go wrong correspond to a list of features of the rule of law: generality, publicity, non-retroactivity/prospectivity, comprehensibility, non-contradictoriness, feasibility of compliance, stability, and administrability.[46] As others, particularly positivists like Hart and Raz, have pointed out, systems of law can satisfy these criteria and still be bad law.[47] For this reason, some theorists of the rule of law would move toward a more robust version of the rule of law that incorporates a substantive criterion of respect for human rights or a procedural requirement of democratic enactment.

So far so familiar. But I suggest that the rule of law faces an even more immediate threat, one that undermines it on its own narrow terms: the problem of opportunism. Those promulgating and enforcing law might evade the requirements of the rule of law in a fashion similar to someone who exploits the formal law of property or the formal terms of a contract to achieve a purpose unforeseeably at odds with the purposes of the law. So here, at the macro level in these instances, the rule-of-law criteria themselves serve the same role of benchmark and target for opportunistic evasion (through law-making) that the formal law does in the private law when private actors exploit it in ways that (micro) equity seeks to counter. Interestingly, Fuller hints at this problem with a couple of his examples. So, constitutional provisions against 'private laws' and 'special legislation' (which might be thought related to the generality criterion of the rule of law) have, according to Fuller, 'produced much difficulty for courts and legislatures' because 'their requirements are met by such apparently disingenuous devices as a provision that a particular statute shall apply "to all cities in the state which according to the last census had a population of more than 165,000 and less than 166,000"'.[48] Not willing to give up on formal legality, he strangely remarks that '[b]efore condemning this apparent evasion we should recall that the one-member class or set is a familiar and essential concept of logic and set theory'.[49] Yes, but so what? The real question is whether courts can find proxies—like bizarrely and functionally unmotivated descriptions

[46] Fuller, *Morality* (n 1) 38–91.

[47] HLA Hart, *The Concept of Law* (2nd edn, Clarendon Press 1994) 207 (arguing that rule-of-law principles are 'compatible with very great iniquity'); Joseph Raz, 'The Rule of Law and its Virtue' in *The Authority of Law* (2nd edn, Oxford University Press 2009) 210, 211.

[48] Fuller, *Morality* (n 1) 47 n 4. Perhaps for this reason, Fuller thought it better to view prohibitions on special legislation as not sounding in the generality criterion of the rule of law (his 'internal morality of the law') but in external considerations of fairness.

[49] Fuller, *Morality* (n 1) 47 n 4.

that pick out one city—that can be used to police the generality requirement. Fuller may be right that this particular rule cannot be policed, partly because it is not really a rule, but the problem of evasion here is clear. Or to take a better example invoked by Fuller and relating to retroactivity, a 1938 federal statute contained a rule that if a person meeting the description in the Act received a firearm in interstate commerce, it would be presumed that the receipt was after the effective date of the Act. As Fuller notes, '[t]his piece of legislative overcleverness was stricken down by the Supreme Court in *Tot v. United States*'.[50]

The possibility of evasion suggests the need for some appeal outside the formal system itself. Even if theoretically every loophole could be closed, it is an empirical question whether it is better to prevent evasion *ex ante* with better rules, to rely relatively less on rules and use *ex post* standards to target evasion, or to tolerate evasion. If the history of areas of law like tax, criminal law, and a wide variety of equitable interventions is any guide, some combination of the three is best, and how to compromise is a complex empirical question that will require some guesswork.[51] But the history does suggest that some reliance on a safety valve will be necessary on the macro level, for reasons similar to those that push property on a more micro level to be formal much of the time—but tempered with the equitable safety valve directed at opportunism.

That some safety valve will be necessary is also suggested by the nature of formal systems in general, of which property and private law (micro) and the rule of law (macro) are but two examples. An expression or a system of expressions is formal to the extent that it is invariant to context.[52] If so, then formalism is a matter of degree. Formalism is a property of many systems, from mathematical notation to natural language. The interesting question is when formal expression makes sense, what its costs are, and hence where its limits lie. Francis Heylighen shows that formal systems ultimately have to invoke some context—no context is not possible—in order to serve their functions. That is, no formal system is completely formal.[53] Reasons why not abound. A completely formal system faces an infinite regress of definitions, and a system's primitive terms need to refer to context (something outside the system). Moreover, the process of interpretation of the expressions in a system cannot be completely described within that system.[54] Particularly interesting for present purposes are two of Heylighen's sources of the

[50] Fuller, *Morality* (n 1) 62, citing *Tot v United States*, 319 US 463 (1942). Fuller also notes that the same opinion also struck down the Act's presumption that a person in possession of a firearm meeting the description in the Act received the firearm after its having been shipped in interstate commerce (Fuller, *Morality* (n 1) 62 n 20).

[51] See eg Buell, 'Good Faith and Law Evasion' (n 24); David A Weisbach, 'Formalism in the Tax Law' (1999) 66 *University of Chicago Law Review* 860.

[52] See eg Francis Heylighen, 'Advantages and Limitations of Formal Expression' (1999) 4 *Foundations of Science* 25, 49–53 (equating formality of language with context independence); Smith, 'The Language of Property' (n 4) 1112 ('[A]n expression is formal to the extent that its meaning is invariant under changes in context').

[53] Heylighen sees Heisenberg's Uncertainty Principle and Gödel's Incompleteness Theorem as 'special cases' of this general proposition. Heylighen, 'Advantages and Limitations' (n 52) 25, 37.

[54] Heylighen, 'Advantages and Limitations' (n 52) 37 citing Lars Löfgren, 'Complementarity in Language: Toward a General Understanding' in Marc E Carvallo (ed), *Nature, Cognition and System II*,

limits of formal expression. He points out that many systems rely on a sense of 'normal conditions' as the background context. Specifying these completely is not possible. Likewise, the nature of causation in different realms makes some systems of description less formal. The law, on both the micro and macro scale, raises these problems to a large degree because it governs actors who can evade. The possibility of evasion will make rules based on *ex ante* specifications of context and cause inadequate. I suggest that equity in private law and macro equity in the service of the rule of law anchor the formal systems of property and the rule of law, respectively. Equity at both levels prevents evasion of the basic ground rules, allowing those to function properly.

Which is not to say that law cannot be formal. It is a common fallacy of Legal Realism and its progeny to argue that because the law is not—or cannot be—totally formal it cannot be formal at all.[55] This would be true if formalism were all or nothing, but it is not. Formalism comes in degrees, and different parts of the law can be further towards the formal end of the spectrum than others. For functional reasons, we should expect—and do find—that the most in rem aspects of property are more formal than those that are closer to being in personam.[56] We can also hypothesize that parts of the law can be as formal as they are because they are backed up with a safety valve of equitable intervention against evasion.

4. Law as a Semi-open System

It has often been remarked that respect for the rule of law ultimately has to be rooted in a culture of the rule of law.[57] In this section, I make a narrow (but strong) version of that argument: on the macro level as well as the micro level, law is too vulnerable to evasion by opportunists to succeed in its goals of providing definiteness and certainty and stability of expectation without some invocation of purpose outside the system.

Macro equity is necessary for scaled-up versions of the reasons for micro equity in private law. If so, law must be a semi-open system. The information cost theory converges with a thin version of natural law, one version being Fuller's account of the rule of law. As in previous work, I am not arguing that explanations in private law should be grounded in utilitarianism or non-consequentialist morality.[58] Instead, once information costs are added to the economic analysis of law, that analysis tends to converge with certain kinds of morality-based accounts of the law, in particular those that stress local interpersonal morality, like corrective justice and Kantian mutual freedom, rather than more global theories of distributive justice or

vol ii (Kluwer 1992) 73; Lars Löfgren, 'Towards System: From Computation to the Phenomenon of Language' in Marc E Carvallo (ed), *Nature, Cognition and System i* (Kluwer 1988) 129.

55 Smith, 'The Language of Property' (n 4) 1180–2.

56 Thomas W Merrill and Henry E Smith, 'The Property/Contract Interface' (2001) 101 *Columbia Law Review* 773. See also Smith, 'The Language of Property' (n 4) 1110–13, 1150–7, 1180–2.

57 See eg Gerald J Postema, 'Fidelity in Law's Commonwealth' this volume.

58 Merrill and Smith, 'Morality of Property' (n 22), Smith, 'Modularity and Morality' (n 14).

very unconstrained versions of utilitarianism.[59] Equity, was historically associated with 'natural equity' or 'natural justice',[60] and something along these lines can be justified within a (tactically chosen) version of high-level utilitarianism. In other words, an economic account of the equitable decision-making mode tends to converge with a limited version of the morality of law, based on a mixture of custom combined with relatively uncontroversial notions of commercial morality, mostly sounding in anti-deception.[61] Perhaps the supposed conflict between equity and the rule of law is overblown.

In private law, when equity serves as a safety valve against opportunism, it employs moral language. This is no accident. As I have argued elsewhere, the reliance on a very basic and uncontroversial morality is one of the constraints on equity.[62] Furthermore, equity was not supposed to conjure up new property rights out of moral whole cloth. Instead, it used a procedurally and substantively limited version of morality to protect the structures of property in the common law. For example, rights to land defined by the *ad coelum* rule would be protected with injunctions, but the presumption would flip in cases of disproportionate hardship.[63] (The same approach can and should be applied to patent trolls.[64]) Broad versions of equity seem at first glance to animate the areas of misappropriation and unfair competition. But even here, there were limits: misappropriation is based on what is sometimes called quasi-property (as opposed to full-blown in rem property).[65] Equity also traditionally focused on enforcing custom, which poses a

[59] See Merrill and Smith, 'Morality of Property' (n 22); Smith, 'Modularity and Morality' (n 14); Andrew S Gold and Henry E Smith, *How Private Law Is Simply Moral* (MS 2013).

[60] See eg Hugo Grotius, *De Jure Belli ac Pacis* (first published 1646), trans Francis W Kelsey (Hein 1995) pt ii.6 193 ('We must, in fact, consider what the intention was of those who first introduced individual ownership; and we are forced to believe that it was their intention to depart as little as possible from natural equity'); Gulian C Verplanck, *An Essay on the Doctrine of Contracts: Being an Inquiry How Contracts Are Affected in Law and Morals, by Concealment, Error, or Inadequate Price* (first published 1825, photo reprint 1972) 37 (Lord Mansfield made 'the judgments of the law correspond with the actual practice of intelligent merchants, and with those universal usages, founded partly in convenience, and partly in natural equity, which might be considered as the common commercial and maritime law of the civilized world'); see also *Bright v Boyd*, 4 F Cas 127, 132 (CC Me 1842) (No 1, 875); *Moses v Macferlan* (1760) 97 Eng Rep 676, 681 (KB) (Mansfield, J) ('In one word, the gist of this kind of action is, that the defendant, upon the circumstances of the case, is obliged by the ties of natural justice and equity to refund the money'); but see Fred F Lawrence, *A Treatise on the Substantive Law of Equity Jurisprudence* (Bender 1929) § 3 (arguing that it is fallacious to regard equity as based on natural justice). Again, the correlation of jurisdictional equity with equity as a decision-making mode is not complete. As Joseph Story noted, even common law courts would 'administer justice with reference to principles of universal or natural justice'. Story, 'Commentaries on Equity Jurisprudence' (n 34) § 34, at 33–4.

[61] Henry E Smith, 'Custom in American Property Law: A Vanishing Act' (2013) 48 *Texas Journal of International Law* 507, 519–21.

[62] Smith, 'Law versus Equity' (n 2) 28–33.

[63] Smith, 'Law versus Equity' (n 2) 34–6; see also Gergen et al, 'Accidental Revolution?' (n 28) 226–30.

[64] Gergen et al, 'Accidental Revolution?' (n 28) 243–7; Henry E Smith, 'Institutions and Indirectness in Intellectual Property' (2009) 157 *University of Pennsylvania Law Review* 2083, 2125–32.

[65] Henry E Smith, 'Equitable Intellectual Property: What's Wrong with Misappropriation?' in Shyamkrishna Balganesh (ed), *Intellectual Property and the Common Law* (Cambridge University Press 2013) 42; see also Shyamkrishna Balganesh, 'Quasi-Property: Like, But Not Quite Property' (2012) 1560 *University of Pennsylvania Law Review* 1889.

further constraint on equity, both in the sense that it pre-exists its application through equitable decision-making and in the sense that it, along with the most basic forms of commercial morality, enjoys a wider and easier acceptability and accessibility than other types of morality or comprehensive notions of justice. While it is true that the use of socially accepted morality of this sort does not guarantee the morality in a deep sense of law itself, the type of morality involved here is also not likely to be very controversial (except in the sense of how it should fit into a larger picture of justice).

This morality and good faith would be applied not directly but typically through the mediation of custom.[66] On the one hand, the reliance on custom should be appealing to positivists because it is rooted in social conventions. On the other hand, custom has often been identified with natural law and reason. Indeed, one of the reasons for the decline in the invocation of custom in the law can be traced to the falling out of fashion of natural law and natural rights (and the blurring of the traditional limits on equity with its fusion into law culminating in the Realist era).[67]

Post-Realism has called forth a number of attempts to harmonize equity with the rule of law. Interestingly, the Legal Realists both harboured scepticism about the value of the rule of law and at the same time worked to extend equity, partly through fusion with the law. The Realists believed in context-sensitive decision-making but did not subscribe to the feasibility or the desirability of the traditional limits on equity. The extension of equitable procedural devices, remedies, and discretion beyond their historic limits led to a 'triumph' of equity over law.[68]

Nevertheless, there have been attempts to reconcile equity—or something very much like it—with the rule of law. Lawrence Solum has argued that equity and law are consistent despite their being in some tension.[69] Particularism and discretion that come from trying to do justice in an individual case might seem to undermine the rule of law. He attempts to reconcile equity with the rule of law through a theory of virtuous judging. Virtuous judges will exercise integrity and wisdom and this will make equity predictable. Solum notes that his account is somewhat related to Ronald Dworkin's, in which application of moral principles yields right answers that are in principle predictable. For Dworkin the stability comes from principles, and for Solum from the virtue of the judge. In response, Steven Burton argues that a direct aim for justice on the part of a virtuous judge is not constraining enough to lead to stability, predictability, and notice.[70] Simply put, this amount of discretion is incompatible with the rule of law. Similarly, Dworkin's account of

[66] Emily Kadens, 'The Myth of the Customary Law Merchant' (2012) 90 *Texas Law Review* 1153, 1193–4.

[67] Smith, 'Custom in American Property Law' (n 61) 521–2.

[68] See eg Laycock, 'Triumph of Equity' (n 43) 53 ('The distinctive traditions of equity now pervade the legal system. The war between law and equity is over. Equity won.').

[69] Lawrence B Solum, 'Equity and the Rule of Law' in Ian Shapiro (ed), *The Rule of Law* (NYU Press 1994) 120.

[70] Steven J Burton, 'Particularism, Discretion, and the Rule of Law' in Shapiro (ed), *The Rule of Law* (n 69) 178.

right answers from principles and a heroic holistic legal–moral enquiry has met with a similar scepticism that morality can constrain to the degree asserted.[71]

Part of the problem of equity's impact on the rule of law traces all the way back to Aristotle.[72] In the *Nicomachean Ethics*, Aristotle calls equity (*epieikeia*) an invocation of justice where law fails on account of its generality.[73] Particularism is needed,[74] but why? One interpretation is that *epieikeia* calls for a totally open-ended gap filling wherever space opens up between the law and its purposes. But a narrower version of Aristotelian equity is possible. (Alternatively, one might say that equity as an all-purpose fixing up of the law in the name of justice might be the outer bound of the concern of equity, while within this broader domain, anti-opportunism is an especially compelling rationale for intervention in the name of equity.) Law can fail because its generality allows opportunists to evade it, subvert it, and misuse it. Dennis Klimchuk shows that a narrower interpretation of *epieikeia* based on this narrower focus on the problem of law's generality is consistent with Aristotle's discussion.[75] This is especially true of the 'stickler in a bad way' who exploits the law's generality for illegitimate purposes.[76] I have argued that a theme of anti-opportunism makes sense of much equity practice, and that a theoretical case can be made (in line with some traditional thought quoted above) that equity strengthens the law through its protection of the law against opportunists.[77] Equity is targeted at a certain kind of *intentionally created and hard-to-foresee gap* between the law and its purposes.

A good illustration of the stakes involved comes from the oft-discussed case of *Riggs v Palmer*.[78] In that case, a grandson (Elmer) killed his grandfather because he knew that the grandfather was planning to change his will to provide for his new wife. Elmer killed his grandfather before that could happen, in order to get his inheritance in full. The court held that Elmer could not take under the will or as the grandfather's heir at law. Although the court invoked a 'common law' principle, the

[71] For a discussion of a variety of views on Dworkin's Right Answer Thesis, see Robert Justin Lipkin, 'Beyond Skepticism, Foundationalism and the New Fuzziness: The Role of Wide Reflective Equilibrium in Legal Theory' (1990) 75 *Cornell Law Review* 811, 841–9.

[72] See Aristotle, *Nicomachean Ethics* (n 35) and accompanying text.

[73] Aristotle, *Nicomachean Ethics* (n 35) 133.

[74] Aristotle likens equity to the leaden rule of the builders of the island of Lesbos that unlike an iron measure was moulded to stones allowing a fitting next one to be chosen (Aristotle, *Nicomachean Ethics* (n 35) 133). Later he notes that 'What is called judgement, in virtue of which men are said to be "sympathetic judges" and to "have judgement", is the right discrimination of the equitable' (Aristotle, *Nicomachean Ethics* (n 35) 152).

[75] Dennis Klimchuk, 'Is the Law of Equity Equitable in Aristotle's Sense?' (June 2011) (unpublished manuscript) ('Correction is sometimes necessary because all law is universal and, owing to its universality, can lead to error in particular cases.').

[76] Dennis Klimchuk, 'Equity and the Rule of Law' in this volume. Broader versions of the equitable anti-opportunism depend on the notion of legitimate leverage and abuse of the law. These seem broader than the notion of opportunism I am employing, but they still fall short of equity as an all-purpose fix-it principle.

[77] Smith, 'Law versus Equity' (n 2).

[78] 22 NE 188 (NY 1889) (Earl J). For an excellent discussion of the case itself and the vast jurisprudential commentary to which it has given rise, see Daniel A Farber, 'Courts, Statutes, and Public Policy: The Case of the Murdering Heir' (2000) 53 *SMU Law Review* 31, 31–3.

case is taken as the classic formulation of the equitable principle that '[n]o one shall be permitted to profit by his own fraud, or to take advantage of his own wrong, or to found any claim upon his own iniquity, or to acquire property by his own crime'.[79] To get there the court applied equitable reasoning directly and as a method of interpreting the wills statute. The dissent raised the classic formalist position that the statute did not call for any such exception and so should be applied according to its terms,[80] which is particularly important where stability and notice are important. The dissent on the surface is more consistent with classic formulations of the rule of law.

What can be said for the majority opinion, and the equitable mode of decision-making for which it has come to stand? Many defences of 'equity' are quite expansive. As with equity in general, the usual anti-formalist position either celebrates context-sensitive decision-making and downplays the rule of law, or denies that basing decision-making on general notions like fairness or morality really involves discretion, instability, and arbitrariness. As we have seen, Dworkin's and Solum's approaches fall in the latter camp. Dworkin sees in *Riggs* an exercise in morally informed legal decision-making that goes beyond a narrow model of rules. It is a holistic and heroic exercise, and very much opposed to the narrower view of rules put forth by positivists. Dworkin showcases *Riggs* (as well as *Henningsen v Bloomfield Motors, Inc*[81]) in his development of a principles-based approach to law in which morally informed enquiry leads to right answers.[82] But as the history of equity and the tenor of the rule-of-law literature indicate, a direct application of a potentially large set of principles is not very comforting from the point of view of the rule of law as classically formulated.

Riggs and the reasoning it exemplifies are subject to a narrower interpretation. Rather than being an invitation for a wide-open moral enquiry or an unconstrained exercise in ensuring fairness, *Riggs* stands for a version of the anti-opportunism principle. Courts will not aid people in profiting from their own wrongs. The wrongs involved are defined by criminal law, tort law, custom, and proxies for opportunism. This principle against profiting from one's own wrong comes under the heading of restitution for wrongs and often finds a place (especially in the United States) in the law of unjust enrichment.[83] The wills statute did not need to state that murderers were not to take under a will or by intestacy, because the

[79] 22 NE 188 (n 78) 190. Perhaps the court labelled the principle a 'common law' one in order to promote the fusion of law versus equity begun in New York in the Field Code in 1848. See Note, 'Can a Murderer Acquire Title by his Crime?' (1890) 4 *Harvard Law Review* 394, 395 (attributing decisions like *Riggs v Palmer* to the confusion of law and equity as a result of their jurisdictional fusion).

[80] 22 NE 191 (Gray J, dissenting).

[81] 161 A2d 69 (NJ 1960).

[82] Ronald Dworkin, *Taking Rights Seriously* (Harvard University Press 1977) 17–45; Ronald Dworkin, 'The Model of Rules' (1967) 35 *University of Chicago Law Review* 14.

[83] Restatement (Third) of Restitution and Unjust Enrichment (American Law Institute 2011) s 45 ('A slayer's acquisition, enlargement, or accelerated possession of an interest in property as a result of the victim's death constitutes unjust enrichment that the slayer will not be allowed to retain'); see also Nili Cohen, 'The Slayer Rule' (2012) 92 *Boston University Law Review* 793.

equitable safety valve could ensure it.[84] But that is all it is: a safety valve. As the problem of the murdering heir became well known to legislatures, anti-slayer statutes were passed.[85] What was once an equitable problem has now been partially crystallized, or *sedimented*, into a well-known rule.[86] Equity still has a role to play if a bad actor tries to take unforeseen advantage of this or some other rule, but the core of the 'slayer problem' has been solved. Equity is like a moving frontier: what was an equitable problem at one time is not unforeseeable anymore and so is no longer a proper matter for equity.

Does this mean that equity is just another version of the law, and nothing special? In this chapter, all I argue is that equity points to something beyond the more formal parts of law. Whether it is part of the law in a positivist sense (pedigreed from the proper authority) or not, can be left open.[87] What the foregoing argument suggests is that even if equity is part of the law, it cannot be part of a formal part of the law and it gains strength from drawing on extra-legal morality. Elsewhere I argue that the opportunism problem, based as it is on an element of unforeseeability from the opportunist's superior knowledge, cannot be a matter purely of rules.[88] Nonetheless, equity need not lead to an all things considered approach in all cases, because specific albeit fuzzy-edged proxies for opportunism trigger the presumption against the possible opportunist who will then have the burden of showing fairness.[89] The *ex post* discretion and other features of equity may be limited, but they cannot be done away with. Among these irreducible features is the moral flavour of equity.

Why is equity based so directly on a certain kind of fairness and morality? Historically, equity grew out of traditions of Aristotelian justice and elements of

[84] This is especially true if one adopts the traditional solution to the slayer problem of allowing the property to pass to the slayer under the will and then to impose a constructive trust. See Restatement (Third) of Restitution and Unjust Enrichment (n 83) s 45 cmt c; Jesse Dukeminier and Robert H Sitkoff, *Wills, Trusts, and Estates* (9th edn, Aspen Publishers 2013) 136–7; James Barr Ames, 'Can a Murderer Acquire Title by his Crime and Keep It?' (1897) 45 *American Law Review* 225.

[85] See Restatement (Third) of Restitution and Unjust Enrichment (n 83) s 45 cmt b; Dukeminier and Sitkoff, *Wills, Trusts, and Estates* (n 84) 137–8. The current rule is in part a matter of such statutes and partly a matter of well-settled unjust enrichment, with equity in the sense of the equitable decision-making mode left over for novel situations and those like insurance proceeds not covered by some states' statutes.

[86] Smith, 'Rose's Human Nature of Property' (n 32) 1052–3.

[87] For a discussion of *Riggs* and positivism, see Frederick Schauer, *Playing by the Rules: A Philosophical Examination of Rule-Based Decision-Making in Law and in Life* (Oxford University Press 1991). Positivists have defended positivism against Dworkin's use of *Riggs* by insisting that principles like 'no one shall profit from his own wrong' can be regarded as a non-rule-like but pedigreed part of the law (Schauer, *Playing by the Rules* (n 87) 201–6); see eg Schauer, *Playing by the Rules* (n 87) 12–14; Joseph Raz, 'Legal Principles and the Limits of Law' in *Ronald Dworkin and Contemporary Jurisprudence*, ed Marshall Cohen (Rowman & Allanheld 1984) 73, 82; Rolf Sartorius, 'Hart's Concept of Law' in *More Essays in Legal Philosophy*, ed Robert S Summers (Blackwell 1971) 131, 156; Frederick Schauer, '(Re)Taking Hart' (2006) 119 *Harvard Law Review* 851, 873–4. Schauer calls the question whether these principles are part of the law or not both terminological and deep (Schauer, *Playing by the Rules* (n 87) 205–6).

[88] Smith, 'Law versus Equity' (n 2).

[89] On presumptions, see Joseph Raz, *The Morality of Freedom* (Oxford University Press 1986) 11; Schauer, '(Re)Taking Hart' (n 87) 204–5.

canon law, and always was identified with natural law before it fell out of fashion. Indeed the phrase 'natural equity' was often invoked when courts acted against opportunists.[90] Custom and equity have tended to be identified with 'reason' in the natural law tradition.[91] By this was meant a minimum reason-based type of morality that would receive universal assent. Not profiting from one's own wrong (as defined by other relatively uncontroversial sources) would be a good example. Moreover, appeals to widely shared moral notions may not render equity determinate all on their own without equity's characteristic structure of proxies and presumptions, but such reliance on morality does make notice and acceptance easier to achieve.[92]

Micro equity thus rested on a limited invocation of morality and fairness that come from outside the formal law. But what of macro equity? Let me suggest that in a somewhat similar fashion, the rule of law itself depends on the limited ability to invoke moral considerations against potential opportunism. In its need for an equitable safety valve on both the micro and macro levels, law demonstrates a familiar limit to formal systems. Even if we could create a wholly formal rule of law, might that meta-meta system itself be subject to opportunistic evasion? The potential regress of opportunism can only be broken by a shared culture and morality. In general, formal systems need to rest on something outside the system itself. In the case of law, where interests are often antagonistic, this appeal must happen in part because of the possibility of opportunistic misuse of the criteria set up by the law.

Legal culture is the backstop to the rule of law in a specific way: the rule of law depends on macro equity to counter opportunism.[93] But the possibility of a macro equity to prop up the rule of law in the face of potential opportunism depends on

[90] See eg *Moses v Macferlan* (1760) 97 Eng Rep 676, 681 (KB) (Mansfield J).

[91] James Bryce, *Studies in History and Jurisprudence* (Clarendon Press 1901) 127–86 (discussing history of the notion of the Law of Nature); Charles Grove Haines, 'The Law of Nature in State and Federal Judicial Decisions' (1916) 25 *Yale Law Journal* 617, 622 ('Natural justice, or the reason of the thing, which the common law recognized and applied was a direct outgrowth of the law of nature which the Romans identified with jus gentium and the mediaeval canon lawyers adopted as being divine law revealed through man's natural reason'); cf James Q Whitman, 'Why Did the Revolutionary Lawyers Confuse Custom and Reason?' (1991) 58 *University of Chicago Law Review* 1321 (arguing that confusion of custom and reason was a seventeenth- and eighteenth-century development arising out of an evidentiary crisis of custom).

[92] Something similar may be true of property and torts. See Merrill and Smith, 'Morality of Property' (n 22); Smith, 'Modularity and Morality' (n 14). Larry Alexander and Emily Sherwin raise the concern that overriding rules, as in equity (versus law), involves objectionable and self-defeating deception: Larry Alexander and Emily Sherwin, *The Rule of Rules: Morality, Rules, and the Dilemmas of Law* (Duke University Press 2011) 88–91. For an account of how equity can appeal to multiple audiences without deception see Yuval Feldman and Henry E Smith, 'Behavioral Equity' (2014) *Journal of Institutional and Theoretical Economics* 137.

[93] See eg Oliver E Williamson, 'Calculativeness, Trust, and Economic Organization' (1993) 36 *Journal of Law & Economics* 453, 476 ('The main import of culture, for purposes of economic organization, is that it serves as a check on opportunism'); but see Richard Craswell, 'On the Uses of "Trust": Comment on Williamson, "Calculativeness, Trust, and Economic Organization"' (1993) 36 *Journal of Law & Economics* 487, 495–6 (critiquing notion of non-calculative trust as a source of explanation and criticizing Williamson for not pushing calculative theories to explain emergence of norms).

there being a sufficient consensus, enough of such a culture, to serve this function. Is there such a consensus? That is an empirical question to which I have no ready answer. Based on the argument of this chapter, however, one can make two predictions. The first is that doing without any equitable safety valve will be very difficult, and the aspiration to be totally contextual or totally formal will not lead in the end to stability and the other rule of law virtues in practice.[94] The second is that if the consensus on morality or the overall legal culture shrinks, and particularly if disingenuous use of the system to further policy ends comes to be celebrated, one can expect a polarization in views about the rule of law. Either it will be discarded as an obstacle, or the reaction will be to emphasize formalism more than ever, to try to plug the loopholes on the micro and the macro levels as best one can. That can never be wholly successful, but if formalism is a matter of degree and the safety valve works less well for lack of consensus, more formalism is one of the possible responses. Perhaps the current polarization of views about the rule of law can be traced to the damage that lack of consensus is doing to the possibility of the equitable safety valve.

5. Conclusion

Law and equity are not so opposed after all, if equity acts as a safety valve aimed at preventing opportunism. Instead, an information cost theory of property and private law points to a limited role for equity to protect the formal rules of the law against opportunistic exploitation. Thus, within the law, micro equity need not undermine the rule of law, but rather reinforces it. And at the level of the legal system itself, the problem of opportunistic and disingenuous satisfaction of thin notions of the rule of law points to a similar need for macro equity—a limited invocation of standards outside the system of formal law. At both levels, the information cost theory converges with a morality of the law that requires both formalism and equitable intervention against opportunistic evasion of formal systems.

[94] Replacing this cooperative element that involves context with a formal system completely would be analogous to a natural language trying to do without pragmatics and relying solely on semantics. Again, there are limits to formal expression. One of these limits stems from evasion. At a high enough level, operation of a system of law has to be cooperative. It cannot be adversarial all the way up (down?). In this, law is a little like conversation. For conversation to work, the participants have to be cooperating at least in a general way, as in Grice's Cooperative Principle: 'Make your conversational contribution such as is required, at the stage at which it occurs, by the accepted purpose or direction of the talk exchange in which you are engaged': Paul Grice, *Studies in the Ways of Words* (Harvard University Press 1989) 22, 26. Aristotelian equity is the pragmatics (as opposed to semantics, in terms of context dependence) of the rule of law.

11

Equity and the Rule of Law

*Dennis Klimchuk**

1. Introduction

In this chapter I want to make a case against two views that are widely held, though for the most part only implicitly. The first is that the rule of law is essentially a public law doctrine or ideal, expressed principally in constraints on government action—so Hayek claims, for example, that '[s]tripped of all its technicalities, the rule of law means that government in all its actions is bound by rules fixed and announced beforehand'[1]—and in principles of constitutional design: so the Constitution of Massachusetts, for example, declares that the legislative, executive and judicial branches of the state shall be kept separate 'to the end it may be a government of laws and not of men'.[2] On this view, the rule of law reaches private law only through rules governing legislation and adjudication, and does not bear directly on the rights and duties it upholds and imposes. Thus, for example, statutes bearing on contracts must, no less than any others, apply prospectively and be publicized. More significantly in common law jurisdictions—where much private law is judge-made law—the rule of law bears on private law, on this view, most directly through its direction to the judiciary to respect *stare decisis*.[3]

This view of the rule of law underlies the longstanding complaint (not always voiced explicitly in these terms) that the law of equity is suspect from the perspective of the rule of law, owing, initially, to Chancery's claim to be unbound by precedent and, more relevant to contemporary law, to the claim of equity for greater space for judicial discretion owing to the open-endedness of its constitutive principles. I want to challenge the received view of the rule of law by challenging

* Earlier versions of this chapter were presented at the Obligations VI conference at Western University (London, Ontario), the Department of Philosophy at Western University, and the workshop from which this volume proceeds. I learned a great deal from the audiences each time, and from many others with whom I've discussed the issues in this chapter. I am particularly indebted to Lisa Austin, Chris Essert, Evan Fox-Decent, Ben McFarlane, Paul Miller, James Penner, Alexander Pless, Irit Samet, Henry Smith, Lionel Smith, and Ernie Weinrib.

1 Friedrich Hayek, *The Road to Serfdom* (University of Chicago Press 1944) 72.

2 *Mass Const* pt 1, art XXX.

3 On the idea that respect for *stare decisis* is a requirement of the rule of law, see *Planned Parenthood v Casey* 505 US 833 (1992) at 854 and Jeremy Waldron, 'Stare Decisis and the Rule of Law: A Layered Approach' (2012) 111 *Michigan Law Review* 1.

this view of equity. I will argue that if we ask to what the rule of law is opposed we can find behind the various principles it is commonly held to entail a more basic principle that is expressed in some substantive doctrines of private law, including a number of distinctly equitable doctrines. The doctrines I have in mind are those that are, in a way I will explain, equitable in Aristotle's sense.

Two quick points of terminology. First, I will adopt the convention of using 'Equity' to refer to the doctrines that descend from the courts of Equity and 'equity' to refer to the principles or ideals that they are said to distinctively embody. So we can ask whether a particular Equitable doctrine is equitable, or what makes it so, or whether it is equitable in Aristotle's sense. Second, I will use 'right' in its pre-disaggregated sense to comprise claim-rights, powers, and privileges.

I will proceed as follows. I will (1) isolate the basic ideal underlying the variously enumerated principles of the rule of law, (2) briefly outline the aspects of Aristotle's account of equity that bear on the law of equity, (3) explain how a doctrine that is equitable in Aristotle's sense upholds the rule of law, and then finally (4) explain how some distinctively Equitable doctrines are equitable in Aristotle's sense, and so uphold the rule of law.

2. The Rule of Law

Notwithstanding substantial disagreement over issues such as whether conformity with the rule of law is a criterion of legality and how substantive are the implications of a commitment to the rule of law, there is, I'd say, fairly substantial consensus on what it requires. It requires, first, that laws be such that it is possible for citizens to obey them and plan their lives around them. Thus laws must be, for example, public, clear, and applied prospectively, and they must be what persons are actually held to in court. It also requires that government be structured in such a way that it and its agents are themselves subject to the law. Thus, for example, powers must be separated. Finally, it requires that justice be administered in a way that makes it more than a hollow ideal. Thus, for example, courts must be at least reasonably accessible and litigants and persons accused of crimes must enjoy the benefit of natural justice and due process.

Now, what ties these together? What makes these requirements of the rule of law? We can get to the answer to this question by first asking another: To what is the rule of law opposed? There are two answers. The first is anarchy. This is the idea invoked, for example, when it is said of a group re-establishing political institutions in a country emerging from a civil war that it is trying to re-establish the rule of law. In this sense the rule of law is contrasted with the absence of rule or order altogether.

That is not the idea implicit in the view around which I claimed there to be a consensus. Conformity with the desiderata of the rule of law in this sense secures rule of one kind rather than another. The sort of rule to which the rule of law in this sense is opposed has been variously characterized. One characterization is found in the provision from the Constitution of Massachusetts I quoted above: again, the powers of government ought to be separated 'to the end it may be a government of laws and not of men'. So one way to put the contrast is between the rule of law and the rule of persons.

Now this is at first puzzling, because in an obvious and important sense all rule is the rule of persons (what else could it be?). So what is meant by this? Let's begin by asking what the drafters might have had in mind in saying that the separation of powers would secure a government of laws rather than of men. The idea, I take it, is the one articulated by Locke when he argued that were executive and legislative power placed in one body its members could simply choose to exempt themselves from the laws they made and in this way be above the law.[4] This would be a government of persons merely because those who govern would not be subject to law. This only gets us part of the way to understanding the idea, however, because such a government could otherwise be in exemplary compliance with the standard principles of the rule of law. In what sense is a government that rules through, for example, insufficiently publicized laws, or whose courts uphold laws other than those publicized, a government of persons rather than of law?

We can see the answer if we put ourselves in the position of citizens in such a polity. So far as they would know, they are subject not to law but rather to the will of the persons who act under its authority and who occupy offices constituted by it. Putting it this way—'so far as they would know'—might be taken to imply the possibility that a citizen could be treated as the rule of law requires though that be unknown to or unknowable by her. But while part of the lesson is that arguably the rule of law imposes on judges and adjudicators generally a duty to give reasons,[5] there isn't really a possible gap between appearance and reality here. To be subject to the rule of law rather than of persons requires that there be a particular sort of justification available for the actions taken by officials to those subject to their decisions and orders, namely one cast in terms of the law to which they are subject. The principles of the rule of law serve to secure the availability of such a justification.

This, I suggest, shows the link between the idea that the rule of law in the sense in which we are interested can be contrast with the rule of persons and the idea that its opposite is subjection to the arbitrary will of others, or, more simply, arbitrary rule. What makes rule arbitrary? There is more than one idea here.[6] In one sense

[4] John Locke, *Two Treatises of Government*, ed Peter Laslett (Oxford University Press 1988) 364 (bk II ch 12 para 143). One might reply that legislators could still seek to exempt themselves from law by building their exemption into the statutes they adopt. Locke's answer would be that it is a condition of their legitimacy that laws be general; the legislature may only pass laws 'not to be varied in particular cases, but to have one rule for rich and poor, for the favourite at court, and the countryman at plough'. Locke, *Two Treatises* 363 (bk II ch 11 para 142).

[5] On which see David Dyzenhaus and Michael Taggart, 'Reasoned Decisions and Legal Theory' in Douglas E Edlin (ed), *Common Law Theory* (Cambridge University Press 2007) 134–67. The duty to give reasons has been late to receive judicial recognition. In Canadian administrative law that came in *Baker v Canada (Minister of Citizenship and Immigration)* [1999] 2 SCR 817.

[6] See Gerald J Postema and William Lucy's contributions to this volume for further disentangling of the senses of 'arbitrariness'. The one I claim to find behind the various principles of the rule of law is not quite identical with any of the many they collectively distinguish, though it is close to the one that Postema endorses.

rule is arbitrary if it is capricious. But rule needn't be capricious in the sense of unreasoned or pointless or random to be arbitrary in the sense that matters here. Again Locke can illuminate. Throughout the *Two Treatises* Locke opposes legitimate rule to the exercise of absolute, arbitrary power, the two nearly invariably conjoined. He distinguishes them with an example that will help elucidate the sense of arbitrariness in which we are interested here. The power of superior officers in the army is absolute, Locke says, in the sense that it is always wrongful to disobey them, but it is not arbitrary. A soldier may be commanded to march to certain death, but not to give up a single penny to his commander '[b]ecause such a blind Obedience is necessary to that end for which the Commander has his Power, *viz.*, the preservation of the rest; but the disposing of his Goods has nothing to do with it'.[7] So in this sense arbitrary rule is unauthorized, in a particular way: it cannot be justified in terms of the law constitutive of the office through which it is exercised.

Rule that is arbitrary in this sense needn't be capricious, and indeed might be exercised in the interest of those subject to it. But it may well be the former and needn't be the latter. This shows the sense in which persons subject to arbitrary rule in this sense are subject to the rule of persons rather than of law. This point needs to be made carefully, so we don't end up collapsing this sense of the rule of law into the sense that opposes it to anarchy. The taxing army commander is not *just* a thief. It is important to the example that the commander's authority is absolute, so in a sense he could not act beyond it. But he can abuse it. Respect for the rule of law here requires imposing constraints on the manner in which rights are exercised.

This sense of the rule of law and the corresponding sense of arbitrariness are well illustrated in Justice Rand's opinion in the leading Canadian administrative law case *Roncarelli v Duplessis*.[8] The plaintiff Roncarelli ran a successful restaurant in Montreal, Quebec. At the direction of the defendant Duplessis,[9] who was then premier and attorney-general of Quebec, the Liquor Commission cancelled Roncarelli's liquor licence, declaring that no future licence would be issued to him. This action was taken, Duplessis had expressly announced, because the defendant had posted surety bail in hundreds of cases for persons arrested for distributing material published by the Church of Witnesses of Jehovah, of which Roncarelli was a member. The Church's criticisms of Catholicism had made it unpopular in Quebec.

While the relevant enabling statute provided that 'the Commission may cancel any permit at its discretion', Justice Rand held that that did not put its decisions beyond review. While '[a] decision to deny or cancel such a privilege [as the holding of a liquor license] lies within the "discretion" of the Commission', he argued, 'that

[7] Locke, *Two Treatises* (n 5) 361–2 (bk II ch 11 para 139).

[8] [1959] SCR 121. In fact *Roncarelli* involves a claim in tort, but one that rests on certain principles of administrative law and of public law more generally.

[9] Or so found many of the judges at the three levels at which the case was heard, including Justice Rand; others found that the Manager of the Commission had made his decision prior to consulting Duplessis. For a helpful sorting though the various opinions and the questions of fact and of law around which they were divided see David Mullan, '*Roncarelli v Duplessis* and Damages for Abuse of Power: For What Did it Stand in 1959 and For What Does it Stand in 2009?' (2010) 55 *McGill Law Journal* 587.

means that decision is to be based upon a weighing of considerations pertinent to the object of the administration'.[10] Here, however, the decision to cancel the permit was on the grounds of Roncarelli having exercised 'an unchallengeable right totally irrelevant to the sale of liquor in a restaurant... Under the statutory language here, that [decision] is not competent to the Commission and *a fortiori* to the government or the respondent [Duplessis].'[11] In 'bringing about a step by the Commission beyond the bounds prescribed by the legislature for its exclusive action', the premier committed 'a gross abuse of legal power' and 'converted what was done into his personal act' and thereby made himself liable under tort for damages.[12]

The link to our themes comes in a famous passage from Justice Rand's judgment:

> That, in the presence of expanding administrative regulation of economic activities, such a step and its consequences are to be suffered by the victim without recourse or remedy, that an administration according to law is to be superseded by action dictated by and according to the arbitrary likes, dislikes and irrelevant purposes of public officers acting beyond their duty, would signalize the beginning of disintegration of the rule of law as a fundamental postulate of our constitutional structure.[13]

The defendant brought it about that the Manager of the Liquor Commission exercised his authority in service of an end outside of that for which sake the authority was constituted, and so in a way that could not be justified in terms of the law constituting the office he occupied. He thus exercised his authority arbitrarily in the sense relevant here, and therefore in a manner unacceptable in a polity committed to the rule of law. This was so notwithstanding that the statute by which the Manager's authority was constituted provided that the Commission could cancel liquor licences 'at its discretion', just as Locke's army commander's claim to tax was arbitrary and an abuse of his authority, notwithstanding that that authority was absolute.

I'll conclude this section by filling in one last piece of the picture I'm sketching here. Why, on this view of what lies at the heart of the rule of law, ought we to uphold it? The answer, I suggest, is that it is required by equality. This would have been Locke's answer, but the idea is much older. In a discussion of democracy in the *Politics*, Aristotle considers the view that among equals

> everyone should be ruled as well as rule, and therefore that all should have their turn. We thus arrive at law; for an order of succession implies law. And the rule of the law, it is argued, is preferable to that of any individual.[14]

10 *Roncarelli* (n 8) 140.

11 *Roncarelli* (n 8) 141.

12 *Roncarelli* (n 8) 143. *Roncarelli* thus marks an important point of contact between private law and the rule of law that I am not discussing in this chapter, namely the idea from Dicey that civil liability can in this way serve to mark the limits of the authority within which office-holders may act pursuant to their mandates. In his concurring opinion, Abott J quotes Dicey approvingly on this point. *Roncarelli* (n 8) 184.

13 *Roncarelli* (n 8) 142.

14 Aristotle, *Politics*, trans B Jowett in *The Complete Works of Aristotle*, ed Jonathan Barnes, vol ii (Princeton University Press 1984) 2042 (3.16, 1287a15–20).

The idea is that if my claim to rule follows from its being my turn, then my authority derives from the rule of succession, not from my being the person I happen to be. Now, Aristotle thinks the idea that each should have their turn ruling is an instance of the general mistake that democrats make, namely thinking that persons equal in one respect, being free-born, are equal in all, including aptitude to rule.[15] But what this line of thinking gets right is that the only sort of polity appropriate to a society of equals is one structured by the rule of law.

Its foundation in equality is reflected in what we might call the moral–expressive content of the rule of law. The exercise of authority is consistent with equality if it is structured by law. Among equals, legal authority is exercised through offices constituted by laws forming part of a legal order to which all are subject. So by abusing authority conferred by law, and in that way acting in violation of the rule of law,[16] an office-holder violates equality. She uses the law as an instrument for her ends while expecting others to regard themselves as subject to it. (This would be true even if her motives were other-directed, as I suggested the army commander's might be. By acting in service of an end other than that for which sake the office he occupies was constituted, the commander arrogates to himself the authority to determine the scope of his office. That makes the law his instrument even if he chooses to use it to help others.)

Hold these thoughts. I will leave them behind for now and turn to outline Aristotle's account of equity. Then in the sections following I will draw these two starting points together in a discussion of the place of the rule of law in private law in general and in Equity in particular.

3. Aristotle's Account of Equity

'The nature of the equitable', on Aristotle's account, is 'a correction of law where it is defective owing to its universality'.[17] Sometimes the defect is owing to the legislator's imprecision, but sometime it is owing to the nature of practical affairs. '[A]ll law is universal', Aristotle says, 'but about some things it is not possible to make a universal statement which shall be correct.'[18] This is so in two kinds of case. In the first

[15] The oligarchs' mistake is the mirror image: they believe that those unequal (superior) in one sense, the ability to make money, are unequal in all (and are thus more capable of ruling). Aristotle, *Politics* (n 14) 2031 (3.9, 1280a22–4).

[16] I put the point in a deliberately qualified ('in that way') and rather circuitous ('acting in violation of…') way because one might reasonably say an individual cannot strictly speaking violate the rule of law. I take up this issue in the beginning of Section 4.

[17] Aristotle, *Nicomachean Ethics*, trans JO Urmson and WD Ross in *The Complete Works of Aristotle*, ed Barnes, ii. 1796 (bk 5.10, 1137b27–8). I believe the interpretation of Aristotle's account of equity I sketch here is correct, but strictly speaking nothing in this chapter turns on that being so. What matters is that I'm correct that (1) a doctrine that is equitable in the sense that I claim to find in Aristotle upholds the rule of law and (2) some doctrines of Equity are equitable in this sense. I make a case in favour of the soundness of this interpretation of Aristotle's account of equity in more detail in 'Aristotle and the Foundation of the Law of Equity' (MS).

[18] Aristotle, *Nicomachean Ethics* (n 17) 1795 (bk 5.10, 1137b13–14).

they [legislators] find themselves unable to define things exactly, and are obliged to legislate as if that held good always which in fact only holds good usually; or [secondly] where it is not easy to be complete owing to the endless possible cases presented, such as the kinds and sizes of weapons that may be used to inflict wounds—a lifetime would be too short to make out a complete list of these.[19]

So it could be impossible to make a universal statement which shall be correct either because certain things (rules, for example, such as the rule that one ought to return borrowed goods to their owner) hold only usually (you ought not to return a weapon to someone who had gone mad since you'd borrowed it) or because the list of particulars collected by a general term such as 'weapon' cannot feasibly be drawn up ('a lifetime would be too short'). Aristotle's one example is an instance of the second class:

If, then, a precise statement is impossible and yet legislation is necessary, the law must be expressed in wide terms; and so, if a man has no more than a finger-ring on his hand when he lifts it to strike or actually strikes another man, he is guilty of a criminal act according to the written words of the law; but he is innocent really, and it is equity that declares him to be so.[20]

My guess is that the written words of the statute at issue make it an offence to strike another with a weapon and that it is written in such a way as to catch the finger-ring. The defendant is innocent, perhaps, only of this charge and not of a lesser one, say assault *simpliciter*. We get to this result by asking what the legislator would say were she present.[21] Because equity is a kind of justice,[22] we have to suppose that this test is in a sense objective. In this example by asking what the legislator would say we are really asking whether on its best interpretation the end served by the law in question would be served by convicting the ring-wearer of assault with a weapon.

So far, then, equity is something directed at judges, a kind of principle of or approach to legislative interpretation that aims to get the law right in a particular way.[23] Aristotle also sometimes uses 'equity' to name a set of directives issued not to judges but rather complainants, asking them, for example, to remember benefits

[19] Aristotle, *Rhetoric*, trans W Rhys Roberts in *The Complete Works of Aristotle*, ed Barnes, ii. 2188 (bk 1.13, 1374a30–4).

[20] Aristotle, *Rhetoric* (n 19) (1.13, 1374a34–1374b2).

[21] Though sometimes, Aristotle tells us, we can only take recourse to a fact-specific decree. He doesn't give us an example of such a case.

[22] Aristotle, *Nicomachean Ethics* (n 17) 1795 (bk 5.10, 1137b6–9).

[23] Coke called equity a kind of construction, and described the idea from Aristotle just sketched without naming him, plainly drawing, however, on Plowden's comments to *Eyston v Studd*, in which he explicitly draws on Aristotle. See Sir Edward Coke, *Commentary on Littleton* (Robert Small 1857) 327 (L.1.C.2.24.b) and *Eyston v Studd* 2 Plowden 465, 75 ER 695. Since at least Coke 'equitable construction' has referred to the kind of purposive statutory interpretation illustrated by Aristotle's example. We see this in *Riggs v Palmer*, discussed below.

Lawrence Solum argues that seeing what Aristotle's account of equity tells us about judging shows that equity and the rule of law are not in conflict. See Lawrence B Solum, 'Equity and the Rule of Law' in Ian Shapiro (ed), *The Rule of Law* (NYU Press 1994) 120. In what follows I claim to find a different path in Aristotle leading to the same conclusion.

rather than injuries and to be patient when wronged.[24] And he claims that from the account outlined above, according to which equity is a correction of errors arising from the universality of law, 'it is plain' who the equitable person is: the person who 'is no stickler for justice in a bad sense but tends to take less than his share though he has the law on his own side'.[25] So equity requires of the claimant that she refrain from being a stickler in a bad sense, and to be content with taking less than her due though she has law on her side.

Now, there is a puzzle here. The first side of equity, that directed at judges, leads them to get the law right: to ensure, we might say, that each gets her due. But the second, that directed at complainants, asks them to be content with *less* than their due. We can reconcile these ideas if we take the law on which the stickler insists to be the strict letter of the law, uncorrected by equity. This suggests that we can find in Aristotle a second sort of problem to which the generality of law may lead and that equity corrects, along with over-inclusivity (illustrated as we saw by his one example). The generality of the law can also be exploited by those who are sticklers for their rights in a bad way.[26]

This second role of equity on Aristotle's account can be nicely illustrated by the reasoning and outcome of the much-discussed case of *Riggs v Palmer*.[27] Elmer Palmer stood to inherit a valuable piece of property from his grandfather, but feared that he was going to change his will. So he murdered him, and claimed the property. The puzzle facing the court was that, in the words of Justice Earl, writing for the majority, '[the] statutes regulating the making, proof and effect of wills, and the devolution of property, if literally construed, and if their force and effect can in no way and under no circumstances be controlled or modified, give this property to the murderer'.[28] The majority found, however, that the statutes could be controlled, in either of two ways. The first is that they, like all statutes, are subject to equitable construction, described by Matthew Bacon in a passage quoted by the court as follows:

> By an equitable construction, a case not within the letter of the statute is sometimes holden to be within the meaning, because it is within the mischief for which a remedy is provided. The reason for such construction is that the law-makers could not set down every case in express terms. In order to form a right judgment whether a case be within the equity of a statute, it is a good way to suppose the law-maker present, and that you have asked him this question, did you intend to comprehend this case? Then you must give yourself such answer

[24] Aristotle, *Rhetoric* (n 19) 2189 (bk 1.13, 1374b10–23). Aristotle does not say that equity in these two senses is directed at different parties. That's a solution to the interpretative puzzle posed by his shift between these two sets of ideas in his account.

[25] Aristotle, *Nicomachean Ethics* (n 17) 1796 (bk 5.10 1137b35–1138a1).

[26] In his contribution to this volume, Henry Smith argues that equity serves to prevent opportunism arising in certain sorts of circumstances, among them the exploitation of the generality of particular laws. Perhaps this is the same idea as I claim to find in Aristotle. Arguably they come apart in some cases. For example the defendant in *Hollywood Silver Fox*, discussed in the next section, was, it seems to me, a stickler in a bad way but not an opportunist. He did not seize a chance made available by the letter of the law. He just acted badly, and then sought immunity under a strict and narrow interpretation of his rights.

[27] 115 NY 506 (1889).

[28] *Riggs* (n 27) 509.

as you imagine he, being an upright and reasonable man, would have given. If this be that he did mean to comprehend it, you may safely hold the case to be within the equity of the statute; for while you do no more than he would have done, you do not act contrary to the statute, but in conformity thereto.[29]

The court finds it 'inconceivable' that 'it was the legislative intention in the general laws passed for the orderly, peaceable and just devolution of property, that they should have operation in favor of one who murdered his ancestor that he might speedily come into the possession of his estate',[30] and so on this basis finds against Riggs.

'Besides', Justice Earl continues,

all laws as well as all contracts may be controlled in their operation and effect by general, fundamental maxims of the common law. No one shall be permitted to profit by his own fraud, or to take advantage of his own wrong, or to found any claim upon his own iniquity, or to acquire property by his own crime.[31]

Each of these maxims describes a rich and complex idea or set of ideas, but I don't think it oversimplifies to suggest that each in its own way describes and forbids one from being a stickler for one's rights in a bad way. This is because presumably each must be called upon only because the prohibition of the wrong the wrongdoer seeks to exploit to her advantage is in itself inadequate to deny her the gains she seeks. It follows that there must behind the sorts of cases to which each might be applied be a strict right on which the wrongdoer seeks to stand.

So though Justice Earl does not use this language, he in effect offers as an alternative rationale for denying Riggs's claim that to allow it would work an inequity in the second as well as the first of the two senses that comprise Aristotle's account. What Justice Earl represents as alternative means to reach the court's decision, Aristotle, I am arguing, would see as two sides of the same coin. On an Aristotelian reconstruction, in reaching the judgment that a finding in Riggs's favour would permit him to be a stickler for his rights in a bad sense the court respects the ends for which the legislature passed the legislation Riggs sought to exploit and corrects for the generality in which it was expressed.

4. Equity and the Rule of Law

Now let me draw the first two parts of this chapter together. My suggestion is that a doctrine or a judgment that is equitable in Aristotle's sense can be seen to uphold the rule of law in the sense outlined in Section 2 of this chapter. Before defending this claim I'd like to respond to what might seem to be a dispositive preliminary objection, namely that it is simply a category error to think that the rule of law is put at issue by law that governs the interactions between individuals. Just as, try as I might, I cannot violate your constitutional right to freedom of expression as a

29 Matthew Bacon, *A New Abridgment of the Law* vol iv (Luke White 1783) 649.

30 *Riggs* (n 27) 511.

31 *Riggs* (n 27) 511.

private citizen, the objection goes, I cannot violate the rule of law. That, so put, seems right. Nonetheless, the rule of law in the sense isolated in the first part of this chapter is upheld by certain private law doctrines, and their justification is anchored in that fact. I'll make the case for this claim by invoking what I think is a clear example of a doctrine that has these properties.

What I have in mind is the bar against contracts for slavery. Nowadays lawyers would say that such a contract is contrary to public policy. But political philosophers in the early modern tradition sought to explain how as a matter of substantive principles of contract and, according to some, its very structure, such a contract was not only impermissible but in a sense impossible. We can construct a powerful instance of the latter sort of argument by conjoining a claim of Rousseau's with a claim of Kant's. Each aimed to show that a contract of slavery, once entered into, undoes itself. Rousseau makes the claim from the perspective of the master, Kant from the slave. For both a contract of slavery confers on one party (or, rather, purports to confer on one party) absolute and arbitrary power over the other.[32] Rousseau's argument is that such a contract leaves the master incapable of bearing duties to the slave. 'Is it not clear', he asks, 'that we can be under no obligation to a person from whom we have the right to exact everything?'[33] Kant's argument is that such a contract would turn the slave into a thing, and so into an entity incapable of bearing duties to another. '[A] contract by which one party would completely renounce its freedom for the other's advantage would be self-contradictory, that is, null and void, since by it one party would cease to be a person and so would have no duty to keep the contract but would recognize only force.'[34] It is analytic that parties to a contract owe duties to one another. Thus, the Rousseau/Kant argument shows, a contract for slavery—understood as subjection to the absolute and arbitrary control of another—is impossible.

The lesson I want to draw from this argument here is that we can make sense of the idea that a rule that purports to permit persons to enter into arrangements among themselves that accord arbitrary power to one party is not just suspect from the perspective of principles of substantive justice or morality, but from the perspective of legality itself. Try as one might, the argument claims, one cannot via contract confer upon another a legal right to arbitrary control over one's life. My suggestion is that we can cast the conclusion of this argument as holding that slavery contracts—or, we should say, so-called slavery 'contracts'—are suspect from the perspective of the rule of law. The claim is not that the master in such an arrangement would violate the rule of law; that, perhaps, is not something that individuals can do. It is rather that were we to allow that a contract for slavery were possible, we would allow that a party can by right be subject to the arbitrary will of another, and that is just what the rule of law in the sense in which we are interested

32 Who enters into it, we might imagine, for the benefit of third parties—say to release his family from poverty.

33 JJ Rousseau, *On the Social Contract*, trans DA Cress (Hackett 1987) 21 (I, 4).

34 Immanuel Kant, *The Metaphysics of Morals*, trans M Gregor (Cambridge University Press 1996) 66 (6:283).

here is set against. And so in this way the rule against contracts of slavery upholds the rule of law.[35]

Let's turn now to equity, though not quite yet to Equity. My claim is that a doctrine or judgment that prevents someone from being a stickler in a bad way, by exploiting the generality of a legal rule, upholds the rule of law. It does so because it prevents (or undoes the effects of) an abuse of right, just as would a court that denied Locke's army commander the right to tax those under his command, and just as did the court in *Roncarelli*. It is a matter of controversy whether the common law should be understood to recognize a doctrine of abuse of right. Probably the balance of opinion weighs against it. Still I would like to make the conceptual point about the connection between equity and the rule of law with a look at a case that arguably stands for the proposition that the common law of tort makes actionable at least some forms of abuse of property right, *Hollywood Silver Fox Farm v Emmett*.[36] I say *Hollywood* arguably stands for this proposition because the court does not use the phrase 'abuse of right'. An argument based on a controversial interpretation of a doctrine that does not on balance enjoy the support of authority (to put the case against it rather strongly) will of course have its limits. The line is nonetheless worth pursuing here, because *Hollywood* illustrates particularly clearly how in seeking to prevent a defendant in a civil suit from benefiting from an abuse of right a court could be understood to do equity in Aristotle's sense and so uphold the rule of law.

Here are the facts. The plaintiff established a business breeding foxes adjacent to land owned by the defendant. The defendant Emmett asked the plaintiff to remove a sign the plaintiff had erected on his own land advertising his farm, because Emmet thought it would be detrimental to his plans to develop his land into residential properties. The plaintiff refused. The defendant then had his son fire a gun on the property line with the aim of disrupting the breeding of the foxes, as indeed it did. The plaintiff sued for damages and sought an injunction. He won, on the grounds that though the defendant was entitled to shoot on his land, in this case he did so maliciously, with the end of harming the plaintiff, and so thereby committed a wrongful nuisance.

Counsel for the defendant argued, and the court accepted, that the plaintiff cannot convert his neighbour's permissible use of his land into a nuisance by establishing a business that requires an unusual degree of quiet (as fox breeding does). The defendant denied malice, but added that it didn't matter either way because malice cannot make a lawful action unlawful. (While Aristotle does not tell us what makes someone a stickler for her rights in a bad way, I think that however that should be unpacked Emmett will qualify.)

[35] I think this gives some support to Fuller's claim that while conformity with the rule of law does not guarantee that a given legal system is just in all or even most respects, it does not follow that '*any* substantive aim maybe adopted without compromise of legality', though this is of course controversial and let me add that nothing in my argument here turns on its being so. See Lon L Fuller, *The Morality of Law* (rev edn, Yale University Press 1969) 153.

[36] [1936] 2 KB 468.

The court did not accept the evidence led in support of Emmett's first argument and rejected the second as a matter of principle. Thus *Hollywood* is taken to stand for the proposition that, put in general terms, motive matters in tort; put more narrowly, otherwise permissible uses of land can become nuisances if the end of the use is merely harming the interest of another owner. In using his property as he did, some commentators say—though the court does not—the defendant abused his rights.[37] A recent and compelling account of just how this is so has been defended by Larissa Katz.[38]

On Katz's view, ownership is a kind of office. What a system of private property does is grant owners the right to determine what is a worthwhile agenda for the thing they own. They act within their authority when the use to which they put their property is or expresses an answer to that question. They exceed that authority, and abuse their rights as owners, when they make decisions to use their property for reasons unconnected to this end, as did Emmett. On this view Emmett is like the defendant in *Roncarelli* and abuses his authority in a structurally parallel way. In denying him the right to do so, then, the court refuses to allow him to exercise his authority arbitrarily in the sense I explained above, and in that way upholds the rule of law.

Katz's analysis of *Hollywood* lends itself readily to representation in the terms of Aristotle's account of equity. Emmett could claim that ownership granted him a licence to act as he did only by insisting on a particularly (and misleadingly) general description of the right he enjoys as property owner: as the right to determine the use of his property *simpliciter* rather than, as Katz argues, the right to determine a worthwhile agenda for it. By insisting on this description of his rights—one that omits the end for which sake an owner enjoys the rights he does—Emmett is a stickler for them in a bad way; equity intervenes by filling in the details.

On this analysis both the links among the idea of an abuse of right, the Aristotelian conception of equity and the rule of law, and the parallels among the cases of Locke's commander, *Roncarelli*, and *Hollywood* are borne by the idea of an office whose mandate constrains the exercise of the rights its occupants bear in virtue of their occupancy. Looking ahead, this suggests a link to many core, distinctly Equitable doctrines, for example those through which are imposed fiduciary duties that constrain the powers of office-holders such as company directors and trustees. However, many no less equally distinctly Equitable doctrines, for example promissory estoppel and *laches*, are not similarly structured by the idea of an office. And, indeed, one might take issue with its deployment in the context of ordinary property ownership. Let's start there; I'll turn to Equity in the next section.

[37] Note that this analysis does not imply that the plaintiff would have had a case only were Emmett the owner of the property (as he was). What matters is that Emmett defended himself by saying he was acting within his rights as a property owner.

[38] Larissa Katz, 'Spite and Extortion: A Jurisdictional Principle of Abuse of Property Right' (2012) 122 *Yale Law Journal* 1444.

Let me sharpen the issue. The worry is that the parallel I've drawn between *Hollywood* and the public law cases—through which I have undertaken to make the case for treating the control of the abuse of right in the private law context as a matter of upholding the rule of law—rests on a controversial characterization of ownership. How controversial this characterization is depends on how much we find in the idea of an office. According to what I will call the formal conception, the claim that ownership is an office amounts to little more than the claim that certain rights and duties attach to ownership and are enjoyed and borne by owners in that capacity, both in the abstract (say qua holder of an estate in fee simple) and in particular cases (say qua owner of this piece of reality, subject as it is to this easement, etc).[39] It seems to me that there is nothing one could take issue with in the formal conception. More controversial is the idea that the office of ownership is teleologically structured in the way that Katz's argument suggests—ie that there is some end to which owners qua owners must be taken to be acting in the use to which they put their property. One might argue that this is exactly what ownership is *not* like: that, instead, it is a kind of *dominium* subject to no such constraints.

The question whether these more controversial claims are sound needn't be settled here. To the extent that the parallels between *Hollywood* and the public law cases that I've claimed to be analogous to it rest on the idea of an office, they do so on an understanding of an office only slightly more robust than that on which the formal conception of the office of ownership relies. The crucial idea is that an office is something subject to abuse. To abuse an office is to act in a sense within its bounds—to exercise the rights that attach to it—but to do so improperly. Analogously, one who is a stickler for her rights in a bad way acts within her rights, but exercises them 'in bad way'. The point of analogy is a common structure, one, I suggest, implicit in Aristotle's account of equity. Let me explain.

Aristotle does not draw attention to the idea that I am invoking here, but attributing it to his account is the only way to make sense of a pivotal step in his argument. That is the step at which, after explaining that equity corrects for the over-generality of the law, Aristotle claims that 'it is plain' that the equitable person is one who is not a stickler for her rights in a bad way. The question is how, exactly, to represent being a stickler for one's rights in terms of the generality or specificity of the formulation of the rule under which one seeks to justify one's actions. There must be a sense in which one gets that rule right, otherwise one is not a stickler for one's rights, but simply wrong about what those rights are. Above I cast Emmett's defence as insisting on a particularly thin or general description of his basic right as an owner: as the right to determine the use of his property *simpliciter* rather than (as Katz argues it is) the right to determine a worthwhile agenda for it. Put this way, what Emmett seeks to do is not so much cast the scope of his rights too widely, but rather deny that they must be exercised in the service of a particular end. He claims not to be subject to a kind of second-order constraint on the exercise of his rights. Note, now, that this is true on the court's own analysis of the case, according to

[39] I'm indebted here to Chris Essert's argument in 'The Office of Ownership' (2013) 63 *University of Toronto Law Journal* 418.

which it turns on the principle that one's bad motives may turn a permissible use of property into a nuisance. My neighbour's reasons for using her land as she does cannot interfere with the enjoyment of my land the way that the shadows her buildings cast or the noise her mills may make. So if my rights constrain the former they do so at a level different from the one at which they constrain the latter.

So we might say that to be a stickler for one's rights in a bad way is to seek to exploit the generality of a law in a particular sort of way. It is to act as though one's rights are not subject to second-order constraints on their exercise of the sort to which Emmett denied he was subject, to insist on a level of description that denies those limits. Put another way, the stickler in a bad way acts as though her rights are subject in their exercise only to those constraints *she* recognizes, or, at least, as though she has final say in the interpretation of those constraints. This, at the most basic level, is what she has in common with Locke's army commander and the defendant in *Roncarelli*: and it this that puts the rule of law at issue in each case.

Cast this way, the account linking equity and the rule of law is purely formal. It rests on but does not explicate the substantive content implicit in the judgment that someone is being a stickler in a *bad* way. Sometimes, one might argue, one ought to be a stickler for one's rights. 'Do not let others tread with impunity on your rights', says Kant, in a list of injunctions issuing from the duty to treat oneself with respect.[40] In some Equitable doctrines, the substantive content is expressive of Equity's concern with a particular kind of exploitation or advantage-taking. In others the analogy with the public law cases carries through on this point as well, and what provides this substance is the term of an office, such as that occupied by a trustee. Let's turn now to consider some examples of each.

5. Some Doctrines of Equity

In the final step of my argument I want to make the case that some Equitable doctrines are equitable in Aristotle's sense, and so, following the argument above, can be seen to uphold the rule of law. I will begin with estoppel and *laches*. Each, I will argue, exhibits the structure that I suggested in the last section was common among the cases of Locke's commander, *Roncarelli*, and *Hollywood*, and neither turns on the idea of an office. I will then turn to consider two Equitable doctrines that do.

A number of doctrines have answered to the name of a kind of estoppel over the years,[41] and it is a complex matter on what terms they should best be sorted. Most important in sharpening my focus here are two distinctions. The first is that between estoppel by representation, the paradigmatic common law estoppel, and equitable estoppel. Estoppel by representation arises when a party denies through some manner of representation some matter of fact that she had formerly

[40] Kant, *Metaphysics* (n 34) 188 (6:436).

[41] For a very helpful survey see Elizabeth Cooke, *The Modern Law of Estoppel* (Oxford University Press 2000) chs 2 and 3.

affirmed—or, rather, seeks or undertakes to deny it: that is what she will be estopped from doing. It was held for some time that, as expressly settled in *Jordan v Money*,[42] estoppel cannot apply in respect of representations concerning the future (for example concerning as yet unexercised rights secured under contract). The emergence of a distinctively equitable form of estoppel is often attributed to the rejection of this restriction by Lord Denning in his opinion in *High Trees v Metropolitan Railway*.[43] It has been common to distinguish within equitable estoppel between promissory and proprietary estoppel; as *Snell's Equity* has it, between cases in which 'E is precluded from resiling from his representation or promise to C' and those in which 'E is precluded from denying C's supposed rights in E's property'.[44] My concern here is with equitable rather than common law estoppel (for obvious reasons) and with promissory rather than proprietary estoppel (just to help set a limit to the discussion). So: is promissory estoppel equitable in Aristotle's sense?

It depends on just what one takes promissory estoppel to amount to, because a number of doctrines are collected under that name.[45] If one takes the doctrine in *High Trees*, as it turns out, then the answer would be no. It will be helpful here, I think, to see why. Let's start with the facts. High Trees had leased a set of flats from Central London in London in 1937. Occupancy fell considerably as the second world war began and the parties reached an agreement to reduce the rates by half. By 1945 the flats were full and Central London sued for payment for the full rent beginning in June 1945. The court held that they were entitled to it because the condition that motivated the reduction in rent had passed. Denning added in *obiter* that had Central London sued for full rent for a prior period they would have lost. Had they sued then, standing as they would have been on the persisting contract right under the lease, I think Central London could have been fairly cast as sticklers in a bad way. So we can see at least the outlines of the case in favour of the analysis of *High Trees* as a case in which equity in Aristotle's sense was done. But we need to be careful, and to attend to the details. Let's start with the question—a surprisingly open one, given its place in the history of the doctrine—whether *High Trees* really is a case in promissory estoppel.

To begin, on the facts, one might think that it is really a case about partial consideration, that is, that we ought to say that Central London had accepted partial payment as consideration for not insisting on full payment, in which case all we need to understand the case are principles of contract.[46] But let's set that aside. The more serious problems come from Denning's opinion itself. The first is his

42 (1854) 5 HLC 185. 43 [1947] KB 130.

44 John McGhee (ed), *Snell's Equity* (33rd edn, Sweet and Maxwell 2005) 257.

45 See Ben McFarlane's helpful conceptual disentangling in McFarlane, 'Understanding Equitable Estoppel: From Metaphors to Better Laws' (2013) 66 *Current Legal Problems* 267, 281–90.

46 Of course, it begs the question to say that if we conclude that this what *High Trees* is really about—as does McFarlane (McFarlane, 'Understanding' (n 45) 281–2)—that it is not really a case of promissory estoppel. That rests on a claim about what is essential to promissory estoppel. I can't begin to defend a view on that here, but take it that one can take the formulation in *Snell's*, above at n 44, as stating something like the received view.

comment that *High Trees* is not really a case in estoppel. By that he meant in part, I think, just that it violated the rule in *Jordan*. But that's just to say it's not a case in common law estoppel, and we might set this concern aside by saying that notwithstanding his caution on this point what Denning did was introduce an equitable species of the doctrine. Perhaps, however, he meant to register that the principle he invoked to justify his decision differed from common law estoppel not only in content but also in structure. According to what I will call the *High Trees* principle, 'a promise intending to be binding, intended to be acted on and in fact acted on, is binding so far as its terms properly apply'.[47] If it is essential to estoppel that it operates to prevent someone from asserting or upholding something—a factual claim, a right—then the *High Trees* principle does not articulate a doctrine of estoppel. Now, of course, perhaps this feature is not essential to estoppel. That arguably follows on the view that what estoppel does most essentially is protect reliance.[48] That's not what the *High Trees* principle does. But what the *High Trees* principle and the principle that (let's say) one may be compelled to make good on those representations to which others have been induced to rely to their detriment share is the fact that each marks a rejection of the doctrine that, excepting those made under seal, only promises for which consideration has been given in exchange will be binding.

All this matters here because it follows that the *High Trees* principle is not equitable in Aristotle's sense. That is because it does not serve to prevent the defendant from being a stickler in a bad way by correcting for the imprecision of the law. Instead it adds to the list of terms on which she, through her conduct, may become subject to a duty owed to the plaintiff. Put another way: the *High Trees* principle does not prevent the abuse of a right; instead it creates a new condition under which a right may be acquired.

More squarely an instance of estoppel and more clearly equitable in Aristotle's sense is the principle articulated in one of the cases that Lord Denning cited as contributing to tempering the rule in *Jordan*, *Hughes v Metropolitan Railway*.[49] There Lord Cairns held that 'it is the first principle upon which all Courts of Equity proceed' that

> if parties who have entered into definite and distinct terms involving certain legal results—certain penalties or legal forfeiture—afterwards by their own act or with their own consent enter upon a course of negotiation which has the effect of leading one of the parties to suppose that the strict rights arising under the contract will not be enforced, or will be kept in suspense, or held in abeyance, the person who otherwise might have enforced those rights will not be allowed to enforce them where it would be inequitable having regard to the dealings which have thus take place between the parties.[50]

The *Hughes* principle, as I will call it, articulates a set of conditions under which persons will, owing to representations they have made (or at least understandings

[47] *High Trees* (n 43) 136.
[48] On which see Michael Spence, *Protecting Reliance: The Emergent Doctrine of Equitable Estoppel* (Hart 1999).
[49] (1877) 2 App Cas 439. [50] *Hughes* (n 49) 448.

they have permitted to form), disentitle themselves from making assertions of one kind or another that they would otherwise be entitled to assert. And in displaying this structure, we can see how the *Hughes* principle is equitable in Aristotle's sense. It expressly prevents persons from being sticklers in a bad way. And unlike the *High Trees* principle, the *Hughes* principle does not add to the ways that persons may acquire rights but rather sets conditions on which others may exercise the rights they hold against them. Importantly, on the sort of facts under contemplation, the rights persons are estopped from enforcing in a sense persist throughout. Say a landlord permits a tenant to pay her rent past the date by which the lease would permit her eviction owing to transitory special circumstances. Once those circumstances pass, nothing need be done for the landlord to recover the right to enforce the suspended term of the lease (just as once the war had ended Central London was entitled to full rent). In short, when it acts to uphold the *Hughes* principle, equitable estoppel prevents persons from being sticklers in a bad way by setting conditions under which their rights may be exercised—and thus makes the law more fine-grained—and so is equitable in Aristotle's sense.

The Equitable doctrine of *laches* bears a parallel structure. Its distinctively equitable character can be brought into relief by comparing it to its common law analogue, statutory limitation periods.[51] *Laches* does not (or at least does not only) protect the defendant's interest in getting on with her life, as is often said on behalf of limitation periods, or make determinate the rights of the parties to the dispute at hand, as Arthur Ripstein argues limitation periods serve to in this volume.[52] Instead it protects her against a particular sort of exploitation, or at least inequitable advantage-taking, by the plaintiff.

A classic formulation of the basic principles of *laches* was given in the case of *Lindsay Petroleum v Hurd*.[53]

> [T]he doctrine of *laches* in Courts of Equity is not an arbitrary or a technical doctrine. Where it would be practically unjust to give a remedy, either because the party has, by his conduct, done that which might fairly be regarded as equivalent to a waiver of it, or where by his conduct and neglect, though perhaps not waiving that remedy, yet put the other party in a situation in which it would not be reasonable to place him if the remedy were afterward to be asserted, in either of these cases, lapse of time and delay are most material.[54]

On the first arm, the passage of time is material if in the context it can reasonably lead to the conclusion that the plaintiff has waived her right to press her claim—or if, as it is sometimes put, she has acquiesced in the conduct or state of affairs in respect of which she now brings suit. In that case *laches* is in effect a kind of estoppel, as acquiescence has sometimes been characterized,[55] and so the analysis of estoppel above would apply. The second arm—'where by his conduct and neglect, though perhaps not waiving that remedy, yet put the other party in a situation in

[51] As Sarah Worthington suggests in *Equity* (2nd edn, Clarendon Press 2006) 34–40.
[52] Arthur Ripstein, 'The Rule of Law and Time's Arrow' this volume.
[53] (1875) LR 5 PC 221. [54] *Lindsay* (n 53) 239–40.
[55] See Graham Virgo, *The Principles of Equity and Trusts* (Oxford University Press 2012) 565.

which it would not be reasonable to place him if the remedy were afterward to be asserted'—describes circumstances in which plaintiffs may no less clearly be characterized as being sticklers in a bad way. For example, the defence of *laches* will disentitle those who stand by knowingly allowing another to make profitable but unauthorized use of their land from then seeking to recover those profits.[56]

As with estoppel, *laches* here serves to qualify the exercise of a second-order right, a right to enforce one's rights, and so, following my argument, is equitable in Aristotle's sense, and thereby upholds the rule of law. So much follows as a matter of its formal structure. But it seems to me—and I can only gesture to the point here—that *laches* in the second form articulated in the passage from *Lindsay Petroleum* particularly clearly reflects what in Section 2 I argued was the moral-expressive content of the rule of law. According to a line of thought running back at least to Aristotle, recall, the only sort of polity appropriate to a society of equals is one structured by the rule of law. One who uses the law as a mere instrument for her ends in the way that the profiteer in our example does acts at odds with the equality expressed through this ideal.

Now let's consider the case, simpler in a sense, of Equitable doctrines that constrain the exercise of office-holders' rights. A company director may be found to have abused her authority if, for example, she issues shares so as to alter the voting majorities in a company, rather than to raise capital. I say 'may' because this area of law is contested, and whether in a particular case this will be found may, and why it would be found if it were will, depend on which of two approaches a court takes. The first is represented in the judgment in *Teck Corp Ltd v Millar*.[57] There Berger J held that the question turned on the motive for which the directors took the steps they did. In a case in which directors issue shares so as to undermine a takeover bid '[they] ought to be allowed to consider who is seeking control and why. If they believe there will be a substantial damage to the company's interests if the company is taken over, then the exercise of their powers to defeat those seeking a majority will not necessarily be categorized as improper.'[58] What settles the question is, first, whether the directors were acting in what they took to be the best interests of the company and, second, whether there were reasonable grounds for their belief: 'if they say that they believe there will be substantial damage to the company's interests, then there must be reasonable grounds for that belief. If there are not, that will justify a finding that the directors were actuated by an improper purpose.'[59] Let's call this the *Teck* approach to improper purposes.

The *Teck* approach thus tracks *Hollywood* in, to use the language of the last section, holding that one acts in abuse of right if one's motives are of a particular sort; and so the rest of the rule-of-law analysis carries over. Trickier, at least at first glance, is the second approach to cases of this sort, represented by the judgment of the court in *Howard Smith Ltd v Ampol Petroleum Ltd*.[60] There the House of Lords upheld a lower court judgment and order that an allotment and issuance of shares for the purpose of altering the voting majorities of shareholders was invalid and

[56] Worthington, *Equity* (n 51) 37.
[57] (1972) 33 DLR (3d) 288.
[58] *Teck* (n 57) para 99.
[59] *Teck* (n 57) para 103.
[60] [1974] AC 821 (PC).

must be set aside. What sets the approaches apart is that the Lords so decided notwithstanding that they had accepted the lower court finding that the directors in this case were not motivated by self-interest and had acted in what they took to be the company's best interests. That was not dispositive, the court held, because

> [j]ust as it is established that directors, within their managerial powers, may take decisions against the wishes of the majority of shareholders, and indeed that the majority of shareholders cannot control them in the exercise of these powers while they remain in office . . . so it must be unconstitutional for directors to use their fiduciary powers over the shares in the company purely for the purpose of destroying an existing majority, or creating a new majority which did not previously exist.[61]

Thus on the *Teck* approach the directors did not act in pursuit of improper purposes. Therefore *Ampol* does not track the structure of *Hollywood* in the way *Teck* does.

A second, and potentially more difficult aspect of the *Ampol* decision is the Lords' approval of the finding that the disputed issuing of the shares was invalid. If 'invalid' means 'void', then this might be read to declare that the action was beyond, rather than a wrongful exercise of, the company director's authority (as, indeed, might be read the characterization of the disputed issuance of shares as 'unconstitutional' in the passage quoted above). The general point about invalidity is made well by Lionel Smith, who casts it in terms of the duties imposed by Equity on trustees; on this point nothing turns on the differences between trustees and company directors and other agents.

> If a trustee has a fiduciary power to give property to any or all of A B and C, a disposition to D will be void (in equity at least) as outside the power. If she gives all the property to A and B because she does not like who C has married, the disposition if voidable . . . This is *not* because she did not have the power to do so; she clearly did; it is because she exercised the power improperly.[62]

Three things might be said in response. The first is that elsewhere language in the judgment arguably points to interpreting invalidity as avoidance. The court concludes that 'an action to set aside the allotment' of the shares was properly brought by the plaintiff.[63] If it were void, one might argue, it would not have to be set aside.[64] Supporting this reading—this is the second point—is the court's finding that the issue of the shares was *intra vires* the directors: and so, it follows, it had legal effect. Finally, in cases involving analogous (mis)exercises by directors of their powers so as to deter a bidder for their company's shares, the law seems to be that resulting transactions are merely voidable.[65] The *Ampol* approach, then, stands for the view that the exercise of a power for at least some ends—those, we might

[61] *Ampol* (n 60) 837.
[62] Lionel Smith, 'Can We Be Obliged to be Selfless?' in Andrew Gold and Paul Miller (eds), *Philosophical Foundations of Fiduciary Law* (Oxford University Press forthcoming) n 63.
[63] *Ampol* (n 60) 838. [64] I owe this point to Lionel Smith.
[65] See Peter Watts, 'Authority and Mismotivation' (2005) 141 *Law Quarterly Review* 4.

say, sufficiently unconnected to those for which sake the power was conferred[66]—may be *intra vires* but an abuse of that power. Such an exercise is thus, in the sense explained in Section 2, arbitrary after the manner of Duplessis's order to the Manager of the Liquor Board. Thus its constraint can be understood to uphold the rule of law.[67]

It is a short step from this example to the trust. We can see the basic elements of standard story of the trust and its development in the Aristotelian account. In the paradigmatic case, the trustee holds legal title to the trust property but is limited in the exercise of the rights she thereby has by obligations imposed on her by Equity. These obligations are not limits on the scope of those rights but rather on their exercise. The trustee must exercise them in the interests of the trust beneficiary, to whom she is said to owe a duty of loyalty.[68] So a trustee found in breach of fiduciary duty may, at least in some cases, aptly be said to have stood on her rights.

So far so good. But things get controversial as we dig a bit deeper, on two points. The first is that the Aristotelian model inclines us away from treating the beneficiary's rights as proprietary, as they are most commonly reckoned. It invites us to think of the right as a right that the trustee exercise her rights and power in a particular way, that is, as directed toward a particular end or set of ends. This makes the right personal or, better,[69] neither proprietary nor personal but rather, as Ben McFarlane and Robert Stevens argue, a third sort of right, namely a right against a right,[70] or, as Lionel Smith casts it, a right in a right.[71]

[66] The Lordships hold that while 'it is . . . too narrow an approach to say that the only valid purpose for which shares may be issued is to raise capital for the company' (*Ampol* (n 60) 835), nonetheless the purpose pursued in this case was improper because it 'cannot be related' to the ground for which the power was granted (*Ampol* (n 60) 838).

[67] Here a concern might be raised about the analogy, reflecting back on the public law cases. *Roncarelli*, recall, was a tort case. Duplessis was found personally liable for his misconduct. Presumably this reflects the judgment that his conduct was *ultra vires* his authority. But this is not quite so dispositive as it seems. In Canada, the federal government provides legal assistance and indemnification to Crown servants subject to civil claims 'despite the fact that they are acting in good faith, within the scope of their duties or in the course of their employment' (*Policy on Legal Assistance and Indemnification* 3.1). The inclusion of the second disjunct—'or in the course of their employment' and so not 'within the scope of their duties'—implies that the government regards some actions that are strictly speaking *ultra vires* their agents to nonetheless be in a sense within the scope of their employment. (This is not to say that Duplessis's actions would have been so regarded.)

Similarly the worry might be raised that in attempting to take money from those under his command, Locke's army commander is acting outside of his mandate and so simply outside of, rather than in abuse of, his authority. This is why it is essential to the example that his authority is absolute, though exercised arbitrarily. Being absolute (I take it), it is always wrongful to resist it. In a way, it cannot be exceeded: but it can be abused. As I suggested in Section 2 of this chapter, Locke's commander is not *just*, or even just like, a thief.

[68] For a compelling argument that the duty of loyalty is not, strictly speaking, a duty after all see Smith, 'Obliged' (n 62).

[69] Better because many aspects of the beneficiary's rights cannot be explained if take them to be personal; nor can they be if we take them to be proprietary in the ordinary sense. Measures one would think would settle the matter, for example the position of third parties, are equivocal. For a helpful survey of the issues see Virgo, *Principles* (n 55) 51–7.

[70] Ben McFarlane and Robert Stevens, 'The Nature of Equitable Property' (2010) 4 *Journal of Equity* 1.

[71] Lionel Smith, 'Trust and Patrimony' (2008) 38 *Revue générale de droit* 379.

The second point is that the Aristotelian account invites us to treat the constructive rather than the express trust as the core case. Consider a case in which a trust is imposed to prevent or—depending on your view on some complicated matters—remedy an unjust enrichment. Here Equity, treating as done what ought to be done, imposes on a person who bears legal title to an asset the obligation to exercise her rights to the benefit of another (in the limit, we might say, of that obligation: by transferring the asset to her). This squares in all details with the Aristotelian account. Less easy to explain is the express trust. This is because equity on Aristotle's account more comfortably fits cases in which constraints on a person's rights with respect to their exercise arise by operation of law so as to prevent the sort of advantage-taking in which those who are sticklers in a bad way engage. We are led from this perspective to adopt the idea that in setting up a trust one acts in a way calculated to bring it about that the law designates someone as a trustee and imposes on her fiduciary obligations with respect to another party it designates as a beneficiary. This view faces the objection that the power to set up a trust seems naturally thought of as an incident of ownership. It seems like something, in short, that a property owner can choose to do.[72] The alternative view in contrast seems like a contrivance.[73]

For what it's worth, I think that there are answers to the objections to these implications of the Aristotelian model. But I'm not going to wade into these issues here. They are complex and run very deep. And each side of the first debate in particular can, it seems to me, fairly claim to be defending orthodoxy. As outlined above, the trustee's duties with respect to the exercise of the rights she has in and with respect to the trust property exhibit the abuse of right-preventing structure of an equitable doctrine in Aristotle's sense. The point stands whether or not we chose to accept the draw of the Aristotelian model toward thinking of the beneficiary's rights as in or against rights, and regarding the constructive trust as the core case.

Behind these somewhat technical concern about trusts, however, arguably lies a more basic worry about the Aristotelian model in the Equitable and broader contexts to which I've applied it.[74] It is, the objection goes, misleading to say that the trustee is first granted general rights that are then corrected by Equity—just as it would be misleading to say that the Manager of the Liquor Control Board was first granted unconstrained discretion which was then corrected by an equitable construction of the enabling statute. Instead the trustee's and Manager's authority are constituted, from the beginning so to speak, by the ends for which sake it must be exercised.

[72] See James Penner 'The (True) Nature of a Beneficiary's Equitable Proprietary Interest Under a Trust' (2014) 27 *Canadian Journal of Law and Jurisprudence* 473.

[73] The line here may seem fine, but there's an important conceptual point to it. Once more there is an illuminating parallel in Locke. According to Locke, while one cannot sell or give away one's life, one can forfeit it, by committing a capital offence. The former are things one does; the latter something to which one is subject, even if one brings it about that one will be so subject. The Aristotelian model arguably requires us to think of settling a trust as akin to forfeiture rather than gift or sale.

[74] Raised to me by Ernie Weinrib.

I think two things can be said to this objection. First, while he puts it that way, it is in a sense misleading to say that for Aristotle equity 'corrects' the law. On Aristotle's view equity gets, rather than makes, things right. In his one example, equity shows the ring-wearing assaulter, he tells us, to be innocent 'really' and on the standard that was already in place. Second, my claim is that what is essential to the Aristotelian model is the idea that the law sometimes imposes duties on right-bearers in circumstances in which insisting that one has an unencumbered right makes one a stickler in a bad way. This structure is most clearly revealed if we reconstruct someone's normative position in two steps: as her bearing a right and then being subject to the duty to exercise it to certain ends and refrain from exercising it to others. But that is a merely analytic tool, and its use is compatible with its being the case that subjection to the limiting duties is a condition of bearing the right to begin with.

6. Conclusion

I will by way of conclusion review the principal claims and main steps in the argument of this chapter.

First: the rule of law. Though on the received view the rule of law appears to be a public law doctrine, we can identify an ideal underlying the various principles commonly adduced in its name that show that it is not essentially so. This ideal contrasts the rule of law with the rule of persons or with subjection to the arbitrary will of another. When cast at this level of abstraction, we can see that the rule of law is not essentially a public law ideal but ranges over the legal system as a whole. In this sense the rule of law represents the only sort of rule compatible with the equality of persons.

Second: Aristotle's account of equity. On Aristotle's account equity serves to correct the errors that arise owing to the generality of legal rules. In the sort of case that interests us here, in doing so it prevents persons from being sticklers in a bad way: from standing on the strict interpretation of their rights.

Third: Equity and the rule of law. Doctrines or judgments that are equitable in Aristotle's sense serve to prevent the abuse of rights and in that way uphold the rule of law. They do so by constraining the way in which persons exercise their legal rights, as do a number of doctrines of Equity, such as estoppel and the fiduciary duties imposed on trustees. Sticklers act as though their rights are unconstrained by these equitable (and in some cases Equitable) rules. They are in this way like public officers, such as Locke's taxing military officer and the Manager of the Liquor Commission in *Roncarelli.* This common structure entails a shared moral-expressive content: each doctrine or judgment aims to prevent persons from treating others as unequals by using the law as an instrument while supposing others to be subject to it. In doing so, those doctrines of Equity that are equitable in Aristotle's sense uphold rather than, as the received view has it, run afoul of the rule of law.

12

The Power of the Rule of Law

*Lisa M Austin**

1. Introduction

The place of property rights within a conception of the rule of law has been largely taken up in the past decade in the multidisciplinary literature relating to development, where the debate focuses on the role of the rule of law in promoting development around the world, and whether this should include substantive elements such as property rights, political and civil rights, or human rights.[1] Many who advocate the inclusion of private property rights within a substantive account of the rule of law seek to give these rights a privileged status that is meant to demarcate constraints on governmental authority—including legislative authority. Such accounts are part of a much older story in which private property, twinned with contract law, expresses and secures individual freedom, and on that basis should be protected against state intervention. There are many historical versions of this view in liberal theory, with differing accounts of the scope of legitimate state intervention. Because of his extreme anti-interventionist view, Hayek is perhaps the most prominent historical defender of such an account of private property in which property is part of a predictable legal structure that allows individuals to plan their actions in light of potential legal sanctions. More recently, and within the legal literature, Richard Epstein has taken up a version of this position.[2]

In this chapter I argue that the relationship between property and the rule of law is much more complex than this kind of traditional picture suggests. The law of private property does not protect a sphere of individual liberty from interference from others and the state, it confers legal powers to secure legal consequences not otherwise possible. The important role played by the guidance function of law, traditionally understood to be part of the rule of law, is not to allow individuals to

* I would like to thank Andrew Gold, Dennis Klimchuk, Arthur Ripstein, and the participants in the Private Law and the Rule of Law workshop for their many helpful comments on earlier drafts of this chapter.

[1] James J Heckman, Robert L Nelson, and Lee Cabatingan, *Global Perspectives on the Rule of Law* (Routledge 2010).

[2] Richard A Epstein, *Design for Liberty: Private Property, Public Administration, and the Rule of Law* (Harvard University Press 2011). See also Allan, this volume ch 3.

plan their actions in order to avoid legal sanctions but to ensure that they can follow instructions to exercise their legal powers. These powers enlarge the scope of individual action by securing a future horizon for action. Although this suggests a strong constitutive relationship between property and the rule of law, as well as between both and a kind of liberty, in another sense private property lies in tension with the rule of law. Although the guidance function of law is important, the core of the rule of law is non-arbitrariness. This points to a deep tension between private property and the rule of law: if the rule of law constrains the arbitrary exercise of power, private ownership seems to involve legal powers that can be exercised arbitrarily. I argue that this is a worry about whether private property secures equal liberty or private domination and that which of these prevails depends on context. Ideas of juridical equality and substantive equality are central to such contextual enquiries.

My argument proceeds as follows. First, I argue that private law theory in general does not pay enough attention to the role of legal powers, focusing instead on ideas of wrongdoing and liability. Drawing heavily upon Raz's work on the nature of legal powers, while also offering a critique, I revive a focus on powers and outline several important features in order to set the stage for reinterpreting private ownership in terms of legal powers. Second, I then offer a powers-based account of the basic components of private ownership. I claim that exclusive possession should be understood in terms of the conferral of a legal power, that alienability involves the exercise of this power, and that use is a consequence of having this power. Third, I show how this account of powers indicates that Raz's claim regarding the guidance function associated with the rule of law requires revision. The principles associated with the rule of law do not make powers more effective, as Raz argues, they make the exercise of legal powers *possible*. Moreover, this constitutive relationship between powers and the rule of law shows us how law can provide a temporal horizon for action, facilitating a kind of freedom. This calls into question Raz's claim that the rule of law is a negative virtue, preventing problems to freedom that the law itself creates; the rule of law does not correct a problem that legal powers create, it helps to constitute them as legal powers and in doing so helps to secure freedom. Finally, I address how private property may also be critiqued from within a rule-of-law perspective by discussing both the relationship between the rule of law and non-arbitrariness and the relationship between property and arbitrariness. I argue that the authority conferred by ownership is arbitrary in the sense of unreviewable and that this authority shifts away from protecting individual liberty and towards securing private domination in contexts where either claims of juridical or substantive equality are in question.

2. Wrongdoing, Powers, and Private Law

Many theories of private law are dominated by accounts of the nature and structure of private law liability, where liability is understood broadly to encompass the structure of private law litigation rather than in the narrower Hohfeldian sense of the jural correlative of a legal power.[3] For example, Weinrib's account of private law focuses on the correlative structure of private law liability and its implications for our understanding of private law.[4] Similarly, Lucy argues that the core structural elements of private law are those 'within which private law litigation takes place and which give it its shape'.[5] These structural elements include the fact that plaintiff and defendant are linked through ideas of wrongdoing and compensation for damage, and that litigation is backward-looking, 'forcing claimant, defendant and judge to account for a relevant past event, to demonstrate that it certainly is, or is clearly not, a legal wrong'.[6] Many other examples could be given. The point is that this emphasis on liability leads to a focus on ideas of rights and wrongdoing, as well as litigation and the courts.

Here I want to question this by highlighting a number of features of private law that this focus on liability obscures. In particular, it obscures the forward-looking and facilitative role of private law that is particularly important for understanding core features of private ownership, such as alienability. If a liability focus most often centres on the idea of wrongdoing, a facilitative focus most often centres on the idea of legal powers. As Hart argues, legal rules such as those that define how to make a valid will do not impose obligations but instead confer powers to create structures of rights and duties and so 'provide individuals with *facilities* for realizing their wishes'.[7] Legal rules regarding the alienability of property are classic examples of legal powers. Harris points to such examples as the kinds of control powers that help to define ownership, and Dorfman has recently argued that such powers are what centrally define private ownership.[8]

If we examine these facilitative moments through a liability-lens, distortion results. Take the example of the power to transfer one's property rights. One can certainly look to private law litigation to understand how a transfer of title can *fail*, such as when courts determine that there has not been a legally valid delivery of a gift.[9] But the central issue in such litigation is not compensation for damages arising out of wrongdoing but rather the determination of who has superior title to the object of property. Moreover, to try and capture what is important about title through an emphasis on a backward-looking claim is misleading. The point of determining title is to determine who is entitled to exercise control powers in relation to the object of property. Although the determination of title might require investigating past events, the exercise of control is forward-looking. Its central case should be understood in its routine everyday exercise away from the courts (but not

[3] W Hohfeld, 'Some Fundamental Legal Conceptions as Applied in Judicial Reasoning' (1913) 23 *Yale Law Journal* 16, 30.

[4] See generally Ernest J Weinrib, *The Idea of Private Law* (Harvard University Press 1995).

[5] William Lucy, *Philosophy of Private Law* (Oxford University Press 2007) 22. Lucy distinguishes this from substantive core concepts, although these turn out to be the same but to have different functions (23–5).

[6] Lucy, *Private Law* (n 5) 23.

[7] HLA Hart, *The Concept of Law* (2nd edn, Clarendon Press 1994) 27.

[8] JW Harris, *Property and Justice* (Oxford University Press 2002); Avihay Dorfman, 'Private Ownership' (2010) 16 *Legal Theory* 1.

[9] *Thomas v The Times Book Co, Ltd* [1966] 2 All ER 241 (Ch).

necessarily away from the lawyer's office) and not in the cases of breakdown that lead to litigation. The point of exclusive control is to enable people to *do* things—sell their land, enter into leases, draft wills—that they would not otherwise be able to do. Therefore to fully understand legal powers, and their role in private law, we need to move away from private law's traditional liability focus.

Hohfeld defines legal powers as the ability to effect a change in legal relations.[10] One set of examples he gives concern property—an owner changes his legal interests, and that of others, through abandonment or through transfer.[11] Its jural correlative is a legal liability, where liability means being vulnerable to having your legal relations changed through another's exercise of a legal power. Raz argues that although this definition is helpful, it is 'not precise and may mislead'.[12]

Raz offers four clarifications of Hohfeld. The first is that '[a] legal power is normatively, not causally, effective'. The point is not that I cause a change in legal position, such as by persuading you to transfer your property to me; 'my act' must effect the change.[13] Second, the type of act performed is important. An offender does not have a legal power even though committing an offence is a voluntary act that changes the offender's legal relations by making 'the offender liable to a sanction'. The act performed has to be one that entails legal consequences and is 'standardly performed *only if* the person concerned wants to secure these legal consequences'.[14] Raz argues:

> This is the most important feature of legal powers, which is all too often neglected. It explains why they are exercised either by special formal and ceremonial acts as in making a deed or getting married, or by ordinary actions whose legal consequences approximate to their non-legal and obvious consequences, as in making a contract. It also explains why most legal powers are exercised by acts with only negligible non-normative consequences, like signing, so that there are few reasons for or against them apart from their legal or other normative consequences.[15]

Third, Raz disputes Hohfeld's claim that the legal changes at issue must be changes in rights and duties and instead construes the nature of the relevant legal change as 'a change in the existence, content or application of a law or legally recognized norm'.[16] For example, 'norm-creating' powers include the power of making a contract.[17] 'Regulative' powers include the power to transfer property, as this does not affect the content of the norms of ownership but does affect their application (by changing the identity of the owner and non-owner).[18] Fourth,

[10] Hohfeld, 'Fundamental Legal Conceptions' (n 3) 44.

[11] Hohfeld, 'Fundamental Legal Conceptions' (n 3) 45. Agency provides him with another set of examples.

[12] Neil MacCormick and Joseph Raz, 'Voluntary Obligations and Normative Powers' (1972) 46 *Proceedings of the Aristotelian Society*, Supplementary Volumes 59, 80. Hart also suggested reservations with Hohfeld—see HLA Hart, 'Bentham on Legal Powers' (1972) 81 *Yale Law Journal* 799.

[13] MacCormick and Raz, 'Voluntary Obligations' (n 12) 81.

[14] MacCormick and Raz, 'Voluntary Obligations' (n 12) 81.

[15] MacCormick and Raz, 'Voluntary Obligations' (n 12) 81. See also Raz's discussion of non-mandatory norms in *Practical Reason and Norms* (Oxford University Press 1975) 103.

[16] Raz, *Practical Reason* (n 15) 103.

[17] Raz, *Practical Reason* (n 15) 82.

[18] Raz, *Practical Reason* (n 15) 82.

Raz argues that we should not think of powers as a species of right, since it is possible to have a power but be under obligations that restrict its use (and therefore have no right to exercise the power).[19]

I want to underscore the importance of legal consequences for understanding the exercise of legal powers. From the perspective of the power-holder, the securing of legal consequences is the very point of exercising the power. Moreover, it is upon this basis that Raz distinguishes duty-imposing and power-conferring rules. Duty-imposing rules are requirements or prohibitions that, according to Raz, 'defeat the agent's other reasons for action'.[20] In contrast, power-conferring rules guide action in a different manner, because 'the law itself attaches legal consequences to an action in order to determine the considerations for or against that action on the basis of which the power-holder will decide what to do'.[21] In other words, it is the legal consequences that attach to the exercise of a legal power that are important: if the agent 'has reason for securing the result the power enables him to achieve then he has reason to exercise it'.[22]

It is the role played by legal consequences that shows both why legal powers are facilitative as well as how the law may perform a facilitative function distinct from that associated with legal powers. The point of a legal power is to provide the normative ability to create legal consequences, which allows for security in relation to some result. However, the law can play a facilitative role outside of the context of legal powers when the law itself (or the state acting through the law) secures some state of affairs that then makes possible other consequences. For example, consider the role played by legal identity documents such as passports. These provide a certification of identity and this certification can then make it possible for others to ascertain that you are indeed a person eligible for certain rights, privileges, etc. Such formal legal documents are therefore facilitative—you cannot, for example, cross the border without one—but their use is not the exercise of a power nor does having a passport in itself confer any legal powers. Laws can create a stable environment in other ways, such as through providing additional support to settled expectations that are themselves created outside the framework of the law. The facilitative function of law therefore includes legal powers but is not coextensive with it.

3. Property and Powers

I have outlined elsewhere my agreement with the position that the central organizing principle of ownership is exclusive possession.[23] Many accounts of private

[19] Raz, *Practical Reason* (n 15) 82.

[20] Joseph Raz, *The Concept of a Legal System* (2nd edn, Clarendon Press 1980) 228.

[21] Raz, *Legal System* (n 20) 228.

[22] Raz, *Legal System* (n 20) 228.

[23] Lisa M Austin, 'Possession and the Distractions of Philosophy' in James Penner and Henry E Smith (eds), *The Philosophical Foundations of Property Law* (Oxford University Press 2013) 182–201. Others have also argued for this basic point, most prominently Penner and Smith although Penner sometimes talks in terms of exclusive *use*, which I think is a mistake.

ownership that place exclusion at their centre focus on the significance of the obligation of non-owners to exclude themselves from the object of property.[24] In other words, they use what I have been calling a liability framework and its emphasis on wrongdoing in order to capture the significance of exclusion to property law. Similarly, the owner's interest is most often described as a right, rather than a power, for it is correlated with this duty, on the part of non-owners, of non-interference with the object of property.

In this section I question this predominant approach and argue that we should think of ownership in terms of legal powers and not rights. However, even within the literature on legal powers there is support for the claim that exclusive possession should be understood as a right, not a power, and I want to start by canvassing this literature and indicating its flaws.

For example, as already indicated, Hart claimed that legal powers permit individuals 'to create, by certain specified procedures and subject to certain conditions, structures of rights and duties within the coercive framework of the law'.[25] Exclusive possession permits me to control the object of property (I get to decide, not you) but these decisions do not, in themselves, create a structure of rights and duties in the way that contract might be said to create new legal rights and duties.[26] Nor are the categories of rights and powers interchangeable. For example, as indicated in the previous section, Raz argues that powers are not a kind of right, since one does not necessarily have a right to exercise the power. By this he means that there might be restrictions on its exercise.

Even if we switch from a focus on rights (the right of exclusive possession) to a focus on obligations (the obligation to refrain from interference), the literature on powers suggests that the language of power is misplaced in relation to possession. Raz argues that the idea of legal powers is key to understanding the distinction between voluntary obligations and obligations imposed by authority, where voluntary obligations are those created through the exercise of legal powers and obligations imposed by authority are not.[27] However, the obligation of non-owners to 'keep off' is not voluntary in the way that a contractual obligation is. It might be that Raz's later refinement of distinguishing between norm-creating and regulative powers already calls this distinction between voluntary and imposed obligations into question somewhat, for regulative powers affect the application but not the content of obligations. One could argue, however, that the kind of regulative powers he has in mind are things like my ability to transfer my property to you—the exercise of which is voluntary on my part. But trespass rules do not involve voluntary choices in any sense; trespass liability arises as a consequence of the legal fact that it is the owner who has authority in relation to the object of property, not the non-owner.

[24] See eg JE Penner, *The Idea of Property in Law* (Oxford University Press 1997). For a different account based on authority, see Larissa Katz, 'Exclusion and Exclusivity' (2008) 58 *University of Toronto Law Journal* 275.

[25] Hart, *The Concept of Law* (n 7) 27–8.

[26] Contracts are one of Hart's key examples of legal powers.

[27] MacCormick and Raz, 'Voluntary Obligations' (n 12) 97ff.

Hart also suggests a sharp distinction between power-conferring rules and duty-imposing rules. He argues that legal powers have been under-theorized and that 'much more than Hohfeld gives us is needed to display the notion fully and to analyze legal powers in their variant forms, and to exhibit the character of the laws which create or confer them'.[28] His key criticism of Bentham's account of powers is that Bentham represented powers such as the power to dispose of property as a kind of 'permission' to do something that is otherwise illegal. In this way, he argues that Bentham turned power-conferring rules into 'fragments of duty-imposing rules', thus obscuring 'their distinct normative character'.[29] As he argues, 'they are more like *instructions* how to bring about certain results than mandatory impositions of duty'.[30] Hart's characterization might work as a description of alienability rules, but the 'keep off' of trespass is imposed and mandatory.

Despite these hurdles, I want to suggest that exclusive possession is indeed best characterized in terms of legal powers. The key is to distinguish between having a power and exercising a power. Possession, as I have claimed elsewhere, is best understood in terms of exclusive control, which is different from exclusive *use*.[31] Thus if I have exclusive possession with respect to some object, I am the one who has exclusive control over that thing. What this means is that I get to decide about access to the object, not you. The decision-making authority, not the use, is what is central. Use is a side-effect, or consequence, of having this authority. If I am the one who has decision-making authority with respect to some object, then I interfere with nobody else's authority by using that object; I have a use-privilege. Having this authority is also distinct from exercising it through related powers of alienability that allow me, in various ways, to transfer my control.

If we switch to thinking about possession in terms of conferring control powers, then the liability rules associated with possession actually become more understandable. The key is to understand these control powers as protected by trespass liability. Indeed, JW Harris describes private ownership in terms of control powers protected, in part, through trespassory rules.[32] Much like contract rules, which protect expectation damages, trespass rules are not loss based. If you trespass on my property, I can get an injunction to prevent this or I can recover damages in the amount of the 'rent' I would have charged you to use my property. This reflects the idea that I get to decide, not you, and so you need my permission to use it. Whether you have injured me in some way is simply not relevant.[33] It is an interference with my authority that is at issue and which the liability structure reflects.[34]

It bears emphasis that the kind of power an owner has is a legal power, not a natural power. One of the key aspects of the right of possession is that you have

[28] Hart, 'Bentham' (n 12) 801.
[29] Hart, 'Bentham' (n 12) 821–2.
[30] Hart, 'Bentham' (n 12) 821–2.
[31] Austin, 'Possession' (n 23).
[32] Harris, *Property* (n 8).
[33] See Arthur Ripstein, 'Beyond the Harm Principle' (2006) 34 *Philosophy & Public Affairs* 215.
[34] As Stephen Smith argues in ch 8 of this volume, trespass is better understood if we drop the idea of an associated duty altogether. On my account, trespass liability is correlated with the power of exclusive control; it is not triggered by the breach of a *duty*.

control over the object of property even when you are not in actual possession.[35] In other words, you do not have to continue to actually exert control over an object but can put it down and still be the one entitled to control it. Trespass, theft, and conversion all presuppose this idea; in each case another factually controls the object when the owner is the one entitled to do so, giving rise to either tort or criminal liability.

But more than this, the fact that I have a power of exclusive control secures a set of legal consequences for me independently of whether I actually exercise this power. If I do not have the power of exclusive control then all I can have are present uses of things: once I am no longer in actual control of something I have no claim to control over the object. The whole point of legal control is that I get to put the object down. The importance of this is that it opens up new uses. More specifically, it makes possible future uses of the object. In this way, the future legal consequences—that the thing remains under my control—are important and can factor in my reasons for acting even though I do not create these consequences through the exercise of a power.

This account therefore construes the standard property trilogy of possession, use, and alienability in the following way. Exclusive possession is a legal power that confers exclusive control in relation to the object of property; interference with this power gives rise to trespass liability. Alienability involves the exercise of this power to transfer my control. Use is a consequence of having this power but should not be confused either with the conferral of the power or its exercise.

4. Guidance, Powers, and Freedom

This focus on legal powers rather than ideas of liability can show why the guidance function of law is not fully captured by the idea that the law provides guidance to individuals by allowing them to plan their lives so as to avoid legal sanctions. Instead, I argue here, guidance is essential to the possibility of *exercising* legal powers. In turn, this shows that property, understood in terms of legal powers, and the rule of law, understood in terms of its guidance function, facilitate a form of freedom in securing a temporal horizon for action. Unlike the 'freedom-from' implied in the understanding of avoiding legal sanctions, this is a 'freedom-to'. In making this argument, I take up and critique Raz's account of the relationship between the rule of law and guidance, as well as the relationship between the rule of law and freedom.

In Raz's famous knife analogy, he compares the sharpness of a knife to the rule of law: just as sharpness is a virtue that makes a knife effective at cutting, the rule of law is a virtue that makes the law effective at guiding individual action. Although this means that the rule of law 'is a necessary condition for the law to be serving directly any good purpose at all', conformity with the rule of law does not mean

[35] Austin, 'Possession' (n 23).

that the law serves any good purpose. The value of the rule of law (generality, clarity, prospectivity, etc) lies in *preventing* dangers to freedom and dignity that can be caused by laws that do not conform to these values. A law that is retroactive is one that will not guide effectively and, because of this, will also violate autonomy and dignity interests. In this way, 'the rule of law is a negative virtue in two senses: conformity to it does not cause good except through avoiding evil and the evil which is avoided is evil which could only have been caused by the law itself.'[36]

For Raz, the central idea of the rule of law is that individuals obey the law, and obeying the law and being guided by the law are closely linked. As he argues:

> A person conforms with the law to the extent that he does not break the law. But he obeys the law only if part of his reason for conforming is his knowledge of the law. Therefore, if the law is to be obeyed it must be capable of guiding the behaviour of its subjects. It must be such that they can find out what it is and act on it.[37]

This description of obeying the law resonates most strongly with duty-imposing rules. Duty-imposing rules impose constraints on what we otherwise have a reason to do. This is why it is possible for my actions to conform to the law even if I have no knowledge of these rules—I have other reasons for my actions and the fact that my actions also conform with my legal duty is a happy coincidence. However, this is not the case with legal powers. Unlike duty-imposing rules, individuals *follow*, rather than obey, power-conferring rules. Power-conferring rules both secure desirable legal consequences and specify the actions that are to be taken in order to obtain these legal consequences. Individuals might have a variety of reasons to desire and choose these consequences; rather than impose constraints, power-conferring rules give instructions regarding how to secure these consequences. Because of this, in relation to powers we cannot talk about conforming to the law without knowledge of it—we need to know the instructions in order to follow them. Moreover, as Raz points out, these instructions usually involve acts that individuals would have few reasons to engage in, apart from securing the desired legal consequences.[38]

We might say that a liability-focus highlights how an otherwise permissible and desirable act might be constrained by the law whereas a powers-focus shows how an act might be defined by law and its consequences made possible through law. But if one cannot exercise a legal power unless one knows what actions constitute exercising that power, then guidance will function differently. This, in turn, calls into question Raz's claim that the rule of law is what makes law effective. That the law is capable of guiding behaviour does not make the exercise of a power more effective—it makes it *possible*.

This constitutive relationship between legal powers and legal guidance helps explain the centrality of ideas of publicity and clarity to many areas of property law.

[36] Joseph Raz, 'The Rule of Law and its Virtue' in *The Authority of Law* (2nd edn, Oxford University Press 2009) 210, 225. He makes the same claim in relation to the value of non-arbitrariness: the law creates the problem of arbitrariness and the rule of law is a solution to this problem.

[37] Raz, 'Virtue' (n 36) 214–15.

[38] MacCormick and Raz, 'Voluntary Obligations' (n 12) 81.

Take the example of powers of alienability, or the power to transfer one's exclusive control either entirely or in part. Powers of alienability rely upon clear title rules for their exercise—a system of powers of alienability can only function when people know who own which things. This is sometimes confused with the issue of giving people notice in order to avoid trespass liability. However, as Penner points out, in order to know to 'keep off' some land all you need to know is that it is not yours—you do not need to know *who* owns it.[39] If we switch instead to a focus on the guidance function associated with legal powers, particularly when thought of in systemic terms, then we can see that property powers require more demanding notice requirements regarding title. For example, in order to obtain title from you, I need a means of ensuring that you are the person entitled to transfer it.[40] A system of title requires clear and public means to determine both what is owned and who owns what.

Sometimes the guidance concern lies with the exercise of property powers to create new legal obligations. For example, an owner might impose an obligation on another through the devise of a conditional estate, such as testamentary gift of a fee simple subject to a condition subsequent where the breach of the condition gives rise to a right of re-entry by the decedent's estate. Or an owner might enter into an agreement with a neighbour, like a restrictive covenant, burdening the neighbour's property with an obligation to refrain from doing something on her land. In both cases these obligations can be found to be void if they are too uncertain. The concern is not with *what* the owners are trying to do so much as *how*, or their form—the exercise of legal powers to create new obligations must conform to basic rule-of-law concerns regarding guidance.[41]

The fact that legal powers have this constitutive relationship with the guidance function of law shows that property, understood in terms of legal powers, has a constitutive relationship with the rule of law. As I outline below, it also shows that it has a constitutive relationship with one form of freedom through helping to secure a temporal horizon for action.

Private ownership is often thought to enlarge the range of choices available to individuals.[42] One way to think about how it does this is to suppose that the trespass rules associated with ownership protect the owner's use of a thing from interference from another, thus enlarging the scope of our effective choices. However, as I have already outlined, the right of possession associated with private ownership does not simply protect our pre-legal abilities to use the objects of property—importantly, it *creates* uses that are simply not possible without legal possession. The point of legal possession is that one does not have to be in factual possession of a thing in order to remain in legal control of it. The possibility that this creates is that of future use: I can pick an apple and put it down in a basket and

[39] Penner, *Idea of Property* (n 24).

[40] This can explain why Merrill and Smith's information cost approach to property law is so helpful. See, for example, Thomas W Merrill and Henry E Smith, 'The Property/Contract Interface' (2001) 101 *Columbia Law Review* 773.

[41] Austin, 'Property and the Rule of Law' (2014) 20 *Legal Theory* 79.

[42] See Harris, *Property* (n 8) ch 13.

not have to continue to hold it or guard it in order to make an apple pie the next day.[43] In this way, I 'have' the apple and it is already (but need not be) tied up with my future plans even though I make no present use of the apple—indeed, this is the very point of a future use.

This is a legal consequence of tremendous importance if we want to think about the enabling and facilitative aspects of property law. It is this feature, which is a *consequence* of the power but should not be confused with its exercise, that shows how private ownership can enlarge the scope of autonomy. Instead of simply being agents who act in the world, the kind of future uses secured by legal possession is one of the things that provide us with a temporal horizon for our actions and this temporal horizon is what transforms abstract agents into individuals with concrete identities and abstract choices into individual life plans.

The second way in which private ownership provides a temporal horizon for action lies in the powers associated with alienability. As already outlined, alienability involves the exercise of legal powers. Here both the acts at issue and the consequences that follow from them are constituted through law. For example, it is not that you sell your land and the law then protects this sale—you can only sell your land by doing the acts prescribed by law as constituting a valid sale. Selling your land might secure any number of non-legal consequences (money in your pocket, for example) but the key consequence is legal—the transfer of title. In fact, it is artificial to separate the act and its consequences—to do the acts prescribed by law as constituting a valid sale simply *is* to transfer title. In this way, legal powers enlarge the scope of autonomy by creating and constituting new actions and future consequences not otherwise possible.

The third way in which private ownership provides a temporal horizon for action arises out of the impersonal nature of ownership. Many people have argued, including myself, that impersonality is central to the idea of private ownership in that the particular identity of the owner does not matter. This permits ownership to change hands without affecting the normative position of anyone other than the parties involved in the transfer. In other words, legal possession attaches to the owner (whoever that happens to be) and so private ownership has a temporal dimension in the sense that it continues to exist independently of any particular individual who happens to be the owner. The common law doctrine of estates is one legal method for dealing with this temporal aspect of ownership. This temporal dimension to ownership, also a consequence of legal possession, provides property law with a number of its distinctive elements. Peñalver has called this land's 'memory'.[44] Others have pointed to the importance of reliance interests in property law.[45] I do not mean to take up these accounts here, or indicate my agreement or disagreement with their particulars. But I do want to suggest that these persistent themes in property law are best illuminated in relation to the manner in which legal possession secures a temporal horizon for action.

[43] Austin, 'Possession' (n 23) for this argument in more detail.
[44] Eduardo M Peñalver, 'Land Virtues' (2009) 94 *Cornell Law Review* 821.
[45] Joseph Singer, 'The Reliance Interest in Property' (1988) 40 *Stanford Law Review* 611.

Private ownership is not unique in securing a temporal horizon for action. This is what law does generally and is the way in which law does not simply protect individuals and actions that can be understood entirely in pre-legal terms but is in many ways constitutive of the selves we become. Taking ownership as an example we can therefore say that law does not simply protect actions that are intelligible in non-legal terms but it also constitutes actions that are only possible and intelligible through reference to the law.

This account of powers, freedom, and the rule of law strongly echoes a number of claims that Raz makes in relation to the rule of law. For example, Raz acknowledges law's function in securing 'the existence of stable, secure frameworks for one's life and actions'.[46] This is freedom understood in the sense of 'an effective ability to choose between as many options as possible'.[47] The rule of law facilitates this freedom through making the law itself 'a stable and safe basis for individual planning'.[48] However, for Raz this function is connected to what he considers the negative virtue of the rule of law. If the rule of law helps to secure freedom on Raz's account, it is only in the sense that it minimizes the harms to freedom that the law itself creates.

However, if we accept that the rule of law helps legal powers to *function* as powers, and that these powers facilitate a 'freedom-to', then Raz's claim that law creates problems for freedom that the rule of law solves looks rather strange. The rule of law does not correct a problem that legal powers create, it helps to constitute them as legal powers and in doing so helps to secure that freedom.

This constitutive relationship between the rule of law and at least some forms of freedom makes the *means* of law, and not just the *ends* of law, morally significant rather than morally neutral. The rule of law is not just of instrumental value, ensuring the effectiveness of the law as an instrument, or of negative virtue in preventing the harms that law itself creates. However, one can still argue that the full moral significance of the rule of law needs to be evaluated in multiple ways. Not all of these ways involve appeals to broad principles of political morality. Importantly, as I argue in the next section, there are rule-of-law grounds to critique private ownership rather than embrace it.

5. The Arbitrariness of Ownership and the Rule of Law

Traditionally, the rule of law is associated with two core ideas: constraints on the arbitrary exercise of power and the guidance function of law. Different accounts usually give primacy to one over the other as the central organizing idea. Whereas the guidance function of law is important to fully understand the relationship between property and the rule of law, it is non-arbitrariness that presents the deepest challenge to private ownership. If non-arbitrariness involves some idea of constraints on power, and private property involves the conferral and exercise of

[46] Raz, 'Virtue' (n 36) 220.

[47] Raz, 'Virtue' (n 36) 220.

[48] Raz, 'Virtue' (n 36) 220.

powers that appear arbitrary, then property and the rule of law look like they are on a collision course. One way around this collision course is to adopt an account of the rule of law that accepts the centrality of guidance over non-arbitrariness, such as Raz's influential account. However, I disagree with this account and in this section outline both my disagreement and the nature of the rule of law challenge to the arbitrariness of ownership.

Raz accepts that the rule of law should be, at least in some senses, contrasted with arbitrary power. However, he notes that '[a]rbitrary power is broader than the rule of law.'[49] For example, he rejects the idea that a law based on the whim of a ruler violates the rule of law. Another sense of arbitrariness is when its exercise is 'done either with indifference as to whether it will serve the purposes which alone can justify use of that power or with belief that it will not serve them', which Raz argues is too subjective for the rule of law to have any bearing upon.[50] Instead, Raz argues that the *application* of laws must be non-arbitrary, not that laws must be non-arbitrary in relation to their content or purpose; therefore the rule of law has strong traction in relation to the judiciary or delegated powers. In relation to this law-applying function, Raz argues that what is at stake is guidance, for 'distorted enforcement' deprives law of its ability to guide.[51] However, then he also states the idea that 'it is universally believed that it is wrong to use public powers for private ends' so any such use would be arbitrary and caught by the rule of law. As others in this volume emphasize, many have argued that this universal belief is in fact the core idea of the rule of law.

Raz's rejection of the centrality of non-arbitrariness is connected to his claim that the idea that the rule of law means government authorized by law is a tautology: 'Actions not authorized by law cannot be the actions of the government as a government. They would be without legal effect and often unlawful.'[52] The way around this tautology, he argues, is to understand that the lay understanding of law is 'a set of open, general and relatively stable laws' rather than the broader set of constitutions, statutes, regulations, and orders that form the lawyer's professional understanding of the law.[53] The rule of law is a meaningful political ideal if we understand that particular laws must be subject to 'general, open and stable ones'. Instead of developing this view at length, Raz then goes on to say that this does not in fact provide much insight into the central importance of the rule of law. Instead, he argues, the 'basic intuition' underlying the rule of law is that 'the law must be capable of guiding the behaviour of its subjects'.[54] If it cannot fulfil this guidance function, then the law cannot be obeyed for, according to Raz, someone obeys the law if knowledge of the law is part of her reason for conforming to the requirements of the law.[55]

This shift to obedience to the law as the place to anchor the guidance function of law is a misstep and it begins with Raz's dismissal of the 'tautology' of government authorized by law. Let me illustrate with the example of unconstitutionally vague

[49] Raz, 'Virtue' (n 36) 219.
[50] Raz, 'Virtue' (n 36) 219.
[51] Raz, 'Virtue' (n 36) 220.
[52] Raz, 'Virtue' (n 36) 212.
[53] Raz, 'Virtue' (n 36) 213.
[54] Raz, 'Virtue' (n 36) 214.
[55] Raz, 'Virtue' (n 36) 214.

laws. Both the Canadian Supreme Court and the United States Supreme Court have emphasized the two general aspects of the rule of law in their void for vagueness jurisprudence: a vague law neither gives individuals fair notice of liability nor is capable of constraining enforcement discretion.[56] According to the Canadian Supreme Court, 'guidance' is involved in both of these aspects. As the court states, 'a law will be found unconstitutionally vague if it so lacks in precision as not to give sufficient guidance for legal debate' where relevant 'legal debate' encompasses both the idea of fair notice to individuals as well as providing the judiciary with the means to control the exercise of law enforcement discretion.[57] Guidance is involved, therefore, even when the rule of law functions as a constraint—but the guidance is not simply to allow law enforcement agents to understand the boundaries of their authority but to allow for review of discretion.

A police officer arresting an individual under the authority of such a vague law does not act *ultra vires* that authority—his action is not outside the law and without legal effect. Indeed, that is precisely why the *law* is challenged as defective and not the officer's actions under the law. The problem is that it is unclear what should or should not fall under the law and so this leaves a large area of discretion for the police officer. This can open up the potential for personal prejudices to enter in, allowing the police officer to pursue her own 'personal predilections', and also means that the treatment of any particular individual will vary greatly depending upon the officer involved, violating law's aspiration to generality. There is something defective with the law itself and its ability to function as law.

To be clear, it is not the case that too much official discretion is the only way in which private purposes might subvert the function of law as law. For example, laws governing the state's power of expropriation are concerned with constraining the state's ability to unfairly and abusively single out a particular individual, and typically require both compensation and a public purpose. There are many ways in which we might say that private purposes enter into the uses of law in a manner that offends the rule of law.

Instead of the tautology of government authorized by law, we could think of the core elements of the rule of law as united by the idea that together they help to *constitute* legal authority by preventing it from being used as an instrument of private power. In this way, the rule of law does not make the law (or legal power) more effective, it is constitutive of it as the kind of thing that it is. If law is an instrument, then the rule of law is what makes it the particular kind of instrument it is. It is not a virtue of the means, as Raz claims, but constitutive of the means; not a negative virtue but still negative in the sense that what is distinctive of the means lies in what it is not.

Where does that leave the guidance function of the rule of law? As already outlined, Raz's account of the guidance function is tied to his argument about the importance of obeying the law. But this too can be recast in terms of the centrality

[56] See eg *R v Nova Scotia Pharmaceutical Society* [1992] 2 SCR 606; *Kolender v Lawson*, 461 US 352 (1983).

[57] *Nova Scotia Pharmaceutical* (n 56) 643.

of the idea that legal authority is regulative of private power and not its instrument. A system governed by the rule of law must have a way of ensuring that public officials indeed follow the law and do not use it as an instrument of private power. One aspect of this involves guidance to those who would hold public officials accountable—for example, the judges. Another aspect is guidance to the officials themselves so that they can be to some extent self-regulating. Private citizens must also follow the law and we can characterize this in similar terms—if the law is not followed then private power is effectively unregulated and this guidance contemplates both guidance to individuals who can then be self-regulating and guidance to those entrusted to hold them accountable.

Despite the fact that legal powers have a constitutive relationship with the guidance function of law, if we understand the rule of law to be primarily concerned with non-arbitrariness then a tension emerges between property and the rule of law. Unlike the powers associated with public office-holders, the legal powers associated with private ownership can be used for private ends—indeed this is their *point*. However, this makes them look 'arbitrary' in Postema's sense of 'unaccountable, exercised at the pleasure of its agent'.[58] This concern lies at the heart of many critical accounts of property. For example, Robert Gordon has argued that despite the efforts of many critics, the 'authoritarian connotations' historically associated with property understood as 'lordship over one's demesne or household' have been lost in a transition to a vocabulary of autonomy and liberty, of power over things rather than power over people. He writes: 'Thus, absolute dominion is left unrestrained within a sphere of right, an unreviewable *fiat* authority defined as freedom.'[59] What are we to make of this unreviewable authority, from a rule-of-law perspective?

Consider the *Anchor Brewhouse* case.[60] The defendant had been using a tower crane that swung over the property of the plaintiffs. This overswinging did not interfere with any use the plaintiffs were making of the property but they sought to have it restrained and were granted an injunction. In granting the injunction, the judge made it clear that he thought the result unreasonable:

> There is a sense in which the grant of an injunction against trespass enables a landowner to behave like a dog in a manger. I am not suggesting that these plaintiffs are so behaving but the conclusion that even if they are, they are nonetheless entitled to their injunction sticks a little in my gullet. It would be possible for the law to be that the court should not grant an injunction to restrain a trifling trespass if it were shown to be reasonable and sensible that the trespass be allowed to continue for a limited period upon payment of substantial and proper damages. But I do not think it is open to me to proceed on that footing. There is too much authority in the way.[61]

[58] See Gerald J Postema, 'Fidelity in Law's Commonwealth' in this volume ch 1, 18.

[59] Robert W Gordon, 'Paradoxical Property' in John Brewer and Susan Staves (eds), *Early Modern Conceptions of Property* (Routledge 1996) 95–110 at 101–2.

[60] *Anchor Brewhouse Developments v Berkley House (Docklands Developments) Ltd*, 2 EGLR 173 (1987).

[61] *Anchor Brewhouse* (n 60) 178.

The owner is permitted to act entirely 'at pleasure', even when clearly unreasonable and even when the owner is not advancing any discernible personal interest—the dog in the manger from Aesop's fable cannot eat the straw, he just wants to make sure that others cannot get it.

We might say, therefore, that owners are permitted to arbitrarily exercise the legal powers associated with ownership. The difficulty with this lies in what it means to exercise a legal power. If I grant you permission to enter my land, or my airspace, then we could say that this is the exercise of a power because it affects a normative change—you are no longer liable to an action in trespass. Your legal position has changed. If I refuse to grant you permission, then this is a refusal to exercise my power to change your normative position. The law's protection of this refusal is not a vindication of the arbitrary exercise of a legal power, it is a restatement of the terms of the conferral of that power—that I am the one who gets to decide rather than you. However, even when the law protects my granting of permission it protects the authority of the owner to decide. If there is a concern about arbitrariness then it lies with the basic terms of the authority of the owner, who is not answerable to another for that decision, rather than with the exercise or refusal to exercise that authority.

The question is whether this is the kind of arbitrariness that the rule of law is concerned about and I think the answer is: maybe and sometimes. One answer is to say that private property rights are in fact a response to the more general concern about private power, protecting individuals in relation to each other as well as in relation to the state.[62] But claiming that this arbitrary authority is not arbitrary power in a more general, and negative, sense requires us to posit both the equality of ownership and the equality of persons more generally. Understood in terms of juridical equality, or what some might call formal equality, a system of private ownership that treats all as equals is one of equal freedom rather than unequal domination. The exercise of legal powers that undermine this ideal of juridical equality is therefore suspect from a rule-of-law perspective. More generally, we might also examine property from the perspective of substantive rather than formal equality and ask whether the exercise of the legal powers associated with property, at least in some contexts, actively contributes to social and economic conditions of domination. Let me illustrate each type of concern with an example.

Suppose that I refuse to give you permission to use my airspace, you do so anyway, and I go to court to seek an injunction. Although this is a refusal to exercise a power, it also requires the exercising of a different legal power in order to make it effective. As Goldberg and Zipursky argue, all private claims involve legal powers—the power to bring a claim in court.[63] There are a number of situations where courts will prevent individuals from bringing otherwise legitimate claims, such as in proprietary estoppel cases. If the plaintiff in *Anchor Brewhouse* had been involved in representing that permission had or would be given, and had the defendants relied

[62] See TRS Allen, 'The Rule of Law as the Rule of Private Law' in this volume ch 3.

[63] John CP Goldberg and Benjamin C Zipursky, 'Civil Recourse Revisited' (2011) 39 *Florida State University Law Review* 341.

upon this to their detriment and to the knowledge of the plaintiffs, then the outcome would have been different. The defendants would still have been trespassing with their oversailing crane, but the trespass would not be actionable. Why restrain the ability to bring a legal claim in these circumstances? A full discussion of equitable doctrines, or even proprietary estoppel, is beyond the scope of this chapter. However, I think that both Smith and Klimchuk are correct to stress that equity restrains a kind of opportunism and that this can be understood in terms of rule-of-law values.[64] In the example I have outlined here, modifying the facts of *Anchor Brewhouse*, the plaintiff exploits his position as the individual legally authorized to decide about the use of the airspace. By representing to another that his power would be exercised to allow the oversailing crane, and then standing by watching while this representation is relied upon, the owner uses the fact of having a legal power to create a vulnerability in another: the defendant's interests are bound up with the plaintiff's decision-making authority, but it is the plaintiff who has created this dependency. In bringing a trespass claim the plaintiff then exploits that vulnerability through relying upon her formal legal powers in the very way she had represented she would not. This exploitation violates respect for juridical equality by using legal powers as the very instrument of both creating and exploiting a vulnerability in another and does so in a manner that treats another as a means for entirely personal ends. By preventing the ability to bring a claim to court in such circumstances, equity preserves the basic position that it is the owner who has the authority to decide about access to the airspace while preventing the owner's ability to use this position to undermine the very idea of law (that it is not a tool of private power) upon which ownership depends.[65]

The systemic effects of private ownership must also be taken into account and show the limits of ideas of juridical equality for evaluating the question of whether the arbitrary authority of ownership involves arbitrary power in the negative rule-of-law sense. For example, the perfectly lawful exercise of powers of alienability can create widespread distributional disparities in relation to who owns what. And this can lead to problems in relation to who gets access to what. For example, as an owner a shopping mall owner can revoke her invitation to a member of the public and charge her with trespass. Given the mall owner's social and economic position, should the law permit this for any reason at all?[66] To take another example, the owner of a grocery store seeking to relocate might wish to impose a restrictive covenant on the land when selling it so that the new owner cannot operate a grocery store on that location and compete with their new location. If this creates an inner city food desert, can the covenant be invalidated on the grounds of public policy?[67]

[64] See Henry E Smith, 'Property, Equity and the Rule of Law' and Dennis Klimchuk, 'Equity and the Rule of Law' in this volume chs 10 and 11.

[65] There is no need to think that this is confined to equity—Ernest J Weinrib gives many examples that work in a similar two-step fashion in 'Private Law and Public Right' (2011) 61 *University of Toronto Law Journal* 191.

[66] *Harrison v Carswell* [1976] 2 SCR 200.

[67] *Davidson Bros v D Katz & Sons*, 643 A 2d 642 (NJ Super AD 1994).

Often the types of concerns that these examples might raise get lumped together into 'distributive justice' with the debate then framed in terms of whether distributive justice can feature within the private law or whether it is essentially a public law idea. But if the issue is the domination concern that centres on 'the influence over the lives of others which large property-holdings afford'[68] then this fits within a rule-of-law framework. As Harris elaborates, this domination concern is only a potential effect of private ownership:

> Without reference to the social context in which any particular property institution holds sway, we cannot tell whether owners of particular items will, in practice, be in a position, by virtue of their ownership, to exercise unjust restraints over the liberties of non-owners. The practical significance of domination-potential depends on questions of relative scarcity, the extent to which a society discharges those just obligations to meet basic needs which we have yet to discuss, and the comparative merits of non-ownership alternatives.[69]

One can say that this kind of domination concern is a non-necessary but possible consequence of private ownership but that does not dispel it as a rule-of-law concern for it shows that a legal relation between persons (private ownership) can help create a situation where these legal relations directly facilitate the exercise of private power over others rather than simply fail to address a social context with power dynamics that can be understood independently of legal relations. The issue is not whether this is a legal concern, rather than one of political morality, or a properly private law concern, rather than public law. Rather, the issue is one of institutional roles and this makes it difficult for judges to address within private law adjudication. As Harris's comments make clear, at least some of the questions involved look more like the considerations Fuller flagged as involving polycentric problems that are ill suited to adjudication.[70] Courts do grapple with these issues, but they are notoriously difficult for they seem to pull in two directions: rule-of-law concerns engage judicial intuitions that there are fundamental legal problems at issue while institutional competence concerns suggest that courts are often—but certainly not always—ill placed to resolve these more structural problems.

6. Conclusion

Private ownership has a complex relationship with the rule of law. As I have argued throughout this chapter, private ownership is best understood in terms of legal powers. Powers are tied to the facilitative function of law, and secure legal consequences that would otherwise not be possible. The guidance function of law is essential to legal powers, for qualities like the publicity and clarity of the law ensure that individuals understand both the consequences to be secured through legal powers and the acts needed to accomplish this. These consequences, in turn, help

[68] Harris, *Property* (n 8) 265.
[69] Harris, *Property* (n 8) 265.
[70] Lon L Fuller, 'The Forms and Limits of Adjudication' in Kenneth I Winston (ed), *The Principles of Social Order: Selected Essays of Lon L. Fuller* (Hart Publishing 2001) 101.

constitute a temporal horizon for action which is better understood in terms of 'freedom to' than 'freedom from'. The rule of law is therefore bound up with both property and freedom but not in the traditional sense of protecting individuals against arbitrary exercises of governmental power or through providing individuals with predictable rules in order to plan their lives so as to avoid legal sanctions.

However, at the same time the legal powers associated with private ownership confer an authority on owners to act arbitrarily in the sense of being unaccountable for their decisions in relation to their exclusive control over the objects owned. Whether this raises a rule-of-law problem depends on whether the authority of owners is best characterized in terms of equal liberty or in terms of unequal domination. This, in turn, depends on context. Therefore private ownership might secure some aspects of freedom while at the same time undermining others.

13

Boilerplate

A Threat to the Rule of Law?

*Margaret Jane Radin**

1. Introduction

In today's United States, transactions between firms and consumers routinely include fine-print terms ('boilerplate') containing multiple rights deletions[1]: extravagant exculpatory clauses; distant choice of forum/choice of law clauses; unlimited unilateral modification clauses; waivers of privacy rights and copyright rights; pre-dispute mandatory arbitration clauses; severe curtailment of statutes of limitation; waivers of consequential damages; and more.[2] This chapter raises the question whether or to what extent this practice of rights deletion is contrary to the rule of law.

To begin an enquiry into this question, this chapter will consider these inter-related avenues of thought and analysis: Are there rights granted or maintained by the state that are inherently within the care of the polity, and non-waivable by individuals? If so, what kinds of rights might fit into this category? To what extent, if any, does the validity of waiver of such rights vary with the extent of its social

* Portions of Sections 3.1, 4.1, 4.2, and 5 of this chapter recapitulate and build upon earlier work; see Margaret Jane Radin, *Boilerplate: The Fine Print, Vanishing Rights, and the Rule of Law* (Princeton University Press 2013). Permission from Princeton University Press to use this material is hereby gratefully acknowledged.

[1] See Margaret Jane Radin, *Boilerplate, Vanishing Rights, and the Rule of Law* (Princeton University Press 2013); see also Margaret Jane Radin, 'An Analytical Framework for Legal Evaluation of Boilerplate' in George Letsas, Gregory Klass, and Prince Saprai (eds), *Philosophical Foundations of Contract Law* (Oxford University Press 2014 (forthcoming)).

[2] The use of boilerplate sets of fine-print terms to delete consumers' legal rights has swept markets in the USA. (Within the term 'consumers' I mean to include businesses in the position of consumers, because those who receive these boilerplate deletions are often small businesses, such as an accountant who purchases several computers for her office.) The situation is different in other countries. Boilerplate rights deletion is found to some extent in Canada, though not on the scale with which it is deployed in the USA. The clauses that concern me most in this chapter cannot be used against consumers in the European Union under the EC Directive on Unfair Contract Terms of 1993 and subsequent developments relating to it. See eg Christian von Bar et al (eds), *Principles, Definitions and Model Rules of European Private Law: Draft Common Frame of Reference (DCFR)* (European Law Publishers 2009). Many of these clauses are disallowed in other countries as well, though I cannot produce a survey here.

dissemination? And how are such rights connected with the rule of law? Does widespread deployment of boilerplate destroy commitment to law itself—that is to government by law rather than arbitrary power—and, if so, should we conclude that boilerplate undermines the rule of law? If certain rights granted or maintained by the state should be considered to be situated within the public realm because they are inherently within the care of the polity, what should we now make of the public/private distinction?

2. Remedies as Integral with the Rule of Law

A system of legal remedies is an integral feature of the rule of law, and the existence of remedies actually available in practice is necessary for an actual legal system to be characterized as one instantiating the rule of law.

2.1 Remedies and the rule of law in theory

Various writers have elaborated principles of the rule of law. There is no single canonical formulation, and my own view is that the rule of law should probably be considered a contested concept.[3] Whatever formulation of the principles and precepts of the rule of law we adopt, however, I think it must be true that inherent or pre-political background rights maintained by the state, as well as rights granted by the state, must have remedies available to subjects in case the rights are transgressed.[4] Jeremy Waldron states, for example, following Dicey, that the rule of law requires 'that people have access to the courts to settle their disputes and to hold the government accountable'.[5] Dicey also held equality before the law as a first principle of the rule of law: the same law must apply to everyone, regardless of class or position. From this position we can infer that people must have equal access to the courts to settle their disputes and to hold the government accountable.

One might argue, contrary to Waldron's adaptation of Dicey, that the need for accountability goes only against government transgressions, and not to disputes or claims between private parties. But I believe this argument would be wrong, because the background rules of the institutions of private law, including contract, property, and tort, must be maintained and properly enforced by government, if these institutions are to be said properly to exist.[6]

[3] See Margaret Jane Radin, 'Reconsidering the Rule of Law' (1989) 69 *Boston University Law Review* 781.

[4] The connection between remedy and the ideal of law goes back a long way: my colleague Bruce Frier reminds me of the Roman maxim *ubi jus, ibi remedium*, and my colleague Elizabeth Anderson reminds me that the idea that power must be non-arbitrary, therefore made accountable through remedies, is 'a pretty standard idea in the canon of political philosophy'.

[5] Jeremy Waldron, 'Stare Decisis and the Rule of Law' (2012) 111 *Michigan Law Review* 1, 3–4, and n 4 (stating that his precis of the rule of law is adapted from AV Dicey).

[6] See John Goldberg's argument that redress of grievance for torts is constitutionally required because it was part of the Ancient Constitution and has always been accepted as necessary for the rule of law. Goldberg, 'The Constitutional Status of Tort Law: Due Process and the Right to a Law for the Redress of Wrongs' (2005) 115 *Yale Law Journal* 524.

In other words, legal rights cannot be empty vessels. If they are empty vessels, if the rights of subjects are merely for show, or merely posters pasted over lawlessness, then they are a merely a sort of 'as if' representation of what kind of state exists, a picture that hides reality, a curtain that hides the real nature of the state from the observer, and provides no bastion against arbitrary power.

If we take Lon Fuller's list of precepts describing what constitutes rule of law as an example,[7] the precepts of the rule of law boil down to the idea that its basis is a structure of legal directives that are knowable, doable, and useful or beneficial for human beings understood as equals before the law. Knowable, meaning the directives cannot be kept secret, cannot change every three minutes, cannot be contradictory. Doable, meaning human beings can actually implement the directives, unlike a command not to sneeze. Useful or beneficial for human beings, in light of the fact that mainstream liberal thought has it that we are to exit a state of nature because a state (at least a well-ordered state) will be beneficial to human beings. Understood as equals before the law, because law that is ignored or applied capriciously or selectively lapses back into arbitrary power.

Background rights or state-granted rights without available remedies in case the rights are transgressed are not useful for human beings. Human beings make mistakes and break rules, so they should not be conceptualized otherwise. An ideal set of principles of precepts that describes a system meant to govern a society of human beings must have a place for remedies when that system's rules (directives, principles) are transgressed. Moreover, if we grant that an infrastructure of remedies supporting background rights or state-granted rights must exist, then, just as rights cannot be empty vessels, but must have remedies attached, neither can the remedies be completely unusable by human subjects. For example, most theorists who have considered the rule of law would say that a right whose statute of limitations for claiming legal remedy expires before the right is violated would not be usable by human beings, and therefore not an instance of rule of law, for the same reason that retroactivity is contrary to the rule of law. Complying with a law when the date of the designated behaviour is in the past is not doable by human beings.

In sum, if legal rights cannot be empty vessels, and if the principle of equality before the law is honoured in practice, all rights holders must have reasonable access to remedies. That means that availability of legal redress of grievances must be a basic principle of the rule of law if the rule of law is to be of possible use in evaluating, even in theory or ideally, what a legal system should look like.

[7] Lon L Fuller, *The Morality of Law* (rev edn, Yale University Press 1969) 33–94. Although Fuller spoke of rules, I do not mean to accept that law is made up only of rules; I think we should consider any kind of directive or principle as potentially part of law. Fuller's formulation of rule of law is usually considered formal, whereas formulations by Rawls and others are considered more substantive, including due process, separation of powers, and perhaps democracy. See eg John Rawls, *A Theory of Justice* (Harvard University Press 1971) ch 4, ss 38–9. The distinction between formalist and substantive conceptions of the rule of law is (I believe) not crucial for the present chapter. I believe even a formalist conception of the rule of law should admit the basic importance of redress of grievances, and it seems this would follow *a fortiori* for a substantive conception, which would include (*inter alia*) due process.

2.2 Remedies and the rule of law in practice

But further, what if we want to consider whether a specific system satisfies the requirements of the rule of law in practice? For a system to satisfy the requirements so as to be described as exhibiting the rule of law, in actual practice rather than in theory, remedies must be reasonably available in practice, not just in theory. In other words, it is not quite enough to admit that the rule of law in theory requires a remedial infrastructure. Rather, that premise should be elaborated with the understanding that the remedies, in order to be usable, must be actually reasonably available to subjects in practice.

The question arises here, as it always does with ideals in political theory: How far can a practice deviate from the ideal under which it is to be evaluated as just or unjust, and still count as justified? This is the problem of 'fit' between a theory of justification and a practice to which we seek to apply it. If we admit that no system in practice must coincide perfectly with a proferred justificatory theory in order to be acceptably considered justified, then how much can a practice deviate from the proferred justification before we declare it unjustified?

With regard to the rule of law, how far can a system of rules (directives/principles) and enforcement thereof depart in practice from the theoretical precepts of the rule of law and still be justifiably said to belong to a system that instantiates the rule of law? For example, can a system enforce retroactive rules some of the time? How often? Can a system implement a one-week statute of limitations? One month? What if the government doesn't create and maintain a court system, or any other system for performing redress of grievances? What if the government does have such a system, but it refuses to fund it or appoint adjudicators, so claimants must wait in line for years? What if the filing fee is $1,000,000? And so on.

I tend to think there is not going to be a general theory that can tell us when a system is close enough to instantiating the rule of law in practice to be called a system abiding by the rule of law, and when it is not. Perhaps that just means I have not found such a theory. So, rather than trying to lay out such a general theory, I think it is going to be easier, but still controversial, to look at the negative end of the continuum from justification to non-justification: at least we can decide that some practices are too far from fitting the justificatory theory to count as justified by that theory. Thus, I seek to identify circumstances or situations where the lack of availability of remedies in practice is not consistent with the rule of law.

That brings me to the specific circumstances I want to examine: widespread use of mass-market boilerplate by private firms to delete recipients' remedies necessary to vindicate basic rights.

3. The Rule of Law and the Problem of Default Rules

I want to argue that certain kinds of rights are permanently in the care of the polity (which I will sometimes refer to as 'permanently situated in the public realm'). Such rights are not to be treated as default rules waivable by individuals, when they are deployed against recipients on a mass-market basis. And I want to argue that the reason this is so is that these kinds of rights are required to be in the care of the polity (permanently situated in the public realm) in order to fulfil the rule of law. Thus, a society in order to be recognized as instantiating the rule of law should keep certain rights in the care of the polity and not allow them to degenerate into default rules changeable by firms through deployment of mass-market boilerplate. In other words, the rule of law at its most basic level requires that some rights not be privatized such that they can be curtailed and sometimes eradicated by firms. This non-waivability can be understood as a species of inalienability.[8]

In previous work I have argued that mass-market boilerplate rights deletions of certain kinds cannot (that is, should not) qualify as enforceable contracts.[9] One reason that some waivers in boilerplate do not qualify as enforceable contracts is that they purport to treat as default rules, waivable by individuals, that which belongs to civil society as a whole. In that context I suggested these characteristics of rights that remain in the care of the polity, not subject to waiver by individuals: (1) the rights are important to collective well-being, or indeed (2) constitutive of civil society; and (3) the rights are not salient for individuals.

In deciding whether or not the privatized ('contractual') deletion of such rights should be disallowed by a system that wants to be understood as respecting the rule of law in practice, it would also be significant to consider (4) the extent of social dissemination of waivers of such rights. That is because the rule of law, as applied to characterize a system in practice, can perhaps tolerate one individual relinquishing with consent a legal right necessary for the collective good—or even tolerate the wrong of depriving one individual of such a right without consent if consent turns out to be lacking—much more readily than it can tolerate a socially widespread scheme of rights waivers. An isolated single instance in which an individual waives a right that should be considered non-waivable because it is a right belonging to civil society as whole would not necessarily undermine the rule of law. Moreover, in cases where it is not prima facie clear that a right is important to collective well-being or constitutive of civil society—and debate about this is to be expected—it could turn out to be preferable to resolve doubt in favour of allowing the single instance of waiver. These conclusions follow from the idea that 'fit' with an ideal of justice need not be perfect.[10] It would be a mistake, and a wrong, for a judge to

[8] Often it should be understood as market-inalienability, at least according to the argument made by firms that recipients are selling them their legal rights in return for lower prices. In light of my argument here that remedial rights of consumers (and firms in the position of consumers) are probably market-inalienable in the context of mass-market boilerplate attempts to delete them, the question arises whether a less than widespread deployment of a waiver, or a waiver by a single individual, should be treated the same. I consider this in Section 3.1.

[9] See Margaret Jane Radin, works cited in n 1.

[10] See Section 2.2. Two caveats: (1) A court faced with what looks like only a single deviation from a rule whose basis may be the well-being of society as a whole should at least treat the issue with strict scrutiny, including (a) a serious enquiry whether the rule in fact is part of a regime aimed to benefit society as a whole, and (b) a serious enquiry whether a single decision in favour of waiver would cause a destructive avalanche of like clauses deployed against consumers en masse, relying on this precedent.

validate a single 'contract' in which consent is really lacking, but this mistake, even though there is a wrong, need not implicate the rule of law.

3.1 Coordination rules

It seems useful to break down the topic of rights related to collective well-being into those rights that are best understood as the solution to a coordination problem, and those that are related to other kinds of collective goods or shared interests. Some kinds of rights enacted by the state can be understood as the solution to a coordination problem. The purpose of this kind of right is defeated if it is understood as a default rule waivable by individuals. Consider a few fanciful examples. Imagine boilerplate fine-print terms in a contract for sale of a car. What if the car purchaser, through the operation of fine print, could waive the rule that he must drive on the right side of the road? What if, through the operation of fine print, he could waive the speed limit, the obligation to obey traffic signals, etc?

These kinds of regulations can be considered as solutions to various kinds of coordination problems. If society wants to maintain the coordination solution, then it has to disallow waivers, at least if the waivers are massively imposed, or even more than de minimis. The rule about which side of the road to drive on is an easy example of non-waivability related to coordination, because unless there exists such a rule, and it is enforced, and it is non-waivable, chaos results.

For those who reason about matters belonging to the collective in terms of individual choice only, all instances of rules benefiting the collective would be analysed as solutions to coordination problems.[11] For example, suppose the car purchaser, through the operation of fine print, could waive air quality standards, or could waive regulatory standards for braking function. If auto purchasers could waive air quality standards, everyone would suffer from worse air quality. In public choice theory terms, extra precautions by individuals could not be organized well enough to take care of the problem, because there would be free riders (those who could take advantage of breathable air without having to contribute to the cost of maintaining its breathability). If auto purchasers could be held to have waived regulatory rights to proper functioning of the vehicle, and the waiver becomes widespread, then society as a whole would be harmed; even those who did not waive the rights would be injured in accidents, and everyone would have to take extra precautions. When legislation can be considered a solution to a coordination problem, then firms that try to undercut it with mass-market waivers are defecting from the collective solution.

An example of this reasoning that may seem more plausible is US copyright law. One could view the copyright regime as a legislative compromise embodying

(2) It should be understood that I am not talking here about individual consent to waive a remedial right after a dispute arises, as part of a settlement of that dispute, but rather pre-dispute waivers.

[11] Such reasoning is usually called public choice theory or political economy theory. For comments on its relationship to the rule of law, see Section 5.2.

acceptance of firms' second-best choices for restraining themselves provided everyone else does so. In that case, when a firm deploys a boilerplate scheme in its transactions with customers that deletes user rights arrived at in the compromise, it is defecting from its commitment to the compromise.

This possibility can be seen as a standard coordination problem of the kind usually labelled a 'prisoner's dilemma'. Suppose a situation in which each firm would prefer to keep all of the information it possesses from being used by others, but at the same time would prefer to have access to the information possessed by others. In other words, the firm would prefer strict copyright enforcement for itself, but expansive fair use as regards others. This situation very probably would occur, because a firm needs access to others' information as inputs to further innovation and information asset creation, but at the same time wishes to lock up the information assets it already has.

It would be impossible to implement for all firms their first-best solution (in which everyone says, 'Free access for me to your—everyone else's—information assets, but no access for you—everyone else—to my information assets'). Suppose further, then, that the second preferred option is that everyone be allowed access to a certain portion of information disclosed and copyrighted by others. Here we suppose that as a fall-back option, a firm would be willing to allow other firms access to some portion of its information in return for free access to some portion of the information of all other firms. This second preferred solution could be achieved through coordination—agreement among all firms. Spontaneous coordination agreement is unlikely, however, and also unstable if it does occur, because each individual firm will be tempted to defect by trying to lock up its own information while still having access to the information of others.

The classic prescription for securing the second-best solution is pre-commitment through legislation. Firms agree in advance to have the state require them to cooperate in this rational manner, and the state's threat of enforcement deters defection after the deal is imposed. Under this coordination rationale, copyright law can be understood as setting out some rules for when information developed by one entity is to be available for use by others, rules that all entities have an interest in supporting. Firms have a rational incentive to organize and get copyright legislation enacted that will allow each firm to have access to some portion of the information held by others, on a reciprocal basis.[12]

Copyright law establishes rules, such as fair use, that permit others some uses of works owned by others. If the law treats such rules merely as default rules, however, then an individual firm will be able to contract around these access rules. If individual firms are allowed to deploy mass-market boilerplate waivers to cancel such rules allowing for user rights, they are defecting from the compromise and seceding from the coordination that is working for the benefit of everyone.

If the waiver occurs in the unread fine print that accompanies the transaction, is that a worse situation than if an individual really understands the waiver and really

[12] In the case of US copyright law, this seems in fact to be what firms actually did. See Jessica Litman, *Digital Copyright* (2nd edn, Prometheus Books 2006).

intends to agree to it? When we are considering just one individual, it seems that consent would validate the transaction, or at least that with consent waiver would be more defensible than without consent. Yet regulations that represent a solution to a coordination problem should not be easily waivable even by one individual recipient, because if one individual can be used to implement the firm's defection, so can many. That is an explanation for keeping these types of regulation in the care of the polity, for the benefit of society as a whole.[13] And to drop out of the realm of theory for a moment, we should note that the waivers that would seriously concern us with regard to cancelling of remedies are deployed in fine-print 'contracts' given not to one individual, but to millions.

3.2 Rights benefiting society as a whole

One need not adopt the language of political economy—prisoner's dilemma games, defection, and so forth—in order to analyse rights that benefit the collective as a whole and should not be waivable by individuals, at least not without serious scrutiny, and not on a mass-market basis. For all but the committed public choice theorist, the air quality example is better viewed from the standpoint of human rights rather than prisoner's dilemma games. It is better viewed from the standpoint of enabling better health for everyone rather than avoidance of free riders.

Indeed, we can consider copyright as a whole as an engine that is supposed to foster innovation for the benefit of society as a whole, rather than as an initial bargain among firms from which individual firms later wish to defect. That is indeed a standard rhetoric of copyright justification. Over-propertization of knowledge can undermine innovation, because follow-on innovators need to work with the innovations of the past. Copyright provisions that allow user rights can be viewed as establishing rights that should not be easily dispensed with by individual waivers, because individual waivers undermine the collective purpose of copyright, impinging on society's present and future well-being.

3.3 Rights constitutive of civil society

Some rights can be considered pre-political background rights, such that the state does not enact them but rather has the duty to recognize that they exist and has the duty to maintain them. (These rights are often thought to have become embedded in common law.) A standard argument of liberal theory, of course, is that the state must come into being so that such rights can be properly maintained and fostered.

[13] The rule of law, when it is being evaluated as applied to a particular system in practice, might permit one person one time to defect or implement defection, because in order for a system in practice to instantiate the rule of law, the adherence to the ideal need not—cannot be—perfect. See discussion of 'fit' in Section 2.2. But defection, once it starts, cascades. In an individual case involving waiver of user rights, or other rights that relate to coordination, a judge should apply strict scrutiny to consider whether the case is unusual and will not start a cascade, bearing in mind that one defection or implementation of defection normally leads to others. See n 10, and text accompanying n 10.

Such rights can be regarded as constitutive of civil society and for that reason inseparable from the rule of law. (No civil society, no law.)

As I have argued above, the rule of law implies that legal rights in general must not be empty vessels in practice, but must be accompanied by sufficiently available avenues for redress of grievance when they are transgressed. This argument applies especially with regard to rights that operate for the society as a whole as necessary background rights that the state is obligated to maintain. Which rights in particular are necessary background rights can be—will be—a matter for contention. At least I can make a start on the problem by proposing that necessary background rights relate to preservation of civil society; that is, to avoiding lapsing into a condition akin to anarchy—which I will call quasi-anarchy[14]—through loss of legal remedies (in the traditional metaphors of western political thought, lapsing back into the state of nature). So, to speak in general, necessary background rights include rights to be free of harm to one's person or property, or indeed to one's basic freedom of action, either caused by the state or caused through the intent or fault of others.

The need to safeguard redress of grievances with respect to necessary background rights calls into question many boilerplate clauses prevalent in the USA that in practice make viable remedy unattainable for large swaths of the public. These clauses include choice of law/choice of forum clauses, exculpatory clauses, waivers of consequential damages, mandatory pre-dispute arbitration clauses, and waivers of aggregative relief. Of particular concern to me is the gathering trend in the USA—and to a lesser extent in Canada—allowing boilerplate to waive liability for harm caused by negligence.[15] Unless a society adopts some other method of compensation and deterrence, it is important not to allow the basic right to be free of injury from others' negligence (and *a fortiori* gross negligence, recklessness, and intentional harm) to degenerate into a default rule routinely cancelled by boilerplate. I take note that some business advocates do not believe that any legal regime of deterrence is necessary, because the threat of harm to a firm's reputation

[14] This is rather a fanciful label, because, of course, to the extent that the boilerplate gives the firm remedies against the recipient, the recipient is not in a state of anarchy but in fact will be held to them. The recipient is in a state that resembles the state of nature only with regard to lost remedies on its own side of the transaction. Still, I think the label can help characterize in what kind of position recipients of mass-market boilerplate rights deletions tend to find themselves.

[15] See eg *Loychuk v Cougar Mountain Adventures Ltd*, 2012 BCCA 122. Consider the following exculpatory clauses that appeared on a sign at the entrance to a public park in which the city permitted a private promotion event:

> By entering these premises, you, on behalf of yourself and any minor accompanying you . . . (ii) VOLUNTARILY ASSUME ALL RISK AND DANGER of personal injury (including death) and all hazards arising from, or related in any way to, this event, whether occurring prior to, during, or after this event, however caused and whether by negligence or otherwise; release, waive and discharge [the promoters] from any and all liability and covenant not to sue . . . for any and all loss or damage on account of injury to your person or property, whether caused by negligence or otherwise.

This example might be extravagant, but it is by no means unique. A large proportion of fitness, sports, and recreation facilities, tour companies, summer camps, and the like, will deploy something like this. Exculpatory clauses are also being used by daycare centres and nursing homes. (I suspect that insurers require that their insureds use these with customers, but I am not an investigative reporter, so this is mere suspicion.)

will suffice to keep it from mistreating those who deal with it.[16] And some believe that legal deterrence measures do not actually operate to deter negligence or other wrongdoing. But at least if we believe deterrence is necessary and efficacious, such degeneration of background rules into default rules allows firms to be irresponsible and leaves recipients on their own for avoiding harms that may threaten them in their everyday lives. It leaves to recipients sole responsibility for avoiding all harms that threaten them from careless activities of others. One way to put this is that lapse into a quasi-anarchy—akin to the pre-political condition—puts recipients into a condition of super-responsibility.

Such super-responsibility violates a duty of the state—supposedly a core reason why it came into being and why it is justified in exerting power—to recognize and protect background rights. People cannot watch their backs every hour of every day. They cannot find out which firms hire employees that are trustworthy and competent and supervise them properly, which firms use machines that are well made and routinely maintained and implement safety standards for their use, which firms do not use toxic substances, and so on. This is a core reason why such rights are permanently or inherently in the care of the polity, and not mere default rules.[17]

Moreover, the use of private law—boilerplate 'contracts'—to place recipients in a position where they are in practice deprived of remedy creates a situation in which one segment of the private sector (large firms) has power over other segments of society (smaller firms and consumers). Those in a position to deploy mass-market boilerplate deleting recipients' remedies against them are using and reinforcing their power over recipients by doing so. This is a form of power that should be seen as inconsistent with the rule of law, both because it is arbitrary power and because it is contrary to the precept of equality before the law. It is arbitrary because deployed at the will of firms for firms' benefit. It is contrary to equality before the law because society becomes divided into groups that retain legal redress of grievances and those that do not. As Gerald Postema has argued, advancing a Kantian thesis, the rule of law is not limited to activities of government but instead extends to reciprocal obligations among all members of the polity.[18] Private entities that delete legal remedies to enhance their economic position may well (depending on circumstances) be exercising arbitrary power and undermining the rule of law.

[16] This may be true in some market circumstances, but certainly cannot be true as a general assertion about all markets, because it depends upon specific circumstances, not a priori reasoning. It will not be true in markets where recipients lack sufficient information, and will be unlikely to be true in circumstances where recipients have no real choice about which firms to deal with, either because of market power or because of sociological circumstances, or circumstances giving rise to industry-wide boilerplate, especially in circumstances in which the product or service is a necessity.

[17] I do not address here whether or under what circumstances an individual can consent to be harmed by another individual. (The question whether sado-masochism is illegal is outside the scope of this chapter.) Also, as mentioned earlier in Section 3.1, mass-market harm is worse than a single harm from a rule-of-law perspective, though when even one individual gives up a right without consent that is still a wrong.

[18] See Gerald J Postema, 'Fidelity in Law's Commonwealth' Section 2.3 in this volume.

3.4 Salience

There is a further concern aroused by boilerplate deletion of rights that should be inherently in the care of the polity. These rights are often not salient for individuals. An individual about to click 'I agree', for example, does not readily consider whether she will ever need any redress of grievances. If she thinks about it, she is likely to think that serious harms happen to other people.[19]

And they most often do. But they do happen to some unlucky people some of the time, and that is one reason why the rights are needed for all of us. The existence of the rights, moreover, is supposed to deter individual actors from harming other people when the harm could have been avoided. And, moreover, the existence of the rights is supposed to grant the public the confidence and comfort to lead their individual lives free from the super-responsibility of quasi-anarchy or the subjection to arbitrary power. The fact that rights beneficial to society as a whole are not usually salient to individuals underscores the point that such rights, though couched as attaching to individuals, should not be waivable by individuals. At least, not so easily, and not in mass-market boilerplate.[20]

4. Democratic Degradation

Boilerplate rights deletion schemes can undermine the significance of political debate and procedures, which results in a form of degradation of democratic ordering affecting the rule of law.

4.1 Democratic processes

Some of the rights regimes that widespread boilerplate cancels have been enacted through democratic processes, often after extended debate and political struggle, whereas erasing them only requires drafting boilerplate (or indeed just copying someone else's boilerplate).[21] When firms can easily divest recipients of rights that are part of a legislative regime arrived at only with much public input, debate, and compromise, it makes a sham of the apparatus of democratic governance.

[19] Psychological research has determined that human beings reason and choose for themselves in ways that are not fully rational (at least in the traditional definition of rationality, or as economists would have hitherto defined rationality). Sometimes this is called 'bounded rationality', or the particular types of biases in reasoning to which we are subject are known as 'heuristic biases'. We are not good at assessing risk (we do not think that serious harm will befall us, but we do think we might win the lottery); we tend to stick with the status quo; and we make choices according to particular surrounding circumstances that are salient to us, ignoring others that may be more pertinent. See Daniel Kahneman, *Thinking, Fast and Slow* (Farrar, Straus and Giroux 2011).

[20] I have argued earlier in this section that mass-market boilerplate rights deletions are worse for the rule of law than waiver by one individual; on this point see text accompanying n 10.

[21] I have met law students whose job as a summer intern for a firm was to copy other firms' boilerplate.

Democratic ordering as we know it is certainly not ideal. Indeed, in the USA, the worst form of democratic degradation is not the erasure of legislated rights through boilerplate deployment, but rather the role of big money paying off legislators to enact laws that the public does not favour, and that do not benefit the public. (The devolution of war to private contractors is worse, too.) Nevertheless, democratic procedures at least give citizens a voice in the structuring of the regimes they must live under; not in the ideal sense of voice that will be accurately heard, but not wholly theoretically, either. An aroused public can 'vote 'em out' if it doesn't like what 'they' enact. In contrast, when a boilerplate rights deletion scheme replaces the state's legal rights regime with a scheme desired by a firm, citizens have a means of exit, at least in theory, because they can refuse to buy the product or service—but they have no voice. That is why these boilerplate 'contracts' are called 'take-it-or-leave-it contracts'.

Exit from a boilerplate scheme is frequently thought not to be difficult. Business advocates routinely tell me, sometimes rather vituperatively, that if I don't like the boilerplate, I don't have to buy the product that comes with fine-print waivers.[22] But in reality, exit is often impossible. Recipients most likely will not read the terms of boilerplate, primarily because they would not understand them if they did read them, so it isn't worth their time, and also because, very often, heuristic bias makes people think that they will never have need of legal rights. When individuals are placed in a situation of decision before a personal need for legal rights arises, such as when they are confronted with the need to click 'I agree', some of the most basic rights are the least salient for individuals.

Exit may be almost impossible for market structural reasons, too. Many products that consumers need to purchase are sold by only one supplier, or by a group of suppliers who all use the same set of terms. Industry-wide standardization of a boilerplate rights deletion scheme prevents consumers from choosing terms they would prefer.[23] They have no exit from onerous terms except for products and services that are not necessities.

4.2 Undermining the rule of law through over-privatization

So much for democratic degradation wrought by boilerplate. But how does such mass-market rights deletion through boilerplate 'contracts' undermine the rule of law? Primarily because these 'contracts' purport to privatize rights that must remain public. Such privatization results in a lapse back toward the state of nature for recipients (which I have dubbed quasi-anarchy), subjection of recipients to arbitrary

[22] These advocates often defend boilerplate by claiming that firms save money by selling products without remedial rights, that firms pass on these savings to consumers, and that consumers choose (or would choose, if rational) to sell off their legal rights to the firm for the amount of the passed-on price reductions. This rationale cannot be true in a general, blanket way, because it depends on empirical assumptions, which depend on the market we are evaluating, but which most often in consumer boilerplate markets involving rights deletions probably will not be valid.

[23] Industry-wide standardization is not per se bad in theory, nor always bad in practice; see Section 5.1.

power of large firms, and treatment of recipients contrary to the principle of equality before the law.

At the risk of being tediously repetitive, let me recognize here, once more, that the system of private ordering is a treasured centrepiece of liberal political thought, and freedom of contract is a revered ideal. A core commitment of political liberalism understands freedom of contract as enabling and enhancing individual freedom through voluntary individual exchanges that produce gains to each party.[24] Enforcement of exchanges by private ordering is legitimate only within a state that underwrites a background legal infrastructure by which contracts that lack voluntariness will be denied enforcement, and by which contracts that are legitimately made under the rules of the state's background legal infrastructure will in fact be enforced. Enforcement is state coercion, and this is the infrastructure that is supposed to justify it. The rules of the background legal infrastructure must remain substantially within the care of the polity. Factions or powerful firms should not be able to change the rules whenever they wish by a simple expedient such as deployment of boilerplate.

Excessive privatization of functions that are situated in the public realm—whether it is done by private armies, private prisons, or private police forces—undermines the safeguards of civil society. Establishing and maintaining such safeguards of civil society is the reason that such functions are situated within the care of the polity in the first place From this it follows that excessive privatization of the legal infrastructure of contracts undermines the possibility of private ordering by contract as envisioned in the ideal liberal story, and as it must exist in actuality to some significant extent if it is to justify the coercive power of the state in enforcing contracts. Large firms' mass-market restructuring of the background rules of remedies for breach, to their own advantage and the public's disadvantage, when it becomes widespread, undermines the legal infrastructure of private ordering, and becomes a scheme of arbitrary power. Thus, firms that deploy mass-market boilerplate schemes for the purpose of erasing core legal rights of redress are undermining a crucial part of the legal infrastructure that makes contractual private ordering possible.

Deploying 'contract' against contractual ordering in practice undermines the rule of law. As I mentioned earlier, the bedrock precepts of the rule of law may be encapsulated as know-ability, do-ability, equality, and benefit to human beings. Prior to the basic precepts, and underlying them, must be the notion of commitment to law itself, to the sovereignty of the political constitution set up and maintained for the very reason of underwriting a government by law. That underlying commitment is what makes it the rule of *law* we are talking about.

[24] I recognize that there are longstanding strands of critical thought that consider the notion of voluntary exchanges as ideological and not descriptive of what happens in the real world. (In other words, critics say that 'fit' between justification and practice is lacking.) But current legal systems have not superseded this traditional justificatory notion for coercive transfers by the state from one party to another when they enforce contracts deemed to meet (closely enough) this idea. We lack an alternative justificatory story, and our legal systems remain seriously devoted to the notion of private ordering. Revolutionary global reinterpretations cannot take hold in practice.

Firms that use contract to destroy the underlying basis of contract, that deploy contract against itself, are using contract to destroy the ideal of contractual ordering, which the rule of law is formulated to protect. In this way, they not only undermine the idea of a regime of private ordering, they effectively undermine the rule of law.

5. Reconsidering the Public/Private Distinction

If we are to affirm the rule of law, it seems that we must also maintain some semblance of a public/private distinction, simply because some rules must remain in the care of the polity; that is, remain stably (non-waivably) public, the situation I sometimes refer to as being permanently situated in the public realm.

5.1 Standardization and privatization

In the abstract, not all mass-market fine-print terms are bad. The mere fact that a form is standardized is not in and of itself problematic. Sometimes standards promote knowledge and ease of use, reduce uncertainty, and lower transaction costs for all parties. There can be beneficial network externalities produced by standardization in some circumstances. A firm that uses a fair set of terms with its customers might find its terms copied by others, in many jurisdictions, and could find its terms widely validated. If a fair set of terms occupies a market, in a setting in which it makes sense to think that consumers understand the terms and choose to buy the product with the terms, it might seem, at least at first, that the normative acceptability of the terms need not turn at all upon whether the standard came about through 'bottom-up' market forces or through 'top-down' legislation or administrative order.

Courts, nevertheless, have sometimes looked askance at the legal standardization that results from 'bottom-up' market forces while deferring readily to the legal standardization implemented by means of governmental ordering. This occasional judicial tendency is not readily understandable through the lens of welfare maximization theory, because, through that lens, a situation is to be judged by its social results rather than its origins. I suggest, however, that judges (and others) who make this distinction are re-enacting the traditional public/private distinction. In that traditional view, whatever becomes law-like belongs to the public realm and not to the private realm. Therefore, standardization of terms, especially industry-wide standardization, may be seen as fine if the government enacts it, but not fine if it comes about by operation of the market (private ordering).

It is overkill to suppose that any standardization that comes about by market ordering is suspect. Sometimes beneficial standards do come about through market evolution.[25] Nevertheless, there is a grain of truth to be seen here. Bottom-up

[25] It is also overkill to suppose, as many boilerplate defenders do, that anytime a standardized set of terms occupies a market, it must be efficient. See eg Douglas G Baird, 'The Boilerplate Puzzle' (2006)

standardization is indeed troubling when it amounts to privatization of an arena of social ordering whose parameters and oversight are properly the duty and exclusive province of the polity, when that oversight must in practice be administered by the infrastructure of the state.

5.2 Dissolution of the public realm from the Right

In the past decades there has been vigorous critique of the public/private distinction, particularly from the Left. It is easy to deconstruct (or at least destabilize) the public/private distinction if it is viewed as consisting of two hard-and-fast conceptual categories, or as consisting of a pure binary opposition. As the legal realists of the first half of the twentieth century pointed out, property and contract as the legal backdrop of private ordering must—as must all legal infrastructures—stem from the state. In the latter part of the twentieth century, the 'crits' of the Critical Legal Studies movement mounted a similar critique. Legal realists would say that even if one thinks that the details of property and contract are conceptually or metaphysically delineated (although they did not think that way), it is still the case that those systems cannot function without state enforcement.

Although these critiques from the Left aimed to dissolve the public/private distinction, at the same time, and just as significant (if not more so), there has been dissolution of the public/private distinction from the Right. This dissolution has been less explicit, but probably more far-reaching. Theorists belonging to the school of thought known as 'political economy' or public choice theory, along with numerous lay followers, reason in exactly the same terms about the purchase of legislation or agency regulation by market actors as they reason about the purchase of contractual obligations or of any other 'good' advantageous to the actor. In the public choice model, a firm would ask itself whether to purchase contractual obligation (in the private 'marketplace') or to purchase legislation (in the public, governmental 'marketplace') just as it would ask itself which firm it should buy its inputs from, or whether indeed it should produce them in-house. When it comes to remedies it wishes to avoid, the firm would ask itself, 'Shall we purchase legislation that bars class actions for antitrust violations and makes it impossible for consumers to get into court with such actions, or shall we deploy a boilerplate scheme waiving recipients' entitlement to bring class actions?' In this calculus, there is no distinction in kind between political (public) action and market (private) action. The premises on which political economy theory is based have obliterated the public/private distinction central to the traditional liberalism upon which our political system is based. The public realm collapses into the private.

104 *Michigan Law Review* 933. I call this the 'Everybody Does It' defence. It is not true that when everybody does something, it must be right; sometimes it's wronger than ever. Markets can be non-competitive or suffer from severe information asymmetry, which could bring about inefficient industry-wide boilerplate. See Radin, *Boilerplate* (n 1) ch 6. The fine print may also, as argued in the current chapter, represent an attempt to delete rights that should not be waivable, at least not by means of mass-market boilerplate.

How can the realm of private ordering be maintained by the public order in a way that enhances the freedom of individuals, if the public order is itself dissolved into the private? Political economy, in particular, because it holds that firms and groups purchase legislation for their own private benefit, undermines the liberal justification of the state. That justification supposes that there is such a thing as the public interest, and that the state can restrain the war of all against all by creating and enforcing rules that are in the public interest. That is, in the interest of everyone.

Earlier I mentioned that political economists tend to think of collective goods in terms of solution to coordination problems. Sometimes the liberal justification of the state is itself couched as a species of coordination problem. Each firm is supposed to give up its untrammelled quest for profit to the extent that it harms society as a whole, provided that all other firms will also do so. It is hard to mesh this cooperative coordination version of justification of the state with the standard political economy reasoning that legislation is bought for self-interested reasons by firms or interest groups, and that each firm or interest group may buy anything it wants and can pay for. If all legislation is thought to reflect such purchases, then the state has not distanced itself much from the war of all against all. The notion that the state enables an exit from anarchy in the state of nature to a realm of governance in the public interest does not make sense in this theoretical framework. So, the prevalence of political economy reasoning in contemporary discourse (and, in some important instances, in action) seems to contribute to the undermining of the rule of law.

5.3 Reviving a (non-global) public/private distinction

I have argued that some functions necessary for the rule of law, particularly modalities for legal redress, must be permanently in the care of the polity, situated in the public realm, and not default rules. This revives a species of public/private distinction.

Legal enforcement means, as the legal realists argued, that the state is involved willy-nilly in the functioning of private ordering, because the state must sustain and police its constitutive rules. To a certain extent, this realist position is consonant with the position that certain rights, especially rights to redress, are permanently and non-waivably in the care of the polity. To be functional, state enforcement must meet criteria that relate to the rule of law, with predictable and even-handed application of the law to keep transactions within the bounds of free exchange. Moreover, public oversight must be in place as an ever-present deterrent for actors who might otherwise transgress. In short, the legal realists realized that a public aspect of law is pervasive, and must undergird a functioning system of private ordering.

But, rather than concluding that all private law is 'always already' inherently permeated with the public aspect, as the 'crits' might say, I would rather say that we can delineate certain specific functions of the state that must be permanently in the care of the polity (that is, remain public), and that these are necessary for the rule of law to obtain in practice, and for private ordering to function as it is supposed to.[26] In other words, the legal realist—and certainly the 'crit'—dismissal of the public/private distinction was global, urging that we give up the distinction altogether, whereas I would urge that we should understand its specific (non-global) role in maintaining the rule of law. Some rules (principles/directives) are permanently situated in the public realm. These are the ones that are not waivable on an individual-by-individual basis when imposed in mass markets. First and foremost, as I have argued in this chapter, are rights to redress of grievances.

6. Conclusion

The problem for the rule of law posed by mass-market boilerplate waiving of legal rights to redress is not just that the waivers by individual recipients of the boilerplate lack meaningful consent. That is a problem, to be sure. A deeper issue—or at least one that has been less noticed—is that pre-dispute waiver of remedial rights is suspect under the rule of law, and undermines the rule of law when these waivers are used on a mass-market basis. Equality before the law cannot exist in practice when one portion of the public has redress of grievances available and another portion (maybe the larger portion) does not. The law is not useful and beneficial for human beings if human beings cannot see to it that it is enforced properly. Firms that impose boilerplate rights deletions on recipients are exercising arbitrary power over them.

The contemporary Supreme Court of the United States—that is, its five-justice conservative activist bloc—does not take much note of the rule of law.[27] It has made short work of retroactivity,[28] and has allowed unlimited corporate money to flood into the political arena.[29] Most recently, the conservative bloc, in opinions by Justice Antonin Scalia, has ruled that the Federal Arbitration Act of 1925 entails that pre-dispute mandatory arbitration clauses prevail over state consumer protection,[30] and also that such clauses prevail over other federal rights, such as antitrust

[26] Because the polity as a whole is responsible for maintaining the rule of law, fidelity to the rule of law is not a 'we–it' proposition ('we,' the subjects, as rule-takers and 'it,' the state, the government, as rule-giver)—with 'it' (the state) in charge. Rather, accepting Gerald Postema's thesis regarding reciprocal responsibilities of everyone for maintaining the rule of law (this volume, see n 18), maintenance of legal remedies and other rights important to the rule of law are in the care of the polity as a whole. In practice, however, it is legal infrastructure set up and maintained by modalities of the state that in the first instance implements the requirements of the rule of law.

[27] In *Bush v Gore*, 531 US 98 (2000), the court by 5–4 vote handed the contested presidential election of 2000 to George W Bush, in an ad hoc decision explicitly declared to be non-precedential. See Margaret Jane Radin, 'Can the Rule of Law Survive Bush v. Gore?' in Bruce Ackerman (ed), *Bush v. Gore: The Question of Legitimacy* (Yale University Press 2002) 110.

[28] *Eldred v Ashcroft*, 537 US 186 (2003) (retroactive copyright term extension).

[29] *Citizens United v Federal Election Commission*, 558 US 310 (2010) (although corporations are not 'natural persons', they have the same rights under the first Amendment as 'natural persons', 558 US at 26, and thus have a free speech right to expend unlimited amounts to influence elections).

[30] *AT&T v Concepcion*, 563 US 321,131 S Ct 1740 (2011).

law.[31] Scalia says openly (though couched in legalese) that it is of no moment that these immunized mass-market arbitration clauses will deprive injured parties of any way of vindicating legal rights, especially in situations where no remedy is possible except through aggregative relief, which these clauses waive. The rule of law is not mentioned. Justice Elena Kagan, in her dissent to the 2013 case denying remedy for breach of federal rights, recapitulates the holding in vernacular: Kagan explains that the majority holds that a monopolist can escape liability under federal antitrust law by the simple expedient of deploying an arbitration clause against its customers; and, she says, the majority's holding, which is 'admirably flaunted rather than camouflaged', is that such immunization of the accused monopolist is just 'too darn bad'.[32]

Too darn contrary to the rule of law, too.

As historians will know, the present is not the only time in the history of the US Supreme Court that it has been out of touch with the rule of law. Still, the contemporary lack of concern for the rule of law may indicate that the rule of law is no longer considered important in American jurisprudence. The widespread waiver of redress of grievances by means of boilerplate deployed against consumers—and against businesses in the position of consumers—is only one symptom of disregard for the rule of law. It is laudable, at least, that so far other countries have not followed the lead of the USA in allowing such widespread deployment of boilerplate rights deletion schemes to eliminate access to meaningful remedies for wide swaths of the public.

[31] *American Express Co v Italian Colors Restaurant, et al,* 570 US ____, 133 S Ct 2304 (2013). The Court has wildly expanded the meaning of the Federal Arbitration Act of 1925 to pre-empt state attempts at redress for consumers, and to elevate its importance over other federal rights. In reality, it seems to me that what is being elevated by the conservative bloc may be the magic idea of 'contract', much as it existed in the Lochner era. (In *Lochner v New York,* 198 US 45 (1905), the Court found 'liberty of contract' to be implicit in the federal constitution such that it trumped New York's regulation limiting workers' hours to 60 per week. The workers' 'liberty of contract' in *Lochner* is about as fictional as the 'contract' that imposed mass-market waivers of remedial rights on those who wished to do business with Amex.) As this chapter is being drafted, a statutory 'overruling' of the Court is pending before the US Congress, which would amend the Federal Arbitration Act to make clear that the Act does not cover employment disputes, antitrust disputes, civil rights disputes, or consumer disputes. Unless Congress passes this legislation (and the bill's previous incarnations have died in committee for some years now), the decision in *Italian Colors* will most likely apply to all of these kinds of actions, including—much as it may surprise those who haven't been following this development in the USA—preclusion of court enforcement and class actions for vindication of federal anti-discrimination rights.

[32] *American Express Co v Italian Colors Restaurant, et al,* 570 US ____, 133 S Ct at [to be supplied] (Kagan and Breyer, JJ, dissenting).

14

The Rule of Law and Time's Arrow

*Arthur Ripstein**

My aim in this chapter is to explain why private rights change with the passage of time. This essay is part of a larger project about private wrongs. The overarching aim of that project is to defend the position that rights are not reducible to interests. To do so, I must provide a positive account of rights, but I also need to do something that may have an objectionable 'objections and replies' feel to it: I respond to what are widely considered to be clear cases in which private law focuses on interests. The role of limitation periods in private actions is an especially prominent case; my aim is to show that they are an expression of an organizing idea of justiciable rights—an idea about the rule of law—and do not need to be explained in terms of interests.

Another organizing theme of the larger project is that the generality of concepts of right is conceptual rather than empirical. Instrumental accounts of private rights suppose that they are expressed in terms of general rules for reasons of simplicity and economy, but that the underlying moral reality lacks this generality. Statutes of limitation provide a particularly clear case of this conception: as I will explain, prominent accounts of them seek to explain or justify them in terms of factors that hold for the most part, and explain or justify the extension of the general rule to cases in which they do not hold from considerations of simplicity and ease of application. My view is that the generality is constitutive of a system of private legal rights. The thought that rights are only secure in the context of institutions authorized to adjudicate them is familiar. I take that idea one step further, and argue that the possibility of institutions giving effect to rights presupposes that most claims are already settled, and so creates a space within which a limitation on stale claims is possible.

This chapter engages with the larger project in another way as well: one of that project's central arguments is that private rights survive their own violation. If one person wrongs another, the aggrieved party's right still survives. That does not

* A proper part of this chapter (if not a proper paper) was presented at a conference on Private Law and the Rule of Law at the University of Toronto in 2012; the penultimate version was presented at Yale Law School in April 2014. I am grateful to members of those audiences for their comments and questions, and to Lisa Austin, Shelley Kagan, Leora Katz, Dennis Klimchuk, Scott Shapiro, Gideon Yaffe, Ernest Weinrib, and Ben Zipursky for further discussion.

mean that, if I breach a contract with you, I still perform, nor that if I destroy your property you still own it. There are some wrongs, such as violations of contracts to deliver a parcel of land, or tort of conversion, in which a decree of specific performance or an order of *vindicatio* or *replevin* can restore the factual thing to which the plaintiff was entitled. In many cases, however, the plaintiff is entitled only to a remedy of money damages, and in a significant class of these, such as damage to reputation or bodily injury, the object of the plaintiff's right may never be able to be properly restored. But the claim that rights survive their own violation is not a claim about the object of the right surviving, but about the right itself: a right is a constraint on the conduct of others. If I violate your entitlement to constrain my conduct, you do not thereby cease to be entitled to constrain it. If I could eliminate it by violating it, it would be no constraint at all. The very idea of an interpersonal constraint requires that its violation does not change the legal relationship between the parties. The plaintiff is still entitled to constrain the defendant's conduct. Thus the plaintiff is entitled to hold the defendant to account.

Statutes of limitation raise a puzzle for the idea that rights survive their own violation, because they limit the time for which rights survive. I will argue that the systematic realization of a system of private rights creates a place for limitation periods. I will not argue that they are essential in every case; I offer no objection to the abolition of limitation periods for sexual assault, for example. In the same way, I will use adverse possession as an example of how systematic requirements underwrite limitations on the availability of a legal action, but the analysis I will offer is consistent with systems of title registration that abolish most cases of the action for adverse possession.

Cast in its most general terms, the organizing thought is that private disputes can only be subject to the rule of law if private parties have determinate rights as against each other. The determinacy of these rights is not in the service of anything else. It is not a matter of finding 'simple rules for a complex world'[1] where the simplification makes it easier for private parties severally to plan their affairs, for courts to process cases, or for behaviour to be coordinated so as to produce an optimal outcome.

People can only enjoy private rights if courts are available to resolve disputes; the possibility of our all enjoying our rights turns on the thought that everyone can only enjoy their rights if rights form a consistent set. From the perspective of a system of private rights, unresolved disputes are a pathology, even if less so than unresolvable ones. Thus the procedure for resolving a dispute must be available, and if a plaintiff does not avail himself of the procedure, the dispute is resolved.

I will begin by situating my account in relation to prominent views about limitation periods. The first of these treats limitation periods as a response to changes in the underlying rights. This idea presents itself as intuitively plausible in the following remark by Oliver Wendell Holmes, 'The true explanation of title by prescription seems to me to be that man, like a tree in the cleft of a rock,

[1] Richard Epstein, *Simple Rules for a Complex World* (Harvard University Press 1995).

gradually shapes his roots to his surroundings, and when the roots have grown to a certain size, can't be displaced without cutting at his life.'[2] More recently, Jeremy Waldron has developed this line of thought, adding a comparative dimension by arguing that with the passage of time, the previous owner's attachment fades, while the new owner comes to integrate the thing into his or her life. So, on this view, limitation periods reflect the fact that rights themselves change with time.[3]

The other line of argument I will consider supposes that limitation periods constitute a legitimate restriction on the operation of rights, rather than reflecting a change in those rights. The most familiar form of this analysis treats limitation periods as a response to the difficulty that defendants have in finding evidence with the passage of time. A more general version of the second approach is often associated with the work of Frederick Hayek.[4] It emphasizes the importance of planning, and represents the closure provided by statutes of limitation as enabling people to plan for the future by removing uncertainty.

Each of these arguments contains an important insight. The first recognizes that a person's connection to a thing changes with the passing of time, but inverts this insight by supposing that the right reflects the connection, rather than vice versa. The second draws on the thought that a person should be able to clear his or her name, and places the burden of alleging a wrong where it belongs, namely on the one who says another has done wrong. The more abstract version of the second argument captures the importance of people standing in relations of private right, but then mistakes that for the idea that it is useful to know where you stand.

Despite significant differences, the Holmes/Waldron view and the Hayekian view are alike in their acceptance of the idea that legal rules enable people considered severally to exercise something—for Waldron, autonomy, for Hayek, planning—that can be understood without reference to specific concepts of private law. Both approaches reduce the question of whether someone has an enforceable right to a comparative exercise, looking at the relative strength of competing claims.

On the view I will defend, the requirement of closure does not emerge on empirical comparative grounds, but is inherent in the very idea of a system of justiciable rights. In order for a plurality of persons to enjoy private rights against each other, disputes about right must be subject to closure, either through procedures or through the passage of time. The passage of time acts as a part of the procedure.

1. Fading Rights

On the first of the prominent views I will consider, rights 'fade' with the passage of time. If somebody wrongs you, you are initially entitled to a remedy, but, with the

[2] Oliver Wendell Holmes, 'The Path of the Law' (1897) 10 *Harvard Law Review* 457, 476–7.

[3] Jeremy Waldron, 'Superseding Historic Injustice' (1992) 103 *Ethics* 4.

[4] Frederick Hayek, 'Planning and the Rule of Law' in *The Road to Serfdom* (University of Chicago Press 1944).

passage of time, your claim to a remedy diminishes and, eventually, fades away to nothing. Jeremy Waldron has developed this intuitive picture in some detail. His basic thought is that as people adapt to the fact of a wrong, and come to rely on its effects, they will eventually have a more important interest in the status quo, and in getting on with their lives, than the original right-holder will have in a remedy. Waldron makes this point in a discussion of historic injustices, but presents it as an implication of a general analysis of rights. He also notes that many of those who have come to rely on the new status quo are completely innocent in relation to the past wrong. With the passage of enough time, everyone who benefits from the past wrong was innocent in its creation, because not yet born. The only way to make them answerable for it would be to show that they are implicitly benefiting from it. Even that becomes difficult to establish, because once the original right has faded, nobody does wrong by benefiting from its violation. The great-grandchildren of settlers did not participate in any colonial enterprise, wrongful or otherwise; new immigrants to Canada or Australasia, who came in the twentieth century, arrived long after any wrongs that the initial conquest visited on aboriginal inhabitants. Their interests in relation to the land in question are legitimate, are not tainted by past wrongdoing, and are more important because stronger than the interests of the descendants of those who were wronged. Moreover, those who were wronged once had a significant attachment to the land, but their descendants no longer have that attachment. Waldron is not denying that they might feel an attachment, and understand their lives in terms of reclaiming the land. His claim instead is that the land does not figure in their day-to-day lives in the way that it figured in the lives of their ancestors. Thus their claim has faded, while, at the same time, the claim of the descendants of settlers and other newcomers has brightened.

In formulating his claim in this way, Waldron relies for intuitive support on the thought that this sort of structure shows up in other contexts as well. All private rights are subject to statutes of limitation, and Waldron regards this as recognition of the way in which rights fade and other claims brighten.

He illustrates with the example of a private transaction:

> Think of the . . . theft of my automobile. Certainly, the car should be returned if the thief is discovered within weeks or months of the incident. But what if she is never caught? What if the stolen car remains in her family for decades and is eventually passed down as an heirloom to her children and grandchildren? Are we so sure that when the circumstances of its acquisition eventually come to light, it should be returned without further ado to me or my estate?[5]

He also notes the pragmatic basis for this in discussing statutes of limitations:

> Statutes of limitation are inspired as much by procedural difficulties about evidence and memory, as by any doctrine about rights. It is hard to establish what happened if we are enquiring into the events that occurred decades or generations ago. There are nonprocedural pragmatic arguments also. For better or worse, people build up structures of expectation around the resources that are actually under their control. If a person controls a resource over

[5] Waldron, 'Historic Injustice' (n 3) 15.

a long enough period, then she and others may organize their lives and their economic activity around the premise that that resource is 'hers,' without much regard to the distant provenance of her entitlement.[6]

But he holds that there are also principled grounds:

The other reason entitlements may fade has to do with the basis of the rights themselves. Theories of historic entitlement, like the theory of John Locke or the theory sketched more recently by Robert Nozick, focus on the establishment of an intimate relation between a person and a resource as the basis of property rights. A person works with an object, shaping and modifying it, so that it becomes imbued with part of her personality; it comes to contain a part of herself. But if the right is taken out of her hands for a long period, the intimacy of that relation may evaporate.[7]

He concedes that the Lockean idea of mixing labour may be difficult to render precise or attractive, but in its place suggests that relationship to property can be understood in terms of the integration of an object into a person's plans:

She shapes it in a certain way—ploughing it, for example, or practicing good husbandry in her hunting over it—so as to allow it to perform a certain role in her life and activity not only now but in the future. If someone else, Q, comes along and seizes the land, taking it from P without her consent, then the whole structure of action is disrupted. P's planning and the structure of P's action are destroyed and replaced by that of Q. Moreover, P did not have to do anything equivalent to this disruption.[8]

He sums up the implications as follows, 'if something was taken from me decades ago, the claim that it now forms the center of my life and that it is still indispensable to the exercise of my autonomy becomes less credible'.[9] Waldron also notes that, with the passage of time, claims of loss become more difficult to establish. Had you not wronged me a decade ago, I might have made a foolish investment with the money I still had, and ended up losing much of it.[10]

Addressing the same issue from the opposite direction, Waldron also contends that judgments about rights, especially to property, must also be sensitive to the interests of others:

[6] Waldron, 'Historic Injustice' (n 3) 16.
[7] Waldron, 'Historic Injustice' (n 3) 16.
[8] Waldron, 'Historic Injustice' (n 3) 18.
[9] Waldron, 'Historic Injustice' (n 3) 18–19.
[10] Part of his argument turns on the implications of Derek Parfit's 'non-identity problem' which is supposed to show that anyone who would not have been born but for a wrong taking place cannot complain of that wrong, since that person is better off having been born. See Derek Parfit, 'Future Generations: Further Problems' (1982) 11 *Philosophy & Public Affairs* 113. So many contingencies enter into who is in fact born that it is all but certain that nobody could claim to have been disadvantaged by a wrong done in an earlier generation. I want to put this aspect of Waldron's argument aside, because legal systems have familiar ways of dealing with such issues, and actuarial tables can make the measurement of consequential loss more nearly tractable. So too can the fact that there are other histories with which to compare it, and the fact that the standard of proof in civil matters is the balance of probabilities. But the other reason for putting to one side is that difficulties of calculation may make it impossible to compensate, without in any way making the wrong fade. If someone leaves behind no survivors, there may be no one to compensate. It doesn't follow that there is no ground for compensation.

if some individual makes a claim to exclusive use of some resources in our territory, then the difficulty of sustaining that claim will clearly have some relation to the level of our concern about the plight of other persons who will have to be excluded from the resources if the claim is recognized. The only theory of property entitlement that would be totally immune to variations in background circumstances would be one that did not accept any burden of justification in relation to our real concerns.[11]

The nub of the 'fading' argument is to be found in its analysis of the ground of the initial right: On Waldron's view, a right is an instrument for protecting an interest that can be specified without any reference to the concept of a right, and the existence of the right is conditional on the degree of the interest. With respect to land the relevant interest is in the 'intimate relation' between person and place. If the right itself is 'based on' the centrality of the use of the object to my life, then, as my use of it becomes peripheral, for whatever reason, my right to it fades accordingly. Because interests are specified without reference to the idea of a right, the existence of the right does not depend on how the object lost its centrality to my life, whether it is because my priorities changed or because someone else does wrong to me. What matters is that it no longer figures centrally in my life.

The initial strength of such a view is also its fundamental weakness, however. The difficulty comes from the thought that rights admit of degree. The suggestion that something can fade presupposes that the thing in question admits of degrees. Certainly things can fade—friendships, memories, blue jeans. When they do, a thing persists while the degree to which it has a given property changes. The same analysis can be made to apply to interests. As circumstances change, someone can come to have less of an interest in something that was once vital to her, to the point of having no interest at all—an interest can fade away to nothing.

The first difficulty with applying such a view to rights is that it would seem to entail that their existence is always a matter of degree, and in so doing, eliminate their distinctive role in moral and legal discourse. The fact that you have a right to something means that others may not interfere with it. Defenders of interest theories of rights sometimes describe rights as occupying an 'intermediate' level in moral reasoning, but supposing that rights themselves have a degree deprives them of this intermediate role, because it collapses the distinction between a right and the interest that is supposed to ground it. Again, there is a lively debate about whether or in extreme circumstances rights can be overridden by competing moral concerns, whether they have 'thresholds'.[12] But even if such a view could be made out successfully, it would not entail that every right is a matter of degree. If a person has a right not to be tortured, any argument that aspired to establish that, if enough lives were at stake, this right must be overridden, would not thereby show that the right against torture admits of degrees. It would show, instead, that it admits of exceptions. Such a claim could be modified to lead to the conclusion that whether torture is permissible in some circumstance simply depends upon balancing the

[11] Waldron, 'Historic Injustice' (n 3) 20.

[12] See, for example, Frances Kamm, 'Rights' in J Coleman and S Shapiro (eds), *The Oxford Handbook of Jurisprudence and Philosophy of Law* (Oxford University Press 2002).

competing interests against each other. If that is the model, however, the concept of a right is left with no work to do; it is just a way of packaging a conclusion reached on the grounds of a balance of interests.

It is more, rather than less, difficult to make more prosaic rights, such as property rights, admit of degrees. If someone has a right to property, others are not permitted to interfere with the property without the owner's consent. Whether someone has a right in a particular case does not depend on whether the owner or some other person is more invested in its use. To the contrary, that is exactly what a property right contrasts with: the owner gets to decide, and what the owner says goes, even if it would have been better for the owner to have made a different decision. Although some people find this aspect of rights distasteful or troubling, the appropriate way to articulate such distaste or concern is not to use the word 'right' in a way that makes it go away. Your right that others not trespass on your land holds generally, and does not change or weaken if your connection to the land is limited. Nor will it do to respond to this sort of argument by saying that you should not have a right to your property if you lack sufficient connection to it. Such a response concedes the point at issue. To say that someone should not have a right to something requires the concept of *what a right is* that is not equivalent to the interest-based grounds for attributing it.

So it turns out that on Waldron's analysis, time is just a proxy for something having nothing to do with time. As a proxy, it is by its nature imperfect. Although Waldron does not consider this possibility, his view has the surprising consequence that in cases in which the current owner of an object has not integrated it into his or her life, an intruder who comes along and integrates it has a superior claim. More generally, since integration into a person's life is just one interest among many, even without the passage of time it may be that a non-owner has a greater interest in an object than the owner. In the same way, it may be that one person has a greater interest in the sum of money than another and, taken to the extreme, a wealthy person who is injured by a poor person may have less interest in receiving damages than the poor person does in avoiding paying. There are those who would welcome these consequences, and it is not my purpose to engage them here. My point is only that such consequences sit poorly with the way in which the law normally thinks about either rights or limitation periods. The law focuses exclusively on time, and does not enquire into the underlying interests. Moreover, although much Legal Realist writing has insisted that the law is really secretly and indirectly considering interests when it purports to do otherwise, limitation periods look like a particularly poor example for such insistence. They focus exclusively on a single factor and prevent the court from considering the underlying interests.

I want to suggest, instead, that rights are not the kind of things that admit of degrees. That does not entail that the passage of time or change in institutional context cannot modify a right; I will argue that the way in which rights can disappear if not enforced is a conceptual requirement imposed by the structure of a system of justiciable rights. But rather than conceptualizing this as a matter of competing interests reaching an eventual tipping point, the law instead supposes that the change is abrupt.[13]

One further difficulty for Waldron's approach is worth mentioning. He introduces statutes of limitation in order to make a point that is supposed to be fundamentally about land and secondarily about chattels. Yet limitation statutes are found throughout private law. In a tort or contract claim, the standard remedy is money damages; in an action for debt money is the subject matter of the dispute in question. There is no reason to suppose that the plaintiff's interest in money has faded, while the defendant's interest in keeping his or her money has deepened or strengthened. Money is fungible, and whatever role it plays in a person's life is not in any way tied to its specificity. In some cases of personal injury the plaintiff adjusts to a disruption and makes new plans—some studies report people who suffer serious injuries and disabilities report no loss in welfare.[14] It may be that in such cases being made to pay damages is more of a disruption to the defendant, who will have made other plans. Such changes, however, typically take longer than the standard limitation periods. Further, in the case of the plaintiff's adaption, the fact that the plaintiff adapted would only be relevant to the extent of the defendant's liability, rather than to the plaintiff's entitlement to sue; in the case of the defendant's changed situation, legal devices such as a defence of change of position would seem to be better suited to handle the details of such cases. Further, many injured plaintiffs do not adjust to their injuries, many actions are for property damage or breach of contract, and many defendants who are sued are businesses or carry liability insurance. Of course it is true that a wrongdoer may make other plans after a certain amount of time, in the belief or expectation that he will be able to avoid paying damages. But that account seems to turn on the defendant having some legitimate basis for so assuming. It does not seem appropriate to allow the defendant's thought that he has got away with wronging the plaintiff, and is not going to be held liable, to count as an interest that the law must protect *and so* as a reason against holding him liable.

2. 'Pragmatic' Justifications

Standard treatments of statutes of limitation regard them as a response to a problem about absent or deteriorated evidence. Thomas Merrill summarizes this line of thought:

[13] To be fair to Waldron, his principal concern is with historic injustices, not with private transactions. Nonetheless, his argument is predicated on an explanation of the nature of the statutes of limitation. Further, Waldron's argument has a structural feature that is familiar, but, for all that, highly problematic. Waldron assumes that the way to explain statutes of limitation is to focus on limitation, rather than on statutes; to find an underlying moral structure that institutions only need to make precise.

[14] Peter Ubel, George Loewenstein, Norbert Schwarz, and Dylan Smith, 'Misimagining the Unimaginable: The Disability Paradox and Health Care Decision Making' (2005) 24 *Health Psychology* S57, S60.

The concern about lost evidence is common-sensical. As the quality and quantity of evidentiary material deteriorates over time, the process of fact-gathering and proof becomes more difficult. Surrogate witnesses and documents generally are not as accessible or as reliable as originals; consequently, more resources must be expended in finding them and corroborating their veracity. A rule requiring prompt resolution of claims is thus efficient in that it helps to minimize the costs of litigation and trial.[15]

There is also a fairness concern underlying the lost evidence rationale. Requiring that disputes be resolved promptly prevents the plaintiff from unfairly surprising the defendant with a claim that may be difficult or impossible to refute because evidence that would allow the defendant to defeat the claim no longer exists.

The same view is developed in more detail in a recent treatise on civil procedure:

Limitation periods exist for three purposes: (1) to promote accuracy and certainty in the adjudication of claims; (2) to provide fairness to persons who might be required to defend against claims based on stale evidence; and (3) to prompt persons who might wish to commence claims to be diligent in pursuing them in a timely fashion... It can be difficult for triers of fact to determine what happened with the passage of time because memories fade and documentary records may be lost or destroyed... Limitation periods provide fairness because with the passage of time, it may be unfair for a person accused of causing harm to be required to defend a claim where the evidence to do so has been lost or destroyed. In some situations, potential defendants may be unaware of the need to preserve evidence that might vindicate them or that might assist the court in arriving at an accurate determination of the facts and a just determination of the case.... As for diligence, limitation periods recognize the societal need to provide an incentive to plaintiffs to act diligently to commence a claim within a reasonable time after becoming aware of it.[16]

Although the frankness of an emphasis on pragmatic factors and compromise may seem refreshing, its explanatory reach exceeds its grasp. It fails to capture most of the familiar features of limitation schemes. First, most such schemes have clocks too short for the cited factors to weigh heavily. In Ontario, the jurisdiction the law of which the treatise purports to explicate, the limitation period on debts and tort actions is two years.[17] Even if evidence does become stale or difficult to find after decades, and even though some sharp line would need to be imposed within an extended time period, two years is not a credible place to draw such a line. This point is even clearer in the case of debts, where the relevant evidence is much easier to find. In the case of wrongs, however, the statute of limitation runs from the point at which the wrong is discovered (or the plaintiff was in a position to discover it). Here, again, the clock begins to run based on a factor independently of the availability

[15] Thomas Merrill, 'Property Rules, Liability Rules and Adverse Possession' (1984) 79 *Northwestern University Law Review* 1122, 1128. For a more detailed development of a similar line of thought see Robert Ellickson, 'Adverse Possession and Perpetuities Law: Two Dents in the Libertarian Model of Property Rights' (1986) 64 *Washington University Law Quarterly* 723.

[16] John W Morden and Paul M Perell, *The Law of Civil Procedure in Ontario* (1st edn, LexisNexis 2010) 98. In *Deaville v Boegeman* (1984) 48 OR (2d) 725 (CA) in discussing the purpose of limitation periods, the Court of Appeal noted that it was in the public interest that there be an end to the threat of litigation.

[17] Limitations Act, SO 2002, c 24, s 4.

or deterioration of evidence. Some jurisdictions have introduced statutes of repose that focus on the date of the actual wrong. But even here, the point is that they are not ordinary limitation periods. Further, the availability of exculpating evidence is at least in part a function of the limitation period. How long it makes sense to keep potentially exculpating records depends on how long the limitation period is. Many people keep their tax records for the length of the potential audit period, and it is difficult to see why the same reasoning would not influence the conduct of potential defendants.

It is perhaps open to defenders of this pragmatic account to contend that the current law has it wrong, and that the statutory limitation period should be much longer than it is. Such a defence, however, raises a puzzle about the nature of the account that it purports to defend. Ordinarily, economic and doctrinal writing about law seeks to explain or rationalize the law as it is. An account that seeks to explain the law as it is, but does not fit its actual contours, cannot be vindicated by complaining that the law should be modified so as to conform with it. My point here is not that what the positive law says is always correct, but rather that general features of the positive law that seem surprising, such as statutory limitations on bringing a cause of action, are not successfully explained by saying that they are a response to factors that are absent or irrelevant to the law as it actually exists. Nor would I deny that a variety of factors might properly be taken account of by a legislature charged with determining the appropriate limitation period. My point is only that the power of the legislature to limit the time within which an action can be brought needs to be explained in general terms.

That said, such accounts do pick up on something important about private rights. It is a structuring idea of a system of law that everyone is presumed to have done no wrong, and the onus always lies with the person who alleges another has done wrong to establish. The focus on the difficulty the defendant has in finding evidence may or may not be genuine; the entitlement of the defendant to have any allegations brought forward in a timely manner, by contrast, is part of the organizing structure of private rights. It shapes the general requirement that the plaintiff must bring a cause of action against the defendant, and establish each of its elements; the defendant is presumed to have done no wrong unless the plaintiff has established otherwise. In a related context, it structures the otherwise puzzling tort of defamation: if the plaintiff establishes that the defendant has published something that damages his or her reputation, it falls to the defendant to establish an affirmative defence. The plaintiff does not need to clear his or her own name. Instead, the person who represents it in a bad light needs to affirmatively establish his or her claim.

Your right to your own good name is of tremendous moral importance, but it is above all a structuring principle of a legal system. A court presupposes it in framing and resolving disputes; my suggestion is that it, rather than concerns about the quality of evidence, structures the legal system's readiness to hear a case. Indeed, once the structuring role of your right to your own good name is in focus, concerns about the deterioration of evidence lose their force; as evidence deteriorates, it becomes harder for the plaintiff to meet the burden of coming forward with it and to meet the burden of proof. In some cases, the defendant will have a hard time remembering or finding witnesses who do, but that can equally well happen to the plaintiff, and there is no reason to believe that the passage of time systematically disadvantages one party. Within that context, the plaintiff has ample incentive for diligence, and the defendant does not need extra help in defending against ill-supported claims.

When it is understood in terms of the defendant's right to his or her own good name, the way in which the limitation period runs from the discovery of the wrong rather than its commission comes into clearer focus. The time within which someone can allege that you have done wrong is limited, not by worries about lost records, but because your name should, as a general matter, be clear unless someone can establish that you have committed a wrong. That means that someone has a limited opportunity to allege that you have done wrong, running from the point at which the person making the allegation knew or should have known of your potential role in the wrong. If no allegation is made, your name is clear.

3. Legal Certainty

A more general approach, with the same general thrust, has been developed in detail in the writings of Frederick Hayek, and finds expression in much other legal scholarship. On this view, the fundamental value that statutes of limitation serve is legal certainty: the ability of parties to know exactly where they stand in relation to the law. The fact that private actions are always launched at the initiative of the plaintiff means that a certain amount of uncertainty is unavoidable. As Richard Epstein puts it, 'The major cost associated with the passage of time is uncertainty.'[18] However, on this view, statutes of limitation minimize the time span within which such uncertainty prevails. The potential defendant can achieve repose once sufficient time has elapsed, and so is better positioned to make plans, secure in the knowledge that there is no longer any risk of legal proceedings.

In a slightly different context, Gustav Radbruch argued that the law has two core values, justice and certainty;[19] statutes of limitation can be seen as a compromise between them. This more systematic characterization of the rationale for statutes of limitation has the advantage of explaining why a very short limitation period could be appropriate; rather than seeing lost or corrupt evidence as the problem, this account sees the problem is just as severe where the evidence is available, because the problem is not that it is hard for a defendant to defend themselves, but rather that parties need to know where they stand.

Whatever the merits of Radbruch's bifurcated account elsewhere, limitation periods are a difficult customer for it. If justice and certainty are competing values,

[18] Richard Epstein, 'Past and Future: The Temporal Dimension in the Law of Property' (1986) 64 *Washington University Law Quarterly* 667, 667.

[19] Gustav Radbruch, 'Der Zweck des Rechts' in *Gustav Radbruch: Gesamtausgabe*, ed Arthur Kaufmann, vol iii (CF Müller 1990) 39–50.

certainty figures on both sides, but justice on only one. The statute of limitation prevents an aggrieved plaintiff from enforcing a right. If justice is on the plaintiff's side, it would appear that the grounds for limiting the plaintiff's right would have to be that certainty is more important. To such a response, however, a plaintiff would do well to ask why certainty of having rights vindicated, by means of a longer statutory period, wouldn't do adequate justice to the demands of certainty. That is, certainty is on both sides, provided by any fixed rule; the plaintiff is advantaged by a long period, the defendant by a short one. Certainty isn't advanced more by one than the other.

Still, it might be thought that potential defendants have an especially urgent interest in knowing whether they are at risk of litigation.

This more systematic formulation requires a more systematic response. The root of its difficulty is not that it cannot be made to fit the legal doctrine that it seeks to explain. Indeed, it is more or less guaranteed to fit pretty much any legal doctrine: by setting up two competing values, any result can be characterized as a particular 'balance' between them. Instead, the problem is that the rationale is introduced through a contrast with an imaginary case. To treat limitations periods as a response to a difficulty imposed by a lack of information, the account implicitly appeals to a contrasting situation in which full information is available. The thought, then, is that in such a world, no limitation periods would be required. It would simply be open to everyone to decide whether to pursue a claim in future.

Perhaps I am putting too much weight on the role of information in such accounts; perhaps the intended contrast could be introduced differently, without explicit appeal to information, by appealing instead to an independent value of repose. Perhaps the idea is supposed to be that in addition to imperfect information as to whether others will sue you, you also have a further interest in resting easy. I do not mean to deny that everyone has such an interest, but once the account is so modified, the putative interest is not in *knowing* where you stand but in *standing* somewhere secure. To bring that interest in is not to add something new to the balance, but rather to reframe the entire issue.

Hayek's emphasis on knowing where you stand presents itself as a reductive account of the importance of clear legal rules. On closer inspection, however, it rests on an equivocation between two ways of thinking about the importance of being able to plan. On the first of these, the interest in planning and predictability is perfectly general, but legal rules, especially the rules of private law, are not particularly well suited to advancing it. On the second, legal rules have a much tighter connection with planning; so tight, indeed, that the importance of planning cannot be expressed except through juridical concepts.

There is, no doubt, a non-juridical conception of planning: if I can reliably predict the weather, I can plan my weekend. An airline that knows what the prevailing winds are is in a position to plan its flight schedules. Without knowing those things, planning becomes more difficult. This sense of planning is not completely irrelevant to the law: having predictable legal rules makes planning easier. If legal rules change frequently, or if changes take retroactive effect, planning in this weekend and airline sense becomes more difficult for legal actors. In that sense, then, the law can contribute to predictability, although its main contribution lies in not making itself unpredictable. That is, its contribution to predictability in the weekend/airline sense is largely negative. Further, by laying down rules, it can contribute to the predictability of other people. If you know that other people are not allowed to do certain things, and that you have forms of recourse against them if they do, then you can organize your affairs accordingly. In this sense, law makes social life more predictable.

The difficulty with this way of characterizing the relation of law to planning is that the virtue of law operates entirely independently of the content of law and, indeed, would work exactly the same way with laws that were very different. As Joseph Raz has emphasized, there is something illuminating but also artificial about characterizing this as the virtue of the rule of law. Raz argues that the disease to which clear, prospective and consistently applied rules is the cure is itself an artefact of the system of legal rules. That is, the epistemic virtues of the rule of law are virtues in relation to a pathology specific to legal rules. If public officials are going to enforce rules, it is much easier to plan if the rules are set out prospectively and consistently, but that fact gives us no insight into the way in which they are supposed to govern private interaction.[20]

In particular, private law's organizing distinction between nonfeasance and misfeasance is merely incidental on this account of private law rules as making planning more effective or easier. Some have sought to explain some version of this distinction itself in terms of information costs: Henry Smith has argued that the basic rule of property reflects the ease with which someone is able to ascertain whether something belongs to him or her. Thus the law gives priority to what people already have because doing so makes planning easier.[21] However, putting aside the particular difficulties of this account, there is a more general problem: the requirement that people know what they are and are not permitted to do is only one among many ways in which information might be relevant to planning in the neutral, non-juridical sense. Knowing what is permitted is important to people's ability to plan, but so is knowing what other people are going to do. The law has a special purpose device for getting people to commit to future courses of action. It is called contract. Absent a contract, however, nobody has a right that the conduct of others be predictable. People need to know what they are entitled to do, no doubt, if they are to arrange their own affairs consistent with the rights of others to do so; they need to have a consistent set of entitlements. If legal rules are to guide action, it is not that they are supposed to guide this person, that person, and the other person. Instead, they are supposed to set out the rights of everyone.

Rather than helping you to plan and separately helping me to plan, the law protects your interest in exercising your (legal) rights; and thereby protects your

[20] Joseph Raz, 'The Rule of Law and its Virtue' in *The Authority of Law* (2nd edn, Oxford University Press 1981) 210.

[21] Henry E Smith, 'Property as the Law of Things' (2012) 125 *Harvard Law Review* 1691, 1706.

interest in planning only insofar as you have a right to be certain about various matters. You have no protected interest in certainty except with respect to things to which you have private rights. Indeed, even with respect to those things, you have at most a protected predictability that falls far short of certainty. Private law tolerates a high degree of uncertainty about certain things—in common law systems, courts follow leading precedents, which make it to appellate courts because both parties thought they had a chance of success; the law was unclear, but the court was able to decide the case in a way that disappointed and may have even surprised one of the parties. These elements of uncertainty lead the parties to go to court, and often settle based on their likelihood of success in litigation. There is no reason to suppose that there is a special problem of uncertainty with respect to the period within which you can be sued.

Limiting the value of certainty to things to which you already have a right, identified in some other way, might seem to still leave certainty with some role. To revise the account in this way, however, uses the vocabulary of planning to express a point that is fundamentally about private rights: people are entitled to organize their affairs within their rights. Talk about people planning makes it sound as if it is in the service of some activity that can be characterized without reference to rights. But that is merely an appearance.

The difference manifests itself in the context of limitation periods. The repose that is supposedly provided by a limitation statute sits uneasily with the weekend/airline model of planning. It would be easier for me to plan my weekend if I could be sure that you would not exercise your right to book a room at the resort that I plan to go to; and it would be easier for an airline to plan its flights if it could be sure that other airlines would not exercise their rights to fly on similar routes. Certainty could be increased, and planning facilitated if there were restrictions on the entitlement of people to exercise their rights. The defender of planning would rightly point out that this is not the sort of planning that the Hayek account has in mind; instead, the point of the account is to let people plan severally, not to let some particular person plan his or her affairs with certainty in a way that puts restrictions on the freedom of others. All of this seems exactly right, but generates a difficulty for any attempt to use Hayek's general strategy to explain limitation periods: a statute of limitation prevents plaintiffs from exercising what would otherwise be their rights. Standing to sue runs out, as a result of which the plaintiff's long-term plans for the things to which he or she has a right are also disrupted. No doubt it becomes easier for a defendant to plan, because once the relevant time period has lapsed, the plaintiff may no longer sue. That does not make things better for everyone, planning-wise; it just makes things better for defendants, the very one-sidedness that we saw in the earlier formulation of Hayek's account. Nor will it do to say that creating a statute of limitation also allows plaintiffs to plan because it tells them how long a window they have in deciding whether to litigate. The same could be true of a requirement that potential competitors of established businesses have restricted times within which they can launch new competitive initiatives. It would also be true of a system that would just change the rule about which people were certain.[22] No doubt there are other reasons that could be found to tip the balance against such proposals. The same perhaps could be said in the case of statutes of limitation, however. That countervailing reasons can be found to claim that the intuitively plausible rule is also the rule with the best consequences is always possible. But to shift ground in this way is to give up on the idea that the point of a statute of limitation is to enable people to plan in favour of the generic claim that the point of every legal rule is to bring about the best balance of consequences. The idea of planning, then, is left with no actual work to do; either planning follows the concept of a right rather than explaining it or, alternatively, it is brought in as a makeweight in order to conclude that legal rules are explicable in other terms.

The second difficulty concerns the concept of knowing where you stand. The importance of knowing where you stand with respect to others in relation to objects of possible use is not a composite of two things, namely standing in certain relations and knowing that. Instead, it is a formal requirement of standing in certain relations that there be a procedure available for determining where you stand. That is the role of legal institutions in making private rights legally effective: in order for a plurality of separate persons to enjoy their private rights together, the legal system must provide a way of determining where each person stands in relation to each other person. The point of such procedures is not to discover something that is entirely determinate apart from it; it is to make private rights members of a single determinate system. Such procedures need to be public in a juridical rather than epistemic sense; courts need to be entitled to make decisions that bind all parties to appear before them, and to have authority over both disputants in each public dispute. The only way a plurality of private persons can enjoy their private rights together is if there are public legal procedures for determining what those rights are. I shall now argue that these procedures open the space within which statutes of limitation operate. Legal procedures provide closure with respect to rights, but procedures themselves must take operate on claims of right that they can treat as settled.

[22] Hayek was certainly correct that having stable rules consistently enforced would make planning easier. Simple rules make things easier still. But legal rules do not take certainty as their object; they take certainty about things to which a person has a right. Private law rules of conduct also carry secondary remedial rules with them. Yet some primary rules are useful for planning purposes but do not have remedial rules. If you know that others are prohibited from interfering with property on which you depend but do not own, you can plan accordingly. But you cannot plan on receiving a remedy should someone breach a duty, which is owed only to the property owner. From the point of view of planning, this is puzzling; tugboat operators have all the information they need to know that they should avoid damaging bridges, and that many people depend on the bridges. There would be no loss of certainty if the bridge user also received a remedy. No doubt the legal rule enables planning in the sense that parties purchase insurance based on the liability it entails. Yet as Jane Stapleton has pointed out, insurance cannot figure in determining the legal rule, as the amount of insurance rational parties will carry depends on the liability rule that is in place. See Stapleton, 'Tort, Insurance and Ideology' (1995) 58 *Modern Law Review* 820. It is open to the defender of planning to say that it governs only primary rights, not remedial ones. The difficulty with such a strategy is that there are always other values available to generate any result at all, depriving planning of its explanatory purchase.

4. Unresolved Disputes

On the view I will defend limitation periods are essential to the possibility of specific private rights being members of a more general system of private rights. On the views of both Waldron and Hayek, limitation periods are a symptom of features of the interests that rights are supposed to promote and protect. On the view I will defend, limitations periods are a response to the regulative demands of a system of private rights, and it is a mistake to read the regulative demands of systematic enforcement back into the rights being enforced.[23] A system of enforceable private rights necessarily seeks closure of all claims, but it does not cease to be such a system if a claim is unsettled for a period of time, or even if a special class of claims is not subject to closure. Like so much else in private law, specification must be done through positive law; their regulative role requires that there be a limitation period, but does not specify what it should be.

The organizing thought is this: people can only enjoy their private rights if there are procedures in place for determining who has which rights as against whom. Procedures are not epistemological, but rather partially constitutive: you only have a legal right if there is a procedure for determining its bounds and its enforcement. This constitutive role is only partial because private rights fall into standard categories across procedurally different legal systems. Nonetheless, without a legal system in place, private rights are not merely insecure (as John Locke might have put it) but incomplete. Procedures that make private rights peremptory cannot be completely open-ended; they must be capable of providing closure, but the system of rights as a whole necessarily seeks closure. Consider, for example, a system in which every dispute could be reopened. In such a system, once the claim has been decided, the disappointed party can simply renew his or her claim. Such a system of 'procedure' would not be a procedure at all, because that would leave everything open, and so provide no closure.

The same difficulties would haunt a system in which a single dispute could be reopened indefinitely, with no requirement that parties respond to claims and counterclaims within a specified period of time. Neither of these imagined systems has the precise problem that statutes of limitation solve; both face problems with the inability of legal proceedings to bring closure. Limitation periods operate differently, because they restrict the time within which legal proceedings can be initiated. They thus seem to be external to the particular proceedings that are supposed to provide closure and thus secure private rights. So long as the procedure itself has a finite number of steps, why would there be a problem if it could always be invoked? Why wouldn't it be more important that the length of actual proceedings be brief, once they have been commenced, rather than a limitation on the time within which they can be initiated?

[23] See Ernest J Weinrib, 'Private Law and Public Right' (2011) 61 *University of Toronto Law Journal* 191.

I want to suggest, however, that the exact same issue arises not at the level of the particular procedure, but rather at the level of the system of private rights as a whole: not only must every claim be capable of being settled through public procedures; the system as a whole must treat claims as settled, and so as no longer subject to dispute. Once a claim is in the system, it is fully determinable, even if its determination takes many steps.

Let me make this point with the example of adverse possession, which provides a familiar example of a limitation period, albeit one that is distinctive in several respects. The operation of adverse possession is often characterized in terms of the features on which the Waldron and Hayek accounts focus: the benefits of certainty, the advantages of seeing to it that land is used effectively, the attachment that people develop to particular locations, and the difficulty of tracing ownership over extended periods. Instead, I want to suggest that the structure of adverse possession is internal to property law. A trespasser becomes an owner simply by taking possession because the only way things can make it into a system of property is by people taking possession of them. That is, the acquisition of property always operates through a procedure. The default and traditional procedure of acquisition is taking possession; in the case of land that is a matter of occupation. Adverse possession is acquisition through occupation. The fact that there was a previous 'true' owner matters in the short term, but eventually becomes irrelevant, simply because the true owner's title was also acquired through satisfying procedures, and no title can be superior to the procedures that establish title. On this understanding, the adverse possessor gets good title because the procedure has been satisfied.

Many legal systems have partially abolished adverse possession in favour of systems of title registration. In doing so, however, they have simply changed the procedures through which things can be acquired or, strictly speaking, changed those procedures in a purely forward-looking way through a sort of mass action for adverse possession in which all prior claims are extinguished. Once a system of title registration takes effect, nothing can be acquired except through specified procedures.

Despite superficial similarities to a view focused on certainty, the account I am proposing is constitutive rather than epistemic. The difficulty is not that we cannot know things about the distant past, and so must give up on them. It is instead that any possible challenge to title presupposes the possibility of a person establishing publicly defensible title. That is, it presupposes that title can be established conclusively through a procedure, which is sufficient to establish it. The problem posed by a previous owner coming along is not that this possibility is going to actualize, but rather that the possibility of priority attaching to earlier title precludes the possibility of any procedure establishing secure title. If so, then the earlier owner cannot come along and establish secure title, because the earlier owner could not have acquired secure title. The only way to show that you have secure title, then, is to show that you complied with the relevant procedures. But if procedures are rendered defective by the possibility of someone coming along with earlier title, then procedures are impossible, and there is no secure title.

The principle organizing adverse possession, then, is that if a private-law claim is uncontested for long enough, it stands. If you have satisfied the procedure for acquiring land, the land is yours. The procedure is just uninterrupted possession, which in cases of adverse possession, the 'true owner' can contest. But it could not be yours if it was always open to contest. That is, the procedure can only generate good title provided that the quality of title can only be called into question for a limited time.[24]

The example of adverse possession is in a certain way unrepresentative. Three features in particular stand out. The first is that in other cases in which statutes of limitation operate, there is no issue of title, but only the issue of a claim that there is an obligation as between the parties. Adverse possession concerns claims in rem, and so they might be thought to be distinctive on the grounds that there must be a single answer to the question of who owns a given piece of land. By contrast, statutes of limitation operate on claims in personam, and so might be thought to be less in need of a single answer. Second, in the case of adverse possession, the original owner's claim to ownership is extinguished by the subsequent owner's claim. The new owner has satisfied a procedure, which is time-bound. By contrast, in other cases, such as an action for debt, the plaintiff's right is not extinguished; only his or her standing to sue is.[25] Third, the defendant who benefits from the statute of limitation has not satisfied a procedure; rather, the plaintiff has simply failed to invoke a procedure in time.

The differences can be summed up this way: both adverse possession and statutes of limitation entail that rights can be lost through the passage of time; in the case of adverse possession, however, the loss of a right depends upon the fact that rights can be acquired through the passage of time. But in the case of an action of limitation on a debt or tort, a right is not acquired.

Despite these differences, the cases are alike in one important respect: both turn on the requirement that rights be determinate. Legal procedures provide closure on disputes. In so doing, they make rights determinate. But they do not simply make this or that particular right determinate; the legal system as a whole makes it possible for all rights to be determinate or, when they are subject to dispute, determinable through a procedure. Indeterminacy is not a matter of insufficient information; if they are indeterminate, then there is no answer to how things stand as between persons. Procedures can only operate, however, by taking the background of how things stand between persons as already settled.

In this light, consider the introduction of title registration systems. They provide a procedure for determining who owns a particular parcel of land: look it up in the official records. However, they can only operate provided that the starting records are taken to be correct, not in the sense of getting all of human history correct, but

[24] I concede that I am oversimplifying here: in English law, for example, adverse possession doesn't generate good title, but merely extinguishes title, which then means that the adverse possessor has possessory title by default.

[25] Thus a stale claim may count as a juristic reason for what would otherwise be an unjust enrichment action.

in the more strictly juridical sense of being determinative. The introduction of a title registration system says that whenever wrongs led to the particular holdings of land at the date that the system takes effect are irrelevant.

Now I want to generalize this idea, and say that procedures for addressing questions about rights must begin with a background in which claims of right are settled. The legal system as a whole must simply take the past as settled. That does not mean that particular claims cannot be litigated or particular disputes cannot be opened; it means only that this can only be done against the background of everyone already having what they have. The role of legal procedures is to provide closure; they do so against the background assumption that the past is already closed.

Understood in this way, we can see what both Waldron's view and the familiar textbook view overlook; the situation does not need to change in order for the pressure for closure to apply. That is why the limitation period can be short and also why it properly runs from when the wrong is or could be discovered, rather than from when it occurs. The period can be short because all disputes must be regarded as settled. The limitation period cannot be so short that it extinguishes a cause of action before it can be brought—that would make it impossible for any dispute to be resolved on its merits—or so long that a potential claim can be open for significant portion of a person's life. Beyond that, the appropriate amount of time during which proceedings can be brought is properly set based on factors related to the bringing of proceedings alone, such as investigating the facts pertinent to it, and seeking legal advice on its viability. It runs from when the wrong is discovered because that is the point at which rights come into potential dispute. The rule of law operates symmetrically for both plaintiffs and defendants, because the rule of law operates not to make the case easier or harder to prove, but rather to provide systematic closure.[26]

I am also now in a position to make good on my earlier distinction between the importance of knowing where you stand for purposes of planning and the importance of where you stand in relation to the rights of others. The view I attributed to Hayek focused on the advantages of certainty for purposes of planning. As I noted, it was unable to explain why the advantages of certainty applied asymmetrically in the case of statutes of limitation, as a special instance of its inability to explain why certainty about rights had a special significance. I suggested that certainty about rights has special significance simply because rights do; knowing where you stand matters because standing in rightful relations to others does. The lack of certainty is a symptom of the underlying issue: the problem it manifests is not being unsure of what you may permissibly do; it is not having a fully determinate set of rights. Your rights to what you have are determinate if they are unencumbered by the actionable but not yet acted upon claims of others. Whether the usefulness of the things to

[26] A discussion of the ways in which limitation periods operate in the criminal law is beyond the scope of this chapter. It is worth noting, however, that their operation is graded to the seriousness of the crime in a way that limitations periods in private law are not. I suspect that this reflects the way in which they concern the relation between the accused and the state.

which you have rights can be changed by the actions of others is an entirely different matter; having them be legally unencumbered may or may not make it easier for you to plan, but it means that you stand in determinate relations to others with respect to your rights. That will have the consequence that there will be fewer legal surprises; but surprised or not, the legal system as a whole works to see to it that everyone is able to enjoy their rights, which requires that where they stand in relation to each other be already settled. That is the material on which procedures for the resolution of particular disputes can operate.

I am also now in a position to make good on my earlier contention that a limitation on actions against you is part of your right to your own good name. If nobody challenges you, you are presumed to have done no wrong; anyone who alleges you have done wrong must establish the truth of his or her allegation. Allegations of wrongdoing can sometimes be established, but your right to be free of accusations is only secure if there is a limit on the time within which someone can allege you to have done wrong.

Finally, I am also in a position to explain why the legal system's pressure towards closure focuses on when proceedings commence, rather than on how long the proceedings take to resolve an issue. From the point of view of planning and uncertainty, slow proceedings may well be worse than the possibility of proceedings being initiated. But all that a legal system has to do is provide processes for the resolution of disputes; once they have commenced, the dispute is fully determinable. From a systematic perspective, the prospect of a dispute that can always be opened is a more serious problem than a dispute that is on its way to being resolved.

To sum up: the point is not that procedures need *known* particulars on which to operate; it is instead that procedures are able to fully do justice between private parties only if those private parties already have determinate rights to what is theirs. As I noted above, this requirement is regulative rather than constitutive; a system of private rights necessarily seeks closure, even if other pressures mean that it will not fully achieve it. That means that disputes must always be capable of being settled, and, if nothing is done, they must simply go away.

5. Are Limitation Periods Required for All Private Rights?

The account I have proposed explains why the legal system would treat time as a procedure for resolving disputes about rights, so that the plaintiff's failure to assert a claim eventually settles the dispute in the defendant's favour. It does not, however, require that courts do so in every case, and I do not mean to suggest that a rule-of-law problem arises whenever there is an exception. Once more, the point is that the requirement is regulative, not constitutive.

Some are straightforward; in many jurisdictions the statute of limitation does not run while the plaintiff is a minor or incapacitated and without a legal guardian. In such circumstances, the plaintiff cannot lose by inaction a right on which he or she was incapable of acting.

This is a feature of the following Ontario rule on assault:

> 10(1) The limitation period established by section 4 does not run in respect of a claim based on assault or sexual assault during any time in which the person with the claim is incapable of commencing the proceeding because of his or her physical, mental or psychological condition.[27]

Other exceptions appear to be focused more on the nature of the specific wrong:

> a proceeding arising from a sexual assault if at the time of the assault one of the parties to it had charge of the person assaulted, was in a position of trust or authority in relation to the person or was someone on whom he or she was dependent, whether financially or otherwise; unless the contrary is proven, a person with a claim based on an assault is to be presumed to have been incapable of commencing the proceeding earlier than it was commenced if at the time of the assault one of the parties to the assault had an intimate relationship with the person or was someone on whom the person was dependent, whether financially or otherwise.[28]

The presumption brings a specific range of cases under a general provision concerning competence, and places the burden of proving competence on a potential defendant in a class of cases in which the very bringing of proceedings is typically extraordinarily traumatic for plaintiffs. The intended effect of such provisions is to dissuade defendants in such cases from arguing statues of limitation, but it operates by replacing the standard presumption according to which 'A person shall be presumed to have been capable of commencing a proceeding in respect of a claim at all times unless the contrary is proved.'[29] It is worth noting that the more familiar rationales for statutes of limitation can either treat this sort of exception as a case in which 'the balance' comes out differently, perhaps claiming that interests do not fade in the same way with respect to sexual assault, or that the added difficulty for defendants is somehow outweighed by the difficulty faced by plaintiffs in bringing suit, or that certainty is not so important in this range of cases. That such ad hoc solutions are available does not speak in favour of the accounts that would provide them. Of course, it is open to defenders of any of these accounts to say roughly what I have said: this is an exception that was carved out to deal with the specific situation and problem.

Such cases are distinctive, however, on several grounds. Most significantly, the wrong in question is distinctive, namely sexual assault of a person in the assailant's custody or control, whether factual or legal. Not only does this make it a narrow class of cases; more significantly, it makes it a case in which initiating an action is itself potentially incapacitating for the plaintiff. Those features suggest that the cases are distinctive because of the tension between two organizing principles for a system of private rights. The system must provide closure: no less urgently, it must also enable those who have been wronged, or believe themselves to have been wronged, to have their day in court and have their claim assessed on its merits.

[27] Limitations Act (n 17) s 10 (1).

[28] Limitations Act (n 17) s 10 (3).

[29] Limitations Act (n 17) s 7 (2).

Rather than one interest balanced against another, instead, two regulative principles pull the system in different directions. I noted above that a limitation period needs to be long enough for claims to be assessed on their merits; the exceptions noted here can be understood as special applications of that general principle. Ordinarily the person who believes that he or she has been wronged is in a position to have his or her day in court. In cases of legal or factual incapacity to bring an action, the clock does not begin to run until the plaintiff brings the action.

6. Conclusion

Limitation periods are sometimes paraded as an example of the priority of substance over form, of the need for the law to be practical, or of the need for 'bright line' rules. On such accounts, the law's use of general rules is a strategy in the service of values that do not display the same generality; rules are introduced to simplify an underlying situation that is messy and particular. I have sought to explain them in a different way. The law's generality reflects the requirement that a plurality of persons be able to enjoy their rights together. In the first instance, this requirement underwrites primary legal rights constraining the conduct of others, and secondary, remedial rights. The systematic application of this requirement explains why all rights must be settled, and so why the passage of time can extinguish remedial rights. That is why my title is 'the rule of law and time's arrow' rather than 'the rule of law and the calendar'. The rule of law requires that the past be settled.

Bibliography

Alexander, GS and H Dagan (2012) *Properties of Property* (Aspen Publishers)
Alexander, L and E Sherwin (2001) *The Rule of Rules: Morality, Rules, and the Dilemmas of Law* (Duke University Press)
Alexander, L and E Sherwin (2007) 'Judges as Rule Makers' in DE Edlin (ed), *Common Law Theory* (Cambridge University Press)
Allan, TRS (2001) *Constitutional Justice: A Liberal Theory of the Rule of Law* (Oxford University Press)
Allan, TRS (2013) *The Sovereignty of Law: Freedom, Constitution and Common Law* (Oxford University Press)
Althusius, J (1995) *Politica*, ed FS Carney (Liberty Fund)
Altman, A (1986) 'The Legacy of Legal Realism: A Critique of Ackerman' 10 *Legal Studies Forum* 167
Aquinas, T (1947–8) *Summa Theologica* (American edn, Benziger Bros)
Arendt, H (1977) *Between Past and Future* (Penguin Books)
Aristotle (1980) *The Nicomachean Ethics*, trans D Ross, ed JL Ackrill and JO Urmson (rev edn, Oxford University Press)
Aristotle (1984) *Nicomachean Ethics*, trans JO Urmson and WD Ross in *The Complete Works of Aristotle*, ed J Barnes, vol ii (Princeton University Press)
Aristotle (1984) *Politics*, trans B Jowett in *The Complete Works of Aristotle*, ed J Barnes, vol ii (Princeton University Press)
Aristotle (1984) *Rhetoric*, trans W Rhys Roberts in *The Complete Works of Aristotle*, ed J Barnes, vol ii (Princeton University Press)
Austin, JL (1961) *Philosophical Papers* (Clarendon)
Austin, LM (2013) 'Pluralism, Context and the Internal Life of Property: A Response to Hanoch Dagan' 63 *University of Toronto Law Journal* 22
Austin, LM (2013) 'Possession and the Distractions of Philosophy' in J Penner and HE Smith (eds), *The Philosophical Foundations of Property Law* (Oxford University Press)
Austin, LM (forthcoming) 'Property and the Rule of Law' *Legal Theory*
Baird, DG (2006) 'The Boilerplate Puzzle' 104 *Michigan Law Review* 933
Baker, JH (1990) *An Introduction to English Legal History* (3rd edn, Butterworths)
Bar, C von et al (eds) (2009) *Principles, Definitions and Model Rules of European Private Law: Draft Common Frame of Reference (DCFR)* (European Law Publishers)
Baum, L (2006) *Judges and their Audiences: A Perspective on Judicial Behavior* (Princeton University Press)
Bennett, M (2011) 'Hart and Raz on the Non-Instrumental Moral Value of the Rule of Law: A Reconsideration' 30 *Law and Philosophy* 603
Besson, S and JL Marti (eds) (2009) *Legal Republicanism* (Clarendon Press)
Bingham, T (2011) *The Rule of Law* (Penguin)
Blank, Y (2011) 'Legalizing the Barrier: the Legality and Materiality of the Israel/Palestine Separation Barrier' 46 *Texas International Law Journal* 309
Bobbio, N (1993) *Thomas Hobbes and the Natural Law Tradition*, trans Daniela Gobetti (University of Chicago Press)

Bone, RG (1989) 'Mapping the Boundaries of the Dispute: Conceptions of Ideal Lawsuit Structure from the Field Code to the Federal Rules' 89 *Columbia Law Review* 1
Bork, RH (1990) *The Tempting of America: The Political Seduction of the Law* (Free Press)
Bowen, OR (1987) Congressional Testimony on Senate Bill S 1804, 257 JAMA 816, 818
Brooks, CW (1993) 'The Place of Magna Carta and the Ancient Constitution in Sixteenth Century Legal Thought' in E Sandoz (ed), *The Roots of Liberty: Magna Carta, Ancient Constitution, and the Anglo-American Tradition of Rule of Law* (University of Missouri)
Brudner, A (1995) *The Unity of The Common Law: Studies in Hegelian Jurisprudence* (University of California Press)
Brudner, A (2011) 'Private Law and Kantian Right' 61 *University of Toronto Law Journal* 279
Brudney, D (1993) 'Two Links of Law and Morality' 103 *Ethics* 280
Bryce, J (1901) *Studies in History and Jurisprudence* (Clarendon Press)
Buell, SW (2011) 'Good Faith and Law Evasion' 58 *UCLA Law Review* 611
Burton, SJ (1994) 'Particularism, Discretion, and the Rule of Law' in I Shapiro (ed), *The Rule of Law* (New York University Press)
Chafee Jr, Z (1933) *The Suffolk County Court and its Jurisdiction, Introduction to 29 Publications of the Colonial Society of Massachusetts, Records of the Suffolk County Court 1671–1680* (Colonial Society of Massachusetts)
Clinton, RL (2000) 'Classical Legal Naturalism and the Politics of John Marshall's Constitutional Jurisprudence' 33 *John Marshall Law Review* 935
Cohen, GM (1992) 'The Negligence–Opportunism Tradeoff in Contract Law' 20 *Hofstra Law Review* 941
Cohen, N (2012) 'The Slayer Rule' 92 *Boston University Law Review* 793
Coke, Sir E (1853) *Commentary on Littleton* (Robert Small)
Cole, D (2010) 'Getting Away with Torture' *The New York Review of Books* (New York, 14 January) 39
Cole, D (2010) 'He was Tortured but he Can't Sue' (*New York Review Blog*, 15 June)
Coleman, JL (1988) *Markets, Morals, and the Law* (Cambridge University Press)
Commission of Inquiry into the Actions of Canadian Officials in Relation to Maher Arar (2006) *Report of the Events Relating to Maher Arar: Analysis and Recommendations* (Public Works and Government Services Canada)
Cook, WW (1993) 'Scientific Method and the Law' in WW Fisher III et al (eds), *American Legal Realism* (Oxford University Press)
Cooke, E (2000) *The Modern Law of Estoppel* (Oxford University Press)
Cover, R (1986) 'Violence and the Word' 95 *Yale Law Journal* 1601
Craig, P (1997) 'Formal and Substantive Conceptions of the Rule or Law: An Analytical Framework' 21 *Public Law* 467
Craswell, R (1993) 'On the Uses of "Trust": Comment on Williamson, "Calculativeness, Trust, and Economic Organization"' 36 *Journal of Law and Economics* 487
Dagan, H (1997) *Unjust Enrichment: A Study of Private Law and Public Values* (Cambridge University Press)
Dagan, H (1999) 'The Distributive Foundation of Corrective Justice' 98 *Michigan Law Review* 138
Dagan, H (2009) 'Political Money' 8 *Election Law Journal* 349
Dagan, H (2011) *Property: Values and Institutions* (Oxford University Press)
Dagan, H (2013) 'Autonomy, Pluralism, and Contract Law Theory' 76 *Law and Contemporary Problems* 19
Dagan, H (2013) 'Inside Property' 63 *University of Toronto Law Journal* 1

Dagan, H (2013) *Reconstructing American Legal Realism & Rethinking Private Law Theory* (Oxford University Press)

de Bracton, H (1968) *On the Laws and Customs of England*, trans SE Thorne (Belknap Press)

de Saussure, F (1983) *Course in General Linguistics*, trans R Harris (Duckworth)

Dibble, CM (1994) *The Lost Tradition of Modern Legal Interpretation* (unpublished manuscript)

Dicey, AV (1959) *Introduction to the Study of the Law of the Constitution* (10th edn, Macmillan and Co)

Dickens, C (1978) *Bleak House* (Oxford University Press)

Dorfman, A (2010) 'Private Ownership' 16 *Legal Theory* 1

Dukeminier, J, RH Sitkoff, and J Lindgren (2009) *Wills, Trusts, and Estates* (8th edn, Aspen Publishers)

Dukeminier, J et al (2010) *Property* (7th edn, Aspen Publishers)

Dworkin, RM (1967) 'The Model of Rules' 35 *The University of Chicago Law Review* 14

Dworkin, RM (1977) *Taking Rights Seriously* (Harvard University Press)

Dworkin, RM (1986) *Law's Empire* (Belknap Press)

Dworkin, RM (2004) 'Hart's Postscript and the Character of Political Philosophy' (2004) 24 *Oxford Journal of Legal Studies* 1.

Dworkin, RM (2011) *Justice for Hedgehogs* (Harvard University Press)

Dyzenhaus, D (1999) 'Fuller's Novelty' in W Witteveen and W van der Burg (eds), *Rediscovering Fuller: Essays on Implicit Law and Institutional Design* (Amsterdam University Press)

Dyzenhaus, D (2000) 'Form and Substance in the Rule of Law: A Democratic Justification of Judicial Review' in C Forsyth (ed), *Judicial Review and the Constitution* (Hart)

Dyzenhaus, D (2006) *The Constitution of Law* (Cambridge University Press)

Dyzenhaus, D (2009) 'Schmitt v. Dicey: Are States of Emergency Inside or Outside the Legal Order?' 27 *Cardozo Law Review* 2005

Dyzenhaus, D (2012) 'Hobbes on the Authority of Law' in D Dyzenhaus and T Poole (eds), *Hobbes and the Law* (Cambridge University Press)

Dyzenhaus, D (forthcoming) 'Freedom under an Order of Public Law: From Hobbes through Hayek to Republicanism' in Andras Sajo and Renata Uitz (eds), *The Tragedy of Liberty* (Eleven Publishing)

Dyzenhaus, D and M Taggart (2007) 'Reasoned Decisions and Legal Theory' in DE Edlin (ed), *Common Law Theory* (Cambridge University Press)

Ellickson, R (1986) 'Adverse Possession and Perpetuities Law: Two Dents in the Libertarian Model of Property Rights' 64 *Washington University Law Quarterly* 723

Emmerglick, LJ (1944–5) 'A Century of the New Equity' 23 *Texas Law Review* 244

Endicott, TAO (1999) 'The Impossibility of the Rule of Law' 19 *Oxford Journal of Legal Studies* 1

Endicott, TAO (2000) *Vagueness in Law* (Oxford University Press)

Endicott, TAO (2009) *Administrative Law* (Clarendon)

Endicott, TAO (2011) 'The Value of Vagueness' in Andrei Marmor and Scott Soames (eds), *Philosophical Foundations of Language in the Law* (Oxford University Press)

Epstein, RA (1973) 'A Theory of Strict Liability' 2 *Journal of Legal Studies* 151

Epstein, RA (1975) 'Unconscionability: A Critical Reappraisal' 18 *The Journal of Law and Economics* 293

Epstein, RA (1986) 'Past and Future: The Temporal Dimension in the Law of Property' 64 *Washington University Law Quarterly* 667

Epstein, RA (1988) 'Covenants and Constitutions' 73 *Cornell Law Review* 906
Epstein, RA (1995) *Simple Rules for a Complex World* (Harvard University Press)
Epstein RA (2011) *Design for Liberty: Private Property, Public Administration, and the Rule of Law* (Harvard University Press)
Essert, C (2013) 'The Office of Ownership' 63 *University of Toronto Law Journal* 418
Fallon Jr, RH (1997) '"The Rule of Law" as a Concept in Constitutional Discourse' 97 *Columbia Law Review* 1
Feldman, Y and HE Smith (forthcoming) 'Behavioral Equity' *Journal of Institutional and Theoretical Economics*
Ferguson, A (1995) *An Essay on the History of Civil Society*, ed F Oz-Salzberger (Cambridge University Press)
Fiss, OM (1979) 'The Supreme Court, 1978 Term—Foreword: The Forms of Justice' 93 *Harvard Law Review* 1
Forsyth, C (ed) (2000) *Judicial Review and the Constitution* (Hart Publishing)
Fox-Decent, E (2011) *Sovereignty's Promise: The State as Fiduciary* (Oxford University Press)
Fox-Decent, E (2012) 'Hobbes's Relational Theory: Beneath Power and Consent' in D Dyzenhaus and T Poole (eds), *Hobbes and the Law* (Cambridge University Press)
Frankfurt, H (1988) 'Freedom of the Will and the Concept of a Person' in *The Importance of What We Care About* (Cambridge University Press)
Fried, C (1981) *Contract as Promise* (Harvard University Press)
Fuller, LL (1955) 'Freedom: A Suggested Analysis' 68 *Harvard Law Review* 1305
Fuller, LL (1958) 'Positivism and Fidelity to Law—a Reply to Professor Hart' 71 *Harvard Law Review* 630
Fuller, LL (1969) *The Morality of Law* (rev edn, Yale University Press)
Fuller, LL (2001) 'The Forms and Limits of Adjudication' in KI Winston (ed), *The Principles of Social Order: Selected Essays of Lon L. Fuller* (Hart Publishing)
Fuller, LL and M Eisenberg (1947) *Basic Contract Law* (1st edn; 8th edn, West: St Paul 2006)
Fuller, LL and WR Perdue (1936) 'The Reliance Interest in Contract Damages: 1' 46 *Yale Law Journal* 52
Fuller, LL and WR Perdue (1937) 'The Reliance Interest in Contract Damages: 2' 46 *Yale Law Journal* 373
Gardner, J (1994) 'Rationality and the Rule of Law in Offences against the Person' 53 *Cambridge Law Journal* 502
Gardner, J (1996) 'The Purity and Priority of Private Law' 46 *University of Toronto Law Journal* 459
Gardner, J (2001) 'Obligations and Outcomes in the Law of Torts' in P Cane and J Gardner (eds), *Relating to Responsibility: Essays for Tony Honoré on his Eightieth Birthday* (Hart Publishing)
Gardner, J (2003) 'The Mark of Responsibility' 23 *Oxford Journal of Legal Studies* 157
Gardner, J (2007) *Offences and Defences* (Oxford University Press)
Gardner, J (2011) 'What is Tort Law For? Part 1. The Place of Corrective Justice' 30 *Law and Philosophy* 1
Gardner, J (2012) *Law as a Leap of Faith: Essays on Law in General* (Oxford University Press)
Gardner, J (2013) 'Reasons and Abilities: Some Preliminaries' 58 *The American Journal of Jurisprudence* 63
Garnett, G (trans and ed) (1994) *Vindiciae Contra Tyrannos* (Cambridge University Press)
Gerber, S (2003) 'Corbin and Fuller's Cases on Contracts (1942?): The Casebook that Never Was' 72 *Fordham Law Review* 595

Gergen, MR, JM Golden, and HE Smith (2012) 'The Supreme Court's Accidental Revolution? The Test for Permanent Injunctions' 112 *Columbia Law Review* 203

Gold, AS (2011) 'A Moral Rights Theory of Private Law' 52 *William and Mary Law Review* 1873

Goldberg, JCP (2005) 'The Constitutional Status of Tort Law: Due Process and the Right to a Law for the Redress of Wrongs' 115 *Yale Law Journal* 524

Goldberg, JCP and BC Zipursky (2002) 'Unrealized Torts' 88 *Virginia Law Review* 1625

Goldberg, JCP and BC Zipursky (2006) 'Seeing Tort Law from the Internal Point of View: Holmes and Hart on Legal Duties' 75 *Fordham Law Review* 1563

Goldberg, JCP and BC Zipursky (2007) 'Tort Law and Moral Luck' 92 *Cornell Law Review* 1123

Goldberg, JCP and BC Zipursky (2011) 'Civil Recourse Revisited' 39 *Florida State University Law Review* 341

Gordley, J (1981) 'Equality in Exchange' 69 *California Law Review* 1587

Gordon, RW (1996) 'Paradoxical Property' in J Brewer and S Staves (eds), *Early Modern Conceptions of Property* (Routledge)

Grice, P (1989) *Studies in the Ways of Words* (Harvard University Press)

Grotius, H (1995) *De Jure Belli ac Pacis*, trans FW Kelsey (William S Hein & Co)

Haines, CG (1916) 'The Law of Nature in State and Federal Judicial Decisions' 25 *Yale Law Journal* 617

Hampton, J (1988) *Hobbes and the Social Contract Tradition* (Cambridge University Press)

Harris, JW (1996) *Property and Justice* (Oxford University Press)

Hart, HLA (1958) 'Positivism and the Separation of Law and Morals' 71 *Harvard Law Review* 593

Hart, HLA (1965) 'Book Review of *The Morality of Law*' 78 *Harvard Law Review* 1281

Hart, HLA (1968) *Punishment and Responsibility: Essays in the Philosophy of Law* (Oxford University Press)

Hart, HLA (1983) 'Problems of the Philosophy of Law' in *Essays in Jurisprudence and Philosophy* (Clarendon Press)

Hart, HLA (1994) *The Concept of Law* (2nd edn, Clarendon Press)

Hart, HLA (2008) *Punishment and Responsibility* (2nd edn, Clarendon Press)

Hart, HLA and T Honore (1985) *Causation in the Law* (2nd edn, Clarendon Press)

Hayek, FA (1944) *The Road to Serfdom* (University of Chicago Press)

Hayek, FA (1960) *The Constitution of Liberty* (Routledge & Kegan Paul)

Hayek, FA (1978) *Law, Legislation and Liberty* ii: *The Mirage of Social Justice* (University of Chicago Press)

Hayek, FA (1981) *Law, Legislation and Liberty* iii: *The Political Order of a Free People* (University of Chicago Press)

Hayek, FA (1982) *Law, Legislation and Liberty* i: *Rules and Order* (Routledge & Kegan Paul)

Hays, MJ (2008) 'Where Equity Meets Expertise: Re-Thinking Appellate Review in Complex Litigation' 41 *University of Michigan Journal of Law Reform* 421

Heckman, JJ, RL Nelson, and L Cabatingan (2010) *Global Perspectives on the Rule of Law* (Routledge)

Heylighen, F (1999) 'Advantages and Limitations of Formal Expression' 4 *Foundations of Science* 25

Hobbes, T (1971) *A Dialogue Between a Philosopher and a Student of the Common Laws of England*, ed J Cropsey (University of Chicago Press)

Hobbes, T (1990) *Behemoth or The Long Parliament*, ed F Tönnies (University of Chicago Press)

Hobbes, T (1994) *Leviathan with Selected Variants from the Latin Edition of 1668*, ed E Curely (Hackett Publishing Co)
Hobbes, T (1996) *Leviathan*, ed R Tuck (Cambridge University Press)
Hobbes, T (1998) *On the Citizen*, ed R Tuck and M Silverthorne (Cambridge University Press)
Hohfeld, W (1913) 'Some Fundamental Legal Conceptions as Applied in Judicial Reasoning' 23 *Yale Law Journal* 16
Holmes, OW (1897) 'The Path of the Law' 10 *Harvard Law Review* 457
Honoré, T (1988) 'Responsibility and Luck: The Moral Basis of Strict Liability' 104 *Law Quarterly Review* 530
Honoré, T (1993) 'The Dependence of Morality on Law' 13 *Oxford Journal of Legal Studies* 1
Horwitz, M (1992) *The Transformation of American Law* (Harvard University Press)
Hunt, M (1997) *Using Human Rights Law in English Courts* (Hart Publishing)
Hyde, A (1997) *Bodies of Law* (Princeton University Press)
Kadens, E (2012) 'The Myth of the Customary Law Merchant' 90 *Texas Law Review* 1153
Kahneman, Daniel (2011) *Thinking, Fast and Slow* (Farrar, Straus and Giroux)
Kamm, F (2002) 'Rights' in J Coleman and S Shapiro (eds), *The Oxford Handbook of Jurisprudence and Philosophy of Law* (Oxford University Press)
Kant, I (1996) *The Metaphysics of Morals in Practical Philosophy*, trans M Gregor (Cambridge University Press)
Katz, L (2008) 'Exclusion and Exclusivity' 58 *University of Toronto Law Journal* 275
Katz, L (2012) 'Spite and Extortion: A Jurisdictional Principle of Abuse of Property Right' 122 *Yale Law Journal* 1444
Kelsen, H (1945) *General Theory of Law and State*, trans A Wedberg (Harvard University Press)
Kelsen, H (1992) *Introduction to the Problems of Legal Theory*, trans BL Paulson and SL Paulson (Clarendon Press)
Kelsen, H (2009) *The Pure Theory of Law*, trans M Knight (The Law Book Exchange, Ltd)
Kennedy, D (2008) *Legal Reasoning: Collected Essays* (The Davies Group Publishers)
King Jr, ML (2010) 'Letter from the Birmingham Jail' in *Why We Can't Wait* (Beacon Press)
Klimchuk, D (2012) 'Hobbes on Equity' in D Dyzenhaus and T Poole (eds), *Hobbes and the Law* (Cambridge University Press)
Klimchuk, D 'Is the Law of Equity Equitable in Aristotle's Sense?' (unpublished)
Komesar, NK (1994) *Imperfect Alternatives: Choosing Institutions in Law, Economics, and Public Policy* (University of Chicago Press)
Konskenniemi, M (2007) 'Constitutionalism as Mindset: Reflections on Kantian Themes About International Law and Globalization' 8 *Theoretical Inquiries in Law* 1
Kramer, MH (1999) *In Defence of Legal Positivism: Law without Trimmings* (Oxford University Press)
Kramer, MH (2003) *The Quality of Freedom* (Clarendon Press)
Kreitner, R (2005) 'Multiplicity in Contract Remedies' in N Cohen and E McKendrick (eds), *Comparative Remedies For Breach of Contracts* (Hart Publishing)
Kronman, AT (1979–80) 'Contract Law and Distributive Justice' 89 *Yale Law Journal* 472
Krygier, M (2011) 'Four Puzzles about the Rule of Law: Why, What, Where? and Who Cares?' in JE Fleming (ed), *Getting to the Rule of Law* (New York University Press)
Krygier, M and W Mason (2011) 'Violence, Development and the Rule of Law' in George Mavrotas (ed), *Security and Development* (Edward Elgar)
Lawrence, FF (1929) *A Treatise on the Substantive Law of Equity Jurisprudence* (Bender)
Laycock, D (1993) 'The Triumph of Equity' 56 *Law and Contemporary Problems* 53

Laycock, D (2012) 'The Neglected Defense of Undue Hardship (and the Doctrinal Train Wreck in *Boomer v. Atlantic Cement*)' 4 *Journal of Tort Law* 1
Lee, BA and HE Smith (2012) 'The Nature of Coasean Property' 59 *International Review of Economics* 145
Lemley, MA (2004) 'Ex Ante versus Ex Post Justifications for Intellectual Property' 71 *University of Chicago Law Review* 129
Lipkin, RJ (1990) 'Beyond Skepticism, Foundationalism and the New Fuzziness: The Role of Wide Reflective Equilibrium in Legal Theory' 75 *Cornell Law Review* 811
Litman, J (2006) *Digital Copyright* (2nd edn, Prometheus Books)
Llewellyn, KN (1940) 'The Normative, the Legal, and the Law-Jobs: The Problem of Juristic Method' 49 *Yale Law Journal* 1355
Llewellyn, KN (1960) *The Common Law Tradition* (Little Brown)
Llewellyn, KN (1962) *Jurisprudence: Realism in Theory and in Practice* (University of Chicago Press)
Lobban, M (2011) 'Legal Theory and Judge Made Law in England, 1850–1920' 40 *Quaderni Fiorentini* 553
Locke, J (1988) *Two Treatises of Government*, ed P Laslett (Oxford University Press)
Löfgren, L (1988) 'Towards System: From Computation to the Phenomenon of Language' in ME Carvallo (ed), *Nature, Cognition and System i* (Kluwer Academic Publishers)
Löfgren, L (1992) 'Complementarity in Language: Toward a General Understanding' in ME Carvallo (ed), *Nature, Cognition and System II* (Kluwer Academic Publishers)
Lucy, W (2007) *Philosophy of Private Law* (Oxford University Press)
Lucy, W (2011) 'Equality Under and Before the Law' 61 *University of Toronto Law Journal* 411
Lyons, D (2008) 'The Legal Entrenchment of Illegality' in MH Kramer et al (eds), *The Legacy of H.L.A. Hart* (Oxford University Press)
McBride, N (2004) 'Duties to Take Care—Do They Really Exist?' 24 *Oxford Journal of Legal Studies* 417
MacCormick, N and J Raz (1972) 'Voluntary Obligations and Normative Powers' 46 *Proceedings of the Aristotelian Society, Supplementary Volumes* 59
McFarlane, B (2013) 'Understanding Equitable Estoppel: From Metaphors to Better Laws' 66 *Current Legal Problems* 267
McFarlane, B and R Stevens (2010) 'The Nature of Equitable Property' 4 *Journal of Equity* 1
McGhee, J (ed) (2005) *Snell's Equity* (33rd edn, Sweet and Maxwell)
Macnair, M (2007) 'Equity and Conscience' 27 *Oxford Journal of Legal Studies* 659
Marcus, R (1990) 'Are Punitive Damage Awards Fair to Firms? Supreme Court Finally Agrees to Referee High-Stakes Dispute' *Washington Post* (Washington, 23 September) H1
Marmor, A (2004) 'The Rule of Law and its Limits' 24 *Law and Philosophy* 1
Martin, M (1997) *Legal Realism: American and Scandinavian* (P Lang)
Merrill, T (1984) 'Property Rules, Liability Rules and Adverse Possession' 79 *Northwestern University Law Review* 1122
Merrill, TW and HE Smith (2000) 'Optimal Standardization in the Law of Property: The Numerus Clausus Principle' 110 *Yale Law Journal* 1
Merrill, TW and HE Smith (2001) 'The Property/Contract Interface' 101 *Columbia Law Review* 773
Merrill, TW and HE Smith (2007) 'The Morality of Property' 48 *William and Mary Law Review* 1849
Miller, J (1984) *Rousseau: Dreamer of Democracy* (Yale University Press)
Morden, JW and PM Perell (2010) *The Law of Civil Procedure in Ontario* (1st edn, LexisNexis)

Moreau, S (2010) 'What is Discrimination' 38 *Philosophy and Public Affairs* 143
Mullan, D (2001) *Administrative Law* (Irwin Law)
Mullan, D (2010) '*Roncarelli v Duplessis* and Damages for Abuse of Power: For What Did it Stand in 1959 and For What Does it Stand in 2009?' 55 *McGill Law Journal* 587
Muris, T (1981) 'Opportunistic Behavior and the Law of Contracts' 65 *Minnesota Law Review* 521
Murphy, C (2005) 'Lon Fuller and the Moral Value of the Rule of Law' 24 *Law and Philosophy* 239
Murphy, J and C Witting (2012) *Street on Torts* (13th edn, Clarendon Press)
Nadler, J (2007) 'Hart, Fuller and the Connection between Law and Justice' 27 *Law and Philosophy* 1
Nagel, T (1979) *Mortal Questions* (Cambridge University Press)
Nozick, R (1974) *Anarchy, State, and Utopia* (Basic Books)
Oakeshott, M (1975) *On Human Conduct* (Clarendon Press)
Oakeshott, M (1999) *On History and Other Essays* (Liberty Fund)
Oliphant, H (1928) 'A Return to Stare Decisis' 14 *American Bar Association Journal* 71
Parfit, D (1982) 'Future Generations: Further Problems' 11 *Philosophy & Public Affairs* 113
Parkin-Speer, D (1983) 'John Lilburne: A Revolutionary Interprets Statutes and Common Law Due Process' 1 *Law and History Review* 276
Peñalver, EM (2009) 'Land Virtues' 94 *Cornell Law Review* 821
Penner, JE (1997) *The Idea of Property in Law* (Oxford University Press 1997)
Penner, JE (2014) 'The (True) Nature of a Beneficiary's Equitable Proprietary Interest Under a Trust' 27 *Canadian Journal of Law and Jurisprudence* 473
Pettit, P (1997) *Republicanism: A Theory of Freedom and Government* (Clarendon Press)
Pettit, P (2001) *A Theory of Freedom: From the Psychology to the Politics of Agency* (Polity Press)
Pettit, P (2012) *On the People's Terms: A Republican Theory and Model of Democracy* (Cambridge University Press)
Phillipson, G and A Williams (2011) 'Horizontal Effect and the Constitutional Constraint' 74 *The Modern Law Review* 878
Pitkin, H (1988) 'Are Freedom and Liberty Twins?' 16 *Political Theory* 523
Plucknett, TFT and JL Barton (eds) (1974) *St. German's Doctor and Student* (Selden Society)
Polanyi, M (1965) *The Logic of Liberty; Reflections and Rejoinders* (University of Chicago Press)
Posner, RA (1990) *The Problems of Jurisprudence* (Harvard University Press)
Posner, RA (1998) *Economic Analysis of Law* (5th edn, Aspen Law & Business)
Posner, RA (2008) *How Judges Think* (Harvard University Press)
Postema, GJ (1999) 'Implicit Law' in WJ Witteveen and W van der Burg (eds), *Rediscovering Fuller: Essays on Implicit Law and Institutional Design* (Amsterdam University Press)
Postema, GJ (2008) 'Conformity, Custom, and Congruence: Rethinking the Efficacy of Law' in M Kramer (ed), *The Legacy of Hart* (Oxford University Press)
Postema, GJ (2010) 'Law's Ethos: Reflections on a Public Practice of Illegality' 90 *Boston University Law Review* 1847
Postema, GJ (2011) *A Treatise of Legal Philosophy and General Jurisprudence* xi: *Legal Philosophy in the Twentieth Century: The Common Law World* (Springer)
Postema, GJ (2014) 'Law's Rule: Reflexivity, Mutual Accountability, and the Rule of Law' in Z Xiaobo (ed), *Bentham's Theory of Law and Public Opinion* (Cambridge University Press)

Pound, R (1911) 'Puritanism and the Common Law' 45 *American Law Review* 811

Pound, R (1913) 'The End of Law as Developed in Legal Rules and Doctrines' 27 *Harvard Law Review* 226

Powell, RR (2013) *Powell on Real Property*, ed MA Wolf (Matthew Bender).

Rabin, EH (1984) 'The Revolution in Residential Landlord–Tenant Law: Causes and Consequences' 69 *Cornell Law Review* 517

Rachlinski, JJ (2006) 'Bottom-Up Versus Top-Down Lawmaking' 73 *University of Chicago Law Review* 933

Radbruch, G (1990) 'Der Zweck des Rechts' in A Kaufmann (ed), *Gustav Radbruch: Gesamtausgabe*, vol iii (CF Müller)

Radin, MJ (1982) 'Property and Personhood' 34 *Stanford Law Review* 957

Radin, MJ (1989) 'Reconsidering the Rule of Law' 69 *Boston University Law Review* 781

Radin, MJ (2002) 'Can the Rule of Law Survive Bush v. Gore?' in B Ackerman (ed), *Bush v. Gore: The Question of Legitimacy* (Yale University Press)

Radin, MJ (2012) *Boilerplate: The Fine Print, Vanishing Rights, and the Rule of Law* (Princeton University Press)

Radin, MJ (forthcoming) 'An Analytical Framework for Legal Evaluation of Boilerplate' in G Letsas, G Klass, and P Saprai (eds), *Philosophical Foundations of Contract Law* (Oxford University Press)

Rawls, J (1971) *A Theory of Justice* (Belknap Press)

Raz, J (1977) 'The Rule of Law and its Virtue' 93 *Law Quarterly Review* 195

Raz, J (1984) 'Legal Principles and the Limits of Law' in M Cohen (ed), *Ronald Dworkin and Contemporary Jurisprudence* (Rowman & Allanheld)

Raz, J (1986) *The Morality of Freedom* (Oxford University Press)

Raz, J (1994) *Ethics in the Public Domain* (Oxford University Press)

Raz, J (1994) 'The Relevance of Coherence' in *Ethics in the Public Domain: Essays in the Morality of Law and Politics* (Oxford University Press)

Raz, J (2009) 'Incorporation by Law' in *Between Authority and Interpretation: On the Theory of Law and Practical Reason* (Oxford University Press)

Raz, J (2009) 'The Rule of Law and its Virtue' in *The Authority of Law* (2nd edn, Oxford University Press)

Reid, JP (2004) *Rule of Law: The Jurisprudence of Liberty in the Seventeenth and Eighteenth Centuries* (Northern Illinois University Press)

Rheinhart, L (1971) *The Dice Man* (W Morrow)

Ripstein, A (2006) 'Beyond the Harm Principle' 34 *Philosophy & Public Affairs* 215

Ripstein, A (2009) *Force and Freedom: Kant's Legal and Political Philosophy* (Harvard University Press)

Ripstein, A and BC Zipursky (2001) 'Corrective Justice in an Age of Mass Torts' in GJ Postema (ed), *Philosophy and the Law of Torts* (Cambridge University Press)

Rodell, F (1939) *Woe Unto You, Lawyers!* (Reynal and Hitchcock)

Rogers, WVH (2002) *Winfield & Jolowicz on Tort* (16th edn, Sweet & Maxwell)

Rose, CM (1988) 'Crystals and Mud in Property Law' 40 *Stanford Law Review* 577

Rose, CM (2004) 'Shelley v. Kraemer' in G Korngold and AP Morriss (eds), *Property Stories* (Foundation Press)

Rose, N (1999) *Powers of Freedom* (Cambridge University Press)

Rosen, M (2012) *Dignity: Its History and Meaning* (Harvard University Press)

Rothbard, MN (1982) *The Ethics of Liberty* (Humanities Press)

Rousseau, JJ (1987) *On the Social Contract*, trans DA Cress (Hackett)

Rundle, K (2009) 'The Impossibility of an Exterminatory Legality: Law and the Holocaust' 59 *University of Toronto Law Journal* 65

Rundle, K (2012) *Forms Liberate: Reclaiming the Jurisprudence of Lon L Fuller* (Hart Publishing)

Sage, NW (2012) 'Original Acquisition and Unilateralism: Kant, Hegel, and Corrective Justice' 25 *Canadian Journal of Law and Jurisprudence* 119

Sartorius, R (1971) 'Hart's Concept of Law' in RS Summers (ed), *More Essays in Legal Philosophy* (Blackwell)

Scalia, A (1989) 'The Rule of Law as a Law of Rules' 56 *University of Chicago Law Review* 1175

Schauer, F (1989) 'Is the Common Law Law?' 77 *California Law Review* 455

Schauer, F (1991) *Playing by the Rules: A Philosophical Examination of Rule-Based Decision-Making in Law and in Life* (Oxford University Press)

Schauer, F (2000) 'Incentives, Reputation, and the Inglorious Determinants of Judicial Behavior' 68 *University Cincinnati Law Review* 615

Schauer, F (2004) 'The Failure of the Common Law' 36 *Arizona State Law Journal* 765

Schauer, F (2006) 'Do Cases Make Bad Law?' 73 *University of Chicago Law Review* 883

Schauer, F (2006) '(Re)Taking Hart' 119 *Harvard Law Review* 852

Schauer, F (2011) 'Editor's Introduction' in KN Llewellyn, *The Theory of Rules*, ed F Schauer (University of Chicago Press)

Selden, J (1689) 'Equity' in *Table-Talk: being the discourses of John Selden, Esq.* (2nd edn, JM Dent & Co) 43

Shakespeare, W (1914) *The Winter's Tale* (Oxford University Press)

Shanske, D (2005) 'Four Theses: Preliminary to an Appeal to Equity' 57 *Stanford Law Review* 2053

Shapiro, SJ (2011) *Legality* (Belknap Press)

Sherwin, E (2005) 'Rule-Oriented Realism' 103 *Michigan Law Review* 1578

Simmonds, N (2007) *Law as a Moral Idea* (Oxford University Press)

Simmons, AJ (1992) *The Lockean Theory of Rights* (Princeton University Press)

Singer, J (1988) 'The Reliance Interest in Property' 40 *Stanford Law Review* 611

Singer, JW (2009) 'Normative Methods for Lawyers' 56 *University of California Law Review* 899

Skinner, Q (1998) *Liberty Before Liberalism* (Cambridge University Press)

Skinner, Q (2002) 'Hobbes and the Purely Artificial Person of the State' in *Visions of Politics* iii: *Hobbes and Civil Science* (Cambridge University Press)

Smith, HE (2002) 'Exclusion Versus Governance: Two Strategies for Delineating Property Rights' 31 *Journal of Legal Studies* S453

Smith, HE (2003) 'The Language of Property: Form, Context, and Audience' 55 *Stanford Law Review* 1105

Smith, HE (2009) 'Institutions and Indirectness in Intellectual Property' 157 *University of Pennsylvania Law Review* 2083

Smith, HE (2011) 'Modularity and Morality in the Law of Torts' 4 *Journal of Tort Law* 1

Smith, HE (2011) 'Property Is Not Just a Bundle of Rights' 8 *Economics Journal Watch* 279

Smith, HE (2011) 'Rose's Human Nature of Property' 19 *William and Mary Bill of Rights Journal* 1047.

Smith, HE (2011) 'Standardization in Property Law' in K Ayotte and HE Smith (eds), *Research Handbook on the Economics of Property Law* (Edward Elgar)

Smith, HE (2012) 'Custom in American Property Law: A Vanishing Act' 48 *Texas Journal of International Law* 507

Smith, HE (2012) 'On the Economy of Concepts in Property' 160 *University of Pennsylvania Law Review* 2097
Smith, HE (2012) 'Property as the Law of Things' 125 *Harvard Law Review* 1691
Smith, HE (2013) 'Equitable Intellectual Property: What's Wrong with Misappropriation?' in S Balganesh (ed), *Intellectual Property and the Common Law* (Cambridge University Press)
Smith, HE 'An Economic Analysis of Law versus Equity' (unpublished)
Smith, L (2008) 'Trust and Patrimony' 38 *Revue générale de droit* 379
Smith, L (2014) 'Can We Be Obliged to be Selfless?' in A Gold and P Miller (eds), *Philosophical Foundations of Fiduciary Law* (Oxford University Press)
Smith, SA (2004) *Contract Theory* (Oxford University Press)
Smith, SA (2012) 'Duties, Liabilities, and Damages' 125 *Harvard Law Review* 1727
Smith, SA (2012) 'A Duty to Make Restitution?' 26 *Canadian Journal of Law and Jurisprudence* 157
Solum, LB (1994) 'Equity and the Rule of Law' in I Shapiro (ed), *The Rule of Law* (New York University Press)
Spence, M (1999) *Protecting Reliance: The Emergent Doctrine of Equitable Estoppel* (Hart Publishing)
Stapleton, J (1995) 'Tort, Insurance and Ideology' 58 *Modern Law Review* 820
Sterk, SE (1997) 'Minority Protection in Residential Private Governments' 77 *Boston University Law Review* 273
Stevens, R (2007) *Torts and Rights* (Oxford University Press)
Story, J (1836) *Commentaries on Equity Jurisprudence: as Administered in England and America* (Hillard, Gray & Co)
Stromseth, J, D Wippman, and R Brooks (2006) *Can Might Make Rights? Building the Rule of Law After Military Interventions* (Cambridge University Press)
Taggart, M (ed) (1997) *The Province of Administrative Law* (Hart Publishing)
Tamanaha, BZ (2004) *On the Rule of Law: History, Politics, Theory* (Cambridge University Press)
Tamahana, BZ (2006) 'How an Instrumental View of Law Corrodes the Rule of Law' 56 *DePaul Law Review* 469
Thompson, EP (1975) *Whigs and Hunters: The Origin of the Black Act* (Pantheon Books)
Thorburn, M (2008) 'Justifications, Powers and Authority' 117 *Yale Law Journal* 1070
Tierney, B (1963) '"The Prince is Not Bound by the Laws": Accursius and the Origins of the Modern State' 5 *Comparative Studies in Society and History* 378
Ubel, P, G Loewenstein, N Schwarz, and D Smith (2005) 'Misimagining the Unimaginable: The Disability Paradox and Health Care Decision Making' 24 *Health Psychology* S57
Ullman-Margalit, E and S Morgenbesser (1977) 'Picking and Choosing' 44 *Social Research* 757
Verplanck, GC (1972) *An Essay on the Doctrine of Contracts: Being an Inquiry How Contracts Are Affected in Law and Morals, by Concealment, Error, or Inadequate Price* (Arno Press)
Virgo, G (2012) *The Principles of Equity and Trusts* (Oxford University Press)
von Bar, C et al (eds) (2009) *Principles, Definitions and Model Rules of European Private Law: Draft Common Frame of Reference (DCFR)* (European Law Publishers)
Wade, W and C Forsyth (2009) *Administrative Law* (10th edn, Oxford University Press)
Waldron, J (1992) 'Superseding Historic Injustice' 103 *Ethics* 4
Waldron, J (1994) 'Why Law—Efficacy, Freedom, or Fidelity?' 13 *Law and Philosophy* 259
Waldron, J (1996) 'Kant's Legal Positivism' 109 *Harvard Law Review* 1535
Waldron, J (2002) 'Is the Rule of Law an Essentially Contested Concept (in Florida)?' 21 *Law and Philosophy* 137

Waldron, J (2008) 'Hart and the Principles of Legality' in M Kramer et al (eds), *The Legacy of H.L.A. Hart: Legal, Political and Moral Philosophy* (Clarendon Press)

Waldron, J (2008) 'The Concept of Law and the Rule of Law' 43 *Georgia Law Review* 1

Waldron, J (2008) 'Positivism and Legality: Hart's Equivocal Response to Fuller' 83 *New York University Law Review* 1135

Waldron, J (2011) 'The Rule of Law and the Importance of Procedure' in J Fleming (ed), *Getting to the Rule of Law* (New York University Press)

Waldron, J (2012) *Dignity, Rank and Rights* (Oxford University Press)

Waldron, J (2012) 'How Law Protects Dignity' 71 *Cambridge Law Journal* 200

Waldron, J (2012) 'Stare Decisis and the Rule of Law: A Layered Approach' 111 *Michigan Law Review* 1

Walker, G de Q (1988) *The Rule of Law: Foundation of Constitutional Democracy* (University of Melbourne Press)

Watts, P (2005) 'Authority and Mismotivation' 141 *Law Quarterly Review* 4

Weinrib, EJ (1985) 'The Insurance Justification of Private Law' 14 *The Journal of Legal Studies* 681

Weinrib, EJ (1987) 'The Intelligibility of the Rule of Law' in A Hutchinson and P Monahan (eds), *The Rule of Law: Ideal or Ideology?* (Carswell)

Weinrib, EJ (1988) 'Legal Formalism: On the Immanent Rationality of Law' 97 *Yale Law Journal* 949

Weinrib, EJ (1995) *The Idea of Private Law* (Harvard University Press)

Weinrib, EJ (2002) 'Corrective Justice in a Nutshell' 52 *University of Toronto Law Journal* 349

Weinrib, EJ (2011) 'Private Law and Public Right' 61 *University of Toronto Law Journal* 191.

Weinrib, EJ (2012) 'Poverty and Property in Kant's System of Rights' in *Corrective Justice* (Oxford University Press)

Weinrib, J (2013) 'Authority, Justice, and Public Law: A Unified Theory' DPhil thesis (University of Toronto)

Weisbach, DA (1999) 'Formalism in the Tax Law' 66 *University of Chicago Law Review* 860

West, R (2011) 'The Limits of Process' in JE Fleming (ed), *Getting to the Rule of Law: NOMOS L* (New York University Press)

Whitman, JQ (1991) 'Why Did the Revolutionary Lawyers Confuse Custom and Reason?' 58 *University of Chicago Law Review* 1321

Wilkerson, I (2010) *The Warmth of Other Suns* (Vintage Books)

Williamson, OE (1985) *The Economic Institutions of Capitalism: Firms, Markets, Relational Contracting* (Collier Macmillan)

Williamson, OE (1993) 'Calculativeness, Trust, and Economic Organization' 36 *Journal of Law and Economics* 453

Winner, L (2012) *Still: Notes on a Mid-Faith Crisis* (HarperOn)

Winston, KI (1994) 'Legislators and Liberty' 13 *Law and Philosophy* 389

Worthington, S (2006) *Equity* (2nd edn, Clarendon Press)

Zahnd, EG (1996) 'The Application of Universal Laws to Particular Cases: A Defense of Equity in Aristotelianism and Anglo-American Law' 59 *Law and Contemporary Problems* 263

Zipursky, BC (1998) 'Rights, Wrongs, and Recourse in the Law of Torts' 51 *Vanderbilt Law Review* 1

Zipursky, BC (2005) 'A Theory of Punitive Damages' 84 *Texas Law Review* 105

Zipursky, BC (2011) '*Snyder v. Phelps*, Outrageousness and the Open Texture of Tort Law' 60 *DePaul Law Review* 473

Zipursky, BC (2012) '*Palsgraf*, Punitive Damages, and Preemption' 125 *Harvard Law Review* 1757
Zipursky, BC (2013) 'The Inner Morality of Private Law' 58 *American Journal of Jurisprudence* 27
Zipursky, BC (forthcoming) 'Civil Recourse and the Plurality of Wrongs' *New Zealand Law Review*
Zuckerman, A (2006) *Zuckerman on Civil Procedure* (2nd edn, Sweet & Maxwell)

Index of Subjects

Index of Names